DECOLONIZING THE CRIMINAL QUESTION

Decolonizing the Criminal Question

Colonial Legacies, Contemporary Problems

Edited by
ANA ALIVERTI
University of Warwick

HENRIQUE CARVALHO
University of Warwick

ANASTASIA CHAMBERLEN
University of Warwick

MÁXIMO SOZZO
National University of Litoral

OXFORD
UNIVERSITY PRESS

OXFORD
UNIVERSITY PRESS

Great Clarendon Street, Oxford, OX2 6DP,
United Kingdom

Oxford University Press is a department of the University of Oxford. It furthers the University's objective of excellence in research, scholarship, and education by publishing worldwide. Oxford is a registered trade mark of Oxford University Press in the UK and in certain other countries

First Edition published in 2023

Published in the United States of America by Oxford University Press
198 Madison Avenue, New York, NY 10016, United States of America

British Library Cataloguing in Publication Data
Data available

Library of Congress Control Number: 2023936570

ISBN 978–0–19–289900–2

DOI: 10.1093/oso/9780192899002.001.0001

Printed and bound by
CPI Group (UK) Ltd, Croydon, CR0 4YY

Foreword: Decolonizing Critique

Mark Brown

It is with pleasure that I write these opening words for *Decolonizing the Criminal Question: Colonial Legacies, Contemporary Problems*. I had the good fortune to participate as a discussant in the workshop from which these chapters emerged and I am sure their present form has profited not only from this book's fine editors but also from the wide-ranging and productive discussions that unfolded over those two days in September 2021.

Decolonizing the Criminal Question contributes to a burgeoning literature within criminology that, in different ways, attempts some form of critical reckoning with history, geography, and the powerful forces—colonialism and imperialism among them—that have shaped the world we live in today. The collection draws on voices, perspectives, and locations that reflect the wide diversity of colonial and imperial forms and as such reinforces the danger of speaking of either term in a general sense. There is, in other words, no singular colonialism from which we should today decolonize. In fact, even within empires and no less in their enduring formations and reverberations, diversity and accommodation are salient features. Still, that does not limit our capacity to critique colonization nor to offer thoughts or prescriptions for how its deleterious impacts might be challenged. At the heart of this collection, therefore, is the act of critique: an exercise in exploring limits, inconsistencies, and impacts. Yet at the same time, and as readers of this collection might usefully contemplate, all work in this area seems necessarily to tread a delicate line. This is the balance between, on the one hand, recruiting the established forms and practices of critique—traditions, it should be noted, born of the same European thought that also gave us colonialism, imperialism, slavery, and a liberal order founded on private property, capital, and 'free' labour—and on the other, rescuing other forms of critique that disrupt the former.

This invites us to think carefully about the role, purpose, and limits of critique, something which all contributors to this collection engage with in some way. For without such in view, we seem bound to be drawn back inwards by the powerful centripetal forces that shape criminology and other scholarly disciplines alike. As Siraj Ahmed (2017, p. 243) has observed, 'Whereas critical reason originally questioned institutional authority in order to foster autonomy in its strict sense, it eventually came merely to question institutional procedures in order to devise more effective ones.' As such, critique has emerged within criminology as elsewhere across the academy and in praxis as a key tool for legitimizing norms via subtle fine-tuning rather than as a method paving the way for transgressive ideas or visions of potential futures. If, as Ahmed suggests, critique's original purpose was to foster autonomy—by which he means release from subjection to external laws or forces, be that dogma, sovereign command, colonial logic, or the like—what might this constitute in the various registers on which criminology operates?

One answer might begin by observing that the critique the book's title demands, of *Decolonizing the Criminal Question*, must surely have at least two targets. One is the epistemic and ethical horizons of this edifice we call criminology; the other, the nature of the field in terms of its tendency for homogeneous reproduction. The first is dealt with squarely by contributors. Yet at the broader analytic level, we should also observe that autonomy in the strict sense of freedom from heteronomy will mean different things in different places. This is, indeed, reflected by the wide variety of colonialisms contemplated in these chapters and to which different peoples were subject. In this respect, a particular schism that divides visions of autonomous decolonial futures or other forms of alterity is that which runs between scholars whose focus lies primarily in settler colonial states (past and present) and those whose analysis and transgressive imagination falls upon states that experienced (at least formal) postcolonial liberation. The former typically include Australia, Canada, New Zealand, and the United States, where indigenous communities live through a seemingly indefinite colonial moment. The latter take in much of the new nation-states formed in the nineteenth century in Latin America and, in the twentieth, in South and Southeast Asia and Africa (though this is, of course, to gloss over other empires and regions, such as the Ottomans and the Balkan region, as one example). Transgressive imaginations of autonomy through return to some pre-colonial figuration of, variously, rights to land, political authority, and the like characteristic of critiques of settler colonialism may not hold anything like the same resonance in, for example, contemporary South Asia (though cf. the experience of Adivasi tribal groups in India: see Kapoor, 2021).

Yet in contemplating autonomous futures, (post)colonial peoples and societies of all stripes face challenges of both method and imagination. The latter reflects a practical constraint based on what Hans Georg Gadamer (1960/2013) termed our historical situation, or locatedness in history. 'The very idea of a situation,' observes Gadamer, 'means that we are not standing outside of it and hence are unable to have any objective knowledge of it' (p. 312). Indigenous knowledge and thought traditions, many of which are discussed in this collection, might offer some way out of this labyrinth wherein, as Gadamer goes on to note, we are left unable to see or imagine that which is possible, simply by dint of our situatedness, 'a standpoint that limits the possibility of vision' (p. 313). Methodologically, we face at least two challenges. To begin, and on a minor key, our field faces a challenge in the deep historical research that understanding the applicability of Northern concepts to Southern lives and worlds entails. For example, Prathama Banerjee (2018, p. 81) has argued that despite the extremely productive use to which Foucault's ideas have been put in understanding how 'colonial governmental techniques—reform, education, medicine, enumeration, classification, codification, survey and representation—came to produce in India critical social categories such as caste, religion, gender and ethnicity', in fact attention to pre-colonial history and the endurance of its social and political categories renders Foucault's schema unfit for purpose in modern India. Intimations of the same are to be found throughout this volume. How should this be solved, while also keeping in sight the goal of autonomous futures? On a major key, we should note that to resolve such problems we typically fall back on rational analysis and critique. But while this might make sense methodologically in mainstream approaches, here we need to recognize the powerful conservative forces exerted by such critique. Or as Ahmed (2017, p. 249) pithily observes:

> Enlightenment critique leads inevitably, if subtly, to a colonial logic. If, according to the terms tacitly set out by the Enlightenment, the ultimate goal of critique is 'autonomy,' the path to autonomy must, conversely, pass through a specifically European tradition of critical reason. This is one conundrum in which anticolonial revolution became trapped.

It is also a conundrum that faces those of us attempting to decolonize the criminal question.

Returning, then, to the question of how we might seek release from the grid of colonial logic within which our field itself is embedded, we should reflect on how the many insights and transgressive proposals made by contributors to this collection may enter the wider field. This, too, would seem to have at least two parts. The first is the receptivity of institutional (academic) criminologists to the ideas contained in this collection. Most criminology academics in most institutions that teach it—i.e. those of the Global North—are tightly and narrowly focused on domestic concerns. And most of these concerns, as Stanley Cohen (1988, p. 4) long ago and perhaps even rather generously diagnosed, can be seen as but 'a series of creative, even brilliant, yet eventually repetitive variations on ... late-nineteenth-century themes' centred upon the European state and its effectiveness. Here, perhaps, colleagues who grumble that their critical insights into domestic policing or other criminal justice agencies or practices are routinely ignored (or trivially accommodated) by practitioners and policy makers may find themselves, in the face of the challenges posed in this collection, unexpected bedfellows of such agents of inertia. For, as their own experience has shown, the presence of critical insight and new visions does not in any way imply ready uptake. If that proves to be the case, how might criminology transform?

Arguably, the field is most reliably reproduced by its constant production of new graduating students. The second part of the question of how insights and proposals contained in this volume might find their way into the wider field may, therefore, be addressed by considering what is taught in classrooms. While curricular offerings remain the preserve of academic judgement and institutional strategy, almost all programmes nevertheless recognize the need to teach what might loosely be termed the core and frontiers of criminological knowledge. A brief desk-based review of undergraduate offerings in Australia, Hong Kong, the Netherlands, and UK reveals how the strong inward-looking domestic focus that one might predict from criminological research is indeed replicated in teaching. At the same time, however, in the UK a new benchmark statement for criminology released by the Quality Assurance Agency for Higher Education in March 2022 includes for the first time reference to 'colonialism (past and present)' (QAA, 2022, p. 5). As decolonization gains traction at the institutional level too, greater demand will arise for teaching resources to support academic colleagues to integrate the sorts of questions addressed in this collection into their course- and module-level curricula. The path to autonomy—freedom from subjection to an external, oppressive force—may thus in important ways run through the students we teach, in the diversity of their voices, the diversity of the teaching they receive, and in the capacity of criminology to accommodate and adapt to these challenges. This fine collection paves the way towards all of these goals.

References

Ahmed, S. (2017) 'Thinking at the Enlightenment's limit', *Cultural Critique*, 96, pp. 235–60.

Banerjee, P. (2018) 'The Abiding Binary: The Social and the Political in Modern India', in Legg, S. and Heath, D. (eds) *South Asian Governmentalities: Michel Foucault and the Question of Postcolonial Orderings*. Cambridge: Cambridge University Press.

Cohen, S. (1988) *Against Criminology*. New Brunswick, NJ: Transaction Publishers.

Gadamer, H.-G. (1960/2013) *Truth and Method*. London: Bloomsbury.

Kapoor, D. (2021) 'Anticolonial Participatory Action Research (APAR) in Adivasi-Dalit Forest-Dweller and Small Peasant Contexts of Dispossession and Struggle in India', in Kapoor, D. and Jordan, S. (eds) *Research, Political Engagement and Dispossession: Indigenous, Peasant and Urban Poor Activisms in the Americas and Asia*. London: Bloomsbury.

Quality Assurance Agency for Higher Education (2022) *Criminology Benchmark Statement*, 4th edn. Gloucester: QAA.

Acknowledgements

This collection is the culmination of a long-standing collaboration that started in 2019. Due to the many obstacles and delays caused by the global Covid-19 pandemic, five years on, we know that the collection has finally come to fruition due to the commitment and help of several people to whom we are immensely grateful.

First, as co-editors we are wholeheartedly thankful to the fantastic contributors in this collection. The richness of their accounts, their passion, and critical insights have made this collection a diverse, detailed, and, we feel, important effort to decolonize the criminal question. We are also grateful to the contributors for being so patient with the editorial process, being open and responsive to our feedback, and for being committed to producing high-quality scholarship. We met virtually most of the contributors at a workshop in September 2021 which focused on this book and helped us to lay out the many synergies among our individual projects. While that workshop was an important means for pulling together ideas and key arguments in this collection, and while since then we have had many conversations with individual contributors, we hope that we will soon meet the authors of this collection in person so that we can more properly celebrate their achievements in this book.

We are immensely grateful to our proofreader and editor Bel Rawson. Bel has expertly reviewed drafts of all chapters and has been incredible at meeting our often-unrealistic deadlines; we have been truly lucky to have benefited from her support and the book's polished look is certainly a result of her hard work. We are also thankful to Mark Brown for writing such an insightful Foreword to this collection; his broader work in the area, but also his comments on this project, have been inspirational. Furthermore, we would like to thank Vanessa Barker, Roxana Cavalcanti, Sacha Darke, David Santos Fonseca, Beatrice Jauregui, and Raza Saeed for acting as discussants at the book's workshop, for their insightful comments on the chapters, and the project more broadly.

We are also lucky to have received institutional and financial support for this project since its inception. We received support to organize an in-person international workshop, which unfortunately never materialized due to Covid-19. Nonetheless, we are grateful to the British Society of Criminology, the Socio-legal Studies Association, Warwick Law School, and to the Social Theory Centre and Criminal Justice Centre at Warwick for offering to financially sponsor the project's intellectual activities.

We are especially grateful that we can publish this collection Open Access. It has been politically and intellectually important for us as editors and for the contributors in this collection to make this book as accessible as possible and in doing so challenge and overcome the many institutional and other barriers that prevent free and open intellectual exchange globally. The financial support to pursue an Open Access agreement was generously offered by the Library Open Access Fund, Warwick Law School, and the Department of Sociology at the University of Warwick; we are thankful to colleagues in these departments for helping us to make this collection more democratically accessible.

Finally, we are thankful to the editorial team at Oxford University Press for commissioning the collection, showing faith in its content, and for guiding us through the editorial and copy-editing stages.

We very much see this collection as a collaborative exchange that we hope will continue for years to come—thank you to all who with their criticisms and feedback, insights, patience, collegiality, and solidarity helped us to put this project out into the world.

Ana Aliverti
Henrique Carvalho
Anastasia Chamberlen
Máximo Sozzo
October 2022

Contents

List of Contributors

Editors

Ana Aliverti, University of Warwick, UK

Henrique Carvalho, University of Warwick, UK

Anastasia Chamberlen, University of Warwick, UK

Máximo Sozzo, Universidad Nacional del Litorial, Argentina

Contributors

Biko Agozino, Virginia Tech, USA

Ahmed Ajil, University of Lausanne, Switzerland

Mahuya Bandyopadhyay, Indian Institute of Technology Delhi, India

Kwan-Lamar Blount-Hill, Arizona State University, USA

Lucia Bracco Bruce, Pontificia Universidad Católica del Perú, Peru

Melanie Collard, Royal Holloway, University of London, UK

Chris Cunneen, University of Technology Sydney, Australia

Rod Earle, Open University, UK

Sarah Ghabrial, Concordia University, Canada

Lucy Harry, University of Oxford, UK

Manuel Iturralde, Universidad de los Andes, Colombia

Omar Phoenix Khan, University of Bath, UK

J. M. Moore, Independent Scholar, UK

Conor O'Reilly, University of Leeds, UK

Alpa Parmar, University of Cambridge, UK

Coretta Phillips, London School of Economics and Political Science, UK

Maayan Ravid, Tel Aviv University, Israel

Hugo Leonardo Rodrigues Santos, Universidade Federal de Alagoas, Brazil

Gail Super, University of Toronto, Canada

Zoha Waseem, University of Warwick, UK

Amanda Wilson, University of Warwick, UK

Introduction

Ana Aliverti, Henrique Carvalho, Anastasia Chamberlen, and Máximo Sozzo

Overview

This collection engages with debates within 'criminology'—understood as a complex and polyvalent field of knowledge (Sozzo, 2006; 2021; Lacey and Zedner, 2017; Sparks, 2021)—and about matters of colonial power, which have come to be conceptualized through the language of 'decolonization'. In many ways, these efforts are not new; as far back as the 1970s and 1980s, significant critical contributions introduced, in various ways, the connection between colonialism—in its various forms—and the criminal question with the intention of devising theoretical and practical tools to better understand contemporary processes of social control and rethink their foundations. For example, in the Global North, the pioneering work of Stanley Cohen (1982) focused on the processes of 'transfer' of institutions, discourses, and practices of crime control from the metropoles to postcolonial contexts, and sought to offer different interpretive keys to read these dynamics and their political implications, which he articulated into different 'models' ('benign transfer', 'malignant colonialism', and 'paradoxical damage'). In the Global South, the influential work of Rosa del Olmo (1975; 1981) and Eugenio R. Zaffaroni (1988; 1989) placed colonialism and neocolonialism at the centre of their understanding of the history and present of criminology and penal systems in Latin America. Colonialism in its different forms, they argued, has contributed to reproducing the dependence and submission of peripheral countries with respect to those at the centre, both in the production of knowledge and in the institutions and practices of social control. In Zaffaroni's own theoretical and political position, defined as a 'marginal criminological realism', such power dynamics take centre stage in an effort to produce alternative logics and practices from the periphery (García and Sozzo, forthcoming).

In recent years, however, there has been an increasing and sustained interest in this connection, with an exponential growth of scholarship advocating for and advancing 'counter-colonial', 'postcolonial', 'decolonial', and 'Southern' criminological perspectives.[1] Such work denounced the many silences and absences in this field of knowledge,

[1] See among others Aas, 2012; Agozino, 2003; 2004; 2010; 2018; 2021; Alagia and Codino, 2019; Aliverti et al., 2021; Anderson et al., 2020; Ben-Natan, 2021; Black et al., 2020; Blagg, 2008; Blagg and Thalia, 2019; Bracco Bruce, 2022; Brown, 2001; 2005; 2014; 2017; 2018; 2021; Brown et al., 2021; Cain, 2000; Carrington and Hogg, 2017; Carrington et al., 2016; 2018; 2019; Cavalcanti, 2020; Chartrand, 2019; Ciocchini and Greener, 2021; Cunneen, 2011; 2018a; 2018b; Cunneen and Tauri, 2017; Darke and Khan, 2021; Davis and

Ana Aliverti, Henrique Carvalho, Anastasia Chamberlen, and Máximo Sozzo, *Introduction* In: *Decolonizing the Criminal Question.* Edited by: Ana Aliverti, Henrique Carvalho, Anastasia Chamberlen, and, Máximo Sozzo, Oxford University Press.
 DOI: 10.1093/oso/9780192899002.003.0001

criticizing what Cunneen has sharply characterized in the opening chapter of this book as 'criminological innocence'. This active process of 'unknowing' and 'ignorance' has been reproduced in vast sectors of the criminological field up to the present, including in its teaching (Aliverti et al., 2021, pp. 299–300). However, the growth of these critical voices in recent years has made the maintenance of such innocence more difficult and problematic for those writing in this field (Cunneen, this volume, pp. 19–35).

This collaborative project builds on such works while expanding conceptual and methodological tools to uncover the coloniality of crime, criminal justice, and social control more broadly, and reflects on their implications for doing research in these areas. We decided to frame the subject of this collective project using the idea of the 'criminal question', an expression born within the framework of the construction of a 'critical criminology' in the Italian scene of the 1970s. In 1975, a group of intellectuals, including Alessandro Baratta, Franco Bricola, Dario Melossi, Tamar Pitch, and Massimo Pavarini, created an academic journal, *La Questione Criminale*, which promoted that critical tradition. The same expression has been rescued more recently by Italian critical researchers in the title of a new journal, *Studi Sulla Questione Criminale*, which was first published in 2006. In giving conceptual depth to this expression, Tamar Pitch's intellectual contribution was crucial. In one of the first texts in which this idea circulated in English, she pointed out more than twenty-five years ago that:

> To study the criminal question is different from studying crime. It means that crime is not considered independently from the procedures by which it is defined, the instruments deployed in its administration and control and the politics and debates around criminal justice and public order.
>
> (Pitch, 1995, p. 45; see also Pitch, 2022, p. 14)

This concept implies moving away from the idea that 'crime' is a 'natural fact', as the various 'substantialist' positions have presented throughout history—from its association with the notion of 'sin' to the positivist elaboration of a concept of 'natural crime'. But it also implies moving away from 'formalist' positions, which define it with reference to the law, and are strongly associated with the Enlightenment and liberal thought (Pitch, 1995, p. 46). The allusion to the criminal question means adopting a 'constructionist' point of view which critically analyses not only the social and political dynamics of the processes of 'primary criminalisation'—the creation of criminal law—but also those of 'secondary criminalisation'—the application of criminal law (Pitch, 2022, p. 14). This involves recognizing the centrality of state agencies and practices, including their extra-legal modes of action, but also the importance of non-state actors (from corporations to social movements) in these social and political dynamics (Pitch, 1995, p. 46). In turn, this frame also involves scrutinizing the role that researchers play in the construction of the criminal question, producing knowledge from different methodological and theoretical perspectives, creating discourses,

Gibson-Light, 2020; Dimou, 2021; Evans, 2021; Fonseca, 2018a; 2018b; Lee and Laidler, 2013; Medina, 2011; Moosavi, 2019a; 2019b; Morrison, 2006; Pfingst and Kimari, 2021; Phillips et al., 2020; Porter, 2016; Rodriguez Goyes, 2018; 2019; Saleh-Hanna, 2008; Sozzo, 2011; 2021; Stambøl, 2021; Travers, 2019; Zaffaroni, 2022; Zaffaroni and Codino, 2015.

concepts, and arguments. Furthermore, it highlights the importance of the representations disseminated in 'the public', themselves the result of an intricate process of elaboration (Pitch, 1995, p. 47; 2022, p. 14).[2]

In other words, the idea of the criminal question foregrounds the breadth and politics of criminological knowledge. It sheds light on structures of inequality, injustice, and domination, with their various racist, classist, and patriarchal axes, in the functioning not only of social control institutions (see many chapters in this volume, such as Cunneen, Iturralde, Moore, Phoenix Khan, Wilson, among others) but also of academia (Parmar, 2016; Phillips et al., 2020; 2022; Blount-Hill and Ajil, this volume). When, how, why, by whom, and with respect to whom certain behaviours are effectively defined as crimes in social life become fundamental interrogations (Pitch, 1995, p. 47; 2022, p. 14), as does the question of how such a selective process has shaped the study of 'crime' and 'punishment'. Indeed, from its origins, the reliance of criminology on state categories, processes, and funding (Zedner, 2003) had made those interrogations both urgent and forceful if criminology is to serve a critical, decolonial purpose. Thinking of crime as a social and political construction, however, does not imply treating it as a mere illusion. This viewpoint does not ignore the existence of singular acts or more complex activities that have violent, harmful, and damaging consequences, and their unequal impacts on socially disadvantaged groups, nor does it neglect the fact that many of these harms are not acknowledged as such by contemporary criminal law (Pitch, 1995, p. 47; 2012, p. 14).

Thus, the word 'question' in the notion of the 'criminal question' simultaneously serves two roles—coinciding with the meanings it has in Italian, French, Portuguese, and Spanish:[3] to refer to and recognize a 'subject' or 'problem' and, at the same time, to 'interrogate', to 'call into question' (Sozzo, 2009, p. 2). In this way, the criminal question identifies a complex area of institutions and actors, discourses and practices whose borders are mobile and porous, and which has multiple dimensions and levels (Pitch, 1995, p. 45; 2022, p. 14). The translation of this concept into English and its centrality for this collective project seek in part to destabilize the existing geographical, linguistic and epistemological hierarchies in the processes of knowledge production within criminology. More importantly, in rescuing the critical potential of this concept, we aim to denaturalize and deconstruct the criminological core of mainstream scholarship about these issues, locating this core within political, economic, and cultural structures forged through colonialism (Aliverti et al., 2021, pp. 298–299; see also Melossi, Sozzo, and Sparks, 2011, pp. 2–3; Loader and Sparks, 2011, pp. 5–6; 2013, pp. 60–61). As the contributors to this volume have documented, race articulated and gave meaning to colonial encounters and conquests. The traces of these encounters are vivid in the bodies, memories, and life trajectories of racialized groups in contemporary sites of confinement and practices of control (Phillips, 2012; Bosworth, 2014; de

[2] Conceiving 'crime' as a social and political construction implies assuming that it is a human invention, what Pavarini—another key researcher initially involved in that intellectual movement in the Italian context—has ingeniously called the 'consciousness of fiction' (2006, p. 16; see also, for a similar position in the French language debate, Pires, 2006).

[3] It is no coincidence that this expression has also been widely used in critical literature in this field of knowledge in Spanish, from the early 1980s (Bergalli, 1982) to the present (Sozzo, 2009; Zaffaroni, 2012; Caimari and Sozzo, 2017).

Noronha, 2019; Bracco Bruce, Phillips, Ravid, Rodrigues Santos et al., this volume). Simultaneously, as a category formed by 'mobile essentialisms' (Stoler, 1995; 2016), racial thinking, imageries, and feelings remain critical for understanding the contemporary shapes, travels, and academic production of the criminal question (Gilroy, 2003; Bonilla-Silva, 2019; Sekimoto, 2018; Blount-Hill and Ajil, Ghabrial, Phoenix Khan, this volume).

Given this complexity, decolonizing this field is admittedly a very ambitious project, due to its multifaceted character. This in turn opens up different fronts, a plurality of paths that can only be taken through an immense collective and collaborative effort by researchers from a multiplicity of disciplines working on geopolitical locations ascribed both to the Global South and the Global North. Although we return to these paths in more detail in the concluding chapter, some fundamental axes of the plural project we pursue in this collection should be outlined at this stage:

(a) This project seeks to trace the multiple impacts of colonialism, in its various forms, both in the past and in the present, on the dynamics of knowledge production on the criminal question. This exercise involves identifying and disarming the mechanisms of hierarchy, subordination, and dependence of researchers who work in the Global South, in postcolonial scenarios, with respect to the problems, concepts, and arguments emerging from work conducted within the Global North, in metropolitan contexts, which are frequently presented as universal, timeless, and placeless.
(b) It also scrutinizes the multifaceted relationship between colonialism and social control institutions, processes, and practices by state actors—police, courts, prisons, etc.—and non-state actors—private security, vigilante groups, etc.—with the aim of exposing recurring processes of the racialization and marginalization of diverse social groups, in the Global South and North.
(c) The project tracks, elaborates, and expands on the different forms of resistance and struggles against colonialism in the field of the criminal question, both in terms of knowledge and action, as well as via the construction of decolonial practical alternatives, in the past and in the present, in the Global North and South.

Thus, this project has a number of ambitions. First, it aspires to take stock and reconstruct critical traditions through efforts done by others; second, it wants to map the intellectual richness of the work being done within and beyond this field of studies; and, third, it sketches a way forward that foregrounds these theoretical, methodological, political, and ethical insights to craft an emancipatory programme of research and action. We believe and hope that this dialogue (across disciplines, among scholars working in the Global South and the North) not only deepens the critical potential of the project but provides some much-needed intellectual freshness and vitality to a field stagnated by tired and inadequate conceptual, methodological, and theoretical frameworks.

Decolonizing criminology, in this sense, involves not only looking back and looking South, but also, as contributors to this volume suggest, understanding how ideas and concepts travel in a sort of 'imperial feedback loop', and not necessarily in a North–South trajectory (Collard, Harry, O'Reilly, Wassem, this volume), which is fundamental for appreciating contemporary global dynamics beyond the frame of the nation-state (Aas, 2011; 2017; Bosworth et al., 2018; Aliverti, 2016). Above all, it entails breaking open these frameworks and exploring actors, institutions, discourses, and practices with fresh eyes, questioning Northern hegemonies through methodological and epistemological shifts; that is, doing theory from the 'South' (Comaroff and Comaroff, 2012b; 2012a). This demands, as Bandyopadhyay articulates in her chapter, an ethnographic sensibility to the diversity, chaotic, and messy nature of crime and its control, unencumbered by Northern representations and explanatory frameworks, which impinge on our capacity to hear and see well. The empirical findings and reflections presented here, then, seek to unsettle concepts (nation-state, punishment, violence, legitimacy), dichotomies (society and the state, the prison and the street, official and unofficial, private and public violence, law and disorder, metropole and periphery, South and North), and boundaries in criminological and penological scholarship.

This project is the product of a long process that started five years ago. In 2019, we first launched a call for papers for a conference at the University of Warwick. There was a positive response to that initial call, but with an overrepresentation of researchers based in universities of the Global North, in many cases studying scenarios of the Global South. Such response reflected the existing inequalities in contemporary global academia in terms of access to resources and opportunities for conducting research, particularly for empirically based projects (Carrington et al., 2019; Travers, 2019; Moosavi, 2019a; Aliverti et al., 2021). Another obstacle for securing contributions from academics who carry out their research predominantly in other languages was the fact that the call for papers and the announced conference were in English (Faraldo Cabana, 2018; Faraldo Cabana and Lamela, 2019; Aliverti et al., 2021). To generate a greater balance in contributions, at a second stage, we directly invited contributors from a wide range of contexts. Despite our efforts to include marginalized voices in this academic field, our achievements have been limited. We are convinced that it is essential to redouble future efforts, with institutional and academic inventiveness, to broaden the sphere of theoretical and political discussion, involving more actively researchers who work in the Global South and in languages other than English, to enrich and strengthen the various perspectives in relation to the project of decolonization. As such, this volume contributes to building and imagining the 'decolonizing horizon'; thus, rather than an outcome we see it primarily as a contribution to a broader collective conversation, process, and praxis.

Because of the Covid-19 pandemic and the limitations it imposed on global mobility, we decided to suspend the conference and hold it in 2021. Meanwhile, the various authors prepared the first versions of their chapters. Due to the prolongation of the effects of the pandemic, finally the contributions were presented and discussed in an online two-day workshop held in September 2021. The editors and other non-contributing academics were discussants of the papers, in an environment which fostered an invaluable opportunity for a productive collective conversation. Following the workshop, the editors compiled key pieces of feedback for each author. The results of our revisions of each chapter were sent in writing to the authors, who produced second versions that were revised again. In this sense, this volume can be considered the result of a truly collective and collaborative effort that has involved researchers from North America, Latin America, Africa, Europe, Asia, and Oceania.

We have sought to ensure that the contents of this collective and collaborative effort reach as many readers as possible. To this end, thanks to the financial support of the University of Warwick, this book is Open Access.[4] This can ensure that all those who want to access these materials can do so freely, without this access being mediated by a commodification process. We believe that this form of publication is one of the crucial ways to start reversing the existing inequalities in the academic world, particularly in relation to the democratization of the circulation of knowledge. Rather paradoxically, making this publication open access is also possible because of the financial resources available in Northern, neoliberal universities. Despite its relevance, we are conscious that open access to academic research by itself does not solve the enormous and enduring inequalities in the production of knowledge. Ameliorating these inequalities requires profound changes in the material and institutional bases of its production (as we briefly pointed out earlier and is a point we return to in the concluding chapter), which reflect the contemporary broader and extreme economic imbalances between central and peripheral countries and the institutions within them (Moosavi, 2019a, p. 258; Travers, 2019, p. 11; Carrington et al., 2019, p. 185). A next step, which is within our plans, is to start to address language and other dissemination and communication barriers that stand in the way of more democratic and inclusive discussions of these indispensable questions.

The book is structured in five parts. The first, 'Unsettling Concepts and Perspectives', includes chapters that address the theoretical challenges entailed in decolonizing the criminal question, in a general way, although with reference to particular contexts and regions and from different points of departure. In the first chapter, Chris Cunneen explores the coloniality of power as it is exercised through the material practices, discourses, and underlying epistemological assumptions of the criminal legal system and sets out the necessity of and potential parameters for decolonizing criminology. There are three broad ideas which underpin this chapter and provide a structure to the analysis. The first is the importance of understanding colonialism and the coloniality of power. The second is the relevance of subaltern knowledges, epistemologies, and methodologies, and how criminal justice and criminology have failed to move beyond imperialist and colonialist ways of representing and understanding the world. The third and final section of the chapter considers whether criminology might play a role in the strategies for a decolonial abolitionist activism, and what role that might be. The chapter argues the need for, and the challenges facing, decolonization in the context of policing and penal power, and the compromised position of criminology.

In Chapter 2, John Moore takes us back to the colonial origins of criminology and highlights that to overcome its history of bias, racism, and state-sponsored endorsements of criminalization, we ought to take seriously the idea that abolition is a viable, decolonial project. Moore reminds us that crime is a European concept that was (and is) central to its colonial project, whilst criminology's key innovation, the discovery of the criminal Other, has its origin in the racial Other, a project central to European colonialism. This intimate link between colonialism and both crime and criminology—a

[4] We would like to thank the Library's Open Access Fund (particularly, João Vicente), the Law School, and the Sociology Department of the University of Warwick for making this possible by providing the necessary funding.

Gordian Knot—is so embedded that it requires a radical restructuring and rethinking. Both decolonization and abolition require, Moore argues, revolutionary changes to our established social structures; taking such revolutionary action seriously promises to break us free from existing power relations and can be the main way to comprehensively develop new ways of living.

In Chapter 3, Manuel Iturralde examines the contributions of Southern criminologists in decolonizing criminological thinking in Latin America while critiquing their invisibilization in global discussions. He focuses on some of the most salient features of Latin American crime control during the last three decades and shows that they are deeply connected to Latin American countries' historical trajectories and the dynamics of colonialism and neocolonialism. The latter is not just a remnant of the past but, as Iturralde suggests, is a live, acting force that profoundly affects the political economy of Latin American societies today.

In Chapter 4, Biko Agozino shows us how readings of colonial histories and rationales ought to be revisited in order to properly and critically decolonize criminological thinking and practice. Focusing on anti-colonial resistance in Nigeria, Agozino shows that, to the astonishment of the colonizers, it was women who led the uprising against autocratic colonizing powers and their appointed chiefs in what was known as the Women's War in Nigeria. In response, the colonizers commissioned anthropologists to conduct 'intelligence reports' for the purpose of determining if the women were drunk or under the influence of the men to make them oppose despotic colonial rule. This chapter reflects on one such report by C. K. Meek (1937) on *Law and Authority in a Nigerian Tribe* and its implications for the retention of despotic authoritarianism in neocolonial African states today.

The second part of the collection, titled 'Contextualizing the Criminal Question', includes three chapters, each offering a unique perspective on criminal justice institutions in three particular contexts. In Chapter 5, Zoha Waseem looks at policing and social movements to shed new light on the idea that state police forces in many postcolonial countries are notorious for militarized and informal policing practices. Her chapter comparatively explores postcolonial policing in Pakistan and Nigeria and develops the notion of the 'postcolonial condition of policing' to capture how regime insecurity fosters reliance upon colonially designed policing structures within which professional and financial insecurities of officers enable punitive practices which in turn exacerbate public insecurity. This framework also helps to explain the emergence and development of activism against state and policing institutions in these scenarios.

In Chapter 6, Gail Super explores extrajudicial punishment in South Africa. In questioning criminologists' tendency to study predominantly state-sponsored punishment, Super argues that extrajudicial punishment plays a central role in penality and that, particularly in postcolonial contexts, rates of imprisonment do not adequately reflect levels of penal punitiveness. She uses the term 'extrajudicial punishment' to refer to punishment-like phenomena which are inflicted by civilian or state actors, in response to an allegation of criminality or lawbreaking. In South Africa, extrajudicial punishment plays out on multiple scales, across space and time, in and through varying jurisdictions, and disproportionately targets and affects poor black people. While this is also the case in Western (and other) contexts, it is more exaggerated, more visible, and more violent in the postcolony. Thus, she reminds us that studying penality in postcolonial contexts is instructive for theorizing about the more general contradictions of liberal penal forms.

Mahuya Bandyopadhyay reflects on carceral cultures in India in Chapter 7. She questions the ability of the hegemonic Western framework to comprehend criminality, violence, and imprisonment in India, and considers the constraints of doing prison ethnography within the established requirements and infrastructure of a state science. Is the solution to transcend the restrictive limitations of crime prevention and embrace different, culturally sensitive perspectives to develop an understanding of social harm in numerous public and private spaces? In this context, her chapter deconstructs an inherently chaotic carceral culture manifested in prisons and outside through carceral spillovers. It explores how conceptions of chaotic sites and everyday lives, as well as the decentring of research questions from their obvious presence and occurrence, can contribute to the study of crime, violence, and incarceration in contemporary India.

The third part of the collection, 'Locating Colonial Duress', offers four chapters specifically on the impact of different forms of colonialism in past and present social control institutions and practices in an array of contexts. In Chapter 8, Sarah Ghabrial writes about border criminality in Algeria and France. Paying close attention to historical events (from 1844 to the present), she sketches a trans-Mediterranean genealogy of 'border criminalization'—defined as the de-legalization, bureaucratization, racialization, and policing of particular modes of mobility—from the French colonial occupation of Algeria through to the present neocolonial relationship between Europe and the Maghreb. In so doing, Ghabrial seeks to understand how mobility and illegality inform, rationalize, and reproduce each other to sustain continued North–South asymmetries of power and difference. The chapter unpacks these categories through a range of data including penal, judicial, and bureaucratic instruments which are situated temporally within a governmental continuum. In doing so, this chapter foregrounds the figure who undertakes *harraga* ('clandestine migration' in Maghrebi colloquial Arabic), whose sojourns reveal state law to be *arbitrary*—an inorganic and violently imposed externality—even as they keep alive memories of ancestral geographies and chart possible futures rooted in non-normative epistemologies of justice.

In Chapter 9, Omar Phoenix Khan examines the coloniality of criminal justice in Brazil by focusing on decisions during pre-trial hearings. Phoenix Khan exposes how colonial logics inform contemporary justice mechanisms. The chapter begins by discussing the hierarchized and bounded nature of citizenship during the Portuguese empire and charts how white-supremacist power structures were sustained beyond the abolition of slavery and into the post-colonial period. Thematic analysis of interviews with judges, prosecutors, public defenders, and specialists in Rio de Janeiro reveals the white-centred nature of citizenship and how stigmatized spaces are considered criminogenic. Inhumane treatment of racialized groups is thus naturalized at an ontological level for judges. The high rates of pre-trial detention in Brazil can, he concludes, be understood as a product of the coloniality of criminal justice.

In Chapter 10, Maayan Ravid tackles racialized exclusion and criminalization in Israel. By looking at the policing of Israeli Ethiopian citizens and the detention of Sudanese and Eritrean asylum seekers, she carves out a comparative lens through which to navigate and categorize the prejudice of the state towards different categories of racialized 'Others'. Ravid argues that racialization, criminalization, and exclusion of non-white groups emanates from a Eurocentric postcolonial social order of racial differentiation that accompanied the occupation of Palestine. She argues that this hierarchical order became ingrained in the state and has evolved over time to exclude different groups of 'Others' (Palestinians, Ethiopian Jewish citizens, and African asylum seekers) highlighting how racial formations and hierarchies animate both penal and citizenship regimes.

Hugo Leonardo Rodrigues Santos in Chapter 11 historically locates the criminalization of black and indigenous groups in Brazil, mapping the enduring facets of colonialism and structural violence in contemporary Brazilian criminal justice. Rodrigues Santos illustrates how structural racism engenders contemporary punitive practices. By imposing punishments that disregard their ethnic and cultural characteristics, he shows how criminal law provided an authoritarian inclusion of indigenous people within broader society. The chapter also looks at how Brazilian policing developed in a racially selective manner, which contributes to the recrudescence of the treatment of black people and aggravates the problems of police lethality and mass incarceration. He argues that the foundation of penal practices upon a colonial rationality favours the naturalization of the subalternity of Brazilian black and indigenous peoples.

Part 4 of the collection, 'Mapping Global Connections', includes three chapters that particularly address the travels of ideas and practices of social control across the Global North and South, the metropolis and colonies and ex-colonies, but also beyond that divide. Chapter 12 by Conor O'Reilly explores global policing mobilities through the Atlantic archipelago of Cape Verde, shedding light on how colonial legacies intersect with contemporary policing of global insecurities. It charts how Cape Verdean policing actors are increasingly more than mere passive beneficiaries of foreign security expertise that flows unidirectionally from North to South but rather manifest increasing agency and ambition within regional and transnational policing arrangements. In so doing, Cape Verdean policing disrupts dominant Western-centric assumptions about the unilateral nature and direction of policing and security mobilities. Indeed, whilst ostensibly peripheral to the global policing web—and much neglected within policing scholarship—this chapter spotlights how policing in this West African archipelago is, in fact, highly integrated within transnational networks. It also brings into sharp focus both the postcolonial pitfalls and the emancipatory pathways that are furnished through subaltern engagement with the transnational policing community.

In Chapter 13, Melanie Collard considers the transnational institutionalization and ideological legitimation of torture as a counterinsurgency practice. Through a case study illustrating the transfer of torture techniques from Algeria to Argentina, this chapter explains that torturers were nurtured, trained, and supported by their own and foreign governments. It also argues that France became a 'torture trainer' after its own decolonization wars to expand its imperial interests by maximizing its military influence abroad through the development of militarization and, more specifically, counterinsurgency strategies. Collard posits that this French military *savoir-faire* was not transferred to help Argentina protect its territory from potential threats, but rather served the same main function that it did in Algeria: the repression of its own population. As she shows, this type of state crime, which illustrates the *persistence*—and not the *resurgence*—of torture, is directly related to neocolonial settings.

In a similar vein, Chapter 14 by Lucy Harry highlights the transfer and endurance of colonial patriarchy in the Malaysian penal context. Harry examines the double colonial history of, on the one hand, the death penalty, and on the other, the criminalization of drugs, and explores their convergence and legacy in contemporary Malaysian penal culture. Utilizing the concepts of 'colonial patriarchy' and 'hyper-sentencing', this chapter maps the British colonial legacies of criminalization that have now been reappropriated to bolster nationalist discourses of moral purity; particularly by exposing foreign national women of a socio-economically marginalized status to the remnants of this hostile penalty. Harry alerts us to the intersections of race, class, and gender when locating the legacies of empire and of their contemporary articulations that perpetuate and extend global inequalities.

The last part of the book, 'Moving Forward', looks to the future of these investigations and explores new methods and approaches for decolonizing the criminal question. By focusing on personal experience testimonies as a means to decolonize and empirically show the legacies of empire and colonialism, Rod Earle, Alpa Parmar, and Coretta Phillips in Chapter 15 argue that there is methodological and theoretical merit in seeking to understand contemporary experiences of criminalization through the lens of race and colonialism. While accepting that categorical or aetiological links between colonial dynamics and contemporary experiences of criminal justice may be hard to specify empirically, they suggest that our understanding of the relationship between race and crime can be enriched by connecting personal biography, criminological analysis, and historical colonial experience. Drawing on Althusser's ideas about symptomatic reading (Althusser and Balibar, 1970)—a strategy for interpreting the 'latent content' behind the 'manifest content' of a text—they suggest that if we want to appreciate the magnitude of race and racism in questions of crime, social order, and disorder, a simple or 'innocent' reading of the criminal question is not enough. The specific contribution of this chapter, then, is to supplement and encourage diverse approaches to decolonizing criminology through revisiting empirical studies, developing collaborative analyses to better inform our understanding of otherwise obscured colonial dynamics.

In Chapter 16, Lucia Bracco Bruce's ethnography of the largest women's prison in Peru, Santa Monica, crafts a decolonial, feminist approach to prison research, by focusing on two subaltern, Southern categories. She introduces the term *Ayllu* as an Andean category that may be helpful for understanding women's communitarian organization during imprisonment. Second, she considers the concept of *Mestizaje* as a non-precise identity category arguing that the intertwining of both concepts is helpful for accounting for women prisoners' relational dynamics inside Santa Monica. She contends that a decolonial feminist epistemology may provide a more well-suited theoretical lens through which to analyse punishment and imprisonment in criminalized communities. This perspective, as she shows, highlights the domination processes at play while simultaneously focuses on the subjects' capacity to strategically incorporate and use to their benefit discourses and practices of resistance.

In Chapter 17, Amanda Wilson looks at colonial discourses within therapeutic jurisprudence. Therapeutic jurisprudence advocates have suggested that this field can deliver benefits to criminalized indigenous people because it does without the criminal justice categories and practices of crime and punishment. Taking the most widely recognized example of applied therapeutic jurisprudence—the drug court—as a case study, Wilson draws from observational fieldwork and interview data to show how the structure and operations of these courts perpetuate colonial legacies thus questioning how far such practices can deliver healing for indigenous people.

Kwan-Lamar Blount-Hill and Ahmed Ajil close this part of the collection with a reflection on early career, minority academics' exposure and vulnerability to cognitive imperialism. They document cognitive imperialism's operation in the professional lives of five academics, bolster their stories with support from other narrative works, and specify an ideology that clashes with non-archetypal individuals at the level of identity, perception, experience, and connection. For these young academics, understanding cognitive imperialism at work arises through a process of recognition, reorientation, response, and recovery by seeking reform of an inherently colonized, imperial intellectual space.

Finally, in the edited collection's concluding chapter, we take stock of the discussions and issues raised by the many contributions and then use the reflections raised by them to set an agenda for future efforts in decolonizing the criminal question. More specifically, this chapter outlines a theoretical and methodological framework that aims to take seriously the task of thinking critically about the colonial underpinnings, elements, and legacies of criminological knowledge.

References

Aas, K. F. (2011) 'Victimhood of the National? Denationalizing Sovereignty in Crime Control', in Crawford, A. (ed.) *International and Comparative Criminal Justice and Urban Governance: Convergence and Divergence in Global, National and Local Settings*. Cambridge: Cambridge University Press.

Aas, K. F. (2012) '"The Earth is one but the world is not": Criminological theory and its geopolitical divisions', *Theoretical Criminology*, 16(1), pp. 5–20.

Aas, K. F. (2017) 'Criminology, Punishment, and the State in a Globalized Society', in Liebling, A., Maruna, S., and McAra, L. (eds) *The Oxford Handbook of Criminology*. Oxford: Oxford University Press.

Agozino, B. (2003) *Counter-Colonial Criminology: A Critique of Imperialist Reason*. London: Pluto Press.

Agozino, B. (2004) 'Imperialism, crime and criminology: Towards the decolonisation of criminology', *Crime, Law and Social Change*, 41, pp. 343–358.

Agozino, B. (2010) 'What is criminology? A control-freak discipline!', African Journal of Criminology and Justice Studies, 4(1), pp. 1–20.

Agozino, B. (2018) 'The withering away of the law: An indigenous perspective on the decolonisation of the criminal justice system and criminology', *Journal of Global Indigeneity*, 3(1), pp. 1–22.

Agozino, B. (2021) 'Reparative justice: The final stage of decolonization', *Punishment & Society*, 23(5), pp. 603–620.

Alagia, A. and Codino, R. (2019) *La descolonización de la criminología en América Latina*. Buenos Aires: eDIAR.

Aliverti, A. (2016) 'Researching the Global Criminal Court', in Bosworth, M., Hoyle, C., and Zedner, L. (eds) *Changing Contours of Criminal Justice: Research, Politics and Policy*. Oxford: Oxford University Press.

Aliverti, A., Carvalho, H., Chamberlen, A., and Sozzo, M. (2021) 'Decolonizing the criminal question', *Punishment & Society*, 23(3), pp. 297–316.

Anderson, C., Ifill, M., Adams, E., and Moss, K. (2020) 'Guyana's prisons: Colonial histories of post-colonial challenges', *Howard Journal of Crime and Justice*, 59 (3), pp. 335–349.

Ben-Natan, S. (2021) 'The dual penal empire: Emergency powers and military courts in Palestine/Israel and beyond', *Punishment & Society*, 23(5), pp. 741–763.

Bergalli, R. (1982) *Crítica a la criminología*. Bogota: Temis.

Black, L., Seal, L., and Seemungal, F. (2020) 'Public opinion on crime, punishment and the death penalty in Barbados', *Punishment & Society*, 22(3), pp. 302–320.

Blagg, H. (2008) *Crime, Aboriginality and the Decolonisation of Justice*. Annandale: Federation Press.

Blagg, H. and Thalia, A. (2019) *Decolonising Criminology*. London: Palgrave Macmillan.

Bonilla-Silva, E. (2019) 'Feeling race: Theorizing the racial economy of emotions', *American Sociological Review*, 84, pp. 1–25.

Bosworth, M. (2014) *Inside Immigration Detention*. Oxford: Oxford University Press.

Bosworth, M., Franko, K., and Pickering, S. (2018) 'Punishment, globalization and migration control: "Get them the hell out of here"', *Punishment & Society*, 20, pp. 34–53.

Bracco Bruce, L. (2022) *Prisons in Peru: Ethnographic, Feminist and Decolonial Perspectives*. London: Palgrave.

Brown, M. (2001) 'Race, science and the construction of native criminality in colonial India', *Theoretical Criminology*, 5, pp. 345–368.

Brown, M. (2005) 'Colonial History and Theories of the Present: Some Reflections upon Penal History and Theory', in Godfrey, B. and Dunstall, G. (eds) *Crime and Empire 1840–1940: Criminal Justice in Local and Global Context*. Cullompton: Willan.

Brown, M. (2014) *Penal Power and Colonial Rule*. Abingdon: Routledge.

Brown, M. (2015) 'Postcolonial penality: Liberty and repression in the shadow of independence, India c. 1947', *Theoretical Criminology*, 21(2), pp. 186–208.

Brown, M. (2017) 'The Birth of Criminology in South Asia: 1765–1947', in Shahidullah, S. (ed.) *Crime, Criminal Justice and the Evolving Science of Criminology in South Asia: India, Pakistan and Bangladesh*. London: Palgrave Macmillan.

Brown, M. (2018) 'Southern Criminology in the Post-Colony: More than a "Derivative Discourse"?', in Carrington, K., Hogg, R., Scott, J., and Sozzo, M. (eds) *The Palgrave Handbook of Criminology and the Global South*. London: Palgrave Macmillan.

Brown, M. (2021) 'Truth and method in Southern criminology', *Critical Criminology*, 29, pp. 451–467.

Brown, M., Jadhav, V. K., Raghavan, V., and Sinha, M. (2021) 'Imperial legacies and southern penal spaces: A study of hunting nomads in postcolonial India', *Punishment & Society*, 23(5), pp. 675–696.

Caimari, L. and Sozzo, M. (2017) (eds) *Historia de la Cuestión Criminal en América Latina*. Rosario: Prohistoria.

Cain, M. (2000) 'Orientalism, occidentalism and the sociology of crime', *British Journal of Criminology*, 40, pp. 239–260.

Carrington, K. and Hogg, R. (2017) 'Deconstructing *criminology's origin stories*', *Asian Journal of Criminology*, 12(3), pp. 181–197.

Carrington, K., Hogg, R., and Sozzo, M. (2016) 'Southern criminology', *British Journal of Criminology*, 56, pp. 1–20.

Carrington, K., Hogg, R., Scott, J., and Sozzo, M. (eds) (2018) *The Palgrave Handbook of Criminology and the Global South*. London: Palgrave.

Carrington, K., Hogg, R., Scott, J., Sozzo, M., and Walters, R. (2019) *Southern Criminology*. New York: Routledge.

Cavalcanti, R. (2020) *A Southern Criminology of Violence, Youth and Policing. Governing Insecurity in Brazil*. London: Routledge.

Chartrand, V. (2019) 'Unsettled times: Indigenous incarceration and the links between colonialism and the penitentiary in Canada', *Canadian Journal of Criminology and Criminal Justice*, 61(3), pp. 67–89.

Ciocchini, P. and Greener, J. (2021) 'Mapping the pains of neocolonialism: A critical elaboration of Southern criminology', *British Journal of Criminology*, 61(6), pp. 1612–1629.

Cohen, S. (1982) 'Western crime control models in the third world: Benign of malignant?', *Research in Law, Deviance and Social Control*, 4, pp. 85–119.

Comaroff, J. and Comaroff, J. (2012a) Theory from the South: Or, how Euro-America is Evolving Toward Africa. Abingdon: Routledge.

Comaroff, J. and Comaroff, J. (2012b) 'Theory from the South: Or, how Euro-America is evolving toward Africa', *Anthropological Forum*, 22, pp. 113–131.

Cunneen, C. (2011) 'Postcolonial Perspectives in Criminology', in Bosworth, M. and Hoyle, C. (eds) *What is Criminology?* Oxford: Oxford University Press.

Cunneen, C. (2018a) 'Indigenous Challenges for Southern Criminology', in Carrington, K., Hogg, R., Scott, J., and Sozzo, M. (eds) *Palgrave Handbook on Criminology and the Global South*. London: Palgrave Macmillan.

Cunneen, C. (2018b) 'Sentencing, punishment and indigenous people in Australia', *Journal of Global Indigeneity*, 3(1), pp. 1–22.

Cunneen, C. and Tauri, J. (2017) *Indigenous Criminology*. Bristol: Policy Press.

Darke, S. and Phoenix Khan, O. (2021) 'Coloniality, just war & carceral injustice in Brazil', *Punishment & Society*, 23(5), pp. 723–740.

Davis A. P. and Gibson-Light, M. (2020) 'Difference and punishment: Ethno-political exclusion, colonial institutional legacies, and incarceration', *Punishment & Society*, 22(1), pp. 3–27.

De Noronha, L. (2019) 'Deportation, racism and multi-status Britain: Immigration control and the production of race in the present', *Ethnic and Racial Studies*, 42(14), pp. 2413–2430.

Dimou, E. (2021) 'Decolonizing Southern criminology: What can the "decolonial option" tell us about the modern/colonial foundations of criminology', *Critical Criminology*, 29, pp. 431–450.

Evans, J. (2021) 'Penal nationalism in the settler colony: On the construction and maintenance of "national whiteness~" in settler Canada', *Punishment & Society*, 23(4), pp. 515–535.

Faraldo Cabana, P. (2018) 'Research Excellence and Anglophone Dominance: The Case of Law, Criminology and Social Science', in Carrington, K., Hogg, R., Scott, J., and Sozzo, M. (eds) *The Palgrave Handbook of Criminology and the Global South*. London: Palgrave Macmillan.

Faraldo Cabana, P. and Lamela, E. (2019) 'How international are the top international journals of criminology and criminal justice?', *European Journal on Criminal Policy and Research*, 27, pp. 151–174. Fonseca, D. S. (2018a) 'Punishment at the Margins: Groundwork for a Revisited Sociology of Punishment', in Carrington, K., Hogg, R., Scott, J., and Sozzo, M. (eds) *The Palgrave Handbook of Criminology and the Global South*. London: Palgrave Macmillan.

Fonseca, D. S. (2018b) 'Reimagining the sociology of punishment through the global south: Postcolonial social control and modernization discontents', *Punishment & Society*, 20(1), pp. 54–72.

Garcia, N. and Sozzo, N. (forthcoming) 'For a "marginal criminological realism". Zaffaroni and the birth of a critical perspective on the criminal question from the Global South', *Justice, Power and Resistance*.

Gilroy, P. (2003) 'After the Great White Error ... The Great Black Mirage', in Moore, D., Kosek, J., and Pandian, A. (eds) *Race, Nature, and the Politics of Difference*. Durham, NC: Duke University Press.

Hogg. R. and Brown, D. (2018) 'Rethinking Penal Modernism from the Global South: The case of Convict Transportation to Australia', in Carrington, K., Hogg, R., Scott, J., and Sozzo, M. (eds) *The Palgrave Handbook of Criminology and the Global South*. London: Palgrave Macmillan.

Lacey, N. and Zedner, L. (2017) 'Criminalization: Historical, Legal, and Criminological Perspectives' in Liebling, A., Maruna, S., and McAra, L. (eds) *The Oxford Handbook of Criminology*. Oxford: Oxford University Press.

Lee, M. and Laidler, K. J. (2013) 'Doing criminology from the periphery: Crime and punishment in Asia', *Theoretical Criminology*, 17(2), pp. 141–157.

Loader, I. and Sparks, R. (2011) *Public Criminology?* London: Sage.

Loader, I. and Sparks, R. (2013) 'Knowledge Politics and Penal Politics in Europe', in Daems, T., Van Zyl Smit, D., and Snacken, S. (eds) *European Penology?* Oxford: Hart Publishing.

Medina, J. (2011) 'Doing Criminology in the "Semi-Periphery" and the "Periphery"', in Arberet, R., Smith, C. J., and Zhang, S. X. (eds) *Routledge Handbook of International Criminology*. New York: Routledge.

Melossi, D., Sozzo, M., and Sparks, R. (2011) 'Introduction. Criminal Questions: Cultural Embeddedness and Diffusion', in Melossi, D., Sozzo, M., and Sparks, C. (eds) *Travels of the Criminal Question. Cultural Embeddedness and Diffusion*. Oxford: Hart Publishing.

Moosavi, L. (2019a) 'A friendly critique of "Asian criminology" and "Southern criminology"', *British Journal of Criminology*, 59(2), pp. 257–275.

Moosavi, L. (2019b) 'Decolonising criminology: Syed Hussein Alatas on crimes of the powerful', *Critical Criminology*, 27(2), pp. 229–242.

Morrison, W. (2006) *Criminology, Civilisation and the New World Order*. Abingdon: Routledge.

Parmar, A. (2016) 'Intersectionality, British criminology and race: Are we there yet?', *Theoretical Criminology*, 21(1), pp. 35–45.

Parmar, A., Earle, R., and Phillips, C. (2022) 'Seeing is believing: How the layering of race is obscured by "white epistemologies" in the criminal justice field', *Journal of Criminal Justice Education*, 33(2), pp. 289–306.

Pavarini, M. (2006) '¿Vale la pena salvar a al criminología?', in Sozzo, M. (ed.) *Reconstruyendo las criminologías críticas*. Buenos Aires: Ad-Hoc.

Pfingst, A. and Kimari, W. (2021) 'Carcerality and the legacies of settler colonial punishment in Nairobi', *Punishment & Society*, 23(5), pp. 697–722.

Phillips, C. (2012) *The Multicultural Prison. Ethnicity, Masculinity, and Social Relations among Prisoners*. Oxford: Oxford University Press.

Phillips, C., Earle, R., Parmar, A., and Smith, D. (2020) 'Dear British criminology: Where has all the race and racism gone?', *Theoretical Criminology*, 24, pp. 427–446.

Pires, A. (2006) 'Consideraciones preliminares para una teoría del crimen como objeto paradojal', in Sozzo, M. (ed.) *Reconstruyendo las criminologías críticas*. Buenos Aires: Ad-Hoc.

Pitch, T. (1995) *Limited Responsibilities*. London: Routledge.

Pitch, T. (2022) 'Introduzione', in Pitch, T. (ed.) *Devianza e Questione Criminale*. Rome: Carocci.

Porter, A. (2016) 'Decolonizing policing: Indigenous patrols, counter-policing and safety', *Theoretical Criminology*, 20(4), pp. 548–565. Rodriguez Goyes, D. (2018) 'Green Criminology as a Decolonial Tool: A Stereoscope of Environmental Harm', in Carrington, K., Hogg, R., Scott, J., and Sozzo, M. (eds) *The Palgrave Handbook of Criminology and the Global South*. London: Palgrave Macmillan.

Rodriguez Goyes, D. (2019) *A Southern Green Criminology: Science Against Ecological Discrimination*. Bingley: Emerald.

Saleh-Hanna, V. (ed.) (2008) *Colonial Systems of Control: Criminal Justice in Nigeria*. Ottawa: University of Ottawa Press.

Sekimoto, S. (2018) 'Race and the senses: Toward articulating the sensory apparatus of race', *Critical Philosophy of Race*, 6(1), pp. 82–100.

Sozzo, M. (2006) '"Tradutore Traditore": Traducción, Importación Cultural e Historia del Presente de la Criminología en América Latina', in Sozzo, M. (ed.) *Reconstruyendo las criminologías críticas*. Buenos Aires: Ad-Hoc.

Sozzo, M. (2009) 'Introducción', in Sozzo, M. (ed.) *Historia de la Cuestión Criminal en Argentina*. Buenos Aires: Editores del Puerto.

Sozzo, M. (2011) 'Cultural Travels and Crime Prevention in Argentina', in Melossi, D., Sozzo, M., and Sparks, C. (eds) *Travels of the Criminal Question: Cultural Embeddedness and Diffusion*. Oxford: Hart Publishing.

Sozzo, M. (2021) 'Public and Southern Criminologies: A Possible Encounter', in Daems, T. and Pleysier, S. (eds) *Criminology and Democratic Politics*. New York: Routledge.

Sparks, R. (2021) 'What Are We Going to Do Now? Criminology and Democratic Politics All Over Again', in Daems, T. and Pleysier, S. (eds) *Criminology and Democratic Politics*. New York: Routledge.

Stambøl, E. M. (2021) 'Neo-colonial penality? Travelling penal power and contingent sovereignty', *Punishment and Society*, 23(4), pp. 536–556.

Stoler, A. (1995) *Race and the Education of Desire: Foucault's History of Sexuality and the Colonial Order of Things*. Durham, NC: Duke University Press.

Stoler, A. (2016) *Duress: Imperial Durabilities in Our Times*. Durham, NC: Duke University Press.

Travers, M. (2019) 'The idea of a Southern criminology', *International Journal of Comparative and Applied Criminal Justice*, 43(1), pp. 1–12.

Zaffaroni, E. R. (1988) *Criminologia, aproximación desde un margen*. Bogota: Temis.

Zaffaroni, E. R. (1989) *En busca de las penas perdidas*. Buenos Aires: Ediar.

Zaffaroni, E. R. (2012 *La cuestión criminal*. Buenos Aires: Planeta.

Zaffaroni, E. R. (2022) *Colonialismo y derechos humanos: Un ahistoria criminal del mundo*. Madrid: Taurus.

Zaffaroni, E. R. and Codino, R. (2015) 'Notas para una criminología del sur', *Revista de Derecho Penal y Criminologia*, V(11), pp. 17–27.

Zedner, L. (2003) 'Useful Knowledge? Debating the Role of Criminology in Post-War Britain', in Zedner, L. and Ashworth, A. (eds) *The Criminological Foundations of Penal Policy: Essays in Honour of Roger Hood*. Oxford: Oxford University Press.

PART 1
UNSETTLING CONCEPTS AND PERSPECTIVES

1
Decoloniality, Abolitionism, and the Disruption of Penal Power

Chris Cunneen

Introduction

This chapter explores the coloniality of power as it is exercised through the material practices, discourses, and underlying epistemological assumptions of the criminal legal system and sets out the necessity for and potential parameters for decolonizing criminology. In short, the coloniality of power refers to the way in which colonial relationships are reproduced in the contemporary world, and more specifically in the context of this chapter through the various laws, institutional policies, and practices of the criminal legal system. The coloniality of power begs the question of decoloniality: how we understand, contribute to, and participate in processes for decolonization. More precisely, it confronts us with the question of whether criminology can contribute to this process. Does it have a role in subverting the coloniality of power? Or is it so intellectually and politically compromised that the best we can hope for is that it is either rendered irrelevant, or that its more progressive and critical insights can be incorporated into the broader political and theoretical project of decoloniality?

This chapter is contextualized by the global uprising in 2020 against police violence, oppression, and racism. It is contextualized by the resurgence in the ideas and politics of abolitionism; that is, penal abolitionism in its broadest sense to include the prison, other systems of carcerality, and the police and security forces. It is a struggle which has been foregrounded in the US by the Black Lives Matter (BLM) movement and a range of calls, including for the abolition of the prison industrial complex and to 'Defund the Police' (Kaba, 2021; Davis et al., 2022). However, the popular challenge to police violence and unaccountability extended in various forms across most parts of the world (Cunneen, forthcoming). An important linkage for the argument of this chapter is the connection between the political and intellectual programmes of abolitionism and decoloniality. Indeed, it can be argued that the historical roots of both are linked to the struggle against slavery and colonial subjugation and dispossession. It is an argument that recognizes that the foundations of the contemporary institutions of penal power are found in the interplay between the centre and periphery of the colonial experience. For Mignolo (2011, p. 16), the colonial matrix of power is the 'very foundational structure of Western civilization', and it is also a defining feature of the colonized to the extent that the colonial encounter altered and reconstituted colonized societies internally and externally into global systems under imperialism. Further, and fundamental to the historical and contemporary experiences of penal power, the

Chris Cunneen, *Decoloniality, Abolitionism, and the Disruption of Penal Power* In: *Decolonizing the Criminal Question.*
Edited by: Ana Aliverti, Henrique Carvalho, Anastasia Chamberlen, and Máximo Sozzo, Oxford University Press.
 DOI: 10.1093/oso/9780192899002.003.0002

modern idea of 'race' was founded in the colonial encounter which codified the differences between the colonized and the colonizer into 'a natural situation' of biological inferiority and superiority (Quijano, 2000, p. 533). The other significant change that emerged through the colonial encounter was the control of labour based on racial division and determined by capital production for an emerging world market (Quijano, 2000, pp. 535–536). Slavery and forced labour were core to the accumulation of capital, and specifically for indigenous peoples, dispossession from their lands was the 'irreducible element' of settler colonialism (Wolfe, 2006, p. 388).

There are three broad ideas which underpin this chapter and provide a structure to the analysis. The first is the importance of understanding colonialism and the coloniality of power. The modern state is a colonial state or, in Mignolo's (2011; 2017) terms, coloniality is constitutive of modernity. It is argued that a core site for the operation of colonial power is (and historically has been) the law and criminal legal systems of the colonizer—which have remained within both settler colonial societies and former colonies post empire. Central to this process has been the racialization of the colonized subject. The second is the importance of subaltern knowledges, epistemologies, and methodologies, and how criminal justice and criminology have failed to move beyond imperialist and colonialist ways of representing and understanding the world. The final section of the chapter considers whether and what role criminology might play in the strategies for a decolonial abolitionist activism.

The argument is not meant to be prescriptive: either theoretically or in relation to the substantive matters which are identified. As decolonial, postcolonial, abolitionist, and indigenous critiques of crime and the meaning of justice take hold more firmly in our understanding of the way police and security forces, the judiciary, and carceral systems operate, others will undoubtedly offer differing theoretical insights and set different priorities for research and political action. To a significant extent, our praxis stems from the combination of theory, experience, and engagement, and mine has been influenced by being a non-indigenous white male living in a settler colonial society and working with First Nations individuals, communities, and organizations. To paraphrase Angela Davis and her colleagues (Davis et al., 2022, pp. xiii–xiv), we should always question particular accounts, narratives, and renditions and seek to expand dialogue, praxis, and reflection. Further, the praxis of decolonialism cannot be universally prescribed and will be differentiated along a range of axes, determined by historical and contemporary contingencies. For example, Coulthard has argued that the theory and practice of indigenous anticolonialism:

> … is best understood as a struggle primarily inspired by and oriented around *the question of land*—a struggle not only *for* land in the material sense, but also deeply *informed* by what the land *as system of reciprocal relations and obligations* can teach us about living our lives in relation to one another and the natural world in nondominating and nonexploitative terms.
>
> (Coulthard, 2014, p. 13)

Indeed, the indigenous struggle over land and resources exposes them to the violence of police and penal power globally from, for example, North America (Estes et al., 2021) to Brazil (Carvalho et al., 2021) to India (Kakati, 2021).

Further, Coulthard's statement raises the point that simple distinctions between the material and the epistemic do not hold—they are deeply intertwined for both colonial systems of power and the resistance of the colonized. The material practices of colonial violence, for example, expressed and reconstituted racialized hierarchies and epistemic 'truths' about biological and cultural differences, as do contemporary systems of punishment, risk, and penal power where algorithms and risk-based technologies reproduce the racialized subject as non-conforming and dangerous (Ugwudike, 2020). Conversely the calls to decolonize police and penal institutions are both material and epistemic—that is, the need to fundamentally change systems of power and reimagine public safety through an ethic and practice of community solidarity.

Global State Violence and Unknowing Criminology

Goenpul scholar Aileen Moreton-Robinson (2015, p. xi) has noted that, 'It takes a great deal of work to maintain Canada, the United States, Hawai'i, New Zealand and Australia as white possessions. The regulatory mechanisms of these nation states are extremely busy reaffirming and reproducing this possessiveness.' The same could be said of various regimes across the world where indigenous, black, brown, and other racialized peoples continue to be oppressed. It is this busy work of criminal legal institutions that is of concern to us here. The global nature of state violence has been a core driver of contemporary protest movements. Police and prison officers can kill the racialized and criminalized subject at will with little or no fear of repercussions. They can have their actions captured on video and broadcast across the globe, and yet still the legal system of the colonial state manages to explain that the force was reasonable and necessary in the circumstances, the shooting was justified, or the cause of death was positional asphyxia as if that was somehow unrelated to the actions of the police or prison guards kneeling on a person's throat.

Decolonialism centres state violence. For most of the world's population, policing, courts, and prisons have been historically synonymous with colonial state violence and are still experienced as violent enterprises today. Criminalization and differing forms of carcerality were and are key to the maintenance of colonial power. As Fanon so clearly articulated, colonialism is a divided world built on violence. 'The dividing line, the frontiers are shown by barracks and police stations. In the colonies it is the policeman and the soldier who are the official, instituted go-betweens, the spokesmen of the settler and his rule of oppression' (1967, p. 29). Colonial violence drew no more than a 'shrug of the shoulders' in the metropolitan centres of empire (Memmi, 1965, p. 130; Cesaire, 1972). Modern penality developed in the context of colonialism—what has been referred to as penal colonialism (Saleh-Hanna, 2008) and a penal/colonial complex (Cunneen et al., 2013). A decolonial perspective also enables appreciation of the historical foundations of criminological knowledge as part of the colonialist project (Agozino, 2003; Morrison, 2006) and deepens our understanding that the modern political state developed through the systematic abuse of peoples at the hands of state *justice* institutions.

However, as important as it is to understand the historical foundations of colonial violence, the overwhelming levels of contemporary state violence completely unhinge the conceptual and explanatory frames of most criminologists. The international protests over police violence in mid-2020 highlighted the profound levels of violent repression people face on a global scale. In opposition to the oppressive apparatus of the state are the multiple and intersecting forms of people's resistance by black, indigenous, people of colour, women, disability activists, LGBTQI organizations, and others. Demonstrations around the world acknowledged the death of George Floyd in the US, but they were more importantly part of ongoing domestic protest movements against state violence. In Africa, Asia, Latin America, North America, Australasia, Europe, and Britain, protests against police killings and deaths in custody have been common (Cunneen, forthcoming). There were a set of commonalities across many countries, which spanned the Global North and South:

- the routine nature of lethal police violence, torture, and intimidation;
- the failure of systems of state accountability—although there might be differences in the excesses of violence in different countries, police impunity is a global issue;
- the histories of colonialism, slavery, racism, and indigenous dispossession are fundamental to understanding the contemporary targets of police violence;
- the failure to 'decolonize' policing and penal institutions post 1945 independence, particularly in Africa and South Asia, and in Latin America after dictatorships;
- the role of policing and penal powers in maintaining structural inequalities which were exacerbated by the Covid-19 pandemic (e.g. the Nigerian National Human Rights Commission reported that more people were killed by the police than by Covid-19 in the first few months of the lockdown in 2020);
- the hypocrisy of governments from Africa, India, Australia, and elsewhere condemning the death of George Floyd while ignoring the hundreds of deaths by police and security forces within their own countries.

The colonial underpinnings of police violence and its ubiquitous nature in the contemporary world throws into question criminological enterprises, particularly in 'police studies'.

Historians have argued that the racist ideologies underpinning colonialism and the motive of ruthless economic exploitation meant that the ideas of police accountability, legitimacy, and popular consent were irrelevant (e.g. Tankebe, 2008; Killingray, 1991). Colonial policing was defined by wide discretionary powers and an absence of accountability. In Tankebe's memorable words, to speak of colonial policing and police legitimacy or policing by consent is a 'contradiction in terms; it is oxymoronic' (2008, p. 74). Given policing's foundational role in the colonial project, the question is whether policing as we know it can ever be 'decolonized' without being fundamentally reimagined. Certainly, there are many abolitionists who would dispute the possibility of reforming the police (Davis et al., 2022; Anti-Security Collective, 2021; Kaba, 2021; Neocleous, 2021; Maher, 2021; Schrader, 2019; Vitale, 2017). The abolitionist argument is that liberal reforms of the police have continually failed and more of the same will not alter their fundamental role. The police cannot be reformed—indeed, liberal reforms often strengthen the institution.

However, the precise relationship between abolitionism and decolonialism develops differently in diverse historical and contemporary contexts, as shown in the three examples which follow. In South Africa, abolition is framed in the historical context of apartheid and the policing and penal system that enforced racism. Contemporary policing continues to enforce a racial hierarchy of white supremacy, relying on militarized repressive force. As in many other African countries, policing has remained largely caught within pre-independence, colonial structures which rely on violent oppression (CopsAreFlops, n.d.; McMichael, 2016). As argued elsewhere, in Australia Aboriginal resistance to settler colonialism is simultaneously anti-colonial and abolitionist. It directly challenges settler colonial definitions of crime, policing, punishment, law, and sovereignty and exposes the illegitimate foundations of the Australian nation-state—invasion forged under a banner of *terra nullius*, land theft, and genocide (Porter, 2019). In the US, the roots of abolitionism are in the demise of slavery, the work of W. E. B. Du Bois and his concept of abolition democracy. Abolition democracy called for a more expansive programme than simply abolishing the modern colonial practice of slavery, it was aimed at ensuring social democracy and abolishing the conditions and institutions that enabled slavery—an institutional legacy that is continued today through policing and carceral systems (Davis, 2005). Abolitionism in the US is a movement that has recognized anti-colonialism as a core domestic and international strategy from Du Bois to the Black Panther Party to the contemporary abolitionist movement (Davis et al., 2022).

Many criminologists have played a role in bolstering oppressive criminal justice institutions. It has been noted in relation to policing:

> The range of laughably predictable questions that they (criminologists) ask: what increases police efficiency, what are the right police numbers, what makes for police professionalism, what will improve police performance, how might the police best relate to the public ... ? Each question leads in its own way to what is, for police science and criminology, the ultimate question: how can we make the police work best? The necessity of the police power is taken for granted; all that remains is for a doffing of scholarly caps and an offering of the very support and knowledge on which the police power insists.
>
> (Anti-Security Collective, 2021, p. 2)

In contrast to criminology's role as a handmaiden of police and penal power, we might envisage a decolonial criminology focused on disrupting state violence. For all the never tiring academic work on policing, how much of it challenges state violence? How much has focused, for example, on police killings in the Philippines—now the subject of an International Criminal Court investigation for crimes against humanity (ICC, 2021); or Brazil—where the UN High Commissioner for Human Rights called for an independent investigation of a recent police massacre (Neuman, 2021); or in Venezuela—where the civilian death rate through police fatal violence is higher than the *general* homicide rate in the vast majority of countries of the world (Centro de Investigación y Docencia Económicas, 2019, p. 167); or the routine use of torture by police in India—where the Chief Justice of India recently referred to the police as the most significant threat in the country to human rights and bodily integrity (Dhillon, 2021)?

Criminological Innocence

Connected to the silences and absences noted earlier, there is a disavowal (or repudiation) of colonialism which permeates political and intellectual life and is reproduced endlessly in academic work on crime and justice—policing being but one example. As Yuin scholar Amanda Porter has noted:

> Despite centuries of colonisation and imperialism, despite deep structural inequalities, racial discrimination and high rates of victimisation and over-representation in the criminal and juvenile justice systems as well as deaths in police and prison custody, much criminology continues to operate without an acknowledgement of colonialism and its effects.
>
> (Porter, 2019, p. 124)

For decolonial and critical scholars the discussion *begins* with an understanding of colonialism and its long-term outcomes. However, the argument here seeks to push the matter beyond the recognition of colonialism. Indeed, in what might appear as something of a paradox, it is not that colonialism is simply unknown to criminology, it is rather that its explanatory value and political importance is vigorously denied (Agozino, 2003). The disavowal of colonization in relation to indigenous, formerly colonized, and enslaved peoples is not a matter of a forgotten past—it is well remembered by those communities who were and are subjected to its ongoing practices. However, for the colonizers and the elites that profit from the exploitative arrangements in 'former colonies', it is in fact an active process of 'unknowing' and ignorance:

> This act of ignoring is aggressively made and reproduced ... in ways that conform [to] the social relations and economies of the here and now. Colonial unknowing endeavours to render unintelligible the entanglements of racialization and colonization ... attributing finality to events of conquest and dispossession.
>
> (Vimalassery et al., 2016, p. 1)

For example, a leading criminologist in Australia explains that First Nations' mass incarceration is simply the result of indigenous criminal offending (Weatherburn, 2014). He argues that colonization and dispossession are only of historical interest and have no place in explaining contemporary indigenous crime and over-representation in prison (2014, p. 150); similarly, the incidence of institutional racism is denied as an explanation for indigenous contact with the criminal legal system (2014, pp. 41–54, 150). Furthermore, according to Weatherburn, indigenous knowledges are unimportant for explaining the mass imprisonment of First Nations people which is 'entirely amenable to explanation in conventional scientific or western terms' (2014, p. 65). This denial of the ongoing effects of colonialism contrasts directly with and *silences* the work of black, First Nations, and other minoritized academics and activists that place the long-term colonial experience at the centre of explaining the contemporary position of indigenous and racialized peoples in (settler) colonial states (e.g. Rodriguez,

2019; Porter, 2019; Dunbar-Ortiz, 2014; Tauri, 2014; Davis, 1998). As Vimalassery and colleagues go on to say:

> This needing not to know is requisite to the pretence of white innocence. It is both the privileged position of not being the target of racism and colonial dispossession and benefitting from the circumstances that are themselves sustained through the disavowal of racism and colonial dispossession.
>
> (Vimalassery et al., 2016, p. 2)

The benefits for criminologists of *not knowing* have been manifold. At the very least, they can go on asking 'laughably predictable questions' and continue to arrive at equally predictable answers, while ensuring their privileged position within the criminological enterprise is guaranteed.

What is of specific importance for developing decolonial and abolitionist critiques is the distinctive manner through which dispossession, racialization, and colonial unknowing (or innocence) are instantiated and materially reproduced through criminal legal policies and practices. Although it has been stated often enough, talking about 'race' is complex to the extent that it has no objective, inherent, or fixed quality (Delgado and Stefancic, 2007). The concept of *racialization* usefully directs attention to the social, political, economic, and legal processes through which race is made meaningful (Murji and Solomos, 2005, p. 3). The criminal legal system is an essential site that makes 'race' intelligible: it produces racialized outcomes both through social practices and the production of knowledge that define the behaviours and pathologies of the racialized Other and which justify criminalization. While crunching numbers and determining correlations, the criminologist carries on with the colonizer's task to 'paint the native as a sort of quintessence of evil . . . the enemy of values . . . the absolute evil . . . corrosive . . . destroying . . . disfiguring' (Fanon, 1967, pp. 31–32).

One example of these racializing processes can be seen in the use of various risk-based algorithmic and other assessment tools. Risk assessment technologies remove the history and contemporary impact of colonialism and reduce the world of racialized oppression to a series of preconceived, measurable, and individual dysfunctions (Ugwudike, 2020). At the same time, risk assessment technologies embody and privilege assumptions about whiteness and class—particularly in the expectations of what constitutes the law-abiding, socially conforming, and economically engaged citizen (Cunneen, 2020). The technologies produce and maintain white innocence through their appeal to neutral decision-making and scientific objectivity, in much the same way as Weatherburn's account discussed earlier insists on the absolute primacy of 'conventional scientific or western terms' (note how the two terms are conflated). In other words, the knowledge of the oppressed is irrelevant to their oppression and what to do about it. Just as importantly, the appeal to science relieves the colonizer of responsibility—their innocence is maintained. Although the modalities and processes of racism have changed over the decades, an abiding characteristic of colonial power has been the continuing creation of the inferiority of the colonial subject—their lack of deservedness to be treated as equal.

The 'unknowing' of colonialism leaves criminology as a discipline with only individualized deficit-based accounts of dysfunction—crime prone, drug addicted, incompetent parent, poorly educated, work-shy, with cognitive deficits, and so on. We are left with criminology's *dysfunctional native*. In this situation, the requirement for remedial and carceral interventions by the state is justified. The historic civilizing mission of the colonizer finds expression today, for example, in cognitive behavioural therapy programmes within the cages of the prison. Even in those accounts that might recognize that criminalization is connected to social disadvantage there is little appreciation that contemporary poverty, chronic health issues, overcrowded housing, imprisonment, lower life expectancies, and poor educational outcomes were *created* through policies of enslavement, dispossession, and forced labour and are *maintained* through institutionalized racism. Colonialism, by definition, has been a constant process of immiseration for the many, and the generation of wealth and privilege for the few.

Decolonial Knowledges

If criminology as a discipline and criminal 'justice' as a state ideology and practice developed within the confines of colonialism, then decentring Eurocentric approaches to crime and crime control and their embeddedness within associated intellectual and popular discourses is imperative. The denial and attempted eradication of the voice of the colonized is captured in Spivak's (1988) concept of *epistemic violence* and Santos's (2007) concept of *epistemicide*. Epistemic violence and epistemicide are the denial of a position from which the subaltern, the marginalized, and the oppressed can speak and the active obliteration of different ways of knowing. Like the forceful 'unknowing' of colonialism, the denial of other ways of speaking is an exercise in the coloniality of power. It establishes the limits of what 'can count as evidence, proof, or possibility' (Vimalassery et al., 2016, p. 2).

Challenging the epistemological privilege of Eurocentric understandings of crime decentres primary criminological concepts. The answers to the questions of what is crime and who is criminal are dependent on positionality. For people who are the victims of genocide, dispossessed of their lands and their livelihoods and forced into slavery, the answer to these questions is not self-evidently those who are arrested, convicted in the courts, and imprisoned by the state. A decolonial lens must break hegemonic constructions of victimization and criminalization by re-centring the worldviews, understandings, and responses of the colonized. For criminology, there are imperatives for the decolonization *of* research, as well as research *for* decolonization. The former is a challenge to dominant research methods: stretching from fundamental questions of research ethics through to ways of thinking about and describing the world and the value we place on certain forms of evidence and knowledge. Research *for* decolonization requires us to re-evaluate and address the question, *for whom* are we doing research? This is an old question for criminology, and we need to be asking it again, more so than ever. Positivist claims of the scientific neutrality of the researcher hold little value in a world where mass imprisonment is targeted against racialized minorities and state killings go unanswered. As Fanon succinctly stated, 'for the native, objectivity is always directed against him' (1967, p. 61).

The privileging of Western epistemological claims and cultural assumptions concerning the validity of knowledge and truth are deeply embedded in criminological theory and practice. For example, dominant approaches to victimology are limited in understanding the complex forms by which the coloniality of justice continues to impact on black, indigenous, and racialized communities, in regard to both victims and offenders. Alternatively, a critical decolonial lens can disrupt hegemonic constructions of victimization and criminalization by re-centring subaltern understandings and responses. One example relates to domestic violence, where mainstream crime control policies and initiatives have proved deficient in protecting indigenous, black, and other racialized women and have material effects of greater imprisonment of both minoritized men and women. Decolonial, abolitionist, and First Nations women have argued strongly against 'carceral feminists' who seek to expand the criminal legal system (Davis et al., 2022). The decentring of Eurocentric approaches requires challenging the hegemonies of knowledge production and their material impact. Legal, criminological, and various statistical accounts continue to construct and legitimize particular forms of knowledge about the racialized Other. These accounts authorize the knowledge holders (who rarely come from the class and/or minoritized group under investigation) and privilege their interpretation of the world and their prescriptions for intervention, social engineering, and compliance. Reworking a phrase from C. Wright Mills (1963 [1943]), these are the 'racial and class pathologists' who uncritically accept existing social structures, lack historical awareness, and rake over social problems constructed within narrowly defined frameworks, bolstered by an array of assessment technologies and 'what works' programmes (which, given ever increasing police personnel, high recidivism rates, more prisons, and burgeoning prison populations, do not appear to work very well at all unless the goal is a more expansive carceral state).

In the context of coloniality, power, and knowledge, there is a contrast between the prevailing dominant theories of colonial penality and the language that dominates decolonial approaches. On the one side, there are the various professionalized and individualized behaviour modification programmes and risk/need paradigms in offender management which dominate state criminal justice interventions, and which reproduce narrowly defined individual 'deficits' (Ward and Maruna, 2007). These deficit approaches ultimately blame the individual for their failings and punish them accordingly, while disavowing the systems of classed, raced, gendered, and ableist oppression which create the definitions of and conditions for 'crime'. In contrast, decolonial approaches use concepts such as healing, Ubuntu, reparation, and restorative and transformative justice. I am not suggesting that these five concepts are all the same—they are not. For example, some activists draw distinctions in meaning between restorative and transformative justice (Kaba, 2021). However, they are broadly underpinned by a different motivation of repairing harm compared to the institutional demands for retribution and punishment. The process of change is both individual and collective: the process relies on inter-relationality rather than individualism, and enables communities to respond holistically to harm; and it brings into account the needs of victims, offenders, and the community affected by harm to repair the effects of trauma in its various individual, structural, and historical manifestations.

These processes overturn the material practices and discursive concepts that surround the 'responsible' penal or carceral subject and underpin contemporary approaches to punishment. It recognizes that punishment is not the resolution of harm. Rather than punishing and imprisoning individuals, these approaches to justice seek to transform the conditions that make harm possible. Individual harms and wrongs are placed within a context of collective experiences (e.g. racism, institutional violence, dispossession, forced removal) and are thus connected to the process of decolonization. By affirming a collective understanding of individual experience, it directly opens the door to seeing the historical, structural, and material conditions of trauma and oppression as they impact on the life experiences of people, both individually and collectively.

In this discussion of decolonial knowledges and the decentring of Eurocentric approaches, another area to consider is the modes of redefinition and resistance that destabilize the taken-for-granted validity and truth claims of criminology (and, indeed, law and social science research more generally). For example, there is a long history of the use by indigenous, black, and other racialized and minoritized communities of visual and performative art in challenging colonialism and its representations. Consideration of these 'arts of resistance' opens up a decolonizing politics, a different way of seeing, being, and understanding in a world deeply structured by colonial effects (Cunneen, 2017). This counter-vision is the affirmation of subaltern sovereignty: acts of survival in the face of ontological denial and physical genocide. Perhaps more prosaically, these ways of knowing and representing the world challenge the positivist underpinnings of criminology and related disciplines and motivate our thoughts to the *value* we attach to different types of knowledge which challenge criminological certainties.

Strategies for Decolonial Activism

This chapter has argued the necessity for, and the challenges facing, decolonialism in the context of policing and penal power. It has repeatedly pointed to the compromised position of criminology. It is not surprising that questioning the definitions of crime, the right to punish, kill, and cage people, and the nature and legitimacy of state power strongly inflect the political demands of indigenous, black, and other racialized communities in colonial states. There are also clear connections with an abolitionist agenda. Abolitionists and colonized and minoritized peoples challenge the state's right to punish, and deny the efficacy of state criminal justice systems in achieving community safety. Indeed, the role of state-centred policing and punishment is about something quite different: it is a system of violent control of poor, marginalized, racialized, and colonized peoples. Criminalization and incarceration are seen as devastating processes that cause further individual, family, and community disintegration. As I have argued elsewhere (Cunneen, 2021), abolitionist, indigenous, black, and decolonial critiques of policing, the prison, and punishment emerge from a radical *disbelief* in the ability of colonial state systems of policing and penality to achieve positive long-term changes for either individuals or communities. Disbelief in colonizer justice systems as fair, reformatory, or rehabilitative is hardly surprising given that colonized peoples have had first-hand experience over many generations of destructive, violent, and deadly intervention by various carceral agents and institutions: police, courts, prisons, welfare workers, and 'Native' managers and agents.

Decolonialism challenges core criminological concepts, including our understandings of legitimacy and consent, crime, victimization, violence, rehabilitation, and risk, to name only some. It challenges the way we do 'justice' through the institutional responses of policing, courts, and prisons and associated carceral and punishing enterprises such as child welfare and disability services, and at its broadest, the nation-states' exclusive claim to sovereignty. It challenges the criminological profession as an organized system of intellectual labour that silences the voices of minoritized members (e.g. Sadiki and Steyn, 2022; Deslandes et al., 2022; Russell-Brown, 2021; Phillips et al., 2020; Tauri, 2017). Having said that, there has been progress among the critically minded within criminology over the last two decades (and longer) in thinking through the long-term, ongoing, multiple, and intersecting effects of colonialism—to the extent that there is a significant body of decolonial and abolitionist literature.

The reappraisal brought about by this decolonial turn includes recognition, at a minimum, that the dominant intellectual frameworks of criminology were established in the West (and are not universal); the identification of the historical connections between the development of criminology in the nineteenth century and the projects of colonialism and imperialism; the acknowledgement that policing and penality were foundational to the colonial enterprise and the material practices of policing and penal power were constituted in both the colony and the metropole interdependently; and the recognition that intellectual definitions, categorizations, periodizations, and explanatory frameworks cannot claim legitimacy while ignoring the majority of world's population and their historical and contemporary experiences. This is not to argue that there has been a revolution in criminology—in its foundations, or its day-to-day operations—however, the parameters of the challenge to the orthodox accounts of the discipline are clearly articulated.

Outside academia, the decolonial and abolitionist political struggles against contemporary police and penal power are well established. The important role that popular protest has played in confronting oppressive criminal legal systems was shown during the 2020 uprising. For example, in the US in changing police budgets in some cities, in developing practical community-based alternatives to policing, and more broadly in thinking through the importance of community control and community regeneration as part of an abolitionist agenda for replacing police and penal power. As indicated at the beginning of the chapter, the 2020 uprising was global and demonstrated the depth of resistance against police and penal power as it is experienced in multiple countries. It is important to consider the productive alternatives that have been generated in these acts of resistance. Mignolo (2017, p. 15) has argued that the first step in thinking through decolonial possibilities is to imagine the many and rich possibilities of governance that exist as alternatives to state institutions. He warns that 'we must not confuse the State form with the variegated forms of governance that are open to people'. These questions of governance go to the heart of thinking about alternatives to contemporary systems of police and penal power which enhance community-safety and community-defence initiatives.

Community-safety and defence initiatives have a long history, including those developed by the Black Panther Party for Social Defense, the American Indian Movement, and the Black Power movement in the US and Australia during the late 1960s and early 1970s to protect communities against police violence. These organizations saw themselves in the context of colonialism and imperialism and connected to the international Black Power movement. They were quintessentially about positive interventions for community protection, advocacy, and the building of community-led initiatives to support black, indigenous, and oppressed peoples. Their work gave rise to various 'survival programmes', including for schooling, adult education, housing, medical treatment, and legal and social security advice. The contemporary BLM and abolitionist movements in the US have generated a great deal of discussion and activist solutions to decrease and ultimately eliminate reliance on policing and carceral systems. These include, by way of example, community-based interventions and programmes to respond to domestic violence, gun violence, and mental health crises, the development of local dispute-resolution mechanisms, and supportive approaches to homelessness rather than criminalization (e.g. Agbebiyi et al., 2021; Kim et al., 2021; Human Rights Watch, 2020; Vitale, 2017). It is certainly not suggested that these are transferable to other decolonizing struggles outside the US which, as indicated at the beginning of this chapter, have their own historical and contemporary decolonial struggles and organic solutions (e.g. Agozino, 2020).

Community-safety patrols and committees as alternatives to policing have developed in various locations. For example, community-safety patrols in First Nations communities in Australia question the way state policing is built on bureaucratic authority and the threat or use of violence. The patrols represent a different vision of community engagement and authority to state-based police: the external authority of the state is replaced by local cultural authority; and bureaucratized state-centred methods of crime control are replaced by an organic approach to community need which focuses on assistance and prevention rather than force. In South Africa, the Zwelethemba model draws on the idea that governance can be built locally and rely on people within their community to solve local problems. The establishment of community peace committees (and subsequent iterations) have allowed people to have their complaints resolved by local peace committees rather than by the police (SaferSpaces, 2022). Porter (2016) suggests that the way community patrols work (and, by extension, local peace committees) enables us to rethink the concept of policing as it is understood within dominant criminological discourses. The colonial logic of policing founded in the constant potentiality of state violence and imprisonment is replaced by a different logic of care, of thoughtfulness and sensitivity to community and individual needs, and is consistent with decolonial and abolitionist calls to replace current policing practices with community control, harm reduction, and social justice.

While decolonizing criminal legal systems may be a common objective for various approaches that challenge police and penal power, there are also complex questions about the ability to reform or substantially change the legal institutions of the colonial society. The attempts to modify/change criminal courts in settler colonial states through the growth in indigenous courts in Canada, Australia, New Zealand, and the US are a case in point. These courts are the long-term outcome of the struggle between indigenous activism and official accommodation. The tribal courts in the US exercise the greatest autonomy, while the others are essentially modified non-indigenous courts where community input is enabled through the presence non-judicial indigenous court members. The yet-to-be determined political question is whether these courts are 'part of an imperfect and incomplete decolonizing trend' (Proloux, 2005, p. 92) and a form of postcolonial cultural and legal creativity, or whether they simply prolong the trend of indigenization whereby symbolic initiatives of incorporation substitute for meaningful self-determination (Tauri, 1998). How we understand these developments raises broader issues around both the meaning and possibility of reform, as well as the political strategies of decoloniality and abolitionism.

Conclusion

I want to conclude by perhaps stating the obvious. Both decolonialism and abolitionism are deeply political processes. As such they are open to multiple definitions and interpretations, strategies, and priorities. They are embedded in ongoing processes of power and resistance which at one level are subject to global imperatives of capital for markets, labour, and resources, while simultaneously playing out in localized historical and cultural milieus. One of the fundamental political questions which arises, and is particularly relevant to police and penal power, is that of reformism. The problem has been confronted by abolitionists who speak of an abolition horizon—the future point of police and carceral abolition. As Ruth Wilson Gilmore states, abolition is about 'building the future from the present' (cited in Emerge, 2020). This work of building involves strategic decision about reform—about understanding which reforms take us closer to the horizon of abolition (Kaba, 2021, pp. 93–98). It is about being able to distinguish between 'reformist' and 'non-reformist' reforms. The lesson also applies to strategies for decolonization of police and carceral agencies.

There is a fault line which ultimately separates abolitionism/decolonialism from reformism and that is whether the proposed changes expand or contract the criminal legal system. Abolitionist and decolonizing reforms shrink or retract the system. By way of example, these might include redirecting calls for service away from police, developing community safety programmes that do not rely on police and penal power, disarming police, legal and policy changes that decriminalize behaviours or otherwise reduce prison populations, and shrinking police and carceral budgets. The importance of any one of these changes is that they are seen in the context of an overall abolitionist/decolonial strategy rather than an end in themselves. 'Reformist' reforms expand and strengthen the existing carceral/policing system (e.g. anti-bias training, use of force training, technological fixes such as body cams, non-lethal alternatives, and community policing). Reformism reinvigorates and reinforces the centrality of police and penal power rather than challenging it. Indeed, criminal legal institutions are able to command ever greater resources through reformism, and police and penal power is enhanced rather than diminished or contested.

The insights of abolitionism have resonance for thinking through approaches to decolonizing police and penal power. While decolonializing/abolishing criminal legal institutions might be a common objective, the strategies and processes through which this can be achieved may be contested. At the mid-point on the spectrum between abolition/decolonialism on one side and reformism on the other, there are multiple ambiguous grey areas. For example, is the democratic control of existing police institutions and an effective system of accountability achievable? As Kaba (2021, pp. 97–98) has suggested, there are not always clear-cut answers to these questions. A further point of differing analysis hinges on the role of the state and whether the state is seen as inevitably carceral and colonialist. For theorists like Mignolo, there is no hope for reforming state processes because the state is a fundamental dimension of the colonial matrix of power. 'Delinking from the colonial matrix of power is what I call decoloniality, but this is not a task that States could enact. States are a fundamental dimension of the colonial matrix of power. Consequently, decolonizing the State (or democratizing the State) is non-sense' (Mignolo, 2017, p. 16). However, others are committed (or at least neutral) to the possibility of building democratic institutions that equitably distribute social goods through the capture, transformation, and democratization of the state (Davis, 2005). We know from the day-to-day experiences of political activism around abolition and decolonialism that there are constant engagements with widely varying attempts at change and reform of police, judicial and penal ideologies, and practices. To return to a point made at the beginning of this chapter, we need to engage in dialogue and reflection that works to build solidarity across these various endeavours.

References

Agbebiyi, K., Shepherd, K., and Sered, D. (2021) *Solutions to Violence: How to Create Safety Without Policing or Prisons*. New York: Common Justice.

Agozino, B. (2003) *Counter-Colonial Criminology: A Critique of Imperialist Reason*. London: Pluto Press.

Agozino, B. (ed.) (2020) *The Routledge Handbook of Africana Criminologies*. Abingdon: Routledge.

Anti-Security Collective (2021) 'Introduction to the Special Issue: A critical theory of police power in the twenty-first century', *Social Justice*, 47(3–4), pp. 1–7.

Carvalho, S. de, Goyes, D. R., and Vegh Weis, V. (2021) 'Politics and indigenous victimization: The case of Brazil', *British Journal of Criminology*, 61(1), pp. 251–271.

Centro de Investigación y Docencia Económicas (2019) *Monitor del uso de la fuerza letal en América Latina: Un estudio comparativo de Brasil*, Colombia, El Salvador, México y Venezuela, 2019. Aguascalientes, Mexico: Centro de Investigación y Docencia Económicas.

Cesaire, A. (1972) *Discourse on Colonialism*. New York: Monthly Review Press.

CopsAreFlops (n.d.) 'Reimagining Justice in South Africa Beyond Policing'. Available at: www.drive.google.com/file/d/1krNcg_saPFABqjuFkQvtVKUpIjivd8Es/view (accessed 12 May 2022).

Coulthard, G. (2014) *Red Skin White Masks*. Minneapolis: University of Minnesota Press.

Cunneen, C. (2017) 'Visual Power and Sovereignty: Indigenous Art and Colonialism', in Brown, M. and Carrabine, E. (eds) *The Routledge International Handbook of Visual Criminology*. Abingdon: Routledge, pp. 376–388.

Cunneen, C. (2020) 'Youth justice and racialization: Comparative reflections', *Theoretical Criminology*, 24(3), pp. 521–539.

Cunneen, C. (2021) 'A Disbelief in Colonial Penality: Settler Colonialism and Abolitionism', in Coyle, M. and Scott, D. (eds) *The Routledge International Handbook of Penal Abolitionism*. London: Routledge, pp. 269–279.
Cunneen, C. (forthcoming) *Defunding the Police*. Bristol: Bristol University Press.
Cunneen, C., Baldry, E., Brown, D., Brown, M. et al. (2013) *Penal Culture and Hyperincarceration: The Revival of the Prison*. Aldershot: Ashgate.
Davis, A. Y. (1998) 'Racialised Punishment and Prison Abolition', in J. James (ed.) *The Angela Y. Davis Reader*. Oxford: Blackwell, pp. 96–107.
Davis, A. Y. (2005) *Abolition Democracy*. New York: Seven Stories Press.
Davis, A. Y., Dent, G., Meiners, E., and Richie, B. (2022) *Abolition. Feminism. Now.* Dublin: Penguin Random House.
Delgado, R. and Stefancic, J. (2007) 'Critical race theory and criminal justice', *Humanity & Society*, 31(2–3), pp. 133–145.
Deslandes, A., Longbottom, M., McKinnon, C., and Porter, A. (2022) 'Women's police stations down under: A proposal without evidence?' *Decolonization of Criminology and Justice*, 4(2) (in print).
Dhillon, A. (2021) 'India's police stations are human rights threat, says chief justice', *The Guardian*, 10 August. Available at: www.theguardian.com/world/2021/aug/10/india-police-stations-human-rights-threat-chief-justice (accessed 11 May 2022).
Dunbar-Ortiz, R. (2014) *An Indigenous Peoples' History of the United States*. Boston, MA: Beacon Press.
Emerge (2020) 'The Abolitionist Horizon. Building a World without Police or Prisons', 24 June. Available at: www.dsaemerge.org/the-abolitionist-horizon-building-a-world-without-police-or-prisons/ (accessed 11 May 2022).
Estes, N., Gilmore, R. W., and Loperena, C. (2021) 'United in struggle', *NACLA Report on the Americas*, 53(3), pp. 255–267.
Fanon, F. (1967) *The Wretched of the Earth*. Harmondsworth: Penguin.
Human Rights Watch (2020) 'A Roadmap for Re-Imagining Public Safety in the United States', 12 August. Available at: www.hrw.org/news/2020/08/12/roadmap-re-imagining-public-safety-united-states (accessed 11 May 2022).
International Criminal Court (ICC) (2021) *Decision on the Prosecutor's request for authorisation of an investigation pursuant to Article 15(3) of the Statute, Situation in the Republic of the Philippines*, Pre-Trial Chamber 1, 15 September 2021, No. ICC-01/21.
Kaba, M. (2021) *We Do this Till We Free Us*. Chicago, IL: Haymarket Books.
Kakati, B. (2021) 'Conflict and development in Northeast India. Stories from Assam', Transnational Institute, 16 May. Available at: www.tni.org/en/article/conflict-and-development-in-northeast-india (accessed 11 May 2022).
Killingray, D. (1991) 'Guarding the Extended Frontier: policing the Gold Coast, 1865–1913', in Anderson, D. M. and Killingray, D. (eds) *Policing the Empire: Government, Authority and Control—1830–1940*. Manchester: Manchester University Press, pp. 106–125.
Kim, M. E., Chung, M., Hassan, S., and Ritchie, A. J. (2021) 'Defund the Police—Invest in Community Care: A Guide to Alternative Mental Health Response Crisis Responses', Interrupting Criminalization. Available at: www.interruptingcriminalization.com/s/Crisis-Response-Guide.pdf (accessed 11 May 2022).
Maher, G. (2021) *A World Without Police*. New York: Verso.
McMichael, C. (2016) 'Police wars and state repression in South Africa', *Journal of Asian and African Studies*, 51(1), pp. 3–16.
Memmi, A. (2003 [1965]) *The Colonizer and the Colonized*. London: Earthscan.
Mignolo, W. (2011) *The Darker Side of Western Modernity*. Durham, NC: Duke University Press.

Mignolo, W. (2017) 'Interview with Walter Mignolo', in Woons, M. and Weier, S. (eds) *Critical Epistemologies of Global Politics*. Bristol: E-International Relations Publishing, pp. 11–25.

Mills, C. W. (1963 [1943]) 'The Professional Ideology of the Social Pathologist', in Mills, C. W. (ed.) *Power, Politics and People*. New York: Oxford University Press.

Moreton-Robinson, A. (2015) *The White Possessive. Property, Power and Indigenous Sovereignty*. Minneapolis, MN: University of Minnesota Press.

Morrison, W. (2006) *Criminology, Civilisation and the New World Order*. Abingdon: Routledge-Cavendish.

Murji, K. and Solomos, J. (2005) 'Racialization in Theory and Practice', in Murji, K. and Solomos, J. (eds) *Racialization: Studies in Theory and Practice*. Oxford: Oxford University Press.

Neocleous, M. (2021) '"Original, absolute, indefeasible": Or, what we talk about when we talk about police power', *Social Justice*, 47(3–4), pp. 9–32.

Neuman, S. (2021) 'U.N. Calls For Investigation As Police in Brazil Kill At Least 24 in Rio Drug Raid', National Public Radio, 7 May, Available at: www.npr.org/2021/05/07/994588467/u-n-calls-for-investigation-as-police-in-brazil-kill-at-least-24-in-rio-drug-rai (accessed 11 May 2022).

Phillips, C., Earle, R., Parmar, A., and Smith, D. (2020), 'Dear British criminology: Where has all the race and racism gone?', *Theoretical Criminology*, 24(3), pp. 427–446.

Porter, A. (2016) 'Decolonizing policing: Indigenous patrols, counter-policing and safety', *Theoretical Criminology*, 20(4), pp. 548–565.

Porter, A. (2019) 'Aboriginal sovereignty, "crime" and criminology', *Current Issues in Criminal Justice*, 31(1), pp. 122–142.

Proloux, C. (2005) 'Blending justice: Interlegality and the incorporation of Aboriginal justice into the formal Canadian justice system', *Journal of Legal Pluralism*, 37(51), pp. 79–109.

Quijano, A. (2000) 'Coloniality of power, Eurocentrism, and Latin America', *Nepantla: Views from South*, 1(3), pp. 533–580.

Rodriguez, D. (2019) 'Abolition as praxis of human being: A foreword', *Harvard Law Review*, 132(6), pp. 1575–1612.

Russell-Brown, K. (2021) 'Black lives matter in criminology? Let's prove it', *Race and Justice*, 11(3), pp. 328–337.

Sadiki, L. and Steyn, F. (2022) 'Decolonising the criminology curriculum in South Africa: Views and experiences of lecturers and postgraduate students', *Transformation in Higher Education*, 7, pp. 1–9. Available at: https://doi.org/10.4102/the.v7i0.150 (accessed 11 May 2022).

SaferSpaces (2022) 'Peace Committee Model'. Available at: www.saferspaces.org.za/be-inspired/entry/peace-committee-model (accessed 11 May 2022).

Saleh-Hanna, V. (2008) 'Penal Coloniality' in Saleh-Hanna, V. (ed.) *Colonial Systems of Control: Criminal Justice in* Nigeria. Ottawa: University of Ottawa Press, pp. 17–54.

Santos, B. de S. (2007) 'Beyond abyssal thinking: From global lines to ecologies of knowledges', *Research Foundation of State University of New York*, 30(1), pp. 45–89.

Schrader, S. (2019) *Badges Without Borders: How Global Counterinsurgency Transformed American Policing*. Berkeley, CA: University of California Press.

Spivak, G. C. (1988) 'Can the Subaltern Speak?' in Nelson, C. and Grossberg, L. (eds) *Marxism and the Interpretation of Culture*. London: Macmillan.

Tankebe, J. (2008) 'Colonialism, legitimation and policing in Ghana', *International Journal of Law, Crime and Justice*, 36(1), pp. 67–84.

Tauri, J. (1998) 'Family group conferencing: A case-study of the indigenisation of New Zealand's justice system', *Current Issues in Criminal Justice*, 10(2), pp. 168–182.

Tauri, J. (2014) 'Settler colonialism, criminal justice and Indigenous peoples', *African Journal of Criminology and Justice Studies*, 8(1), pp. 20–37.

Tauri, J. (2017) 'Imagining an Indigenous Criminological Future' in Deckert, A. and Sarre, R. (eds) *The Palgrave Handbook of Australian and New Zealand Criminology, Crime and Justice*. London: Palgrave Macmillan, pp. 769–783.

Ugwudike, P. (2020) 'Digital prediction technologies in the justice system: The implications of a "race-neutral" agenda', *Theoretical Criminology*, 24(3), pp. 482–501.

Vimalassery, M., Hu Pegues, J., and Goldstein, A. (2016) 'On colonial unknowing', *Theory and Event*, 19(4). Available at: https://muse.jhu.edu/article/633283 (accessed 12 May 2022).

Vitale, A. (2017) *The End of Policing*. London: Verso.

Ward, T. and Maruna, S. (2007) *Rehabilitation*. London: Routledge.

Weatherburn, D. (2014) *Arresting Incarceration: Pathways out of Indigenous Imprisonment*. Canberra: Aboriginal Studies Press.

Wolfe, P. (2006) 'Settler colonialism and the elimination of the native', *Journal of Genocide Research*, 8(4), pp. 387–409.

2

Abolition and (De)colonization

Cutting the Criminal Question's Gordian Knot

*J. M. Moore**

Introduction

In this chapter I explore the prospect for decolonizing both criminology and the broader criminal question. This challenge occurs at a time of widespread calls to decolonize. Although these calls are not restricted to academia, universities have often been a prime site for this debate (Bhambra et al., 2018). However, it is important to recognize that the debates, and associated activism, emerging from calls to decolonize have been much wider, encompassing campaigns like Black Lives Matter which has identified that struggles against racism need to recognize its roots in European colonialism (Elliott-Cooper, 2021). Despite this growing prominence, it is not always clear what is meant by decolonization or, indeed, what it entails. So, in the first section of this chapter, I define what I understand by decolonization and explore how it has been addressed in the criminological literature. Understanding decolonization is impossible without understanding colonization. The next section of the chapter addresses this, emphasizing colonialism's violent and destructive nature. In particular, this section highlights how law, particularly penal law, was not only central to colonialism, but also embedded racism at its core. Disputing the universality often ascribed to the concept of crime, the chapter identifies its European origin, arguing that this means the criminal question is ultimately a colonial question.

Criminology, like the modern capitalist state, emerged during the period of European colonialism. This is, the next section argues, no coincidence. The dramatic changes in social structure required by capitalism and colonialism generated problems which needed new ways of thinking. It is in this context that criminology and many of the disciplines we see in today's university were born. Criminology was, however, unique as its subject matter—crime—was exclusively determined by the state. The limitations of criminology as a tool of decolonization, given its dependence on

* Earlier versions of this chapter were delivered to a Centre for Crime and Justice Studies academic seminar in May 2017, the British Sociological Association conference in April 2019, and the workshop organized by the editors of this collection. The generous and constructive feedback received at all of these has greatly helped my thinking and the arguments presented in this chapter. Sections of the finalized version benefited from being reviewed in a session of the *Abolitionist Futures* writing group—thank you, comrades. Finally, can I record my thanks to the editors of this collection for all their work on the project and for helpful and constructive feedback on this chapter in particular.

J. M.Moore, *Abolition and (De)colonization* In: *Decolonizing the Criminal Question*. Edited by: Ana Aliverti, Henrique Carvalho, Anastasia Chamberlen, and Máximo Sozzo, Oxford University Press.
DOI: 10.1093/oso/9780192899002.003.0003

the capitalist/colonial state, are detailed. These problems are compounded in the next section which explores how criminology's discovery of the criminal was grounded in the racism of colonialism. Europe's creation of the racialized Other created a model through which early criminologists were able to invent the criminal Other. Having established that both the criminal question and criminology are so intimately tied to colonialism that separating them is impossible—the criminal question's Gordian Knot—the final section argues that decolonization requires the adoption of an abolitionist praxis. Both decolonization and abolition are utopian in the sense that they are unachievable within the existing social structure. To achieve them requires developing new ways of living and escaping existing power relations. Decolonization therefore requires abolition to sever the Gordon Knot that ties the criminal question and criminology to colonialism.

A Decolonized Criminal Question? A Decolonized Criminology?

Decolonization can mean many things to different people, these range from those who advocate a performative decolonization involving only minor, token changes, to those who argue for a revolutionary decolonization requiring fundamental change to the whole social structure. My own understanding is that, firstly, decolonization requires recognizing the harms colonialism caused and continues to cause. Secondly, it entails taking positive steps to repair this damage, and, thirdly, it necessitates the development of new ways of doing things that do not replicate colonialism. Much of what is presented as decolonization focuses on recognizing colonialism's historic impact (Blagg and Anthony, 2019; Cunneen and Tauri, 2016). Whilst this is important, limiting the scope of decolonization to a historical exercise can compromise attempts to undo the social structures perpetuating the rationales and legacies of colonialism; the ways of thinking and economic inequalities colonialism created. Such approaches are vulnerable to being absorbed into institutions where, inevitably, they become watered down (Dhillon, 2021). As Franz Fanon (1967, p. 28) has argued, decolonization is, 'the meeting of two forces, opposed to each other by their very nature'. It cannot, through compromises or accommodations, be mainstreamed within fundamentally colonial institutions. It has been defined by Joel Modiri (cited by Adebisi, 2019) as:

> an insatiable reparatory demand, an insurrectionary utterance, that always exceeds the temporality and scene of its enunciation. It entails nothing less than an endless fracturing of the world colonialism created.

It requires action that achieves real change, ultimately leading to the dismantling of the world created by colonialism (Adebisi, 2019). It is about returning what was stolen: sovereignty, land, and power (Tuck and Yang, 2012). It is not a process that involves adding something—books to a reading list—but it is, as Franz Fanon (1967, p. 27) made clear, 'always a violent phenomenon'.

Critiques of penal law and criminology from a colonial perspective are not new. Writing in 1955, Fanon (2018, p. 416) concluded that attempts to achieve 'a criminological understanding' in the context of colonial North Africa 'proves impossible'. Stan Cohen (1982) critiqued the transfer of Western crime control techniques to 'Third World' countries highlighting the dangers Western criminology presented to African postcolonial societies. The need for a postcolonial criminology was identified by Chris Cunneen (1999, p. 125) who argued that it was 'required to theorise … [criminology's] disciplinary foundations within a colonial project which involved systematic and gross abuse of human rights'. Biko Agozino (2003, p. 228) identified that '[c]riminology was developed primarily as a tool for imperialist domination'. In response to these critiques, a number of new strands of the discipline have been proposed, including: Black criminology (Russell, 1992; see also the contributions of Unnever et al., 2019); postcolonial criminology (Cunneen, 1999); counter-colonial criminology (Agozino, 2003); Pan-African criminology (Agozino, 2004); Asian criminology (Liu, 2009); Indigenous criminology (Cunneen and Tauri, 2016); Southern criminology (Carrington et al., 2016); and a decolonized criminology (Agozino, 2018; and, from a different perspective, Blagg and Anthony, 2019). A detailed review of these new criminological paradigms, and the literature from which they have emerged, is beyond the scope of this chapter; however, what they all—irrespective of their critique of their parent discipline—have in common is a focus on the potential of postcolonial and decolonial interventions to 'develop and enrich criminology' (Cunneen, 2011, p. 263). The editors of this collection have referred to 'the difficult ongoing task of decolonising criminology' (Aliverti et al., 2021, p. 299) whilst the authors of *Indigenous Criminology* have argued for 'the possibilities of a decolonised postcolonial relationship between criminal justice institutions and Indigenous communities' (Cunneen and Tauri, 2016, p. 160). For Kerry Carrington et al. (2016, p. 1), their proposed Southern criminology is not intended 'to dismiss the conceptual and empirical advances in criminology, but to more usefully de-colonize and democratize the toolbox of available criminological concepts, theories and methods'. This literature has in common both a harsh critique of contemporary criminology, based on its colonial history, and a belief in the urgent need to engage in a process of decolonizing both the discipline and the wider criminal question. However, these scholars have tended to assume that it is possible to identify colonial influences and legacies within both criminology and criminal justice policies, practices, and institutions and, somehow, remove these to produce a decolonized criminology and criminal question. Although this approach does recognize the harms of colonialism, this chapter argues that, through their continued commitment to both criminology and answering the criminal question, such approaches fail to develop new ways of doing things, and leaves them at risk of replicating colonialism.

Colonialism, Justice, and the Concept of Crime

The British and other European empires were created by conquest. Across the globe, lands were invaded, Indigenous people's resistance crushed or otherwise overcome—the use of deceit, by, for example, signing treaties that the British had no intention of honouring, was common—and the invaded territories' social structure demolished to make way for a new capitalist order. This violence was largely endorsed by liberal philosophy which deployed its intellectual powers to provide a range of justifications (Losurdo, 2011; Mehta, 1999). These varied from the concept of *terra nullius*—seeing the lands as empty spaces despite their habitation by a people with their own culture, society, and economy—through to the concept of a just war (Chatterjee, 2012, p. 52). Liberal theory legitimized not only invasion but the remaking of colonized places and people. It justified the violent demolition of established social relations and moral economies and their replacement with new arrangements based on liberal political economy, a capitalist social structure, and regulation by Western criminal and penal law (Loomba, 2005, p. 9). The colonized people found their 'cultures trampled underfoot, institutions undermined, lands confiscated, religions smashed, magnificent artistic creations destroyed' (Césaire, 2000, p. 43). To satisfy the pursuit of 'Christianity, Commerce and Civilization' (David Livingstone cited in Rijpma, 2015, p. 26), a new order was created, often through 'the application of Black people's labour to Red people's land producing the White man's property' (Wolfe, 2016, p. 3).

Two central and inter-related aspects of the colonial project—racism and law—need to be highlighted. In Europeans' interaction with Indigenous populations racism was ever present and the concept of race was deployed as a primary register of difference that established and naturalized inequality (Kolsky, 2010, p. 14). Within the British Empire, race provided 'the primary grid for the organisation of power, possession and knowledge' (Sen, 2012, p. 300). This racism was institutionalized in the law. For example, the 1661 Barbados Slave Code established clear legal distinctions between negro slaves—the terms negro and slave were used interchangeably, emphasizing how both meant the same to its authors—and white servants (Olusoga, 2016, pp. 69–70). Under the code: 'Mutilation of the face, slitting of nostrils, branding of cheeks and foreheads and castration were all deemed acceptable punishments (reserved exclusively) for Africans' (Olusoga, 2016, p. 70). Four centuries later, the deployment of laws explicitly based on race continued to operate. The United States, established as a settler and slave colony by Britain, still maintained segregation and apartheid South Africa maintained a racist legal code established when it was a British colony. These early twentieth-century British laws had, as well as restricting the franchise to the white settler population, institutionalized:

> 'job color bars' that legally reserved certain jobs for whites only, residential segregation, a pass system for controlling the mobility and involuntary servitude of blacks, and a bifurcated legal system that subjected blacks to draconian administrative control . . .
>
> (Evans, 2005, p. 191)

For the Indian nationalist Bal Gangadhar Tilak, it was clear that the 'goddess of British Justice, though blind, is able to distinguish unmistakably black from white' (cited in Kolsky, 2010, p. 4).

In a critique of criminology, Paddy Hillyard and Steve Tombs identified nine principal criticisms of the discipline. These included that crime had no ontological reality, consists of many petty events, excludes much serious harm, legitimizes the expansion of crime control, and maintains power relations (Hillyard and Tombs, 2004). Criminology, they argue, 'perpetuates the myth of crime' (ibid, p. 11). Whilst sympathetic to their critique, I would argue for going beyond the no ontological reality/social construct critique of crime to argue that the concept is best understood as both a legal construct and an exercise in state power. Crime is created by the state both through legislation (technically making something a crime) and through action (the infliction of blame and pain). Nowhere is this clearer than in the operation of colonialism where law, both civil and criminal, was deployed both to establish the colonies and subsequently in their governance (Moore, 2014). As I have argued previously, penal law has its roots in the slave societies of European antiquity, and this equipped penal law, and the associated processes of criminalization, for its role in colonial domination (Moore, 2016). Crime is so imbedded in our culture that we forget that it is not a universal concept but has a European history. I was struck when reading Oyérónké Oyěwùmi's brilliant *The Invention of Women* that not only are gender and sex not the natural categories they are often presumed in Western feminist discourse, but the same could also be argued with respect to the concepts of crime and the criminal Other. Indeed, Oyěwùmi (1997, p. 4) points out how the 'omnipresence of biologically deterministic explanations in the social sciences can be demonstrated within the category of the criminal or criminal type'. Just as gender was seen from a particular Western biological deterministic perspective, so too was crime (and, indeed, race). Crime, criminal justice, and criminology are all European colonial impositions that replaced a wide variety of mechanisms for conflict resolution and the maintenance of social order long established prior to colonization. Pre-colonial African societies, for example, were characterized by 'accountability, forgiveness and reparative justice' (Agozino, 2004, p. 243). Unlike penal law which focuses on individuals, allocating blame, and enforcing shame (Christie, 2004), African models of justice 'not only seek to restore relationships broken due to conflict, but also seek to understand and address the underlying causes of the conflict' (Elechi, 2004, p. 160). Whereas Agozino, Elechi, and others have seen these traditions as having the potential to reform criminal justice, both in Africa and elsewhere, I would argue that they are fundamentally incompatible with criminal justice. Their potential lies not in reform but in promoting an alternative paradigm. As Nọnso Okafọ (2006, p. 37) concludes, it is important for former colonized societies to recognize 'indigenous social control systems as superior and preferable to foreign systems'. To illustrate this, let us consider this example:

> Igbo legal procedures aim essentially at re-adjusting social relations. Social justice is more important than the letter of the law ... The resolution of a case does not have to include a definitive victory for one of the parties involved. Judgement among the Igbo ideally involves a compromise and consensus ... This implies a 'hostile' compromise in which there is neither victor nor vanquished, a reconciliation to the benefit of—or a loss to both parties.
>
> (Uchendu, 1965, p. 14)

It is an approach that implies a rejection of core criminal justice concepts. There is no division between offender and victim and the case is dealt with on its own terms without needing to be defined as a crime, or with the associated need to single out an individual for blame and the infliction of pain. This is recognized by Okafọ (2012) in his study of justice in an Igbo community, whereby the effectiveness of the indigenous system is compromised by its need to coexist with the postcolonial Nigerian criminal justice system. He argues that Igbo justice offers greater potential for effective social control and for the abolition of the colonial legacy of criminal justice. For most of the world, the criminal justice systems operating today were imposed by colonialism. They have not become infected by a bit of colonialism, an infection that can be cured by a dose of decolonization, they are fundamentally colonial. The criminal question, therefore, is itself inherently colonial.

Criminology, its Colonial Origins, and its Relationship with the State

Whilst crime and punishment had been the subject of European intellectual discourse since antiquity, the emergency of criminology as a discipline in the modern sense occurred as part of a broader movement to reorganize knowledge. A range of disciplines (e.g. economics, geography, phrenology/psychology, anthropology, sociology, statistics) appeared, broadly simultaneously, in the early part of the nineteenth century. These initially took the form of the establishment of learned societies and their journals, before, often much later, the disciplines embedded themselves in the academy. Whatever their institutional incarnations, what was significant was that they represented a new way of organizing and producing knowledge (Foucault, 2002). It was no coincidence that this reorganization of intellectual thought across such a wide range of social subjects occurred at roughly the same time. The emergence of industrial capitalism, beginning in Great Britain in the 1780s, and the dramatic changes in social structure that, as a consequence, occurred in both the metropole and its colonies, were generating an extensive range of social problems requiring a response from liberal thought (Beckett, 2014; Moore, 2014). It was necessary to create bodies of knowledge that took at their 'object man as an empirical entity' (Foucault, 2002, p. 375).

The philosophical glue that held together these disciplines of the individual was liberalism (Losurdo, 2011). Whilst the word liberal is routinely used promiscuously to refer to a range of ideas and attitudes (Bellamy, 1992), my deployment of the term 'liberal' refers to those mainstream liberal philosophers—Hobbes, Locke, Rousseau, Smith, Kant, Bentham, Hegel, and J. S. Mill—whose work provided the intellectual underpinning of, and justification for, the capitalist and colonial projects of modernity. Alongside those other disciplines we now call the social or human sciences, criminology emerged to provide strategies of liberal governance. Indeed, as Michel Foucault (2002, p. 376) has pointed out, 'the historical emergence of each one ... was occasioned by a problem, a requirement, an obstacle of a theoretical or practical order'. This function, in respect to criminology, Foucault (1980, p. 47) was later to identify as 'entirely utilitarian' after he asked:

> Have you read any criminological texts? They are staggering ... I fail to comprehend how the discourse of criminology has been able to go on at this level. One has the

> impression that it is of such utility, is needed so urgently and rendered so vital for the working of the system, that it does not even need to seek a theoretical justification for itself, or even simply a coherent framework.

This 'entirely utilitarian' character of criminology may, at least in part, be a direct result of it being unique among disciplines in having its subject matter—crime—determined by the state.

The institutional history of British criminology is complex and still awaits its historian. Activity until the second half of the twentieth century was a mix of national and international conferences organized through governments, networks of individuals working inside policing and penal institutions, and scholars working in other disciplines (Garland, 1988). What all these had in common was an acceptance of the necessity and naturalism of criminal justice; a commitment to a liberal individualistic approach and a willingness to operate within agendas set by the state. This connection between criminology and the state is so intimate that it is often unrecognized by criminologists. As Mark Neocleous (2021, p. 47) has observed, criminology as a discipline has 'ambled along without any real concept of the state, let alone a theory of it'. The oppressive and violent nature of the state, so obvious in the colonial context, tends to escape criminological discourse unnoticed. Most criminology has an implicit, rather than explicit, understanding of the state as a natural and necessary collection of institutions working for the general social good. Parts may be performing poorly or in problematic ways, but these issues are correctable through a reform agenda. Such a consensus perspective is fundamentally ahistorical. Radical, critical, and Marxist criminology do, on occasions, engage with the problematic nature of the state from a class perspective, however, there is little or no recognition of how the modern state—in the metropole, settler colonies, and the postcolonial independent states—has been shaped by the requirements of colonial governance (Chatterjee, 2012, p. 55). All these states have an interlinked history and have developed to impose and maintain unjust social orders. What is crime—criminology's subject matter—is determined by the state. Indeed, what is prosecuted and sanctioned as crime is also determined by state institutions—the courts, the police, prosecutors, probation services, and prisons. But it is not only that criminology's subject matter is determined by the state that is problematic. It is also that as a discipline criminology, throughout its history, has consistently sought to serve the state. It has regularly assisted the state by identifying 'criminals' and developing proposals for reforming the institutions of penal law. From its birth, criminology has been 'a selective science' endorsing a focus on the criminalization of a narrow selection of harms, an emphasis legitimizing the targeting of the most vulnerable and powerless whilst simultaneously largely ignoring the far greater harms caused by the powerful (Forero, 2017, p. 196). Criminology's adaption to the Nazi Party's rise in twentieth-century Germany, and the ease with which it incorporated Nazi ideology into its theorizing, demonstrates its ability to accommodate the needs of the state (Rafter, 2008).

To claim, as Emmanuel Onyeozili (2004, p. 225) does, that the British occupation of Lagos was 'international terrorism and a violation of international law', or as Biko Agozino (2004, p. 234) does, that the 'enslavement of Africans was a crime against humanity', is to attach an ahistorical meaning to the word crime. In reality, however harmful, vile, and repugnant the behaviours of British colonialism were, they were not crimes. The British state took great care to craft the law in ways that legitimized its conduct. Rather than being crimes, these abuses of human rights show the limitation of the concept. As I have previously argued, criminology, by adopting the state's language and power to define its foundational concepts, is a paradigm ill-equipped to generate useful explanations of 'the *legal* enslavement of Africans, the *legal* genocide of indigenous peoples, the *legal* looting of India, the racist colonial *legal* codes, and the wide range of other *legalised* (and *legally* enforced) injustices and harms that characterised colonial governance' (Moore, 2020, p. 492, emphasis in original).

'Race' and the Invention of the Criminal

Social entrepreneurs of the late eighteenth-century understood what they considered crime as having its origins in 'deficiencies of the laws' rather than any 'general depravity of the human character' (Colquhoun, 1796, p. 440). Influenced by Beccaria and Bentham, their focus was on creating a suitable apparatus of effective policing and the imposition of appropriate penal sanctions. However, in the nineteenth century this changed and by its end Raffaele Garofalo (1914, p. xxvii, emphasis in original) was able to declare that criminology had discovered 'an enemy mysterious, unrecognized by history ... the CRIMINAL'. How was this discovery possible? 'In Europe,' Clare Anderson (2004, p. 181) has pointed out, 'ideas about criminal typology were inextricably linked to readings of race and social evolution'. This association used the criminal's alleged similarities with non-Europeans (i.e. colonial subjects) to legitimize their exclusion and denial of citizenship rights. For example, in 1861 Henry Mayhew (2008, p. 3) declared that all human beings could be divided into two races: 'the wanderers and the settlers—the vagabond and the citizen—the nomadic and the civilised tribes' each of which had its own 'peculiar and distinctive physical as well as moral characteristics'. This Othering characterized much criminological discourse with, for example, Garofalo declaring that '[t]he typical criminal is a monster in the moral order who has characters in common with the savages and other characters that make him descend below humanity' (cited by Forero, 2017, p. 181). This link, between the criminal and the 'savage' was a recurring theme in nineteenth-century criminological discourse. From its foundation, criminology—to establish the criminal as a distinct identifiable type—drew on racist myths of racial difference.

Alejandro Forero (2017, pp. 180–181) has highlighted this link by pointing out that 'the birth of criminology emerged in openly racist texts'. Lombroso's racism was not some unfortunately personal defect but provided the intellectual unpinning and social context of his theories. As Willem Bonger (1943, p. 71) has argued, for Lombroso 'race, explains everything'; a conclusion confirmed by Lombroso (2006, p. 175) arguing that 'few have understood the behavior of savages to be criminal or recognized in it the origin of modern criminality'. As Agozino (2003, p. 69) has highlighted, the 'dominant assumption in criminology is that prisoners are not normal people'. This required theorizing to differentiate the criminal from the non-criminal, a process 'premised on assumptions of superior and inferior races representing white and non-white races respectively' (Kalunta-Crumpton, 2004, p. 7). 'Race' was therefore not only 'the organising grammar' of the imperial project (Stoler, 1995, p. 27) but it was a grammar eagerly adopted by criminology. Racism, and the understandings of the concept of race it promoted, was central to the imperial project (Solomos et al., 1982, p. 11). Constructions of race were deployed to legitimize occupation, slavery, genocide, and other colonial violence (Wolfe, 2016). Race, or more specifically white European racism, was deployed to distinguish the colonizer from the colonized and subsequently 'to establish and naturalize imperial inequality' (Kolsky, 2010, p. 14). Racism therefore challenged the concept of the universal human being. Difference, the superiority of some types and the inferiority of racialized Others, was naturalized.

As Catherine Hall (2002, p. 7) has pointed out, constructions of race 'depend on the production of stereotypes which refuse full human complexity'. Through cartoons, newspapers, periodicals, and books, often written by slavers, racist caricatures of Black and other non-white people were relentlessly repeated to create the racialized Other. A West Indian Planter (1788, p. 9) in an attempt to justify slavery, wrote that Africans 'do no more work, than they are compelled to do by the terrors of punishment'. An unwillingness to work was one of the innate characteristics consistently claimed for the African, another was their insatiable sexuality. Bryan Edwards (1793, pp. 82–83), slaver and politician, claimed that the African, 'both men and women', was possessed of a 'passion' that is 'mere animal desire'. In 1788, the *Gentleman's Magazine*, which James Walvin (1982, p. 60) has described as 'perhaps the most popular and influential periodical of the day', claimed:

> The Negro is possessed of passions not only strong but ungovernable; a mind dauntless, warlike and unmerciful; a temper extremely irascible; a disposition indolent, selfish and deceitful; fond of joyous sociality, riotous mirth and extravagant shew ... Furious in his love as in his hate; at best, a terrible husband, a harsh father and a precarious friend.
>
> (Cited in Walvin, 1982, p. 60)

For William Cobbett (1829, pp. 144, 344), champion of the rural labouring classes, enslaved Africans, 'the unhappy creatures whom nature has marked out for degradation', were 'always lazy and saucy; nothing but the lash will extort from them either labour or respectful deportment'. Although Black and brown people have lived in Britain, particularly its ports and cities, throughout history, for many white English people these discourses would have been how they learnt about non-white people (Olusoga, 2016). Through publications like the 1810 edition of the *Encyclopaedia Britannica*, they would have learnt that 'the Negro' was 'an unhappy race' whose characteristics included 'idleness treachery, revenge, cruelty, impudence, stealing, lying, profanity, debauchery, nastiness and intemperance' (cited in Walwin, 1982, p. 70). Racism and its stereotype of the racialized Other, subsequently reinforced by racist pseudoscience, legitimized Britain's slavery and colonialism (Saini, 2020).

For the founders of criminology, racist ideas of difference and the racialized Other meant that new forms of 'knowledge and theory become possible' (Foucault, 2002, p. xxiv). Whereas Beccaria, Colquhoun, Howard, Bentham, and their European predecessors knew their criminals not as the Other, but as rational beings, motivated by the same forces and influences as anyone else, racist ideas made possible new ways of thinking and seeing the world. In respect of the criminal question, the criminal as the Other could be born. Initially, the criminal was morally defective, a damaged creature requiring reformation. Hence, the references in the mid-nineteenth century to prisons as 'moral hospitals' (see, e.g., Hill, 1857, p. 103). The focus had moved on from discovering the appropriate police arrangements and penal sanctions to deter *all* from crime, to an attempt to *know* the criminal and the particular regime of treatment they required. This search was to lead to the discovery by Lombroso (2006), and other early criminologists, of the *born criminal*, an incurable primitive being beyond reform, sub-human, and entirely unlike the *normal* person. What better way to express the discovery of the criminal than by establishing, scientifically, differences in the skulls of the criminal Other. Criminology mirrored race pseudoscience drawing on its Othering to establish a new truth.

Beyond the Criminal Question: The Need for a Decolonial Abolitionist Praxis

Criminology and the criminal question's relationship with decolonization is best described as a Gordian Knot, a problem that is impossible to resolve in its own terms. It cannot be untied but requires cutting. In this section, I argue that the tool allowing us to sever this knot is abolition. What distinguishes abolition from other perspectives on the criminal question is that it does not see the criminal justice system as having (ultimately resolvable) problems but that it is *the* problem. Rather than seek ways to correct its failures, for example by decolonising it, abolition seeks to dismantle criminal justice. From an abolitionist perspective, 'the criminal question' is the wrong question. As the activist group Critical Resistance (undated) highlights: 'abolition isn't just about getting rid of buildings full of cages. It is also about undoing the society we live in.' It is this commitment to revolutionary social change that echoes Fanon's (1967, p. 27) recognition that at its core decolonization 'sets out to change the order of the world'. Whilst abolition's initial focus is on addressing the needs of those who have been harmed, it recognizes that this ultimately necessitates 'transforming the power structures and immediate social relations that breed harm in the first instance' (McLeod, 2019, p. 1623). Abolition and decolonization have in common a recognition that they can only be achieved by transforming the world we live in.

Abolition is often dismissed as utopian and therefore a distraction from immediate reforms needed by the criminal justice system. Such a critique not only ignores reform's long history of failure (Moore, 2009) but misunderstands utopian thinking. What makes an idea utopian is not that is not achievable, but that 'it is incongruous with the state of reality within which it occurs' (Mannheim, 1936, p. 173). Perspectives such as abolition (or, indeed, decolonization) seem impossible because a critic 'who has consciously or unconsciously taken a stand in favor of the existing and prevailing social order' has blurred 'the distinction between absolute and relative unrealizability' (ibid, p. 177). In the sense that abolition or decolonization cannot be attained within the current unjust social order, they are correct. Both require a new social order. This does not mean ignoring the injustices and sufferings of the present. Abolitionists, whilst ultimately aspiring to a radically changed society, recognize and contribute to addressing immediate concerns, for example by engaging in prisoner solidarity and campaigning for reforms (PSN, 2021). However, whilst most reformers are motivated by a desire to see the criminal justice system function better, and thereby often contribute to strengthening and expanding the system, abolitionists focus on reforms that contract the system and improve the rights and living standards of those ensnared by the penal state. Abolitionist reforms ultimately aim to undermine the system and expose the contradictions between penal law's stated objectives and the reality of how it functions. For abolitionists, the institutions of criminal justice—courts, police, and prisons—do not function in a just manner, they may claim to protect us, respond to those who harm us, and distribute justice, but these are alibis designed to mask penal law's real function, maintaining an unjust social order. Whilst reformers focus on criminal justice's failure to deliver on its stated aims, abolitionists highlight that in reality it is a success, delivering its real function (Moore, 2015; Kaba, 2021, pp. 6–13). Decolonization similarly perceives contemporary social structures, both within and beyond penal law, as products of colonialism, designed to facilitate oppression, exploitation, and genocide. Colonialism's legacy of racism is an inherent feature of both the economic structure and the superstructure which sustains it. It is not something that can be reformed; decolonization 'entails nothing less than an endless fracturing of the world colonialism created' (Modiri, cited by Adebisi, 2019). Like abolitionism, it necessitates the replacement of the contemporary colonial/capitalist social order.

When faced with the question of the feasibility of living without police and prisons, abolitionists have argued that this is the wrong focus; abolition is ultimately 'about abolishing the conditions under which prison became the solution to problems' (Gilmore and Murakawa, 2020). Colonialism has contributed to the making of our unjust society. Decolonization is a demand for justice. But not the justice of the courtroom or penal law. What is required is much more akin to how abolitionists perceive justice, as 'an integrated endeavour to prevent harm, intervene in harm, obtain reparations, and transform the conditions in which we live' (McLeod, 2019, p. 1615). This approach allows us to imagine a different world, where conflict can be resolved, and harms addressed, without recourse to penal law's focus on locating an individual who can be allocated blame and pain. Indeed, abolitionists are already seeking to develop such approaches outside the agencies of penal law. Through transformative justice interventions, abolitionists have developed responses that have a commitment to, first, avoiding causing more harm and violence (including systemic harms/violence) whilst, subsequently, addressing immediate needs—for safety, healing, accountability, etc. (Bay Area Transformative Justice Collective, 2013). Many of these initiatives have emerged in Black and Indigenous communities, for whom they represent decolonization as much as abolitionist organizing.

As this chapter has previously detailed, penal law and the institutions of criminal justice were designed to maintain an unjust social order. Their imposition on colonized societies swept away long-established customs that had maintained their moral economies social order to facilitate the imposition of colonialism's capitalist political economy. Today, in the metropole, penal law disproportionately impacts on the most powerless and marginalized communities, including the descendants of those colonized. In settler colonies, penal law continues the ongoing process of colonization, by sustaining settler dominance and targeting Indigenous communities. In the independent postcolonial states, the retention of colonialism's penal law functions as an impediment to achieving decolonization. Given penal law's complicity with colonialism historically and its contemporary role sustaining colonial relations and institutions, it is impossible to decolonize the criminal question. Likewise, criminology's commitment to both explaining crime and the existence of the criminal Other makes it impossible to decolonize. Crime is a European concept; a legal construct determined by the state to reflect the values and interests of the dominant class; colonialism was built using penal law to legitimize and enforce European rule. Criminology emerged in the late nineteenth-century and established itself by its creation of the criminal Other, utilizing the racism of race pseudoscience, which had invented the racialized Other to justify European colonialism. Criminology has from its birth been intimately linked with colonialism and racism, indeed as Juan Tauri (2018, p. 5) has argued, 'criminologists often contribute to the political enterprise of inclusion/exclusion through the very act of *doing* criminology'. As with the criminal question, to talk of its decolonization is inherently contradictory. This does not mean that criminologists (or other academics) can ignore the decolonization agenda. But it does require them to approach decolonization from an abolitionist perspective. In particular, they need to draw on the work undertaken by abolitionists to distinguish between reforms which strengthen the system and reforms that are consistent with an abolitionist objective (Mathiesen, 1974). We need to ensure that we prioritize the needs of those oppressed by colonialism, and those engaged in the ongoing struggles to decolonize our society, rather than the needs of our careers, our discipline, our institution, the state, or (for many of us) our whiteness.

Writing about abolition, Mariame Kaba (2021, p. 4) has argued that 'if we keep building the world we want, trying new things, and learning from our mistakes, new possibilities emerge'. Abolitionism is a very different way of thinking but, possibly more importantly, it is also a practice (Lamble, 2021). Decolonization also requires us to work and live in ways which allow new possibilities to emerge. European colonization was incredibly destructive, 'elaborate systems worked out to cope with nature and with one another were often destroyed, leaving human beings at the mercy of a social order more cruel and more incomprehensible in its chaos, its illogicality and its contradictions than nature itself' (wa Thiong'o, 1986, p. 66). Both criminology and the criminal question are ultimately part 'of the world colonialism created' and as such they need 'fracturing' (Modiri, cited in Abebisi, 2019). But as well as 'fracturing', we need, as Kaba has advocated, to be 'building the world we want'. It will be a very different world and include possibilities we cannot yet imagine. It will also allow the recovery of many of the 'elaborate systems' colonialism destroyed. Abolitionist and decolonizing praxis can work together to create this new world. Let us be inspired by Franz Fanon's (1967, p. 254) conclusion to *The Wretched of the Earth*:

> So, comrades, let us not pay tribute to Europe by creating states, institutions and societies which draw their inspiration from her. Humanity is waiting for something other from us than such an imitation, which would be almost an obscene caricature.

To seek to decolonize the criminal question or to create a decolonized criminology, without abolition at its heart, is to risk creating such 'an obscene caricature'.

References

'A West India Planter' (1788) *Considerations on the Emancipation of Negroes*. London: J. Johnson.

Adebisi, F. (2019) 'Why I say "decolonisation is impossible"', *African Skies*, 17 December. Available at: https://folukeafrica.com/why-i-say-decolonisation-is-impossible/ (accessed 17 June 2022).

Agozino, B. (2003) *Counter-Colonial Criminology: A Critique of Imperialist Reason*. London: Pluto Press.

Agozino, B. (2004) 'Reparative Justice: A Pan-African Criminology Primer', in Kalunta-Crumpton, A. and Agozino, B. (eds) *Pan-African Issues in Crime and Justice*. Aldershot: Ashgate, pp. 228–248.

Agozino, B. (2018) 'The withering away of the law: An indigenous perspective on the decolonisation of the criminal justice system and criminology', *Journal of Global Indigeneity*, 3(1), pp. 1–22.

Aliverti, A., Carvalho, H., Chamberlen, A. et al. (2021) 'Decolonizing the criminal question', *Punishment and Society*, 23(3), pp. 297–316.

Anderson, C. (2004) *Legible Bodies: Race, Criminality and Colonialism in South Asia*. New York: Berg.

Bay Area Transformative Justice Collective (2013) 'Transformative Justice and Community Accountability'. Available at: https://batjc.files.wordpress.com/2014/06/tj-ca-one-pager.pdf (accessed 17 June 2022).

Beckett, S. (2014) *Empire of Cotton*. London: Penguin.

Bellamy, R. (1992) *Liberalism and Modern Society: An Historical Argument*. Cambridge: Polity Press.

Bhambra, G. K., Gebrial, D., and Nişancioğlu, K. (2018) 'Introduction: Decolonising the University', in Bhambra, G. K., Gebrial, D., and Nişancioğlu, K. (eds) *Decolonising the University*. London: Pluto Press, pp. 1–18.

Blagg, H. and Anthony, T. (2019) *Decolonising Criminology: Imagining Justice in a Postcolonial World*. London: Palgrave Macmillan.

Bonger, W. A. (1943) *Race and Crime*. Montclair, NJ: Patterson Smith.

Carrington, K., Hogg, R., and Sozzo, M. (2016) 'Southern criminology', *British Journal of Criminology*, 56(1), pp. 1–20.

Césaire, A. (2000) Pinkham, J. (trans.) *Discourse on Colonialism*. New York: Monthly Review Press.

Chatterjee, P. (2012) *The Black Hole of Empire: History of a Global Practice of Power*. Princeton, NJ: Princeton University Press.

Christie, N. (2004) *A Suitable Amount of Crime*. London: Routledge.

Cobbett, W. (1829) *Advice to Young Men and (Incidentally) to Young Women*. London: Mills, Jowett & Mills.

Cohen, S. (1982) 'Bandits, rebels, or criminals: African history and western criminology', *Africa: Journal of the International African Institute*, 56(4), pp 468–483.

Colquhoun, P. (1796) *A Treatise on the Police of the Metropolis*, 3rd edn. London: C. Dilly.
Critical Resistance (n.d.) 'What is the PIC? What is abolition?'. Available at: http://criticalresistance.org/about/not-so-common-language/ (accessed 17 June 2022).
Cunneen, C. (1999) 'Criminology, genocide and the forced removal of indigenous children from their families', *The Australian and New Zealand Journal of Criminology*, 32(2), pp. 124–138.
Cunneen, C. (2011) 'Postcolonial Perspectives for Criminology', in Bosworth, M. and Hoyle, C. (eds) *What is Criminology?*. Oxford: Oxford University Press.
Cunneen, C. and Tauri, J. (2016) *Indigenous Criminology*. Bristol: Policy Press.
Dhillon, S. (2021) 'An immanent critique of decolonisation projects', *Convivial Thinking*, 25 September. Available at: https://convivialthinking.org/index.php/2021/09/25/critique-of-decolonisation-projects/ (accessed 17 June 2022).
Edwards, B. (1793) *The History, Civil and Commercial of the British Colonies in the West Indies*, vol. II. London: John Stockdale.
Elechi, O. O. (2004) 'Women and (African) Indigenous Justice Systems', in Kalunta-Crumpton, A. and Agozino, B. (eds) *Pan-African Issues in Crime and Justice*. Aldershot: Ashgate, pp. 157–179.
Elliott-Cooper, A. (2021) *Black Resistance to British Policing*. Manchester: Manchester University Press.
Evans, I. (2005) 'Racial Violence and the Origins of Segregation in South Africa', in Elkins, C. and Pedersen, S. (eds) *Settler Colonialism in the Twentieth Century*. New York: Routledge.
Fanon, F. (1967) *The Wretched of the Earth*. London: Penguin Books.
Fanon, F. (2018) Corcoran, S. (trans.) 'Conduct of Confession in North Africa (2)', in Khalfa, J. and Young, R. J. C. (eds) *Alienation and Freedom*. London: Bloomsbury Academic, pp. 413–416.
Forero, A. (2017) 'Old and new discourse: The role of positivist criminology in the criminalisation of anarchism', *Justice, Power and Resistance*, 1(2), pp. 178–199.
Foucault, M. (1980) 'Prison Talk', in Foucault, M. *Power/Knowledge: Selected Interviews and Other Writings 1972–1977*. New York: Harvester Wheatsheaf, pp. 37–54.
Foucault, M. (2002) *The Order of Things*. London: Routledge.
Garland, D. (1988) 'British criminology before 1935', *British Journal of Criminology*, 28(2), pp. 1–17.
Garofalo, R. (1914) *Criminology*. Boston, MA: Little, Brown & Co.
Gilmore, R. W. and Murakawa N. (2020) 'Covid 19, Decarceration, and Abolition', Haymarket Books, 28 April. Available at: www.youtube.com/watch?v=hf3f5i9vJNM (accessed 17 June 2022).
Hall, C. (2002) *Civilising Subjects: Metropole and Colony in the English Imagination, 1830–1867*. Cambridge: Polity Press.
Hill, M. D. (1857) *Suggestions for the Repression of Crime, contained in Charges Delivered to Grand Juries of Birmingham*. London: John W. Parker.
Hillyard, P. and Tombs, S. (2004) 'Beyond Criminology', in Hillyard, P., Pantazis, C., Tombs, S. et al. (eds), *Beyond Criminology: Taking Harm Seriously*. London: Pluto Press.
Kaba, M. (2021) *We Do This 'Til We Free Us*. Chicago, IL: Haymarket Books.
Kalunta-Crumpton, A. (2004) 'Criminology and Orientalism', in Kalunta-Crumpton, A. and Agozino, B. (eds) *Pan-African Issues in Crime and Justice*. Aldershot: Ashgate, pp. 5–22.
Kolsky, E. (2010) *Colonial Justice in British India: White Violence and the Rule of Law*. Cambridge: Cambridge University Press.
Lamble, S. (2021) 'Practising Everyday Abolition', in Duff, K. (ed.) *Abolishing the Police*. London: Dog Section Press, pp. 147–160.
Liu, J. (2009) 'Asian criminology—challenges, opportunities, and directions', *Asian Journal of Criminology*, 4, pp. 1–9.

Lombroso, C. (2006) *Criminal Man*. Durham, NC: Duke University Press.
Loomba, A. (2005) *Colonialism/Postcolonialism*. Abingdon: Routledge.
Losurdo, D. (2011) *Liberalism: A Counter-History*. London: Verso.
Mannheim, K. (1936) *Ideology and Utopia*. London: Routledge.
Mathiesen, T. (1974) *The Politics of Abolition*. New York: Wiley.
Mayhew, H. (2008) *London Labour & the London Poor*. Ware: Wordsworth Classics.
McLeod, A. M. (2019) 'Envisioning abolition democracy', *Harvard Law School*, 132, pp. 1613–1649.
Mehta, U. S. (1999) *Liberalism and Empire: A Study in Nineteenth-Century British Liberal Thought*, 2nd edn. Chicago, IL: University of Chicago Press.
Moore, J. M. (2009) 'Penal reform: A history of failure', *Criminal Justice Matters*, 77, pp. 12–13.
Moore, J. M. (2014) 'Is the empire coming home? Liberalism, exclusion and the punitiveness of the British State', *Conference Papers from the British Criminology Conference*, 14, pp. 31–48. Available at: http://britsoccrim.org/volume14/pbcc_2014_wholevolume.pdf#page=35 (accessed 17 June 2022).
Moore, J. M. (2015) 'Reframing the "Prison Works" debate. For whom and in what ways does prison work?', *Reclaim Justice Network*, 10 March. Available at: https://downsizingcriminaljustice.wordpress.com/2015/03/10/reframing-the-prison-works-debate-for-whom-and-in-what-ways-does-prison-work/ (accessed 17 June 2022).
Moore, J. M. (2016) 'Built for inequality in a diverse world: The historic origins of criminal justice', *Conference Papers from the British Criminology Conference*, 16, pp. 38–56. Available at: www.britsoccrim.org/wp-content/uploads/2016/12/pbcc_2016_moore.pdf (accessed 17 June 2022).
Moore, J. M. (2020) '"Law", "order", "justice", "crime": Disrupting key concepts in criminology through the study of colonial history', *The Law Teacher*, 54(4), pp. 489–502.
Neocleous, M. (2021) *A Critical Theory of Police Power: The Fabrication of Social Order*. London: Verso.
Okafọ, N. (2006) 'Relevance of African traditional jurisprudence of control, justice and law: A critique of the Igbo experience', *African Journal of Criminology and Justice Studies*, 2(1), pp. 36–62.
Okafọ, N. (2012) 'A justice void filled: Explaining the endurance of extreme tradition-based laws in Nigeria', *African Journal of Criminology and Justice Studies*, 6(1–2), pp. 121–142.
Olusoga, D. (2016) *Black and British: A Forgotten History*. London: Macmillan.
Onyeozili, E. C. (2004) 'Gunboat Criminology and the Colonization of Africa', in Kalunta-Crumpton, A. and Agozino, B. (eds) *Pan-African Issues in Crime and Justice*. Aldershot: Ashgate.
Oyėwùmi, O. (1997) *The Invention of Women: Making an African Sense of Western Gender Discourses*. Minneapolis, MN: University of Minnesota Press.
PSN (Prisoner Solidarity Network) (2021) 'Retrospective 2020–2021', *PNS*, 28 December. Available at: https://prisonersolidarity.wixsite.com/psnldn/post/retrospective-2020-2021 (accessed 17 June 2022).
Rafter, N. (2008) 'Criminology's darkest hour: Biocriminology in Nazi Germany', *Australian & New Zealand Journal of Criminology*, 41(2), pp. 287–306.
Rijpma, S. (2015) *David Livingstone and the Myth of African Poverty and Disease: A Close Examination of His Writing on the Pre-Colonial Era*. Leiden: Brill.
Russell, K. K. (1992) 'Development of a black criminology and the role of the black criminologist', *Justice Quarterly*, 9(4) pp. 667–683.
Saini, A. (2020) *Superior: The Return of Race Science*. London: 4th Estate.
Sen, S. (2012) *Disciplined Natives: Race, Freedom and Confinement in Colonial India*. Delhi: Primus Books.

Solomos, J., Findlay, B., Jones, S. et al. (1982) 'The Organic Crisis of British Capitalism and Race: The Experience of the Seventies', in Centre for Contemporary Cultural Studies (ed.) *The Empire Strikes Back: Race and Racism in 70s Britain*. London: Routledge.

Stoler, A. L. (1995) *Race and the Education of Desire: Foucault's History of Sexuality and the Colonial Order of Things*. Durham, NC: Duke University Press.

Tauri, J. M. (2018) 'The master's tools will never dismantle the master's house: An indigenous critique of criminology', *Journal of Global Indigeneity*, 3(1), 6, pp. 1–18.

Tuck, E. and Yang, K. W. (2012) 'Decolonization is not a metaphor', *Decolonization: Indigeneity, Education & Society*, 1(1), pp. 1–40.

Uchendu, V. C. (1965) *The Igbo of Southeast Nigeria*. New York: Holt, Rinehart and Winston.

Unnever, J. D., Gabbidon, S. L., and Chouhy, C. (2019) *Building a Black Criminology: Race, Theory, and Crime*. New York: Routledge.

Walvin, J. (1982) 'Black Caricature: The Roots of Racialism', in Husband, C. (ed.) *'Race' in Britain: Continuity and Change*. London: Hutchinson, pp. 59–72.

wa Thiong'o, N. (1986) *Decolonising the Mind: The Politics of Language in African Literature*. London: John Curry.

Wolfe, P. (2016) *Traces of History: Elementary Structures of Race*. London: Verso.

3

The Weight of Empire

Crime, Violence, and Social Control in Latin America—and the Promise of Southern Criminology

Manuel Iturralde

Introduction

During the last two decades, Latin American scholars working from different perspectives have shown an increasing interest in the region's crime control fields as an object of study. Nonetheless, the analysis of crime, violence, and social control in Latin America is still marginal in Global North discussions; scholars seldom engage with their Global South colleagues in a constructive debate (Faraldo-Cabana, 2018; Liu, 2009). On the other hand, in the cases that Global North criminologists and theories recognize the knowledge production of the Global South, some of them still use it as a source to exemplify 'primitive', 'pre-modern', or 'tribal' societies, as well as extreme expressions of violence, social disorder, and penal excess[1] (Connell, 2007, p. 66; Carrington, Hogg, and Sozzo, 2016, p. 2). Social and criminological phenomena of Global South jurisdictions are depicted as an imperfect realization of universal theories and laws of development. This rhetorical device marshals the unstated assumption that Global South countries are bound to follow the path of Global North societies to reach modernity as a superior stage of development (Carrington, Hogg, and Sozzo, 2016, p. 2).

This state of affairs creates an epistemological gap between Global North and Latin American worldviews on crime and punishment as social realities and concepts (Carrington, Hogg, Scott et al., 2019; Carrington, Hogg, and Sozzo, 2016; Carrington, Hogg, Scott et al., 2018; Carrington, Dixon, Fonseca et al., 2019). Nevertheless, Global North scholars often advise Latin American governments and international organizations on policy and institutional changes to confront crime and violence in the region. Their influence increases proportionally to the degree to which local elites are amenable to external pressure and find them helpful to secure their privileges and preserve the status quo (Blaustein, 2016; Fonseca, 2018; Iturralde, 2019).

This set-up has cleared the way for the 'standard' perspectives and highly punitive penal policies that predominate in Latin American societies. Such penal policies have come to be known under diverse labels (and with different accents)—*zero-tolerance*,

[1] Eg for discussions regarding prisons in Latin America and their comparison with Global North countries' prisons, see Birkbeck, 2011.

Manuel Iturralde, *The Weight of Empire* In: *Decolonizing the Criminal Question.* Edited by: Ana Aliverti, Henrique Carvalho, Anastasia Chamberlen, and Máximo Sozzo, Oxford University Press. © Manuel Iturralde 2023.
DOI: 10.1093/oso/9780192899002.003.0004

mano dura, and *seguridad ciudadana* (Dammert and Salazar, 2009). Additionally, the war on drugs, the expansion of the prison system,[2] procedural penal reforms,[3] and the militarization of law enforcement (Flores-Macías and Zarkin, 2021; Solar, 2021) have contributed to the authoritarian configuration of Latin American crime control fields. To a significant degree, these policies and practices are not simply the reproduction and adaptation of discourses and practices that travel from Global North countries. Instead, they lay roots in a colonial past that is still felt in the present-day realities of many Global South countries through global hierarchical market relations, extreme forms of inequality, injustice, and violence that constitute neocolonial forms of unequal power relations (Ciocchini and Greener, 2021; Carrington, Hogg, Scott et al., 2019).

In this chapter, I will focus on some of the most salient features of Latin American crime control during the last three decades. I discuss the following hypothesis: these fields of crime control are deeply connected to Latin American countries' historical trajectories and the dynamics of colonialism and neocolonialism. The latter is not just a remnant of the past but an acting force that profoundly affects the political economy of Latin American societies. The colonial matrix of power, shared by Global North and South countries, is still felt nowadays through extreme forms of violence, exclusion, and discrimination. Crime control fields play an essential role to uphold, rather than eradicate, different forms of oppression. Additionally, within an unequal and hierarchical global order, the international agenda on crime control topics plays a crucial role in defining the options available to Latin American countries to achieve significant political, economic, and social transformations. Such an agenda has been predominantly set by Global North countries, which impose their worldviews and interests.

In the first section of the chapter, I will briefly expose some of the central arguments of Southern criminology to decolonize the predominant criminological discourse and to develop a Southern perspective. In the second section, I will discuss the debate within Southern criminology regarding its theoretical and political aims. In the third part of the chapter, I will map some of the main features of Latin American crime control fields in recent decades—with an emphasis on Colombia—from the perspective of Southern criminology to exemplify the critical criminological analysis of neocolonization in Global South contexts.

By neocolonization, I mean the political and economic processes that configure asymmetrical power structures and economic relations between Global North countries (most of them former colonial powers) and Global South countries (former colonies), despite their juridical sovereignty. Such asymmetrical power relations may stem from a shared colonial past, but also from contemporary dynamics resulting from the transformations and positioning of Global North capitalism and liberal democracy as the dominant forms of economic and political regimes around the globe. Nowadays, Global South countries' state sovereignty is compromised by Global North countries

[2] Sometimes following the US model of supermax prisons, like the so-called 'new generation' prisons in Colombia (de Dardel and Söderström, 2015).

[3] Many of these reforms have introduced the accusatorial model following the pattern of Global North countries, like the United States and Germany (Langer, 2004; 2007).

and international institutions' co-option and influence, under the auspices of free markets and the rule of law. From this outlook, neocolonialism is a useful theoretical framework for assessing external influences and pressures in Global South countries' crime control fields that contribute to perpetuate the dependence of the Global South on the Global North (Stambøl, 2021).

Additionally, in this third section of the chapter, I will briefly discuss how the authoritarian trends of many Latin American countries' crime control fields have heightened in recent times, and particularly as a response to the economic and social crisis unleashed by the Covid-19 global pandemic. I will also present three key features of Latin American societies often overlooked and that have the potential to explain some of the most relevant dynamics and transformations of Latin American crime control fields and their interconnections with Global North societies: state-building and its relationship to colonialism; the strengthening of state capacity; and the role that Global North countries, institutions, and discourses have played in the configuration of crime control in the region.

In the fourth section, and by way of concluding the chapter, I will stress the importance of studying the historical and contextual trajectories, as well as the processes of state-building and social control of Global North and South countries to make sense of their differences, but also their similarities and connections. This perspective may contribute to criminological theory by providing a more comprehensive picture of global political, social, and economic relations, still based on the inequality and oppression of the colonial matrix of power.

The Southern Criminology Project

Different scholars have developed a body of research to decolonize criminology epistemologically and methodologically, as well as to assess current dynamics and structures of neocolonization (see, among others, Aliverti, Carvalho, Chamberlen et al., 2021; Carrington, Hogg, Scott et al., 2019; Carrington, Hogg and Sozzo, 2016; Carrington and Hogg, 2017; Carrington, Hogg, Scott et al., 2018; Carrington, Dixon, Fonseca et al., 2019; Ciocchini and Greener, 2021; Iturralde, 2010). Despite its different approaches, one of southern criminology's main features is its critique towards mainstream criminology, which naturalizes the *modernization project*. As part of the modern social sciences (Connell, 2007), mainstream criminology presents itself as universal, timeless, and placeless. However, from a political economy perspective, like all modern social sciences, criminology is, in fact, a contingent product of Global North societies' historical, political, and economic processes towards modern capitalism, where violent conquest and colonialism played a constitutional role.

As Carrington, Hogg, Scott et al. (2018, p. 4) point out, through the narrative of modernity, the Global North is regarded as the normative benchmark of Global South countries to reach capitalist modernity and therefore economic, political, and social development. The term 'Southern' refers not only to geographical divides in the world (i.e. the metropolitan states of Western Europe and North America, on the one hand, and the countries of Latin America, Africa, Asia, and Oceania, on the other); it is a metaphor for the unequal and exploitative power relations embedded in 'periphery–centre' rapports in the realm of knowledge (Connell, 2007, p. viii); it is also a metaphor for the other, the invisible, the subaltern, the marginal, and the excluded (Carrington, Hogg, Scott et al., 2018, p. 5). In this sense, the South is also part of Global North societies, which increasingly exclude and exercise different forms of violence against marginal groups.

As an academic discipline, mainstream criminology provides Global South countries with theoretical and methodological tools to understand and confront social dislocation, crime, and violence, common in countries undergoing modernization processes. Under this narrative, 'underdeveloped' countries are experiencing similar challenges to those that Global North countries faced during the processes of urbanization and industrialization in the nineteenth century. This narrative implies that Global South countries are backward; they live in the past of developed countries and must follow their path to become modern, developed, civilized. It also naturalizes the dichotomic forms in which modern social sciences organize and categorize social realities, which in turn legitimize a hierarchical world order through adjectives that fix societies' identities (i.e. developed/underdeveloped, industrialized/industrializing, modern/pre-modern; first world/second world/third world countries).

The modernization narrative also builds the image of a Weberian state, characterized by internal peace and which effectively holds the monopoly of legitimate violence. This ignores the historical role of state-violence in nation-building, the idea of empire and the violent expansion of colonialism across the Global South as constituent aspects of modernity. Colonialism is not simply an echo of the past but a driving force of hierarchical and unequal relations between North and South (Aliverti, Carvalho, Chamberlen et al., 2021; Carrington, Hogg, Scott et al., 2018; Iturralde, 2010). As Connell stresses, the Global North supremacy was built upon the violent subjugation and exploitation of the Global South, and its consequences still resonate today (2007, p. 38). Despite the formal decolonization of Global South societies, they are still wrestling with the legacies of colonialism and Global North intervention and control, including the United States as a neocolonial power (Carrington, Hogg, Scott et al., 2018, p. 5).

Southern criminology seeks to unearth these events and relations as an essential part of the analysis of current phenomena related to crime, violence, and social control—and the epistemic and methodological construction of criminology itself. Standard criminological Global North narratives do not offer a theoretical framework sensitive to the phenomena of crime, violence, and social control outside Global North 'advanced capitalist economies', and do not acknowledge the interconnectedness of Global North societies with other national and regional contexts, which could help to explain the former's domestic situation (Fonseca, 2018, p. 55). Southern criminology aims to redress the power relations embedded in the hierarchical production of criminological knowledge that privileges theories, assumptions, and methods based largely on empirical specificities of the Global North. This does not entail dismissing the theoretical, methodological, or empirical relevance of Northern criminology but rather transforming it into a more plural and inclusive discipline by democratizing the toolbox of available criminological concepts, theories, and methods. Also, one of Southern criminology's goals is to establish a horizontal collaboration with Global North criminology, not only in epistemic terms but also in the discussion of pressing criminological issues that affect both the North and South, and which are commonly dismissed by the metropolitan hegemony of criminological thought (Carrington, Hogg, Scott et al., 2018, p. 3).

Likewise, discourses, strategies, and technologies of social control—some of these echoing colonial practices and anxieties that spring from the fear of an 'exotic other' (Fonseca, 2018, p. 62)—have travelled, not only from the North to the South but also across Northern societies to buttress the subordinated inclusion of 'Southern others' through the excess of penal practices. Thus, the configuration of some significant features of many Global North countries' crime control fields (despite relevant differences among them) is not completely foreign to the forms of social control of postcolonial societies (Fonseca, 2018, pp. 55–56).

Southern criminology stresses that social disorder, violence, and crime, and the different forms of social control to confront them in the Global South, are also relevant in the Global North. This is because they are interconnected in today's global order and have long-standing historical links to the colonial past. Additionally, Global North countries and the global capitalist system are still, at least partially, responsible for them; in this sense, both the North and South share similar features and challenges.

A Critical Elaboration of Southern Criminology: Capitalism, Colonialism, and Empire

Southern criminology is a compelling project that has not been exempt from internal debates. Ciocchini and Greener (2021) have recently exposed a series of objections and proposed a critical elaboration of this project to advance its emancipatory agenda. According to Ciocchini and Greener, Southern criminology has concentrated on the transformation of hegemonic and hierarchical epistemological practices while leaving in the background the development of a critical focus on actual structures and dynamics of neocolonization integral to the current global social order (see also Aliverti, Carvalho, Chamberlen et al., 2021). This may be a contestable point of view, since Southern criminologists are increasingly developing theoretical and empirical analyses underscoring and questioning the ties between contemporary global capitalism and neocolonialism, on the one hand, and different forms of exploitation, subordination, crime, and violence that disproportionately affect the Global South, particularly vulnerable groups and common goods (such as women, migrants, ethnic minorities, and the environment; see, e.g., Carrington, Hogg, Scott et al., 2019).

Internal debates aside, Ciocchini and Greener make the important claim that colonialism is not simply a legacy of the past that casts a shadow over the present, but an ongoing process. Furthermore, the categories of *capitalism* and *imperialism* are crucial to making sense of colonialism and how it creates and sustains the hierarchical categories of class, gender, and race. These are critical components of the debate in Southern criminology and postcolonial studies (2021, p. 3). The concept of 'empire' highlights the historical, and current, role of state violence in the expansion of colonialism (Ciocchini and Greener, 2021, p. 3; Carrington, Hogg, Scott et al., 2019). From this, it follows that colonialism and empire are at the centre of Southern criminology's research agenda as living forms that still shape social relations and geographies of inequality and oppression. These are not simply historically rooted phenomena that manifest themselves through the inertia of the past; they are enforced by state-led dynamics of disempowerment of social groups under gender, class, and race criteria, with the support of local, regional, and global market forces (ibid; Aliverti, Carvalho, Chamberlen et al., 2021).

One of the most emancipatory aspects of Southern criminology is its critical assessment of the connection of empire and neocolonialism with current systems of criminalization and subjugation of specific social groups, as well as the unjust outcomes of North/South unequal exchanges (Ciocchini and Greener, 2021, p. 4; Carrington, Hogg, Scott et al., 2019). Following this route, in the next section of this chapter, I will concentrate on the critical analysis of some features of Latin American crime control fields as supporting structures of neocolonization and empire. These fields facilitate violent forms of inequality and accumulation in the global capitalist system, practices of exploitation and oppression in the Global South, and the imposition of brutally unequal social orders (Ciocchini and Greener, 2021, p. 8).

The Latin American Crime Control Fields: A Southern Perspective

The study of Latin American crime control fields may advance the critique of the global political economy at the base of modernity that, since colonial times, has produced and legitimized forms of oppression and exploitation in the Global South (Ciocchini and Greener, 2021, p. 8). Neocolonial powers, multilateral and international institutions, multinational and local corporations, as well as local elites, have exercised these unequal forms of power to their benefit. Thus, the travels of punitive institutions, practices, and discourses aimed at the social control of the 'unruly' or the 'dangerous classes' is not simply an imposition from the Global North or a legacy of a colonial past. It is also a complex translation, negotiation, and adaptation process of such techniques that configure a rather punitive 'postcolonial penality' (Brown, 2017, p. 189), which in some cases also benefits local elites who want to consolidate their hold on power and to participate in the exploits of an unequal global order whose logic and dynamics are felt on a local scale (Aliverti, Carvalho, Chamberlen et al., 2021; Stambøl, 2021; Agozino, 2005).

This is not to say that the travels of Global North ideas and practices of crime control are a monolithic and unidirectional process, exclusively oriented towards the benefit of local, regional, or global elites. This is a complex process with different outcomes. Indeed, progressive social and political movements have taken advantage of Global North discourses, technologies, and practices to confront forms of crime and violence committed by elites against the bulk of the population or particular social groups to protect or increase their power (i.e. human rights violations, corruption, crimes against the environment). Likewise, there are also significant penal transfers from the Global South to the Global North and between Global South countries. Indigenous forms of justice—which have provided an important body of experiences and theoretical insight to the construction of transitional justice and restorative justice as concepts and an institutional devices—are a case in point (Carrington, Hogg, Scott et al., 2019, pp. 188–189).

To avoid a deterministic and simplistic understanding of colonialism as the global expansion of capital imposed from the North, it is better to frame it through the concept of the 'colonial power matrix'—a complex network of multiple and heterogeneous hierarchies, operating on a global, regional, and local scale, that exert different forms of domination and exploitation (Grosfoguel, 2006; Ciocchini and Greener, 2021, p. 8). Neocolonialism is different from the kind of colonialism that constituted modernity because it has changed strategy: it no longer aims at foreign territories' direct occupation and governance. Instead, it has become de-territorialized thanks to the ascendancy of global financial markets and the institutions that control them. Nevertheless, both forms of colonialism pursue the same goal: 'the exertion of political power over another territory or group in the interests of economic gain' (Ciocchini and Greener, 2021, p. 8).

A clear example of neocolonialism is the 'Washington consensus' imposed by international financial institutions, especially on Latin American countries, which brought about radical economic, institutional, and political reforms in the region, under the mantra of the rule of law, free markets, the global economy, and development. In a traumatic way, the Washington consensus, wrapped in neoliberal discourses and practices, shaped the Latin American political economy of the late twentieth and early twenty-first centuries. It produced economic, social, and political crises, contributed to increases in inequality and the concentration of power among local elites, as well as boosted Latin America's dependency on the Global North, especially the United States and international financial institutions (such as the International Monetary Fund (IMF), the World Bank (WB), and the Inter-American Development Bank (IDB) (Iturralde, 2019).

Crime and Violence Under the Colonial Matrix of Power

This brand of neocolonialism also came at a price regarding the upsurge of social conflict in the region. As poverty remained extremely high, while inequality and social exclusion increased, crime and violence spread in pandemic proportions. As a result, Latin America has been for decades the most violent region of the world and displays the highest crime rates: though Latin America's population represents 8 per cent of the global population, it is a victim of 33 per cent of the world's homicides; the homicide rate in the region is 21.5 per 100,000 inhabitants, three times the global average; seventeen of the twenty countries (and forty-three of the fifty cities) with the highest homicides rates are Latin American; South America and Central America display the highest levels of reported physical assaults and violent robberies in the world—426.28 and 364.84 robberies per 100,000 inhabitants, respectively, while the average in Western Europe is 226.60 (Muggah and Aguirre Tobón, 2018, pp. 2–9).

Crime and violence are depicted as an obstacle to sustainable development and economic growth in the region, making them a central object of political debate, policy reforms, public spending, and different kinds of international intervention (Iturralde, 2019; 2021). The 'crime control and development' rationale is a vital component of the neocolonial project. It reproduces and legitimizes the predominantly economic and geopolitical interests of Global North countries and the international organizations they control (Iturralde, 2021, p. 178; Stambøl, 2021, p. 5). Global North governments and organizations also exert a strong influence on the framing of and responses to crime, violence, and development in Latin American countries, as zero tolerance and law and order policies, as well as the war on drugs, attest (Iturralde, 2019). Despite progressive discourses and practices that have contributed to oppose the colonial legacy, the so-called 'modernization' of Latin American countries' penal institutions during the last three decades has been largely affected by the neocolonial project.

Imprisonment as a Form of Penal Excess Against Marginalized Groups

In spite of the seemingly progressive and humanitarian discourse of the prison as a modern and civilized institution, the incapacitation (rather than the rehabilitation) of marginalized social groups regarded as threatening has been a long-lasting feature of Latin American prisons, almost since their inception in the region in the nineteenth century (Darke and Garces, 2017; Carrington, Hogg, Scott et al., 2019, p. 189). During the last three decades, such incapacitation ethos has intensified, as the vertiginous increase of imprisonment rates attests. The expansion of many Latin American countries' prison systems and populations is, to a significant degree, the result of the modernizing efforts of Latin American countries to comply with international standards and join the global order and market economy. According to the predominant doxa, a key component of the strengthening of the rule of law and the modernization of state institutions is the reform of criminal justice systems to improve the security for the markets as preconditions for development (Iturralde, 2021). The scale of this expansion is visible in trends in prison statistics.

Imprisonment rates rose sharply in almost all Latin American countries; on average such rates doubled (107 per cent), reaching 237 inmates per 100,000 inhabitants. At the beginning of this period, it had been 126 per 100,000 inhabitants (Iturralde, 2019, p. 478). This is one of the highest prison population rates in the world, compared to the global average of 145 inmates per 100,000 inhabitants; Latin America's population represents 8 per cent of the world's population and houses 12 per cent of the globe's total prison population—around 1.2 million—(Marmolejo, Barberi, Bergman et al., 2020). Including the US imprisonment rates (639 prisoners per 100,000 inhabitants), the Americas display the highest imprisonment rates globally. The US penitentiary model has influenced Latin American countries—like Colombia—to expand, modernize, and even partially privatize—in the case of Chile, Brazil, and Peru (Dammert and Salazar, 2009, p. 39)—their carceral systems, and to adopt incapacitation and disciplinary techniques, epitomized in the supermax prison model (Hathazy, 2016; de Dardel, 2015; Ariza and Iturralde, 2021).

Militarized Policing and the Upsurge of Police Brutality in Recent Times: The Covid-19 Pandemic

Even though it is hard to have complete and reliable information regarding police brutality in Latin America, the Lethal Force Use Monitor initiative has gathered data from five countries (Brazil, Colombia, El Salvador, Mexico, and Venezuela). The number of civilian deaths in 2017 at the hands of Venezuelan police forces was extremely high—it exceeded fifteen per 100,000 inhabitants (4,998 civilians killed; 25.8 per cent of the total number of intentional homicides), a rate higher than the intentional homicide rate in most countries. Venezuela was followed by El Salvador, with a rate of six civilians per 100,000 inhabitants (407 civilians killed; 10.3 per cent of the total number of intentional homicides). In third place came Brazil with a rate of just over two civilians per 100,000 inhabitants (4,670 civilians killed; 7.3 per cent of the total number of intentional homicides); Colombia had a rate below one (0.3; 169 civilians killed; 1.5 per cent of the total number of intentional homicides). In Mexico, 0.3 civilians per 100,000 inhabitants were killed by state security forces (371 civilians killed; 1.2 per cent of the total number of intentional homicides) (Monitor Fuerza Letal, 2019, pp. 25–26).[4]

Since the Coronavirus pandemic, poverty, unemployment, and the death toll in Latin American countries are among the highest in the world. This harrowing situation has led to social unrest and violence, as well as spreading protests and riots, that police forces have repressed with extreme violence in countries like Colombia, Chile, Brazil, El Salvador, Peru, and Nicaragua (Human Rights Watch, 2022a; 2022b; 2021; 2020a; 2020b; 2019). I will succinctly refer to the cases of Chile, Colombia, and Brazil to illustrate this point.

At the end of 2019 in Chile, just before the pandemic broke out, students and young people demanded cheaper public transport and better education and health care. Security forces repressed the social protests; reportedly, they killed more than thirty people and injured hundreds of demonstrators (Eisele, 2020). Of 3,449 protesters injured during the strike between October and November 2019, 352 suffered severe eye injuries because police fired rubber bullets directly at their faces (Amnesty International, 2021, p. 21); this is seemingly becoming a recurrent police tactic in Chile and Colombia.

On 28 April 2021, a national strike was declared in Colombia by trade and student unions to protest different government policies that affected the middle and popular classes in the middle of the pandemic. Colombia is one of the Latin American countries with the highest rates of deaths and infections due to Covid-19 (Semana, 2021a), and where poverty increased the most during the pandemic (ECLAC, 2021; CEPAL, 2021, p. 21). According to the Economic Commission for Latin America and the Caribbean (ECLAC), the pandemic brought approximately 22 million people below the poverty line in the region in 2020. That year, the extreme poverty rate was 12.5 per cent, while the poverty rate affected 33.7 per cent of the population. Thus, the

[4] Nonetheless, at least in the cases of Colombia and Mexico, the available data is not trustworthy and may lead to underestimation (Monitor Fuerza Letal, 2019, pp. 25–26).

total number of poor people rose to 209 million; 78 million people lived in extreme poverty—8 million more than in 2019. The countries with the highest increases in poverty rates were Honduras (from 52.3 to 58.6 per cent), Bolivia (from 31.1 to 39 per cent, Colombia (from 31.7 to 38.7 per cent, and El Salvador (from 30.4 to 38 per cent) (ECLAC, 2021).

The response of the Colombian government to the national strike was to deploy the police forces, particularly the militarized anti-riot police unit (known as ESMAD for its Spanish acronym) and even the military to confront the protesters. According to Temblores (a Colombian NGO), between 28 April and 31 May at least twenty people died, and firearms shot by police forces injured seventy; three persons were killed and 167 were wounded by non-lethal weapons used by the antiriot police—sixty-two of them suffered severe eye injuries. Additionally, 1,649 protesters were arbitrarily detained by police forces, and two of them died in detention (Temblores, Indepaz, and Paiis, 2021). Human Rights Watch (2022a) reported that between late April and mid-June 2021, police forces killed twenty-five people, including protesters and bystanders, in most cases with live ammunition; it also reported complaints of five cases of rape and over 100 cases of gender-based violence by police officers. Indigenous groups that joined the national strike were also targeted by police forces and even by armed civilians, especially in Cali, the most populous city in south-west Colombia. Cali's social order is characterized by a closed, white elite that mistrusts indigenous peoples politically organized in south-western Colombia and Afro-Colombians who live in the city's slums in extreme poverty conditions and with the highest levels of unemployment, crime, and violence. These stigmatized groups led mobilizations and road blockages; feeling under siege, members of Cali's elite, heavily armed (as they proudly showed in social networks), acted as vigilante forces, patrolled their neighbourhoods, and, with police complicity, assaulted and even shot at the demonstrators (Human Rights Watch, 2021).

Regarding Brazil, in Rio de Janeiro, between January and April 2020, the police killed 606 people. In April 2020, as isolation measures came into place due to the pandemic and crimes dropped, police violence increased. During this month, police forces were responsible for 35 per cent of all killings in Rio de Janeiro state, killing around six people a day on average—a 43 per cent increase from April 2019. Nationwide, Brazilian police forces have killed more than 33,000 people in the last ten years (Human Rights Watch, 2020a).

The racialized and classed excessive use of lethal force in Brazil is manifest—more than three-quarters of the 9,000 people killed by the Rio de Janeiro police in the last decade were black men. Most of them lived in *favelas* and were killed during police operations allegedly conducted to bust gangs and drug cartels, but that serve to control and eliminate 'dangerous' populations living on society's fringes. While this was happening, President Jair Bolsonaro and Rio de Janeiro Governor Wilson Witzel, during press conferences, encouraged the police to kill even more (ibid). The most recent and brutal of such massacres occurred in the *Jacarezinho favela* in Rio de Janeiro. The police killed twenty-five inhabitants during a police crackdown operation to allegedly arrest twenty-one suspects for minor drug offences; three were arrested, and three were killed. There were one policeman and sixteen neighbours of the *favela* among the dead, all men between 18 and 41 years of age (Olliveira and Betim, 2021).

As these examples show, militarized and lethal policing, together with the expansion of prisons, are central features of Latin American crime control efforts to maintain punitive and exclusive social orders that exert subordinated forms of control along racial and class lines. Police brutality is a structural and long-standing problem historically connected with the central role police forces played during the military dictatorships and the authoritarian democratic regimes (like Colombia) that swept the region during most of the second half of the twentieth century (González, 2020; Iturralde, 2019). Even though police reforms were attempted in some countries during the democratization period starting in the 1990s, many members and high-ranking officers of the police and military forces, formed under the cold war, anti-communist ideology, kept their posts and influence (González, 2020). Their authoritarian mindset sees criminals, human right activists, members of workers and student unions, social protesters, and members of ethnic minorities as a threat to the established order, an indistinguishable internal enemy that must be defeated (González, 2020; Sozzo, 2016).

This exclusionary way of making sense of the political, economic, and social order is also promoted from the top of Latin American governments. During the protests that occurred in Chile and Colombia between 2019 and 2021, both presidents made vague statements that referred to the demonstrators, especially young people, as vandals, criminals, and even as terrorists; a relentless enemy that was at war with the state and society. They also pointed the finger, without concrete evidence, at foreign forces that supposedly support a communist and socialist agenda, and which pretend to overthrow democratic regimes and free markets (Semana, 2021b; Navarro and Tromben, 2019). These examples from different Latin American countries reveal how criminal justice and police institutions spearhead state repression and criminalization to maintain exclusive social orders and sustain racialized, classed, and gendered hierarchies (Ciocchini and Greener, 2021, p. 13), both between the Global North and South and within each of them.

State Building, State Capacity, and Links with Crime and Punishment in Latin America

These salient features of Latin American crime control have contributed to Latin American states being labelled as weak and fragmented, controlled by elites. These authoritarian regimes are seen as not having the necessary institutions, infrastructure, resources, and capabilities to confront social conflicts (Pearce, 2018; Miller, 2021). From this perspective, Latin American states are lacking adequate capabilities to respond to social dislocation through social policies tending thus to resort to punitive measures as the default response.

This narrative overlooks aspects that are crucial to understanding the dynamics of the discourses, practices, and institutions of social control in Latin America, particularly during the last four decades. First, it ignores the extreme inequality, as well as the widespread forms of crime and violence, that affect the region and that pose a great challenge, not only to Latin American states but also to Global North countries and institutions in a globalized world, where crime and violence travel across frontiers. Many of these phenomena find their roots in the historical trajectories and colonial past of Latin American societies, as well as in the processes of state-building in the region, where highly racially segregated political and social orders developed, and where a white and exclusive elite consolidated, thus limiting the state's capacity to act as a legitimate intermediary to negotiate social and economic conflicts.

Second, despite such a historical trajectory, since the 1980s Latin American countries have experienced a profound process of democratization and transformation of their economic regimes that sought to adapt to globalization and the predominant forms of political and economic organization—liberal democracies and market economies. Even though high levels of inequality and poverty are still primary features of the region, and despite neoliberal economic and institutional reform policies aimed at downsizing the state by privatizing many of the services and goods it provides (with the notable exception of the penal state, which has swelled), the Latin American middle class has expanded, mainly because of economic growth, as well as increased taxation. As a result of these changes, many Latin American states increased their capabilities and resources for spending on public goods such as social security, health, education, and security—although these are increasingly provided by the private sector. Therefore, despite neoliberalism (but also because of it vis-à-vis the penal state), state capacity has increased in most Latin American countries during the last four decades, though this has not necessarily resulted in more inclusive societies. The growth of state capacity has impacted security and penal institutions, which have been a focus of institutional reform, and which now have more resources and capabilities to confront crime and violence—even though they still do it mainly through authoritarian and repressive means. This is a central aspect that explains the increase of punishment in different Latin American countries, regardless of their political economies.

Third, the increase of state capacity in Latin American crime control fields has been, to an important degree, influenced by Global North countries and institutions that finance, and pressure for, institutional and policy changes. Global North countries and institutions also provide the discourses, toolkits, and experts to design and implement the new policies and institutions to strengthen the rule of law and the capitalist market economy (Stambøl, 2021). They do so according to their worldviews and interests, which may be aligned with those of Latin American elites, but not with those of the majority of the population, particularly the excluded and marginalized social groups who commonly suffer the consequences of economic structural adjustments, as well as crime, violence, and law and order policies.

These three broad aspects are all related to the colonial legacy and neocolonial forms of power characterized by the exploitation, oppression, and subordination of significant groups of the population (segregated along racial, class, and gender lines) to the benefit of local and global elites. To understand the configuration of crime control fields in the Americas, it is necessary to study the relationship between violence, its unequal distribution among social groups, and state-building. Moreover, it is essential to consider colonialism and slavery's legacies, together with the specific political and institutional forms they produced, which are fragmented, multilayered, often incoherent, and uneven (Miller, 2021).

Conclusion: From the Punitive Turn to the Decolonial Turn

The Latin American crime control fields reproduce the colonial power and knowledge matrix, directing their material and symbolic violence against 'the Other'. This colonial subject is constructed and subordinated through categories based on race, class, and gender. Such forms of subordinated inclusion produce violent reactions from the excluded who have little reason to trust state rules and authorities, perceived as foreign and unjust, lacking the legitimacy to punish (Gargarella, 2016). In this way, the excluded are trapped in a vicious circle in which they exert and suffer violence as a way of life. As Pearce (2018, p. 5) notes, young and poor men in Latin America constitute most of the victims and perpetrators of lethal violence. There is a 50 per cent chance that a low-income young man will die before he turns 31. Furthermore, more than half of the twenty-five countries with the highest femicide rates are Latin American; most victims are poor, young women (ECLAC, 2020; UNODC, 2019).

These interlocked problems of violence, crime, and exclusion that lacerate Latin American societies result from the subordinate and unequal relations that neocolonial forms of power impose at local, regional, and global levels. The dominance of capitalism, liberal democracy, and the rule of law, from a Northern perspective, has conditioned and legitimized unfair, and even violent, forms of exchange, between Global North countries and institutions, and their Southern counterparts. International institutions provide the seal of approval for policies and reforms that Latin American countries must adopt to receive financial aid and technical support. In turn, such endorsement is supposed to point Latin American countries in the right direction to be a part of the global market and the international community, and ultimately to being incorporated into 'civilization' and modernity (Carrington, Hogg, Scott et al., 2019, p. 188). But, in many instances, such policies and reforms are biased, for they respond to the worldviews and interests of Global North countries, while the needs and local knowledge of Global South countries are often ignored.

This type of interference has had a long-lasting impact on Latin American crime control fields, which share a history with their Global North counterparts, building a relation that is entrenched in the dynamics of colonialism and neocolonialism (Carrington, Hogg, Scott et al., 2019, p. 190). Many of the policies enforced to confront violence and crime, as well as the discourses, knowledges, technologies, and institutions that support them, are commonly devised by Global North governments and experts. They conceptualize the crime problem, and the responses to it, from their realities and interests, without knowing, or even acknowledging, the significant differences and varieties of the Latin American context. As a result of this process, 'common sense', 'technical', and 'politically neutral' policies, not only do not work on Latin American ground but can be counterproductive.

The war on drugs is a compelling example; after decades of enforcing a prohibitionist and punitive approach towards the drugs problem, not only has the illegal drugs trade not decreased, but the criminal organizations behind it have multiplied, are extremely violent, with great corrupting power, and the capacity to seriously disrupt fragile states that do not hold the monopoly of violence in their territories. Latin

American countries take most of the burden of the human and economic costs of the war on drugs. Such war has caused thousands of deaths, environmental disasters, the weakening of democratic institutions, and has propelled the expansion of an authoritarian penal and carceral system that disproportionally punishes the most vulnerable social groups (young males and women from urban peripheries, single mothers, ethnic minorities, impoverished peasants).

Likewise, and equally important, penal transfers, such as the war on drugs, are embraced in various ways by dissimilar local actors in the recipient countries, according to the different conditions, problems, and interests of their contexts. During the process, penal transfers experience a true metamorphosis that produces, not simply adaptations, but new forms of penality, with a series of peculiarities that sets them apart from the 'originals' (Carrington, Hogg, Scott et al., 2019, p. 190).

Mainstream, Northern criminology has been, for the most part, blind to the contextual construction of the problems of crime and violence—and the responses to them—beyond Global North countries. Southern criminology has provided innovative epistemological perspectives to shed light on these forms of structural injustice and has questioned the legitimacy of Northern criminology as the dominant knowledge of crime and social control phenomena. Additionally, Southern criminology has emphasized how the political, economic, and cultural elites segregate and oppress the colonial subjects, both in the North and the South.

Taking inspiration from the most critical strands of criminology, Southern criminology bears the promise of being an emancipatory enterprise, potentially bringing down the divisive and exclusive foundations on which modern forms of social control are based. To fulfil this promise, Southern criminology must unearth the structural political, economic, and cultural causes of violence and crime in the Global South, their connection to the Global North, as well as the forms of social control they elicit. Moreover, it must show how the power relations that emerged with colonialism and neocolonialism produced specific forms of government and state-building. Together with these, it must reveal the discourses and practices of social control that reproduce and legitimate the exclusion and oppression of certain social groups who are the main targets of penal excesses, many of which are still travelling from Global North countries.

Southern criminology is not the opposite, or the successor, of Northern criminology. Rather, it is a globally oriented criminology envisioned with a Southern look, which is particularly sensitive to the inclusion of multiple subaltern voices (Carrington, Hogg, Scott et al., 2019, p. 182), but without excluding Northern perspectives. This is also the expression of a conceptual pragmatism that understands that the bedrock of criminological thinking is to be found in the Global North (ibid, p. 184), together with its dark side—the colonial matrix of knowledge and power upon which it was built—and which cannot be dismissed.

The Southern perspective seeks to engage with Northern criminology to democratize, pluralize, open, and de-centre the criminological discipline (ibid), making it more innovative adaptative, and varied. This inclusive perspective seeks to place Southern criminology *in relation to*—instead of *in opposition to*—Northern criminology. Its aim is to help to build—on an equal footing—a transnational criminology that bridges global divides (ibid, p. 188), rather than broadening the existing gaps. Just as the metamorphosis and hybridization of penal transfers processes from the North to the South—and vice versa—are an essential object of study of Southern criminology, the hybridity of cognitive and methodological frameworks to make sense of crime, violence, and social responses to them in an increasingly globalized and interconnected world is a key component of the Southern perspective.

By turning its gaze to the South, geographically and metaphorically speaking, Southern criminology has opted to find new paths instead of following the Anglo-European trail of civilization. Hopefully, this search will lead to innovative ways of devising political, social, economic, and cultural projects that may construct a different, more inclusive regime. One that embraces difference and is better equipped to confront crime and violence without systematically inflicting pain and humiliation upon the most vulnerable social groups.

References

Agozino, B. (2005) 'Crime, Criminology and Post-Colonial Theory: Criminological Reflections on West Africa', in Sheptycki, J. and Wardak, A. (eds) *Transnational & Comparative Criminology*. London: Glasshouse Press.

Aliverti, A., Carvalho, H., Chamberlen, A. et al. (2021) 'Decolonizing the criminal question', *Punishment & Society*, 23(3), pp. 297–316.

Amnesty International (2021) 'Tiros a la vista: Traumas oculares en el marco del paro nacional'. London: Amnesty International. Available at: www.amnesty.org/es/documents/amr23/5005/2021/es/ (accessed 30 June 2022).

Ariza, L. and Iturralde, M. (2021) 'Las prisiones y las transformaciones del campo del control del crimen en Colombia', in Ariza, L., Iturralde, M., and Tamayo, F. L. (eds) *Cárcel derecho y sociedad. Aproximaciones al mundocarcelario en Colombia*. Bogotá: Uniandes, pp. 21–53.

Birkbeck, C. (2011) 'Imprisonment and internment: Comparing penal institutions North and South', *Punishment & Society*, 13(3), pp. 307–332.

Blaustein, J. (2016), 'Exporting criminological innovation abroad: Discursive representation, "evidence-based crime prevention" and the post-neoliberal development agenda in Latin America', *Theoretical Criminology*, 20(2), pp. 165–184.

Brown, M. (2017) 'Postcolonial penality: Liberty and repression in the shadow of independence, India c. 1947', *Theoretical Criminology*, 21(2), pp. 186–208.

Carrington, K. and Hogg, R. (2017) 'Deconstructing criminology's origin stories', *Asian Journal of Criminology*, 12(3), pp. 181–197.

Carrington, K., Hogg, R. and Sozzo, M. (2018) 'Criminology, Southern Theory and Cognitive Justice', in Carrington, K., Hogg, R., and Sozzo, M. (eds) *The Palgrave Handbook of Criminology and the Global South*. Cham: Palgrave, pp. 3–17.

Carrington, K., Dixon, B., Fonseca, D. et al. (2019) 'Criminologies of the Global South: Critical reflections', *Critical Criminology*, 27, pp. 163–189.

Carrington, K., Hogg, R., Scott, J. et al. (2019) *Southern Criminology*. Abingdon: Routledge.

Carrington, K., Hogg, R. and Sozzo, M. (2016) 'Southern criminology', *The British Journal of Criminology*, 56(1), pp. 1–20.

Ciocchini, P. and Greener, J. (2021) 'Mapping the pains of neo-colonialism: A critical elaboration of Southern criminology', *The British Journal of Criminology*, 61(6), pp. 1612–1629.

Comisión Económica para América Latina y el Caribe (CEPAL) (2021) 'La paradoja de la recuperación en América Latina y el Caribe Crecimiento con persistentes problemas estructurales: desigualdad, pobreza, poca inversión y baja productividad'. Santiago de

Chile: CEPAL. Available at: https://repositorio.cepal.org/bitstream/handle/11362/47043/5/S2100379_es.pdf (accessed 29 June 2022).

Connell, R. (2007) *Southern Theory: The Global Dynamics of Knowledge in Social Science*. Sydney: Allen & Unwin.

Dammert, L. and Salazar, F. (2009) *¿Duros con el delito?: populismo e inseguridad en* América Latina. Santiago de Chile: FLACSO.

Darke, S. and Garces, C. (2017) 'Surviving in the new mass carceral zone', *Prison Service Journal*, 229, pp. 2–9.

De Dardel, J. (2015) 'Resistiendo la "nuda vida": las prisiones como agentes en la era de la nueva cultura penitenciaria en Colombia', *Revista Crítica Penal y Poder*, 8, pp. 47–65.

De Dardel, J. and Söderström, O. (2009) 'The rise and fall of Supermax: How the US prison model and ultra punitive penal policy travelled to Colombia', MAPS Working Papers 3. Neuchâtel: University of Neuchâtel.

Economic Commission for Latin America and the Caribbean (ECLAC) (2020) 'ECLAC: The Persistence of Violence against Women and Girls in the Region and Femicide, its Maximum Expression, is Troubling', 24 November. Available at: www.cepal.org/en/pressreleases/eclac-persistence-violence-against-women-and-girls-region-and-femicide-its-maximum (accessed 30 June 2022).

ECLAC (2021) 'Pandemic Prompts Rise in Poverty to Levels Unprecedented in Recent Decades and Sharply Affects Inequality and Employment', 4 March. Available at: www.cepal.org/en/pressreleases/pandemic-prompts-rise-poverty-levels-unprecedented-recent-decades-and-sharply-affects (accessed 30 June 2022).

Eisele, I. (2020) 'Police violence in Latin America "out of control"', *Deutsche Welle*, 11 October. Available at: www.dw.com/en/police-violence-in-latin-america-out-of-control/a-55231675 (accessed 29 June 2022).

Faraldo-Cabana, P. (2018) 'Research Excellence and Anglophone Dominance: The Case of Law, Criminology and Social Science', in Carrington, K., Hogg, R., and Sozzo, M. (eds) *The Palgrave Handbook of Criminology and the Global South*. Cham: Palgrave, pp. 163–181.

Flores-Macías, G. A. and Zarkin, J. (2021) 'The militarization of law enforcement: evidence from Latin America', *Perspectives on Politics*, 19(2), pp. 519–538.

Fonseca, D. (2018) 'Reimagining the sociology of punishment through the global-south: Postcolonial social control and modernization discontents', *Punishment & Society*, 20(1), pp. 54–72.

Gargarella, R. (2016) *Castigar al prójimo. Por una refundación democrática del derecho penal*. Buenos Aires: Siglo XXI.

González, Y. (2020) *Authoritarian Police in Democracy: Contested Security in Latin America*. Cambridge: Cambridge University Press.

Grosfoguel, R. (2006) 'World-systems analysis in the context of transmodernity, border thinking, and global coloniality', *Review (Fernand Braudel Center)*, 29(2), pp. 167–187.

Hathazy, P. (2016) 'Remaking the prisons of the market democracies: New experts, old guards and politics in the carceral fields of Argentina and Chile', *Crime Law Social Change*, 65, pp. 163–193.

Human Rights Watch (2019) 'Crackdown in Nicaragua. Torture, Ill-Treatment, and Prosecutions of Protesters and Opponents'. Available at: www.hrw.org/report/2019/06/19/crackdown-nicaragua/torture-ill-treatment-and-prosecutions-protesters-and (accessed 29 June 2022).

Human Rights Watch (2020a) 'Brazil Suffers its Own Scourge of Police Brutality', 3 June. Available at: www.hrw.org/news/2020/06/03/brazil-suffers-its-own-scourge-police-brutality (accessed 29 June 2022).

Human Rights Watch (2020b) 'Peru: Serious Police Abuses Against Protesters', 17 December. Available at: www.hrw.org/news/2020/12/17/peru-serious-police-abuses-against-protesters (accessed 29 June 2022).

Human Rights Watch (2021) 'Colombia: Egregious Police Abuses Against Protesters', 9 June. Available at: www.hrw.org/news/2021/06/09/colombia-egregious-police-abuses-against-protesters (accessed 29 June 2022).

Human Rights Watch (2022a) 'Colombia: Events of 2021', in *World Report 2022*. Available at: www.hrw.org/world-report/2022/country-chapters/colombia#583016 (accessed 29 June 2022).

Human Rights Watch (2022b) 'El Salvador: Evidence of Serious Abuse in State of Emergency', 2 May. Available at: www.hrw.org/news/2022/05/02/el-salvador-evidence-serious-abuse-state-emergency (accessed 29 June 2022).

Iturralde, M. (2010) 'Democracies without citizenship: Crime and punishment in Latin America', *New Criminal Law Review*, 13(2), pp. 309–332.

Iturralde, M. (2019) 'Neoliberalism and its impact on Latin American crime control fields', *Theoretical Criminology*, 23(4), 490.

Iturralde, M. (2021) 'The Emperor's New Clothes: A Critical Reading of the Sustainable Development Goals to Curb Crime and Violence in Latin America', in Blaustein, J., Fitz-Gibbon, K., Pino, N.W. et al. (eds) *The Emerald Handbook of Crime, Justice and Sustainable Development*. Bingley: Emerald Publishing, pp. 175–196.

Langer, M. (2004) 'From legal transplants to legal translations: The globalization of plea bargaining and the Americanization thesis in criminal procedure', *Harvard International Law Journal*, 45(1), pp. 1–64.

Langer, M. (2007) 'Revolution in Latin American criminal procedure: Diffusion of legal ideas from the periphery', *The American Journal of Comparative Law*, 55(4), pp. 617–676.

Liu, J. (2009) 'Asian criminology—challenges, opportunities and directions', *Asian Journal of Criminology*, 4(1), pp. 1–9.

Marmolejo, L., Barberi, D., Bergman, M. et al. (2020) 'Responding to Covid-19 in Latin American prisons: The cases of Argentina, Chile, Colombia, and Mexico', *Victims & Offenders*, 15(7–8), pp. 1062–1085.

Miller, L. L. (2021) 'American Exceptionalism or Exceptionalism of the Americas? The Politics of Lethal Violence, Punishment and Inequality', in Lacey, N., Soskice, D., and Cheliotis, L. et al. (eds) *Tracing the Relationship between Inequality, Crime and Punishment*. Oxford: Oxford University Press, pp. 133–162.

Monitor Fuerza Letal (2019) 'Monitor del uso de la fuerza letal en América Latina: un estudio comparativo de Brasil, Colombia, El Salvador, México y Venezuela'. Aguascalientes: Monitor Fuerza Letal. Available at: www.monitorfuerzaletal.com/app/9SfbJ2os932UW8Af5wn8qspLl3S6fRN1SRItTN3x.pdf (accessed 30 June 2022).

Muggah, R. and Aguirre Tobón, K. (2018) 'Citizen security in Latin America: Facts and Figures'. Rio de Janeiro: Igarapé Institute. Available at: https://igarape.org.br/wp-content/uploads/2018/04/Citizen-Security-in-Latin-America-Facts-and-Figures.pdf?utm_campaign=2018_newsletter_10&utm_medium=email&utm_source=RD+Station (accessed 30 June 2022).

Navarro, F. and Tromben, C. (2019) '"Estamos en guerra contra un enemigo poderoso, implacable": los discursos de Sebastián Piñera y la revuelta popular en Chile', *Literatura y Lingüística*, 40, pp. 295–324.

Olliveira, C. and Betim, F. (2021) 'La ONU pide una investigación independiente de la masacre en una favela de Río de Janeiro', *El País*, 7 May. Available at: https://elpais.com/internacional/2021-05-07/la-onu-pide-una-investigacion-independiente-de-la-masacre-en-una-favela-de-rio-de-janeiro.html (accessed 30 June 2022).

Pearce, J. (2018) 'Elites and violence in Latin America: Logics of the fragmented security state', in Violence, Security, and Peace Working Papers, 1. Available at: www.lse.ac.uk/lacc/publications/PDFs/VSP1-Pearce-Elites-Violence-Latin-America-web.pdf (accessed 30 June 2022).

Semana (2021a) 'Colombia es el tercer país de América Latina más afectado por el coronavirus', *Semana*, 27 May. Available at: www.semana.com/vida-moderna/articulo/colombia-es-el-tercer-pais-de-america-latina-mas-afectado-por-el-coronavirus/202145/ (accessed 30 June 2022).

Semana (2021b) 'Duque dice que el vandalismo durante el paro nacional es "terrorismo urbano de baja intensidad"', *Semana*, 30 April. Available at: www.semana.com/nacion/articulo/el-presidente-ivan-duque-dice-que-el-vandalismo-durante-el-paro-nacional-es-terrorismo-urbano-de-baja-intensidad/202158/ (accessed 30 June 2022).

Solar, C. (2021) 'Militarism and the militarization of public security in Latin America and the Caribbean', *Research Publications*, 38, pp. 1–26.

Sozzo, M. (2016) 'Policing after Dictatorship in South America', in Bradford, B., Jauregui, B., Loader, I. et al. (eds) *The Sage Handbook of Global Policing*. London: Sage, pp. 337–355.

Stambøl, E. M. (2021) 'Neo-colonial penality? Travelling penal power and contingent sovereignty', *Punishment & Society*, 23(4), pp. 536–556.

Temblores, Indepaz, and Paiis (2021) 'Informe de Temblores ONG, Indepaz y Paiis a la CIDH sobre la violación sistemática de la Convención Americana y los alcances jurisprudenciales de la Corte IDH con respecto al uso de la fuerza pública contra la sociedad civil en Colombia, en el marco de las protestas acontecidas entre el 28 de abril y el 31 de mayo de 2021'. Available at: https://4ed5c6d6-a3c0-4a68-8191-92ab5d1ca365.filesusr.com/ugd/7bbd97_691330ba1e714daea53990b35ab351df.pdf (accessed 30 June 2022).'

United Nations Office on Drugs and Crime (UNODC) (2019) 'Global Study on Homicide. Gender-related killing of women and girls'. Vienna: UNODC. Available at: www.unodc.org/documents/data-and-analysis/gsh/Booklet_5.pdf (accessed 30 June 2022).

Wacquant, L. (2003) 'Toward a dictatorship over the poor? Notes on the penalization of poverty in Brazil', *Punishment & Society* 5(2), pp. 197–205.

4
From Genocidal Imperialist Despotism to Genocidal Neocolonial Dictatorship
Decolonizing Criminology and Criminal Justice with Indigenous Models of Democratization

*Biko Agozino**

Introduction

Colonizers tend to adopt the ideology of the Empire of Law to normalize the despotic means of domination that characterize imperialism. They tend to believe that the colonized were living under Asiatic despotism before the colonizers arrived with the civilizing mission or the white man's burden of bringing Enlightenment to dark natives. Records of genocidal crimes organized by the colonizers tend to be rationalized as essential for the purpose of teaching the natives some moral lessons through pacification and sadistic domination. This legalistic interpretation of colonial plunder was framed by Henry Maine (1861) in his book about the rule of law under British colonization in India where the common law was relied upon to directly govern areas with significant European presence while the vast expanse of the subcontinent was allowed to be ruled under what was defined as customary laws. Such a 'dual mandate' seemed to work well enough to maintain conditions suitable for the exploitation of the natives in India and so the method was adopted by Frederick Lugard who applied it to parts of Africa, including Nigeria (Mamdani, 2012). As expected by the colonial administrators, there were African national groups such as the Igbo of Nigeria and the Kikuyu of Kenya who did not have chiefs and could not be easily defined as part of the dual mandate system. Rather than recognize indigenous democratic systems of self-determination and republican representative governance as advanced systems of governmentality, according to Walter Rodney (1970), the non-monarchical African cultures were called 'headless societies' and represented as the most backward 'tribes' who were desperately in need of being civilized by having chiefs appointed and imposed on them.

* As a faculty member of the Virginia Tech community, I acknowledge the Tutelo/Monacan peoples who are the traditional custodians of the land upon which we work and live, and recognize their continuing connection to the knowledge, land, water, and air that Virginia Tech consumes each day. As a land grant university established for white men only on a plantation where hundreds of enslaved Africans were forced to labour for hundreds of years without pay, we collectively pay our respects to these Nations, and to their elders past, present, and emerging generations for helping to increase inclusive excellence.

Biko Agozino, *From Genocidal Imperialist Despotism to Genocidal Neocolonial Dictatorship* In: *Decolonizing the Criminal Question.* Edited by: Ana Aliverti, Henrique Carvalho, Anastasia Chamberlen, and Máximo Sozzo, Oxford University Press.
 DOI: 10.1093/oso/9780192899002.003.0005

For thousands of years before Africans came into contact with Europeans, we had our own laws and rules that ensured peaceful coexistence without the need for prisons, professional judges and lawyers, armed police officers, and even without a standing professional army. The Europeans arrived with assumptions of white superiority to justify enslavement, conquest, conversion, and colonization. Cheikh Anta Diop (1991) dismissed such assumptions of white supremacy with the documentation of evidence that Africa was civilized and was held in high esteem before contact with the Europeans and he suggested that the Europeans were the ones who appeared to be barbaric by contrast. That was what made Mahatma Gandhi reportedly say that Western civilization would be a good idea if it meant that the West would act in a more civilized manner around the world. Meanwhile, the colonized have never ceded their freedom, humanity, wisdom, spirituality, and equality, nor have they ceded their land; and our scholars have no intention of ceding any discipline to the colonizers and settlers. The struggle for decolonization is an ongoing process epistemologically but also politically and economically in the efforts to deepen democracy and abolish policy despotism and terrorism. The struggle continues against the continuation of European attempts to recolonize the world in alliance with the phantom bourgeoisie and their servile pseudo intellectuals who lack the nationalism of the European bourgeoisie (Said, 1993; Fanon, 2004).

To the astonishment of the colonizers, it was the women who led the uprising against the autocratic powers of the colonizers and their appointed chiefs in what was known as the Women's War in Nigeria (Agozino, 1997; Falola and Paddock, 2011). In response, the colonizers commissioned anthropologists to conduct 'intelligence reports' for the purpose of determining if the women were drunk or under the influence of the men to make them oppose despotic colonial rule. This chapter reflects on one such report by C. K. Meek (1937) on *Law and Authority in a Nigerian Tribe* with implications for the retention of despotic authoritarianism in neocolonial African states today.

The book by Meek was prefaced with a quotation from a Scottish Unionist and colonial administrator, Lord Tweedsmuir (John Buchan) stating that 'If we are to found another Rome ... we should carry our fathers on our shoulders.' This says a lot about the intentions of the colonizers and their intellectuals who believed that Rome represented a classical or model civilization based on the rule of law and less on the force of conquest, a precursor to the concept of hegemony by consent as elaborated by Gramsci who applied it to the ruling class under capitalism. The invocation of Rome in colonial jurisprudence is very apt for a genocidal British Empire that relied mainly on what Onyeozili (2020) identified as 'gunboat criminology' to conquer and exploit millions of people around the world or subject them to genocide if they were not ready to sign treaties of 'protection' so that their land could be seized, and their resources expropriated.

Rome was a brutal military dictatorship that did not pretend to be democratic despite the existence of a Senate at the capital where slavery, blood sports, assassinations, bloody pogroms, and mass rape were nevertheless the more notable aspects of their history (Gibbon, 2016 [1776]). European jurisprudence sanitizes the despotism of Rome by recognizing the foundational codification of law that went on to influence the Napoleonic Code and the family of law known as the civil law tradition while retaining the assumption of force or violence in 'law enforcement', according to Derrida (1992). The same picture fits the British Empire perfectly even though it claims to be under the common law tradition but was forced to adopt codification for the administration of the empire by few officials in far-flung places. Historians still celebrate Rome and the British Empire as if they were glorious, yearning to build another Rome as if one barbarous empire was not enough—whereas Fanon (2004) called on colonized peoples to avoid trying to build another Europe that talks so much about humanity but commits abominations against human beings wherever they found them. Being an OBE (Order of the British Empire, otherwise known as obedient boy of the empire) or a KBE (Knight of the British Empire, also called the knave of the British empire) is still a valued status among the British even though the British Empire has since been defeated by forces of decolonization and despite the rejection of the 'honour' by many people with conscience, like John Lennon and Phil Scraton, among others.

The Westminster parliamentary democracy that the British practised at home was denied to the colonized who were persuaded by means of bayonets and canons to accept British rule around the world. But like the Romans, the British also tried to pretend that their oppressive and exploitative domination was based on the rule of law in a civilized manner that should attract the gratitude of the colonized. Karl Marx critiqued this assumption with the concept of Oriental Despotism which was regarded by previous writers as a reference to the inferiority or barbarism of the colonized. Marx flipped the concept back at Europeans by using the concept to indicate the fact that European culture was despotic and such despotism was being extended to people in the Orient by strengthening traditional systems of authority suitable for colonial domination. Edward Said (1978) pointed this out in *Orientalism* by noting that what Marx critiqued as oriental despotism was also to be found in Western despotism. Evidence for this can be found in *Ancient Law* by Maine (1861) who documented the patriarchal despotism that characterized life in Europe but Maine assumed that such patriarchal despotism was natural and universal. African women were struggling to challenge racist-imperialist-patriarchy to show that despotism is neither natural nor universal in ancient societies structured in democracy without race-class-gender hierarchies and where social status was based more on generation than on gender contrary to the Eurocentric notion that all women were inferior to all men under patriarchy (Nzegwu, 2006; Oyewumi, 1997). Diop (1991) also pointed out that what Marx and Engels called the Asiatic Mode of Production is better referred to as the African Mode of Production because it developed first in Africa for the purpose of collective labour to control the annual overflows of the Nile river through irrigation for agriculture in collectively owned land but not necessarily with despotic state power nor with patriarchy given the widespread practice of matriarchy and matrilineal descent in African societies.

In his interpretation of *Ancient Law*, Mamoud Mamdani (2012) agreed with Maine that colonial domination was implemented mainly through legal definitions and classifications of people than through the application of military force. In his Harvard University Lectures, *Define and Rule*, Mamdani reflected on what it means to be classified as neither native nor settler, how the colonized were defined and subjected to indirect rule, and how they struggled for decolonization. According to him, many

Africans did not have national consciousness until the colonizers came to define them as tribes based on their languages. He cited the doctoral dissertation of Kenneth Dike (1956) on *Trade and Politics in the Niger Delta* to assert that the Igbo of Nigeria did not have a pan-Igbo identity in their semi-autonomous villages before the British came to define them as an 'Ibo tribe'. Similarly, he cited the selected writings of Bala Usman (2006) to insist that the Hausa did not identify themselves by their common language but by their hometowns while the name given to the Yoruba was attributed to the Hausa and Fulani who called them Yariba or unreliable. Hausa people from Kano identified as Kanawa and not as Hausa until the colonizers came to define them as belonging to a Hausa–Fulani tribe—a combination of two different ethnic groups, according to Usman.

Mamdani neglected to point out that, as Walter Rodney (1972) observed in *How Europe Underdeveloped Africa*, there are no tribes in Africa despite colonial attempts to define Africans in tribal terms. According to Rodney, it is false to define the Hausa, Yoruba, or Igbo, numbering about 50 million people each, as tribes when they do not have a common leader or a common story of origin despite each sharing a common language. The genocidal war that was waged against the Igbo in Biafra was often called a tribal war but Rodney disagreed because there was no genocidal war against the Igbo by their neighbours before colonization, and there is no African tribe called Shell BP or the British Labour Party Government or the Soviet Union that supported the genocidal war with weapons and a food blockade that claimed 3.1 million lives in thirty months, mainly through the use of starvation as a 'legitimate weapon of war' (Ekwe-Ekwe, 2019).

Although Mamdani identified the fact that unlike the centralization of authority of white men under colonialism, the indigenous societies had decentralized power sources that allowed women and different social classes to define what was legitimate, his book of lectures neglected the struggle of African women against the dual mandate system of colonial rule. Instead, Mamdani devoted some attention to the opposition of educated women in Tanzania against a mutiny by soldiers whereas the Igbo and Ibibio Women's War, Abeokuta women's uprising, Kikuyu Women's anti-forced labour in Kenya, anti-pass law protests by South African women, Algerian, Guinean, Mozambican, Zimbabwean, South African, and Angolan women involved in the wars of national liberation, Igbo women in Biafra serving in the military, providing food, directing traffic, running schools, and raising children under starvation and air bombardments, and the Liberian Women 'Praying the Devil Back to Hell' would have been more appropriate for the focus of his book (Agozino, 1997; Achebe, 2012; Falola and Paddock, 2011).

This chapter will not conduct a detailed discourse analysis of the well-known militancy of African men and women against the definition of Africans as tribal for the purpose of domination, the maintenance of such definitions in post-colonial Africa by the phantom bourgeoisie identified by Frantz Fanon (2004), and the continuation of the struggle to negate colonialist definitions of Africans for domination and the push towards intensified decolonization and for the withering away of the colonial state structures imposed on Africans and maintained by neocolonialism. Instead, this chapter focuses on the lessons that criminologists could learn from the history of actually existing decolonization struggles for the decolonization of criminology which emerged as the social science most closely tied to colonialism as a tool for the domination of others (Agozino, 2003).

Decolonization as Resistance Against Colonization

We know that indigenous peoples resisted and continue to resist racism-sexism-imperialism on their own land and suffered genocide at the hands of European invaders in many parts of the world. Irene Watson (2015) analysed the legal aspect of the resistance struggles by the Aboriginal peoples of Australia by pointing out that before being conquered and dehumanized by the settlers, the indigenous peoples had their own 'naked law' or 'raw law' for people who were innocent enough not to obsess about covering their nakedness with clothes or wear fake hair as wigs to signify the authority of judges and lawyers. She illustrated the law-abiding nature of the indigenous people with the indigenous folklore of the giant frog that drank all the water in the world and did not have any qualms if all other animals and plants died of thirst. The indigenous people discussed this environmental crisis and considered spearing the giant frog to let out the water for everyone to enjoy. They decided not to spear the frog but instead to tickle him until he laughed and let all the water out for every creature to enjoy. Catherine Bell (1997) stated that section 35 of the Canadian Constitution guarantees the rights of indigenous peoples to be governed under indigenous law just as the rights of French Canadians to be governed under civil law and English Canadians to be governed under common law are supposedly protected by the Constitution except when one system infringes on the rights of others, indigenous rights being the ones that are routinely infringed upon without much redress. Hence, Maria Giannacopoulos (2017) warned that the 'campaign seeking "recognition" of Aboriginal people in the Constitution effaces the foundational debts of dispossession that structure both economy and sovereignty'.

The New Zealand Treaty of Waitangi contains a criminological lesson in non-violent jurisprudence because the treaty stated that the Māori were ready to share their land and knowledge equally with the Pakeha, but it turned out that the British Crown did not keep to the bargain, allowing the settlers to wage wars of conquest against the indigenous people of Aotearoa who only wanted to exercise the right to continue farming their gardens but were racially profiled as having 'warrior genes' and 'criminal genes' to justify genocidal policies against them (Jackson, 2016; Cunneen and Tauri, 2016; Blagg and Anthony, 2019). American Indian Natives saved the pioneers by sharing their food and knowledge of healing herbs with them. But the visitors turned around and almost completely wiped out the indigenous populations in order to steal their land for plantations run by enslaved Africans who continued to wage liberation struggles—sometimes in alliance with the American Indian Natives and some white abolitionists—everywhere there was enslavement, forcing Europeans to outlaw slave trading and eventually to end enslavement during the Civil War out of fear of uprisings (Du Bois, 1906; 1935).

Marx remarked that the memories of past traditions of struggle inform current ones and so criminologists should not be quick to ignore the past traditions of colonized people in the struggle to decolonize the discipline not simply by claiming to borrow family conference methods of dispute resolution or criminology as peacemaking from indigenous communities without adequate commitment to reparative justice and decolonization (Pepinsky and Quinney, 1991; Morris and Maxwell, 1998; Moyle and Tauri, 2016). As Marx put the imperative for tradition in change:

> The tradition of all dead generations weighs like an Alp on the brains of the living. And just as they seem to be occupied with revolutionizing themselves and things, creating something that did not exist before, precisely in such epochs of revolutionary crisis they anxiously conjure up the spirits of the past to their service, borrowing from them names, battle slogans, and costumes in order to present this new scene in world history in time-honored disguise and borrowed language.
>
> (Marx, 1852)

The indigenous philosophy of law that is devoid of militarized policing and mass incarceration must have puzzled Sigmund Freud (1919) when he observed that the indigenous peoples regulated incest taboos with the threat of death by spearing, and yet such killing was rare to indicate that indigenous people avoided breaking the incest taboo more than Europeans who were fond of marrying their close cousins just to keep the family inheritance in the family. Instead of recognizing the scientific wisdom of indigenous peoples who avoided breaking the incest taboo for obvious reasons of not weakening the gene pool, Freud turned it around to assume that the indigenous people must be neurotic to enforce such common-sense rules more strictly than 'normal' Europeans.

Nelson Mandela exemplified indigenous jurisprudence after the abolition of apartheid in South Africa by constituting the Truth and Reconciliation Commission under Archbishop Desmond Tutu instead of seeking the punitive justice model of the Nuremburg Principles (Dastile and Ndlovo-Gatsheni, 2020). Derrida called this model the forgiveness of the unforgivable in contrast to Abrahamic religions that preached forgiveness only for things that are forgivable (Derrida, 1997). Desmond Tutu and Mpho Tutu maintained that the philosophy of Ubuntu or 'a bundle of humanity' shows that there is nothing that is unforgivable and that there is no one who does not deserve to be forgiven for something (Tutu and Tutu, 2014). Achebe agrees that African culture is a culture of tolerance symbolized by the Igbo with Mbari sculptures of a miniature house populated with figurines representing people, animals, plants, and spirits from different parts of the world (Achebe, 2012; Elechi, 2020). Martin Luther King Jr repeatedly referred to a similar symbol of 'the beloved community' as 'the World House' that was constructed by a common ancestor for us all to share if we do not fight and burn it down with foolish chaos (King, 1968).

In other words, the struggle against racism-sexism-imperialism is in the interest of the vast majority of people who suffer the consequences of oppressive ideologies directly or indirectly. Such a global struggle for social justice involves coalitions and alliances in line with the theory of articulation in societies structured by dominance (Hall, 1980). It is mistaken to dismiss such struggles as special interests that involve only those directly affected. Moreover, when the struggle against injustice is won—for example in the abolition of slavery, the right of women to vote, independence for colonies, and the anti-apartheid movement—it is not only the victimized who benefit for oppression is a world system and liberation contributes to social justice globally. In this regard, Onyeozili et al.'s (2021) discussion of the protests against the Special Armed Response Squad of the Nigerian police shows that the whole world would benefit from democratic policing even in poor countries where militarized policing is the preferred policy. Priyamvada Gopal's book, *Insurgent Empire*, offers an analysis of insurgent movements and struggles against the British Empire as struggles beneficial for British people too, where workers did not win the struggle for the eight-hour day until slavery was abolished, women did not get the right to vote until Ireland regained independence, and the welfare state emerged at the height of the anti-colonial insurgency in India and Africa (Gopal, 2020).

European Colonial Despotism and Resistance

Following the 1857 mutiny against British rule in India, Henry Maine was invited to study ancient society and identify what made it different from Western society. The result was his influential work on *Ancient Law* that was published in 1861 to wide acclaim, earning him a position as the legal expert in the governing council of colonized India. In the book, he asserted that there are two types of society—those based on the status of individuals (race, caste, gender, generation, and class) and those based on the social contract that modernist Europeans claimed to be the basis of their civilized social organization in contrast to oriental societies that were presumably still under despotic authorities of patriarchs, just like ancient Europeans presumably used to be before the Enlightenment era.

It is a matter of record that colonized people resisted as best they could in order to defend their independence and they continued the struggle for the restoration of their independence. The battles between the warriors of Shaka Zulu and the Boers and the British in South Africa are the stuff of legends (Rodney, 1972). The indigenous peoples of Mozambique were not defeated until the invaders who were known as 'locusts' by the people, managed to recruit fighters from one ethnic group to be used in the defeat of another (Rodney, 1970). Similar long-drawn-out battles were recorded by the Igbo in Nigeria against the British invaders during the Ekumeku war documented by Ohadike (1991). The anti-colonial wars of national liberation in Angola, Mozambique, Zimbabwe, Kenya, and Algeria hold lessons for criminologists who should include them in texts about deviant colonizers and social control by liberation activists. The wars in Latin America led by Simon Bolivar, the war led by Jose Marti against Spanish rule in Cuba, the Chinese revolution, the wars in Vietnam and Korea, and the Cuban revolution are all well documented and could serve as teachings for the decolonization of criminology to make it less of a technology for imperialist domination (Chomsky, 1975).

A lot has been published on the Women's War of 1929 that the colonizers tried to demean by defining it as the Aba Women's Riot as if it was localized in one town, and as if it was only a riot rather than a war, battle, or fight as seen by the women (Afigbo, 1972; Echewa, 1992; Agozino, 1997; Falola and Paddock, 2011). There is no need to rehash the details here, but it will be helpful to highlight the theoretical lessons that can be learnt from the militancy of African women against colonial despotism. The history of the struggle was documented by Adiele Afigbo (1972) in *Warrant Chiefs* to demonstrate that the attempt by the colonizers to tax women in Eastern Nigeria without representation in the colonial government was what prompted the women to declare war against the warrant chiefs appointed by the colonizers over the traditionally democratic people. The women burned the homes of those chiefs, burned down the trading posts of colonial merchants, and burnt down the corrupt native courts imposed by the colonizers. In response, the colonial police opened fire and killed dozens of unarmed women. Two public enquiries were held to find out what led to the uprising. Following that, the entire communities were fined to recover the costs of the properties destroyed, but the colonizers bowed to the pressure of the women by deciding to abolish the corrupt warrant chief system of indirect rule in Eastern Nigeria while the taxation of women was also discontinued, unless they were civil servants who paid as they earned.

To understand what gave African women the courage to rise up against the might of the colonial authorities, intelligence reports were commissioned from colonial anthropologists to conduct ethnographies on the system of government among 'acephalous' people who lived in what the colonizers called 'headless' societies. One such report was compiled by a theologian, C. K. Meek (1937) who was trained at Oxford University. He started from the assumption that the Igbo were among the most primitive people in Africa because they proudly claimed that the Igbo knew no king (*Igbo ama Eze*) or that the Igbo had no king (*Igbo enwe Eze*). The colonizers believed that they were doing them a favour by trying to civilize them with the imposition of warrant chiefs. They were surprised to learn that respected men like Ezulu in *The Arrow of God* by Chinua Achebe (1964) would rather starve than accept being appointed as a warrant chief to serve the colonizers. Consequently, only ne'er-do-wells accepted such appointments and immediately proceeded to rule oppressively as all feudal lords tend to do (Afigbo, 1972).

The colonizers must have wondered if the women were drunk to make them declare war against colonialism. A lot of the investigations by Meek were about the drinking of alcoholic wine tapped from the palm oil tree and naturally mixed with water. However, he found that Igbo women did not indulge in this habit as much as the men, and that even the men did not drink to get drunk but instead shared drinks ceremoniously and as part of religious rituals. The people drank more water than wine and used water to pour some of their libations to the spirit of the morning sun. They could be said to have turned water into wine by drinking it and enjoying it like wine (Agozino, 2021). Meek also examined warrior traditions like headhunting but found that women did not indulge in that, nor did every man do so given that the achievement symbolized by the buying and killing of cows to be shared by all was also respected as headhunting. In search of patriarchy, he considered the symbol of the right hand, *Ikenga*, as the authority symbol for men who qualified as successful headhunters but he did not know that every woman also has *aka ikenga* or the right hand; everyone does because the Igbo make a moral distinction between the food hand, *aka nri*, as opposed to the left hand, *aka nsi*, that was regarded as unclean and must not be used to take or give food. He really could not find anything wrong with the women who declared war against colonialism, and so he recommended that the people were too difficult to be subjected to indirect rule because they were backward. He concluded that they should be governed directly by the District Commissioners, and this remained the case even after some colonial constitutions allowed the appointed House of Chiefs to sit with a legislative assembly in other regions of Nigeria, however the South East region remained unicameral with only an elected legislative assembly.

Looking broadly at the history of the confrontations between women of African descent and colonial law and order policies, it becomes clear that the militancy of Igbo and Ibibio women during the Women's War was observed in different eras as was documented in *Black Women and the Criminal Justice System* (Agozino, 1997) to illustrate what Stuart Hall (1980) theorized as race-class-gender articulation, disarticulation, and rearticulation in societies structured by dominance. Although the systems of enslavement, colonialism, neocolonialism, and internal colonialism were represented by dominant social forces as part of the civilizing process, Edward Said (1993) warned that we must never forget that the New World was announced by the conquerors and settlers with a sense of white supremacy, presumptions of the white man's burden of bringing what even the relatively backward Portuguese called *illuminismo* to the dark peoples, and with moral crusades about the savages that needed to be saved from hell fire. Yet, it was the genocidal colonizers who exhibited the worst forms of devilish immorality based on greed, theft, plunder, and genocidal warfare, racism, sexism, and imperialism (Rodney, 1972; Chinweizu, 1975; Fanon, 2004; Agozino, 2003). Criminologists have remained reluctant to include such huge organized crimes in the subject matter of the discipline despite abundant literature in other disciplines.

A classic treatment of the topic was offered by C. L. R. James (1980, pp. 2–26) in *The Black Jacobins*, but criminologists have largely ignored the text. Whereas apologists of white supremacy suggested that the enslaved Africans were happier than their ancestors in Africa, James presented evidence to show that the Africans lived in more humane peaceful societies before the commencement of the raids that forced some of the chiefs to wage wars for the capture of men and women to be sold into slavery. African women had high social status as wives and mothers, but they were soon debased to the status of sex slaves and breeders of people to be enslaved while also having their labour stolen on the plantations. James narrated the endless revolts waged by Africans against the raiders from the interiors to the coasts and aboard the ships to show that what was going on was plunder, force, warfare, kidnapping, and human trafficking but not trade as such. If there was no resistance, then there would have been no need to chain the kidnapped Africans to prevent them from running away. The resistance continued on the plantations despite efforts to promulgate laws exclusively applied to the enslaved Africans. The 1685 Negro Codes authorized whipping of rebellious Africans and this must have been used excessively to necessitate 'reforms' aimed at regulating the number of lashes allowable, but still no one kept count and people were frequently beaten to death. Some scholars discovered a mental illness that caused the enslaved to keep running away and they prescribed the cure or 'punishment' for the 'crime' of running away from their kidnappers to be the chopping off of the foot and other forms of brutality (Paton, 2001). Note that the people being collectively punished were the enslaved African victims of a huge organized crime and the criminals were the ones given the power to victimize the innocent Africans. According to James, in the rare case of a white man being found guilty of torturing enslaved Africans to death, the colonial governor of Saint Domingo ordered that he should be retried and found not guilty because the fate of the whole island depended on a not guilty verdict. That was what led to the Haitian Revolution during which enslaved Africans defeated the armies of France, Spain, and Britain in quick succession to establish the first republic proclaimed by formerly enslaved people and thereby hastening the abolition of slavery. Angela Davis (1981) pointed out that it was possible for enslaved African women to participate equally in the uprisings with enslaved African men because the material conditions under enslavement were relatively equal despite the additional burden of systematic raping of enslaved women for the reproduction of enslaved labour.

Walter Rodney (1972, p. 46) supports this analysis by pointing out that there was no slave mode of production in Africa because no African society relied on slave labour for major economic activities. Rodney maintained that the few Africans who collaborated with the Europeans were the chiefs who saw the Europeans as class allies whereas the majority of Africans, including men and women, waged fierce struggles against the capture and enslavement of their beloved. Rodney (1969), therefore, cautioned that it is wrong to study African history only from the points of view of the few chiefs and kingdoms when the study of direct democracies like the Igbo could yield better lessons for people of African descent living in democracies today.

Under colonial legal systems, Africans were subjected to cruel oppressive rules designed to facilitate the extraction and evacuation of surpluses produced by African workers and peasants for the dialectical process of the development of Europe, at the expense of the underdevelopment of Africa. Just as in the hundreds of years of slavery, colonized Africans were not passive victims of colonial oppression and exploitation, they mobilized against their victimization. Agozino (1997, p. 27) remarked that the resistance against victimization should be recognized by criminologists as an original contribution to the decolonization paradigm rather than theorizing everything done by the criminal justice system as 'the punishment of offenders'—the first four words in the influential text by David Garland (1990). Under the colonial condition, what is sometimes referred to as punitive expeditions represent organized plunder, looting, child abuse, and massacre of innocent Africans, Māori, Aboriginal and Torres Strait Islander peoples of Australia, American Indian Natives, and Asians who defiantly resisted colonial injustice or were just abducted and massacred as children to be buried in mass graves by churches that pretended to be educating them on behalf of the despotic state.

The killing of indigenous scholars and the exclusion of their contributions to knowledge can be theorized as epistemicide, according to Santos (2014). Others have added that there can be no decolonization without epistemic decolonization (Carrington et al., 2019; Cavalcanti, 2020). To these truisms, it should be added that the struggle for decolonization in Africa and elsewhere is not simply an epistemic 'decolonial' struggle but also, and primarily, a practical struggle of the people to regain their sovereignty and self-determination in the face of determined efforts by imperialism to recolonize the world of knowledge, economy, culture, and politics with the tools of despotism. Moosavi (2018) is right to caution that those who propound theories from the South should be careful not to use the turn of phrase as an alibi to continue privileging the knowledge and lives of people who descended from the North and who may steal the knowledge and wealth of the world without sufficient acknowledgement of the originators from the South.

Conclusion

The Women's War shows that the militancy of the women was not proof that the men were not brave enough to fight against colonization or vice versa, contrary to the views of some historians cited by Agozino (1997). Rather, both men and women engaged in the struggle for the restoration of independence sometimes separately and sometimes jointly, as was the case in other parts of Africa. There was no gender separatism in the struggle against colonialism unlike the struggle of British women against nuclear arms at Greenham Common when they also demonstrated against men joining the protest because they saw men as part of the problem of militarism (Young, 1990).

African women always include demands in the interest of African men instead of treating all men as the enemies of all women. For instance, the women demanded that women must not pay taxes but they also demanded that men must not pay taxes to a colonial government that did not represent them. Up until today, tax collectors do not bother the women in the villages while the men are likely to flee into the bushes to avoid being arrested for tax avoidance. The women are aware that when their sons or husbands are arrested for tax evasion, the women will be forced to use their own savings to pay the taxes and bail them out. As discussed earlier to show that anti-racism-imperialism-sexism is in the interest of all, the strategy of gender separatism among Western feminists is counter-productive because the challenges facing men and women under racist-imperialist-patriarchy are articulated, disarticulated, and rearticulated in societies structured by dominance in such ways that the suitable strategy for resistance is coalition and alliance building as Stuart Hall (1980) insisted and Kimberley Crenshaw (1989) theorized.

The marginalization of women in decolonization struggles serves to weaken the decolonization efforts. Frantz Fanon (2003) theorized the role of women in the war of national liberation in Algeria, and Thomas Sankara (2007) and Samora Machel (1985) both emphasized that the liberation of women is not an act of charity but a necessary condition for the liberation of Africans (Agozino, 1997; 2020). Consequently, the African Union Commission Parliament adopted the principle of gender parity in the make-up of the Parliament, but this principle is yet to be adopted and implemented in every state in Africa and at every level of government. Walter Rodney reminds us that educated African women are still discriminated against in public appointments to the disadvantage of Africans as a whole, who need to support gender equity in education at all levels. Mahmood Mamdani (2012) reported that one of the political parties opposed to Julius Nyerere supported the mutiny against his government on the ground that educated married women were being offered employment when there were many unemployed African men.

The defeat of the warrant chief systems of indirect rule by women during the Women's War should have encouraged Africans to incorporate the principle of representative democracy in the constitution of every level of government. This principle was approximated by Nnamdi Azikiwe, the leader of the struggle for the restoration of independence in Nigeria, who negotiated for an elected single camera legislative body in the Eastern Regional Government where he was the Premiere during the self-rule transition to independence. The Northern Region remained under what the colonizers defined as House of Natural Rulers who reigned beside the Northern Legislative Assembly. The Western Region also retained what was imposed by the colonizers as the House of Chiefs that ruled alongside the Western Legislative Assembly. Only the Eastern Region lacked a legislative house made up of what the colonizers defined as traditional rulers. In hindsight, Azikiwe should have negotiated for a House of Women to be elected to sit alongside the legislative assembly in the South East. Perhaps, the state assemblies across Africa should adopt this insight by having one chamber for men and another chamber for women to sit and offer checks and balances in lawmaking, while the archaic feudal institutions that the colonizers imposed on Africans should be abolished in the way that India abolished such after regaining independence.

In the case of the Igbo, another Oxford colonial anthropologist, Margery Perham (1970), bragged that she was the one who recommended to the military dictatorship that the Igbo may have been rebellious because they were jealous of their monarchical neighbours, and not because they were subjected to genocide by the neocolonial terrorist state. Thus, according to Perham, the way to make the Igbo more governable was to impose traditional rulers on them as the colonizers had attempted and failed. This recommendation was implemented in the Local Government Reform Decree of 1976 by General Olusegun Obasanjo, but the Igbo need to reassert their democratic traditional preference for representative republicanism and replace the imposed traditional rulers with elected town mayors and councillors for limited terms in office given that the constitution promises a republic.

The genocidal state imposed on Africans is made to wither away by deepening democracy and reuniting Africans across the colonial boundaries, abolishing the oppressive feudal structures that the colonizers imposed and by expanding educational opportunities for all Africans, then all Africans, including women, would be happy to pay taxes to support publicly funded education and healthcare at all levels. Ifi Amadiume (2000) theorized that women already tax themselves to build and equip hospitals in African communities because they know that they will at some time need those facilities, while the male-dominated political leadership across Africa continues to indulge in the theft of public funds. Such women should be supported to organize with like-minded men to elect more women into public office and hold them accountable along with the men. The owners of big mansions should be made to pay property tax to go to local government authorities for the purpose of funding schools.

In the final analysis, the true test of the struggle for decolonization in Africa may not lie in the coining of a new cliché such as 'decolonial theory' but in the practical withering away of the colonial boundaries and the despotic colonial laws that are retained in Africa (Agozino, 2018). Nelson Mandela helped to push the African National Congress and the Communist Party of South Africa ruling coalition for a more humane new South Africa by abolishing the boundaries of the apartheid homelands overnight, abolishing the death penalty, granting the right to vote to prisoners, recognizing marriage equality, and legalizing marijuana. The unfortunate spates of violence against fellow Africans who were allegedly attacked for speaking incomprehensible '*makwerekwere*' languages and for 'stealing jobs and women' by fellow Africans in South Africa (Matsinhe, 2016) may end along with the internal attacks on other ethnic groups and the epidemic violence against women throughout Africa and along with penal abolitionism (Dastile and Agozino, 2019). When the ridiculous colonial boundaries are erased to allow Africans the freedom of movement in a People's Republic of Africa united democratically and when women and the working people have proportional representation in governance, then the terrorist state imposed by the colonizers will never again organize genocidal attacks against the masses and foreign ants will be unable to attempt to swallow the African elephant without indigestion.

References

Achebe, C. (1964) *Arrow of God*. Oxford: Heinemann.

Achebe, C. (2012) *There was a Country: A Personal History of Biafra*. New York: Penguin.

Afigbo, A. (1972) *The Warrant Chiefs: Indirect Rule in Southeastern Nigeria, 1891–1929*. Ibadan: University of Ibadan Press.

Agozino, B. (2003) *Counter-Colonial Criminology: A Critique of Imperialist Reason*. London: Pluto Press.

Agozino, B. (2018 [1997]) *Black Women and the Criminal Justice System: Towards the Decolonization of Victimization*. New York: Routledge.

Agozino, B. (2018) 'The withering away of the law: An indigenous perspective on the decolonisation of the criminal justice system and criminology', *Journal of Global Indigeneity*, 3(1), pp. 1–22.

Agozino, B. (2020) 'Africana Liberation Criminologies', in Agozino, B., Saleh-Hanna, V., Onyeozili, E. C. et al. (eds) *The Routledge Handbook on African Criminologies*. London: Routledge.

Agozino, B. (2021) 'Why Did Jesus Turn Water into Wine', in Mason-John, V. (ed.) *Afrikan Wisdom: New Voices Talk Black Liberation, Buddhism, and Beyond*. Berkeley, CA: North Atlantic Books.

Amadiume, I. (2000) *Daughters of the Goddess, Daughters of Imperialism: African Women Struggle for Culture, Power and Democracy*. London: Zed Books.

Bell, C. (1997) 'Metis constitutional rights in section 35(1)', *Alberta Law Review*, 36(1), pp. 180–217.

Blagg, H. and Anthony, T. (2019) *Decolonising Criminology: Imagining Justice in a Postcolonial World*. London: Macmillan.

Carrington, K., Hogg, R., Scott, J. et al. (2019) *Southern Criminology*. London: Routledge.

Cavalcanti, R. P. (2020) *A Southern Criminology of Violence, Youth and Policing: Governing Urban Insecurity in Brazil*. London: Routledge.

Chinweizu, I. (1975) *The West and the Rest of Us: White Predators, Black Slavers and the African Elite*. New York: Random House.

Chomsky, N. (1975) *Turning the Tide: US Interventions in Central Americas and the Struggle for Peace*. Chicago, IL: Haymarket Press.

Crenshaw, K. (1989) 'Demarginalizing the intersections of race and sex: A black feminist critique of antidiscrimination doctrine, feminist theory and antiracist politics', *University of Chicago Legal Forum*, 1, pp. 139–167.

Cunneen, C. and Tauri, J. (2016) *Indigenous Criminology*. Bristol: Policy Press.

Dastile, N. P. and Agozino, B. (2019) 'Decolonizing incarcerated women's identities through the lens of prison abolitionism', *South African Crime Quarterly*, 68, p. 21–32.

Dastile, N. P. and Ndlovo-Gatseni, S. J. (2020) 'Nelson Mandela's Criminology: A Decolonial Interpretation', in Agozino, B., Saleh-Hanna, V. Onyeozili, E. C. et al. (eds) The Routledge Handbook on Africana Criminologies. London: Routledge.

Davis, A. (1981) *Women, Race and Class*. London: The Women's Press.

Derrida, J. (1992) 'Force of Law: "Mythical Foundations of Authority"', in Cornell, D., Rosenfeld, M., and Carlson, D. G. (eds) *Deconstruction and the Possibility of* Justice. London: Routledge.

Derrida, J. (1997) *On Cosmopolitanism and Forgiveness*. London: Routledge.

Dike, K. O. (1956) *Trade and Politics in the Niger Delta, 1830–1885: An Introduction to the Economic and Political History of Nigeria*. Oxford: Clarendon Press.

Diop, C. A. (1991) *Civilization or Barbarism: An Authentic Anthropology*. New York: Lawrence Hill.

Du Bois, W. E. B. (1906) *The Suppression of the African Slave Trade to America*. Cambridge, MA: Harvard University Press.

Du Bois, W. E. B. (1935) *Black Reconstruction in America: 1860–1880*. New York: Harcourt Brace.

Echewa, O. T. (1992) *I Saw the Sky Catch Fire*. New York: Dutton.

Ekwe-Ekwe, H. (2019) *The Longest Genocide: Since May 1966*. Dakar: African Renaissance Press.

Elechi, O. O. (2020) 'Mbari and Ubuntu in Indigenous African Criminologies', in Agozino, B., Saleh-Hanna, V., Onyeozili, E. C. et al. (eds) *The Routledge Handbook on African Criminologies*. London: Routledge.

Falola, T. and Paddock, A. (2011) *The Women's War of 1929: A History of Anti-Colonial Resistance in Eastern Nigeria*. Durham, NC: Carolina Academic Press.

Fanon, F. (2003) 'Algeria Unveiled', in Duara, P. (ed.) *Decolonization: Perspectives from Now and Then*. London: Routledge.

Fanon, F. (2004) *The Wretched of the Earth*. New York: Grove Press.

Freud, S. (1919) *Totem and Taboo: Resemblances Between the Psychic Lives of Savages and Neurotics*. New York: Moffat, Yard and Co.

Garland, D. (1990) *Punishment and Modern Society: A Study in Social Theory*. Oxford: Clarendon.

Giannacopoulos, M. (2017) 'Sovereign debt crises, referendums and the changing face of colonial power', *Continuum*, 31(1), pp. 33–42.

Gibbon, E. (2016 [1776]) *The History of the Decline and Fall of the Roman Empire*. New York: BiblioBazar.

Gopal, P. (2020) *Insurgent Empire: Anticolonial Resistance and British Dissent*. London: Verso.

Hall, S. (1980) 'Race, Articulation and Societies Structured in Dominance', in UNESCO (ed.) *Sociological Theories: Race and Colonialism*. Paris: UNESCO.

Jackson, M. (2016) 'The Abolition of Prisons and Indigenous Self Determination', Keynote Presentation at the Forum for Indigenous Research Excellence, University of New South Wales, Wollongong. Available at: www.youtube.com/watch?v=mPnf0cbFIuo (accessed 28 June 2022).

James, C. L. R. (1980) *The Black Jacobins: Toussaint L'Ouverture and the San Domingo Revolution*. London: Allison and Busby.

King, M. L. Jr (1968) *Where Do We Go From Here: Chaos or Community?*. Boston, MA: Beacon Press.

Machel, S. (1985) Munslow, B. (ed.) *Samora Machel, An African Revolutionary: Selected Speeches and Writings*. London: Zed Books.

Maine, H. S. (1861) *Ancient Law: Its Connection with the Early History of Society, and its Relation to Modern Ideas*. London: John Murray.

Mamdani, M. (2012) *Define and Rule: Native as Political Identity*. Cambridge, MA: Harvard University Press.

Marx, K. (1852) 'The Eighteenth Brumaire of Napoleon Bonaparte'. Marxists.org. Available at: www.marxists.org/archive/marx/works/subject/hist-mat/18-brum/ch01.htm (accessed 28 June 2022).
Matsinhe, D. (2016) *Apartheid Vertigo: The Rise in Discrimination Against Africans in South Africa*. London: Routledge.
Meek, C. K. (1937) *Law and Authority in a Nigerian Tribe*. Oxford: Oxford University Press.
Moosavi, L. (2018) 'A friendly critique of "Asian" and "Southern" criminology', *The British Journal of Criminology*, 59(2), pp. 257–275.
Morris, A. and Maxwell, G. (1998) 'Restorative justice in New Zealand: Family group conferences as a case study', *Western Criminology Review*, 1(1), pp. 1–17.
Moyle, P. and Tauri, J. M. (2016) 'Māori, family group conferencing and the mystifications of restorative justice', *Victims & Offenders*, 11(1), pp. 87–106.
Nzegwu, N. (2006) *Family Matters: Feminist Concepts in African Philosophy of Culture*. Albany, NJ: SUNY Press.
Ohadike, D.C. (1991) *The Ekumeku Movement: Western Igbo Resistance to British Conquest of Nigeria, 1883–1914*. Athens, OH: Ohio University Press.
Onyeozili, E. C. (2020) 'Gunboat Criminology in the History of People of African Descent: Nigeria and Democratic Republic Congo examples', in Agozino, B., Saleh-Hanna, V., Onyeozili, E. C. et al. (eds) *The Routledge Handbook on African Criminologies*. London: Routledge.
Onyeozili, E. C., Agozino, B., Agu. A. et al. (2021) *Community Policing in Nigeria*. Blacksburg, VA: Virginia Tech Publishing.
Oyewumi, O. (1997) *The Invention of Women: Making an African Sense of Western Gender Discourse*. Minneapolis, MN: University of Minnesota Press.
Paton, D. (2001) 'Punishment, crime, and the bodies of slaves in eighteenth-century Jamaica', *Journal of Social History*, 34(4), pp. 923–954.
Pepinsky, H. E and Quinney, R. (eds) (1991) *Criminology as Peacemaking*. Indianapolis, IN: University of Indiana Press.
Perham, M. (1970) *Colonial Sequence: 1949–1969: A Chronological Commentary Upon British Colonial Policy in Africa*. London: Methuen and Co.
Rodney, W. (1969) *The Groundings With My Brothers*. London: Bogle l'Ouverture.
Rodney, W. (1971) 'The year 1895 in Southern Mozambique: African resistance to the imposition of European colonial rule', *Journal of the Historical Society of Nigeria*, 5(4), pp. 509–536.
Rodney, W. (1972) *How Europe Underdeveloped Africa*. London: Bogle L'Ouverture.
Said, E. (1978) *Orientalism*. New York: Penguin.
Said, E. (1993) *Culture and Imperialism*. New York: Penguin.
Sankara, T. (2007) *Women's Liberation and the African Freedom Struggle*. Ottawa: Pathfinder Press.
Santos, B. de S. (2014) *Epistemologies of the South: Justice Against Epistemicide*. London: Routledge.
Tutu, D. and Tutu, M. (2014) *The Book of Forgiving*. New York: HarperCollins.
Usman, Y. B. (2006) *Beyond Fairy Tales: Selected Historical Writings of Yusufu Bala Usman*. Zaria: Abdullahi Smith Centre for Historical Research.
Watson, I. (2015) *Aboriginal Peoples, Colonialism and International Law: Raw Law*. New York: Routledge.
Young, A. (1990) *Femininity in Dissent*. Milton Keynes: Open University.

PART 2
CONTEXTUALIZING THE CRIMINAL QUESTION

5

A Postcolonial Condition of Policing?

Exploring Policing and Social Movements in Pakistan and Nigeria

Zoha Waseem

Introduction

Responding to contemporary calls for decolonizing criminology (Aliverti et al., 2021) and drawing upon Southern and postcolonial perspectives (Carrington, Hogg and Sozzo, 2016), this chapter develops a framework on postcolonial policing by exploring aspects of public policing in two former colonies: Pakistan and Nigeria. It presents what I call the 'postcolonial condition of policing' (PCP). This framework critically captures the legacies, continuities, and impacts of colonial security policies and their postcolonial adaptations, building on scholarship from Asia and Africa (Jauregui, 2016; Owen, 2016a, 2016b; Hornberger, 2013, Comaroff and Comaroff, 2007).

To varying degrees, postcolonial states exhibit traits of regime insecurity, due to persisting state fragility, disputed sovereignty, and contested legitimacy, where the stability of governments, legal frameworks, and policing mechanisms cannot be assumed (Jauregui, 2013).[1] In these states, colonial institutional designs of the police have largely been retained at a macro-level by successive postcolonial regimes to secure the interests of the status quo at large. At a micro level, securitization policies are designed to keep the postcolonial regimes' interests in mind (such as targeting migration, dissent, or political activism) and routinely influence police culture, practice, and policy. Public policing institutions and agents are at the centre of two compulsions: on the one hand, they must meet the security-centric demands of the postcolonial state and its elite patrons, with professional uncertainties and personal vulnerabilities; on the other hand, they continue to face challenges created by their colonial institutional design that has produced a regimented, hierarchical, and coercive apparatus. The PCP captures policework and culture in such contexts.

I maintain that there are two primary effects of the PCP as it applies to public policing. First, is the persistence of *militarism* or police militarization: a direct legacy of the institution's colonial design, and the ethos of colonial governmentality with which the institution was developed.[2] Second, we see the persistence of *informality*: a state in

[1] Indeed, state fragility also depended on experiences with colonial rule across empires (Tusalen, 2016).

[2] As Heath (2021) discusses, colonial governmentality depended upon disciplinary violence, punishment, and a range of oppressive tactics to manage colonial subjects. Over time, this directly evolved into the 'violence work' (e.g. police torture) enabled by the colonial regime through its police.

Zoha Waseem, *A Postcolonial Condition of Policing?* In: *Decolonizing the Criminal Question.* Edited by: Ana Aliverti, Henrique Carvalho, Anastasia Chamberlen, and Máximo Sozzo, Oxford University Press.
DOI: 10.1093/oso/9780192899002.003.0006

which institutional weaknesses and capacity issues are acknowledged, but largely unaddressed; as a result, police work and officer survival is contingent upon the utilization of informal practices, procedures, and networks of interpersonal relations.[3] Here, I briefly explore how the PCP explains police violence in Pakistan and Nigeria and state responses to social movements (specifically, the Pashtun Tahaffuz Movement in Pakistan and the #EndSARS movement in Nigeria). This chapter demonstrates that a continued manifestation of the PCP has aggravated public insecurity and fuelled collective resistance against state violence but suggests, based on state responses to both movements, that the PCP is unlikely to be resolved despite social agitation.

Postcolonial perspectives enable critical analyses of policing, especially in geographies with shared histories and traumas. The enquiry of colonial experiences is essential to see how policing institutions were designed and deployed, and how, even with modernization reforms and professionalization agendas (delivered through new training, technology, and skill sets), historical foundations continue to shape contemporary enforcement (Deflem, 1994). Therefore, both colonial and contemporary histories, studied comparatively, reveal significant political, social, and economic challenges underpinning law enforcement structures, within and beyond the postcolony. Contemporary scholarship has also recognized how ideas, knowledge, and strategies borne out of and designed for the subjugation and suppression of colonial subjects are travelling back to the metropolises, enabling the racial discrimination against minorities—what is sometimes referred to as the 'colonial boomerang effect', 'imperial feedback loop', or 'colonial policing coming home' (Bell, 2013; Elliot-Cooper, 2021; Mukhopadhyay, 1998; Go, 2020). A critical analysis of policing and justice in Southern or postcolonial contexts can therefore better inform criminological scholarship and policymaking globally.

Catering to this agenda, I use two cases for the application of this perspective of postcolonial policing. For my primary case, Pakistan, I draw upon ethnographic and archival research that I have been conducting since 2014. For my secondary case, Nigeria, I consult peer-reviewed publications, open sources, and policy reports (Agbiboa, 2015a; Alemika, 1993, Chukwuma, 1997; Owen, 2012; Cooper-Knock and Owen, 2014; CLEEN, 2013). Pakistan and Nigeria make for an exciting comparison, one previously unexplored. Both are former British colonies, but colonial rule in British India was more direct, centralized, and longer, leading to relatively well-defined institutions after independence. In Nigeria, colonial administration was less centralized, leading to weakly designed and less-cemented institutions (Kohli, 2020). While in both jurisdictions, the British introduced civil services that included the police, these were more developed in British India. Nevertheless, a crisis of police legitimacy has persisted over the decades in both postcolonies. Both have also seen similar sociopolitical trajectories: strained civil–military relations and problematic democratic transitions; rapid population growth and urbanization; demographically

[3] Also see Owen (2016b) on how officers use informal networks and relationships to 'strategically navigate' institutional restraints when it comes to promotions and postings, and Jauregui (2016) on how officers, especially the rank-and-file, innovate to meet demand in the face of limited resources and political interferences. I have further developed the notion of 'procedural informality' in my work on police response to the Covid-19 pandemic in Pakistan (Waseem, 2021).

diverse societies with unresolved ethno-religious conflicts; rampant corruption; police inefficiency and a lack of public accountability; and failed attempts at police reform coinciding with years of extrajudicial violence. Collectively, these factors have stimulated civil society resistance grounded in grievances against authoritarian policing styles.

A Framework for Postcolonial Policing

Colonization produced varied manifestations of governance, policing, and order maintenance. Although certain administrations incorporated or co-opted existing (indigenous) policing and dispute-resolution mechanisms, in accordance with local traditions, creating hybrid and, in some cases, pluralized systems of governance, colonial governmentality relied on top-down repression and coercion. The 'modernization' of formal legal and policing structures (most extensively, in British India) relied on the institutionalization of militarism into policing, to cement a disciplinary and hierarchical structure through which systemic violence could be perpetrated by both elite officers and the subjugated and subservient 'native' rank-and-file (Heath, 2021).

While postcolonial states inherited these structures, these states have also faced peculiar local or regional challenges such as state fragility, political uncertainty, ethno-religious grievances, economic strains, civil–military clashes, and rapid urbanization with underdevelopment, among other factors that have routinely and sometimes collectively challenged the legitimacy and authority of these states. Postcolonial states are thus uniquely insecure regimes (despite 'democratization' efforts undertaken in some cases), where insecure elites have calculatedly retained repressive colonial policing structures. Here, quests for regime security have trumped demands for police accountability to the people, or institutional reform at large (Baxi, 1982), public trust in the police has remained low, and ideas such as procedural justice, popularized in the West, have struggled to take root (Tankebe, 2009). Under such regime insecurity, and with the retention of colonial policing structures, we see a continuity of colonial policing but with uniquely postcolonial constraints, considerations, and challenges.

Capturing colonial continuities in contemporary policing, in a comparative way, is complicated; it is neither accurate to blame the colonial past alone or make claims of an 'unbroken chain', nor simply disregard historical (postcolonial) developments that have taken place in the domains of policing and law enforcement. Therefore, to design a critical perspective on postcolonial policing that can explain contemporary grievances with the police, I build on existing perspectives from Africa (Owen, 2016a; 2016b; Agbiboa, 2015a, 2015b; Hills, 2008; Tankebe, 2009; 2013) and India (Jauregui, 2013; 2016; Lokaneeta, 2020) among others, and develop the framework of the 'postcolonial condition of policing'. What distinguishes PCP from other forms of policing is that postcolonial states have uneven reach and 'contested sovereignty', due to a 'complex choreography of police and paramilitaries, private and community enforcement, gangs and vigilantes' (Comaroff and Comaroff, 2007), much more extensive than the contestation seen in other contexts. In the face of such contested sovereignty, and other informal policing mechanisms, postcolonial policing remains central to the

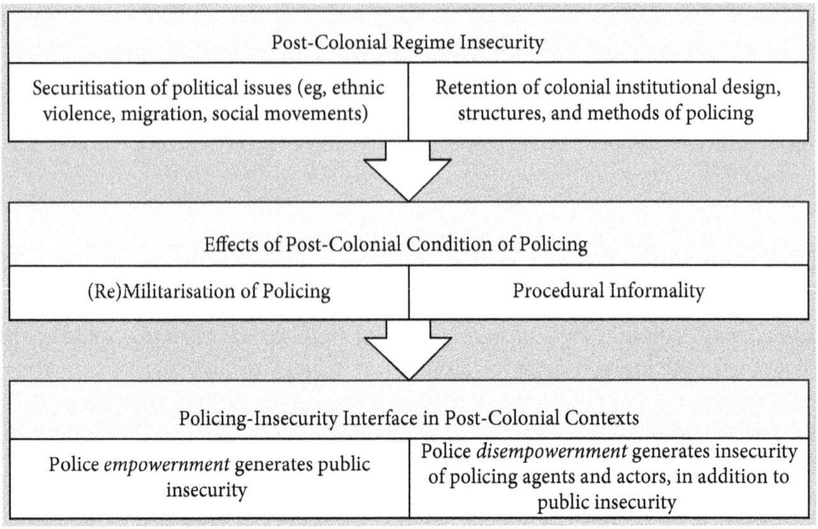

Fig. 5.1 The postcolonial condition of policing

regime's attempts at consolidation and centralization of power. Failure to centralize power in this manner, during both colonial and postcolonial periods, is what feeds regime insecurity in postcolonial politics. The PCP thus takes place under this dynamic of persisting regime insecurity.

No doubt, some key characteristics of the PCP will differ to varying degrees depending upon the cases and contexts in which this condition is explored. Nevertheless, some key components can be outlined before we analyse this condition comparatively (Figure 5.1).

First, as discussed, the condition occurs within an overarching environment of *regime insecurity*, in which state-centric discourses, influenced by political instability, shape the issues being securitized. In addition to the threats generated by contentious politics and strained institutional relationships, regime insecurity may also be exacerbated by ensuing civil wars, insurgencies, and separatist movements experienced extensively in the aftermath of independence. In such contexts, national security becomes conflated with internal and domestic security challenges, leading to emergency provisions, exceptional practices, and 'doctrines of necessity' that enable states to continue with colonial policing practices for addressing 'law and order problems', instead of settling political issues through non-policing (or, in some cases, non-military) means. The same securitization processes have been extended to the state's response to and policing of popular politics under postcolonial regimes (Kumar, 2021, pp. 144–145).

Second, with such persisting political uncertainties, postcolonial states have deliberately retained colonial *institutional designs* of the public police. This means that the vertically hierarchical structure of police continues to entrench divisions between rank-and-file and elite cadres of officers, a divide determined by socio-economic differences, and one with little upward mobility for most officers (especially the constabulary). Because of the resulting financial insecurity of these police officers, their low salaries, exploitation, and the 'labour work' that they need to provide, officers are less loyal towards the institution and instead form selective loyalties towards individual colleagues and/or political patrons in pursuance of particular goals, such as promotions and favourable postings (Jauregui, 2014; Owen, 2016a). Under this hierarchical, class-based, discriminatory structure, relations between junior and senior officers have been strained, with the juniors required to do the 'dirty work' of their superiors or engage in corruption in exchange for lucrative posts and state-subsidized accommodation (Chukwama, 1997; Jauregui, 2013). Class-based divisions, maintained during both colonial and postcolonial periods, have also resulted in the use of lower ranked officers for 'violence work', such as torture and extrajudicial killings (Heath, 2021), fuelling police militarization (discussed later).

This institutional design has also depended not just on the discipline and control of the subjugated masses, but also of the 'native' police officers (Kumar and Verma, 2009; Heath, 2021). During colonial rule, such subjugation of 'native' officers was ensured through training and supervision by 'white' or British administrators, instilling a culture in which 'native' (junior) officers would be restrained from policing members of the white (elite) ruling class (Anderson and Killingray, 1991). Similarly, in postcolonial states (as in Pakistan and Nigeria), the policing of ruling class officers (belonging to an elite cadre, higher educated, and in some ways an indigenous replacement of the formerly white commanding officer), by the rank-and-file remains rare, and often impossible without political patronage afforded to junior officers.

Third, this institutional design has facilitated dependency upon informal policing practices, including petty corruption, creating informal networks to get ahead, and improvising during routine police work (Owen, 2016b; Waseem, 2021). Strained due to the security-centric demands placed upon them, engaged in catering to the socio-economic elite who consume public policing and security goods, and struggling to cope with budgetary constraints and financial insecurities, police officers in postcolonial contexts are not just reliant upon but encouraged (if not expected) to use informal methods and practices, such as for settling disputes (Kyed, 2017). This acknowledgement that officers will strategically use 'off the books' tactics to meet state, elite, and institutional demand is what I call '*procedural informality*' (Waseem, 2021; 2022), building on emerging scholarship on informal police work and practice (e.g. Hornberger, 2004; Kyed, 2017). Procedural informality is the idea that where public officials cannot deliver through legal or formal routes, they will improvise and even engage in extra-legal tactics to meet demand. Procedural informality is thus, to some extent, a sign of police disempowerment, in the sense that such improvisions are symptomatic of institutional weaknesses, individual insecurities, and the limits on an officer's formal authority (Jauregui, 2016).

Fourth, is the persistence of *police militarization*. It is well established that militarism was ingrained into colonial police in varying degrees (Anderson and Killingray, 1991, p. 6) and was one of the defining features of the colonial state, whose very purpose was grounded in conquest. Such militarism ensured that the police were not only repressive but also disliked and distrusted, so as to alienate them from the 'native' communities (beyond simply moving the officers into the barracks), institutionalizing a culture of 'policing strangers by strangers' (Alemika, 1993). Militarism in colonial governance influenced the hierarchy of policing institutions, the emphasis on drill and discipline, and a war-like philosophy that was exacerbated during anti-colonial and nationalist struggles, and through the introduction of laws on sedition and terrorism, thus cementing the police as 'an instrument of coercive state power and political intelligence' (Kalhan et al., 2006). This influence continued after colonial rule, with a fixation on maintenance of public order and regime security.

Indeed, in postcolonial contexts, colonial policing structures have been further militarized, especially where countries have seen authoritarian politics and military regimes over the decades (e.g. Pakistan, Bangladesh, Ghana, Nigeria, South Africa, and Myanmar), but also in postcolonial democracies suffering from unresolved conflicts (e.g. Jammu and Kashmir in India). This is evident not just by the continued weaponization of the police and creation of various militarized units and intelligence-collection teams, but also through pluralized policing policies that generate competition between state police and other para/military forces. This was evidenced during military rule in Nigeria, and in parts of Pakistan that have seen sustained periods of co-policing by both 'civilian' and paramilitary organizations.

Collectively, such militarization coupled with procedural informality has produced a 'culture of predation' in former colonies such as Nigeria and Pakistan (Agbiboa, 2015a), deployed most starkly through the insecure street-level officers. The most glaring manifestation of such 'cultures of predation' is the practice of extrajudicial killing—also referred to as 'police encounter killings' (simply, staged shoot-outs) in India, Pakistan, and Bangladesh (Jauregui 2016; Kamal Uddin, 2018). In Pakistan and Nigeria, such violence has contributed to the rise of social movements and resistance to atrocities.

Finally, this simultaneous empowerment (through militarized practices) and disempowerment (through persisting institutional weaknesses and officers' insecurities) creates a dynamic that makes officers insecure workers *and* producers of public insecurity, turning them into what Baxi (1982) called 'a despised minority'. This type of policing-insecurity interface is useful for understanding police–society relations in postcolonial contexts. As discussed later, the policing-insecurity interface—in which public grievances and citizen insecurity are fuelled by insecure officers who engage in militarized and informal practices to meet state and elite demand—has been central to the social movements in contemporary Pakistan and Nigeria.

Hence, the PCP captures and contextualizes how both public and police insecurity is generated, and in some ways coproduced, making both entities *distrustful* and *despicable* to the other. This is exacerbated through securitization processes that criminalize entire population groups based on ethnicity, class, and physical appearances (such as the Pashtuns in Pakistan or young activists in Nigeria). The PCP, therefore, frames a contentious state–police–society relationship in its unique contexts.

Pakistan

In their initial years in the Indian subcontinent, the British worked alongside existing administrative and bureaucratic mechanisms. The ground for 'professionalized' policing was laid in the 1700s when the East India Company began experimenting with existing traditional systems of justice, but one of the earliest attempts at formal policing was in the nineteenth century with the criminalization of thugee and the creation of the 'Thug police'. The successful repression of thugee and other tribes under the Criminal Tribes Act of 1871, provided legitimacy to the Raj's plans for cementing formal policing structures. By now, there was also a demand for mechanisms that would protect colonial interests, and that could be trusted for 'internal security', maintenance of public order, and revenue collection (Suddle, 2015).

At this point, the British were also looking to make headway in Sindh (now a southern province in Pakistan), and its geopolitically relevant port town of Karachi (now, Pakistan's largest city). The conquest of Sindh, led by Sir Charles Napier in 1843, followed by the 1857 sepoy rebellion that exaggerated the perception of 'threats' posed by natives, stimulated the regime's desire to constitute a coercive policing apparatus that would legally support the colonial state's efforts to collect intelligence and curb rebellions and nationalist resistance.

These factors collectively led to the creation of a police network that spread across Sindh. It was commanded by military officers (mostly British) with a well-armed rank-and-file, inspired by the Royal Irish Constabulary (RIC), cementing its militarized roots. While Napier distrusted the natives, Rajputs and Pathans, who were seen as 'warrior tribes', were inducted to create the impression of an indigenized rank-and-file, potentially for increasing the success of surveillance and intelligence-gathering. Napier's police in Sindh became a model for the rest of the empire in British India and was driven by both economic motives (land and revenue collection) and political calculations (protecting the empire against resistance through intelligence collection and the use of force, including torture that was often a public spectacle) (Heath, 2021). Subsequently, in colonial India the 1861 Police Act cemented a centralized, vertically accountable, hierarchical structure, which continues to be applied (to varying degrees) across territories in contemporary South Asia.

In British India, the development of state institutions was relatively robust. In other words, greater investments were made over a long period of time (approximately eight decades if we consider the development and operations of the modern policing institution in Sindh). This does not discount the fact, however, that the police were still institutionally constrained, with rank-and-file officers poorly paid, and an institutional focus on coercion rather than crime-investigation or prevention, and little interest in addressing complaints of torture and corruption (Heath, 2021).

Chronologically, professionalized police forces in British India predate the efforts undertaken in Africa. Indeed, in colonies such as Kenya, laws, structures, and personnel were transported from colonial India with the idea of modelling policing structures in Africa along the lines of the RIC (Deflem, 1994). While the transportation of police officers between colonies has of course ceased, a process of transferring/posting officers between provinces within Pakistan continues. As per policy, during the first few years after their recruitment into the elite cadre (the Police Services of Pakistan), PSP officers are required to serve in provinces from where they do not belong. Indeed, in Karachi, officers were brought in from Punjab to suppress political opposition during the 1990s; when this was not enough—and the police could not effectively curb political unrest—paramilitary soldiers, also predominantly from Punjab, were deployed. In some ways, therefore, practices of 'policing by alienation' continued in post-colonial Pakistan as in other former colonies.

Primarily, regimes in Pakistan have retained the use of colonial criminal justice structures for economic and political incentives. The most obvious example of this is the preferential treatment given by police officers to public and private elites—the 'VIPs'—a form of class-based discrimination that leaves substandard policing 'goods' for the most marginalized sections of society. By one estimate, between 30–50 per cent of the total police budget in Pakistan is consumed by 'VIP protection' duties (Abbas, 2011). First, this compromises the kind of security provisions available to ordinary citizens (Jackson et al., 2014). Second, this leaves insufficient finances for everyday police work, leading rank-and-file officers to rely upon extortion and other forms of corruption to make ends meet, a process that is tolerated if not encouraged by the elite cadre of officers and the state at large—a manifestation of procedural informality.

With this legacy, policing in postcolonial Pakistan has remained focused on regime security, the maintenance of public order, and the protection of state and elite interests, at the cost of both public security and the well-being of junior officers. Hence, reform efforts have been superficial and largely unsuccessful (Suddle, 2015); those that have taken place have prioritized police militarization without adequately addressing the financial grievances of police personnel. As such, officers have continued to rely upon informality and the use of excessive force. The practice of police 'encounter killings' (extrajudicial killings), that led to the rise of the Pashtun Tahaffuz Movement, must be understood in this context.

Pashtun Tahaffuz Movement

Pashtuns, an ethnic minority, have faced state repression and discrimination both during colonial and postcolonial periods, a discrimination that has been exacerbated by colonial relics and legal frameworks that have led to the erosion of Pashtun 'tribal' culture, indigenous dispute-settlement mechanisms, and suppressed Pashtuns 'tribal' areas (Yousuf, 2019a). Furthermore, policing in the frontier regions has been historically more militarized than perhaps seen in urban areas (Yousaf, 2019b). Nevertheless, while frontier policing has particularly hurt Pashtun culture and society in 'tribal' areas, Pashtuns across Pakistan continue to be discriminated against in urban areas as well, especially after their migration from Afghanistan and their displacement from northern areas of Pakistan increased their population in the cities.

In 2018, the extrajudicial killing of a young Pashtun man in police custody (an incident that was presented as a 'terrorist' killed in a police shoot-out) exemplified the racial lens through which Pashtuns have been policed. Naqeebullah Mehsud moved to Karachi from northern Pakistan in the aftermath of a military operation in his hometown. He was an aspiring model and shopkeeper in Karachi. In January 2018, the police's counter-terrorism department detained Mehsud. Shortly after, a police team led by a notorious 'encounter specialist', Rao Anwar,[4] was involved in Mehsud's

[4] Anwar was removed from service after Mehsud's killing. At the time of writing, his case was ongoing but Anwar was out on bail.

extrajudicial killing. The police team conjured up false evidence to show that Mehsud had links to a banned terrorist organization, Tehreek-e-Taliban Pakistan.

During colonial rule, Pashtuns were perceived as 'warriors' or 'warrior-like', 'savages', and, in the words of Winston Churchill, 'animal-like' (Yousuf, 2019a), and presented as 'lawless and turbulent' 'fanatics' who posed 'special dangers' that 'necessitated special measures' (Kolsky, 2015). The postcolonial representations of Pashtuns in Pakistan have not much improved, being branded since 2001 as 'terrorists', and threats to 'national security', even though many Pashtun communities and elders have found religious militancy incompatible with Pashtun culture (Yousuf, 2019a). Nevertheless, their securitization has directly impacted the way Pashtuns have been seen by state agents, including law enforcement agencies, as suspects. Because of such securitization, law enforcement agencies (including the police and paramilitary and military forces) have continually acted against Pashtuns in repressive ways.[5]

Post-9/11, and the multiple security operations that were carried out in Pakistan's tribal areas, there has been excessive policing of Pashtuns, through military and police checkpoints, curfews, house-to-house searches, the use of landmines, extrajudicial arrests, and secret detentions (Aslam and Neads, 2021, p. 270). The killing of Mehsud, and the public outcry it generated, was a consequence of such colonial and postcolonial racialization and securitization of Pashtuns. They were also products of militarized police actions that resulted from a continued reliance upon extrajudicial practices and political patronage of 'encounter cops' deemed loyal to the political regime (a patronage that has enabled informal networks and relationships to form between police officers and their elite patrons).

Mehsud's killing united Pashtuns across Pakistan against the injustices committed by the state and the prevailing insecurities of this ethnic minority group in the face of extrajudicial violence, illegal detentions and enforced disappearances, and discriminatory profiling at security check-posts. The PTM thus demanded a restoration of peace and stability in Pakistan's northern and tribal areas that had long suffered the assaults of both religious militants and various military-led operations against once-patronized militant groups. The PTM has been defined as 'an indigenous peace and rights movements from the tribal areas, comprising of young tribal Pashtuns, both men and women' (Yousaf, 2019a). The movement sparked nationwide peaceful protests, exerting pressure on law enforcement agencies to arrest one of their own, senior superintendent of police Rao Anwar. Nevertheless, state response to the PTM continues to demonstrate the postcolonial condition of policing at work.

Persistence of PCP in Pakistan

While the rise of the PTM shows how the postcolonial condition of policing generates insecurity for racialized and overpoliced minorities, state response to the movement

[5] This is not to suggest that Pashtuns have not served in law enforcement agencies. Many Pashtun officers have not only served in higher ranks within the Pakistan Police Services but have also been killed in the line of duty.

further demonstrates how postcolonial regime insecurity intersects with colonial policing structural designs to continue repression again dissent, activism, and social movements that challenge state authority and legitimacy. To this end, postcolonial regimes instrumentalize informal and militarized policing practices and the dispensability of junior officers.

First, the incrimination of PTM activists through arrests and illegal, and often long-term, detentions, shows the utility of postcolonial policing mechanisms. State efforts to criminalize PTM leaders, for instance, have included their arrests under the Anti-Terrorism Act (ATA) and the Maintenance of Public Order (MPO) Act. Under the ATA, PTM leaders have been charged with both terrorism and sedition. Sedition has specifically been weaponized to police and suppress the movement. The law of sedition is a colonial-era instrument that has historically been used to criminalize dissent and 'protect imperial sovereignty' (Jan, 2020). In postcolonial South Asia, it has been used against politicians, peaceful protesters, journalists, and students (Jan and Waseem, forthcoming). The application of such charges on PTM leaders is symptomatic of state insecurity in the face of a grassroots movement that challenges its authority. The charge facilitates the detention of PTM activists for prolonged periods for 'conspiring' against state interests. In December 2020, Ali Wazir, and several other PTM leaders, were arrested by the police on charges of sedition. The charge claimed that Wazir and others had use 'derogatory language' against state institutions (including the police and military) and tried to 'create hatred' and 'deteriorate the law-and-order situation'. Wazir's arrest led to detention for over twenty-four months (at the time of writing, he was still imprisoned). Wazir is a member of the National Assembly and has lost seventeen family members in terrorist attacks. Despite the injustices suffered by supporters of the PTM, the postcolonial state continued to unfairly police, survey, and punish Pashtun activists.

Second, state response to the PTM protests on the streets has also demonstrated an insecure regime's intolerance of agitation. On 26 May 2019, a year after its formation, a peaceful PTM demonstration was attacked by security forces who opened fire on unarmed protesters (here, the military was involved in policing the area). In the Khar Qamar Massacre, as it is known, up to thirteen activists were killed and PTM leaders were taken into custody. The escalation in the state's violent response at Khar Qamar was described as a 'logical escalation of deliberate military policy' against the social movement; PTM activists had been warned by military spokesmen that their 'time was up', several activists were arrested prior to this gathering, and surveillance of the PTM leadership had already begun (Aslam and Neads, 2021). Hence, the state's violent crackdown at Khar Qamar is a manifestation of the postcolonial condition of policing: an insecure regime's excessive reliance on militarized policing tactics for political grievances that parallels the colonial regime's handling of anti-colonial resistance in British India in the mid-twentieth century.

Third, state repression of dissent also demonstrates the utility of the colonial design of the police for the postcolonial state. Consider, for instance, that much of the state-mandated violence inflicted upon Pashtuns has happened through an institutional design that relies upon subservient and subjugated rank-and-file officers (across policing and military institutions) who are trained and groomed to follow orders and mete out state violence, and are otherwise also described as 'violence workers' (Heath,

2021). Mehsud's killing, which sparked PTM, was carried out by a team of officers led by Anwar. Anwar had joined the police as a junior officer, quickly climbing the ranks based on his ability to satisfy his patrons by acting as a 'violence worker', an escalation enabled by informal networking and 'strategic navigation' (Owen, 2016b).[6]

Hence, Anwar's case, Mehsud's death, and the policing of PTM protests reveal important trends. First, colonial continuities in the police's institutional design ensure that there is a pool of pliable officers who can be patronized for informal practices, 'dirty work', even 'violence work', which activates the policing-insecurity interface. In other words, the insecurity and disempowerment of junior officers creates their reliance upon practices required, but not legally allowed, by the state and elite, and which compromises citizen security. Second, regime insecurity leads to the racialized policing of minorities who challenge state authority. And. third, a continued reliance upon informal and militarized policing tactics by state institutions (both civilian and military) demonstrates the persistence of the PCP. Therefore, through this case study of the onset of the PTM and the state's response to it, we find observable traits of the postcolonial condition of policing at work. The onset of the #EndSARS in Nigeria, and the response it received, show similar trends.

Nigeria

Historical developments of the Nigerian police during colonial rule are well documented (Johnson, 2013; Owen, 2012; Onoja, 2005). In the pre-colonial period, traditional African policing methods and mechanisms were rooted in community-led initiatives already in place. The British established local and decentralized police forces, largely to protect the person and the property of the colonial authority (Onoja, 2005).

In contrast to British India, the state institution in Nigerian development was relatively less robust. Nigeria was a poorer colony and there was less appetite for investing in its institutions (Kohli, 2020). Hence, the development of 'professional' policing institutions differed as well. Nevertheless, the creation of law enforcement structures was not simply for the maintenance of order, but rather specifically to maintain an order that suited colonial authorities, could protect the imperial regime, and suppress the general population. Even when existing native institutions were co-opted, they were used for colonial governmentality. As Deflem (1994, p. 46) explained, 'acceptance of native political authority always implied a British redefinition and limitation of the role of African political powers and radical mutations of traditional practices whenever they were considered repugnant in light of European conceptions'. The guiding philosophy behind colonial policing mechanisms was thus similar across settings and makes for a powerful analysis of the lasting legacies of colonial repression in large parts of the world, which in many cases continue to be utilized by both authoritarian and 'democratic' postcolonial regimes.

[6] Based on interviews conducted with police officers in Karachi in 2020 and 2021.

In 1861, the first professional police force was established in Lagos colony, southern Nigeria. Strategic decisions by colonial administrators led to the recruitment of culturally distinct Hausa officers (considered to be from the 'martial tribes') and their deployment from the north to the south of the colony to enable a 'policing by alienation' strategy, which continues to date (ibid). These included freed slaves and other Hausa young men to enable the coercive functions of the colonial authority (Owen, 2012b). Basic principles of indirect rule and customary law guided British colonial policies in the early decades of colonial rule in Nigeria (Deflem, 1994). The amalgamation of 'modern' police mechanisms designed by the British came in addition to the Native Authority Police forces. While the former were largely recognized as being established for the protection of colonial interests, the latter were associated with local governments but were neither apolitical nor non-coercive (Daly, 2019).

Post-independence, the police continued to be used for political ends, for which violence and coercion became necessary instruments of state rule. This was evident during Nigeria's first republic (1960–1966) when both local elites and political parties utilized the police for personal and political gain. As Agbiboa (2015b, p. 262) explains, the police were deployed to suppress challenges to the status quo and were 'heavily implicated in election rigging, harassment of voters, and intimidation and/or elimination of political opponents'. Today, as in Pakistan, the police in Nigeria, based on survey data, are one of the most corrupt institutions (Agbiboa, 2015b; Jackson et al., 2014). Both corruption and abuse affect the poorest and most marginalized sections of both societies.

Furthermore, historical analyses also illuminate a discriminatory culture of policing. As in Pakistan, police discrimination in Nigeria is grounded in ethnic, religious, as well as class-based differences. As Chukwuma explains, class-based discrimination means that the elite (including senior public officials) are rarely detained. If they are detained (for political motives, for instance), they are usually privy to 'VIP' treatment, a trend we see across South Asia. The poor, however, are mistreated in almost every interaction with the police (Chukwuma, 1997, p. 50).

In addition to such discrimination and preferential treatment, extrajudicial police killings are also a common theme in the scholarship on Nigeria (Abiodun et al., 2020), some of which highlights that such violence also occurs because of informal police practices (e.g. petty corruption such as non-payment of bribes). Furthermore, the literature suggests that extrajudicial killings also prevail due to institutional shortcomings, including weak investigation techniques, political patronage, and a tolerance for politically motivated murders (a legacy of colonial rule and the inherently political nature of colonial police forces). This scholarship also links police violence back to the colonial origins of the Nigerian Police Force (NPF). Daly (2020) describes how colonial policing in Nigeria was repressive and authoritarian, to suppress dissent and agitation. Ikuteyijo and Rotimi (2014) discuss the exploitation and subjugation of marginalized groups seen during colonial rule, and its continuation in the form of routine, everyday exploitation of the working class, such as transportation drivers (or, in Pakistan's case, police exploitation of migrant communities).

In addition to the colonial foundations that have shaped the delivery of policing, sociopolitical developments in Nigeria have also sustained a climate ripe for police impunity. As Agbiboa (2015b) explains, military governments 'inadvertently strengthened the [state] institutions for arbitrary, oppressive, and insensitive personal rule', of which the NPF has been a prime example, wherein the 'culture of predation' is borne out of authoritarian policing legacies (Agbiboa, 2015a). Also observable in the postcolonial period are legal frameworks (e.g. Force Order 237) that allowed officers to shoot suspects allegedly evading arrest—an excuse frequently used to extrajudicially kill those already in custody, or those who are non-compliant, arguably one of the key causes behind the trigger-happy attitude of SARS police officers.

#EndSARS

The Special Anti-Robbery Squad (SARS) was a heavily armed unit established in the early 1990s as part of the NPF's Criminal Investigation Department (CID), which is rooted in the colonial policing apparatus. Police investigation, including that carried out by the CID, has remained weak and compromised because of its focus on revenue collection. This aim of the police as integral to the maintenance of public order as well as the collection of funds, has over time morphed into creating avenues and opportunities for corruption and extortion, especially among the rank-and-file who have remained historically underpaid and unreasonably burdened. This history of extortion and abuse has directly influenced contemporary behaviours of Nigerians. SARS officers, in particular, were accused of intimidation, predation, extortion, excessive use of force, and torture. The grooming of SARS officers and their public-facing practices must be read in this context.

In 2017, the initial calls for disbanding SARS circulated online in protest against allegations of wide-ranging misconduct. The government responded by promising police reforms and investigating SARS officers; however, these efforts amounted to little, and citizens continued to be subject to police harassment. Over time, SARS brutalities became more evident, especially officers' applications of false accusations and trumped-up charges. Relatedly, it was revealed that SARS officers predominantly singled out innocent young, male Nigerians, perceivably dressed affluently, but often from middle- or working-class backgrounds. These men would be illegally detained during raids, at nightclubs and in their homes, and accused of armed robbery or internet fraud (who they called the 'Yahoo Boys'). Reports of inhumane treatment towards not just suspected individuals in SARS custody, but also their family members who had to pray and pay for miracles, emerged, many of whom had to live with the stigma and trauma of their sons or brothers being arrested or killed by the police (Oduah, 2021).

The #EndSARS protests (as they came to be known and popularized through the Twitter hashtag that was revitalized in October 2020) came in response to such policing practices—and in the aftermath of the shooting of a young man by SARS officers—spreading across Nigeria and gathering national and international support as evidence of other such killings circulated online.

Persistence of PCP in Nigeria

The #EndSARS protests began out of grievances directly related to the PCP in Nigeria: most notably, the militarization of SARS, and the informal practices of its officers. The state's response to the protests and the movement at large, too, depict a continued desire to sustain the PCP. Some of the state's responses in the aftermath of the #EndSARS protests have included the criminalization and over-policing of protesters (including their excessive surveillance, labelling, and arrests). Furthermore, the most infamous example of an insecure regime responding in a heavy-handed and militarized manner to resistance to its authority was the massacre at the Lekki Tollgate, when at least twelve peaceful protesters were shot dead by uniformed officers.

The state's reliance upon such postcolonial policing mechanisms was also observable in its treatment of the SARS unit and officers. In response to the protests, although SARS was disbanded, some of its officers were absorbed into existing departments. Furthermore, the former chief of SARS was appointed as head of security for an opposition party candidate. In addition, the aftermath of the protests saw state-sanctioned restrictions in the civic space, such as bans on social media, blocking of select bank accounts, and censorship of broadcast media. Igwe (2021) warns that such governmental pressures indicate Nigeria's turn towards 'democratic authoritarianism'. Reports have also found that in the year following the protests little change was observable in Nigeria's police culture (Uwazuruika, 2021).

Importantly, the protest movement had made several demands, a brief consideration of which shows the lack of will on the part of the state to prioritize human security over regime security. First, the movement demanded the release of its protesters; a year later, several remained incarcerated without trial. In Lagos alone, nearly 300 protesters remained imprisoned (Uwazuruike, 2021) without fair trial. Second, the protesters had demanded psychological evaluation of SARS officers. After it was disbanded, however, SARS was restructured and renamed as the Special Weapons and Tactical Unit (SWAT), another militarized unit, without retraining and evaluating the officers of law enforcement agencies collectively. Because of the inability of the government to extend such evaluation and training across the country's policing forces, reports of police brutality continued.

Third, the protesters demanded compensation for the victims of police violence. The government did establish state judicial panels to investigate these killings and compensate victims, but these have been criticized for being unrepresentative and compromised, and for delaying justice. Further, the panel investigating police killings in Lagos and the Lekki Tollgate Massacre, in particular, was found to be slow and unsuccessful because of a lack of cooperation from the army (Ukonne, 2021). Fourth, an important demand was the investigation and prosecution of SARS officers. However, although several dozen officers were indicted, a year after the protests none of them had been prosecuted (although several lower ranked officers were nominated for further investigation, prosecution, or dismissal from the service). The Attorney General stated that there was a lack of evidence to prosecute the officers, contrary to the findings of the National Human Rights Commission. The lack of prosecution of police officers for extrajudicial violence in Nigeria resonates with the trends observed in Pakistan.

Lastly, the protesters demanded an increase in police salaries to reduce their insecurities which compelled them to engage in moral and financial corruption, among other informal practices. However, little effort was made to improve the meagre wages (especially, of the lower ranked officers) in Nigeria. A similar trend (the under-payment of rank-and-file officers) can be observed in Pakistan. Such insecurity, especially on the part of rank-and-file officers, risks strengthening patron–client relations between junior officers and elite stakeholders which continues to ensure that police accountability flows upwards (to political bosses and the postcolonial regime) instead of to the public.

Conclusion

This chapter has introduced a framework for postcolonial policing, what I call the 'postcolonial condition of policing' (PCP). The framework captures a state of policing in which public police remain accountable to the regime and in the service of elite interests because of the regime insecurity that prevails in postcolonial contexts. This condition is comprised of two key traits: militarization and informality in police work. I discussed how the PCP can be evidenced through, among other things, the state's response to social movements borne out of grievances against police violence. Through the exploration of contemporary protest movements in Pakistan and Nigeria respectively, this chapter has shown how despite promises of reform, postcolonial states retain colonial structures to ensure institutional loyalty towards the regime, especially in the face of challenges to state authority and legitimacy. To justify this retention, the state securitizes political grievances, thereby criminalizing activism (such as Nigerian youth and social media campaigners) and protest movements demanding respect for ethnic minorities (such as the Pashtuns in Pakistan), and presents these as national security threats. Because of such focus on state security, top-down (state and donor-funded) reforms in postcolonial contexts (across Asia, Latin America, and Africa) overwhelmingly focus on building the military capacity of the police, through the provisions of arms, counterterrorism training, and the creation of special units to investigate political crimes (e.g. sedition). These efforts typically fail to improve the socio-economic insecurity of the police and are largely silent on the class-based inequalities within policing structures that enable officer patronage and corruption.

This chapter is the first attempt to comparatively explore postcolonial policing in Pakistan and Nigeria, and the first to comparatively study civil society activism and non-violent grassroots mobilization in these two contexts based on the rise of the Pashtun Tahaffuz Movement and #EndSARS. It encourages future research on how grassroots mobilization may facilitate change in postcolonial policing—though the extent of such change remains to be seen. What is important is that both #EndSARS and PTM saw repression and state violence used against them, enabled by the PCP, and were able to demand change because of the popular support they generated, across classes and geographies.[7] Both cases show the importance of bottom-up, non-violent,

[7] It is important to mention that while #EndSARS called directly for police reform in Nigeria, such a call has largely been absent in the PTM; the latter more broadly demands reform of the systems of law and governance. Both movements have varied in scope, scale, and timescales.

mobilization and sustained civil society action for generating momentum for transformative police reform.

These examples also demand that we conceive of police reform as a 'bottom-up' process rather than the top-down initiatives typically seen in most countries with limited success. Indeed, in both Pakistan and Nigeria, such reforms have been unable to take root. Reformists who take a critical stand on such state-driven efforts point out that they are unlikely to 'stick' because of a lack of input and consideration from the rank-and-file (Bayley, 2008). This is particularly true in postcolonial societies where rank-and-file officers are traditionally seen as being subservient to the elite, and whose voice is seldom represented in reform efforts, and who are, in many cases, prohibited from collective action themselves.

References

Abbas, H. (2011) *Reforming Pakistan's Police and Law Enforcement Infrastructure: Is it Too Flawed to Fix?* Washington DC: United States Institute of Peace.

Abiodun, T. F., Oloyede, A. O., Ademola, O. E., Abah, O., and Kehinde, O. S. (2020) 'Unlawful Killings of Civilians by Officers of the Special Anti-Robbery Squad (SARS) Unit of the Nigerian Police in Southwest Nigeria: Implications for National Security', *African Journal of Law, Political Research and Administration*, 3(1), pp. 49–64.

Agbiboa, D. E. (2015a) '"Policing is not work: It is stealing by force": Corrupt policing and related abuses in everyday Nigeria', *Africa Today*, 62(2), pp. 95–126.

Agbiboa, D. E. (2015b) 'Protectors or predators? The embedded problem of police corruption and deviance in Nigeria', *Administration and Society*, 47(3), pp. 244–281.

Alemika, E. O. A. (1993) 'Colonialism, state and policing in Nigeria', *Crime, Law and Social Change*, 20, pp. 187–219.

Aliverti, A., Carvalho, H., and Chamberlen, A. (2021) 'Decolonizing the criminal question', *Punishment and Society*, 23(3), pp. 297–316.

Anderson, D. and Killingray, D. (eds) (1991) *Policing the Empire: Government, Authority and Control, 1830–1940*. Manchester: Manchester University Press.

Aslam, W. and Neads, A. (2021) 'Renegotiating societal-military relations in Pakistan: The case of the Pashtun Tahafuz Movement', *Democratization*, 28(2), pp. 265–284.

Baxi, U. (1982) *The Crisis of the Indian Legal System*. Delhi: Vikas Publishing House.

Bayley, D. H. (2008) 'Police reform: Who done it?', *Policing and Society*, 18(1), pp. 7–17.

Bell, E. (2013) 'Normalising the exceptional: British colonial policing cultures come home', *Memoire(s), identité(s), marginalité(s) dans le monde occidental contemporian*, 20(9).

Carrington, K., Hogg, R., and Sozzo, M. (2016) 'Southern criminology', *The British Journal of Criminology*, 56(1), pp. 1–20.

Chukwuma, I. (1997) 'The legal structure of the police and human rights in Nigeria', *Third World Legal Studies*, 14(4), pp. 41–70.

CLEEN (2013) *CLEEN Foundation Annual Report*. Lagos: CLEEN Foundation.

Comaroff, J. L. and Comaroff, J. (2007) *Law and Disorder in the Postcolony*. Chicago, IL: University of Chicago Press.

Cooper, A. E. (2021) *Black Resistance to British Policing*. Manchester: Manchester University Press.

Cooper-Knock, S. J. and Owen, O. (2014) 'Between vigilantism and bureaucracy: Improving our understanding of police work in Nigeria and South Africa', *Theoretical Criminology*, 19(3), pp. 355–375.

Daly, S. F. C. (2019) 'From crime to coercion: Policing dissent in Abeotuka, Nigeria, 1900–1940', *The Journal of Imperial and Commonwealth History*, 47(3), pp. 474–489.

Deflem, M. (1994) 'Law enforcement in British Colonial Africa: A comparative analysis of imperial policing in Nyasaland, the Gold Coast, and Kenya', *Police Studies*, 17(1), pp. 45–68.

Go, J. (2020) 'The imperial origins of American policing: Militarization and imperial feedback in the early 20th century', *American Journal of Sociology*, 125(5), pp. 1193–1254.

Heath, D. (2021) *Colonial Terror: Torture and State Violence in Colonial India*. New York: Oxford University Press.

Hills, A. (2008) 'The dialectic of police reform in Nigeria', *Journal of Modern African Studies*, 46(2), pp. 215–234.

Hornberger, J. (2004) '"My police—your police": the informal privatisation of the police in the inner city of Johannesburg', *African Studies*, 63(2), pp. 213–230.

Hornberger, J. (2013) 'From General to Commissioner to General—on the popular state of policing in South Africa', *Law and Social Inquiry*, 38(3), pp. 598–614.

Igwe, U. (2021) 'The ghost of #EndSARS looms over Nigeria's democratic authoritarianism', *Punch*, 2 December. Available at: https://punchng.com/the-ghost-of-endsars-looms-over-nigerias-democratic-authoritarianism/ (accessed 19 May 2022).

Ikuteyijo, L. and Rotimi, K. (2014) 'The image of Nigeria police: Lessons from history', *Journal of Applied Security Research*, 9(2), pp. 221–235.

Jackson, J., Asif, M., Bradford, B., and Zakar, M. Z. (2014) 'Corruption and police legitimacy in Lahore, Pakistan', *The British Journal of Criminology*, 54(6), pp. 1067–1088.

Jan, A. A. (2020) '"We the (Seditious) People": Repression and revolution in South Asia', *Jamhoor*, 20 January. Available at: www.jamhoor.org/read/2020/1/19/we-the-seditious-people-repression-and-revolution-in-south-asia (accessed 19 May 2022).

Jan, A. and Waseem, Z. (forthcoming) 'Crossing Red Line: Policing Sedition and Dissent in Postcolonial South Asia', in Squires, P., Cavalcanti, R., and Waseem, Z. (eds) *Southern Perspectives on Policing, Security, and Justice*. Bristol: Bristol University Press.

Jauregui, B. (2013) 'Cultures of legitimacy and postcolonial policing: Guest editor introduction', *Law and Social Inquiry*, 38(3), pp. 537–552.

Jauregui, B. (2014) 'Police and Legal Patronage in Northern India' in Piliavsky, A. (ed.) *Patronage as Politics in South Asia*. Cambridge: Cambridge University Press.

Jauregui, B. (2016) *Provisional Authority: Police, Order, and Security in India*. Chicago, IL: Chicago University Press.

Johnson, I. (2013) 'Policing in Contemporary Nigeria: Issues and Challenges', African Journal for the Psychological Study of Social Issues, 16(1), pp. 71–77.

Kalhan, A., Conroy, G. P., Kaushal, M., Miller, S. S., and Rakoff, J. (2006) 'Colonial continuities: Human rights, terrorism, and security laws in India', *Colombia Journal of Asian Law*, 20, pp. 93–234.

Kamal Uddin, M. D. (2018) 'Abductions and disappearances in Bangladeshi policing', *Policing*, 14(3), pp. 643–656.

Kohli, A. (2020) *How Britain and the United States Shaped the Global Periphery*. Oxford: Oxford University Press.

Kolsky, E. (2015) 'The Colonial Rule of Law and the Legal Regime of Exception: Frontier "Fanaticism" and State Violence in British India', *American Historical Review*, 120(4), pp. 1218–1246.

Kumar, R. (2021) *Police Matters: The Everyday State and Caste Politics in South India, 1900–1975*. Ithaca, NY: Cornell University Press.

Kumar, V. and Verma, A. (2009) 'Hegemony, discipline and control in the administration of police in colonial India', *Asian Journal of Criminology*, 4(1), pp. 61–78.

Kyed, M. (2017) 'Inside the Police Stations in Maputo City', in Fassin, D. (ed.) *Police in Africa: The Street-Level View*. London: Hurst & Co.

Lokaneeta, J. (2020) *Truth Machines: Policing, Violence, and Scientific Interrogations in India*. Ann Arbor, MI: University of Michigan Press.

Mukhopadhyay, S. C. (1998) 'Importing back colonial policing systems? The relationship between the Royal Irish Constabulary, Indian policing and militarization of policing in England and Wales', *Innovation*, 11(3), pp. 253–265.

Oduah, C. (2021) 'Gone: The lost victims of Nigeria's "most brutal" police station', Al Jazeera, 20 January. Available at: www.aljazeera.com/features/2021/1/20/gone-the-lost-victims-of-nigerias-most-brutal-police-station (accessed 19 May 2022).

Onoja, A. F. (2005) 'Sustaining a tradition of policing through alienation: An assessment of recruitment and training in the colonial and postcolonial Nigeria police', *Africa Zamani*, 13/14, pp. 137–151.

Owen, O. (2012) 'Maintaining order in Nigeria: Towards a history of state sovereignty', *African Policy*, 4(128), pp. 25–51.

Owen, O. (2016a) 'Policing after Colonialism', in Bradford, B., Jauregui, B., and Loader, I. (eds) *The SAGE Handbook for Global Policing*. London: Sage, pp. 303–319.

Owen, O. (2016b) 'Government properties: The Nigeria police force as total institution?', *Africa*, 86(1), pp. 37–58.

Suddle, S. (2015) 'Police System of Pakistan', PILDAT Position Paper. Islamabad: PILDAT.

Tankebe, J. (2009) 'Public cooperation with the police in Ghana: Does procedural justice matter?', *Criminology*, 47(4), pp. 1265–1293.

Tankebe, J. (2013) 'In search of moral recognition? Policing and eudaemonic legitimacy in Ghana', *Law and Social Inquiry*, 38(3), pp. 576–597.

Ukonne, C. B. (2021) 'The #EndSARS panels one year on: Was justice ever delivered?', *African Arguments*, 20 October. Available at: https://africanarguments.org/2021/10/the-endsars-panels-one-year-on-was-justice-ever-delivered/ (accessed 19 May 2022).

Uwazuruike, A. (2021) '#EndSARS: An evaluation of successes and failures one year later', *Georgetown Journal of International Affairs*, 13 December. Available at: https://gjia.georgetown.edu/2021/12/13/endsars-a-evaluation-of-successes-and-failures-one-year-later/ (accessed 19 May 2022).

Waseem, Z. (2021) 'Policing COVID-19 through procedural informality in Pakistan', *Policing and Society*, 31(5), pp. 583–600.

Waseem, Z. (2022) *Insecure Guardians: Enforcement, Encounters, and Everyday Policing in Postcolonial Karachi*. London: Hurst & Co.

Yousaf, F. (2019a) 'Pakistan's "tribal" Pashtuns, their "violent" representation, and the Pashtun Tahafuz Movement', *SAGE Open*, 9(1), pp. 1–10.

Yousaf, F. (2019b) 'Pakistan's colonial legacy: FCR and postcolonial governance in the Pashtun tribal frontier', *Interventions*, 21(2), pp. 172–187.

6

Extrajudicial Punishment and the Criminal Question

The Case of 'Postcolonial' South Africa

Gail Super

Introduction

Punishment and Society scholars tend to study particular institutions (such as the prison) and spaces where punishment is imposed by the state, usually after a conviction in a criminal court. This chapter questions the boundaries of the field. I argue that extrajudicial punishment plays a central role in penality and that, particularly in postcolonial contexts, rates of imprisonment do not adequately reflect the level of penal punitiveness in a given society. This is very apparent in South Africa where a steep drop in prison population rates, from 403 per 100,000 inhabitants to 259 (World Prison Brief, 2020), has been accompanied by a dramatic increase in prisoners serving life terms (Phelps, 2019, p. 829; Van Zyl Smit and Appleton, 2019) and an increase in recorded cases of extrajudicial punishment—by civilian vigilantes, police officers, and prison wardens (Bruce, 2019; Lancaster, 2021; Knoetze, 2021a; 2021b; Super, 2021b).

With its backdrop of colonial and apartheid rule, history of state toleration of legal pluralism, extrajudicial penal violence, racist mobility restrictions, structural inequality, and weak state capacity (particularly at the local level) (Abrahams, 1998; Alexander and Kynoch, 2011; Brewer, 1994; Glaser, 2005; Chanock, 2001), South Africa presents an excellent case study for the central role of extrajudicial punishment in constituting penal punitiveness. Thus, it should be taken into account together with more liberal forms of punishment, such as long-term imprisonment. As such, traditional conceptions of liberal punishment, as that which is imposed by a judicial offer after a finding of guilt in a criminal court (Zedner, 2016), must be revisited to reflect the reality of what happens in practice.

I use the term 'extrajudicial punishment' to refer to punishment-like phenomena which are inflicted by civilian or state actors, in response to an allegation of criminality or lawbreaking. Not all forms of extrajudicial punishment are unlawful: for example, park exclusion orders, punitive bail conditions, evictions, etc. are lawful (Becket and Herbert, 2010; Sylvestre et al., 2015). In South Africa, extrajudicial punishment plays out on multiple scales, across space and time, in and through varying jurisdictions, and disproportionately targets and affects poor black people. While this is also the

Gail Super, *Extrajudicial Punishment and the Criminal Question* In: *Decolonizing the Criminal Question*. Edited by: Ana Aliverti, Henrique Carvalho, Anastasia Chamberlen, and Máximo Sozzo, Oxford University Press.
DOI: 10.1093/oso/9780192899002.003.0007

case in Western, and other contexts (Beckett and Herbert, 2010; Hannah-Moffat and Lynch, 2012; Fassin, 2018) it is more exaggerated, more visible, and more violent in the postcolony (Mbembe, 1992; Bierschenk, 2014; Brown, 2002). Thus, studying penality in postcolonial contexts is instructive for theorizing about the contradictions of liberal penal forms.

I start by discussing the central role of extrajudicial punishment and legal pluralism during colonialism and apartheid. I then examine how, when the South African Constitutional Court outlawed the death penalty in *Makwanyane*,[1] it facilitated extrajudicial punishment in prison and elsewhere. Second, I argue that arrest, pre-trial detention, bail denial, and the abdication by prosecutors of their jurisdiction to prosecute are all forms of lawful extrajudicial punishment. Lastly, I discuss the unlawful extrajudicial punishments inflicted by civilians in former black townships and informal settlements and the state's 'abdication of jurisdiction'[2] in these marginalized spaces.

Extrajudicial Punishment and the Abdication of Liberal Law During Colonialism and Apartheid

The colonial state relied on exploitation, violence, and political control as central pillars of rule, rather than an effective bureaucracy, in the Weberian sense of the term (Nugent, 2010). Because it was mainly concerned with extracting natural resources from the colonies, its focus was on exploiting and politically controlling colonial subjects, rather than ruling through hegemonic legitimatory processes. It was precisely because the type of state that European colonizers imposed on African colonies was different to that in the metropole (Bierschenk, 2014) that penal excess against racially subordinate populations, rather than accountability, characterized its rule (Brown, 2002; Bierschenk, 2014). Racialized penal violence was a central tactic of control, both directly and indirectly—through state toleration of and sometimes outright complicity in extrajudicial violence (Brown, 2002; Alexander and Kynoch, 2011; Mbembe, 1992; Hansen and Stepputat, 2005).

In South Africa, the law itself created spatial exclusions and spaces of marginality via legislation which not only established, but also compelled, most citizens to live in racially segregated black and 'coloured' townships.[3] Hence, tactics of penal violence and criminalization combined with processes of expulsion and dispossession to produce spaces of marginalization. Black townships were to be situated as far as possible from white neighbourhoods but close to the industrial areas so that residents could provide a source of cheap labour. Prime land, in close proximity to the city centre,

[1] *S v Makwanyane and another* (CCT3/94) [1995] ZACC 3; 1995 (6) BCLR 665; 1995 (3) SA 391; [1996] 2 CHRLD 164; 1995 (2) SACR 1 (6 June 1995).

[2] This term comes from Valverde, 2015.

[3] From the 1920s, South Africa's housing policy focused on demolishing 'native slumyards' (Maylam, 1990, p. 60) and forcibly relocating residents to racially segregated locations on the margins of cities (Smit, 2016). The white minority National Party government, which gained power in 1948, poured enormous resources into continuing these expulsive processes. It constructed racially segregated black townships on urban peripheries and *bantustans* ('homelands') in impoverished rural areas. Enabled by a raft of legislation, it forcibly relocated black Africans to the newly created townships and criminalized their movement (Maylam, 1990; Smit, 2016, Chanock, 2001).

was reserved for whites, while those black people who were permitted to live in urban areas lived on the periphery.

A wide range of non-judicial actors were legislatively enabled to punish lawfully, in support of summary justice. These included mining companies, *indunas* ('commanders'), *baasboys* ('bossboys'), chiefs, and white farmers. Summary (in)justice was further enabled by poorly trained, low-level, administrative officials who exercised judicial, legislative, and executive powers against black subjects, mostly via regulation and hence beyond the reach of judicial oversight (Chanock, 2001; Bierschenk, 2014). Thus, for example, the 1928 Native Administration Act provided that the punishments imposed by native commissioners were 'administrative acts' and as such not subject to review by the courts (Chanock, 2001, p. 289). Thus, black Africans were subjected to a discretionary form of rule in which extrajudicial punishment and penal violence played central roles.

Corporal punishment and various forms of racialized containment played key roles in the development of a specifically South African style of racial capitalism. The myth of 'civilized' whites versus 'savage' blacks underpinned the narrative and practices of corporal punishment as a means to control black subjects (Pavlich, 2018; Chanock, 2001), with violence being presented as an integral mechanism for the 'civilizing mission' in terms of an ethos which framed Africans as 'child-like', only able to comprehend the language of bodily violence, and ruled by customary law because they were 'not yet ready for autonomy' (Alexander and Kynoch, 2011, p. 400; Chanock, 2001, p. 34). To give some examples: during the second British occupation of the Cape (between 1806 and 1910), the judges, applying Roman–Dutch common law, referred to slaves as having 'great numbers' and 'less-civilized dispositions', hence justifying cruel and different punishments in the interests of 'deterrence and the preservation of slave society' (cited in Pavlich, 2018, p. 148); the 1898 Gold Law provided that twenty-five lashes could be imposed on blacks for offences such as 'misbehaving in service' (Chanock, 2001, p. 411); a 1908 Transvaal Supreme Court case held that 'natives' were physically able to cope with more severe corporal punishment than were 'Europeans and Asiatics' (ibid, p. 92), and traditional heads of households in rural areas could lawfully inflict 'reasonable' corporal punishment for the 'purpose of correction and to maintain peace and order' (ibid, p. 320). This authoritarian construct of customary law was explicitly embraced by courts in the 1926 case of *Mokhatle and others v Union Government*, where the court accepted the evidence of white 'native law experts' that all chiefs had 'essentially the same' absolute powers and customs, and could 'act without consultation or consent' (ibid, p. 288). Thus, local chiefs and headmen could impose unreviewable orders and fines, along with imprisonment for non-compliance, over their subjects (ibid, p. 289).

Whereas Africans were presented as savages who were ruled by customary law because they were not yet ready for autonomy, whites were regarded as the 'bearers of a 2,000-year-old legal tradition' in the form of the Roman Dutch common law (ibid, p. 34). The 'myth' was that it (together with the British and Dutch colonial law before it) was rational, scientific, uniform, and humane (Fitzpatrick, 2001) when in fact it was unsettled and based on a mixture of discretionary powers and pluralized, arbitrary violence. This myth of rationality was based on the constitution of the 'irrational black savage' (Fitzpatrick, 1992) as being the constitutive outside modern law, and hence not subject to its protections. Whereas whites were ruled by 'constitutional' law, 'non-whites' were subject to authoritarian law (Chanock, 2001, p. 41). Thus liberal law fulfilled its promises for whites by offering rule of law protections against abuse of power, but it failed for black subjects, not only because these protections were unavailable for them, but also because judges refused to overrule the delegation of discretionary authority to low-level administrative officers. In this way, liberal law played a central role in justifying the racist and oppressive South African state (ibid, p. 20), through abdicating its own jurisdiction.

The apartheid state was not particularly concerned with preventing crime inside black townships and in *bantustans*. Instead, it sought to protect white citizens from the supposed criminal threat presented by black people (Super, 2013). Hence, there were very few police stations in black townships and township residents relied on interpersonal and patronage networks as forms of security. Vigilante associations were common. It is therefore unsurprising that extrajudicial punishment emerged in the face of a criminal justice system that was a tool to control, rather than protect, black people from victimization (Chanock, 2001).

By the time the first democratic elections were held in 1994, there was a deep historical legacy of instant 'justice' in which extrajudicial punishment played a central role (see, e.g., Buur, 2005; Glaser, 2000; Hund and Kotu-Ramoppo, 1983; Super, 2017). At the height of the liberation struggle, shadowy state agents perpetrated multiple executions, torture, and unlawful confinements of anti-apartheid activists. This infliction of horrific and deeply punitive violence by apartheid state operatives produced 'violent subjectivities' (Rueedi, 2015, p. 403) inside township communities, shaping counter-violence against *impimpis*, the police, the hated community councillors, and other apartheid collaborators (Rueedi, 2015; Super, 2010). However, since the line between political and ordinary crime is a porous one, the comrades also imposed extrajudicial punishments on people who had committed non-political crimes such as theft and drug use (Super, 2013; 2022a). As I discuss next, extrajudicial punishment continues to play a central role in contemporary South African penality.

Extrajudicial Punishment (in Prisons and Elsewhere) Post-1994

Makwanyane

The 1995 *Makwanyane* judgment, which was the first case heard by the newly formed Constitutional Court, represented a 'foundational moment' (Davis and Le Roux, 2009, p. 120) for the newly constituted South African democracy. It also, as I argue here, entrenched the use of imprisonment (and punishment in general) as a tool of racial repression without considering its centrality to colonial and apartheid rule. In ruling the death penalty to be unconstitutional, the court relied extensively on the notion of *ubuntu*, a Xhosa word which literally translated means humanness. More metaphorically, it denotes an ethos of reciprocity and mutual aid (Marais, 2001) which were, supposedly, foundational values of the 'new' South Africa.

The court stated that offenders are 'capable of rehabilitation' and should therefore not be put to death, but that since 'heinous crimes' were the 'antithesis of ubuntu', criminals could nonetheless be sentenced to long terms of imprisonment (judgment, para. 225). Thus, the Constitutional Court corralled off those incorrigible offenders who had violated *ubuntu* by virtue of their 'heinous crimes' (para. 225), and legitimated harsh punishment against them.

By stating (at para. 296) that:

> [imprisonment] compels the offender to spend years and years in prison, away from his family, in conditions of deliberate austerity and rigid discipline, substantially and continuously impeding his enjoyment of the elementary riches and gifts of civilized living

it clearly recognized that long-term imprisonment was not a 'soft option.'

The Constitutional Court judges relied heavily on consequentialist arguments that the death penalty was not effective in preventing crime (Davis and Le Roux, 2009, cited in Super, 2013). The judges sought to legitimate imprisonment through its assumed instrumental effect, setting up a binary between two 'deterrents': 'putting the criminal to death' or 'subjecting the criminal to the severe punishment of a long term of imprisonment' (including that of life imprisonment) (para. 123). Without any empirical proof that imprisonment actually achieved its stated goal of being 'reformative', it both claimed this to be the case and also, in a very utilitarian fashion, stated that criminals had to be 'subjected to severe sentences' because it was the likelihood of apprehension, conviction, and punishment 'presently lacking in our criminal justice system' (para. 122) which would be the best deterrent and prevent the law from 'fall[ing] into disrepute' (para. 124). Indeed, Judge Madala stated (at para. 243) that:

> the offender has to be imprisoned for a long period for the purpose of rehabilitation. By treatment and training the offender is rehabilitated, or, at the very least, ceases to be a danger to society.

Following on from this judgement, South Africa's Parliament passed the 1997 Criminal Law Amendment Act, which formally removed the death penalty as a sentencing option and simultaneously encouraged courts to impose life imprisonment more often (Van Zyl Smit and Appleton, 2019, p. 155). To say that it achieved this goal is an understatement. South Africa has the highest recorded growth of life imprisonment in the world and the third highest number of life-serving prisoners in the world (ibid). Not only has the number of prisoners serving life sentences increased by 2,000 per cent, from 433 in 1995 to 13,260 in 2016 (ibid, p. 98; Phelps, 2019), but offences that would not have attracted either the death penalty or life imprisonment during apartheid now attract mandatory life sentences (Muntingh, 2017; Mujuzi, 2008).[4] The jurisdictional bar of who can impose these sentences has also been lowered to include regional court magistrates.

It is safe to say that South African prisons do not provide any form of 'social rehabilitation' (Van Zyl Smit and Appleton, 2019, p. 298) or the rehabilitation based on *ubuntu* that the Constitutional Court referred to. Instead, they are containers for extrajudicial

[4] Unless the court is satisfied that 'substantial and compelling circumstances exist'.

punishment. Department of Correctional Services (DCS) reaction units (Emergency Support Teams) have been known to impose 'collective punishments' (Bruce, 2019, p. 10) inside prisons through the use of excessive force against prisoners, and prisoner allegations of assaults by wardens are common. The most common weapon used by officials is the baton, but prisoners have also been kicked, teargassed, and shocked with electrified shields (ibid). While these are euphemistically categorized as 'non lethal incapacitating devices', in practice they are used as lethal weapons (ibid, p. 40). Since the Correctional Services Act does not stipulate which types of weapons may be authorized, the use of body-worn electric shock devices, electric shock shields, and hand-held electronic stun devices are all legally permitted (ibid, p. 18). This is a classic example of how a lacuna or absence in law ends up authorizing discretionary extra-judicial (in this case, unlawful) violence. Yet, the vast majority of complaints never reach the courts, the police, or even the Judicial Inspectorate for Correctional Services (JICS) (CSPRI et al., 2016, p. 10). Out of 2,341 complaints of official-on-prisoner assaults reported to JICS monitors in 2014–2015, only 109 were recorded, and of these only twenty were investigated by JICS itself. Even in the case of alleged homicides, inflicted as punishments by groups of prison officials on single prisoners, of which JICS has reported twenty-six since 2009, no criminal prosecutions of any departmental officials have been opened. Thus, not only is extrajudicial punishment in prisons the norm but it is enabled by the law, as was the case during colonial rule. By abdicating jurisdiction, the law enables violence by prison officers.

Arrest and bail as extrajudicial punishment

Along with long-term imprisonment and remand detention, police arrests and police violence have also increased since 1994 (Muntingh et al., 2017, p. 29; CSPRI et al., 2016, p. 16; APCOF and SAHRC, 2022). Complaints pertaining to unlawful or arbitrary arrests were among the top five complaints made to the South African Human Rights Commission (SAHRC) between 2012 and 2017 (ibid). Although 1.19 million people were arrested in 2019/20 only 883,611 dockets were referred to prosecutors for a decision on the merits (ibid, p. 2). Thus, over 300,000 SAPS arrests (approximately 25 per cent) were finalized at the station level. At this level, then, the arrest is the punishment. I develop this point in detail later.

Although the vast majority of complaints to the Independent Police Investigative Directorate (IPID) concern allegations of police brutality meted out against the racialized poor, very few result in internal disciplinary sanctions or criminal convictions (CSPRI et al., 2016, p. 6). South Africa is both 'exceptional and exemplary' (Fassin, 2018, p. 16) in this regard. The total number of police killings registered since 1997 stood at more than 10,000 by February 2020 (Knoetze, 2021b), with twenty-seven occurring during the first six weeks of South Africa's first Covid-19 lockdown. As at the end of March 2021, IPID investigations included 794 killings by police, 665 torture cases, 1,635 alleged shootings, and thousands of assault cases. Yet, SAPS failed to initiate nearly half of the watchdog's disciplinary recommendations, and despite the high number of killings and brutality allegations reported to IPID in 2020/21, SAPS only dismissed six police officers after initiating departmental hearings (Knoetze, 2021a).

One out of thirteen adult men is arrested annually in South Africa with half of all arrestees spending three or more months in custody. Of these, the majority are poor, black, and alleged to have committed non-serious statutory offences (CSPRI et al., 2016, p. 18). Since the law no longer provides for after-hours bail applications, a person who has been arrested and detained, particularly over a weekend, will experience punitive treatment without having been found guilty of any offence, least of all one which deserves a period of incarceration.[5] This is tantamount to extrajudicial punishment. Moreover, persons accused of offences referred to in Schedules 5 and 6 to the Criminal Procedure Act are denied bail as a matter of course, unless they are able to satisfy the court that their release is in the 'interests of justice', or they demonstrate 'exceptional circumstances'.[6] Since 'shock and outrage of the community' is one of the grounds on which a court may deny bail, the door is open for an ambiguous and vengeful 'community' to play a central role in bail decisions (Super, 2016b; Redpath, 2019, p. 7).

Denial of bail, and/or the imposition of punitive bail conditions, which are penal phenomena in and of themselves (see, e.g., Sylvestre et al., 2015), are unevenly distributed and mostly experienced by the racialized poor. Thus, for example, more than half of the 20,000 people admitted annually to Pollsmoor Remand Detention Facility (RDF) in Cape Town, come from only six police stations (Redpath, 2019, p. 5) in poor, 'non white' areas, with many being detained because they cannot afford bail (Redpath, 2019, pp. 53–55). The conditions of remand detention at Pollsmoor are appalling, with the majority of detainees accommodated in overcrowded communal cells with a capacity ranging from fifteen to thirty, in some instances housing up to eighty with only one toilet (*Sonke Gender Justice v Government of the Republic of South Africa and one other*, p. 17). A 2016 Public Service Commission inspection of the Pollsmoor RDF found the cells to be 'alarming and not fit for human habitation' (Redpath, 2019, p. 2). At the time of the inspection, the RDF housed 4,358 male detainees in a facility designed for 1,619—some 246.94 per cent over capacity (ibid, p. 19). Prisoners had no more than an hour per week outside their triple-bunked cells, had to urinate in the shower, use a bucket for their ablutions, and received inadequate medical care. The conditions inside the cells included broken windows, filthy blankets, no hot water, and lice infestations (ibid: pp. 33–34, 39).

In most cases, however, after spending time in pre-trial detention, the charges are withdrawn, or struck from the roll, due to lengthy delays in bringing the matter to trial (CSPRI et al., 2016, p. 18). In fact, the overall number of prosecutorial withdrawals has increased steadily since 2003 and annual prosecution rates (compared to the number of police arrests) have significantly decreased (Muntingh et al., 2017, p. 28). This is not because of a lack of police referrals (ibid). Whereas 407,530 cases were finalized by the courts in 2002/3, this had dropped by 22 per cent to 319,149 by 2015/16. Prosecutors ascribe the high rates of withdrawals to Alternative Dispute Resolution Mediation (ADRM) processes. These increased dramatically from 14,808 in 2002/3, to 184,314 in 2014/15. While theoretically based on restorative justice principles[7] in

[5] Section 50(6)(b) of the Criminal Procedure Act provides that an accused person is not 'entitled to be brought to court outside ordinary court hours'.

[6] Section 60(11)(a) and (b).

[7] In terms of the NPA guidelines, charges should only be withdrawn if an accused person accepts responsibility and offers to make amends for the harm caused by the crime.

terms of which withdrawal agreements (drawn up after the accused and victim participate in a formal mediated process) are ratified by the court and entered into a central register, this does not happen in practice. Instead, 75 per cent of ADRMs consist of off-the-record ('corridor') mediations, with prosecutors withdrawing charges (sometimes in the corridors outside the courts) on the condition that the 'accused' pays compensation to the 'victim'—without a formal mediated process (ibid, p. 32). The fact that these are conducted by individual prosecutors without being entered into a central register, and without the accused person having admitted guilt (ibid, p. 33), renders the whole process entirely discretionary. In fact, the courts have no oversight of the process at all. It is also a form of extrajudicial punishment given that the accused has to pay or do something for an alleged crime, without having been found guilty in court.

Given the high rate of withdrawals, it is unsurprising that the bail decision is perceived, by both the accused and the victims of crime, as the last opportunity for the courts to make a decision that *seems like* a punishment (Redpath, 2008; Super, 2020). In this sense, bail denial is an extrajudicial, albeit lawful, form of punishment, even though it is technically not punishment. Thus, the boundaries established by liberal law, between arrest, pre-trial detention, and punishment, are porous and blurred. This disconnect and collapse takes place on multiple spatiotemporal levels: spatially (because the punishment is meted out at the time of the arrest, or in the police cells) and temporally (because it occurs before a judicial finding of guilt). In all cases, however, the 'normal [liberal] framing of criminal justice' (Aas, 2014, p. 522) is destabilized and precarious.

Withdrawals are not included by the National Prosecuting Authority (NPA) for the purposes of calculating its almost 100 per cent conviction rate (ACJR, 2018, p. 8), hence the high rate of 'successful' prosecutions is clearly the result of prosecutors deciding not to prosecute (Redpath, 2016). Thus, the initial accusation itself becomes foundational to the resultant extrajudicial punishment—whether it results in arrest, remand detention, the payment of a fine, or civilian-inflicted punishments. In all of these instances, as was the case during colonial and apartheid rule, non-judicial discretion plays a central role, the effects of which are particularly experienced by the racialized poor. As I discuss next, extrajudicial punishment is not inflicted by the state alone.

Civilian-Led Extrajudicial Punishment in Informal Settlements and Former Black Townships

Given the pluralist legal approach adopted by the colonial and apartheid governments, which subjected black Africans to summary (in)justice and an 'extensive, localized and legally arbitrary [form of] rule' (Chanock, 2001, p. 2), it is unsurprising that extrajudicial punishments played (and continue to play) a central role in the production of violent social orders in marginalized spaces. They are, to use Hutta's words, the 'immediate effects' of the segregation that produced them 'in the first place' (Hutta, 2019, p. 71).

Between January to March 2021, vigilante-related murder cases constituted 15 per cent (the third highest cause) of South Africa's total recorded murders, in those cases where a motive could be detected (Lancaster, 2021). When viewed over time, vigilante murders also seem to have increased.[8] Thus, in Khayelitsha, a former black township on the outskirts of Cape Town with high rates of violent crime, recorded vigilante murders rose from thirty-five in 2003 to 106 in 2012, dropping to sixty-nine in 2016. In Nyanga, another former black township in Cape Town (sometimes referred to as the country's 'murder capital'), they increased from eighteen in 2003 to ninety-seven in 2014, dropping to eighty-two in 2016. Vigilante-related kidnappings in Khayelitsha rose from fifteen in 2010 to twenty-six in 2012, hovering at sixteen in 2016. They also increased steadily in Nyanga, from three in 2003 to fourteen in 2011, dropping to eleven in 2016. In Khayelitsha, vigilante-related attempted murders increased from thirteen in 2002 to thirty-five in 2014, dropping to thirty-two in 2015, and twenty-four in 2016. In Nyanga, they rose from fourteen in 2004 to twenty-six in 2016. These are the recorded cases: in practice, very few are people arrested for vigilante-related violence, and very few of these cases are recorded at all (Super, 2021b).

A perusal of the SAPS Annual Reports creates the impression that, for the most part, murder and attempted murder are the only forms of vigilantism (ibid). Similarly, the Western Cape Crime Report for 2018–2019 (Department of Community Safety, 2019) refers to 'community retaliation/vigilantism' only in the context of murder and attempted murder. Thus, unless lethal collective violence is involved, or large crowds of people act violently, or visibly confront the police, by for example stoning their police vehicles (which would lead to charges of public violence), everyday acts of extrajudicial punishment, such as shack evictions, corporal punishment, interrogations, and kidnappings, etc. are largely ignored. Only rarely does the police database indicate action taken against community members who purportedly exercise 'community arrests', and in the process assault the person suspected of wrongdoing. In certain instances, there is outright complicity, with the police watching (or even assisting) residents to evict (and thereby punish) suspected criminals (Super, 2021a). Even in spectacular cases of violence—which directly threaten the state's sovereignty—perpetrated by large crowds of people who beat and/or burn alleged criminals to death, prosecutions are rare. Thus, between 2000–2016, out of the 746 vigilante-related murder cases recorded at the Lingelethu, Khayelitsha, and Harare police stations (which service the township of Khayelitsha), only 264 (35 per cent) resulted in police referrals to prosecutors. In 469 cases (65 per cent), neither arrests nor suspects were recorded, which means that there was no investigation. When the police do gather evidence and refer vigilante-related cases to prosecuting authorities, more often than not, the matter does not reach the trial stage, and convictions are few and far between. Like the other 'processes of concealment' (Hutta, 2019, p. 66) I discussed in the context of extrajudicial punishment by state actors, these forms of wilful blindness, based on 'non-intervention and non-investigation', end up displacing the protections provided by liberal law (Hutta, 2019). They also displace 'state systems of accountability' and

[8] Because the police do not have a separate category of vigilante-related offences, it is difficult to measure the true extent of civilian punishments and/or vigilante-related violence. The data in this section are drawn from research I conducted on the SAPS computerized crime information system for the period 2000–2016 in respect of six police stations in the Khayelitsha and Nyanga Policing Clusters (Super, 2021b; 2022a). For details on my methods, see Super 2021b and 2022a.

enable 'techniques of camouflage' through the abdication, rather than claim of state sovereignty, over the use of violence (ibid). Thus, contrary to liberal theory, which frames punishment beyond the state as unlawful, as was the case during colonialism and apartheid, illegal practices are regarded as licit and bolster, rather than challenge, the state's penal power, because they assist in keeping a certain form of order—one which does not challenge the state per se (Roitman, 2006; Black, 1983; Super, 2017).

I am not arguing that extrajudicial punishments, including what Roy (2019) refers to as 'racialized banishments', do not occur in the more well-off formerly white areas. To the contrary. However, the affluent have better ways of masking their violence, by for example contracting out to private security companies (Murray, 2020; Diphoorn, 2017; Hentschel, 2015), and they have the financial and social capital to use law as a weapon of protection for their unlawful and/or marginally lawful expulsive violence which is in effect extrajudicial punishment (at the very least banishment, but sometimes also physical assault) for the 'crime' of being out of place.

'Repertoires of violence'

In the post-apartheid era, the number of informal settlements where the very poor (who are all black) erect tin shacks as their homes, has exponentially increased. Insecurity is experienced on many levels in these marginalized spaces—socio-economically (due to racialized poverty and endemic inequality), in terms of the volatile politics of local governance structures, because of the high rates of interpersonal violence, and state violence against so-called 'land invaders' and other 'disposable populations' (Butler, 2012, p. 168). This insecurity is intimately linked to the historical process of racialized expulsion, dispossession, and resistance (Razack, 2014; Maylam, 1990; Smit, 2016; Chanock, 2001). As grand apartheid began to be formally dismantled in South Africa, in the mid-1980s, there was an influx of people from the former homelands to urban areas. Thanks to the current 'post-Fordist era of precarious work' (Hunter and Posel, 2012, p. 287), made worse by Covid-19-related lockdowns, and a massive drop in industrial employment in rural areas, this influx has, together with a limited supply of formal housing, resulted in a significant increase in illegal land occupations in or near former black townships. In the post-1994 era, violent removals of shacks and shackdwellers, at the behest of the local state and/or private companies acting on behalf of the state, have increased (Chance, 2018; Super and Ballasteros-Pena, 2022b)—in other words, expulsions, accompanied by extrajudicial punishments, continue.

The punitive forms of local justice which occur in these spaces are both products of and contributors to the porous boundaries between life and death, between security and insecurity, between law and violence, and between different forms and infrastructures of extrajudicial punishment. To give some examples: decisions by a street committee to evict or expel someone, have the potential to collapse into deadly violence when the crowd (or certain individuals in the crowd) go beyond the initial decision (Super, 2016a; 2017). While 'the community' may have decided to evict but not to assault, to beat but not to kill, to interrogate but not to torture, to torture but not to kill, in practice the boundaries between these unlawful penal forms are porous, and susceptible to collapsing in on each other. Relatedly, the normative lines between community policing and extrajudicial punishment, between 'community' and 'mob', and between 'victim' and 'offender' are also porous, with people assuming contemporaneous identities as members of lawful community structures, as complicit (or innocent) bystanders, as kidnappers, and/or as members of what the media and political elite frame as 'violent mobs' (Cooper-Knock, 2014; Super, 2016a; 2017; 2022a). Sometimes the police arrest someone while they are being beaten 'by the community' and take them to hospital, where they die (in police custody) as a result of their injuries. These deceased are recorded as being suspects in relation to unproven crimes (Super, 2021b).

It is quite common for small groups of men, some of whom get paid for their services, to forcefully place a suspected thief in the trunk of a vehicle and drive them around until they point out the location of stolen goods (Super, 2016a; 2022a). In other instances, suspects are summonsed to meetings in community halls, outside open spaces, and/or in empty containers where they are interrogated (often accompanied by physical violence) in order to locate stolen property. Thus, the space of the trunk, the hall, the container, and empty lot become temporary spaces of confinement, interrogation, vengeance, arbitrary violence, and sometimes death. In this sense, the boundaries between everyday infrastructures and infrastructures of penal violence are also porous—with one space assuming multiple functions. In many instances, these shadowy vigilante formations will not track down stolen goods until their 'client' or the victim of the initial crime, has laid a formal charge at the police station. After the stolen property is retrieved and the suspected thief has been 'massaged', they are sometimes dropped off at a police station in order for the 'law to take its' course' (Super, 2016a, p. 475; 2022a). In this way, judicial and extrajudicial penal violence interact with each other (but in an unpredictable way) in the co-constitution of 'moral communities' (Buur and Jensen, 2004).

Conclusion

Using South Africa as my case study, I have argued that extrajudicial violence plays a central role in penality. I have given examples of the extrajudicial punishments inflicted by prison wardens, police, prosecutors, and civilians in former black townships and informal settlements. There are many more examples, such as the penal violence meted out by heavily armed security company employees (in the affluent and largely white suburbs of Johannesburg (Murray, 2020)) and by municipal police in central business districts (Samara, 2011; Bénit-Gbaffou, 2008). These penal forms target the racialized urban poor, in particular unemployed, young black men. In most instances, the state affirms and legitimates this violence by abdicating its jurisdiction to act against it—there are virtually no arrests, no trials, and sometimes active participation. These must be taken into account when assessing penal punitiveness in a given society, but particularly in South Africa where dropping prison rates are not an indication of decreasing punishments.

Legal pluralism and extrajudicial punishments by the state, settlers, and subjects were central tactics of colonial and apartheid rule (Chanock, 2001; Mamdani, 1996). Indeed, colonialism and apartheid encouraged a plethora of actors to punish extrajudicially, resulting in deeply rooted and multiscalar violent extrajudicial punishments which have shaped current 'repertoires of violence' (Thomas, 2011) and violent forms of extrajudicial punishment in contemporary South Africa (Super, 2022a). From its inception as the Union of South Africa in 1910, the South African state suffered from a lack of capacity, inefficiency was baked into its administration, with low-level administrative officials exercising judicial, legislative, and executive powers against its black subjects, and with the law itself providing for indirect rule (Chanock, 2001). Liberal law failed to protect the racialized subjects of colonial and apartheid rule. Indeed, it was crafted in such a way as to encourage discretionary and arbitrary rule over black subjects, alongside a fairly sophisticated rule of law project which applied to whites only. Thus, the law abdicated its own jurisdiction, producing multiple spatiotemporalities in which extrajudicial violence by state and civilian actors played a central role in a violent form of social control. This extrajudicial punishment was imposed alongside state-imposed punishments (in terms of the criminal justice system) which too distinguished between settlers and subjects, between 'white' and 'non-white'. Given this history of discretionary rule and extrajudicial punishment, discussions of penality in contemporary South Africa (and elsewhere) must incorporate non-state and extrajudicial punishments. These too target poor racialized subjects and actively produce the poor black 'criminal'.

As Aliverti et al. (2021, p. 298) note, there is a need to re-examine stable concepts in criminology such as punishment, and to recognize that it is a 'broad, complex and polyvalent field'. Despite the fact that extrajudicial punishment is an integral component of penality, current measures and definitions of punishment are based on idealized, state, and Western-centric epistemologies. Didier Fassin (2018) has made persuasive arguments about the difference between punishment in theory and in practice, and the need to include the latter in discussions of the former. Failure to do this masks historical and structural forms of violence, and invisibilizes the penal violence that accompanies the formal criminal justice system and its supposed shift to humanization via liberal punishments (such as imprisonment). We must also revisit and reinterpret theoretical concepts such as 'security', 'justice', 'mass incarceration', 'mass supervision', and 'penal punitiveness'. Otherwise, in trying to achieve the promises of liberal justice and punishment, the result will be, like Donzelot's family or Foucault's prison, a perpetually failing project.

Extrajudicial punishment manifests more frequently and/or is more visible in 'post'-colonial contexts because legal pluralism and expulsion were central tactics of colonial rule and hence resulted in more obvious forms of 'necropolitics' (Mbembe, 2003). South Africa, with its history of legal pluralism, tradition of extrajudicial and extralegal violence, high levels of social inequality, comparatively weak state form, and history of colonial and apartheid rule, is markedly predisposed to legal and penal pluralism. Formal processes of decolonization and the transition from apartheid to formal democracy did not result in a dismantling of the deep-rooted trend of extrajudicial punishment and the central role it played in attempts to control the racialized poor. However, the consequences of historic and contemporary racialized mobility restrictions and other expulsive projects (such as urban gentrification and crimmigration) have shaped the tight coupling of spatialization and criminalization in *all* contexts (Global North countries included). This has produced contemporary marginalities on multiple spatiotemporal scales. At the same time, technologies of state violence are always implemented in a scalar way: the greater the inequality, the more scales there are, and the less chance there is of legal challenges to the situation. Thus, it is in informal, fluid, and unstable penal processes as much as in elaborate statutes, constitutions, and judgments that we must 'situate our understanding of'(Chanock, 2001, p. 218) punishment.

References

Aas, K. (2014) 'Bordered penality: Precarious membership and abnormal justice', *Punishment and Society*, 16(5), pp. 520–541.

Abrahams, R. (1998) *Vigilant Citizens, Vigilantism and the State*. Cambridge: Polity Press.

Abrahams, R. (2008) 'Some Thoughts on Vigilantism', in Pratten, D. and Sen, A. (eds) *Global Vigilantes*. New York: Columbia University Press.

ACJR (Africa Criminal Justice Reform) (2018). 'Factsheet 8. Performance of South Africa's National Prosecuting Authority'. Cape Town: African Criminal Justice Reform: Available at: https://acjr.org.za/resource-centre/npa-performance-nov-2018.pdf/view (accessed 12 May 2022).

Agozino, B. (2003) *Counter-Colonial Criminology. A Critique of Imperialist Reason*. London: Pluto Press.

Alexander, J. and Kynoch, G. (2011) 'Introduction: Histories and legacies of punishment in Southern Africa', *Journal of Southern African Studies*, 37(3), pp. 395–413.

Aliverti, A., Carvalho, H., Chamberlen, A., and Sozzo, M. (2021) 'Decolonizing the criminal question', *Punishment and Society*, 23(3), pp. 297–316.

APCOF (African Policing Civilian Oversight Forum) and SAHRC (South African Human Rights Commission) (2022) '2022 Police Human Rights Dialogue Theme: Arbitrary Arrest—Why does it persist?', Concept Paper.

Beckett, K. and Herbert, S. (2010) *Banished. The New Social Control in Urban America*. Oxford: Oxford University Press.

Bénit-Gbaffou, C. (2008) 'Community policing and disputed norms for local social control in post-apartheid Johannesburg', *Journal of Southern African Studies*, 34(1), pp. 93–109.

Bierschenk, T. (2014) 'Sedimentation, Fragmentation and Normative Double-Binds in West-African Public Services' in Bierschenk, T. and De Sardan, J. O. (eds) *States at Work. Dynamics of African Bureaucracies*. Leiden: Brill, pp. 221–249.

Black, D. (1983) 'Crime as social control', *American Sociological Review*, 48(1), pp. 34–45.

Bosworth, M. (2008) 'Border control and the limits of the sovereign state', *Social and Legal Studies*, 17(2), pp. 199–215.

Brewer, J. (1994) *Black and Blue: Policing in South Africa*. Oxford: Oxford University Press.

Brown, M. (2002) 'The politics of penal excess and the echo of colonial penality', *Punishment and Society*, 4(4), pp. 404–423.

Bruce, D. (2019) *The Use of Less-Lethal Weapons in South African Prisons and Crown Management: Monograph 201: November*. Institute for Security Studies, pp. 1–61.

Butler, J. (2012) 'Post one. precarity talk: A virtual roundtable with Lauren Berlant, Judith Butler, Bojana Cvejić, Isabell Lorey, Jasbir Puar, and Ana Vujanović', *Precarity and Performance: Special Consortium Issue TDR*, 56(4), pp. 163–177.

Buur, L. (2005) 'The Sovereign Outsourced: Local Justice and Violence in Port Elizabeth', in Hansen, T. B. and Stepputat, F. (eds) *Sovereign Bodies: Citizens, Migrants, and States in the Postcolonial World*. Princeton, NJ: Princeton University Press, pp. 192–217.

Buur, L. and Jensen, S. (2004) 'Introduction: Vigilantism and the policing of everyday life in South Africa', *African Studies*, 63(2), pp. 139–152.

Cameron, E. (2017) 'Imprisoning the nation: Minimum sentences in South Africa'. Lecture delivered at the University of the Western Cape, 19 October.

Chance, K. (2018) *Living Politics in South Africa's Urban Shacklands*. Chicago: University of Chicago Press.

Chanock, M. (2001) *The Making of South African Legal Culture 1902–1936: Fear, Favour and Prejudice*. Cambridge: Cambridge University Press.

Cooper-Knock, S.J. (2014) 'Policing in intimate crowds: Moving beyond "The Mob" in South Africa', *African Affairs*, 113(453), pp. 563–582.

CSPRI (Civil Society Prison Reform Initiative, LHR (Lawyers for Human Rights), Just Detention International (2016) 'South Africa Thematic Alternate Report on Criminal Justice and Human Rights in South Africa'.

Davis, D. and le Roux, M. (2009) *Precedent and Possibility. The (Ab)use of Law in South Africa*. Cape Town: Double Story.

Department of Community Safety (2019) 'Western Cape Crime Report for 2018–2019'. www.westerncape.gov.za/sites/www.westerncape.gov.za/files/wccs_crime_report_2020-03-25_medres.pdf (accessed 1 November 2020).

Diphoorn, T. (2017) 'The "Bravo Mike Syndrome": Private security culture and racial profiling in South Africa', *Policing and Society*, 27(5), pp. 525–540.

Fassin, D. (2018) 'What is Punishment', in Kutz, C. (ed.) *The Will to Punish*. New York: Oxford University Press.

Fitzpatrick, P. (1992) *The Mythology of Modern Law*. London: Routledge.

Fitzpatrick, P. (2001) *Modernism and the Grounds of Law*. Cambridge: Cambridge University Press.

Fourchard, L. (2011) 'The politics of mobilization for security in South African townships', *African Affairs*, 110(441), pp. 607–627.

Glaser, C. (2000) *Bo-tsotsi: The Youth Gangs of Soweto, 1935–1976*. Cape Town: James Currey.

Glaser, C. (2005) 'Whistles and sjamboks: Crime and policing in Soweto, 1960–1976', *South African Historical Journal*, 52(1), pp. 119–139.

Hannah-Moffat, K. and Lynch, M. (2012) 'Theorizing punishment's boundaries: An introduction', *Theoretical Criminology*, 16(2), pp. 119–121.

Hansen, T. B. and Stepputat, F. (2005) 'Introduction: On Empire and Sovereignty' in Hansen, T. B. and Stepputat, F. (eds) *Sovereign Bodies: Citizens, Migrants, and States in the Postcolonial World*. Princeton, NJ: Princeton University Press, pp. 9–37.

Hentschel, C. (2015) *Security in a Bubble. Navigating Crime in Urban South Africa*. Minneapolis, MN: University of Minnesota Press.

Hopkins, R. (2018) 'Following ConCourt ruling, SAPS continues to arrest people for possession of cannabis', *Daily Maverick*, 8 October. Available at: www.dailymaverick.co.za/article/2018-10-08-following-concourt-ruling-saps-continues-to-arrest-people-for-possession-of-canna bis/ (accessed 11 May 2022).

Hund, J. and Kotu-Rammopo, M. (1983) 'Justice in South African Townships: The sociology of Makgolta', *Comparative and International Law Journal of Southern Africa*, 16, pp. 179–208.

Hunter, M. and Posel, D. (2012) 'Here to work: The socioeconomic characteristics of informal dwellers in post-apartheid South Africa', *Environment and Urbanization*, 24(1), pp. 285–304.

Hutta, J.S. (2019) 'From sovereignty to technologies of dependency: Rethinking the power relations supporting violence in Brazil', *Political Geography*, 69, pp. 65–76.

Knoetze, D. (2021a) 'Parliament rebukes SAPS for poor discipline as watchdog probes 794 killings by police', *GroundUp*, 25 May. Available at: www.groundup.org.za/article/parliam

ent-rebukes-saps-poor-discipline-watchdog-probes-794-killings-police/ (accessed 11 May 2022).

Knoetze, D. (2021b) 'Above the Law. Massive Database of Killings by Police made Public', *Viewfinder*. 20 October. Available at: https://viewfinder.org.za/massive-database-of-killings-by-police-made-public/ (accessed 11 May 2022).

Lancaster, L. (2021) 'South Africa needs a murder reduction strategy', ISS (Institute for Security Studies), 14 June. Available at: https://issafrica.org/iss-today/south-africa-needs-a-murder-reduction-strategy?utm_source=BenchmarkEmail&utm_campaign=ISS_Today&utm_medium=email (accessed 10 May 2022).

Lund, C. (2006) 'Twilight institutions: Public authority and local politics in Africa', *Development and Change*, 37(4), pp. 685–705.

Mamdani, M. (1996) *Citizen and Subject: Contemporary Africa and the Legacy of Late Colonialism*. Princeton, NJ: Princeton University Press.

Marais, H. (2001) *South Africa: Limits to Change: the Political Economy of Transition*. Cape Town: University of Cape Town Press.

Maylam, P. (1990) 'The Rise and decline of urban apartheid in South Africa', *African Affairs*, 89(354), pp. 57–84.

Mbembe, A. (1992) 'Provisional notes on the postcolony', *Africa*, 62(1), pp. 3–37.

Mbembe, A. (2003) 'Necropolitics', *Public Culture*, 15(1), pp. 11–40.

Merry, S. (2004) 'Colonial and Postcolonial Law' in Sarat, A. (ed.) *The Blackwell Companion to Law and Society*. Oxford: Blackwell, pp. 569–589.

Metz, T. (2011) 'Ubuntu as a moral theory and human rights in South Africa', *African Human Rights Law Journal*, 11(2), pp. 532–559.

Mujuzi, J. (2008) *The Changing Face of Life Imprisonment in South Africa*, Research Paper No. 15, CSPRI.

Muntingh, L. (2017) 'Op-ed Rethinking Life Imprisonment', *Daily Maverick*, 2 March. Available at: www.dailymaverick.co.za/article/2017-03-02-op-ed-rethinking-life-imprisonment/ (accessed 11 May 2022).

Muntingh, L., Redpath, J., and Peterson, K. (2017) *An Assessment of the National Prosecuting Authority. A Controversial Past and Recommendations for the Future*. Africa Criminal Justice Reform (ACJR) and Dullah Omar Institute.

Murray, M. (2020) *Panic City. Crime and Fear Industries in Johannesburg*. Stanford, CA: Stanford University Press. 30

Nugent, P. (2010) 'States and Social Contracts in Africa', *New Left Review*, 63, pp. 35-68. Available at: http://newleftreview.org/II/63/paul-nugent-states-and-social-contracts-in-africa (accessed 13 February 2023).

Pavlich G. (2018) *Criminal Accusation: Political Rationales and Socio-Legal Practices*. London: Routledge.

Phelps, K. (2019) 'Book review: *Life Imprisonment: A Global Human Rights Analysis*. By Dirk van Zyl Smit & Catherine Appleton', *South African Law Journal*, 136(4), pp. 825–830.

Razack, J. (2014) '"It happened more than once": Freezing deaths in Saskatchewan', *Canadian Journal of Woman and the Law*, 26(1), pp. 51–80.

Redpath, J. (2008) 'Detention Without Trial is Back in South Africa', *Abahlali baseMjondolo*, 21 April. Available at: http://abahlali.org/taxonomy/term/jean_redpath/jean_redpath/ (accessed 11 May 2022).

Redpath, J. (2016) *Trends in the exercise of prosecutorial discretion: Armchair discussion on the National Prosecuting Authority*. 22 November. University of the Western Cape, Dullah Omar Institute, and CSPRI.

Redpath, J. (2019) *Liberty Not the Only Loss—The Socio-Economic Impact of Remand Detention in the Western Cape*. ACJR and Dullah Omar Institute.

Roitman, J. (2006) 'The Ethics of Illegality in the Chad Basin', in Comaroff, J. and Comaroff, J (eds) Law *and Disorder in the Postcolony*. Chicago, IL: University of Chicago Press.

Roy, A. (2019) 'Racial Banishment' in Antipode Editorial Collective, Jazeel, T., Kent, A. et al. (eds) *Keywords in Radical Geography: Antipode at 50*. Hoboken, NJ: Wiley-Blackwell, pp. 227–230.

Rueedi, F. (2015) 'Narratives on trial: Ideology, Violence and the struggle over political legitimacy in the case of the Delmas Prison Trial, 1985–1989', *South African Historical Journal*, 67(3), pp. 335–355.

Samara, T. (2011) *Cape Town After Apartheid: Crime and Governance in the Divided City*. Minneapolis, MN: University of Minnesota Press.

Smit, W. (2016) 'Informal Settlement Upgrading: International Lessons and Local Challenges' in Cirolia, L. R., Görgens, T., van Donk, M. et al. (eds) *Upgrading Informal Settlements in South Africa. A Partnership Based Approach*. Cape Town: University of Cape Town Press.

SAHRC (South African Human Rights Commission) (2017) 'Annual Trends Analysis Report 2016/17'. Available at: www.sahrc.org.za/home/21/files/SAHRC%20Trend%20Analysis%202016%20-%202017.pdf (accessed 12 May 2022).

Super, G. (2010) 'The spectacle of crime in the "new" South Africa: a historical perspective (1976–2004)', *British Journal of Criminology*, 50(2), pp. 165–184.

Super, G. (2013) *Governing through Crime in South Africa. The Politics of Race and Class in Neoliberalizing Regimes*. Farnham: Ashgate.

Super, G. (2016a) 'Volatile sovereignty: governing crime through the community in Khayelitsha', *Law and Society Review*, 50(2), pp. 450–483.

Super, G. (2016b) 'Punishment and democracy in South Africa', *Punishment and Society*, 18(3), pp. 325–345.

Super, G. (2017) 'What's in a name and why it matters: A historical analysis of the relationship between state authority, vigilantism and penal power in South Africa', *Theoretical Criminology*, 21(4), pp. 512–531.

Super, G. (2021a) Punitive welfare on the margins of the state: Narratives of punishment and (in)justice in Masiphumelele', *Social and Legal Studies*, 30(3), pp. 426–447.

Super, G. assisted by Avila, A. and Teran, J. (2021b) 'Report to SAPS: Vigilante Violence in the Khayelitsha and Nyanga Policing Clusters, 2000–2016'. Unpublished. Report on hand with author.

Super, G. (2022a) 'Cars, compounds and containers: Judicial and extrajudicial infrastructures of punishment in the "old" and "new" South Africa', *Punishment & Society*, pp. 1–19. DOI: 10.1177/14624745221079456.

Super, G. and Ballesteros-Pena, A. (2022b) 'Violence and bordering on the margins of the state: A view from South Africa and the southern border of Spain', *Theoretical Criminology*, pp. 1–21. DOI: 10.1177/13624806221076422.

Sylvestre, M., Damon, W., Blomley, N., and Bellot, C. (2015) 'Spatial tactics in criminal courts and the politics of legal technicalities', *Antipode*, 47(5), pp. 1346–1366.

Thomas, D. (2011) *Exceptional Violence. Embodied Citizenship in Transnational Jamaica*. Durham, NC: Duke University Press.

Valverde, M. (2015) *Chronotopes of Law. Jurisdiction, Scale and Governance*. London: Routledge.

Van Zyl Smit, D. and Appleton, C. (2019) *Life Imprisonment: A Global Human Rights Analysis*. Cambridge, MA: Harvard University Press.

Wilson, R. (2009) *The Politics of Truth and Reconciliation in South Africa, Legitimizing the Post-Apartheid State*. Cambridge: Cambridge University Press.

World Prison Brief (2020). Available at: www.prisonstudies.org (accessed 2 February 2021).

Zedner, L. (2016) 'Penal subversions: When is a punishment not punishment, who decides and on what grounds?', Theoretical Criminology, 20(1), 3–20.

Court Cases

S v Makwanyane and another (CCT3/94) [1995] ZACC 3; 1995 (6) BCLR 665; 1995 (3) SA 391; [1996] 2 CHRLD 164; 1995 (2) SACR 1, Constitutional Court of South Africa (6 June 1995).

Sonke Gender Justice v Government of Republic of South Africa and the Head of Centre, Pollsmoor Remand Detention Facility (24087/15), Western Cape Division of the High Court (23 February 2017).

7
Carceral Cultures in Contemporary India

Mahuya Bandyopadhyay

Introduction

'Carceral turn', 'carceral condition', and 'carceral age' are well-established anchors of enquiry in multidisciplinary research on prisons and punishment (Moran et al., 2017; Bosworth and Kaufman, 2011; Brown, 2014b; Simon, 1998; Schept, 2014; Moran and Schliehe, 2017; Gottschalk, 2015). They emphasize the need for evaluating modern punishment and prison governance outside the obvious confinement sites and institutions. This chapter examines the culture of incarceration or 'carceral culture' in modern India by drawing on ideas of the prison/street interface (Weegels et al., 2020; Bandyopadhyay, 2020).[1]

'Carceral culture' refers to the norms, attitudes, practices, and standards that shape and characterize the prison experience and structures of punishment, surveillance, and confinement. Carceral culture also signifies a variety of traits, experiences, and situations associated with incarceration, punishment, and the carceralizing of bodies and citizens. It allows us to recognize that the carceral experience occurs not just within criminal justice facilities, but also in a variety of settings outside those that are particularly established as carceral (Peter and Turner, 2017; Rannila and Repo, 2017). The term culture is used in this chapter to indicate the ethnographic unravelling of practices and everyday worlds of punishment, confinement, and prisons, while deploying Abu-Lughod's (1996) 'writing against culture' and focusing on the particular. This critiques the self-serving purpose of Western-centric criminology which studies crime and punishment to advance its successful models of dealing with these complex social issues and to fulfil larger ideas of convergence in the project of advancement of industrial capitalism (Kerr et al., 1960; Inkeles, 1981).

The peculiarities of the prison experience in India reveal struggles of meaning-making, practices of order, components of disorder, and the conflicting, paradoxical impulses that make ordinary prison life possible. The prison in India has a colonial past and is modelled after a well-ordered Western prison (Rothman, 1971; Morris and Rothman, 1995; Bandyopadhyay, 2010; 2020). Yet it is surrounded by myriad contaminations in its current practice.

This chapter briefly dwells on some aspects of prison practice to highlight the culture of incarceration in India to demonstrate how this carceral culture manifests itself

[1] Many of the ideas in this chapter have emerged through long and intense discussions with my father, Kalachand Banerjee, over the past few years. Even though I have forever lost his physical presence in my life, I write to feel his presence through my words and ideas, hoping to imbibe a bit of his spirit and his unrivalled capacity to share the lives of others.

Mahuya Bandyopadhyay, *Carceral Cultures in Contemporary India* In: *Decolonizing the Criminal Question.* Edited by: Ana Aliverti, Henrique Carvalho, Anastasia Chamberlen, and Máximo Sozzo, Oxford University Press. © Mahuya Bandyopadhyay 2023. DOI: 10.1093/oso/9780192899002.003.0008

outside the prison walls. Several violent events have taken centre stage in Indian politics and public discourse in the past couple of years, suggestive of the pervasiveness of acts of everyday violence in public spaces and the impunity associated with such everyday violence. Fear, mistrust, anxiety, and a foreboding sense of danger permeates our public lives, paradoxically along with increased surveillance and policing. The unravelling of these events and the consequent shaping of the public discourse around them, express connections between life inside prison and outside its walls. Here I articulate some of these connections and show that they enfold key aspects of the culture of incarceration in India. I present a few such events that have been 'sensational' in the kind of attention they received at the time and critical for the nature of discourse around them. There are several instances that do not find mention in this chapter, but they all indicate aspects of the carceral culture in contemporary India.

The chapter, thus, draws on two registers to explore the particularities of criminality and punishment. I engage with publicly available sources including news reporting, video footage, and television interviews around demonstrations and citizens' prosecutions for challenging government laws and policies. I also reflect on my ethnographic experience in two central prisons over two decades ago. The chapter is divided into three sections. First, I examine what it means to have a decolonial perspective followed by a discussion on carceral spillovers through certain public episodes of violence on the streets in urban India. I then connect these spillovers to aspects of carceral cultures within prisons. In the concluding section, I discuss the implications of carceral culture for thinking about prisons and punishment in India from a decolonial viewpoint.

A Decolonial Perspective—Introductory Remarks

But first, some introductory remarks on the meanings of a decolonial perspective on criminality, punishment, and prisons. In a recent chat with a top prison official, I ran into the usual assumptions and justifications about why policy changes in Indian institutions are difficult. We were discussing how prisons have become closed-off institutions, with access for members of the public severely controlled, if not impossible, in most cases. We agreed that involving civil society in jail reform efforts is difficult. I blamed this on a lack of political will. The officer disagreed, 'I don't believe politicians are concerned about what we do in prisons. They are only concerned with the treatment of some of their own who are incarcerated. Individual officers in charge of prison systems in the state are to blame …' This senior officer, eager for prison reform, emphasized individual initiative, while the conventional responses have centred around institutional difficulties and a lack of political will.

In another conversation, a jail superintendent highlighted the force of structural restraints by pointing out that he and the others were only guards acting as caregivers, doing as instructed. Individual initiative, he believed, had a limited role. He did, however, put a moral spin on their job inside the prison when he declared, '*Kisi ke majboori ko hum apna avsar nahin bana sakte*', which translates to 'We cannot convert someone's compulsion into our opportunity.' These officials' statements reflect the outlines of India's current 'governmentality' of criminality, punishment, and prisons. They enfold the possibility of reimagining prison goals and daily operations differently from conventional perceptions of prisons as rational mechanisms for dealing with social deviance and normative violations. In addition, they demonstrate the need of situating incarceration and the operation of criminal justice institutions within the context of carceral culture.

While it has been relatively easier to write about prisons through archival work (Yang 1985; 1987) and by exposing the colonial 'matrix of power' in representations of crime and criminal justice systems (Agozino, 2003; Brown, 2001; 2014a; 2015), there is a gap in documenting lived experiences in contemporary prison contexts in India and the Global South. Several structural imperatives in the Global South obstruct significant academic involvement with criminal justice institutions. Equally important are the epistemological foundations of criminology. In recreating criminology as a 'broad, multifaceted, and polyvalent field', a decolonial viewpoint exposes these systemic imperatives while also attempting to overcome them (Aliverti et al., 2021). It would necessitate a paradigm shift in prison and punishment research, as well as the adoption of a post-disciplinary epistemology that would push the discipline's bounds with hybrid theories and specific, grounded categories of knowing (Blagg and Anthony, 2019, p. 11). Mignolo (2009) refers to this as 'epistemic disobedience', which the academy must engage in, to expose the power of colonialism and its impact on shaping institutions of confinement, and to question and disrupt the mission of social order through control, confinement, and surveillance.

Researching and writing on the criminal question and prisons in India from an anthropological viewpoint, I consider it equally important to ask what motivations guide this shift in the criminological gaze from the Global North in the production of criminological knowledge. Perhaps there is a saturation of venues, topics, and ideas for producing criminological knowledge and sustaining the discipline of criminology in the Global North. Possibly decolonizing knowledge becomes a new mission of expanding disciplinary contexts, identifying new venues, and looking for fertile ground for postcolonial imperial control over knowledge production. How, then, may the Global North partner with the postcolonial Global South? How can we address the structural obstacles in establishing the field of criminology, within a framework of epistemic disobedience and the mining of ethnographically grounded categories? Such questions are central to any reflexive exercise of knowledge building and understanding regarding crime, punishment, and the criminal justice system.

Carceral Culture and the Chaotic Everyday in Prison

Carceral culture in contemporary India relies on the colonial discourse on prisons and its logic of a repressive state managing resistant, violent, and unruly subjects. The colonial discourse shapes both how the state acts and how it is perceived. The state is viewed by a resistant, rule-breaking subject as severely repressive. Further, the gap between the violent criminal law-breaking subject and the resistant, politically motivated subject is, in practice, often blurred in the face of a repressive state. This temporary blurring of categories of the criminal and the political prisoner aids the state in constructing, isolating, and paradoxically holding up as an example, the identity of the disposable citizen. Carceral culture is also shaped by global terror and in this the prisons of the Global South stand along with the Western prisons, in their increased surveillance and isolation, imprisonment, and conviction of Muslim men and boys (Raghavan and Nair, 2013).

The imprisonment and conviction of Muslim men and boys is one of the key drivers of overcrowding and the consequent architecture of governance that frames carceral culture in contemporary India. Overcrowding[2] allows for messiness in the daily routine. The resulting instability in the jail environment because of limited space adds to the spatial compression. This is, undoubtedly, a physical sensation. Disputes over space, smell, and proximity are prevalent. Constraints on movement, as well as the temporal fixing of bodies and space, pose challenges of everyday discipline, and are substantially impacted by overcrowding. Routine activities such as taking prisoner counts, attending court and 'interview' dates, collecting meals, bathing, and cleaning, and searching wards and prisoner bodies often become sites of chaos. Taxonomic techniques for identifying and separating convicts, as well as fusion of functions (some prisoners take over the task of guarding and managing prisoners, leading to entangled power relations), are critical in attempting to address the indiscipline that results from such overcrowding. Both these ordering processes, however, have an opposite effect—of producing chaotic everyday lives in prison (Bandyopadhyay, 2010; 2020).

Prisoners are classified into groups based on their standing within the criminal justice system and socio-economic factors, which is reminiscent of colonial norms. Classification is enabling for prison personnel as the task of surveillance is distributed rather than centralized. It instils a sense of self-discipline, rigorously monitored by the prisoner hierarchy. However, such classification systems develop and promote a 'culture of lenience' (Bandyopadhyay, 2010). Aggression, violence, discrimination, and benefits for some, and acute marginalization for others, were all possibilities in everyday activities. Continuous limits and monitoring on time, place, and body are imposed through the fusion of functions. As a few selected criminals count, feed, and secure inmates, the boundary between controller and controlled becomes increasingly blurred (Goffman 1961). Inmates who execute these duties, known as the *mate pahara* (*mate* means fellow inmate and *pahara* means guard), get formal and informal privileges. Because control is no longer the realm of warders and prison authorities, the practice of mixing duties leads to power entanglements. This system supports informal prison hierarchies based on type of crime, outside-prison class standing, access to money and other resources, and in-prison relationships. These interconnected duties and power and privilege entanglements produce everyday instability and encourage a lax prison culture, allowing some convicts to face extreme cruelty and punishment while others enjoy relative freedom and privileges.

[2] At the end of 2020, 371,848 people were awaiting trial in India, out of a total of 488,511 convictions. Other inmates included convicted felons (112,589 inmates) and detainees (3,590 inmates). Despite a 16.4 per cent increase in the jail population over the last five years, the number of convicted inmates decreased by 16.1 per cent. However, the number of pre-trial detainees has climbed by 31.8 per cent (NCRB Report, 2021).

Vignettes of Carceral Spillovers

This constant cycle of chaos, culture of lenience, privileges, and brutalities is an essential component of the carceral culture in prisons. Additionally, varying aspects of this cycle may be perceived on the 'street' through the instances presented here. All these public acts of violence have one thing in common: they show how the terror and violence that convicts experience in prison extends outside its walls, marking a carceral spillover.

In Delhi at the Jawaharlal Nehru University in 2016, an event was held to commemorate the 'judicial killing' of one of the convicted persons in the attack on the Indian Parliament in 2001. Some students in masks allegedly raised slogans, which were branded as anti-India slogans in the chargesheet prepared by the Delhi police. While most of the slogans were about '*Azaadi*' (freedom), protestors allegedly used provocative words declaring the breakdown of India into fragments (*tukde*), and suggested using violence to reclaim freedom. Following such slogans, the Students' Union president and two organizers of the event were arrested, and kept in custody for days. For a few weeks after these arrests, the university became both a space of increased surveillance and a site of resistance and protest. The Students' Union president was arrested under the sedition law even though legal experts clearly pointed out that the sedition law did not apply as a few slogans alone cannot constitute a threat to the nation. They also claimed that he was arrested without any clear evidence that he had raised the slogans. When the Students' Union president was produced for a court hearing he was heckled, beaten, and shamed by men dressed as lawyers within the court premises. The narrative of his arrest, the public violence on him in the courtroom, the interviews with hooligans on national television who claimed that they would have no regrets attacking anyone making anti-India slogans—all indicate the fear, unpredictability, violence, and chaotic every day that define the carceral culture in contemporary India.

More recently, in 2020, several cities in India erupted in spontaneous protests against the Citizenship Amendment Act, which claimed to modify the Indian Citizenship Act, in effect for sixty-four years and preventing illegal migrants from becoming citizens of India. Illegal immigrants are foreigners who enter India without a valid passport or travel documentation, or who stay in the country longer than permitted by law. They might be deported or imprisoned. The Act also amended a section that stated that a person must have resided in India for at least eleven years, or worked for the federal government, before they seek citizenship. Members of six religious minority populations—Hindus, Sikhs, Buddhists, Jains, Parsis, and Christians—will now be exempt from the ban if they can demonstrate that they are from Pakistan, Afghanistan, or Bangladesh. They will only need to reside or work in India for six years in order to be eligible for citizenship by naturalization, which is the process by which a non-citizen acquires citizenship or nationality. Protests erupted as there was a general feeling that the law further marginalized the minority Muslim community while making religious faith the basis of granting citizenship, contravening fundamental constitutional values.

In one such protest on 30 January 2020, a young man shot at a group of peaceful protestors in the capital city of Delhi, invoking the '*Azadi*' (freedom) slogan. This slogan had become the rallying cry among many Indians since the controversial amendment to the Citizenship Amendment Act earlier in the year. Many of these protests, led by students, young people, and women, articulated a general feeling of suffocation and a serious alteration in the cultural ethos of the Indian nation and the idea of India, struggling with concerns of diversity, heterogeneity, and inclusion. A competing slogan juxtaposed with the call for *azadi*—'*Desh ke gaddaron ko, goli maaro salon ko*', loosely translated as *shoot the traitors of the country*—was also popularized in several counter-rallies and local election meetings. '*Yeh lo Azadi*' ('Here, take your freedom'), the young shooter is reported to have said as he fired a pistol injuring a student who was approaching the shooter to reason with him and calm him down. The police looked on.

These incidents—the arrest of students following alleged anti-India sloganeering, shots fired at a group of protestors at a sit-in rally against changes in the citizenship laws, along with many others such as the rape and murder of a young child from a nomadic Muslim community in Jammu in 2018 and the murder of a local journalist in Bengaluru writing in the vernacular press against the ruling dispensation in 2017—are not unconnected. They mark out rapidly altering conceptions of freedom and constraint, and a peculiar force with which the notion of freedom is being articulated in the public domain and through our institutional spaces. They narrate connections between apparently discontinuous, segregated institutional spaces—the prison, the university, the police station, and the court.

Some aspects of carceral culture in prison life resonate with these carceral spillovers. The chaos that I observed as central to prison life is also visible in the instance of public violence against the arrested student leader. Walking into the court premises under police protection presented a chaotic scene in a public place. People, journalists, police, and lawyers crowded around him as they jostled for space. The police tried to shield the arrested person and create a barricade between him and the others, but this was not possible. The cordoned-off space and the human chain around the arrested person was broken into and he was heckled and beaten. It was an exemplary chaotic scene in a public space. Violence and its public enactment with guns to threaten, kill, and instate a culture of fear as also through heckling, beating, and obstructing freedom of movement and the freedom to gather to protest are common to both the prison and the street. Such violence is also unpredictable and arbitrary. This arbitrariness transforms the spaces of its occurrence as precarious, inherently dangerous, and devoid of freedom. The defining features of the carceral culture manifested in the prison and the street are as follows: dependence on the chaos and unpredictability of everyday life; recourse to incarceration as a way of dealing with errant and marginal citizens; the possibility of the prison experience in the life of any citizen; the persistent use of violence in the everyday; the blurring of the boundaries between sites of freedom and constraint, for instance, between the prison and the neighbourhood or the street; and the increasing totalizing of the prison and other state-managed spaces of confinement through control of access and minimum civil society interference.

People's attempts to maintain a fragile sense of order in prison are exemplified by the culture of leniency and power entanglements. Focusing on carceral culture in prisons and beyond raises concerns about where and how we locate the contemporary state's aggression on its subjects, which is frequently rendered inexplicable by the chaotic representation of everyday life for its citizens. The accepted conception of the penitentiary as the main institution for the contemporary state restraining and deploying violence against its citizens may be challenged by carceral cultures and their spillover. Torture charges made by citizens are among the most serious allegations levelled against the state. However, such narratives allow the state to hide its far more insidious role in frightening and utilizing violence against its inhabitants in their daily lives. The turmoil of everyday life might hide this kind of hostility. In prison, such violence is encoded in the constant threat of beatings, the violence implicit in the bareness of the facilities provided to some prisoners, the humiliation inscribed into everyday practices such as taking food, eating, sleeping, using the restrooms, and meeting with family and friends, and in the grand acts through which a posturing of a violent prison regime is effected through severe punishments such as public beatings, solitary confinement, social exclusion, and prison transfers.

The deadly aspect of hardwiring violence beyond prison walls is that you no longer need prisons or custodial settings like a lock-up or torture cell to employ violence as a technique of containment of the undesired and the aberrant. It can now be done on the streets—used as a metaphor for 'free spaces', spaces where citizens may feel free to express themselves. The use of violence in these free spaces is what I call carceral spillover for a certain set of people, and the definition of who belongs to that group is expanding. Foucault's (1975) understanding and genealogy of the modern prison conveys the transition from the 'spectacle of the scaffold' to the 'torture of the soul'. Everyday prison life reveals otherwise. The display of violence on the prisoner's body and the agony of the soul through denials of rights and agency are inextricably linked in the prison environment. Carceral culture founded on practices of predictability, negotiations based on identity and social capital, the fusion of functions within the prison, and the reliance on violence as a means of discipline and control, has colonial roots and many historical continuities linked to the postcolonial imperative of independent thought and redesigning institutions. Nonetheless, narratives of order and ordered institutions that characterized British exigencies of governing unruly populations remain significant.

Using statist vocabulary to study prisons as 'coercive organizations', 'total institutions', 'colonial institutions', and against the backdrop of contemporary, reformative transformations lock the understanding of the prison within anthropological 'gatekeeping' ideas (Appadurai, 1986). Such gatekeeping generates 'blind spots' (Rhodes, 2015) in analysing how the prison is positioned in a wider socio-cultural matrix and how the state frames prison policy using the global language of rights and reform. The difficult reality of everyday existence as experienced by citizen prisoner subjects puts the state's language and the narrative of order that we see and impose in our comprehension of these institutions to the test.

Carceral Culture and the Politics of Disposability

The previous anecdotes suggest that the lines between the repressive prison and the free streets have blurred. The prison is no longer the only location for incarcerating disposable persons and employing violence to punish and dissuade rebellious, deviant citizens, just as the street is no longer merely a sanctuary for freedom. The prison's ordinariness in India's modern, postcolonial era becomes clear in three ways. To begin with, every life has the potential to end up in prison. This is manifested in a context in which dissent is criminalized, and the expression of diverse political views or ideas about what makes society possible is challenged not through civil society debates, but through street confrontations, such as those between two groups of protestors, those criticizing the Citizenship Amendment Act, and those, ironically, protesting against the protestors. However, such ordinariness of the prison experience in everyday life is not limited to political prisoners, but is becoming more common as every kind of dissent is sought to be criminalized, often through broad interpretations of the law. As a seemingly non-criminal citizen enters the prison, even if only for a short time, it opens up the possibility that for every other such person, marginalized by religion, community, caste, gender, and sexuality, or disposable, encountering the prison is no longer a distant possibility but a very real one. The line between prison and street appears to be blurring even further as the public dialogue surrounding the detained assumes a level of normalcy. Second, both within and beyond the prison walls, there is a persistent culture of dread. Fear is coupled with arbitrariness in this pervasive carceral culture. Those demonstrating on the street face the arbitrariness of arrest and eventual imprisonment, while those in prison face the arbitrariness of monitoring, coercion, penalties, torture, and privileges. Third, the line between a regular criminal/prisoner and a political prisoner is becoming increasingly blurred. What influence does this blurring have on the creation of the prisoner subject, as well as concepts of disposability and prison culture?

The techniques for identifying, classifying, and categorizing the disposable citizen, as well as the criteria for disposability, are neither stable, set, nor organized. The question of who is disposable and who must be constantly under surveillance is fluid, susceptible to interpretation, and subject to change. In the recent amendment to the Citizenship Act in India, the government attempted to redefine the contours of citizenship by allowing migrants from certain countries of particular religious faiths to apply for citizenship, whereas the government's silence on Muslim migrants was clearly intended to signal disposability. The concepts of erasure and disposability are intertwined. Erasure might be accomplished through confinement and the imposition of barriers to the performance of ordinary daily lives; alternatively, it could be accomplished through dehumanizing behaviours and the policies that led to the diminution of human worth and the value of an individual existence. It resonates with the notion of carceral citizenship (Miller and Stuart, 2017; Miller and Alexander, 2016; Loyd 2015), which begins at the time of a criminal conviction and is distinguished from other forms of citizenship by the limits, duties, and advantages that are only available to people who have criminal histories, as opposed to other citizens. Contemporary carceral culture in India takes an expansive view of carceral citizenship.

Thus, the term 'disposability' has multiple meanings. It entails a state of abandonment on the part of the state and society. It could also refer to the exploitation and use of bodies to only serve the interests of profit and monetary gain until the body is no longer able to serve, after which it is abandoned to wither away (Bales, 1999). Drawing on Nick Couldry (2008, p. 3), disposability under neoliberalism represents a '"system of cruelty" that requires its own theatre'. It must use the rituals of everyday life to legitimate its norms, values, institutions, and social practices. Current forms of neoliberal governance in India where the state is both heavily invested in identifying weak, errant, marginal, and resistant populations, bringing them within the fold of governance while at the same time keeping them on the brink of erasure, forms fertile ground for the enactment of the politics of disposability. Cruel practices of identifying and isolating the disposable, of holding them up as examples, are reproduced daily through everyday public acts and events such as in the vignettes described earlier. These methods of identifying the disposable and taking action to remove them are no longer simply the responsibility of the state, but are now shared by all citizens, willing to be vigilantes. The vigilantes and their actions become what Giroux (2009) would call a 'pedagogical force, shaping our lives, memories, and daily experiences' (ibid, p. 572) while erasing the ability to form critical and emancipatory views and connections about history, justice, solidarity, and freedom.

The blurring of the prison and the street disrupts conceptions of ordered institutions and enables us to critically examine carceral cultures. In my fieldwork experience, many prisoners' narratives dwelled on the idea that prisoners felt more empowered and in charge of their lives and ability to make choices and decisions within the prison than when they reflected on their lives in the neighbourhood in the pre-prison phases of their lives. These connections have been articulated by some prison scholars such as Cunha (2008) and Wacquant (2001). Cunha's (ibid) study on prisons in urban Portugal reveals how the drug culture has dragged the neighbourhood into the institutions. There are networks of pre-carceral links that provide a sense of continuity between the interior and the outside, which modify the nature of carceral sociality. Pre-carceral arrangements impact prisoners' moral world, cultural forms, social structures, and identities behind bars (Cunha, 2008; Crewe, 2009; Trammell, 2012) and the prisoner community can no longer be regarded as an isolated, self-contained structure. The idea of carceral spillover also resonates with Wacquant's idea of the symbiotic relationship between prison and the ghetto, acting on behalf of the criminal justice system in supporting its extra-penological role as an instrument for the administration of dispossessed and dishonoured groups. Previous relations subsist within the prison walls and the symbolic and real separation between the inside and outside can no longer be taken for granted. Therefore, it is critical to move the emphasis of research from the prison to the webs and relations that span the inside and the outside, and the remaking of both these spaces.[3]

As a result, we recognize that incidents of violence in prison and on the street can also be understood in terms of the camp-like structure and the organization of camp life in different institutional spaces—the university, the police station, the prison, and the camp for the surrendered Maoist revolutionaries (or terrorists, as the state labels them). Agamben (2005) has referred to this as a state of exception, an otherwise temporary suspension of the law which becomes, in contemporary India, a

[3] Some of these interlocked and imbricated relationships between prisons and society have been explored in a special issue of the *Cambridge Journal of Anthropology* (2020), connecting prison and urban ethnographies (see Weegels et al., 2020 and others in this volume). For confinement experiences prisons, camps, and ghettos, also see the special edition of *Ethnos* (2019) (Jefferson, Turner, and Jensen, 2019), which uses 'stuckness' to encompass cross-cutting and overlapping experiences of confinement.

more generalized and pervasive state. It is this state of exception where the rule of law and ideas of allegiance to the nation as enshrined in the law are evoked to precisely suspend it to enable state action on certain marked unruly citizens. Agamben (ibid) quoting Arendt (1951) pointed out that the camp is not necessarily defined by the atrocities that take place there, but by the potential that exists for atrocities to be committed. This possibility was realized when a student who was being transported to court under police supervision was severely assaulted. This is an instance where bare life is produced in full view of the public. The interviews with the attackers speak of how the student leader urinated in his pants when he was beaten. They spoke of his cowardice. In effect, the act of violence had made it possible for the camp to be realized in the premises of the court, where bare life, the living, breathing, body soaked in its own bodily waste was being made and displayed, abandoned by law[4].

Is a Decolonial Perspective Possible?

In my in-depth analysis of Indian prisons, I've been struck by the numerous paradoxes that define and shape these institutions—between deterrence and reform, the contradiction between prison voices being silenced and the proliferation of the written word within prisons, and the paradoxical relationship between order and chaos as everyday governance outcomes in prison.[5] To speak about a decolonial perspective, and to work toward decolonizing knowledge about prisons and punishment in modern India, is both ironic and an exercise in intellectual excess. There is a scarcity of scholarship about prisons, punishment, and criminality. Each of these subjects is under-researched, and the available research is overshadowed by disciplinary traditions or dominant discourses such as those of human rights, jail modernization and reform, and institutional transformation in globalized contexts. Criminological thought, visions for how these institutional spaces might look or should look, prototypes for how crime and punishment should be dealt with in modern nations—the answers to all these questions are found in the models of successful Western nations and the colonial roots of institutions such as the prison. Prisoners' voices are hushed, and the prison itself is rendered invisible. Additionally, the prison's opacity from civil society is reflected in the policies of separation and isolation outlined in standards governing prison entry.

This opacity is also evident in judgements on several issues involving inmates' rights. Father Stan Swamy, an eighty-four-year-old political prisoner who dedicated his life to

[4] The contemporary radical left movement in India has a complex history and is perceived as a major threat to internal security. In 1967, Maoist insurgents staged one of their earliest armed uprisings in West Bengal's Naxalbari village. It began as a peasant rebellion but rapidly grew into a student movement that drew the upper and middle classes into a violent conflict against the state. The Naxalbari movement was suppressed, and many accounts of governmental violence, incarceration, and punishment established the tone for how the state would deal with extreme leftists in the years ahead. The movement was largely suppressed until the 1990s, when the state began issuing mining licenses in the mineral-rich states of Chattisgarh and Jharkhand. This sparked a new phase of rebellion against the granting of mining licenses to private corporations and businesses, as well as tribal dispossession. Balagopal (2006), Prasad (2010), and Navlakha (2010) provide field-views and first-person descriptions of the 'Maoist revolt'.

[5] xxx

advocating for and promoting Adivasi rights, was arrested in 2020 and died in captivity from Covid-19 complications in 2021. Father Stan Swamy, along with numerous other campaigners, was detained in the Bhima Koregaon case. Bhima Koregaon is a tiny hamlet in Maharashtra's Pune district. During the bicentennial commemorations of the Bhima Koregaon fight, violent conflicts between two communities resulted in the death of one person and injuries to numerous others. A few hundred Mahar troops of the East India Company, headed by the British, destroyed the Peshwa army in Koregaon two hundred years ago. This conflict has now taken on legendary proportions in Dalit history. Ambedkarite Dalits see this event as transcending a limited conception of nationalist victory over imperialism. It represents a win for the Mahar community's marginalization and exploitation against the Brahminical Peshwas' abuses.

Each year, thousands of Ambedkarites congregate in Bhima Koregaon to pay their respects to the East India Company's victory pillar, which was constructed in remembrance of the Mahar troops who unintentionally brought an end to Peshwa rule in 1818. Violent conflicts ensued during this 2018 event, which were ascribed to inflammatory comments made during a conference surrounding the event. At this occasion, several activists and academics were detained on charges of encouraging the Bhima-Koregaon violence. One of them was Father Stan Swamy, a Jesuit priest and tribal rights crusader. Father Stan Swamy, who suffered from Parkinson's disease, was repeatedly denied a straw for drinking and was refused bail despite the high risk of infection with Covid-19 and his comorbidities. He eventually succumbed to complications from Covid-19 and died on 5 July 2021, even as his requests for a straw and his appeals for bail on medical reasons reverberated through the corridors of India's criminal justice system. As a carceralized citizen, Father Stan Swamy embodied the dangerous potentialities of detention—denial of care, fair treatment, and fundamental rights, and eventual erasure through death for the average citizen. Additionally, the case serves as an illustrative example of what the current Indian prison represents. Violence, torture, and denial of basic rights are shown as the carceral culture's core.

Similarly, against all international standards and human rights frameworks, the persistent refusal of bail to another political prisoner, Safoora Zargar, who was pregnant and vulnerable to Covid-19, conveyed a signal to society about carceral culture. Safoora Zargar was a young student activist who was arrested in connection with Delhi's 2020 Citizenship Amendment Act protests and the rioting that allegedly ensued from those protests. Zargar was denied bail three times before it was granted. The argument was that numerous pregnant women were incarcerated, several children were safely delivered in jail, and Zargar's circumstances or pregnancy did not qualify her for bail.[6] Here, too, the state portrayed the carceralized citizen as ordinary. Though pandemic circumstances were extraordinary, due to lockdowns and other measures, they were not used to give any concessions to carceralized citizens. Contrarily, locked-down prisons entailed denials of several liberties to the incarcerated—including denial of basic necessities, restrictions on movement outside the prison's wards, periods

[6] For a first person account of her time in prison and her work as a student activist followed by her role in the protests against the Citizenship Amendment Act, see Sharma, 2021.

of isolation for new prisoners, and little or no interaction between prisoners and prison staff, making it difficult to obtain information.

Is there a criminological discourse that presents, navigates, and seeks to understand these issues in the contemporary prison? As fields of enquiry and practice, criminology and penology in India are severely limited. Criminology is taught in a few universities and specialized institutions, with a focus on crime prevention, investigative criminology, and forensic sciences. Its position as a state science is not simply in terms of manipulating the narratives of crime and control but it is reinforced by the strict controls on access to criminal justice institutions, increased surveillance on research in institutions such as prisons, and the paucity of funds or academic and research infrastructure to support such research. This is compounded by the hierarchies within disciplines that render the study of crime from within the social science disciplines marginal to the main contours of these disciplines. How, then, can criminology as a field of enquiry and critical thought emerge in the Indian context? How can we rethink the discipline of criminology or the interface of studies of crime and the penal institutions with other social science disciplines such as sociology, social work, anthropology, and political science, for instance? These interfaces can be productive in challenging the dynamics of colonial power, Eurocentrism, ideas of science, and rigorous scientific research, specifically with regard to the study of prisons in the Global South. Such a focus helps to state the continuities in colonial legacies and impulses in how contemporary prisons are governed, understood, and represented (Mignolo 2018).

To decolonize the criminal question, however, I argue that we must move beyond such simplistic formulations of continuity and rupture in the Indian context and examine the motivations for control, regulation, and the resulting stagnation of criminology and other disciplines that have attempted to disrupt hegemonic narratives about the prison as an institution. And it is not just the state that is implicated in this—but also national and international entities, including academia and the university. How can we conceive of a decolonized criminology from where we are now? And how would a decolonized criminology manifest itself in the Indian context? Decolonization as a means of reframing criminality and punishment in India as a break from colonialism and an unravelling of the colonial power matrix is both potent and limited. It continues to cater to existing academic and disciplinary traditions in the Global North.[7] How are we to study and write about our prisons when they are not accessible to researchers in the same way as prisons in the Global North? A decolonial perspective on prisons is also about a methodological orientation to find ways of resisting the hegemonic categories of our disciplines and the decentring of research questions from the sites of their obvious presence and occurrence to other locations. When access to the prison is controlled by the state, how can carceral cultures be made apparent? One of the ways of totalizing the prison has been the somewhat hidden processes of sealing access to the site of the prison. While several countries in the Global North have relatively open policies encouraging and enabling collaborative

[7] Dimou (2021) argues that coloniality is a power matrix comprised of four intricately intertwined domains: control of knowledge and understanding; control of subjectivities and intersubjective relations; control of the economy; and control of authority through the nation state and its institutions.

engagements between administrators, activists, civil society members, academics, and researchers, the state has not only restricted the prison for members of civil society but also signposts a totalizing policy on how bail, parole, and visitation rights are dealt with. The denial of bail to activist Safoora Zargar, in the middle of the pandemic and despite her pregnancy, and the denial of a straw to Father Stan Swamy are instances of such signposting.

How can researchers in the Global South define the parameters of their own societies' study of crime and punishment without being entangled in the intricate networks of acceptance, validation, and acknowledgement that exist within the global, hierarchical, academic context? The answer to this question lies not just in creating contexts for challenging state dominance in criminology, and questioning Eurocentric categories of knowledge, it is about articulating through prison experience the patriarchal and caste-class dominance in these disciplines and the emerging realities of punishment and the prison. The glimpses of everyday chaos within prisons presented here indicate the potentiality of chaos, culture of lenience, and, paradoxically, the culture of fear and violence in moving towards a decolonial understanding of the prison. The postcolonial prison represents colonial modernity, assertive national resurgence, and the embracing of global norms and commitment to human rights. Viewing and theorizing prisons and punishment through these paradoxical registers enfold the capacity to transcend the narrow confines of crime prevention, control, and the production and maintenance of the 'disposable citizen' to deploy multiple, culturally sensitive perspectives on social harm and disposability as expressed in different public and private spaces. Decoloniality would also involve addressing questions of access to the prison to rethink how the prison in the Global South has been represented and how the ruptures in these images may be unravelled. It will entail a focus on the prison everyday and the use of an anthropological perspective to reveal grounded categories of prison experience. They contribute to understanding the negotiations and manoeuvres in grappling with the well-entrenched infrastructure of a state science.

Is a decolonial perspective possible without a complete breakdown and a dismantling of the colonial institutions and the knowledge surrounding these institutions? Arguing along the grain of the potential of Southern criminologies (Carrington et al., 2016; Sozzo, 2021; Dimou 2021), I began with a somewhat affirmative note on the possibility of decolonizing criminological knowledge. Diverse and fractured subjectivities of prison life can contribute towards a decolonial perspective, instead of existing simply as critiques to criminological knowledge and the articulation of relations between power, knowledge, and representation. Decoloniality might imply a desire to eliminate colonial concepts, institutions, and knowledge and explanatory frameworks.

However, Moosavi (2019) and Cunneen (2018) raise reservations about whether decoloniality would be able to disentangle itself from criminology's Western epistemological and ontological underpinnings. I share this scepticism regarding the capacity of decoloniality to launch 'cognitive justice' when researching and writing about prisons and punishment in India. In fact, I would argue that prisons in the Global South, particularly in India, are under-researched and invisible, and that the first step towards cognitive justice would be to open prison spaces for research and encourage academicians, activists, social workers, and journalists to collaborate in order to broaden the public discourse about prisons and punishment. That would be the first course of action if any pluriversality must emerge.

Furthermore, any call for the dismantlement of the colonial prison and the knowledge around it silences the powerful ruptures and moments of resistance to the grand narratives of the prison as a space for confinement and punishment, even before they have been given the opportunity to surface and be heard. A decolonial perspective on prisons in India is not a point to be arrived at, and nor a particular form of articulation of the relationship between colonial power and modern institutions in postcolonial states, but a process and a particular sensitivity—in my case, an ethnographic sensitivity—to the varieties of lived experiences of the prison. These lived experiences allow us to consider how we may theorize about prisons in the Global South. Aspects of carceral culture reveal the disorderliness, informal hierarchies, and chaos in everyday prison life. They indicate new ways of representing the prison, in contradiction to the neat formulations of Western and Eurocentric versions of the prison.

Multilayered subversions can be found in the entangled interactions that occur within prison. Increasingly, prisoners are challenging the restrictive nature of prisons and, by implication, the state. To do so, they engage critically with the everyday by bending rules, working out privileges within the system, through repeated attempts at escape, rioting, and the reporting of human rights abuses. Prisons, labelled as correctional facilities, emerged in many postcolonial countries as spaces for the articulation of dissenting voices, particularly during periods of rapid social upheaval and coordinated efforts to adapt with globalization. As a result, the prison itself becomes a source of dissent, with the goal of establishing, however tacitly, a larger subversive political arena.

Prisons in the Global South have progressed beyond the rhetoric of being relics of colonial institutions by integrating the distinctive cultural quirks of their respective contexts and cultures. They cannot be considered as completely embracing modernity within the criminal justice system. For new theorizations to emerge, social science disciplines in general and criminology, specifically, must perceive and establish independence from Western categories, from the intrigue of expected new possibilities and research agendas set by Western academia, and the dominance of powerful governmental and statist orientations. Simply revealing the colonial matrix of power is not adequate as articulations of a decolonial criminology.

The idea of ethical loneliness (Stauffer, 2015) holds powerful lessons for a decolonial perspective on prisons. Ethical loneliness emerges not just from the harm inflicted on certain populations but a collective inability to hear those who have suffered. When such people emerge out of contexts of suffering, they find that their speech only counts to fulfil certain obligations, and established notions of justice. Ethical loneliness, then, is the experience of being abandoned by humanity, compounded by the cruelty of wrongs not being acknowledged. It is the result of multiple lapses on the part of human beings and political institutions that, in failing to listen well to survivors, deny them redress by negating their testimony and thwarting their claims for justice (ibid). A decolonial perspective on prisons must be free from such a charge of ethical loneliness. If the messy, chaotic interpretations and ideas from prisons of postcolonial contexts are suppressed even as they begin to emerge as vantage points and tentative theorizations on prisons, it would impinge on our ability to hear well, the many voices and perspectives that the prison and the diverse experiences of incarceration articulate. Recognizing, articulating, and then theorizing from these chaotic interactions reveal the intrinsic fragility of the epistemic confidence of our disciplines, and may provide the key to 'epistemic humility' and the beginnings of a decolonial view on criminality and punishment.

References

Abu-Lughod, L. (1996). 'Writing Against Culture', in Fox, R. G. (ed.) *Recapturing Anthropology: Working in the Present*. Santa Fe, NM: School of American Research Press, pp. 137–162.

Aliverti, A. J., Carvalho, H., Chamberlen, A., and Sozzo, M. (2021) 'Decolonizing the criminal question', *Punishment & Society*, 23(3). pp. 297–316.

Agamben, G. (2005) Attell, K. (trans.) *State of Exception*. Chicago, IL: Chicago University Press.

Agozino, B. (2003) *Counter-Colonial Criminology: A Critique of Imperialist Reason*. London: Pluto Press.

Appadurai, A. (1986) 'Theory in anthropology: Center and periphery', *Comparative Studies in Society and History*, 28(2), pp. 356–361.

Arendt, H. (1951) *The Origins of Totalitarianism*. New York: Harcourt.

Balagopal, K. (2006) 'Maoist Movement in Andhra Pradesh', *Economic and Political Weekly*, 41(29), pp. 3183–3187.

Bales, K. (1999) *Disposable People: New Slavery in the Global Economy*. Berkeley: University of California Press.

Bandyopadhyay, M. (2010) *Everyday Life in Prison: Confinement, Surveillance, Resistance*. New Delhi: Orient BlackSwan.

Bandyopadhyay, M. (2020) 'Carceral entrapments: Views from the prison/street interface in India', *Cambridge Journal of Anthropology*, 38(1), pp. 15–32.

Blagg, H. and Thalia, A. (2019) *Decolonising Criminology: Imagining Justice in a Postcolonial World*. London: Palgrave Macmillan.

Brown, M. (2001) 'Race, science and the construction of native criminality in colonial India', *Theoretical Criminology*, 5(3), pp. 345–368.

Brown, M. (2014a) *Penal Power and Colonial Rule*. Abingdon: Routledge.

Brown, M. (2014b). 'Visual criminology and carceral studies: Counter-images in the carceral age', *Theoretical Criminology*, 18(2), pp. 176–197.

Brown, M. (2015) 'Postcolonial penality: Liberty and repression in the shadow of independence, India c. 1947', *Theoretical Criminology*, 21(2), pp. 186–208.

Carrington, K., Hogg, R., and Sozzo, M. (2016) 'Southern criminology', *The British Journal of Criminology*, 56(1), pp. 1–20.

Couldry, N. (2008) 'Reality TV, or the secret theatre of neoliberalism', *Review of Education, Pedagogy and Cultural Studies*, 30(3), pp. 3–13.

Crewe, B. (2009) *The Prisoner Society: Power, Adaptation and Social Life in an English Prison*. Oxford University Press.

Cunha, M. I. (2008) 'Closed circuits: Kinship, neighbourhood and imprisonment in urban Portugal', *Ethnography*, 9(3), pp. 325–350.

Cunneen, C. (2018) 'Indigenous Challenges for Southern Criminology', in Carrington, K., Hogg, R., Scott, J., and Sozzo, M. (eds) *The Palgrave Handbook of Criminology and the Global South*. Cham: Palgrave Macmillan, pp. 19–41.

Dimou, E. (2021) 'Decolonizing Southern criminology: What can the "decolonial option" tell us about challenging the modern/colonial foundations of criminology?', *Critical Criminology*, 29, pp. 431–450.

Foucault, M. (1975) *Discipline and Punish: The Birth of the Prison*. New York: Random House.

Giroux, H. (2009) 'Hard lessons: Neoliberalism, education and the politics of disposability', *Policy Futures in Education*, 7(5), pp. 570–573.

Goffman, E. (1961) *Asylums: Essays on the Social Situation of Mental and Other Inmates*. New York: Garden Books.

Gottschalk, M. (2015) 'Raze the carceral state', *Dissent*, 62(4), pp. 54–56.

Inkeles, A. (1981) 'Convergence and Divergence in Industrial Societies', in Attir, M. O., Holzner, B. H., and Suda, Z. (eds) *Directions of Change: Modernization Theory, Research, and Realities*. Boulder, CO: Westview Press, pp. 3–38.

Jefferson, A., Turner, S., and Jensen, S. (2019) 'Introduction: On stuckness and sites of confinement', *Journal of Anthropology*, 84(1), pp. 1–13.

Kerr, C., Dunlap, J. T., Harbison, F. et al. (1960) *Industrialism and Industrial Man*. Cambridge, MA: Harvard University Press.

Loyd, J. M. (2015) 'Carceral citizenship in an age of global apartheid', *Occasion*, 8, pp. 1–15.

Mignolo, W. D. (2009) 'Epistemic disobedience, independent thought and decolonial freedom', *Theory, Culture & Society*, 26(7–8), pp. 159–181.

Mignolo, W. D. (2018) 'The Decolonial Option', in Mignolo, W. D. and Walsh, C. E. (eds) *On Decoloniality: Concepts, Analytics, Praxis*. Durham, NC: Duke University Press, pp. 105–226.

Miller, R. J. and Alexander, A. (2016) 'The price of carceral citizenship: Punishment, surveillance, and social welfare policy in an age of carceral expansion', *Michigan Journal of Race and Law*, 21(2), pp. 291–314.

Miller, R. J. and Stuart, F. (2017) 'Carceral citizenship: Race, rights and responsibility in the age of mass supervision', *Theoretical Criminology*, 21(4), pp. 532–548.

Moosavi, L. (2019) 'A friendly critique of "Asian criminology" and "Southern criminology"', *The British Journal of Criminology*, 59(2), pp. 257–275.

Moran, D. and Schliehe, A. (2017) 'Co-Production and Carceral Spatiality', in Moran, D. and Schliehe, A. (eds) *Carceral Spatiality*. London: Palgrave Macmillan, pp. 1–9.

Morris, N., and Rothman, D. (1995) *The Oxford History of The Prison: The Practice of Punishment in Western Society*. New York: Oxford University Press.

National Crime Records Bureau (NCRB) (2021) *Prison Statistics India 2020*. Ministry of Home Affairs. Available at: https://ncrb.gov.in/sites/default/files/PSI_2020_as_on_27-12-2021_0.pdf (accessed 18 June 2022).

Navlakha, G. (2010) 'Days and nights in the Maoist heartland', *Economic and Political Weekly*, 45(16), pp. 38–47.

Peters, K. and Turner, J. (2017) 'Carceral Mobilities: A Manifesto for Mobilities, an Agenda for Carceral Studies', in Turner, J. and Peters, K. (eds) *Carceral Mobilities: Interrogating Movement in Incarceration*. London: Routledge, pp. 1–14.

Prasad, A. (2010) 'The political economy of "Maoist" violence in Chhattisgarh', *Social Scientist* 38(3/4), pp. 3–24.

Raghavan, V and Nair-Shaikhh, R. (2013) 'Over-representation of Muslims: The Prisons of Maharashtra', *Economic and Political Weekly*, XLVIII(11), pp. 12–17.

Rannila, P. and Repo, V. (2017) 'Property and carceral spaces in Christiania, Copenhagen', *Urban Studies*, 55(13), pp. 2996–3011.

Rhodes, L. A. (2015) 'Ethnographic Imagination in the Field of the Prison', in Drake, D. H., Earle, R., and Sloan, J. (eds) *The Palgrave Handbook of Prison Ethnography. Palgrave Studies in Prisons and Penology*. London: Palgrave Macmillan.

Rothman, D. (1971) *The Discovery of the Asylum: Social Order and Disorder in the New Republic*. Boston: Little Brown and Co.

Schept, J. (2014) '(Un)seeing like a prison: Counter-visual ethnography of the carceral state', *Theoretical Criminology*, 18(2), pp. 198–223.

Sen, S. (2011) *Disciplined Natives: Race, Freedom and Confinement in Colonial India*. Delhi: Primus.

Sharma, B. (2021) '"Better days are coming. times change very fast. There is always hope": Safoora Zargar', article 14, 4 March. Available at: www.article-14.com/post/better-days-are-coming-times-change-very-fast-there-is-always-hope-safoora-zargar (accessed 18 June 2022).

Singh, U. (1998) *Political Prisoners in India*. New Delhi: Oxford University Press.

Stauffer, J. (2015) *Ethical Loneliness: The Injustice of Not Being Heard*. New York: Columbia University Press.

Trammell, R. (2012) *Enforcing the Convict Code: Violence and Prison Culture*. Boulder, CO: Lynne Rienner.

Wacquant, L. (2001) 'Deadly symbiosis: When ghetto and prison meet and mesh', *Punishment & Society*, 3(1), pp. 95–133.

Weegels, J., Jefferson, A., and Martin, T. (2020) 'Confinement beyond site: Connecting urban and prison ethnographies', *Cambridge Journal of Anthropology*, 38(1), pp. 1–14.

Yang, A. A. (ed.) (1985) *Crime and Criminality in British India*. Tucson, AZ: University of Arizona Press.

Yang, A. A. (1987) 'Disciplining 'natives': Prisons and prisoners in early nineteenth century India', *South Asia Journal of South Asian Studies*, 10(2), pp. 29–45.

PART 3
LOCATING COLONIAL DURESS

8

'Muslims Have No Borders, Only Horizons'

A Genealogy of Border Criminality in Algeria and France, 1844 to Present

*Sarah Ghabrial**

Introduction

In North African dialects of Arabic, the popular term for undocumented migration is *harraga* (الحراقة), which is drawn from the verb 'to burn'. Figuratively, the person who engages in *harraga* 'burns' the border—they pass it without stopping—in a manner similar to the French expression in which one who 'burns the fire' (*brûler/griller le feu*) runs a red light at an intersection. Both figuratively and sometimes literally, the *harraag*[1] burns their visas and identity papers, and with them their traceability. In a more general sense, *harraga* connotes a disregard for bureaucracy, for rules; *harraga* are always already *against* the law. '*Harraga* is thus an activity that *burns* state-rules and messes up boundaries' (M'charek, 2020, p. 429). In contrast, however, to American 'illegals' or Australian 'boat people', the people engaging in *harraga* are not vilified by those who use this term, as their evasion of law does no real harm; 'stowaway' might serve as an equivalent term in English. This practice is understood to be a strategic, dialectical, and even necessary response to state 'monopolization of the legitimate means of movement' (Torpey, 2000, p. 2). Seeing that law is arbitrary (Bourdieu, 1987), they pay it no mind; determined, they press ahead, reducing to ashes whatever made them legible to the state.

Harraga is not a natural phenomenon, but a juridical and political one. The undocumented migrant is in many ways the most recent expression of nearly two centuries of cartographic and carceral projects undergirding state sovereignty and the concomitant monopolization of movement across the Maghrib and between the northern and southern shores of the Mediterranean. Through the nineteenth and into the early twentieth centuries, s/he was prefigured by the '*indigène*', who also took on different

* This research was made possible by a grant from the Social Sciences and Humanities Council of Canada. I would like to thank Elizabeth Perego, Terrence Peterson, and Sara Rahnama, as well as Rohit De, Sara Fruchtman, Alison Guess, and Renisa Mawani, for their engagement and conversations on earlier versions of this chapter. Gratitude, above all, goes to the editors of this volume for their scrupulous revisions, which greatly improved and clarified this chapter.

[1] The locally variable linguistics and poetics of *harraga* (sometimes rendered *hrague* or *harga*) are often ambiguous. *Harraga* refers both to an activity (extra-legal movement across borders) and the people who engage in this activity. Because the term is specific to North-African dialects (*darija*) rather than formal standard Arabic, there is no common transliteration or singular noun. In this chapter, I identify *harraga* in the singular either as the person engaged in it, or as *harraag*, following M'charek (2020).

Sarah Ghabrial, *'Muslims Have No Borders, Only Horizons'* In: *Decolonizing the Criminal Question*. Edited by: Ana Aliverti, Henrique Carvalho, Anastasia Chamberlen, and Máximo Sozzo, Oxford University Press. © Sarah Ghabrial 2023.
DOI: 10.1093/oso/9780192899002.003.0009

mantles according to the preoccupations of the colonial state: the 'enemy' in times of declared war; the 'rebel' or insurgent in times of ostensible peace; the 'vagrant' or vector of disease when disrupting public order. S/he was briefly followed in the late twentieth century by the '*étranger*', on the move but tolerated because their situation was provisional and secondary. Today, s/he is marked by the state as the '*clandestine*' (Zeghbib, 2009, p. 80), the 'irregular' migrant, whose passage from sub-Saharan Africa into Europe warrants urgent 'traceability', deterrence, and punishment—up to and including death. The produced illegality of the migrant, under its various guises and modes of criminalization, is the subject of this chapter.

In the most basic sense, this chapter is concerned with the relationship between mobility, racialization, and (il)legality. It seeks to understand how mobility and illegality inform, rationalize, and reproduce each other in order to sustain continued North–South asymmetries of power and racialized difference. As the editors of this volume have noted, 'decolonizing the criminal question' necessarily begins with accounting for globalized genealogies and geographies of criminalization (Aliverti et al., 2021). As a historian of Algeria during the French colonial period, this is the context and archive in which I ground my contribution to this collective project. I take as my research objects a set of penal, judicial, and bureaucratic instruments—including land sequestration, identity papers, passports, travel permits, house arrests, vagrancy laws, administrative detention, and deportation—and situate them temporally within a disciplinary and governmental continuum. The aggregate effect of this broad array of instruments and techniques formed an institutional tradition through which the mobility of certain subjects was apprehended, racialized, and criminalized by colonial and postcolonial states.

In turn, this historically grounded study has implications for contemporary debates around the 'illegal' alien, a subject whose very body marks the boundaries of law(fulness); a subject produced and reproduced by immigration law, visa regimes, and border policing. Across temporal divides that supposedly cleave 'post' from 'colonial' are knowledge structures and penal technologies that ascribe particularly 'dangerous' modes of mobility to presumed disorderly subjects, requiring, in turn, exceptionally violent modes of suppression. This chapter benefits from Hagar Kotef's (2015) insight that the colonized subject's perceived irrational and uncontrollable movement, which inherently offends and undermines state sovereignty, is precisely what also places them beyond the reach of legal protections. This cyclical process of 'de-legalization' helps to maintain not only a supply of institutional memory that can be drawn upon to meet new demands as they arise but helps to clarify the 'recursive history and uneven sedimentation of colonial practices' that resonate into and reanimate the colonial present (Stoler, 2016, p. ix). In this case, while the colonial figure of the Arab/Muslim has been the prime historical object of these processes—and for numerous reasons remains the archetypical migrant in France—today the full lethality of border criminality across the Mediterranean weighs most heavily on sub-Saharan black life.

The intended intervention of this argument is two-pronged: the first is to inject historical sensibility into the subfield of border criminology, which too often suffers from an overly presentist preoccupation with state deterritorialization under neoliberalism. Scholars working in this subfield commonly accept that, as globalization has increasingly rendered borders permeable and territorial sovereignty incoherent, mobility controls have been both internalized and outsourced, and thus 'reconstituted around the bodies' of migrants (Mountz, 2010, p. xvii; see also Walia, 2021; Wonders, 2006). This is true, but it is not new. Rather, a main premise of this chapter is that such penal modalities and intensified attention to bodies predates or at least emerged *alongside* political territorialization of modern border regimes. Indeed, the management of vast expanses of functionally ungovernable imperial space meant that policing and penalizing measures had to render knowable/traceable bodies even as—and often before—territorial possession could be meaningfully exercised. In de-historicizing contemporary border regimes, border sociologists and criminologists risk naturalizing territorial states; thus a decolonial objective of this chapter is to correct that methodological mistake.

The second aim addresses the question of transplanting criminological discourse and mechanisms 'from metropoles to colonies and ex-colonies' (Aliverti et al., 2021, p. 304). For one, this process of 'importation' was not unidirectional: for example, as French vagrancy laws were transplanted to Algeria, surveillance and public health-management strategies for controlling movement travelled the other way, from Algeria to France. But more importantly, this chapter reveals how these very regimes and techniques *themselves* served to establish geographies of relation and distinction between metropole and colony. Indeed, such centrifugal cartographies had to be *manufactured* through mobility-policing regimes. Algeria was transformed into a French 'borderland' through an elaborate penal architecture centred on the suspect bodies of racialized Muslim subjects. An ancillary aim of this chapter, therefore, is to disentangle the very histories that produced 'centre' and 'periphery' as spatialized coordinates in criminological literature, including 'decolonial' iterations thereof. Insofar as these spatial imaginaries are inherited by postcolonial states—including, as we shall see, all the states that make up the modern Maghrib—this volume occasions attention to the incongruencies between 'decolonial' and 'postcolonial' (on which more later).

Unfolding in three sections, the remainder of the chapter traces the evolution of these logics and instruments in Algeria: the first section begins with a brief contextual discussion of early colonial land policies and privatization schemes that laid the foundation for Muslim criminality *qua* mobility. French actors presumed a Muslim incapacity for civilized, rational attachment to land even as they themselves alienated Muslims from land through sequestration and forced displacement.

The second section turns to the era of civil governance in Algeria (after 1870), which oversaw the regime of internal mobility controls and the height of administrative internment, a 'special' form of punishment particular to Muslims. Internment was a widely used punishment adaptable to a range of imperatives: to facilitate the removal of 'dangerous' individuals; to penalize the vaguest suspicions of subversive activity; to punish any failure to carry a travel permit, thus confining Muslims to their own villages; to establish control over religious pilgrimage; to both displace Algerians from communally-held lands and force them to work the privately held lands of settlers; to prevent the spread of disease; and to manage the rural–urban migration and 'vagrancy' problems generated by these very policies. The demise, in 1914, of this prolific regulatory and punitive regime did not bring about 'emancipation' for Muslims, but inaugurated new disciplinary mechanisms with an emphasis on surveillance.

The next section briefly explores two moments in which colonial mobility controls and sanctions were revitalized in new forms and put to new ends: the first instance took place between 1955 and 1962, when the French military instituted a clandestine 'deportation' policy during the Algerian War of Independence. As a result, up to one-third of the rural Algerian population were forcibly displaced and relocated to what were euphemistically called 'resettlement camps'. The second moment of revival has transpired in the years since the 2008–2009 promulgation of new Algerian immigration laws, at the behest of the EU and in the name of 'counter-terrorism', which invested broad discretionary power in the police and administrative authorities to control 'irregular' migration within Algerian borders and prosecute 'illicit' departures from Algerian soil. Indeed, through a series of laws introduced during that same period in Morocco, Algeria, Tunisia, and Libya, the whole Maghrib has become a 'buffer zone' (De Genova and Puetz, 2010, p. 5), rendering intra-European freedom of movement possible through the deadly interdiction and *refoulement* of trans-Saharan transits.

Imagining and Producing the 'Borderless' Muslim

In the early years of French conquest in North Africa, during the 1830s and 1840s, colonial administrators had a saying: 'Muslims have no borders, only horizons' (Sayagh, 1986). While this masks the truth that Morocco and its Ottoman-governed neighbours to the east had long observed a real political–topographical distinction between them, the Sahara of the eighteenth and nineteenth centuries was certainly characterized by healthy large-caravan traffic, propelled mainly by pilgrims voyaging to and from the *hejaz* (Warscheid, 2018). Nested within this bromide that 'Muslims have no borders' are multiple readings that clarify the colonial state's anxieties over and eventual attempts at regulating the 'borderless' autochtonous subject. Cause and effect became one: the 'rootless' and 'nomadic' Arab/Muslim/*indigène*[2] lacked the capacity for sovereign subjecthood under rule-of-law governance, which, tautologically, authorized their rightlessness and 'deportability' as a mode of governance (De Genova and Puetz, 2010).

Upon declaring dominion in the Sahara, by the mid-nineteenth century French officials grew quickly distrustful of the Muslim religious obligation to perform the *hajj* (pilgrimage to Mecca), as well as the spiritual value placed in travelling for the sake of religious instruction or the benefit of one's community. This association between pilgrimage and resistance to French domination was further entrenched by reports that the rebel leader Emir Abd-el-Kadir had joined the Qadiriyya brotherhood during a visit to Baghdad in 1828, while on *hajj* (Blanchard, 2018, p. 11). Indeed, and as a

[2] After 1865, 'Muslim' became a legal category in Algeria. Algerians with 'Muslim personal status' were barred from French citizenship despite being subject to French laws. This legal designation and ghettoization was further entrenched by the Cremieux Decree of 1873 which forcibly conferred French citizenship upon all Algerian Jews, leaving only Muslims in the category of '*indigènes*'. Thus, only Muslims were subjected to the exceptional penal regime, later codified in the 1881 Code de l'Indigénat.

result, travel for the sake of pilgrimage was one of the earliest forms of Muslim mobility which the French attempted to regulate and contain. In turn, Muslim movement against or beyond the purview of the colonial state, even to a neighbouring village, became suspicious activity warranting extreme and exceptional penal measures. Forms of collective punishment, in particular land sequestration, as well as forced migration and deportation to penal colonies in Corsica and New Caledonia, became primary modes of punishment for anything from organizing rebellion to uttering speech that could be interpreted as opposing French rule (Blanchard, 2018, pp. 13–14).

The figure of the 'borderless' Muslim also animated French land policies of enclosure and privatization. In this view, the 'wandering Arab' lacked the capacity for consent and self-discipline required for sovereign subjecthood under rule-of-law governance. The imperial 'imaginative geography' (Said, 1994) that informed early colonial rule in Algeria was that of a vast frontier, bereft of both law and inhabitants, not unlike the presumed 'vacant' lands of North America or the Australian fantasy of a *terra nullus*, whose indigenous populations nonetheless 'insist[ed] upon being there despite the myth that insists they were not' (Kotef, 2015, p. 106; see also Bhandar, 2018). As Muslim Algerians failed to disappear, and as the French military government came to terms with the need to rely on indigenous labour, these visions were gradually replaced by new justifications for land seizure. Algeria's inhabitants were, like so many others before and since, 'declared as nomads to break the tie between them and the land', a discursive move which subsequently 'produc[ed] irrationality to justify occupation, expulsion, and violence' (Kotef, ibid). The presumed unwillingness or incapacity of Muslims to draw value from the land (*mise en valeur*) became the primary pretext upon which to stage their removal.

In 1848, the North African territories under French control were officially 'departmentalized'—that is, made into three metropolitan administrative units, thus inaugurating the legal fiction of territorial continuity with mainland France. This set the stage for a sequence of later policy shifts aimed at rendering both Muslim labour and lands available for the benefit of incoming settlers. Fifteen years later, the infamous 1863 *senatus-consulte* replaced practices of rural joint land use with a system of individualized property (Halvorsen, 1978). In an essay on the 'clash of civilizations' (*le choc des civilizations*) signified by the imposition of European capitalism on Algerian agrarian society, Pierre Bourdieu noted that promoters of the *senatus-consulte* hoped not only for a 'general liquidation of the land' that might 'attract and receive emigration from Europe', but also a 'disorganization of the tribe, which was seen as a chief obstacle to pacification' (Bourdieu et al., 2013, p. 45). The *senatus-consulte* was followed up by the 1871 Loi Warnier, which abolished the *waqf/hobous* system of religious endowments, an Islamic legal mechanism that had been used by Muslim land-holders to fend off colonial land confiscation (Powers, 1989).

Colonial policies of land expropriation had a devastating effect on indigenous society, particularly of the interior, by weakening collective ties. As Bourdieu argued:

> Handing the fellah French-style property titles was to offer him the opportunity, the possibility and the temptation to give up his holdings. The result... was radically different from that which was supposedly intended, since, *aiming at creating individual possession, it became an instrument of dispossession.*

(Bourdieu et al., 2013, p. 46; emphasis added)

As a direct result, by the closing years of the nineteenth century, intensified restrictions on Muslim movement were driven as much by the objectives of quashing rebellions and maintaining security as the imperative to stem the veritable mass evacuation of colonized subjects. Countless single men and whole kin-groups took up and left, seeking refuge in neighbouring Muslim countries as far as Egypt (Blanchard, 2018, pp. 14–15). So prevalent was this trend that it gave rise to a new Arabic poetic genre on the theme of *el-ghobra*, or exile (Mokhtari, 2005). In this way, the fantasy of *refoulement* was achieved—though in an ironic and unanticipated way—through mass alienation and displacement from lands held collectively by families and tribal communities. Thus, French land-privatization policies produced the very rootless 'nomads' they had imagined to wander the Algerian interior. In response, colonial state actors developed a set of discretionary and exceptional penal practices intended to control the very displacements instigated by their land policies.

The Administrative Internment Regime (1840s–1914)

Colonial Algeria's administrative internment regime had, at the time, no parallel in French law or government (Le Cour Grandmaison, 2008, p. 209). However, by the time it came under scrutiny in Paris, contemporary comparisons to serfdom (and sometimes slavery) appeared in nearly every treatise taking up the subject, whether arguing for or against it (inter alia Larcher, 1902, p. 39; Larcher and Olier, 1899, p. 158; Rozet in Government of Algeria, 1916, p. 72). Indeed, it was discovered that Algeria's exceptional penal regime had rendered Muslim subjects at once alienated from and tethered to the land: though dispossessed, they were held in place by the ornate system of passport controls and travel permits, as well as the constant threat of deportation at the discretion of the local *commune*'s administrative authority or the executive branch. Liberal lawyer Gilbert Massonié (1909, p. 5) described it at the time as a noxious combination of deportation, surveillance, and incarceration.

Administrative internment came gradually into being without the passage of any law, thus its very nature was amorphous and inscrutable. For one, no maximum length of sentence was ever specified; internment could thus last for any duration, and end—or be extended—at any time (Rozet in Government of Algeria, 1916, p. 63). A colonized subject sentenced to internment could be sent either to one of the local 'indigenous' prisons, to a distant *arrondissement* that they could not leave, or to an overseas penal colony or labour camp, usually Calvi (Corsica), but often as far as New Caledonia (ibid). There was no recourse to legal counsel or appeal (Le Cour Grandmaison, 2008, p. 208). Until a circular of 8 June 1903, defendants were not even interrogated before their deportation (Massonié, 1909, p. 6). Perhaps most notably, internment could be applied *in addition* to any sentence issued under the common law by a normal criminal court. Indeed, it could function as a supplement in the case of a guilty verdict, or even as a substitute in the case of a dismissal, or even acquittal (Massonié, 1909, p. 7).

Though the practice endured even when unacknowledged, it was first explicitly recognized by the civilian government in the 1881 '*rattachement*' act which delegated a number of powers, including internment, land sequestration, collective punishment of tribes, managing pilgrimages, surveilling religious brotherhoods, and the purchase of arms, from the colonial governor general to the Ministry of the Interior in Paris, in an effort to centralize Algerian administration (Government of Algeria, 1916, p. 41). This was also the year that internment, and the adjacent collection of crimes and punishments specific to Muslims, were codified in a 'table' of twenty-three offences—the infamous 'Code de l'Indigénat'—including the obligation to carry a passport, travel permit, or work permit to leave their own *arrondissement*, and the interdiction to 'give asylum' to individuals travelling without permits (Larcher, 1902, p. 40). Colonized subjects were also forbidden to take up 'isolated habitation, without the authorization of an administrator ... in territories where individual property has not yet been constituted' as well as 'camping on prohibited grounds' (Rolland, 1914). Muslims were, furthermore, required to present their travel and identity documents at the mayor's office of any commune in which they were present for longer than twenty-four hours (Larcher and Olie, 1899, p. 158). When centralization was abandoned and *rattachement* abrogated in 1897, these powers were, accordingly, delegated back to the Algerian governor general. This cycle of delegations of power without original authorization reveals, in Le Cour Grandmaison's words, the 'banalization' of this regime (2008, p. 207).

At the turn of the century, as settler hysteria grew over perceived endemic Muslim criminality, and as the spectre of pan-Islamism loomed from abroad, the colonial government general, newly empowered and unburdened of the *rattachement*, unleashed a host of new restrictions further curtailing Muslim mobility in Algeria. An 1898 gubernatorial circular reiterated that Muslims needed to obtain passports to leave Algeria; this was followed by a law of 24 December and circular of 15 July 1904 (concerning Algerians living in France), each further augmenting punishments for any Muslim subject found to be travelling without either a passport or travel permit (Combes, 1904). An 1888 circular had required special permissions for Algerians wishing to travel to Mecca to perform the *hajj*, but further circulars were issued in 1902 and in 1910 simply forbidding Muslims to travel to Mecca on sanitary grounds (see Huber, 2023, p. 223; Le Cour Grandmaison, 2008, p. 207).

Within this flurry of circulars, directives, and instructions, not only were offences and punishments enumerated and increased, but their targets—criminalized individuals and comportments—also expanded and their boundaries blurred. Colonial administrative preoccupation with criminality and disease propelled an enlargement of exceptional penal law to encompass a broader range of suspicious persons and activities. In 1896, the Algerian attorney general issued a circular to all prefects and their subordinates noting Governor General Jules Cambon's concern over recent famines and epidemics which threatened to increase the potential 'dangers' posed by vagrancy (*vagabondage*):

> The attention of the governor general has been drawn to the dangers posed to public health by the tendency of the natives of the interior to emigrate, without authorization, to the populated centres and principally Algiers, where they hope to find resources. This emigration augments the number of vagrants, beggars, and thieves;

> besides this, in the cities it creates real hotbeds of pestilence. ... When the articles of the penal code punishing vagrancy do not seem applicable ... it is advisable to apply the Indigenous Code.

He went on, in the same circular, to outline the methods and tools of exceptional penal law prefects were to deploy to trace and punish all unlawful 'native' movement:

> It is crucial, [in order to] to prevent this accumulation of dangerous vagrants in the cities, to arrest those natives who are traveling without having first obtained from the administration the right to move (*le droit de se déplacer*). When [normal law] punishing vagrancy is not applicable—[whenever] the guilty parties (*les inculpés*) are able to demonstrate a serious residence, sufficient resources, or a habitually exercised profession—it is suitable to apply the Code de l'Indigenat. The natives commit infractions against this law when they definitively leave a commune without having notified the mayor's office; ... when they leave their residence without a passport, travel permit, identity card, or regularly-stamped worker's booklet; when they neglect to have their travel permit with them upon arrival, etc.
>
> (Circulaire du procureur général du 25 février 1896, quoted in Larcher, 1902, pp. 40–41)

This method of widening the scope and power of the Code de l'Indigénat to repress undesirable mobility would be taken up later by Governor General Charles Jonnart who, in 1907, issued a directive authorizing the use of administrative internment not only for 'religious and political characters who ... seek to fight our influence', but also 'all those individuals who, deprived of means of an honest existence, sustain all of their needs without finding any work'. He went on to conclude that

> these lawless people (*ces gens sans aveux*[3]) constitute a danger to the population in which they live. [Thus,] if a local authority wants to subject an *indigène* to internment or surveillance, they must ensure that they fit one of these categories, either by their anti-French activities or by their type of existence.
>
> (Jonnart, 5 March 1907, in Government of Algeria, 1916, p. 53)

Through these directives, any colonized subject's lack of official documents, their 'undeclared' status, exposed them to the threat of internment.

The long era of administrative internment came to an end primarily through the efforts of Albin Rozet, the '*indigénophile*' deputy from Haute-Marne, resulting in two laws to this effect. The first law, which suppressed outright the practice of internment in 1909, was passed only after 'lively opposition' by colonial administrators (Rolland, 1914, p. 155). A final version of the law, passed in 1914, permitted travel to Mecca for religious purposes (article 7) and legalized Muslim freedom of movement within Algeria and between Algeria and France (article 8). Though bringing to an end the

[3] It is worth pausing on the governor general's use of '*sans aveux*' here, which carried a double meaning: one medieval, suggesting a vassal without a master's protection, the other modern, suggesting an 'undeclared' or 'unauthorized' person.

colonial pass system and internment regime, these two monumental articles also ushered in a new suite of policing powers premised on biopolitical and disciplinary imperatives.

First, in support of article 7, Rozet reasoned that the public-health rationale for forbidding travel to Mecca was now outdated since both the Ottoman Empire (which then controlled the Hejaz) and the British Empire (which directly and indirectly controlled the largest Muslim jurisdictions and the most travelled long-distance routes to Mecca) had organized quarantine requirements for all pilgrims upon arrival and departure (Huber, 2013; Low, 2008). Thus, punishment for undertaking the *hajj* was limited only to failure to adhere to hygienic standards. As Rozet stated:

> We know that the plausible reasons for interdicting travel to Mecca lies in the fact that this city, the point of convergence of populations from the Asiatic and African worlds, is sometimes a hotbed of epidemics. [But] we must recognize the real and meritorious sanitary efforts in this regard made by the Ottoman government and interested powers. We must attest that the pilgrimage is done each day under the best conditions from a sanitary perspective.
>
> (Government of Algeria, 1916, p. 70)

In similar fashion, article 8 of Rozet's law abolished the travel pass system, citing the inefficient and easily outmanoeuvred approach of this blunt instrument for population control:

> Travel permits appear as naïve and sterile expressions of … the most nitpicking (*tatillonne*) and annoying (*tracassière*) administration. To find the equivalent of what still exists in Algeria, we would have to look in the past of backwards countries like Persia, Turkey, or Russia. … One of the fundamental errors of the Algerian administration is to have the pretention to surveil 5 million people through travel permits. It is materially impossible. We may surveil in Algeria 50,000, 100,000, even 200,000 individuals. But we cannot have the delusion to surveil 5 million … whatever the zeal and patriotism of the Algerian government. It is such a surveillance, effective because limited but possible, which we propose to organize in our [eighth] article.
>
> (Ibid, pp. 73–74)

He thus proposed shifting energies to the more selective and specialized method of *surveillance de l'haute police*—in effect, something between parole and house arrest—which would identify and monitor the activities and whereabouts of particularly 'dangerous' individuals, including the possibility of preventative detention and withheld right to travel. Rozet's law thereby served to fine-tune travel controls through a more precise, insidious, and discrete surveillance and public-health regulation system, befitting a 'benevolent' imperial power and modern state.

We may, in turn, ask what fundamentally changed in the aftermath of Rozet's efforts. Notably, the Code de l'Indigénat remained in effect, though in a new and slightly curtailed form. The list of offences had merely been reduced from twenty-three to twenty. Harbouring vagrants remained penalized, but was now placed under civil judicial authority. The governor general maintained repressive powers, even if limited: instead of internment, he could only command subjects to be '*mise en surveillance*' in a location of his choosing. The types of cases warranting such punishment were also reduced to just three, though their language was left vague enough to allow for a wide berth of interpretation: 'acts of hostility against French sovereignty; giving political speeches and religious sermons of a nature to harm public security; and acts that manifestly favour thefts of harvest or beasts' (Rolland, 1914, pp. 157–158). The governor general also maintained the discretion to deny any passport application for travel overseas, as a measure to prevent 'native youth going to study in [pan-Islamic] centres where Muslim subjects are transformed into adversaries of French domination' (ibid). In sum, as French law professor Louis Rolland reported, 'the new regime is not essentially different from the old one' (ibid).

One further element of the passport regime remained in place, specifically for any travel outside Algeria besides France. This 'was seen as useful,' wrote Rolland, to 'prevent the natives from ceding to suggestions of the agencies of emigration' (Rolland, 1914, p. 159). In other words, in order to maintain French access to Algerian labour, Muslim circulation between Algeria and France was liberalized precisely as travel anywhere besides the metropole was held in check. This happened to coincide with the labour and personnel exigencies of the war effort. And it worked: the surge of single Algerian men emigrating to France during the First World War and the interwar period was unprecedented.

At the same time, 1914 saw the birth of a new securitization regime for Muslims not only in the colony but also in the metropole. As historians of France have shown, this period witnessed the Mediterranean crossing of colonial personnel, expertise, and profiling methods for surveillance and mobility control. Clifford Rosenberg (2006) has uncovered the immigration of policing and surveillance methods directed towards North Africans in interwar Paris, while Mary Dewhurst Lewis (2007) explored concurrent processes and actors in the provinces, and Emmanuel Blanchard (2007) traced these histories into the immediate postwar period. What each of these authors has found is that Algerian colonial subjects in France were, as Étienne Balibar has put it, 'both less foreign than aliens, and yet more different (more "alien") than them' (2002, p. 79). That is, though Algerians were legally French subjects and ostensibly granted free circulation between Algeria and France, their movements were more closely monitored and their numbers in France were subject to stricter controls. The war and interwar years in France and Algeria thus saw the inauguration of a new imperial-transnational border regime designed to funnel and track North African movements while, at the same time, enhancing and further racializing securitization and surveillance mechanisms.

Afterlives of Internment

Though the pass system and internment regime had been formally suppressed in Algeria under the Third Republic, it left a legacy that would be revived in the postwar period and reverberate into the postcolonial era even to the present. During the Algerian War of Independence (1954–1962), a new 'deportation' regime emerged with characteristics bearing an uncanny similarity to internment. In 1955, France famously declared a state of emergency in Algeria, under which any individual deemed a 'threat to public order' could be placed under house arrest. Very quickly, not only guerrilla troops of the *Front de libération nationale-Armée de liberation nationale* (FLN-ALN) but nearly the entire Muslim population of Algeria came to fall within this category, and were thereby subject to removal without warning or recourse. Under the newly created Sections Administratives Spécialisées (SAS), the geography of Algeria was remapped to consist of 'safe zones' and 'forbidden zones' (Siari Tengour, 2010) in which any Muslim inhabitants were considered threatening or potentially threatening. All comings and goings were directed either through '*couloirs de sécurité*' (secure corridors) for Europeans or '*couloirs d'insécurité*' (unsecure corridors) for combatants and their supporters. Under this pretext, whole villages were forcibly uprooted and carted to distant *arrondissements*, where they were grouped en masse into internment camps euphemistically referred to as '*camps de regroupement*' (resettlement camps) (Le Cour Grandmaison, 2008, p. 213). This mass deportation policy was undertaken in secret, without official orders or public recognition (Bourdieu et al., 2013, p. 29). The practice was only revealed to the general public in a 1959 report by civil administrator Michel Rocard, which was published, thanks to a leak, in the mainstream press.

Rocard and his colleague, Kabyle author Jean Amrouche, produced a series of reports detailing the misery that unfolded in these camps, describing them as instruments of genocide. Because the camps did not officially exist, they were allocated no funds. But because their main purpose was to prevent the civilian population from providing material support (food, shelter, etc.) to anti-colonial militants, detainees were forbidden to leave the camp for work, to cultivate any crops, or to tend their flocks. In a cruel twist on earlier colonial displacement policies, the '*mise en valeur* of the land was regarded as beneficial to the rebellion' and was thus prevented by all means (Siari Tengour, 2010, pp. 209–211). At the same time, food and other essential items were blockaded. Thus, the only source of sustenance were rations distributed according to the mood and supply of the SAS captain. This system was replicated across the entire colonial territory, resulting in starvation and death at a staggering scale. By the end of the war, sociologists Pierre Bourdieu and Abdelmalek Sayad estimated that the number of Algerians 'resettled' had reached not less than 2,157,000—or a quarter of the total population—making this displacement 'one of the most brutal in history' (Bourdieu et al, 2013, p. 30). Rocard and Amrouche reported that 'children die by the thousands for lack of food' (ibid). Those who survived woke up in 1962 to a newly independent Algeria whose rural population had been utterly eviscerated and impoverished. 'Thus was achieved the process of dispossession first undertaken in 1830' (Siari Tengour, 2010, p. 211).

In the years immediately after Algeria gained independence from France, free circulation between both countries resumed—indeed, by French request, under the presumption that settlers would choose to remain in Algeria (Weil, 2008, p. 153). Instead, Algerian outmigration of labourers and families to France accelerated and continued apace for two decades. Economic recession, racist backlash, and right-wing electoral victories in the mid-1980s brought new laws restricting Maghribi access to French citizenship, thus creating in France a multi-generational class of permanent migrants and undocumented (*sans papiers*) people. By the 1990s, at the apogee of globalization and trade liberalization, Europe's border-management regime began a major shift with lasting consequences.[4] In 1995, twenty-six European countries, including France, formed the Schengen Zone, which abolished border controls between signatory countries while establishing shared responsibility for securing the zone's external borders, a mandate later formalized as the suprastate border-policing agency FRONTEX (2005).

For its part, Algeria did not pass any immigration laws for over forty years. Shortly after gaining independence, the FLN government passed its first comprehensive law in 1966, which enshrined freedom of circulation within the country and welcomed visitors and asylum seekers in accordance with the then-prevalent spirit of Third-World solidarity and internationalism. Until the turn of the twenty-first century, across the Maghrib, the concepts of 'illegal immigration' and 'irregular stay' were nearly insensible to the state, and the police and the judicial apparatus rarely intervened (Zeghbib, 2009, p. 79). This began to change in the early 2000s as, under pressure from the EU, one by one, each of the countries of the Maghrib—Morocco (2003), Tunisia (2004), and Libya (2005)[5]—passed laws that initiated stricter border securitization, which collectively amounted, in Hocine Zeghbib's words, to a 'moat' that surrounded the 'juridical wall' guarding Fortress Europe (Zeghbib, 2009, p. 75). In June, 2008, after several years of negotiation with the EU and neighbouring countries, Algeria joined its neighbours in the fortification of the southern Mediterranean 'buffer zone' through the passage of its *Loi n°08-11 du 25 juin 2008 relative aux conditions d'entrée, de séjour et de circulation des étrangers en Algérie* (Law 08-11 of 25 June 2008: Regarding the Conditions of Entrance, Stay, and Circulation of Foreigners in Algeria). The threat that Maghribi products (above all, fossil fuels) may not reach European markets was a powerful incentive: it happens that 2008 also marked the formation of the Union pour la Méditerranée, whose mission includes promoting free trade between the EU and the southern Mediterranean nations.

The Algerian Law 08-11 consisted of nine chapters, composed of fifty-two articles, constituting an 'arsenal of penal dispositions' (Zeghbib, 2009, p. 81) to increase the 'traceability' of transits and regulate 'illegal' migration. Though aimed at the newly announced 'problem' of 'irregular' entry and sojourns, it was written in the register of the War on Terror. In the aftermath of Algeria's civil war in the 1990s, the September 11 attacks in 2001 on the US, as well as the ongoing difficulty of securing Saharan oil-extraction operations against Islamist militant groups, Law 08-11 took shape within the paradigm of counter-terrorism. As the bill was being debated in the National Popular Assembly in October 2007, the Minister of the Interior declared that, 'the evolution of organised crime and the phenomenon of terrorism necessitates a perfect mastery of the movements of foreigners' (ibid). This helps to explain the expansive

[4] The 1990s was also the period of the Algerian 'Dark Decade' (1991–2002), a civil war between the FLN government and Islamist groups following a disputed national election, during which an estimated 200,000 Algerian civilians were murdered; this further prompted French border controls specific to Algerians. This period also brought greater mobility restrictions within Algeria, including through the use of forced removals/displacements and security checkpoints.

[5] While Mauritania passed no corresponding law, it cooperates unofficially with the Spanish coastguard on port control, and with FRONTEX on maritime policing (Zeghbib, 2009, pp. 77–78).

policing and administrative powers instantiated by the law, alongside the 'extreme fragility of procedural guarantees' (Zeghbib, 2009, p. 79), resulting in the multiplication of cases of irregularity and illegality (ibid).

Law 08-11 reintroduced to Algerian space a number of hauntingly familiar infractions and dispositions. It promulgated, for instance, a complex system of permits for entry, exit, internal travel, work, residence, and even marriage—without which any of these activities put the foreigner at risk of either administrative or judicial penalties. It outlined three potential modes of punishment for violating these requirements: administrative detention, deportation, and house arrest. The '*centres d'attente*' created by the law are sites of administrative detention under the authority of either the Ministry of Justice or Ministry of the Interior. Like its colonial predecessor, there is no predetermined length of detention at sentencing; rather, detention is executed in infinitely renewable thirty-day periods (Zeghbib, 2009, p. 82). Under this regime, the colonial fantasy of *refoulement* has been realized as the punishment of '*reconduite à la frontière*' (return to the border) which may be pronounced by either the judicial or administrative authority of the *waliya* (municipal unit). Echoing colonial-era administrative internment, it may serve as either a primary *or supplementary* punishment for an infraction committed by a foreigner, having nothing to do with the regularity of their stay. As Medicines Sans Frontiers has reported, the practice of *reconduite à la frontière* has resulted in countless deaths among 'irregular' migrants, driven into the desert and left to their fates:

> According to the testimonies we collected, these people are violently arrested in police raids or even in their own homes. They are then arbitrarily incarcerated in detention centres for days, weeks, months ... Then the Algerian security forces oblige these people to get into buses or trucks and, in turn, depose them at the famous 'point zero.' According to various sources, there are people who have been lost, others found without life, and still more from whom there is never any news.[6]

In 2009, Law 08-11 was 'completed' by an amendment to the Algerian Penal Code (*Loi n°09-01 du 25 février*) that added 'illegal departure from national territory' to the list of offensive displacements, thus criminalizing not only 'irregular' foreigners, but also Algerian nationals who attempt to leave (Souiah, 2016). In this way, the act of *harraga* was expressly targeted and criminalized. In her observation of two criminal processes, in January 2011, prosecuting 109 suspects caught at sea by coastguards, Farida Souiah noted that the *harraga* were tried, convicted, and sentenced collectively. Under this 'expedited and collective process', lasting thirty minutes for half of the group and forty-five minutes for the rest, they were all represented by a single lawyer; no witnesses or experts were called (Souiah, 2016, p. 21).

The objective and cumulative effect of the Algerian immigration laws and their counterparts has been to outsource Europe's border policing to the Maghrib,

[6] Author's translation: Richard, J. (2021) 'Le drame des migrants expulsés par l'Algérie et abandonnés dans le désert', *RFT*, 15 May. Available at: www.rfi.fr/fr/afrique/20210514-le-drame-des-migrants-expuls%C3%A9s-par-l-alg%C3%A9rie-et-abandonn%C3%A9s-dans-le-d%C3%A9sert?fbclid=IwAR1_Hba_efbu3OFprJw52icpyb1qrHcSa1_bWneBqHqbXzI908-uLIflIKU&ref=fb (accessed 15 June 2022).

projecting Europe's external southern border beyond the Mediterranean and deep into the Sahel. The countries of the Maghrib maintained accords of reciprocity that allowed each other's nationals to enter without visas, to the exclusion of sub-Saharan African countries, even abrogating formalized 'free circulation' zones between North and sub-Saharan countries. Thus came to an end the rich, centuries-long history of trans-Saharan crossings and cultural exchange. Along with the European border, Maghribi society has also absorbed and refracted racialized anxieties over 'undesirable' mobility: the more neutral figure of the 'foreigner' (*étranger*) has given way to more maligned, suspicious, and racialized 'migrant' (Zeghbib, 2009, pp. 79–80). In October 2017, one Algerian municipality temporarily forbade African 'illegal immigrants' (Arabic: *muhājrīn ghīr sharʿīīn*), identifiable, of course, only by their skin colour, from using public transportation. Around the same time, the hashtag 'Non aux Africains en Algérie' (Arabic: *la lil' āf ārqat fī al-jazaʾir*) began trending on Algerian social media. Overall, the result has been to increase the lethality of trans-Saharan and trans-Mediterranean voyages along with the exposure of black lives to murderous state violence.

Conclusion: What Is to Be Done?

With a focus on Algeria through the era of French colonization and post-independence, the object of this chapter has been to trace 'unlawful' movement through time and across space to colonial knowledge and power structures. We now arrive at a set of intertwined conclusions. First, the legal and discursive production of unlawful mobility is enduring because it is self-perpetuating: as the preceding text has explored, the French state in Algeria forced colonized subjects off the land where they resided and subsisted, thus transforming them into 'vagrants', in turn rendering such 'undeclared' status illegal and, then, finally, using that criminalized status as a pretext for further displacement/resettlement—whether to prisons, other regions within Algeria, or overseas penal colonies. Second, border criminality, in terms of its racialized targets, modern bureaucratic infrastructures, punitive dispositions, and profiling methods emerged as a colonial paradigm of governance, whose muscle memory can be called upon reflexively when needed. The ghost of the colonial administrative-internment regime haunting Algeria's 2008–2009 immigration laws is a disturbing case in point. Third and lastly, even those moments of seeming liberal 'progress', such as in 1914 (Rozet's law) and 1962 (re-establishment of free circulation between Algeria and France), when travel controls were loosened and mobility rights seemed reaffirmed, fortuitously corresponded with the labour needs of the metropole—to make up manufacturing and military shortages in wartime France, or as the influx of Maghribi *ouvriers* helped to drive French postwar prosperity. As border sociologists and criminologists have argued, selective border porosity and vacillating deployments of power accord with market logics of labour availability and wage suppression (Mezzadra and Neilson 2013; Wonders, 2006).

Where does this history lead us when put to the question of 'decolonizing criminological scholarship'? Unangax̂ scholar Eve Tuck, writing with K. Wayne Wang, remind us that 'decolonization is not a metaphor' (2012). That is, decolonization does not take place solely, or even mainly, on the psychological or discursive plane, but begins with manifest action, including land repatriation and reparations for colonial theft and violence. It is not reducible to other 'social justice' objectives under a liberal paradigm. Indeed, the impulse for and language of 'reconciliation' and sometimes even 'decolonization' is often driven by settlers and other actors who benefit from enduring colonial structures, since it can serve a dangerously palliative function, helping to gloss and thus excuse further injustice. This is notably resonant with an argument made by Lisa Marie Cacho (2012) that the benevolent 'legalization' of select 'illegals' in the United States only serves to reinforce immigration laws by masking their coercive functions. With these reminders, it is instructive, in closing, to turn back to the *harraag*, whose very existence, like that of the illegal alien, indexes unlawfulness. From another perspective, however, their very existence reveals state (border) law to be *arbitrary*—that is, an inorganic and violently imposed externality, as articulated by Bourdieu through dialogue with Algerian interlocutors. Against this arbitrary law, their sojourns keep alive memories of ancestral geographies while also charting new horizons and possible futures rooted in non-normative epistemologies of justice. In burning borders, *harraga* decentres the state and 'expands living space' (M'charek, 2020). If there is any model for the 'decolonization' of border law, it lies here.

References

Aliverti, A., Carvalho, H., Chamberlen, A. et al. (2021) 'Decolonizing the criminal question', *Punishment & Society*, 23(3), pp. 297–316.

Balibar, E. (2002) *Politics and the Other Scene*. New York: Verso Books.

Bhandar, B. (2018) *Colonial Lives of Property: Law, Land, and Racial Regimes of Ownership*. Durham, NC: Duke University Press.

Blanchard, E. (2007) 'L'encadrement des Algériens de Paris, 1944–1954', *Crime, Histoire & Société*, 11(1), pp. 5–25.

Blanchard, E. (2018) *Histoire de l'immigration algérienne en France*. Paris: La Découverte.

Bourdieu, P. (1987) 'The force of law: Toward a sociology of the juridical field', *Hastings Law Journal*, 38(5), pp. 814–853.

Bourdieu, P., Yacine-Titouh, T., and Fernbach, D. (2013) *Algerian Sketches*. Cambridge: Polity Press.

Cacho, L. M. (2012) *Social Death: Racialized Rightslessness and the Criminalization of the Unprotected*. New York: New York University Press.

Combes, E. (1904) 'Direction de l'administration départementale et communale. Délivrance du passeport à l'étranger a des indigènes algériens, 20 juillet'. Bulletin officiel du Ministère de l'interieur. Available at: https://gallica.bnf.fr/ark:/12148/bpt6k55339232/f69.image.r=%22D%C3%A9livrance%20du%20passeport%20%C3%A0%20l'%C3%A9tranger%20a%20des%20indig%C3%A8nes%20alg%C3%A9riens,%2020%20juillet%201904%22 (last accessed 16 June 2022).

De Genova, N. and Peutz, N. M. (2010) *The Deportation Regime: Sovereignty, Space, and the Freedom of Movement*. Durham, NC: Duke University Press.

Government of Algeria, Directorate of General Security (Gouvernement général de l'Algérie, direction de la sécurité générale) (1916) *Recueil des Textes relatifs à l'internement des indigènes et l'application de la loi du 15 juillet 1914 sur la Mise en Surveillance Spéciale*. Alger: Adolphe Jourdan.

Halvorsen, K. H. (1978) 'Colonial transformation of Agrarian society in Algeria', *Journal of Peace Research*, 15(4), pp. 323–343.

Kotef, H. (2015) *Movement and the Ordering of Freedom: On Liberal Governances of Mobility*. Durham, NC: Duke University Press.

Larcher, É. (1902) *Trois années d'études algériennes législatives, sociales, pénitentaires et pénales*. Paris: A. Rousseau.

Larcher, É. and Olier, J. (1899) *Questions criminelles et sociales: Les institutions pénitentiaires de l'Algérie*. Alger: A. Rousseau.

Le Cour Grandmaison, O. (2008) *Coloniser, exterminer: sur la guerre et l'État colonial*. Paris: Fayard.

Lewis, M. D. (2007) *The Boundaries of the Republic: Migrant Rights and the Limits of Universalism in France, 1918–1940*. Stanford, CA: Stanford University Press.

Low, M. C. (2008) 'Empire and the Hajj: Pilgrims, plagues, and pan-Islam under British surveillance, 1865–1908', *International Journal of Middle East Studies*, 40(2), pp. 269–290.

M'charek, A. (2020) 'Harraga: Burning borders, navigating colonialism', *The Sociological Review*, 68(2), pp. 418–434.

Massonié, G. (1909) *La question indigène en Algérie: l'internement des indigènes, son illégalité*. Paris: Ligue des droits de l'homme.

Mezzadra, S. and Neilson, B. (2013) *Border as Method, or, the Multiplication of Labor*. Durham, NC: Duke University Press.

Mokhtari, R. (2005) *Slimane Azem, Allaoua Zerrouki, chantent Si Mohand U Mhand: les Isefra dans la chanson kabyle de l'exil*. Alger: Éditions APIC.

Mountz, A. (2010) *Seeking Asylum: Human Smuggling and Bureaucracy at the Border*. Minneapolis, MN: University of Minnesota Press.

Powers, D. S. (1989) 'Orientalism, colonialism, and legal history: The attack on Muslim family endowments in Algeria and India', *Comparative Studies in Society and History*, 31(3), pp. 535–571.

Richard, J. (2021) 'Le drame des migrants expulsés par l'Algérie et abandonnés dans le désert', RFT, 15 May. Available at: www.rfi.fr/fr/afrique/20210514-le-drame-des-migrants-expuls%C3%A9s-par-l-alg%C3%A9rie-et-abandonn%C3%A9s-dans-le-d%C3%A9sert?fbclid=IwAR1_Hba_efbu3OFprJw52icpyb1qrHcSa1_bWneBqHqbXzI908-uLIfIlKU&ref=fb (accessed 15 June 2022).

Rolland, L. (1914) 'LOI DU 15 JUILLET 1914 RÉGLEMENTANT LE RÉGIME DE L'INDIGÉNAT EN ALGÉRIE', Notice et notes par M. Louis ROLLAND, professeur de droit administratif à la Faculté de droit de Nancy. *Annuare de legislation française*, vol. 32. Available at: https://books.google.ca/books?id=gq4sAAAAIAAJ&pg=RA2-PA153&lpg=RA2-PA153&dq=LE+R%C3%89GIME+DE+L%27INDIG%C3%89NAT+EN+ALG%C3%89RIE+(1).+Notice+et+notes+par+M.+Louis+ROLLAND&source=bl&ots=xWmeIVGBda&sig=ACfU3U0_8niBcbJ2WjbUvlY4aMXH_3H-3w&hl=en&sa=X&ved=2ahUKEwieg-Go6LL4AhU8JDQIHZpWDpUQ6AF6BAgCEAM#v=onepage&q=LE%20R%C3%89GIME%20DE%20L'INDIG%C3%89NAT%20EN%20ALG%C3%89RIE%20(1).%20Notice%20et%20notes%20par%20M.%20Louis%20ROLLAND&f=false (accessed 16 June 2022).

Rosenberg, C. (2006) *Policing Paris: The Origins of Modern Immigration Control between the Wars*. Ithaca, NY: Cornell University Press.

Said, E. (1994) *Culture and Imperialism*. New York: Knopf.

Sayagh, S. (1986) *La France et les frontières Maroco-Algériennes 1873–1902*. Paris: Editions du Centre National de la Recherche Scientifique.

Siari Tengour, O. (2010) 'Zones interdites et camps de regroupement dans l'Aurès 1954–1962', in *Histoire contemporaine de l'Algérie. Nouveaux objets*. Oran: CRASC (Center of Research in Social Action and Cultural Anthropology). Available at: https://ouvrages.crasc.dz/pdfs/2010-histoire-contemporaine-zones-interdites.pdf (accessed 14 June 2022).

Souiah, F. (2016) 'La pénalisation des "brûleurs" de frontières en Algérie,' *Après-demain*, 39(3), pp. 19–21.

Stoler, A. L. (2016) *Duress: Imperial Durabilities in Our Times*. Durham, NC: Duke University Press.

Torpey, J. (2000) *The Invention of the Passport: Surveillance, Citizenship, and the State*. Cambridge: Cambridge University Press.

Tuck, E. and Yang, K. W. (2012) 'Decolonization is not a metaphor', *Decolonization: Indigeneity, Education & Society*, 1(1), pp. 1–40.

Walia, H. (2021) *Border & Rule: Global Migration, Capitalism, and the Rise of Racist Nationalism*. Chicago, IL: Haymarket Books.

Warscheid, I. (2018) 'The Islamic literature of the precolonial Sahara: Sources and approaches', *History Compass*, 16(5), pp. 1–10.

Weil, P. and Porter, C. (trans.) (2008) *How to be French: Nationality in the Making since 1789*. Durham, NC: Duke University Press.

Wonders, N. (2006) 'Global Flows, Semi-Permeable Borders and New Channels of Inequality: Border Crossers and Border Performativity', in Pickering, S. and Weber, L. (eds) *Borders, Mobility and Technologies of Control*. Berlin: Springer, pp. 63–86.

Zeghbib, H. (2009) 'Les Étrangers en Algérie: Quel Statut Juridique?', *NAQD Critique*, 26–27(1), pp. 73–85.

9

The Coloniality of Justice

Naturalized Divisions During Pre-Trial Hearings in Brazil

Omar Phoenix Khan

Introduction

Custody hearings were introduced in Brazil in 2015 with the hope that prompt in-person presentation of detainees before a judge, rather than merely a police report, would decrease the excessive use of pre-trial detention. However, the use of pre-trial detention remains high, especially for young Black men with low to no income. This chapter contributes to the literature by highlighting the coloniality of justice as manifested within judicial decision-making at the pre-trial stage in Brazil. Analysis of twenty-six interviews with judges, prosecutors, public defenders, and specialists in Rio de Janeiro reveals the divergent treatment accorded to those on either side of the dichotomous notions of the *bandido*[1] (criminal) and the *cidadão de bem* (the good citizen). A thematic framework analysis leads to a discussion of the white-centred nature of citizenship and justice and how stigmatized spaces are considered criminogenic. The chapter traces how colonial white-supremacist logic has persisted in naturalizing inhumane treatment of racialized groups in the collective consciousness of the gatekeepers of justice in Brazil.

By any measurement, pre-trial detention is excessive in Brazil. Of countries with the highest number of people held pre-trial, Brazil now sits behind only the US and China, both of which have far larger general populations (Walmsley, 2017b). As of February 2019, there were 243,308 pre-trial detainees in Brazil (ICPR, 2019), representing 33.8 per cent of the overall prison population. This is a considerable increase from 2000, when only 80,775 pre-trial detainees were recorded (ibid). In Rio de Janeiro state, 56,372 people were deprived of their liberty in 2018, with over 52 per cent of this population detained pre-trial (29,498) (GMF, 2018).

This study focuses on judicial decision-making during 'custody hearings', which is the point at which *flagrante delicto*[2] detentions can be converted into preventative detention (referred to in this chapter as 'pre-trial detention').[3] Custody hearings were

[1] The direct translation is 'bandit', but *bandido* has also been translated as 'criminal' or 'thug'. The word denotes an overt tendency towards criminal behaviour as a way of life and can be linked to violence and corruption. I use *bandido* because it is more loaded with meaning than any translation.

[2] *Flagrante delicto*: meaning caught in the act of committing a crime.

[3] Pre-trial detention in Brazil is divided into two sub-categories: either 'temporary detention' or 'preventative detention'. The former refers to a period during investigation, used in the case of 'certain serious crimes to protect the investigation or to prevent flight for five or 30 days (renewable once), depending on the nature of the crime' (Nascimento dos Reis, 2017, p. 6). The latter can be ordered before or after formal

Omar Phoenix Khan, *The Coloniality of Justice* In: *Decolonizing the Criminal Question*. Edited by: Ana Aliverti, Henrique Carvalho, Anastasia Chamberlen, and Máximo Sozzo, Oxford University Press.
DOI: 10.1093/oso/9780192899002.003.0010

introduced in 2015 after much advocacy from civil society and against a backdrop of condemnation from UN agencies over the 'excessive' use of pre-trial detention and the concerning trend that detention was 'being used as the first resort rather than the last' (UN Human Rights Council, 2014, pp. 11–12). The hope was that the introduction of prompt *in-person* presentation of detainees before a judge, rather than merely the police report, would lead to the increased use of alternatives to pre-trial detention and provide an opportunity for detainees to report instances of torture. However, a recent report titled 'Prison as a Rule' found that pre-trial detention remained the most frequent outcome of custody hearings (62.5 per cent) in Rio de Janeiro, even though almost 70 per cent of those detained were suspected of non-violent crimes (IDDD et al., 2020). The report was also clear that those detained were primarily young Black men with little to no income.

Focusing on custody hearings enables examination of how justice practice—at the earliest point of formal detention—intersects with naturalized assumptions relating to multiple levels of citizenship and, thus, how coloniality influences judicial decision-making at an ontological level. The chapter begins by discussing the hierarchicalized and bounded nature of citizenship during the Portuguese Empire. The second section explores the concept of *coloniality* and charts how the same white-supremacist power structures were sustained beyond the abolition of slavery and into the postcolonial period. The themes revealed from an analysis of twenty-six interviews with court actors and specialists on judicial decision-making are then presented and discussed. The chapter contributes by building on Segato's (2007) concept of the 'coloniality of justice'—which has received limited discussion in English—by providing evidence of how contemporary justice practices continue to be influenced by colonial logics. This endeavour responds directly to Aliverti et al.'s (2021) call to 'decolonize the criminal question' by illustrating coloniality across three key dimensions.

Citizenship and the Colonial Period

During the Portuguese Empire, a person reduced to enslaved status in Brazil was considered 'legally *dead*, deprived of every *right*, and possessing *no representation whatsoever*' (Perdigão Malheiro cited in Chalhoub, 2006, p. 76). This hierarchy of humanity was enshrined in law, and any ethical questioning was abated by the Pope—considered the unquestionable font of morality—via the 'Just War' legitimization for slavery. Although Iberian 'Just Wars' had been waged before, with the violent creation and occupation of the Americas, the temporary justification and war-like state of exception transitioned to permanence.[4] As Maldonado-Torres puts it, '[w]hat happens in the Americas is a transformation and naturalization of the non-ethics of war' (2007, p. 247). This hierarchical relational philosophy that framed the conquerors as superior, rights-bearing citizens and the conquered as inferior and disposable did

charges 'to counter procedural risks or risks to the public or economic order, without a predetermined final term' (ibid, p. 7).

[4] For discussion of coloniality and legacies of 'Just War' for Brazil, see Darke and Khan, 2021.

not dissipate or become reconstructed when the laws changed during the Portuguese Empire. Rather, the status difference became naturalized and accepted at an ontological level.

Unlike in Spanish-occupied territories across the Souths of America which saw large-scale revolutions to build republics, in Brazil, the Portuguese-descended Brazilian monarchy declared independence (in 1822) with comparatively little challenge to the regime. The Brazilian elites had no need to change their philosophies and practices and thus maintained their dominance over a largely uneducated underclass. Throughout the periods of Portuguese and Brazilian Empires, elites employed a politics of exclusion and purposefully limited upward social mobility and access to governance. Carvalho explains that although neighbouring Spanish colonies built national universities and invested in creating numerous high courts, 'Portugal refused systematically to allow the organization of any institution of higher learning in her colonies' (1982, p. 383).[5] Records from the Portuguese Overseas Council state that this policy was explicitly created to ensure dependency of the colonies on Portugal for higher learning (Carvalho, 1982, p. 383).

During the nineteenth century, impoverished groups had some space for movement concerning citizenship status, although it was limited and the position always precarious. Beattie uses the term 'intractable poor' (2015, p. 5) to reflect how powerful social actors stereotyped them collectively as unsavoury social categories. He also coins the phrase 'category drift' and uses this to explain how enslaved people, freed Africans, and other subsections of the intractable poor could move—or perhaps more accurately, *be moved*—across low-status categories, largely at the behest of the governing class (ibid, p. 6). He reflects that it reveals the 'degrees of unfreeness' in Brazil, where those enlisted in the military, indigenous people, and even a 'freedman' could not be considered truly *free* to the same extent (ibid, p. 5). Beattie assesses the situation as precarious for all members of the intractable poor, but that category drift 'disproportionally targeted nonwhites' (ibid, p. 234). This disproportionality and structural nature of discrimination did not get wiped from Brazilian society or the collective conscience of those in power when slavery was abolished.

Coloniality and Citizenship

It is clear that although the end of the nineteenth century saw the abolition of slavery and the birth of the Brazilian republic, the hierarchical notions of citizenship that solidified during centuries of colonial rule remained. Quijano's (2000) concept of 'coloniality of power' is helpful for appreciating the particular dynamics of power that persist beyond decolonization on paper. Mignolo and Walsh describe how such dynamics were 'unveiled' when it became clear that the global and domestic domination of the same European-descended elites endured, creating a form of 'internal

[5] During the century 1772 to 1872, 1,242 members of the Brazilian elite from all eighteen captaincies were enrolled at Portugal's University of Coimbra, and 80 per cent attended before 1828, when Brazil's first two law schools opened. See Carvalho, 1982, pp. 383–384.

colonialism' (2018, pp. 5–6). Santos expands on this last phrase to illustrate the importance for all levels of societal interaction across the Souths of America:

> internal colonialism is not only, or mainly, a state policy; it is rather a very wide social grammar that permeates social relations, public and private spaces, culture, mentalities, and subjectivities. In sum, it is a way of life, a form of unequal conviviality that is often shared by both those who benefit from it and those who suffer its consequences.
>
> (Santos, 2016, p. 26)

For Quijano, the coloniality of power revolved around two fundamental pivots. First, the purposeful arrangement of the means of production to serve exploitative global capitalism. Second, the codification of the boundaries between the conquerors and the conquered, according to invented and hierarchicalized racial categories, used as if they were biological truths (2000, p. 216). These key elements of coloniality were notable preoccupations of Brazilian elites in the late nineteenth and early twentieth centuries, as demonstrated via the overt call to whiten the population when recruiting a new labour force to replace those who had won emancipation. Even through the speeches of famed anti-slavery activists such as Nabuco, we can see that elites believed that they still belonged to Europe more than the Americas. That to be European is to be human, and in contrast, the non-European is something less than or other than human:

> We Brazilians (and the same could be said of the other nations of the Americas) belong to the New World as a new, buoyant settlement, and we belong to Europe, at least in our upper strata. For any of us who has the least culture, the European influence predominates over the American. Our imagination cannot but be European, that is, human. It did not cease when Brazil held its first mass but went on, reforming the traditions of the savages who filled our shores at the time of the Discovery. It continued influenced by all the civilizations of humanity, like that of the Europeans, with whom we share the same basis of language, religion, art, law, and poetry, the same centuries of accumulated civilization, and, thus, as long as there is a ray of culture, the same historical imagination.
>
> (Nabuco, 1963, p. 39 in Santos and Hallewell, 2002, p. 67).

The desire for population whitening was based on an ontological position that presented the hierarchicalization of racial groups as self-evident and natural, with scientists and philosophers comfortable in the thought that they were continuing the intellectual path set by Enlightenment thinkers. These philosophical assumptions were supplemented and enhanced in the late nineteenth century with the development of what was framed as scientific evidence that proved these long-held assumptions. Although many contested the ideas, eugenics gained considerable intellectual attention in Brazil in the twentieth century. Support was such that certain sections of the ruling classes wanted to implement substantial eugenic strategies, including the possible replication of Nazi policies to forcibly sterilize criminals and other groups (Souza and Souza, 2016, pp. 11 and 16).

In considering contemporary Brazil, Da Costa states:

> Coloniality refers to the system of power where values, representations, and forms of knowledge production turn racial and other colonial differences into hierarchical classifications and values that dehumanize Afro-descendant and indigenous peoples, and correspondingly turn their worldviews and ways of life into symbols of backwardness vis-à-vis capitalist modernity.
>
> (Da Costa, 2014, p. 196)

This capitalist modernity cannot be divorced from the conditions and consequences of coloniality that have brought us to this point. Modernity and coloniality are 'two sides of a single coin' (Grosfoguel, 2007, p. 218), with coloniality constituting 'the dark side of modernity' (Mignolo and Walsh, 2018, p. 111). Thus, any discussion of the now without due consideration of coloniality overlooks critical causal factors. Critical criminology has long championed the need to free analysis of Eurocentric positionality, with notable interventions from the Souths of America including Aniyar de Castro's (1987) *Criminology of Liberation*, del Olmo's (1990) *Second Criminological Break*, and Zaffaroni's (1988) *Criminology from the Margins*.

The echoing of colonial-era asymmetries of power and privilege through the targeted execution of criminal justice in the Souths of America led Segato (2007) to highlight the 'coloniality of justice'. Segato maintains that race is not the cause of inequality but 'a product of centuries of modernity and the joint work of academics, intellectuals, artists, philosophers, lawyers, legislators and law enforcement officials, who have classified the difference as the raciality of the conquered peoples' (ibid, p. 150). Darke notes that in contemporary Brazil, prison 'is just the latest in a long series of repressive institutions in the post-colonial era that have openly targeted sections of the population deemed criminally dangerous, threats to state sovereignty, or simply poor, idle or dispensable' (2018, p. 70). This chapter contributes to the literature by highlighting the coloniality of justice as manifested within judicial decision-making at the pre-trial stage in Brazil.

Analysis

Analysis included twenty-six semi-structured interviews with seven judges (J), four prosecutors (Pr), eight public defenders (PD), and seven subject matter specialists, such as NGO professionals and academics (S). These took place in Rio de Janeiro over three months in 2019. One of the seven judges interviewed is Black, and all others are white, which should be understood against a backdrop where 99.4 per cent of entry-level judges are white (AMB, 2018, p. 222).

Interview questions were designed to facilitate discussion and allow the interviewee to speak fluidly about the factors that influence judges' decisions during custodial hearings. These interviews were combined with non-participant observation of sixty-four custodial hearings. A 'thematic framework analysis' (Braun and Clarke, 2006) was used to analyse the interviews and arrive at the themes under discussion.

The themes presented here were developed around what interviewees revealed as important factors about detainees for deciding whether to detain pre-trial.

Space and Place

Although the interviews were explicitly framed about judicial decisions during custody hearings, many of the interviewees[6] moved swiftly to discuss how the dynamics of the courtroom and the social relations that play out within them are symptomatic of wider societal issues. Many spoke of boundaries between groups of people or places and presented resulting dichotomous societal relations. Indicative of the ingrained nature of these constructed boundaries was the fact that interviewees across all stakeholder groups—whether presenting with liberal or conservative views—referred to some notion of naturalized division. Some overtly highlighted the disparities, while others talked of differences as logical or without interrogating their validity or significance.

Interviewees regularly mentioned spatial delineators such as favela/*asfalto*[7] and the city/periphery while discussing the differences people experience in their treatment at the hands of state justice representatives. Some mentioned these terms in passing as if they were natural divisions, while others highlighted them as constructed boundaries, symbolizing the places where the reality of citizenship changed. PD1 expanded on the different realities for different groups with particular mention of policing strategies and stated that this illustrated how 'repressive power remains against those in favelas'. He was steadfast in his assertions that what happens during custody hearings is an extension of the divergent realities of those located both physically and socially in different spaces:

> [There is] a logic of different languages, they are different spaces that each of these groups of people occupy. The reality of a guy in a favela is completely different. I don't know if you have heard about the issues of 'violation of domicile'? In the favela, the police arrive with their foot through the door. In the South Zone, where the judges live, it will not be like that, it's completely different. For him, this is inconceivable. Fuck, there the police kill, the police beat, the police violate rights. So, they are different realities . . . completely different worlds. In a country so unequal, putting such a person in a position to judge is problematic, because they cannot understand reality.

For one section of society, it is inconceivable that the police would kick down their door or shoot first and ask questions later; but for others, it is a reality. Several interviewees discussed how this different relationship with the state extends beyond the favela into the courtroom. They suggested that judges already conceptualize favela residents as dehumanized and therefore do not find it incongruous with the passage of justice to choose a further impingement on rights by detaining them in inhuman conditions.

[6] Twenty-two of twenty-six interviews were conducted in Portuguese, and quotations from these interviews are my translations. Where I believe it relevant, I have included the original Portuguese as a footnote. Interviews with J6 and S4 were in English, and quotations attributed to them are their exact statements.

[7] *Asfalsto* translates as *asphalt*. The meaning, in this case, is to compare the planned and paved civic streets with the informal spaces of favelas, unrecognized by the state.

Several interviewees noted the connections between favela residents and assumptions of criminality as part of a perpetual anti-social narrative. They discussed how the favela has become synonymous with crime and, therefore, just being in such a space, even if it is your residence, is enough to presume involvement in crime. The words of J1 provide some insight into this view:

> And even today [referring to the custody hearings that I had witnessed], there were some cases where the seizure of the drugs was in a context of extreme violence. A place where there has been exchange of fire between them and police officers. So, in crime there has been indirect violence. As much as the person was not apprehended with a gun, he is part of a group that is armed, and he was caught ... The vast majority is theft and trafficking. So sometimes the fact of it being the defendant's first offence and having a good background alone does not rule out the need for detention, especially in those contexts we have seen.

Here we gain a glimpse of the judge's beliefs about who is dangerous or likely to commit crime. There is a conflation between a space associated with violence and somebody arrested with drugs but no weapon. J1 described this as 'indirect violence' and presumes the person to be part of a gang with no evidence beyond the space where the person was arrested.

J1 contrasted the situation in the above quote with that of 'a casual trafficker that doesn't present a great risk'. When I asked him to expand on what he meant by this, he provided another example from the set of hearings that I had witnessed that day. One of the hearings was for a truck driver found with drugs, and J1 explained that he 'does not have the context of criminal association'. In this case, J1 granted conditional release until trial, even though the prosecutor asked for conversion to pre-trial detention. This 'criminal association' is what J1 held in mind and led him to decide on pre-trial detention in the initial case discussed, where he deemed there to have been 'indirect violence'. J1 expanded by saying, 'so, we do not look at the crime, we look at the circumstances of arrest and the facts. That's important. The crime itself makes no difference.'

Such a statement reaffirms the assertion that subjective interpretations of circumstances—in this case, as they relate to space—are significant in influencing judicial decisions relating to pre-trial detention. It appears that merely being present in a favela, existing in one's own space—even without a weapon—may be enough to be associated with a gang/faction and thus lead to a greater likelihood of pre-trial detention. The criminalization of the entire marginalized space means that anyone associated with it is vulnerable to the *guilty by association* logic demonstrated by J1.

This subjective narrative about those associated with favelas also fails to acknowledge the structural factors that disadvantage the group. Prosecutors 1 and 2 suggested that the absence of critical documents such as workbooks, proof of address, and CPF[8] numbers are objective indicators of the need to detain. Other studies have

[8] Jobs within the licit market require a CPF 'Cadastro de Pessoas Físicas' (Natural Persons Register), the Brazilian individual taxpayer registry identification. A citizen must be registered to an official residence to gain a CPF, yet the state does not class many homes in favelas as such. Access to CPFs has increased; however, as it is not relevant to daily life for those working outside the official jobs market, many do not recall them when criminal justice officials ask.

also shown that an inability to provide such documentation is frequently interpreted as a regular involvement in crime (Machado et al., 2019, p. 233). However, many people living in favelas work informally, for example as cleaners, do not have formal workbooks, and are less likely to have CPF numbers or a residence recognized as official. Prosecutors did not reflect on how the lack of such documentation is symptomatic of structural discrimination rather than being an objective indication of criminality. Detainees are therefore disadvantaged due to situational factors primarily out of their control.

Boundaried Citizenship

Many interviewees presented the accepted sentiment that it was not merely that particular people occupy specific spaces but that these were the places where they belonged and that these people were deserving of the treatment with which the space was coupled. Several interviewees suggested that there are large portions of the population, including many judges, who believe that there are certain people who are deserving of prison or pain or death. J7 used the phrase 'miserable classes' to contrast with the privileged class who have their rights respected. J7 explained that when challenging other judges on their approach, they have responded with comments such as 'Ah, they deserved it. They did it in that place, so they deserved it. If they're there, it's because they committed crimes.' J7 provided further explanation of his observations that many of his fellow judges have naturalized such differences and taken these assumptions into the courtroom:

> For example, in situations where a boy from the periphery who abuses his girlfriend, he is justifiably called a rapist. A middle-class boy who abuses his girlfriend, he is a boy in training, developing, discovering sexuality. The speech changes. When it's the rights of those unworthy people, in his point of view, it is all about killing. Why arrest? Kill them quickly. Why pay for the prison system? Kill at once. Why judge? Condemn right away.

J7's representation of the popular assumptions about the worth of people demonstrates a connection between the space from which someone comes, the place where they belong, and thus, what they deserve. The sentiment is presented as being held with such virulence that the logic suggests that guilt should be assumed and extrajudicial killing would be the preferable and economic action for society.

The dichotomous notion of the *cidadão de bem* (the good citizen), who deserves fundamental human rights, such as safety, freedom, and justice; and the *bandido* (the criminal), who forgoes such rights, is pervasive in Brazilian society. Many interviewees juxtaposed these two figures to illustrate the imagined divisions between those deserving of rights and protection and those who are imprisonable and killable. Those highlighting this division suggested that adherence to such beliefs at an ontological level influences judges' considerations around fundamental rights such as presumption of innocence, prevention from torture, and liberty. This constructed dichotomy is emblematic of the extreme ends of a continuum of legitimized access to citizenship and rights and can be traced to the orientalizing discourses of colonialism.

S7 linked a deserving/undeserving dichotomy to popular discourse that conflates punishment with a judgement on what value people are perceived to offer society. S7 explained that those adhering to this discourse say things such as 'they don't produce, they don't add to the economy, they don't add value to anything, they just take, they take handouts and they rob ... So no need for them to live.' Several interviewees mentioned that if a person can be labelled as a *bandido* or *traficante*,[9] then that marker can be used to justify pre-trial detention beyond the scope of recommendations during custody hearings (and even extrajudicial killings). The drug dealer/trafficker label goes far beyond a simple financial transaction for illegal substances to a vision of someone much more dangerous. Indeed, a study found that if a question used the description '*traficantes*' rather than 'people who sell drugs', the public were more likely to agree that the police should kill rather than arrest (18.6 per cent vs 10.3 per cent) (Lemgruber et al., 2017, p. 15). This suggests that the figure constructed in the public conscience goes beyond a connection to specific crimes to conjure up an image representing danger to the extent that extrajudicial killing is deemed to be justifiable. Many of the interviewees used the phrase '*bandido bom é bandido morto*' (the only good *bandido* is a dead *bandido*) to illustrate the strength of desire to eliminate groups that are perceived to be unredeemable. PD4 explained how it would be wrong to think that it is merely a throwaway comment used by members of the public,[10] as it has been used regularly by state officials.

Key themes of race and space reoccurred throughout the interviews and, in many cases, they could not be clearly separated. When these two factors are combined (racialized as Black and associated with a favela), the product is not simply double the risk of injustice but the conjuring of a specific character within the societal imagination: the dangerous and legitimately killable *bandido* or *traficante*. S4 illustrates this point:

> The fear! What a thing the drug dealer became in peoples' fantasy! Someone not human, not born from mother and father ... So you can kill 5, 10, 20, 55 on the street or in a prison.

PD1 explained that the slang term '*o freio de camburão*' (the police car's brake) is used to describe a humbly dressed young Black man, implying that the mere appearance of the person in a place deemed to be a white space is enough to cause the officers to react. PD1 explained that the same reaction occurs within the courtroom, whereby on discovering that a detainee is a Black resident of a favela, the judges make immediate assumptions and then look to confirm their impression. Interviewees suggested

[9] *Traficante* is used in the Drug Law (2006) and can refer to drug dealers or drug traffickers. Legislation designed to punish large-scale organized trafficking continues to be used to prosecute those delivering or dealing small amounts of drugs. The common usage of *traficante* is a conflation of the diverse actors within the illicit drug market that leads any involvement with drugs to be associated with gun violence.

[10] Studies have consistently found significant support for the phrase with the Brazilian public: 37 per cent (Lemgruber et al., 2017), 57 per cent (Fórum Brasileiro de Segurança Pública, 2015); and 43 per cent (Secretaria Especial de Direitos Humanos, 2010).

that such assumptions are entirely naturalized and are not stated overtly. Occasionally, however, such views are made explicit. In 2020, a judge was forced to publicly apologize after it was revealed that in justifying a fourteen-year sentence for theft, she used the phrase '[he was] certainly a member of the criminal group, due to his race' (UOL, 2020).[11] This instance of overt association of race and criminality demonstrates the subterranean beliefs described by several interviewees as being held by many judges.

Other interviewees shared similar views regarding the societal-level schema about racialized groups, with several mentioning the extrajudicial police killing of Evaldo dos Santos Rosa[12] by way of illustration. Interviewees made the point that even though Evaldo fitted the profile of a *cidadão de bem*, as an employed heterosexual man, married with a traditional family and a house, he was still identified by police as killable—as a *bandido*—because he was Black and present in an underprivileged neighbourhood. Shooting eighty bullets at a car without any evidence of criminality or threat is not what representatives of a state do to people considered citizens, but an act reserved for an enemy during times of war. The intersectional nature of this scenario means that it is not simply the negative connotations of race plus that of space equating a double negation of citizenship, but that the amalgamation of the two creates something more pungent, more visceral. Whether on the street or in court, the conjured image is not merely of a lesser group to be overlooked but a dangerous Other to be expunged. Despite multiple sites of resistance, during monarchical regimes via uprisings and quilombos, and post establishment of the Brazilian republic (1889) with legal challenges and changes in legislation, it is evident that the boundary between the conquerors and the conquered remains foundational at an ontological level, meaning: central to understanding the *ways of being* in Brazil.

Whiteness as the Point of Departure

All prosecutors interviewed (all white women) showed awareness of historical racialized power structures but almost exclusively denied the relevance of such structures to current proceedings. In the rare moments that there was an acknowledgement of some possible resonance, prosecutors maintained that it was not a factor in their own thinking or actions. Both Pr1 and Pr2 referred to racial inequalities as 'historical' or 'social' issues and distanced the possibility of a difference in contemporary treatment. Both were very clear that any difference is not a question of prejudice, yet at the same time argued that a country only relatively recently free of slavery is bound to carry some residual discrimination. Pr2 ruled out such impact on the prosecutors but suggested that it could be true for judges. S3 spoke to the issue of the cognitive dissonance among court actors, displayed by Pr1 and Pr2. S3 explained:

[11] Judges can increase sentence lengths if the defendant is proven to be part of a criminal organization.

[12] On 8 April 2019, Evaldo dos Santos Rosa was driving his family to a baby shower in Guadalupe, a low-income area of Rio de Janeiro. Evaldo, a security guard and musician, was killed, and two others were wounded, when ten soldiers shot eighty bullets into the car. The military command initially claimed that the patrol was attacked by criminals but later changed its position (Phillips, 2019b).

> We have this discussion: 'I understand that everyone is racist, but *I'm not racist*'. So we have a process of erasing the functioning or racism as something very systemic.

Both Pr1 and Pr2 expressed that it was rational to expect those with fewer resources or less education to commit more crime, yet did not mention how any structural or societal level issues may play a role or relate to racism. S3 described how the phrase 'criminal tendency' was frequently heard during custody hearings. She explained how it was often used in connection with racialized detainees who lived in favelas to suggest that there is a natural or inevitable element to their alleged offending. S3 expanded, 'it is almost a premonition that this person will offend again'. Such statements resonated with J1's comments about events connected to favelas having the 'context of criminal association'. Here, S3's explanation underlines that this association is silently racialized. S3 identifies how many people, including those with influence in custody hearings, recognize that there is a certain level of social disadvantage for racialized groups but overlook the systemic nature as well as the possibility that they may have been conditioned into particular beliefs.

Pr3 explained that when she started her career, it was openly said that the criminal court was 'for "the three Ps": those who are *Black, poor and whores*'.[13] Although Pr3 maintained that there is no longer an overt focus on those previously disparagingly termed the *three Ps*, it appears that the sentiment remains relevant in the shared imaginary of citizens, consequently passing into preconceptions and judgements. However, when asked about why these groups are still detained more than others, Pr3 resorted to the same emphasis on historical and situational factors rather than any consideration of discrimination. Again, we see a natural logic that impoverished Black people are more likely to commit crime, with no attention to a difference in targeted policing practices or treatment within the courtroom.

The overwhelming majority of those presented in court are men, and interviewees almost exclusively spoke about defendants as men. However, the number of women in prison has increased from 10,112 in 2000 to approximately 44,700 in 2017 (Walmsley, 2017a). Alves argues that 'the experience of disadvantaged Black women has become paradigmatic of the rapidly expanding Brazilian penal system' (2016, p. 230). The gendered and racialized figure of the female *drug mule* is perhaps the most recent iteration of the *three Ps* sentiment.

When attempting to explain the history of 'the three Ps', Pr3 conceded that she is not an expert on the 'racial issue' when referencing the reality of Black people's lives. Indicative of the centring of whiteness as an unspoken assumption, many white interviewees discussed race only when speaking about Black or indigenous people or those with multiple heritage. The construction of whiteness was consistently overlooked. There is an inherent ontological positioning in many cases where justice is considered for a core group (i.e. white people) and access to justice for others is part of a racial issue. Pr3 further revealed this thinking when reflecting that it was safer to go out in public in the past while also noting that society was more overtly racist during the same period. It is evident that when talking about generalizations for the wider public,

[13] My translation of '*pobre, preta e puta*'.

Pr3 centred the white experience, and the concerns of racialized groups were seen as peripheral if acknowledged at all.

Normalization of Black Pain and Death

Centring whiteness is just one side of a coin that, on the other, marginalizes blackness and normalizes pain, danger, and death for Black populations. PD6 spoke about the concerted effort from the Brazilian government to whiten the population and how white European immigration was encouraged while noting vagrancy laws and the criminalization of capoeira as examples of overt state oppression directed explicitly at Black populations. PD6 spoke to the legacies of such state policies and stated that 'Colourism in Brazil is very strong. The darker your skin is, the more racism you will suffer.'

The opportunity to disclose torture was a central driver for introducing custodial hearings. However, reflections of several public defenders suggested that such protections are operationalized in ways that both centre whiteness and normalize Black pain. Multiple public defenders commented that judges are so accepting of corporal punishment of Black people and accustomed to the sight of Black pain that it does not affect them. PD6 encapsulated this sentiment most clearly:

> Judges aren't bothered by seeing an injured, tortured, bruised Black prisoner before them. It doesn't cause discomfort. Nor does it bother them to keep that person deprived of liberty and to legitimise this violence suffered, because it's the natural division of power in Brazil ... They're not committed to the rights of that person who is there before them. They're committed to ensuring that the potential iPhone thief will be incarcerated.

Here PD6 is clear in exposing the white supremacy inherent in accepting corporal punishment against Black people and conceded that even progressive fields such as the public defenders' office are 'committed to a white epistemology'. J6 also wanted to underline the relevance of the legacies of colonial violence for understanding contemporary treatment of racialized people. J6 expressed her view that society is conditioned to understand that people have different inherent value. Such belief allows the acceptance of extrajudicial killings in favelas and explains why judges are willing to detain people despite the inhumane pre-trial conditions. J7 also likened the carceral system to 'concentration camps' and 'modern slave quarters' and variously evoked the hierarchical systems of slavery or the systematic approach to removal of the 'undesirable' by the Nazis.

Shortly after my empirical research, a video emerged of a Black teenager in São Paulo, tied-up, gagged, and stripped in public, being whipped with an electric cord by two white security guards after stealing four chocolate bars (Phillips, 2019a). News reports talked of public outrage, while also conceding that scenes of young Black men 'being tied up, tortured and even murdered are common in Brazil' (ibid). The fact that such torture—whipping being the quintessential form during colonialism—could be considered common in contemporary Brazil exemplifies the clear resilience of colonial notions of what it is acceptable to do to people racialized as Black. Whether for an iPhone or food, the protection of white property continues to be prioritized over Black pain and fundamental rights. Here we see the two key elements of coloniality influencing the justice process: the centrality of capitalist interests and racialized hierarchy.

When asked whether people are treated differently in custody hearings, PD2 made himself plain: 'There is [differential treatment]. No doubt!' He then gave an example of a young white man being brought to a custody hearing. PD2 described how other court actors showed great concern, with one saying, 'Gee, I am worried about his mother. She must be losing her mind because she does not know about her son.' This example is representative of sentiments described by multiple interviewees about how certain citizens (white/male/high socio-economic status) evoke a response of concern in a way that is rare for other detainees. PD2 explained that this is because those with power in court are used to considering the detainees (mainly young Black men from favelas) as fundamentally 'different people' and not as 'equal human beings', resulting in the lack of concern in their detention pre-trial. The whiteness of the privileged detainee worked to serve as 'positive racial capital' (Segato, 2007, p. 150) and resulted in preferential treatment. Conversely, the naturalized construction of blackness as inherently criminal and dangerous serves as negative racial capital, resulting in the overuse of pre-trial detention.

Discussion

> It has thus become obvious that the naturalization of difference is the consequence of ontological coloniality, meaning the coloniality of being (what counts as being, including human being), which in turn founds the coloniality of knowledge and power.
>
> (Santos, 2016, p. 178)

After almost 400 years of legalized and naturalized racial inequality, where people were not seen as members of different socio-economic or cultural classes but literally as part of a different subset of humanity, we arrive at a socially constructed yet firm notion of separation by race, which Luiz Eduardo Soares describes as an 'ontological abyss' (in Lemgruber et al., 2017, p. 36). Souza (2017) urges us to consider slavery not as a name for a thing that once was and is no more but rather as a concept that creates an exclusionary and perverse singularity with significant long-term consequences. When the law changed, the hierarchical concepts were not erased from the elites' collective consciousness, and the consequences of this can be seen in the over-representation of Black Brazilians in pre-trial detention. As Segato writes, '[t]he "colour" of prisons is that of race, not in the sense of belonging to a particular ethnic group, but as a mark of a history of colonial rule that continues to this day' (2007, p. 142). She argues that to deny the racialization of prison populations would be to contradict experience, and thus we need to focus on 'the continuity of the colonial structure in the present' (ibid, p. 153).

This chapter has considered how the legacies of these colonial constructs continue to influence decision-making at the pre-trial stage to reveal the coloniality of justice.

The chapter responds directly to Aliverti et al.'s (2021) call to 'decolonize the criminal question' by exposing and explaining how contemporary justice mechanisms are informed by colonial logics across three key dimensions.

Temporal Dimension

The chapter speaks to Aliverti et al.'s (2021, p. 302) 'temporal dimension' by illustrating how colonial logics inform everyday court practice and is thus indicative of the broader coloniality of justice. As J7 explained:

> The situation has not changed because our culture is a culture of violence against poor and Black children. We have a cultural history of slavery. So, although we have decreed the end of slavery, it is still in the subconscious of our population, and we still treat Black people as second-rate people.

As this quote notes, while laws are in place to ensure equality of treatment, the racialized social and civic hierarchy created under colonial hegemony 'is still in the subconscious' of the Brazilian population. According to many interviewees, judicial decision-making cannot be examined in isolation, and due consideration must be given to the assumptions made within the broader public consciousness. The logic of who is deserving/undeserving still upholds divisions between people, invented and introduced to the Souths of America during empire. A logic underpinned by a conqueror/conquered narrative, whereby some are considered '*killable Others*' and for whom due process can be overlooked and legitimated to protect an elite asserted as more deserving (Darke and Khan, 2021, p. 735).

Spatial Dimension

Aliverti et al.'s (2021) spatialized dimension refers to the Euro-American dominance of epistemological space, and this concept maps onto geographical boundaries in Brazil. The divisions are not merely physical markers constitutive of values. Those of the asfalto space are imbued with a 'Europeanness' in Souza's sense (2007, p. 24) and thus considered rational, moral, and of inherent value. Conversely, favela residents are marred with colonial stereotypes, such as assumed dangerousness, criminality, and immorality. Outside the courtroom, this is observable where violation of domicile, violence, and even extrajudicial killings are normalized in the favela and inconceivable in elite neighbourhoods. This division of treatment is extended into the courtroom, where the stigma of the favela as a place synonymous with crime can be enough to overlook fundamental rights such as assumptions of innocence. J1's thoughts relating to a 'context of criminal association' revealed how merely being present in a favela, existing in one's own space—even without a weapon—can be enough for the presumption of guilt by association and, thus, lead to a greater likelihood of pre-trial detention.

Colonial-era assumptions of European epistemic supremacy are thus made manifest within these physical (yet constructed) boundaries.

Subjective Dimension

Interviewees reflected on the evident assumptions that underpin the difference in treatment of those deemed to be a *bandido* or *traficante* in comparison to a *pessoa de bem*. Testimony suggested that judges orientalize those from favelas by presuming a connection to crime if a person is impoverished or does not have a job within the licit market. Interview testimony strongly indicated that the figure of the *bandido* is heavily racialized within the shared imagination, demonstrating the legacies of the racist colonial and eugenics movements associating Black people with crime. These findings relate to Aliverti et al.'s (2021) subjective dimension of 'decolonizing the criminal question'. The notion that the mere appearance of a young Black man is enough for the police to hit the car's brakes also indicates a gendered element to the construction of the *bandido*. While women appear less in custody hearings, interviewees suggested that those who did were also perceived according to long-standing, constructed stereotypes of underserved Black women as immoral, promiscuous, and bad mothers, all of which are inferences with orientalist, colonial origins. In either case, the intersectional nature of race and gender coalesces to create enduring and criminalizing stereotypes.

In making clear the overt relevance to custody hearings, interviewees contended that judges are so accustomed to witnessing the pain of Black people that they have no issue with remanding them to inhumane conditions. For Alves, 'Blackness is ontologically marked as the negation of sociality' (2014, p. 144), and for Black Brazilians, the constant threat of death is intrinsic to life. Alves quotes Sarah Hartman (1997) to explain that Black people are appreciated as citizens or even as humans 'only to the extent of their culpability' (2014, p. 145). This dynamic is observable in the pre-trial context, as those routinely denied the usual trappings of citizenship (according to Euro-American normative conceptualizations) are only acknowledged as citizens when the law is used against them.

Darke relates a common Brazilian expression 'for my friends, everything: for my enemies, the law' (2018, p. 70) to highlight how the powerful have always weaponized the law against the *Other*. White-supremacist ideology forged during colonization of the Souths of America continues to facilitate an asymmetry of power in the Brazilian justice system at the pre-trial stage. The racialized social hierarchy and the prioritization of property of the privileged over the lives of the marginalized illustrate the ongoing coloniality of justice in Brazil. This study suggests that equality of justice will only be achieved after a profound, active reckoning with the naturalized acceptance of the dichotomous constructions of the conquerors and the conquered.

References

Aliverti, A., Carvalho, H., Chamberlen, A. et al. (2021) 'Decolonizing the criminal question', *Punishment & Society*, 23(3), pp. 244–281.

Alves, J. A. (2014) 'Neither humans nor rights: Some notes on the double negation of black life in Brazil', *Journal of Black Studies*, 45(2), pp. 143–162.

Alves, J. A. (2016) 'On mules and bodies: Black captivities in the Brazilian racial democracy', *Critical Sociology*, 42(2), pp. 229–248.

AMB (2018) *Quem Somos: A Magistratura Que Queremos*. Rio de Janeiro: Associação Dos Magistrados Brasileiros.

Aniyar de Castro, L. (1987) *Criminología de la liberación*. Universidad del Zulia, Vice-Rectorado Académico, Instituto de Criminología.

Beattie, P. M. (2015) *Punishment in Paradise: Race, Slavery, Human Rights, and a Nineteenth-Century Brazilian Penal Colony*. Durham, NC: Duke University Press.

Braun, V. and Clarke, V. (2006) 'Using thematic analysis in psychology', Qualitative Research in Psychology, 3(2), pp. 77–101.

Carvalho, J. M. de (1982) 'Political elites and state building: The case of nineteenth-century Brazil', *Comparative Studies in Society and History*, 24(3), pp. 378–399.

Chalhoub, S. (2006) 'The politics of silence: Race and citizenship in nineteenth-century Brazil', *Slavery & Abolition*, 27(1), pp. 73–87.

Da Costa, A. E. (2014) *Reimagining Black Difference and Politics in Brazil: From Racial Democracy to Multiculturalism*. New York: Palgrave Macmillan.

Darke, S. (2018) *Conviviality and Survival: Co-Producing Brazilian Prison Order*. Cham: Palgrave Macmillan.

Darke, S. and Khan, O. P. (2021) 'Coloniality, just war & carceral injustice in Brazil', *Punishment & Society*, 23(5), pp. 723–740.

Del Olmo, R. (1990) *Segunda ruptura criminológica*. Universidad Central de Venezuela, Facultad de Ciencias Jurídicas y Políticas, Instituto de Ciencias Penales y Criminológicas, Consejo de Desarrollo Científico y Humanístico.

GMF (2018) 'Rio de Janeiro conclui cadastro de mais de 56 mil presos no BNMP'. Available at: http://gmf.tjrj.jus.br/noticias/noticia/-/visualizar-conteudo/5265985/5580491 (accessed 10 June 2022).

Grosfoguel, R. (2007) 'The epistemic decolonial turn', *Cultural Studies*, 21(2–3), pp. 211–223.

ICPR (2018) 'World Prison Brief: Brazil'. Available at: www.prisonstudies.org/country/brazil (accessed 5 June 2022).

ICPR (2019) 'World Prison Brief: Brazil'. Available at: www.prisonstudies.org/country/brazil (accessed 5 June 2022).

IDDD, Justiça Global, and OBSAC-UFRJ (2020) 'Prisão Como Regra: Ilegalidades e Desafios das Audiências de Custódia no Rio de Janeiro', Rio de Janeiro: Instituto de Defesa do Direito de Defesa, Justiça Global and Observatório das Audiências de Custódia. Available at: https://iddd.org.br/wp-content/uploads/2020/11/prisacc83o-como-regra_final.pdf (accessed 5 June 2022).

Lemgruber, J., Cano, I., and Musumeci, L. (2017) *Olho por olho? O que pensam os cariocas sobre 'bandido bom é bandido morto'*. Rio de Janeiro: Centro de Estudos de Segurança e Cidadania (CESeC).

Machado, M. R., De Souza Amaral, M. C., De Barros, M. et al. (2019) 'Incarcerating at any cost: Drug trafficking and imprisonment in Brazilian court reasoning', *Journal of Illicit Economies and Development*, 1(2), pp. 226–237.

Maldonado-Torres, N. (2007) 'On the coloniality of being', *Cultural Studies*, 21(2–3), pp. 240–270.

Mignolo, W. and Walsh, C. E. (2018) *On Decoloniality: Concepts, Analytics, Praxis*. Durham, NC: Duke University Press.

Nascimento dos Reis, T. (2017) 'Detainees on Stage: Achievements and Challenges of the Newly-Implemented Bail Hearings in São Paulo State Courts', Thesis, Stanford Law School. Available at: https://law.stanford.edu/publications/detainees-on-stage-achievements-and-challenges-of-the-newly-implemented-bail-hearings-in-sao-paulo-state-courts/ (accessed 5 June 2022).

Phillips, D. (2019a) 'Video of Black teen whipped for stealing chocolate sparks outrage in Brazil', *The Guardian*, 3 September. Available at: www.theguardian.com/world/2019/sep/03/brazil-teenager-whipped-stealing-chocolate (accessed 4 June 2022).

Phillips, D. (2019b) 'Brazil: 10 soldiers arrested after firing more than 80 bullets into family's car', *The Guardian*, 8 April. Available at: www.theguardian.com/world/2019/apr/08/brazil-soldiers-arrested-shooting-car-family (accessed 4 June 2022).

Quijano, A. (2000) 'Coloniality of power and eurocentrism in Latin America', *International Sociology*, 15(2), pp. 215–232.

Santos, B. de S. (2016) *Epistemologies of the South: Justice against Epistemicide*. London: Routledge.

Santos, S. A. dos and Hallewell, L. (2002) 'Historical roots of the "whitening" of Brazil', *Latin American Perspectives*, 29(1), pp. 61–82.

Segato, R. L. (2007) 'El color de la cárcel en América Latina', *Nueva Sociedad*, 208, pp. 142–161.

Souza, J. (2007) 'The Singularity of the Peripheral Social Inequality', in Souza, J. and Sinder, V. (eds) *Imagining Brazil*. Lanham, MD: Lexington Books.

Souza, J. (2017) *A Elite do Atraso: Da Escravidão à Lava-Jato*. Rio de Janeiro: Casa da Palavra.

Souza, V. S. de and Souza, V. S. de (2016) 'Brazilian eugenics and its international connections: An analysis based on the controversies between Renato Kehl and Edgard Roquette-Pinto, 1920–1930', História, Ciências, Saúde-Manguinhos, 23, pp. 93–110.

UN Human Rights Council (2014) 'Report of the Working Group on Arbitrary Detention: Mission to Brazil', A/HRC/27/48/Add.3. Available from: https://digitallibrary.un.org/record/777916?ln=en#record-files-collapse-header (accessed 5 June 2022).

UOL (2020) 'Juíza diz que homem negro é criminoso 'em razão de sua raça' e o condena', 12 August. Available at: https://noticias.uol.com.br/cotidiano/ultimas-noticias/2020/08/12/sentenca-de-cunho-racista.htm (accessed 4 June 2022).

Walmsley, R. (2017a) *World Female Imprisonment List: Women and girls in penal institutions, including pre-trial detainees/remand prisoners*, 4th edn. Institute for Criminal Policy Research. Available at: www.prisonstudies.org/sites/default/files/resources/downloads/world_female_prison_4th_edn_v4_web.pdf (accessed 5 June 2022).

Walmsley, R. (2017b) *World Pre-trial/Remand Imprisonment List*, 3rd edn. Institute for Criminal Policy Research. Available at: www.prisonstudies.org/sites/default/files/resources/downloads/wptril_3rd_edition.pdf (accessed 5 June 2022).

Zaffaroni, E. R. (1988) *Criminología: Aproximación Desde Un Margen*. Bogotá: Temis.

10

Contextualizing Racialized Exclusion and Criminalization in Postcolonial Israel

Policing of Israeli Ethiopian Citizens and Detention of Sudanese and Eritrean Asylum Seekers

Maayan Ravid

Introduction

In this chapter I argue that observing which populations a state excludes and polices sheds light on a state's constitutive order and enables us to confront it. In response to this volume's call of 'decolonizing the criminal question', I use the case study of Israel to demonstrate the racialized ways in which criminal subjectivities are constructed and rooted in postcolonial racial hierarchies and remain ingrained in national orders over time. As the editors have noted elsewhere:

> The identification and construction of dangerous and criminal subjectivities based on notions of otherness has been at the heart of criminological enquiry. Within these processes and discourses, ideas of difference, threat and danger condensed to embody the criminal subject, which in turn traveled and formed the staple to define and deal with colonial subjects—and vice-versa.
>
> (Aliverti et al., 2021, p. 9).

Thus, rereading processes of criminalization and exclusion with a consciousness of race and postcolonial hierarchies, and their co-constitutive relationship, enables us to examine the development of categories and groups in context. It enables us to see how colonial racial categories continue to operate and evolve in present-day settings of exclusion and crime control. Efforts to decolonize the debate require a multiplicity of accounts regarding how such processes have taken place across the globe. I add to the debate by exploring the repeated constructions of racialized groups in Israel over time as threatening, criminal, or deserving of exclusion.

I take a broad view of the 'criminal question' by observing not only legal, state-enforced practices and institutions of crime control, but also wider social structures and systemic inequalities that foreground social categorizations, including socio-economic and socio-spatial exclusion (Aliverti et al., 2021, pp. 12–13; Bauman, 2000;

Maayan Ravid, *Contextualizing Racialized Exclusion and Criminalization in Postcolonial Israel* In: *Decolonizing the Criminal Question*. Edited by: Ana Aliverti, Henrique Carvalho, Anastasia Chamberlen, and Máximo Sozzo, Oxford University Press.
 DOI: 10.1093/oso/9780192899002.003.0011

Garland, 2001). Systemic marginalization through political, social, spatial, and economic structures produces environments and populations more vulnerable to poverty, estrangement, and risk; these factors, in turn, serve to criminalize entire groups based on race, class, status, or neighbourhood (Hall et al., 1978, p. 380; Lipsitz, 2007; Phillips et al., 2003; Young, 1999).

The impacts of colonialism include diverse reverberations of oppressive power relationships stemming from colonialism and imperialism, over time, and towards different populations (Goldberg and Quayson, 2002, pp. xii, 6–7; Stoler, 2016, pp. 45–46). Formations of racial categories, structural inequalities, and hierarchies are deeply entwined with histories of colonial and imperial enterprise (Meer, 2018, pp. 1165–1170; Omi and Winant, 1994; 2008). When states rely on historically entrenched racial categories and hierarchies as road maps for inclusion and exclusion to determine allocation of rights, protections, resources, exemptions, or enforcements, colonial logics are reified in present times (Bhambra, 2014b; Stoler, 2016, p. 41). The state's differential treatment of groups gradually constructs new and evolving iterations of the criminal other—a modern racial criminalization based on historical racism (Gibran Muhammad, 2010).

This argument unfolds through examination of the Israeli case study, by observing how different racialized groups are progressively targeted for exclusion and state control. It begins by situating Israel's establishment in Palestine within postcolonial sociohistorical context and scholarship (Bhabha, 1997; Bhambra, 2014b; Said, 1978; Shohat, 1992). Postcolonial or settler colonial framings have been used in previous studies of racialized exclusion and criminalization in Israel, largely focused on Palestinians and *Mizrahi* citizens,[1] and are discussed after outlining the methods and scope of this enquiry.

The chapter then delves into state treatment of two other racialized groups that have steadily been criminalized and targeted for exclusion, albeit in different ways—Ethiopian Jewish citizens and asylum seekers from Sudan and Eritrea. I begin by describing structural racialized exclusion that contributes to the marginalization and increasingly tenuous relationship of each group with the state and its authorities. I then focus on one aspect of state control disproportionally enforced upon each group, originally developed through state efforts to control Palestinians.

First, I examine the fraught relations between police and Israeli Ethiopian citizens that have resulted in high numbers of police killings of young men from this population over the last two decades. Second, I discuss the administrative detention of Sudanese and Eritrean asylum seekers. Examination of state acts to differentiate and exclude racialized groups through structural and direct violence, using means developed from British colonial structures, indicates that colonial racism and control mechanisms still operate today.

[1] Israel's Jewish society is commonly characterized by a cleavage between two major 'ethnic groups' (in Hebrew, plural—*edot*) that make up most of Israel's Jewish citizenry. Jews from Europe and English-speaking countries are called *Ashkenazim* (Ashkenaz was the medieval Jewish name for Germany). Jews from the Middle East and North Africa are termed *Mizrahim* (literally meaning 'Orientals' or 'Easterners'; historically there existed a distinction from *Sephardim*, literally, of Spanish descent) (Smooha 1976; Ram 2019).

A Note on Methods and Scope

I use socio-historical analysis to consider the role of past events in forming today's social and racial constructs. This choice of method was inspired by select works of W. E. B. Du Bois, Stuart Hall, and Gurminder Bhambra (Bhambra, 2014b; Du Bois, 1897; Hall, 1986; 1992; 2017), as each scholar diagnosed the racist afflictions of their different times and settings. I follow Du Bois who contextualized urban racialization in American legacies of slavery (Du Bois, 1897); Hall who related differential inclusion of racialized citizens in the UK to colonial relationships abroad (Hall, 1986; 1992); and Bhambra who emphasizes the continued impacts of colonialism on 'relations of hierarchy, domination and the inclusions and exclusions that they create' (Bhambra, 2014a, pp. 472–473), urging us to look both backwards to deconstruct events, and forwards in reconstructing explanations for present-day happenings using a race-conscious lens (Bhambra, 2014b, p. 117). I similarly situate the present-day analysis of racialized criminalization in Israel as a socio-historical postcolonial exploration.

The term postcolonial is used here to describe lasting connections between colonialism and its legacies—physical, institutional, discursive, and ideological (Goldberg and Quayson, 2002; Hall, 1992). Most important for this chapter are the colonial practices of population control: policing and administrative detention, first developed to control Palestinians; and colonial racial hierarchies that animated the exclusion and criminalization of distinct groups over the course of time.

Existing scholarship on postcolonial racial dynamics and policing of minority groups in Israel largely focuses on differential enforcement along the internal divide of *Ashkenazi–Mizrahi* dichotomy, and a national cleavage between Israelis and Palestinians (Ben-Porat and Yuval, 2012; Hasisi and Weitzer, 2007; Sa'di, 2014). Group diversity, complexities, and internal dynamics related to these categories cannot be fully addressed in this limited space. A wealth of literature regarding each group and its relationship with the state can be found elsewhere and some is cited in this chapter.

Sparce scholarship exists on how colonial practices of policing and border control have travelled into the state and are used against black subjects, to mark and exclude from within. This chapter starts to fill a crucial gap by connecting the criminalization of Ethiopian Israeli citizens and asylum seekers from Sudan and Eritrea to earlier group criminalization of Palestinians. It does so through a focus on institutional and ideological traces of colonial racism and control.

A final note is needed regarding timeframes discussed in the chapter. Early examples of Palestinian population management and policing in the first years of the state are briefly discussed as historical antecedents of state control. However, one need not go back in time to find omnipresent ways in which Palestinian citizens and non-citizen lives are controlled and devalued by the Israeli state.

At the time of writing, the residents of Gaza struggle with the aftermath of an Israeli military campaign named 'Operation Guardian of the Walls', during which Israeli bombardments killed over 240 Gazans over eleven days (Bateman, 2021). This round of violence erupted following restrictive Israeli policing and obstruction of prayers in the al-Aqsa mosque during the month of Ramadan, as well as efforts to evict Palestinian families in the Sheikh Jarrah neighbourhood of East Jerusalem and homes in Yaffa, that raised tensions and clashes between police and the Palestinian public. Military actions were followed by a police campaign titled 'Operation Law and Order' aimed to 'restore order' in Palestinian towns in Israel. The operation entailed extensive police activity in Arab cities, with the police fitted out in military gear, in order to conduct mass arrests and with a reliance on excessive force. Over 2,000 people were arrested as part of the campaign (Ministry of Public Security, 2021). Arrests were based on racial profiling and inflicted collective punishment intended as a 'deterrent' (Adalah, 2021).

This recent conflict and state violence are consistent with past over-enforcement and excessive use of force against Palestinians by Israeli police. Such dynamics between the police and the Palestinian population have resulted in extrajudicial killings of Palestinians with impunity (Menashe et al., 2017; Schaeffer Omer-Man, 2017). State violence and over-enforcement against Palestinians continues.

Socio-Historical Context—An Ethnonational Settler State

Israel was established as a settler society in the first half of the twentieth century simultaneous to colonial and imperial projects spread across the surrounding Middle East, and throughout the Global South. The state was established by Jews of European descent who, though categorized as non-European 'Others' and rejected in Europe, emulated modern European nationalism throughout the settling process in Palestine (Erakat, 2015; Hirsch, 2009).

Lively debates persist regarding Israel's categorization as a colonial endeavour. Arguments against this categorization cite various characteristics that make Israel distinct from other colonial states or settler movements, including: the persecution and decimation of Jewish communities on European lands, the plight of Jews as motivation for seeking safety in Israel, the arrival of half the Jewish population from Middle Eastern countries, a lack of a metropole or 'mother country', as well as historical connections to the land; and settler intent to live alongside Palestinians. This chapter engages with the literature produced over the last three decades that increasingly examines Israel through postcolonial and settler colonial frameworks, to expand our understandings of colonial and imperial impacts, and resists exceptionalism in this debate (Abdo and Yuval-Davis, 1995; Lentin, 2018; Peled, 2017; Sabbagh-Khoury, 2021; Stoler, 2016; Veracini, 2006).

Like all other settlement movements of that era, Israel's establishment was accompanied by Eurocentric ideological, cultural, and political sentiments. Such sentiments enabled the establishment of 'new' countries in 'empty' lands, a process that required construction of collective self-definition to qualify, evaluate, and differentiate between members, outsiders, and others (Bhabha, 1997; Mendel and Ranta, 2018; Said, 1978; 1992). Colonial 'inventions of the other' (Desai and Nair, 2005, p. 5) elevated European cultures, structures, and ideas as dominant and preferred, as they downgraded non-Western cultures (Hall 1992; 2017, p. 101). Such discourses and ideas accompanied settlement and state-building around the colonized world, and in Palestine (Rouhana and Sabbagh-Khoury, 2015; Lentin, 2018; Sabbagh-Khoury, 2021). They produced unequal, racializing treatment of distinct groups by the state, that in turn created long-term division and inequality (Kedar, 2003; Kimmerling, 2004; Shafir and Peled, 1998; Shenhav, 2006).

Hierarchical racialized orders of belonging and exclusion operate both internally and externally to differentiate groups in relation to the desired national order (Dauvergne, 2016). In Israel, the desired national order of European, modern, Jewishness relied on processes of othering and exclusion of both 'Oriental' Jews and Palestinians:

> In this process the same terms and binaries were adopted from Europe to reshape the Jewish collectivity as a national one, and were applied, albeit in different ways, to the Palestinians and the Jews from Arab countries.
>
> (Raz-Krakotzkin, 2005, p. 166)

External to the Jewish collective, Palestinians were physically, legally, and socially excluded. They were displaced, policed, incarcerated, and controlled through diverse state apparatuses across Gaza, the Occupied Territories, and within the green line. Palestinians who remained within Israel and became citizens were treated by the state as unwanted, the enemy, or second-class citizens (Jamal, 2020; Kimmerling, 2004; Rouhana and Sabbagh-Khoury, 2015; Sultany, 2012). Palestinians remain the most widely detained, controlled, targeted, and racialized population in Israel (Hasisi and Weitzer, 2007; Jamal, 2016; Shalhoub-Kevorkian, 2016; Goldberg, 2021).

Within Israel's Jewish population, ethnic division animated differential institutional treatment between the two largest Jewish ethnic groups—*Ashkenazim* and *Mizrahim*—that manifested in systemic inequality and marginalization (Chetrit, 2010; Shenhav et al., 2002; Smooha, 1976). Ethnic 'group making' emerged in the early years of the state to distinguish and differentiate within the Jewish collective (Zawdu and Willen, 2019). *Mizrahi* citizens were relegated to social, economic, political, and geographic margins of the state and society (Khazzoom, 1999; Massad, 1996; Tzfadia and Yacobi, 2011). As the new, modern state of Israel sought contrast from its Oriental surroundings, the *Mizrahim* were categorized and treated as less valued citizens, in need of modernization due to their countries of origin (Khazzoom, 2003; Shenhav, 2006; Shohat, 1988). Uneven resource distribution and investment created entrenched inequalities that persist today.

Israel's Euro-centric racial order similarly marginalized Jews of African descent. Haim Yacobi and Eitan Bar Yosef elaborate on the ways in which meanings and imaginations of Africa developed over time in Israeli culture and society (Bar Yosef, 2013; Yacobi, 2015). They trace how Africa became an idea and place that provides territorial and cultural boundaries. According to Bar Yosef, African representations in Israeli culture 'say something about ourselves, our whiteness, our racial cleavages, and our national fantasies' (Bar Yosef, 2013, p. 22; author's translation). Yacobi describes how ideas of Africa provided a contrast against which Israeli national identity was defined as modern, Western, and white. Distinction constructed symbolic group borders and a graded order of inclusion and exclusion that stretches from whiteness to blackness within Israel (Yacobi, 2015, p. 12). This framing is important for understanding the positioning of Ethiopian Jewish citizens in Israel's social and racial hierarchies. Ethiopian Israelis remain in an inferior position compared to their *Mizrahi* counterparts, but in a better position than Palestinians and non-Jews. Group differentiation can thus be understood within a relational scale of ethnonational and postcolonial racial ordering.

Beyond colonial racial ideologies, colonial institutions also exist in Israel as many of Israel's state apparatuses, laws, and structures of enforcement were adopted from thirty years of British mandatory rule that preceded the establishment of the state in 1948. Colonial institutional legacies are thus easily identifiable. I focus in this chapter on two examples of colonial apparatuses that are used in present-day enforcement of state control—Israel's National Police force (INP) and the use of administrative detention in border control.

Israel's national police was modelled after European police structures of the eighteenth and nineteenth centuries, to enforce state control and sovereignty of the ruling group against threats from outside and within (Shadmi, 1998, pp. 207–208). The police are highly identified with state interests and those of the hegemonic group, often against or at the expense of minority and racialized groups within it. This is especially the case in deeply divided societies such as Israel where policing serves those in power and 'concentrate[s] misconduct toward subordinate racial and ethnic groups, while members of the dominant group are treated more favourably' producing inequality in law, differential enforcement, and distrust in the police (Hasisi and Weitzer, 2007, p. 737; Mesch and Talmud, 1998, pp. 235–237).

In Israel, police identification with, and service of, state interests meant that policing involved security concerns and enforced the Occupation. Erella Shadmi examined how state interests shaped Israeli policing in its early years by tracing the expansion of police functions beyond conventional roles to national security tasks. Maintaining order, security, and border policing were prioritized (Shadmi, 1998, pp. 216–218). Policing apparatuses and approach were adopted from the British police law and standing orders into the Israeli legal system:

> British colonial police were transplanted into the neocolonial Israel police force. This process was further reflected in the adoption of colonial training material, disciplinary rules, investigative procedures, patrol methods (such as mounted police in rural areas), but especially in the centralized paramilitary structure of the force and the incorporation of the border police within the INP.
>
> (Shadmi, 1998, p. 220)

Application of colonial control systems was especially evident in the first twenty years of military rule over the Occupied Territories (1948–1966), and with INP deployment in the West Bank starting in 1967. Eilat Maoz has researched police operations in the West Bank by observing police failures to enforce crime control, prevent violence, or protect residents; alongside its multiplication of control and enforcement upon Palestinians, and galvanization of settler presence and vigilantism on the land (Maoz, 2020). Though Maoz's analysis focuses on INP operations in the West Bank, she explains that police control in the Occupied Territories reveals much about Israeli policing throughout the country—a state force that operates to ensure racial exclusivity and state sovereignty (Maoz, 2020, p. 8).

Another important front in safeguarding state interests was the border. Exclusive border entry, and extensive policing, were adopted to protect the new state borders and carry out a 'War on Infiltration'—a campaign against border-crossers. The state termed such groups *Fedayeen*—organized groups that presumably entered to commit violent acts, smuggling, or trafficking—and increased military powers to arrest and detain them.

Administrative detention had been used since the founding of the state under the Defense Emergency Regulation of 1945, an Imperial Parliament Act which was adopted by authorities in Palestine and later incorporated into Israeli law (Government and Law Arrangements Ordinance, 1948). British High Commissioner responsibilities were transferred to the Minister of Defense until new legal frameworks were developed (Defense (Emergency) Regulations, 1945; Gil, 2010, p. 11; Shetreet, 1984, pp. 183–187). Most important for this chapter is the 1954 Prevention of Infiltration Law.

During the 1947–1948 war, or *nakba*, hundreds of thousands of Palestinians were displaced and on the move. Those who crossed the newly established border without permits were categorized as 'infiltrators' under the Prevention of Infiltration Law that allowed for extensive administrative detention with little judicial review. Oren Bracha surveyed the legal developments between 1948 and 1954 that preceded the enactment of the Law and cites a diversity of people who crossed the border for different reasons—family reunification, employment, tending to their fields, and more. Police reports from those years showed that less than 10 per cent of 'infiltrators' were involved in criminal activities (Bracha, 1998, p. 339). Nonetheless, all were labelled by the state as security threats, entering to commit crimes, terror, or espionage.

Against this backdrop, in the next two sections I examine how racist over-policing and administrative detention present in Israel today. State acts developed to control and exclude Palestinian populations have been increasingly directed at additional racialized groups. I situate present-day policing and detention of black subjects in the context of colonial technologies of control, and ideology, to historicize racial criminalization.

The Policing of Ethiopian Jewish Citizens

The year 2015 saw unprecedented mobilization and protests by the Israeli Ethiopian community against police brutality, racism, and criminalization. Following decades of political advocacy and focused protests against racist incidents, thousands took to the streets to express mounting discontent, coupled with political consciousness and discourse against racist policing. Speaking about police violence against Ethiopians, Roni Alsheich, the then General Commissioner of Police, explained:

> In all criminological studies around the world it is proven that immigrants are more involved in crime than others, and this should not surprise us ... This was the case in all the waves of immigration [to Israel]. When there is a community that is more involved in crime—also with regard to Arabs or East Jerusalem, and the statistics are

> known—when a police officer meets a suspect, naturally enough his mind suspects him more than if he were someone else. That is natural.
>
> (Beaumont, 2016)

Approximately 155,000 Israeli Ethiopian citizens lived in Israel in 2020 (Central Bureau of Statistics, 2020). A little under half of that population was born in Israel, and a little over half were born in Ethiopia, migrated to Israel, and became citizens based on their Jewish identity and Israel's Law of Return. This group's arrival into the Eurocentric society established in Israel, combined with their shared origins and phenotypical attributes, resulted in distinct standing and uneven treatment from their earliest days in the country. When Ethiopian Jews came to Israel, mostly in the 1980s and 1990s,[2] they were treated as less advanced, less Jewish, and less Western by the established Jewish population and institutions (Raz-Krakotzkin, 2005, p. 171). Ethiopian Jews were met by Orientalist and colonial discourses, similarly to other non-European Jewish populations that had migrated to Israel before them (Chetrit, 2010; Yona, 2005, p. 5).

Guetzkow and Fast compare Ethiopian citizens' standing to that of Palestinian citizens, citing that the two groups: 'are very similar on a range of socioeconomic indicators ... [marginalized] by very different symbolic boundaries: national belonging in the case of Arab Palestinian citizens and ethnoracial inferiority or 'backwardness' in the case of Ethiopians' (Guetzkow and Fast, 2016, p. 156). They and others have compared Ethiopians and Palestinians to examine similar kinds of exclusionary treatment (Lamont et al., 2016, p. 4; Mizrachi and Herzog, 2012).

Discrimination and state failures to equally integrate this group into the wider citizen population have been acknowledged by the state (Israel State Comptroller, 2012; Ministry of Justice, 2018; Palmor, 2016). Systemic marginalization and discriminatory institutional treatment have been identified in education, employment, and housing (Abu-Rabia-Queder, 2019; Mola, 2018; Swirski and Swirski, 2002; Walsh and Tuval-Mashiach, 2012). Differential treatment serves to segregate this group in impoverished geographic or social peripheries, contributing to their distinction from their Jewish citizen peers (Fenster, 1998; Offer, 2007). The spatial manifestation of racialized differentiation is highly visible in cities across Israel, where Ethiopian neighbourhoods are systemically neglected and impoverished.

Accounts of segregation worldwide show that group distinction and separation, though different in each locale, is often entwined with stigmatization and racialization (Nightingale, 2012; Wacquant, 2008). Indeed, in Israel. too, Ethiopian Jewish citizens face exclusion and stigmatization on different fronts of Israeli society and many aspects of their everyday lives (Lamont et al., 2016, p. 224; Mengistu and Avraham,

[2] Ethiopian Jews had arrived in Israel in small numbers since the early years of the state. In 1973, the group's Jewish identity was officially recognized by Israel's Chief Rabinnical Authority, which led to increased entrants. Two major state-sponsored airlifts brought in large groups of this population from Ethiopia in Operation Moses (1984–1985) and Operation Solomon (1991); and entree of smaller groups continues to date. Ethiopian Israelis constitute less than 2 per cent of Israel's population—they became citizens pursuant to Israel's Law of Return—though discrimination and degrading treatment by religious authorities has also hindered citizenship attainment for some by casting doubt on the population's Jewish identity (Anteby-Yemini, 2010; Ben-eliezer, 2004; Mengistu and Avraham, 2015).

2015; Mizrachi and Zawdu, 2012; Salamon, 2003). Processes of social separation, othering, and racialization are also accompanied by group criminalization (Cohen, 2002; Goode and Ben-Yehuda, 1994).

Group criminalization of Ethiopian citizens is reflected in over-policing of their communities and neighbourhoods, and over-representation in the criminal justice system (Fine and Parenti, 2018). According to the Public Defender's Office 2016 report, 88 per cent of Ethiopian Israeli youths who are convicted of a crime are sent to prison, compared to 45 per cent of Arab Israelis and 25 per cent of veteran Israelis (Yaron, 2016). This is the outcome of parole recommendations that send Ethiopian Israeli youths to prison instead of other therapeutic rehabilitative services, at rates twice and three times higher than their non-black counterparts. Such trends indicate a complexity in the racialized logics of belonging and exclusion, as skin colour and other 'racial' attributes cut across different dimensions such as nationality, ethnicity, and religion as criminogenic traits meriting policing or exclusion.

In recent years, large segments of the Israeli Ethiopian population have mobilized in public protests against police violence targeting their community, following disproportionate numbers of police killings of young Ethiopian men. Public protests in May 2015 were met with a harsh police response that included a large number of forces in paramilitary gear, the use of shock grenades, mounted police, and other means of crowd control previously used to police Palestinian mobilizations and protests in the Occupied Territories (BBC News, 2015; 2019; TOI Staff, 2015).

In 2019, Solomon Teka and Yehuda Biadga, two Israeli Ethiopian men, were shot and killed by police officers which resulted in public uproar. Nine other deaths of Israeli Ethiopian men over the last two decades have taken place either at the hand of police, following interactions with the police, or after having spent time in state custody (Eglash, 2019; Halbfinger and Kershner, 2019). Over-policing and excessive violence are evident in police relations with this group, along with the use of military technologies previously used on Palestinians.

Connecting present-day police practices and the racist institutional approach to Ethiopian citizens, with the development of Israeli policing through the control of Palestinian populations, illuminates the ways in which colonial racism and structures of control persist over time. The same INP that was established to police Israel's borders and control the Palestinian threat is also deployed to police Ethiopian neighbourhoods, youths, and political protests. Racial profiling, over-enforcement, and differential sentencing prevail in both groups.

The 2016 statement cited at the start of this section, by then police commissioner Roni Alsheich, is emblematic of the institutional view of this citizen population as suspect based on their blackness. It also makes clear connections to criminological studies and practices around the world that mark minority groups as 'naturally' suspicious through use of statistics, and construct black populations as pathologically criminal or violent. The argument for observing colonial continuities in Israel corresponds with similar efforts to historicize institutional racism elsewhere. In the United States, Khalil Gibran Muhammed explores the 'Condemnation of Blackness' through tracing how statistical discourse on black criminality grew from legacies of slavery (Gibran Muhammed, 2010). Saidiya Hartman reflects on the 'afterlife of slavery' in the ways that black lives remain devalued and impacted by a persistent and deeply embedded racial logic (Hartman, 2007).

Across Western countries, hierarchies of belonging among citizens are constructed upon colonial racism (Bhambra, 2014b; Du Bois, 1897; Hall, 2017). In Israel, structural discrimination and inequalities that disadvantage Ethiopian neighbourhoods, police targeting and excessive use of force against Ethiopian Israeli citizens is telling of a racialized national order. It shows a specific dimension of anti-black exclusion and criminalization within the Jewish collective. I now turn to discuss how anti-black racialized exclusion is applied to non-citizen, non-Jews of African descent.

Detention of Asylum Seekers from Sudan and Eritrea

Some 30,000 Sudanese and Eritrean nationals lived in Israel at the end of 2020 (Population and Immigration Authority, 2020), who the state officially term 'Infiltrators'. Members of this group crossed into Israel through unauthorized border points along Egypt's Sinai desert between the years 2005 and 2012 until construction of a border security fence was completed thus preventing further entry. State categorization of this group as 'infiltrators' is central to their construction as criminalized subjects, and has been discussed at length elsewhere (Duman, 2015; Hochman, 2015; Ziegler, 2015). Socio-economic marginalization and physical exclusion also contribute to this process. Over half of the group have submitted asylum claims that are still pending in Israel's Ministry of Interior and they are therefore termed asylum seekers in this chapter (Israel State Comptroller, 2018).

Sudanese and Eritrean nationals cannot be deported to their home countries under the international law principle of *non-refoulement* and have remained in Israel for over a decade under 'temporary group protection' or the 'collective non-removal' policy (Harel, 2015; Kritzman-Amir, 2012). Other migrant groups' stays in Israel are regulated by the Entry to Israel Law (1952), while Eritrean and Sudanese entrants are dealt with using the Prevention of Infiltration Law. The Prevention of Infiltration Law has been amended four times over the course of five years to control African asylum seekers' presence in the country and limit their rights in order to discourage them from staying.[3] Asylum seekers reside in Israel with a temporary document that grants no social, health, or welfare rights (Ziegler, 2015) and serves to remind them that their residence is temporary, under constant threat, and their presence unwanted.

The Prevention of Infiltration Law was originally drafted to police Palestinians, conceived as security threats, from crossing the border of the newly established state.

[3] Legal contestation of the Prevention of Infiltration Law unfolded between 2010 and 2014 between the state that tried to introduce restrictive measures such as indefinite administrative detention, and human rights organizations that decried basic rights infringements. The state amended the Law four times until it was approved by the court (*Prevention of Infiltration Law (Crimes and Jurisdictions) (Amendment No. 3) 5772*, 2011; *Prevention of Infiltration Law (Crimes and Jurisdiction) (Amendment No. 4 and Temporary Order) 5774*, 2013; *Law for the Prevention of Infiltration and Securing the Departure of Infiltrators from Israel (Legislative Amendments and Temporary Orders) 5775*, 2014). The Law was discussed in three Supreme Court cases (*HCJ 7146/12 Adam v The Knesset*, 2013; *HCJ 8425/13 Gebrselassie, HCJ 7385/13 Eitan et al v The Government of Israel et al*, 2014; *HCJ 8665/14 Desete et al v The Knesset et al*, 2015).

It allows for lengthier enforcement of administrative detention of border-crossers, with fewer procedural protections (Berman 2015; Bracha 1998). Application of this legal category, drawn from security legislation, as a tool for migration control labels this group of African migrants and facilitates a convergence of the migrant and criminal categories (Rosenberg Rubins, 2019).

Over time, the evolution of the infiltrator category from Palestinian border-crossers to African asylum seekers demonstrates how the state apparatuses of both control and punishment can be directed at newly constructed criminal subjects. Sarah Willen has pointed out how Israeli policies towards Palestinians have resonated with state treatment of migrants when: 'certain forms of phenotypic Otherness necessarily indexed criminality and deportability ... [and] these forms of Otherness—like Palestinians' purported "real" Otherness—legitimated verbal abuse, humiliation, and even physical violence' (Willen, 2019, pp. 129–136). State treatment of African asylum seekers, efforts to contain or remove them that are unparalleled with any other migrant group in the state, thus emerge as a form of racist state violence (Ravid, 2022). Importantly, the roots of this treatment emanate from colonial technologies developed to control land and Palestinian populations.

Under the fourth Amendment of the Prevention of Infiltration Law, Israel opened the Holot detention facility in 2013 to detain young, single men from Sudan and Eritrea, many of whom had already resided in the state for several years (Yaron Mesegna and Ramati, 2017). During the five years of its operation, more than 13,000 African men were each held in the Holot facility in the Negev desert for approximately one year. Holot was closed in 2018 due to its high operational costs and reduced efficacy. In preparation for the facility's closure, the state attempted the forced removal of those who remained in Holot to countries in Africa—Uganda and Rwanda (Willen, 2019, p. 205). However, the forced deportation proved illegal and unfeasible and was therefore never realized. The men were then released from Holot and prohibited from residing in several Israeli cities, including Tel Aviv where most services available to this population are provided by NGOs, where men had previously established connections, communities, and networks of support. The men suffered emotional and physical harm during their time in detention, as well as setbacks in their employment and economic and overall well-being (Ravid, 2021).

Physical exclusion by use of detention has become a common strategy of migration control around the globe with the aim of preventing unwanted persons, often from the Global South, from crossing to live, work, or find refuge in the Global North (Bosworth et al., 2018; Franko, 2020; Mountz, 2020, p. 4; Squire, 2009). As in other places, African asylum seekers in Israel had been marked and remarked as unwanted through repeated assertions of their detainability and deportability (De Genova, 2019).

Criminologists have illuminated how racial hierarchies in states' treatment of non-citizens connects border control and penal practices with imperial and colonial legacies (Agozino, 2004; Cunneen, 2011). In Israel, state-enforced exclusion marks black asylum seekers as criminals as it relegates them to the margins of, or away from, Israeli society (Anteby-Yemini, 2017). No other group of migrants has ever been collectively detained or threatened with deportation based on their national origins and mode of entry. While the largest numbers of asylum seekers in Israel are nationals of Russia and East European countries (Population and Immigration Authority, 2020), they were never sent to Holot which was constructed exclusively for the detention of single African men. Detention was an extreme and direct act of state violence to exclude and denigrate a group in its entirety, redrawing the nation's boundary along racial lines grounded in colonial hierarchies.

Connecting Racialized Exclusions

By observing the racialized criminalization of both citizens and non-citizens and indigenous and immigrant populations, I have so far shed light on how the national order is being maintained—a relational racial order that follows a Eurocentric 'grammar of social exclusion' (Yona, 2005, p. 1). Racial distinction thus provides an organizing principle for 'social sorting'. Anne Stoler suggests that we might think of imperial formations 'as scaled genres of rule that in their very making thrive on opaque taxonomies that produce shadow populations—liminally tethered second-class citizens, citizens-in-waiting . . .' (Stoler, 2016, p. 177). She thus highlights an important, productive, aspect of colonial and imperial formations. They not only keep certain groups under constant threat of violence or removal from the polity (whether by way of detainment or expulsion), but also construct them as a threat to the common good or collective order.

When state acts of differentiation are accompanied by control and exclusion, their underpinning logics are revealed:

> Criminalization legitimates excessive policing, the use of state violence, the loss of liberty and diminished social and economic participation. Criminalization also permits an historical and political amnesia in relation to the effects of colonial processes.
> (Cunneen, 2011, p. 257)

Each repeated iteration of racialized exclusion, inflicted upon a different distinct group, is testament to the ongoing and enduring effects of colonialism on both oppressor and oppressed (Cunneen, 2011, p. 249). By connecting the practices of Palestinian population control in the past (and present), with new forms of group criminalization and control of the black populations today, I argue that exclusion and criminalization should be seen as products of racial postcolonial hierarchy. Persistent colonial racism animates the state control that travels across areas and populations to disproportionately target non-white groups.

Conclusion

This chapter has contextualized the present-day dynamics of racialized exclusion and criminalization in Israel's postcolonial situation. Such exclusion is connected to systemic racism directed at Palestinians, but is also part of a broader racialized structure that stems from Israel's Eurocentric approach and persisting coloniality. By examining state exclusion of black citizens and non-citizens in the context of the country's ethnonational and postcolonial racial order, we can better understand how colonial templates of racialized criminalization extend and evolve over time.

The chapter has focused on the exclusion of two racialized groups—Ethiopian Jews, constructed as internal others; and Sudanese and Eritrean asylum seekers, constructed as external threats. Examining the treatment of these two groups in discussion of the criminal question—who the state chooses to exclude or police—and through a postcolonial lens, enables us to trace a coherent line between them and populations racialized and criminalized before them and alongside them. Distinct group exclusions thus emerge as reiterations of the same racialized colonial logics, over time and in evolving forms.

I argue that racialization, criminalization, and exclusion of non-white groups emanate from a Eurocentric postcolonial order of racialized differentiation that was embedded in the Jewish settlement in Palestine. The hierarchical order became ingrained in the state and has gradually evolved to exclude different groups of 'Others': Palestinians, Ethiopian Jewish citizens, and African asylum seekers. The state practices examined above demonstrate how racial formations and hierarchies animate both penal and citizenship regimes. Recognizing their interconnectedness and contextualizing their symbiosis using a postcolonial lens is important for producing a historically situated, critical, and alert criminological enquiry. If we are to decolonize the criminal question, confronting colonial and postcolonial constructs that persist to date is at least a step in the right direction.

References

Abdo, N. and Yuval-Davis, N. (1995) 'Palestine, Israel and the Zionist Settler Project', in Stasiulis, D. and Yuval-Davis, N (eds) *Unsettling Settler Societies: Articulations of Gender, Race, Ethnicity and Class*. London: Sage, pp. 291–322.

Abu-Rabia-Queder, S. (2019) 'The paradox of diversity in the Israeli academia: reproducing white Jewishness and national supremacy', *Race Ethnicity and Education*, 25(2), pp. 231–248.

Adalah (2021) 'Adalah demands Israeli police end mass arrests of Palestinian citizens', *Adalah*, 27 May. Available at: www.adalah.org/en/content/view/10334 (accessed 19 May 2022).

Agozino, B. (2004) 'Imperialism, crime and criminology: Towards the decolonisation of criminology', *Crime, Law and Social Change*, 41(4), pp. 343–358.

Aliverti, A., Carvalho, H., Chamberlen, A. et al. (2021) 'Decolonizing the Criminal Question', *Punishment & Society*, 23(3), pp. 297–316.

Anteby-Yemini, L. (2010) 'On the Margins of Visibility: Ethiopian Olim in Israel', in Lomsky-Feder, E. and Rapoport, T. (eds) *Visibility in Immigration: Body, Gaze, Representation*. Jerusalem: Hakibbutz Hameuchad and Van Leer Institute, pp. 43–67.

Anteby-Yemini, L. (2017) 'African asylum-seekers in Israel: Illegalization, incorporation and race relations', *Hagira*, 7, pp. 7–20.

Bar-Yosef, E. (2013) *Villa in the Jungle*. Jerusalem: Van-Leer Institute and Kibbutz Hameuchad.

Bauman, Z. (2000) 'Social Uses of Law and Order', in Garland, D. and Sparks, R. (eds.) Criminology and Social Theory. Oxford: Oxford University Press.

Bateman, T. (2021) 'Israel-Gaza ceasefire holds despite Jerusalem clash', *BBC News*, 21 May. Available at: www.bbc.com/news/world-middle-east-57195537 (accessed 24 May 2022).

BBC News (2015) 'Israel police clash with Ethiopian Jewish protesters', 4 May. Available at: www.bbc.com/news/world-middle-east-32577452 (accessed 24 May 2022).

BBC News (2019) 'Police clash with Ethiopian Israeli protesters', 3 July. Available at: www.bbc.com/news/av/world-middle-east-48855783 (accessed 23 May 2022).

Beaumont, P. (2016) 'Israel police chief says it is natural to suspect Ethiopians of crime', *The Guardian*, 31 August. Available at: www.theguardian.com/world/2016/aug/31/israel-police-chief-roni-alsheich-natural-suspect-ethiopians-crime (accessed 24 May 2022).

Ben-eliezer, U. (2004) 'Becoming a black Jew: Cultural racism and anti-racism in contemporary Israel', *Social Identities*, 10(2), pp. 245–266.

Ben-Porat, G. and Yuval, F. (2012) 'Minorities in Democracy and Policing Policy: From Alienation to Cooperation', *Policing and Society*, 22(2), pp. 235–252.

Berman, Y. (2015) 'Arrests of Refugees and Asylum Seekers in Israel', in Kritzman-Amir, T. (ed.) *Where Levinsky Meets Asmara: Social and Legal Aspects of Israeli Asylum Policy*. Jerusalem: Van-Leer Institute and Hakibbutz Hameuchad, pp. 147–208.

Bhabha, H. K. (1997) 'The Other Question: The Stereotype and Colonial Discourse', in Newton, K. M. (ed.) *Twentieth-Century Literary Theory: A Reader*. London: Macmillan, pp. 293–301.

Bhambra, G. K. (2014a) 'A Sociological dilemma: Race, segregation and US sociology', *Current Sociology*, 62(4), pp. 472–492.

Bhambra, G. K (2014b) *Connected Sociologies*. London: Bloomsbury.

Bosworth, M., Parmar, A., and Vázquez, Y. (eds) (2018) *Race, Criminal Justice, and Migration Control: Enforcing the Boundaries of Belonging*. Oxford: Oxford University Press.

Bracha, O. (1998) 'Unfortunate or perilous: The infiltrators, the law and the Supreme Court 1948–1954', Tel-Aviv University Law Review ['Iyune mishpat], 21, p. 333.

Central Bureau of Statistics (2020) 'The Ethiopian Population in Israel'. Available at: www.cbs.gov.il/he/mediarelease/DocLib/2020/358/11_20_358b.pdf (accessed 24 May 2022).

Chetrit, S. S. (2010) *Intra-Jewish Conflict in Israel: White Jews, Black Jews*. New York: Routledge.

Cohen, S. (2002) *Folk Devils and Moral Panics: The Creation of the Mods and Rockers*. London: Routledge.

Cunneen, C. (2011) 'Postcolonial Perspectives for Criminology', in Bosworth, M. and Hoyle, C. (eds) *What Is Criminology?* Oxford: Oxford University Press.

Dauvergne, C. (2016) *The New Politics of Immigration and the End of Settler Societies*. New York: Cambridge University Press.

De Genova, N. (2019) 'Detention, deportation, and waiting: Toward a theory of migrant detainability', *Gender a výzkum/Gender and Research*, 20(1), pp. 92–104.

Desai, G. and Nair, S. (2005) *Postcolonialisms: An Anthology of Cultural Theory and Criticism*. Oxford: Berg.

Du Bois, W. E. B. (1897) *The Philadelphia Negro: A Social Study*. Philadelphia, PA: University of Pennsylvania Press.

Duman, Y. H. (2015) 'Infiltrators go home! Explaining xenophobic mobilization against asylum seekers in Israel', *Journal of International Migration and Integration*, 16(4), pp. 1231–1254.

Eglash, R. (2019) 'Police shooting of an Ethiopian Jew prompts a Black Lives Matter moment in Israel', *Washington Post*, 12 July. Available at: www.washingtonpost.com/world/police-shooting-of-an-ethiopian-jew-prompts-a-black-lives-matter-moment-in-israel/2019/07/11/93acbd94-a258-11e9-a767-d7ab84aef3e9_story.html (accessed 23 May 2022).

Erakat, N. (2015) 'Whiteness as property in Israel: Revival, rehabilitation, and removal', *Harvard Journal on Racial & Ethnic Justice*, 31, pp. 69–104.

Fenster, T. (1998) 'Ethnicity, citizenship, planning and gender: The case of Ethiopian immigrant women in Israel', Gender, Place & Culture 5(2), pp. 177–189.

Fine, R. and Parenti, C. (2018) 'Statistical Analysis of Police Data 2007–2017'. Available at: www.iaej.co.il/ wp- cont ent/ uplo ads/ 2019/ 04/נתו נים-משטרת יים-עברית-אגודת-יהודי-אתיו פיה-סופי-Hebrew-Final.pdf (accessed 23 May 2022).

Franko, K. (2020) *The Crimmigrant Other: Migration and Penal Power*. Abingdon: Routledge.

Garland, D. (2001) *The Culture of Control: Crime and Social Order in Contemporary Society*. Oxford: Oxford University Press.

Gibran Muhammad, K. (2010) *The Condemnation of Blackness: Race, Crime, and the Making of Modern Urban America*. Cambridge, MA: Harvard University Press.

Gil, E. (2010) 'A Reexamination of Administrative Detention in a Jewish and Democratic State', in Kremnitzer, M. and Shany, Y. (eds) *Exceptional Measures in the Struggle Against Terrorism*. Jerusalem: Israel Democracy Institute.

Goldberg, D. T. (2021) 'Racial Palestinianization', in Lentin, R. (ed.) *Thinking Palestine*. London: Bloomsbury, pp. 25–45.

Goldberg, D. T. and Quayson, A. (eds.) (2002) *Relocating Postcolonialism*. Oxford: Blackwell.

Goode, E. and Ben-Yehuda, N. (1994) *Moral Panics: The Social Construction of Deviance*. Oxford: Oxford University Press.

Guetzkow, J. and Fast, I. (2016) 'How symbolic boundaries shape the experience of social exclusion: A case comparison of Arab Palestinian citizens and Ethiopian Jews in Israel', American Behavioral Scientist, 60(2), pp. 150–171.

Halbfinger, D. M. and Kershner, I. (2019) 'After a Police Shooting, Ethiopian Israelis Seek a "Black Lives Matter" Reckoning', *The New York Times*, 13 July. Available at: www.nytimes.com/2019/07/13/world/middleeast/ethiopian-israeli-protests-racism.html (accessed 24 May 2022).

Hall, S. (1986) 'Gramsci's relevance for the study of race and ethnicity', *Journal of Communication Inquiry*, 10(2), pp. 5–27.

Hall, S. (1992) 'Chapter 6: The West and the Rest: Discourse and Power', in Hall, S. and Gieben, B. (eds) *Formations of Modernity*. Cambridge: Polity Press, pp. 185–227.

Hall, S. (2017) *The Fateful Triangle: Race, Ethnicity, Nation*. Cambridge, MA: Harvard University Press.

Hall, S., Critcher, C., Jefferson, T. et al. (1978) *Policing the Crisis: Mugging, the State and Law and Order*. London: Macmillan.

Harel, S. (2015) 'Israel's Asylum Apparatus: The Process of Transferring Treatment of Asylum Requests from UNHCR to the State of Israel', in Kritzman-Amir, T., (ed.) *Where Levinsky Meets Asmara: Social and Legal Aspects of Israeli Asylum Policy*. Jerusalem: Van-Leer Institute and Hakibbutz Hameuchad, pp. 43–89.

Hartman, S. (2007) *Lose Your Mother: A Journey Along the Atlantic Slave Route*. New York: Farrar, Straus and Giroux.

Hasisi, B. and Weitzer, R. (2007) 'Police relations with Arabs and Jews in Israel', *British Journal of Criminology*, 47(5), pp. 728–745.

Hirsch, D. (2009) '"We are here to bring the West, not only to ourselves": Zionist occidentalism and the discourse of hygiene in Mandate Palestine', *International Journal of Middle East Studies*, 41(4), pp. 577–594.

Hochman, O. (2015) 'Infiltrators or asylum seekers? Framing and attitudes toward asylum seekers in Israel', *Journal of Immigrant & Refugee Studies*, 13(4), pp. 358–378.

Israel State Comptroller (2012) *Aspects of Ethiopian Jewish Integration-—Substantial flaws in National Program Management*. 63C, Annual Report. Available at: www.mevaker.gov.il/sites/DigitalLibrary/Documents/63c/2013-63c-101-Atyopia.pdf (accessed 24 May 2022).

Israel State Comptroller (2018) *Annual Report 2018—Treatment of Political Asylum Requests*. Annual Reports 68C, 5 August. Available at: www.mevaker.gov.il/he/Reports/Report_627/8eaa80a0-a426-4424-aefa-8fdc4e8b176a/221-zarim-2.pdf (accessed 24 May 2022).

Jamal, A. (2016) 'Mechanisms of Governmentality and Constructing Hollow Citizenship: Arab Palestinians in Israel', in Rouhana, N. N. and Huneidi, S. (eds) *Israel and Its Palestinian Citizens: Ethnic Privileges in the Jewish State*. Cambridge: Cambridge University Press, pp. 159–190.

Jamal, A. (2020) *The Politics of Inclusion and Exclusion in Israeli–Palestinian Relation*. Tel Aviv: The Walter Lebach Institute.

Kedar, A. (2003) 'On the Legal Geography of Ethnocratic Settler States: Notes Towards a Research Agenda', in Holder, J. and Harrison, C. (eds) Law and Geography. Oxford: Oxford University Press, pp. 401–442.

Khazzoom, A. (1999) 'Western culture, ethnic categorisation, and social closure: The backdrop to ethnic inequality in Israel', *Israeli Sociology*, 1(2), pp. 385–428.

Khazzoom, A. (2003) 'The great chain of orientalism: Jewish identity, stigma management, and ethnic exclusion in Israel', *American Sociological Review*, 68(4), pp. 481–510

Kimmerling, B. (2004) *Migrants, Settlers, Natives: The Israeli Society Between Cultural Pluralism and Cultural War*. Tel Aviv: Am Oved.

Kritzman-Amir, T. (2012) 'Refugees and asylum seekers in the State of Israel', *Israel Journal of Foreign Affairs*, 6(3), pp. 97–111.

Lamont, M., Silva, G. M., Welburn, J. S. et al. (2016) *Getting Respect: Responding to Stigma and Discrimination in the United States, Brazil, and Israel*. Princeton, NJ: Princeton University Press.

Lentin, R. (2018) *Traces of Racial Exception: Racializing Israeli Settler Colonialism*. London: Bloomsbury.

Lipsitz, G. (2007) 'The racialization of space and the spatialization of race: Theorizing the hidden architecture of landscape', *Landscape Journal*, 26(1), pp. 10–23.

Maoz, E. (2020) *Living Law: Police and Sovereignty in an Occupation Regime*. Jerusalem: Van-Leer Institute and Hakibbutz Hameuchad.

Massad, J. (1996) 'Zionism's internal others: Israel and the oriental Jews', *Journal of Palestine Studies*, 25(4), pp. 53–68.

Meer, N. (2018) '"Race" and "post-colonialism": Should one come before the other?', *Ethnic and Racial Studies*, 41(6), pp. 1163–1181.

Menashe, D., Kremnitzer, M., and Ghanayim, K. (2017) 'The use of lethal force in effecting arrest', *Bar-Ilan Law Studies*, 3, pp. 703–734.

Mendel, Y. and Ranta, R. (2018) *From the Arab Other to the Israeli Self: Palestinian Culture in the Making of Israeli National Identity*. London: Routledge.

Mengistu, G. and Avraham, E. (2015) '"Others among their own people": The social construction of Ethiopian immigrants in the Israeli national press', *Communication, Culture & Critique*, 8(4), pp. 557–575.

Mesch, G.S. and Talmud, I. (1998) 'The influence of community characteristics on police performance in a deeply divided society: The case of Israel', *Sociological Focus*, 31(3), pp. 233–248.

Ministry of Justice (2018) *Report on the Government Unit for Coordinating the Struggle Against Racism 2018*. Annual Report. Jerusalem: Ministry of Justice.

Ministry of Public Security (2021) 'Summary of "Operation Law and Order" of the Israel Police'. Available at: www.gov.il/en/departments/news/police-restoring-order-030621 (accessed 24 May 2022).

Mizrachi, N. and Herzog, H. (2012) 'Participatory destigmatization strategies among Palestinian citizens, Ethiopian Jews and Mizrahi Jews in Israel', *Ethnic and Racial Studies*, 35(3), pp. 418–435.

Mizrachi, N. and Zawdu, A. (2012) 'Between global racial and bounded identity: Choice of destigmatization strategies among Ethiopian Jews in Israel', Ethnic and Racial Studies, 35(3), pp. 436–452.

Mola, S. (2018) 'I'm Totally Normal: Jewishness, Israeliness and Whiteness as Identity Anchors for Ethiopian Youth's Dealings with Racism in Israel', in Aloni, N. and Amnon, Y. (eds) *Giluy Da'at*, (14), pp. 13–42.

Mountz, A. (2020) *The Death of Asylum: Hidden Geographies of the Enforcement Archipelago*. Minneapolis, MN: University of Minnesota Press.

Nightingale, C. H. (2012) *Segregation: A Global History of Divided Cities*. Chicago, IL: University of Chicago Press.

Offer, S. (2007) 'The Ethiopian community in Israel: Segregation and the creation of a racial cleavage', *Ethnic and Racial Studies*, 30(3), pp. 461–480.

Omi, M. and Winant, H. (1994) *Racial Formation in the United States: From the 1960s to the 1990s*. New York: Routledge.

Omi, M. and Winant, H. (2008) 'Once more, with feeling: Reflections on racial formation', *Publication of the Modern Language Association (PMLA)*, 123(5), pp. 1565–1572.

Palmor, A. (2016) 'Committee against Racism toward Ethiopians Final Report', July. Government of Israel. Available at: http://graphics-lapam.org.il/clients/roam/gizanut/files/assets/common/downloads/A4_migur_report_ALL.pdf (accessed 23 May 2022).

Peled, Y. (2017) 'Delegitimation of Israel or Social-Historical Analysis? The Debate over Zionism as a Colonial Settler Movement', in Jacobs, J. (ed.) *Jews and Leftist Politics: Judaism, Israel, Antisemitism, and Gender*. Cambridge: Cambridge University Press.

Phillips, C., Bowling, B., and Parmar, A. (2003) 'Policing Ethnic Minority Communities', in Newburn, T, (ed.) *Handbook of Policing*. Cullompton: Willan, pp. 528–555.

Population and Immigration Authority (2020) *Data on Foreigners in Israel*. Ministry of Interior. Available at: www.gov.il/BlobFolder/generalpage/foreign_workers_stats/he/ZARIM_q4_2020.pdf (accessed 23 May 2022).

Ram, U. (2019) 'Sociopolitical Cleavages in Israel', in Hazan, R. Y., Dowty, A., Hofnung, M. et al. (eds.) *The Oxford Handbook of Israeli Politics and Society*. Oxford: Oxford University Press.

Ravid, M. (2021) 'Criminalisation and Detention of African Asylum Seekers in Israel: Exclusionary Policies, and the Dynamics of Race and Place', PhD thesis. Oxford: University of Oxford.

Ravid, M. (2022) 'Making their lives miserable: Structural violence and state racism towards asylum seekers from Sudan and Eritrea in Israel', *Journal of State Crime* 11(1), pp. 128–148.

Raz-Krakotzkin, A. (2005) 'Zionist Return to the West and the Mizrachi Jewish Perspective', in Penslar, D. J. and Kalmar, I. (eds) *Orientalism and the Jews*. Waltham, MA: Brandeis University Press, pp. 162–181.

Rosenberg Rubins, R (2019) 'Crimmigration as Population management in the "control society"', *New Criminal Law Review*, 22(3), pp. 236–300.

Rouhana, N. N. and Sabbagh-Khoury, A. (2015) 'Settler-colonial citizenship: Conceptualizing the relationship between Israel and its Palestinian citizens', *Settler Colonial Studies*, 5(3), pp. 205–225.

Sabbagh-Khoury, A. (2021) 'Tracing settler colonialism: A genealogy of a paradigm in the sociology of knowledge production in Israel', *Politics & Society*, 50(1), pp 44–83.

Sa'di, A. H. (2014) *Thorough Surveillance: The Genesis of Israeli Policies of Population Management, Surveillance and Political Control towards the Palestinian Minority*. Manchester: Manchester University Press.

Said, E. W. (1978) *Orientalism*. London: Routledge & Kegan Paul.

Said, E. W. (1992) *The Question of Palestine*. New York: Vintage Books.

Salamon, H. (2003) 'Blackness in transition: Decoding racial constructs through stories of Ethiopian Jews', *Journal of Folklore Research*, 40(1), pp. 3–32.

Schaeffer Omer-Man, E. (2017) 'Extrajudicial killing with near impunity: Excessive force by Israeli law enforcement against Palestinians', *Boston University International Law Journal*, 35, pp. 115–157.

Shadmi, E. (1998) 'Police and Police Reform in Israel: The Formative Role of the State', in Friedmann, R. R. (ed.) *Crime and Criminal Justice in Israel: Assessing the Knowledge Base toward the Twenty-First Century*. Albany, NY: State University of New York Press, pp. 207–244.

Shadmi, E. (2012) *The Fortified Land*. Tel Aviv: Hakibbutz Hameuchad.

Shafir, G. and Peled, Y. (1998) 'Citizenship and stratification in an ethnic democracy', *Ethnic and Racial Studies*, 21(3), pp. 408–427.

Shalhoub-Kevorkian, N. (2016) 'Settler Colonialism, Surveillance, and Fear', in Rouhana, N. N. and Huneidi, S, (eds) Israel and *Its Palestinian Citizens: Ethnic Privileges in the Jewish State*. Cambridge: Cambridge University Press, pp. 336–367.

Shenhav, Y. A. (2006) *The Arab Jews: A Postcolonial Reading of Nationalism, Religion, and Ethnicity*. Stanford, CA: Stanford University Press.

Shenhav, Y. A., Hever, H., and Motzafi-Haller, P. (eds) (2002) *Mizrahim in Israel: A Critical Observation into Israel's Ethnicity*. Jerusalem: The Van Leer Jerusalem Institute and Hakibbutz Hameuchad.

Shetreet, S. (1984) 'A Contemporary Model of Emergency Detention Law: An Assessment of the Israeli Law', in Dinstein, Y. (ed.) *Israel Yearbook on Human Rights*. Aylesbury: Brill, pp. 182–220.

Shohat, E. (1988) 'Sephardim in Israel: Zionism from the standpoint of its Jewish victims', *Social Text*, 19/20, pp. 1–35.

Shohat, E. (1992) 'Notes on the "post-colonial" ', *Social Text*, 31/32, pp. 99–113.

Smooha, S, (1976) *Pluralism and Conflict in Israel: An Anthology on Mizrahi-Ashkenazi, Religious-Secular, Arabs-Jewish Relations*. Haifa: Haifa University.

Squire, V. (2009) *The Exclusionary Politics of Asylum*. London: Palgrave Macmillan.

Stoler, A. L. (2016) *Duress: Imperial Durabilities in Our Times*. Durham, NC: Duke University Press.

Sultany, N. (2012) 'The making of an underclass: The Palestinian citizens in Israel', *Israel Studies Review*, 27(2), pp. 190–200.

Swirski, S. and Swirski, B. (2002) 'Ethiopian Jews in Israel: Housing, Employment, and Education', *Information on Equality*, 11. Available at: https://adva.org/wp-content/uploads/2014/09/gil11.pdf (accessed 24 May 2022).

TOI Staff (2015) 'Ethiopian–Israeli protest against police brutality turns violent, over a dozen hurt', *The Times of Israel*, 30 April. Available at: www.timesofisrael.com/jlem-street-blocked-in-protest-over-police-brutality-against-ethiopian-born-israelis/ (accessed 24 May 2022).

Tzfadia, E. and Yacobi, H. (2011) *Rethinking Israeli Space: Periphery and Identity*. London: Routledge.

Veracini, L. (2006) *Israel and Settler Society*. London: Pluto.

Wacquant, L. (2008) *Urban Outcasts: A Comparative Sociology of Advanced Marginality*. Cambridge: Polity.

Walsh, S. D. and Tuval-Mashiach, R. (2012) 'Ethiopian emerging adult immigrants in Israel: Coping with discrimination and racism', *Youth & Society*, 44(1), pp. 49–75.

Willen, S. S. (2019) *Fighting for Dignity: Migrant Lives at Israel's Margins*. Philadelphia, PA: University of Pennsylvania Press.

Yacobi, H. (2015) *This Is No Africa: Boundaries, Territory, Identity*. Jerusalem: Van Leer Institute Press and Hakibbutz Hameuchad.

Yaron, L. (2016) '90% of Ethiopian adolescents convicted of a crime are sent to prison compared to one quarter of established Israelis', *Haaretz*, 20 September. Available at: www.haaretz.co.il/news/law/1.3073821 (accessed 24 May 2022).

Yaron Mesegna, H. and Ramati, O. (2017) 'Where time stands still: Holot detention facility and the Israeli anti-infiltration law', *Hagira*, 7, pp. 67–83.

Yona, Y. (2005) *In Virtue of Difference the Multicultural Project in Israel.* Jerusalem: Van Leer Institute Press and Hakibbutz Hameuchad.

Young, J. (1999) *The Exclusive Society: Social Exclusion, Crime and Difference in Late Modernity.* London: Sage.

Zawdu, A. and Willen, S. S. (2019) 'Immigration Dynamics and Changing Constructions of Jewish Nativeness in Israel', in Hazan, R. Y., Dowty, A., Hofnung, M. et al. (eds) *The Oxford Handbook of Israeli Politics and Society*. Oxford: Oxford University Press.

Ziegler, R. (2015) 'No asylum for "infiltrators": The legal predicament of Eritrean and Sudanese nationals in Israel', *Journal of Immigration, Asylum and Nationality Law*, 29(2), pp. 172–191.

11

Coloniality and Structural Violence in the Criminalization of Black and Indigenous Populations in Brazil

Hugo Leonardo Rodrigues Santos

Introduction: Coloniality and the Criminalization of the Subaltern

Colonial legacies strongly reverberate in the practices of punitive agencies and in the processes of criminalization of subaltern populations (Spivak, 2010). In Brazil, the long-term enslavement of black and indigenous people and the structural violence that still affects these populations deeply mark the work of the police and criminal justice. In this regard, one can state that the *racialized social stratification* which characterized the colonial society is not a past reality (Quijano, 2009, p. 107). On the contrary, there is a genuine *space of experience* caused by colonial exploitation, which marks the present time and the *horizon of expectation* concerning the changing of penal institutions historically created in a racialized way (Koselleck, 2006).

The consequences of coloniality for black and indigenous people are still experienced today, impacting on their wider vulnerability to violence and to processes of criminalization. Therefore, the future and past of punitive social control are interconnected, which demands that the goals for implementing a more democratic criminal system and for interrupting the dynamics of victimization of these social groups depend on overcoming this structure, by means of a process of decoloniality. The colonial model imposed on Brazil resulted in a kind of sub-citizenship of these marginalized social groups, due to an excluding and authoritarian process of peripheral modernization. Thus, within Brazilian society, there is a *rabble* (*'ralé'*; Souza, 2016) that embraces a significant number of black and indigenous Brazilians. This enormous contingent of the population evidently represents the effects of socio-economic and political inequality in the country, since the representatives of these social strata have huge difficulties in accessing the most elementary rights and are disproportionally subjected to imprisonment and to the dynamics of violence. Following this reasoning, it is worthy of note that coloniality promotes racial stratification, which dehumanizes non-white populations.

These groups represent *the other* in colonial society, the opposite to the intended civility brought by modernity. Without the premise of inequality between, on the one hand, the white/European and, on the other, native and black peoples, essential for the

Hugo Leonardo Rodrigues Santos, Coloniality and Structural Violence in the *Criminalization of Black and Indigenous Populations in Brazil* In: *Decolonizing the Criminal Question.* Edited by: Ana Aliverti, Henrique Carvalho, Anastasia Chamberlen, and Máximo Sozzo, Oxford University Press. © Hugo Leonardo Rodrigues Santos 2023. DOI: 10.1093/oso/9780192899002.003.0012

colonial project, the subjugation or even the destruction of these peoples would not be possible (Todorov, 2019, p. 211). Mark Brown (2002) has a point when he states that, in the colonial context, the increasing severity of punishment, which at first glance would seem strange to the *civilizing progress* proclaimed by the modernity of the penal system, would actually be a consequence of the continuity of modernity, which *includes structural violence and punitive excess in its colonial governance*. The overemphasized analytical approach of criminology in the Global North loses sight of these features, which makes essential the study of punitive control in periphery societies, including for a better understanding of criminal subjects in countries at the hub (Fonseca, 2018, p. 67).

This chapter aims to assess the repercussion of colonization in the structure of the Brazilian punitive system, joining forces to decolonize criminology. It suggests that historic reflections about the criminal issue in Brazil can contribute to a decolonizing agenda for its criminal justice system. To that end, it will first consider how Brazilian colonization drew on social processes of racialization to produce punitive social control of indigenous and black peoples. Thereupon, some changes that occurred at the end of the nineteenth century and the beginning of the twentieth century will be highlighted, such as the formal abolition of slavery and the advent of the republic, in order to demonstrate their effects on punitive practices against racialized groups. In sequence, by means of two paradigmatic examples, the chapter will analyse how these social practices and representations linked to coloniality are connected to the current processes of criminalization of black and indigenous populations. The penultimate section will explain how the criminal punishment of indigenous peoples works as a *mechanism* for their *civilizing inclusion*, by means of neutralizing their ethnic and cultural bonds. Lastly, the chapter will highlight how structural racism distorts police approaches, inciting the racial selection of the main targets of vigilance.

Brazil has a Huge Past Ahead

Since the beginning of the colonization of Brazil in the sixteenth century, the indigenous populations have been subjected to forced labour. Over the years, difficulties of transporting and distributing the natives throughout the vast Brazilian territory and the consolidation of the transatlantic market of enslaved Africans contributed to gradually replace the indigenous workforce with that of black captives. Notwithstanding that history, the enslavement of the natives has not suddenly ceased; in some Brazilian regions, it has remained massively exploited (Monteiro, 2000). Furthermore, an enormous contingent of the population has been eradicated since their first contact with the Europeans, either as a result of wars or due to diseases against which they had no immunity (Alencastro, 2000, pp. 127–133). Some estimates indicate that millions of indigenous people were killed in this process, and in some areas the native populations were completely decimated. The indigenous population of Brazil currently stands at around 800,000 people (Cunha, 2012, p. 14). On the other hand, with regard to the black population, Brazil received around 46 per cent of all the enslaved Africans who landed in the Americas—which represents about 4.8 million people brought to Brazil (Alencastro, 2018, p. 60). With almost half of the enslaved Africans in the Americas as part of its demographic formation, Brazilian mechanisms of social control were developed on the basis of racialized logics, characterized by an intense oppression against the black population (Flauzina, 2008).

Brazil became independent from the Portuguese Crown in 1822 and adopted an imperial regime—in contrast to what happened with its neighbouring countries in South America which opted to establish republican governments. Since the nineteenth century, the indigenous issue has gradually moved its central axis away from the needs of the workforce and has become increasingly related to land disputes (Cunha, 2012, p. 56). The indigenous peoples started to be classified, from a very simplistic point of view, as *tame* or *wild*. With regard to the latter, there was a broad political discussion concerning what should be done about them, with opinions varying from assimilating them into civilization or simply exterminating them. In 1823, José Bonifácio de Andrada e Silva suggested to the Constitutional Assembly that the wild indigenous people should be moved to villages and catechized (Silva, 2002), aiming at inserting them into the Brazilian *modernizing project*. The seeming kindness of this proposition should not overshadow the engagement with an authoritarian solution that intended to submit the native populations to law and to work. However, the proposition was not formally accepted and there was no mention of indigenist policies in the constitutional charter enacted in 1824. Even so, after centuries of bloody exploitation—with the declaration of just wars, the enslavement of indigenous people, and the siege against native tribes—the official discourse recommended the use of *soft means* when dealing with indigenous people, in spite of the establishment of military deployments to fight against rebellious indigenous people in some regions of particular interest (Cunha, 2012, pp. 63–67).

On the other hand, the enslavement of the Africans was the mainstay of the Brazilian socio-economic structure for many centuries, including the nineteenth century. After a fruitless attempt to hinder the slave trade into Brazil in 1831, Law 581—also known as the Eusébio de Queiroz Law—passed on 4 September 1850, was successful in abolishing the slave trade, while simultaneously intensifying the internal trade of the enslaved between different Brazilian provinces (Mamigonian, 2017, p. 292). Resistance by the captives (Moura, 2020), as well as *haitianism*,[1] stimulated the implementation of immigration policies aiming at whitening the Brazilian population concomitant with a gradual—and quite late—emancipation of the captive population (Azevedo, 2004, pp. 50–64).

In relation to the punitive control of the captives, it is important to note that public punishment of slaves coexisted with the power to punish held by their masters in the private domain (Batista, 2012). In 1830, the Empire Criminal Code was published; whilst it reinforced civil rights and promoted legality and proportionality between crime and punishment, highlighting imprisonment as the main criminal sanction and the limited the use of capital punishment (by hanging), it also allowed the imposition of galleys (forced labour) and flogging predominantly of slaves (Machado Neto, 1977, pp. 77–79). The equity which the individualization of punishment relied upon was not observed for the enslaved, who could be subjected to harsh punishments even though they were not considered rights-bearing subjects (Silva, 2004, p. 97). Apart from an apparent paradox, this idiosyncrasy should be understood against the background

[1] *Haitianism* referred to a fear that tormented the elite of an uprising of captives against their masters, such as in the Haitian Revolution (Morel, 2017, pp. 227–240) (Queiroz, 2017).

that the above-mentioned law sought a hard conciliation between the precepts of liberalism and the structures of a patriarchal and slave-based society. In this regard, the history of Brazilian criminal justice supposes a *reinterpretation of the concept of modernity* (Silva, 2004, p. 100).

Assuming that capital punishment should be understood as a complex exercise formed by social practices, institutional arrangements, and cultural shaping (Garland, 2010, p. 14), the peculiarities of the death sentence by hanging in the Brazilian Empire should also be acknowledged. Therefore, *haitianism* and the advent of uprisings by the captives—especially the Carrancas and Malê Revolts, respectively in Minas Gerais and Bahia—stimulated the creation of a law on 10 June 1835 which facilitated the sentencing to death of the enslaved for murder or attempted murder of their masters or foremen. The death penalty could also be applied to free men, but it was more common for those who were convicted and executed to be the enslaved (Ribeiro, 2005, pp. 314–315). Indeed, the last documented judicial execution in Brazil, in 1876, in Pilar in the province of Alagoas, was the hanging of slave Francisco who was convicted for murdering his masters (Lima Júnior, 1979). That notwithstanding, it is noteworthy that, after 1850, Emperor Pedro II often used his reserve power[2] to commute the death penalty of slaves to perpetual galley punishment (Azevedo, 2010, p. 67). As many captives preferred to submit themselves to the galleys than to remain under their masters' domination, there were cases in which the crimes they committed orchestrated risky strategies that aimed to improve their living conditions (Azevedo, 2010, pp. 68–85). For instance, some murderers surrendered and confessed their acts to the authorities immediately after they had committed their crimes. Presumably, some enslaved people believed that penal justice would be more benevolent and fairer to them than the treatment imposed by their masters (Machado, 2014, p. 40).

The next section will explore how coloniality continued to mark Brazilian social practices even after the formal abolishment of the slave-based regime and the establishment of the republican regime. This aims to demonstrate that, with its basis on justification by means of a new scientism-based and supposedly modern paradigm, indigenous and black peoples were still selected as the main targets of the punitive system, by means of racialized processes of criminalization.

The Authoritarian Republican Progress

The elites' need to expand their control over the mass of poor and non-white people increased during the nineteenth century, following the crisis of slavery and the social movements in favour of the emancipation of captives. Thus, on the verge of the formal abolition of slavery, which occurred only with the approval of the Golden Law on 13 May 1888—Brazil was, henceforth, the last country in the *Black Atlantic* (Gilroy, 2012) to abolish slavery—some efforts to intensify policing on the streets were seen. The police institutions sought to keep public order by targeting mainly felons, slaves, freed slaves, and immigrants (Machado, 1994, p. 69). Freed men from subaltern populations

[2] This is a remnant of absolutism inserted in the Imperial Constitution, which granted the monarch the prerogative of *balancing* the executive, legislative, and judiciary powers.

were submitted to intense social control. There were several mechanisms used to enforce discipline, which were not limited to the traditional apparatus of the criminal justice system, such as the police and prison. For many years, the army served to discipline the free workforce, aiding criminal justice by means of forced recruitment and exile (Beattie, 2009, p. 38). Also worthy of note were actions of the private exercise of punishment and justice by means of *mandonismo* practised by landowners and local leaders, who often guaranteed order by imposing violence (Franco, 1997, p. 159).

In a society characterized by centuries of slavery, its formal abolition represented an important and even traumatic rupture, since it dissolved well-settled social arrangements marked by subordination and social control (Albuquerque, 2009, p. 97). In 1889, the imperial regime ended with the Proclamation of the Republic. This period coincided with (and stimulated) the arrival of new positivist ideas in Brazil, which brought with them a set of new *scientific* explanations about criminality as well as suggestions on how to prevent it. These explanations offered by Italian criminal anthropology were welcomed in Latin America and thereafter a new paradigm, which gradually moved away from the precepts of liberalism and used new evolutionist and racial theories to understand and deal with criminality, was established in the country (Del Olmo, 2004, p. 173). Thereby, 'the same models that explained the Brazilian underdevelopment in comparison with the Western World were used to justify new forms of inferiority'[3] (Schwarcz, 2010, p. 28).

This provided a very convenient—as well as a very persuasive, since it was based on the then existing science—excuse for the elite to emerge in that historic moment to support the *unequal treatment of unequal beings* (Alvarez, 2003, p. 240), which promptly contributed to the intensification of punitive controls. The translation of Lombroso's ideas and those of his followers was not a mere reproduction of its original source, since there had often been creative adaptions of the precepts of positivism in accordance with the specific needs of Brazilian society (Sozzo, 2006, pp. 379–384). Thus, the contextualization of the new penal discourse with regard to the demography of Latin American countries fostered the development of racialized theses to legitimate the punitive control of subaltern social segments.

To exemplify the racialized tone of this interpretation, mention should be made of Nina Rodrigues, one of the founders of forensic medicine in Brazil and professor of the Faculty of Medicine of Bahia, whom Lombroso himself called *the apostle of criminal anthropology in the New World* (Corrêa, 1998, p. 82). This author defended a determinist conception of behaviour—refuting what he used to call the *illusion of freedom*—which resulted in a predisposition for delinquency by the *inferior races*—especially, *indigenous, black, and multiracial people* (Rodrigues, 1933 [1894], pp. 111–130). Based on this premise, he criticized the unification of Brazilian criminal law, stating that these Codes should be constituted by taking into account climatic differences and the racial formation in different Brazilian regions (Rodrigues, 1933 [1894], pp. 207–211). His work designed an original model of racial control, based on scientific theories, which responded to the Brazilian white elite's desires (Góes, 2016, p. 23).

[3] Original in Portuguese: 'os mesmos modelos que explicavam o atraso brasileiro em relação ao mundo ocidental passavam a justificar novas formas de inferioridade'.

This criminological discourse was used to subject indigenous and black peoples to existing punitive mechanisms (Del Olmo, 2004, p. 175).

The Brazilian legislation did not closely follow the positivist guidelines—which is also characteristic of Latin America, whose Criminal Codes from this period adopted a *classical tendency* (Del Olmo, 2004, p. 170). Consequently, the first republican Criminal Code, passed in 1890, was severely criticized, especially for being considered anachronistic as it did not establish the modern positivist propositions then in vogue, opting instead for maintaining its *excessively liberal* structure. According to Nilo Batista, the Code failed from a political point of view, since it did not adhere as expected to the propagated need for criminalization of *social targets* from that historical time frame. So much so, that rules that allowed the selective persecution of these undesired groups were created by additional laws or laws that reformed the original Code (Zaffaroni and Batista, 2003, p. 446). Certainly, this did not obstruct the criminalization of conduct practised by the *insignificant people* ('*gente miúda*') who formed the poorest section of the population, including those who had recently been freed from the slavery. In that regard, many criminal offences in the republican Code were directed at the *usual suspects*: the poor and the non-white (Serra, 2017, p. 111). Some examples are the criminalization of begging, vagrancy, alcoholism, *capoeira*,[4] shamanism, among other everyday social practices usually related to black and indigenous Brazilians.

Nonetheless, the *emphasis on reality*, so characteristic of the positivist discourse, resulted in propositions for reform of the punitive system not being predominantly of a juridical nature. Therefore, unlike the legislative structure which kept its traditional features, many institutions related to criminal justice were profoundly changed in accordance with this scientific ideology, which could explain why the positivist paradigm lasted for so long in spite of some severe criticism (Sontag, 2014, p. 216). For example, in the field of healthcare—a particularly important subject within the positivist project—the faculties of medicine created modules for forensic medicine, incorporating content concerning positive criminology, scientific societies and journals, as well as laboratories for criminal anthropology (Schwarcz, 2010, pp. 189–238; Ferla, 2009, pp. 64–154).

The police also underwent sensitive changes during this period. The untrained and unstructured police forces struggled to adapt to social changes and to the urbanization of the cities. A clearer segregation of the population during the empire allowed a less complex selection of social groups to be subjected to policing. In contrast, in the republican regime, the emergence of the middle classes in society hindered the distinction between workers and vagrants that the police were used to, so that a mistake in identifying a felon could have repercussions for the corporation (Bretas, 2018, p. 141). In any event, police control over the *rabble* made use of the enlargement of their scope of action—the police were authorized to prosecute *ex officio* individuals who were considered to have committed several criminal infringements by Law 628 passed on 2h October 1899—and of the inaccurate semantics of some vague categories, such as *vagrancy* and *begging*, to enlarge the set of people who could be classified as delinquent. This allowed the police to discipline the lower classes by imposing rules of conduct in the Brazilian cities (Bretas, 2018, p. 144).

[4] A mixture of dance and martial arts connected to the black culture that was often used as a practice of resistance.

The use of police violence against selected social targets was sometimes contrary to the existing juridic parameters. Indeed, it is characteristic of Latin American criminal justice systems to make use of illicit or non-institutionalized resources, giving rise to a *subterranean punitive control* (Zaffaroni, 2003, p. 15). In this regard, imprisonment in penal institutions and other modern punitive techniques were sometimes considered inappropriate for punishing the *uncivilized masses*, which led to the use of more *traditional* means of punishment for those social groups (Aguirre, 2009, p. 40). This explains the police *habitus* of arbitrary practices which were deemed not to require the observance of due process, such as *varejamentos* (search and seizure without a judicial warrant), correctional imprisonments and custody *for investigation*, and detention in contravention of legal rules (Valença, 2018, pp. 202–207). It is also worthy of note that such police discretion was always taken into account in the identification of people submitted to police control. Therefore, the power of identifying and labelling certain individuals as delinquents or potentially dangerous presumed a specific notion about *individual constitutions*, either expressed by a scientific language or due to *street knowledge* (Cunha, 2002, p. 55).

Racialized criminalization processes, an expression of Brazilian coloniality, continue to produce concrete effects in the punitive system of Brazil, as can be attested from the use of imprisonment to integrate the indigenous people into the Brazilian hegemonic society and from the racial selectivity adopted by the police against the black population.

The Integration of the Indigenous People by Means of Punishment

Coloniality results in systematic violence suffered by indigenous peoples, practised not only by the state itself and its agents, but also by many others interested in maintaining the marginalization of indigenous populations by denying their rights. The wounds inflicted on this population are numerous, covering symbolic violence (by not recognizing their cultural identity and by means of *epistemicide*), the denial of rights that are essential to the survival of these people (such as the non-demarcation of lands, deforestation, and predatory exploitation of their lands by farmers and miners), and, unfortunately, in increasingly numerous cases, personal violence which may result in the assassination of members of their communities (Carvalho et al., 2020). The omission or denial of rights by the state has seriously affected indigenous peoples.

Notwithstanding the enormous importance of understanding these structural processes of victimization, this chapter will focus on the repercussion of the dynamics of criminalization of indigenous peoples relating to their cultural identity. It should be noted, however, that both phenomena are linked, as the denial of rights of indigenous groups and individuals may lead to their marginalization and social deprivation, which in turn leverages criminalization (Nolan et al., 2020, p. 30). The discussion of socio-economic and/or cultural factors (De Maglie, 2017) that engender processes of criminalization against indigenous populations is also beyond the scope of this chapter, as they are diverse and could not even be brought together in a unified analysis. Furthermore, although there are reports of situations in which indigenous leaders have been criminalized with the aim of politically weakening their organization or due to agrarian interests, most of these charges and imprisonments have been linked to the practice of offences by indigenous individuals—such as theft, robbery, homicide, drug-related crimes, sex crimes, among others—with no allusion to political motivation (Silva, 2013, p. 150).

The 'indigenist' policy instituted at the beginning of the republican regime, clearly influenced by positivism, presumes the inferiority of the native population, denying their cultural identity and their dignity. It was believed that the indigenous peoples would gradually disappear as a distinct ethnic group as they would be assimilated into society as a whole (Araújo Júnior, 2018, p. 176). In fact, the opinion that prevailed was that the existence of native populations was a *civilizational lag*. In this regard, the explanation by Nelson Hungria, one of the main authors of the Criminal Code promulgated in 1940—still in force with substantive parts of its original version maintained—regarding the reason for why the status of the '*silvícolas*' ('wild folk') was intentionally not mentioned in the rules of criminal liability, while describing the circumstances of *incomplete or delayed mental development* in Article 22, is instructive. As stated by the author:

> the Revision Committee understood that within such notion would be included, by extensive interpretation, the wild folk, avoiding that an explicit allusion to them would allow others to falsely presume, abroad, that we are still a country infested by heathens.
>
> (Hungria, 1958, p. 337, emphasis added)[5]

The Statute of the Indigenous, a special law passed in 1973—thus, during the most repressive period of the civic–military dictatorship—and still in force, established that indigenous individuals who were convicted of a criminal offence should have their punishment mitigated, and the judge should consider their degree of social integration when sentencing (art. 56, *caput*). It also stipulated that sentences of deprivation of liberty should be served under the special system of 'semi-liberty', in some location next to their communities (art. 56, *parágrafo único*). Moreover, it allowed the adoption of penalties considered to be appropriate by the indigenous culture to which the individual belonged, provided that it was not a cruel or humiliating punishment or the death penalty (art. 57). The seeming benevolence of this legislation—which sounds paradoxical when compared to the treatment that the military regime used to mete out to the native communities[6]—was the origin of the *myth of the non-liability of the indigenous*, which stated that offences practised by indigenous people would be exempt of

[5] Original in Portuguese: '.a Comissão Revisora entendeu que sob tal rubrica estariam, por interpretação extensiva, os silvícolas, evitando-se que uma expressa alusão a estes fizesse supor falsamente, no estrangeiro, que ainda somos um país infestado de gentio'.

[6] Serious violations against the indigenous populations were practised by state agents during the Brazilian civic–military regime which ruled between 1964 and 1985. For instance, in the lands of the Krenak, in Minas Gerais, a reformatory was run between 1969 and 1972 which served as a concentration and forced labour camp for indigenous people from several nations who were arbitrarily labelled as *deviants*. Likewise, the indigenous rural guard, a militarized police force formed by indigenous individuals, was created, moving those recruited away from their ethnic and cultural bonds (Simi, 2021). For a detailed report on the *genocidal integrationist policy* adopted by the military, which included bombardment of indigenous villages, massacres, and decapitations, see Valente, 2017.

penalties as they were considered to have been done by individuals with *incomplete or delayed mental development*, according to the Criminal Code. This notwithstanding, the idea is absolutely wrong, since the previously mentioned special law—the Statute of the Indigenous—sustains the criminal responsibility of the indigenous (Lacerda, 2011, p. 18). In fact, contrary to the myth, the number of indigenous people arrested has increased in recent years (Nolan et al., 2020, p. 33) in spite of the under-reporting of this data, as will be discussed later.

Some scholars have defended the punitive system used as an authoritarian mechanism for integrating the indigenous people into Brazilian society, since the criminal institutions do not recognize the cultural and ethnic differences of the offenders that come from this group (Baines, 2009, p. 184) (Silva, 2013, p. 152). However, specific rights regarding sentences being served without the offender losing their indigenous cultural bonds are not observed. Therefore, the punishment aims to annihilate the offender's ethnic identity. As explained by Tédney Moreira da Silva:

> this, therefore, means the exercise of a *civilising penalty*, i.e., of an ethnocidal political tactic for neutralising or, even, suppressing the ethnic diversity, which is identified in the investigated or accused individual, by means of a juridical discourse that declares their process of assimilation by the *national society* as complete.
>
> (Silva, 2016, p. 58)[7]

Many criminal justice actors are prejudiced against indigenous defendants, adopting a Eurocentric position by not making any effort to understand their cultural differences (Pontes, 2014, pp. 202–203). The classification of indigenous individuals as criminally liable is based on stereotypes in an effort to deprive them of their specific ethnic–cultural nature; to be considered criminally responsible, it is enough that they have mastered the Portuguese language, hold official documents, or perform paid work (Silva, 2016, pp. 58–59), among other circumstantial observations that do not accurately indicate their ethnic identity. This illustrates the importance of the anthropological report, which is usually dispensed with even though it is known that such study could provide deeper insights about matters of identity, understood as dynamic, relational, and situational social constructions (Amorim, 2014, p. 164). The ethnic self-identification of accused individuals is usually ignored from the start of the police investigation through to the execution of the sentence, which disrespects the *special legal status of indigenous peoples* (Silva, 2013, p. 142). At other times, inmates do not identify themselves as members of a different ethnic group, due to the existing prejudice against indigenous people and '*caboclos*' in the society (Baines, 2009, p. 184).

It is thus not surprising that official statistics regarding the imprisonment of indigenous individuals[8] are under-reported—as these are based on classification by skin

[7] Original in Portuguese: '[t]rata-se, assim, do exercício de uma *penalidade civilizatória*, isto é, de uma tática política etnocida de neutralização ou, mesmo, de supressão da diversidade étnica, que se faz presente no investigado ou acusado, por meio da comunicação de um discurso jurídico que afirma completo o seu processo de assimilação à *sociedade nacional*'.

[8] In Brazil, imprisonment data are compiled by the Ministry of Justice in a periodic report titled Infopen (BRASIL, 2019).

colour assigned by third parties rather than on self-declaration. Hence, many indigenous individuals are wrongly classified as '*pardos*' ('browns'), which obscures the punitive reality against indigenous peoples (Silva, 2013, p. 147). Another consequence of the denial of the ethnic identity of the criminalized is the intensification of the *pain of imprisonment* due to disruption of community bonds and being treated as a non-indigenous person, contrary to what is determined by the Statute of the Indigenous (Lacerda, 2011, pp. 21–23). This obstructs visits to offenders while in prison and their access to legal assistance and to court interpreters, among other rights.

The processes of the criminalization of indigenous peoples are thus the reflection of a colonialist logic that imposes an authoritarian integration of the native population into Brazilian society by means of their ethnic disfigurement. Indeed:

> the criminalization of indigenous peoples in Brazil directly follows from centuries of localising, settling, and assimilating indigenous peoples in order to integrate them by means of disciplinary actions and policies that integrate them into the *national fellowship*—and would this not be the generic way of *reintegrating the prisoners* into society?
>
> (Silva, 2013, p. 148, emphasis in original)[9]

Racial Selectivity in Brazilian Policing

The fact that Brazil has relied on colonization and slavery for many centuries has deeply affected how black people are currently placed in society, particularly impacting on the persistent racial inequality in respect of the distribution of poverty (Osorio, 2019, p. 29). Coloniality also affects the emergence of subjectivities. For instance, the thoughts of Frantz Fanon regarding the marks that colonial racism left on the subjectivity of the black population (Fanon, 2008) are well known. It is possible to state, in this regard, that racism is inherently linked to the Brazilian social structure. Thus, 'individual behaviour and institutional processes result from a society whose racism is a rule and not an exception'[10] (Almeida, 2019, p. 50).

As previously stated, Brazilian criminology was historically built on racist precepts, poorly disguised by scientific efforts towards an alleged (exclusionary) modernization of the country. Regarding this matter, it must be highlighted that:

> the racist criminological discourse, by bringing the criminal closer to the savage, acquires new outlines. It might be understood as an ideology that confuses the aggressiveness and the alienation of men subjected to the colonisation process as their intrinsic

[9] Original in Portuguese: 'a criminalização indígena no Brasil vem a reboque de práticas seculares de localização, fixação e assimilação dos indígenas com vistas a integrá-los por meio de ações e políticas de disciplinarização que os integrem à *comunhão nacional*—e não seria esta a forma genérica de *ressocializar os presos* para sua restituição à sociedade?'

[10] Original in Portuguese: 'comportamentos individuais e processos institucionais são derivados de uma sociedade cujo racismo é regra e não exceção'.

> evilness, classifying as a criminal way of life every means of surviving the colonial reality, of adapting to the imposed models and to the selective violence suffered by them, and especially every human biological diversity distinct from the European standards and every cultural expression able to enable responses, even is symbolic, to the loss of identity due to the colonialising process.[11]
>
> (Duarte, 2017, p. 106)

These discourses associated with criminological positivism are compounded on a daily basis by common sense, by producing *regimes of truth* that connect black youth with delinquency and social danger, turning them into *lives that could be killed* (Morais, 2019, p. 219). Putting this together with factors of victimization that affect this social group, it is not surprising that lethal violence in Brazil has focused on black people in recent years, as one of the most harmful effects of structural racism.

In 2018, 43,890 out of 57,956 people murdered in Brazil were black. In percentage terms, the homicide rate per thousand people in Brazil in the same year was 27.8. However, if only the black population is taken into account, this rate would be 37.8, while the number of non-black people[12] murdered in that period would be 13.9. These inequalities in the distribution of lethal violence are even higher if regional aspects are taken in account. In the state of Alagoas, in the north-east of Brazil, in 2018, 1,175 black people and twenty-five non-black people were killed; hence, in this state, black individuals are 17.2 times more likely to be victimized than non-black people (Cerqueira and Bueno, 2020).

With regard to deaths caused by police action, in 2019, the enormous figure of 6,375 fatalities was registered, the highest number since 2013 when the Brazilian Forum of Public Security started recording the data. Focusing on the racial issue, a qualitative analysis of the figures—according to a database that recorded information concerning 5,088 fatalities; that is, 80 per cent of the cases—reveals an over-representation of black people among the victims of police action, since 79.1 per cent of the fatalities were black people or brown people—a percentage higher than the national average of black people who were the victims of intentional violent death, which corresponds to 74.4 per cent of the total (Bueno and Lima, 2020, p. 90). 'It must be highlighted that a similar pattern was identified among police officers that were victims of homicide or armed robbery resulting in death, as 65.1% of the security officers that were killed in last year were black or brown'[13] (Bueno and Lima, 2020, p. 90).

[11] Original in Portuguese: 'o discurso criminológico racista, ao aproximar o criminoso e o selvagem, adquire novos contornos. Ele pode ser visto como uma ideologia que confundirá a agressividade e a alienação do homem sujeito ao processo de colonização com sua intrínseca maldade, classificando como modo de ser criminal todas as formas de sobrevivência à realidade colonial, as adaptações aos modelos impostos e à violência classificatória sofrida, mas, sobretudo, toda a diversidade humana biológica distinta dos padrões europeus e todas as formas de expressão cultural capazes de possibilitar respostas, ainda que simbólicas, à perda de identidade diante do processo colonizador.'

[12] This classification takes into account white people as well as those related to racial and ethnic minorities (Asians and indigenous peoples), excluding *black* and *brown* peoples, both of whom are considered to be *black* according to the criteria adopted by the Brazilian census.

[13] Original in Portuguese: 'É de destacar que padrão similar foi encontrado entre os policiais vítimas de homicídio e latrocínio, sendo que 65,1% dos agentes de segurança assassinados no último ano eram pretos e pardos.'

The racial issue is also evident in the processes of criminalization. Penal agencies reproduce the existing coloniality by developing racialized practices resulting in the differentiated treatment of the non-white population, who are submitted to more rigorous means of control and discipline. These institutions thereby fulfil an elementary role in the *naturalization of subalternity* (Flauzina, 2008, p. 62). This selectivity leads to the overrepresentation of black individuals in the Brazilian prison system. Therefore, although Brazilian society is composed of 55.4 per cent black and brown people, black prisoners account for 63.6 per cent of the Brazilian prison population[14] (Brasil, 2019, pp. 31–32).

It is possible to verify how racism impacts on the functioning of criminal justice by observing how the Brazilian police operate. However, the subject was approached only as a peripheral issue in recent studies on policing (Freitas, 2020, p. 79). This can be understood as a reflection of coloniality, arising from the maintenance of an ideologic equality discourse within criminal institutions. The reality of the criminal justice field and the history of how police agencies were structured to control the *dangerous classes* refute this false premise and stimulate further research focused on this specific aspect. In fact, it is evident that the black youth who live in peripheral areas are still the main targets of policing (Jesus, 2020, p. 96). In this regard:

> It was never necessary to institutionalise in Brazil a legal apartheid system, because, apart from social and economic discrimination, *small authorities* and the system of '*do you know who you are talking to*?' have always performed the role of restraining the black population in civil society. Black children grow within the borders of these micro-despotisms and of the internalisation of the limits imposed by a society ruled by the white.[15]
>
> (Pinheiro, 1991, p. 56, emphases in original)

Studies demonstrate that black people tend to be more frequently selected for police stops as they represent racial stereotypes related to general orthodoxy (Sinhoretto et al., 2020). This has several immediate effects, such as the excessive number of preventive detentions which disproportionally affects that population. The subject of racism still causes discomfort within police agencies. In focus groups, the use—whether consciously or not—of *neutralization techniques* by police officers was identified several times, due to concerns about disguising the racialized character of police stops by means of maintaining other dichotomies which, although also stereotypical, are distanced from the racial criteria—such as police vs outlaw, or civic vs military[16]

[14] It is worthy of note that the data from Infopen are not highly reliable and that the race/colour of an inmate is not informed by self-identification but assigned by third parties.

[15] Original in Portuguese: 'Nunca foi necessário no Brasil institucionalizar um sistema de *apartheid* legal, porque, além da discriminação social e econômica, as *pequenas autoridades* e o sistema do *sabe com quem você está falando* sempre desempenharam um papel de contenção dos negros na sociedade civil. As crianças negras crescem dentro da baliza desses microdespotismos e da interiorização dos limites impostos pela sociedade dos brancos.'

[16] As a rule, ostensive policing in Brazil is carried out by militarized state police forces (military police). This is another remnant of the civic–military dictatorship that ruled the country from 1964 to 1985. There was never a complete political transition after that regime ended and, hence, the police force has never been demilitarized. For further information, see Soares, 2019.

(Ramos and Musumeci, 2005, pp. 47–50). Similarly, at a local level, in Maceió, the capital of the state of Alagoas, it is possible to identify the construction of the idea of the deviant—personified as *mala*[17]—by the police on the basis of traits such as behaviour, dress code, housing, and social class (Martins, 2015, pp. 95–115).

In this way, structural racism can channel criminal stereotypes ostensibly towards black people. The fact that racism is structured in Brazilian society also explains why police institutions develop racialized practices, even though they are composed of a majority of black officers. In the military police, when its members are questioned about this contradiction, it is common to hear among them that the police officer's skin colour should not influence their behaviour, but the culture of the institution should do so—*the police officer has no colour, he has uniform*[18] (Ramos and Musumeci, 2005, p. 83).

The use of preventive detention is common in Brazil; 32.39 per cent of the Brazilian prison population—which totalled 726,354 people in 2017 (Brasil, 2019)—are deprived of liberty before a definitive sentence being passed. This constitutes a poorly disguised anticipation of the sentence, as the vague legal criteria to impose such measures are hardly considered in detail. There are also some noteworthy regional disparities regarding preventive detentions, as some states use this type of measure more frequently than others. For instance, in Alagoas, in May 2021, 54.89 per cent of the prison intake were under the procedural imprisonment regime (Seris, 2021). Preventive detentions are frequently used in the so-called *war on drugs*, which drives mass incarceration especially through the imprisonment of black people (Barreto, 2018; Borges, 2018; Alexander, 2012). In cases of drug-related crimes, the criminal process normally starts with an arrest *in flagrante delicto* and, for this reason, the word of police officers has considerable weight on the resulting conviction and sentence (Jesus, 2020). Therefore, in this kind of offence, racial selection directly contributes to the phenomenon of mass incarceration.

Conclusion

One of the effects of coloniality in Brazil concerns how the punitive system produces selective processes of criminalization against subaltern social groups. The enormous mass of black and indigenous peoples that form the Brazilian *rabble*—the segment of the population that is deprived of its citizen rights and lives in precarious socio-economic conditions—is more intensely subjected to the punitive excesses and the structural violence that mark the coloniality of power. Since the beginning of the Brazilian colonization, the modernizing project used racialized punitive mechanisms. The genocide of indigenous peoples and the need of the elites to control the enslaved black population led to the formation of state structures that worked in a differentiated manner in respect of those populations. After the formal abolition of slavery and the advent of the republican system, the policing of the lower classes and the legal mechanisms of selective repression against black and indigenous peoples were intensified.

[17] An expression that represents the stereotype of a delinquent, especially related to some urban crimes, such as robbery and drug dealing. It derives from *malandro* (trickster).

[18] Original in Portuguese: 'policial não tem cor, tem farda.'

Nowadays, although there are many social factors that stimulate the processes of criminalization of indigenous individuals, criminal charges against these individuals engender their authoritarian integration into society as a whole, inasmuch as this denies their ethnic and cultural differences. The differentiated legal status of indigenous peoples is ignored, as well as their own identity, which results in the under-reporting of this populational group in the official prison statistics. Moreover, this causes an intensification of the *pain of imprisonment*, as their treatment as being non-indigenous distances them from their relations with the ethnic community to which they belong. Therefore, a *civilizing penality* is adopted and criminal law is used as a means of forcefully integrating indigenous people into the supposed modernity of Brazilian society.

On the other hand, the black population is subjected to a form of policing characterized by the racism that structures Brazilian society. Stereotypes that link black and brown people to criminality are present not only in the historical construction of Brazilian criminological discourse but also in society's common sense and seem to be reflected by the police *habitus*. Consequently, there is a disproportionate number of black individuals among those killed by the actions of the police. This inequality also influences the higher proportion of police stops of black individuals. The judiciary similarly reproduces this structural racism, by trivializing authorizations for preventive detention, which given the racial selectivity in the functioning of these institutions, disproportionately affects black populations. This phenomenon can be clearly identified in cases of drug-related crimes. On the basis on these observations, it can be argued that the institutions that form the criminal justice system continue to anchor their practices in coloniality, thereby perpetuating the naturalization of the subalternity of black and indigenous peoples in Brazil.

References

Aguirre, C. (2009) 'Cárcere e sociedade na América Latina', in Maia, C. N., Neto, S. N.de., Bretas, M. L. et al. (eds.) *História das prisões no Brasil*. Rio de Janeiro: Rocco.

Albuquerque, W. R. de (2009) *O jogo da dissimulação*. São Paulo: Companhia das letras.

Alencastro, L. F. de (2000) *O trato dos viventes*. São Paulo: Companhia das letras.

Alencastro, L. F. de (2018) 'África, números do tráfico atlântico', in Schwarcz, L. and Gomes, F. (eds) *Dicionário da escravidão e liberdade*. São Paulo: Companhia das letras.

Alexander, M. (2012) *The New Jim Crow*. New York: The New Press.

Almeida, S. (2019) *Racismo estrutural*. São Paulo: Pólen.

Alvarez, M. C. (2003) *Bacharéis, criminologistas e juristas*. São Paulo: IBCCRIM.

Amorim, E. (2014) 'A perícia antropológica no processo criminal: estudo de caso', in Villares, L. F. (ed.) *Direito penal e povos indígenas*. Curitiba: Juruá.

Araújo Júnior, J. J. (2018) 'A constituição de 1988 e os direitos indígenas: uma prática assimilacionista?', in Cunha, M. C. da and Barbosa, S. (eds) *Direitos dos povos indígenas em disputa*. São Paulo: UNESP.

Azevedo, C. M. M. (2004) *Onda negra, medo branco*. 3rd edn. São Paulo: Annablume.

Azevedo, E. (2010) *O direito dos escravos*. Campinas: UNICAMP.

Baines, S. G. (2009) 'Esperando para ser julgado: indígenas no sistema penitenciário de Boa Vista em Roraima', in Smiljanic, M. I., Pimenta, J., and Baines, S. G. (eds) Faces da *indianidade*. Curitiba: Nexo Design.

Barreto, A. L. L. de A. (2018) 'Prisões cautelares e tráfico de drogas: um estudo a partir de processos judiciais nas varas de tóxicos de Salvador' *Revista brasileira de ciências criminais*, 148, pp. 209–242.
Batista, N. (2012) *Pena pública y esclavismo*. Caracas: UNES.
Beattie, P. (2009) *Tributo de sangue*. São Paulo: USP.
Borges, J. (2018) *O que é encarceramento em massa?* São Paulo: Letramento.
Brasil (2019) *Levantamento nacional de informações penitenciárias (Infopen): junho de 2017*. Brasília: Ministério da Justiça e Segurança Pública/Departamento Penitenciário Nacional.
Bretas, M. (2018) *Guerra das ruas*. Rio de Janeiro: Gramma.
Brown, M. (2002) 'The politics of penal excess and the echo of colonial penality', *Punishment & Society*, 4(4), pp. 403–423.
Bueno, S. and Lima, R. S. de (eds) (2020) *Anuário brasileiro de segurança pública 2020*. São Paulo: FBSP.
Carvalho, S. de, Goyes, D. R., and Weis, V. V. (2020) 'Politics and indigenous victimization: The case of Brazil', *British Journal of Criminology*, 61(1), pp. 251–271.
Cerqueira, D. and Bueno, S. (eds) (2020) *Atlas da violência 2020*. São Paulo: IPEA/FBSP.
Côrrea, M. (1998) *As ilusões da liberdade*. Bragança Paulista: EDUSF.
Cunha, M. C. da (2012) *Índios no Brasil*. São Paulo: Claro enigma.
Cunha, O. M. G. da (2002) *Intenção e gesto*. Rio de Janeiro: Arquivo nacional.
De Maglie, C. (2017) *Crimes culturalmente motivados*. Rio de Janeiro: Revista dos Tribunais.
Del Olmo, R. (2004) *América Latina e sua criminologia*. Rio de Janeiro: Revan.
Duarte, E. P. (2017) 'Ensaio sobre a hipótese colonial', in Carvalho, S. de and Duarte, E. P. (eds) *Criminologia do preconceito*. São Paulo: Saraiva.
Fanon, F. (2008) *Pele negra, máscaras brancas*. Salvador: UFBA.
Ferla, L. (2009) *Feios, sujos e malvados sob medida*. São Paulo: Alameda.
Flauzina, A. L. P. (2008) *Corpo negro caído no chão*. Rio de Janeiro: Contraponto.
Fonseca, D. S. (2018) 'Reimagining the sociology of punishment through the Global-South: Postcolonial social control and modernization discontents', *Punishment & Society*, 20(1), pp. 54–72.
Franco, M. S. de C. (1997) *Homens livres na ordem escravocrata*, 4th edn. São Paulo: UNESP.
Freitas, F. da S. (2020) 'Racismo e polícia: uma discussão sobre mandato policial', Doctoral dissertation, Programa de Pós-Graduação em Direito. Brasília: UNB.
Garland, D. (2010) *A Peculiar Institution: America's Death Penalty in an Age of Abolition*. Cambridge, MA: The Belknap Press.
Gilroy, P. (2012) *O Atlântico negro*. São Paulo: Editora 34.
Góes, L. (2016) *A 'tradução' de Lombroso na obra de Nina Rodrigues*. Rio de Janeiro: Revan.
Hungria, N. (1958) *Comentários ao código penal*, 1(2). Rio de Janeiro: Forense.
Jesus, M. G. de (2020) *A verdade jurídica nos processos de tráfico de drogas*. Belo Horizonte: D'Plácido.
Koselleck, R. (2006) *Futuro passado*. Rio de Janeiro: PUC-RJ/Contraponto.
Lacerda, R. (2011) 'Responsabilidade penal e situação carcerária dos indígenas no Brasil: uma realidade a ser desvelada. Conselho Indigenista Missionário', in *Violência contra os povos indígenas do Brasil: Dados de 2010*. Brasília: CIMI, pp. 17–24.
Lima Júnior, F. (1979) *Última execução judicial no Brasil*. Maceió: Imprensa universitária.
Machado, M. H. (1994) *O plano e o pânico*. Rio de Janeiro: UFRJ/USP.
Machado, M. H. (2014) *Crime e escravidão*, 2nd edn. São Paulo: USP.
Machado Neto, Z. (1977) *Direito penal e estrutura social*. São Paulo: Saraiva.
Mamigonian, B. G. (2017) *Africanos livres*. São Paulo: Companhia das letras.
Martins, C. (2015) *Polícia e estigma*. Maceió: UFAL.
Monteiro, J. M. (2000) *Negros da terra*. São Paulo: Companhia das letras.

Morais, R. F. (2019) *O extermínio da juventude negra*. Rio de Janeiro: Revan.

Morel, M. (2017) *A revolução do Haiti e o Brasil escravista*. Jundiaí: Paco.

Moura, C. (2020) *Rebeliões da senzala*. São Paulo: Fundação Maurício Grabois.

Nolan, M. M., Hilgert, C. D., and Balbuglio, V. (2020) *Relatório: Violência contra os povos indígenas do Brasil: dados de 2019*. Brasília: CIMI.

Osorio, R. G. (2019) *A desigualdade racial da pobreza no Brasil*. Rio de Janeiro: IPEA.

Pinheiro, P. S. (1991) 'Autoritarismo e transição', *Revista da USP*, 9, pp. 45–56.

Pontes, B. C. (2014) 'O índio e a justiça criminal brasileira', in Villares, L. F. (ed.) *Direito penal e povos indígenas*. Curitiba: Juruá.

Queiroz, M. V. L. (2017) *Constitucionalismo brasileiro e o Atlântico negro*. Rio de Janeiro: Lumen juris.

Quijano, A. (2009) 'Colonialidade do poder e classificação social', in Santos, B. de S. and Meneses, M. P. (eds) *Epistemologias do Sul*. Coimbra: Almedina.

Ramos, S. and Musumeci, L. (2005) *Elemento suspeito*. Rio de Janeiro: Civilização brasileira.

Ribeiro, J. L. (2005) *No meio das galinhas as baratas não têm razão*. Rio de Janeiro: Renovar.

Rodrigues, N. (1933 [1894]) *As raças humanas e a responsabilidade penal no Brasil*. Rio de Janeiro: Guanabara.

Schwarcz, L. M. (2010) *O espetáculo das raças*. São Paulo: Companhia das letras.

Seris (2021) *Mapa da população carcerária: plantões de 04/05/2021 a 05/05/2021*. Maceió: Governo do Estado de Alagoas/Secretaria de Estado de Ressocialização e Inclusão Social.

Serra, M. A. de S. (2017) 'Na charneira de dois séculos', Doctoral dissertation, Programa de Pós-Graduação em Direito. Rio de Janeiro: Universidade Estadual do Rio de Janeiro.

Silva, C. T. da (2013) 'O índio, o pardo e o invisível: primeiras impressões sobre a criminalização e o aprisionamento de indígenas no Brasil', *Antropolítica*, 34, Niterói, pp. 137–158.

Silva, J. B. de A. e. (2002 [1823]) 'Apontamentos para a civilização dos índios bravos do império do Brasil', in Caldeira, J. (ed.) *José Bonifácio de Andrade e Silva*. São Paulo: Editora 34.

Silva, M. L. da (2004) 'O código criminal de 1830 e as ideias que não estão fora do lugar', in Cancelli, E. (ed.) *Histórias de violência, crime e lei no Brasil*. Brasília: UNB.

Silva, T. M. da (2016) *No banco dos réus, um índio*. São Paulo: IBCCRIM.

Simi, G. (2021) 'Reformatório, campo de trabalho e colônia penal: o confinamento de indígenas na ditadura militar', in Galeano, D., Corrêa, L. R., and Pires, T. (eds) De *presos políticos a presos comuns*. Rio de Janeiro: PUC/RJ.

Sinhoretto, J., Batitucci, E., Mota, F. R. et al. (2020) *A filtragem racial na seleção policial de suspeitos. Relatório de pesquisa*. São Carlos: UFSCAR, pp. 121–158.

Soares, L. E. (2019) *Desmilitarizar*. São Paulo: Boitempo.

Sontag, R. (2014) *Código criminológico?* Rio de Janeiro: Revan.

Souza, J. (ed.) (2016) *A ralé brasileira*. Belo Horizonte: UFMG.

Sozzo, M. (2006) 'Traduttore traditore: traducción, importación cultural e historia del presente de la criminología em América latina', in Sozzo, M. (ed.) Reconstruyendo *las criminologias críticas*. Buenos Aires: Ad Hoc.

Spivak, G. C. (2010) *Pode o subalterno falar?*. Belo Horizonte: UFMG.

Todorov, T. (2019) *A conquista da América*. São Paulo: Martins Fontes.

Valença, M. A. (2018) 'Soberania policial no Recife do início do século XX', Doctoral dissertation, Programa de Pós-Graduação em Direito. Brasília: Universidade de Brasília.

Valente, R. (2017) *Os fuzis e as flechas*. São Paulo: Companhia das letras.

Zaffaroni, E. R. (2003) *Criminología*. Bogotá: Temis.

Zaffaroni, E. R. and Batista, N. (2003) *Direito penal brasileiro*, 1, 2nd edn. Rio de Janeiro: Revan.

PART 4
MAPPING GLOBAL CONNECTIONS

12

Emancipatory Pathways or Postcolonial Pitfalls?

Navigating Global Policing Mobilities Through the Atlantic Archipelago of Cape Verde

Conor O'Reilly

Introduction

'*Cabo Verde não é bem Africa*' ('Cape Verde is not quite Africa'). This statement—made by the Portuguese police liaison officer (PLO) who greeted us upon arrival at Aeroporto Internacional Nelson Mandela in Praia, Cape Verde, provided our first insight into the anomalies of this small archipelago-state located some 350 miles off the West African coast. Our interlocutor, who was attached to the Portuguese Embassy, and had also served on international policing missions, was quick to single out an atypical African-ness as a defining characteristic of Cape Verde, and by extension of its policing. In essence, he was telling us to prepare for something less expected in our coming fieldwork. He was reiterating how this West African archipelago, and its policing experience, emerge somewhat exceptional to, and indeed can be juxtaposed against, dominant trends across Western and sub-Saharan Africa. On deeper reflection, however, there was more to be taken from this welcoming exchange. First, Cape Verde has been *comparatively* spared—largely by geographic removal—from the conflicts, instabilities, ruptures, and turmoil that have impacted policing in many other postcolonial African settings (see, e.g., Beek and Göpfert, 2015; Beek et al., 2017; Hills 2000; 2014). Indeed, Cape Verdean policing boasts democratic credentials and claims a surprising 150-year historical continuity within its police organization that spans pre-independence colonial policing to the present day. Second, the presence of a Portuguese PLO—there to advise the *Polícia Nacional de Cabo Verde* (PNCV) on training needs and organizational improvements—was a strong signal for the renewed connections between Cape Verde and its former Metropole in Lisbon. Consequently, whilst independence had witnessed separation and later *rapprochement*, the rupture that occurred appears less extreme than that experienced in most other Luso-African postcolonial contexts. Moreover, it also became apparent that transnational policing mobilities through Cape Verde were much more varied and complex than re-engagement with Portugal. Indeed, this eight-island archipelago occupies a space within both flows of policing—expertise, models and practices—and the correlated

Conor O'Reilly, *Emancipatory Pathways or Postcolonial Pitfalls?* In: *Decolonizing the Criminal Question.* Edited by: Ana Aliverti, Henrique Carvalho, Anastasia Chamberlen, and Máximo Sozzo, Oxford University Press.
DOI: 10.1093/oso/9780192899002.003.0013

policing of flows—notably drugs and migrants—that belies its modest 4,000 square-kilometre landmass and population of almost half a million.

We visited Cape Verde in July 2014 to conduct interviews as part of the international research project 'COPP-LAB' (Circulations of Police in Portugal, Lusophone Africa and Brazil). Seventeen interviews were conducted with PNCV officers and site visits undertaken to PNCV headquarters and police stations in Praia and Tarrafal.[1] Whilst this fieldwork was not pursued with the explicit aim of contributing towards decolonizing criminological scholarship, its findings retain significance for such ambitions.[2] Indeed, the general lack of attention towards Cape Verde from within this field reiterates dominant Western-centrism. The archipelago reveals itself to be a significant research blind spot, with the penal and policing structures of these small, but strategically important, Atlantic islands deriving from colonialism, exploitation, and slavery. Moreover, they continue to be marked by multiple external *neo-colonizing* influences. Currently, most evident in a certain recruitment of its crime control and security structures into the (Western) policing of global insecurities.

An important *entrepôt* for the transatlantic slave trade; multifaceted carceral continuities throughout its history; elevated standing through intermediary roles within colonial administration, as well as within racial hierarchies of Portuguese colonialism; serial status as a recipient of multiple policing mobilities that span transcolonial exchange, imperial oppression, foreign police assistance and international training; enlistment as an Atlantic sentinel in efforts to combat irregular migration and drug trafficking: these super-imposed characteristics cumulatively offer insights into the outworkings of policing's historical and transnational co-constitution. In short, the Cape Verdean experience sheds new light on the 'entangled histories, global encounters and uneven power relations' that combine to forge policing in the postcolony, and indeed beyond (Hönke and Müller, 2012, p. 386).

Both rooted within formative structures of colonialism and engaging the voices of senior policing figures from these islands—themselves with diverse transnational experiences—this chapter explores Cape Verde's evolving subaltern role within the global making of policing, temporally, spatially, and subjectively (Aliverti et al., 2021). From former colonial subject and colonial intermediary to contemporary agent of global mobility regimes and global security agendas, it considers how progressive

[1] This chapter results from the research project 'COPP-LAB–Circulations of Police in Portugal, Lusophone Africa and Brazil' (PTDC/IVC-ANT/5314/2012) supported by the Portuguese *Fundação para a Ciência e a Tecnologia*. I am grateful for the fieldwork support provided by Joana Oliveira, who accompanied me to Cape Verde, as well as to Nina Herzog for later research assistance. I also wish to acknowledge support from my COPP-LAB colleagues Susana Durão and Daniel Seabre Lopes during the project, as well as from the editors, for their support and very helpful feedback. This chapter has benefited immensely from comments provided by Sandra Araújo, Jarrett Blaustein, Rita de la Feria, Graham Ellison, Richard Hill, and Beatrice Jaurequi. Previous iterations of this chapter were presented at academic gatherings hosted at the universities of Leeds, Maynooth, Montreal, Porto, and Warwick (virtually). My thanks to all who provided feedback.

[2] Whilst this project had self-evident postcolonial underpinnings, its fieldwork had two broad aims: namely (a) to interview serving PNCV officers who had attended a five-year officer training course at the Academy of Police Science and Internal Security in Lisbon regarding that training experience and subsequent reintegration into police service in Cape Verde; and (b) to interview senior PNCV figures about Cape Verdean policing generally, not least as regards its participation and engagement with transnational policing, and foreign police training in particular. Interviews were conducted in Portuguese and the extracts used have been translated into English by the author.

cooperation with external policing influences has given way to more *knowledgeable* and *knowing* engagement with the agendas, architecture, and networks of transnational policing. These interactions have fostered aspirations within the Cape Verdean policing organization to extend its own agency within regional and transnational policing and pursue a more protagonist role in policing mobilities. In so doing, it further disrupts dominant, Western-centric, assumptions about the unilateral nature and direction of policing and security travels.

The Cape Verdean case provides nuanced insights into the variant ways that police forces in postcolonial settings may harness colonial legacies to gain a foothold in the transnational policing realm. Aware of the prestige and legitimacy to be garnered by elevating policing action and experience out of the domestic setting, Cape Verdean policing holds itself out as a beacon for democratic policing and exemplar for policing change elsewhere in Africa. It is simultaneously regarded as a model regional player within Western efforts to combat transnational insecurities. However, Cape Verdean ambitions and strategies to leverage and mediate postcoloniality afford both emancipatory pathways and postcolonial pitfalls. A less-dependent policing future that offers scope for inter-African co-constitution of policing is also paralleled by the potential recrudescence of Cape Verde's intermediary past through the problematic self-identity it left behind. There are risks that Cape Verde's postcolonial, North-to-South, intermediary role in confronting transatlantic insecurities risks facilitating processes of international postcolonial othering (Brogden and Ellison, 2013) with its crime control structures enlisted into neocolonial policing and security arrangements (Ciocchini and Greener, 2021). Mapping out these potentials for Cape Verde provides valuable insights and reflections into how postcolonial settings seek to carve out their own space, identity, and purpose within the global policing web; one that remains overwhelmingly anchored within Western policing traditions, models, and priorities.

This chapter is divided into six sections that progressively demonstrate how Cape Verdean policing is: contextually/historically embedded; transnationally connected; and, increasingly regionally/globally ambitious. The first section locates this chapter within evolving patterns of criminological and policing scholarship and its contribution in the context of decolonizing ambitions. The next section critiques Cape Verdean exceptionalism by both recognizing embedded divergences from continental African neighbours, whilst also raising important qualifications for positive imagery regarding the archipelago's much vaunted democratic and development credentials. Following this, Cape Verdean policing's progressive engagement with transnational policing is charted through key phases from the colonial to the contemporary: exploring its evolving position; shifting points of policing reference; and the complicated police identity that ensued. The next section sets out how policing patterns in these islands paradoxically demonstrate Occidental traits, but also illuminate archetypal subaltern roles within the architecture of global policing. Next is a closer focus on Cape Verde's role within efforts to combat the illicit mobilities of drug trafficking and irregular migration. It spotlights brokering possibilities within asymmetrical power dynamics that can work in its favour, as well as the risk of (re)emerging as a postcolonial intermediary through such arrangements. The final section reflects on recent plans to construct an international police academy in Cape Verde, as well as the symbolism for its police identity and wider ambitions that this proposal represents.

Cape Verde and Decolonizing Policing Scholarship

Policing scholarship has unquestionably progressed since Brogden (1987a) lamented how '[e]thnocentricity, inadequate comparative knowledge of policing and a-historicism are the hallmarks of the Anglo-American sociology of the police' (p. 4). A range of scholars have built upon pioneering critical observations regarding 'boomerang effects' (Foucault, 2003), 'counter-colonialism' (Agozino, 2007), and 'internal colonialism' (Brogden, 1987b) to develop refined research attention to what Hönke and Müller (2012; 2016) usefully term 'the global making of policing', endorsing approaches that reject conflation of the global with the Western. This has included scholarship explicitly focused on dismantling unidirectional conceptualizations of policing and security traffic (Amar, 2013; Bilgin, 2016; Jones et al., 2021; Newburn et al., 2018), as well as works that recognize nuance within power dynamics, along with more complex ambitions across all parties to these mobilities (Blaustein, 2015; O'Reilly, 2017b; Qadim, 2010; Stambøl, 2021a; 2021b). More integrated disciplinary approaches have paralleled these efforts, notably increased exchange between colonial policing historians and transnational policing scholars (see, e.g., Blanchard et al., 2017; Ellison and O'Reilly, 2008; Sinclair and Williams, 2007) and productive harnessing of conceptual resources from areas such as critical policy studies, advocating for more refined methodologies within the criminological examination of global crime-control mobilities (Newburn et al., 2018; Jones et al., 2021).

Nonetheless, despite such advances, the lens of global policing studies remains blinkered and significantly 'Anglobalised' (Agozino, 2019, p. 13). Swathes of Southern settings remain either problematically approached or comparatively under-examined; neglected not only as sites for research that can contribute novel practical and theoretical approaches towards the criminal question, but also as regards their importance within the global penal and policing web. Cape Verde is a powerful example of this. It is part of the Lusophone community; that postcolonial collection of African, Asian, European, and American settings where some 270 million people—primarily located in the Global South—are linked through legacies of Portuguese colonialism. In terms of policing scholarship, Luso-policing—considered collectively—is a neglected but emerging field (see, e.g., Bretas, 1997; Durão and Lopes, 2015; Gonçalves, 2014; O'Reilly, 2017a). It is also a field that furnishes difference, novelty, and less orthodox outlets and subjects for policing scholarship. For example, during the Portuguese late-colonial era, policing operated under the dual repressive tendencies of imperial power and a fascist regime. Its political police, PIDE, were active both at home and in the colonial *ultramar* (as Portuguese 'overseas' territories were then termed). In parallel, key actors and thinkers within anti-colonial movements—not least Cape Verde's Amilcar Cabral—were at once pan-African, anti-colonial, anti-fascist, and anti-capitalist in their orientation. Indeed, Cabral's own ideals were part-informed by encounters with other political activists whilst attending university in the Metropole of Lisbon through educational structures to integrate promising young scholars from the colonies (Tomás, 2021, pp. 37–43). This inadvertent outcome reiterates how structures of coloniality can create unintended opportunities for agency and resistance to take hold. This chapter later returns to Cabral's revolutionary reflections on the need for critical assimilation of colonial/foreign transplants which usefully informs discussion of opportunities afforded by contemporary policing mobilities.

Whilst Cabralism has an important place within Africana liberation criminologies (Agozino, 2020), Cape Verde itself remains an unfamiliar setting for criminological research, more so for policing scholarship. However, it would be inaccurate to hold it out as untouched for scholarship holding interest for criminologists. Anthropological and sociological research, primarily from Cape Verdean and Portuguese scholars, has made important contributions across a range of salient security issues, notably youth gangs and violence, reintegration of deportees, public security, and penal policy in Cape Verde (see, e.g., Bordanaro, 2010: Lima, 2018; Rocha, 2017; Zoettl, 2016). Building upon these works and recognizing Cape Verde's complex colonial/penal/racial history are fundamental points of orientation for navigating policing mobilities within, through, and out of this postcolonial setting. Cape Verde is not only a node for multiple intersecting policing mobilities, but also a fascinating nexus of both the postcolonial condition (Hönke and Müller, 2012; 2016; Waseem, this volume) and the transnational condition (Sheptycki, 2007a; 2007b). These conditions coalesce, both negatively and positively: shared *othering* processes stretch across time and space; local agency in the postcolony exerts growing influence within transnational policing/security arrangements; and, transnational connections offer both pathways out of postcolonial subordination, as well as pitfalls that obstruct such progress.

Qualifying Cape Verdean Exceptionalism

Intersecting peculiarities of geography and colonial/postcolonial history have witnessed Cape Verde emerge *somewhat* exceptionally to other postcolonial patterns in Africa. It is important to note that this continentally detached setting was not only comparatively sheltered from the worst effects of the war for independence that principally played out in continental Guinea-Bissau, but also subsequently less exposed to the conflict and ethnic, political, religious, and/or tribal ruptures that marked other nations' post-independence emergence. As a result, its governance—particularly as regards security—emerged relatively stable and well defined. Indeed, it sits in contrast to some other West African settings where heterarchical, rather than hierarchical, arrangements dominate, and governance of security is often characterized by fragmented, improvised, and sporadic arrangements (Stambøl, 2021a).

Cape Verde is widely viewed as an embedded, stable democracy that has forged progress in a challenging context (Baker, 2006; 2009). It is consistently ranked amongst Africa's most democratic nations. It is viewed as 'developing', rather than 'less developed'. It is relatively peaceful, culturally rich, and possesses a well-educated population. It has demonstrated traits that have earned plaudits from Western and international policy bodies; one US Ambassador hailing Cape Verde as 'a model in the region for strategic partnership' (Plácido dos Santos, 2014, p. 2). However, this almost idyllic picture bears qualification. These islands retain significant problems of poverty, inequality, and unemployment that have historically been addressed through emigration. Recent decades have also witnessed moral panic around youth gangs and urban crime, as well as an increasingly punitive penal state that has embraced more securitized Western policies (see, e.g., Bordanaro, 2010; Lima, 2018; Zoettl, 2016). The spectre of transatlantic narco-traffic—so toxic in effects upon neighbouring Guinea-Bissau, termed Africa's first narco-state—with its attendant scope for infiltrating corruption and money-laundering into Cape Verdean society, has also prompted action and concern (Kane, 2019).

It must also be underscored that Cape Verdean society was shaped by carceral continuities and penal (im)mobilities that extend beyond the, more acknowledged, slave trade (returned to later). From its earliest colonial settlement, Cape Verde was the final destination for the undesirables expelled from the Metropole and exiled to its inhospitable environment (Lobban Jr, 2019, p. 23). It was later home to the infamous concentration camp at Tarrafal, part of a transcolonial framework of externalized political prisons that foreshadowed more contemporary 'black-site' jails and offshored asylum-processing facilities (Mester, 2016). More recently, this archipelago has become integrated into repressive mobility regimes. Cape Verdean immigrants who have been convicted of gang-related or immigration offences in the USA have been deported back to these islands through a 'corridor of abandonment' (Drotbohm, 2011, p. 392). Public insecurity around these co-called '*Americanos*' was woven into moral panic around gang violence with pursuant Western-inspired tough penal/policing approaches witnessing both doubling of the prison population as well as criticism of heavy-handed policing (Zoettl, 2016, p. 401). Lima (2018) draws historical parallels of dehumanization with the black man exiled to the islands through the slave trade; the folk-devil of the *badio* (fugitive slave) being (re)lived in contemporary urban Cape Verde through the figure of the *thug* (gang member) (p. 15).

The colonial legacy looms large. Not least within the complex psyche of this Creole nation of the 'Brown Atlantic' (Vale de Almeida, 2004, p. 109) where traumatic and stigmatic colonial bequests heavily endure. Slavery and exploitation; the sexual violence of miscegenation; lingering identity issues born of colonial intermediary roles: all retain a shaping influence on the collective subconscious, and indeed on police identity. One senior police officer when asked how history had shaped Cape Verdean policing, reiterated these effects of colonial legacy, highlighting how they both stood in contrast to popular imagery about the archipelago and resonated within policing. Questioning the romanticized Cape Verdean trait of *morabeza*—a term that speaks to an engrained friendliness and hospitality of the people from these islands—he remarked:

> I don't agree with that [the idea of *morabeza*] ... To be honest and sincere. If *morabeza* ever existed in the past, it no longer exists in that form. We must consider that the people of Cape Verde were people that were exchanged in violence ... slavery ... you don't treat a slave with niceties ... the relationship between people was a tense one. Not only between the bosses but also in relation to the slaves themselves. The colonizer was careful enough not to have two people from the same tribe in the same house ... so they don't speak the same language ... Well, that, whether we like it or not, has an influence on the formation of the individual and on the various generations, doesn't it? ... And ... We're going to recruit our [police] agents in this society, not in any other place. So, it comes in the DNA, in people's genes ...

Portuguese cultural imperialism entailed erasure and concealment of Cape Verdean African origin history, replacing it with educational orientation towards the Metropole. This Atlantic colony was the setting for intersecting ambitions that spanned civilization, exploitation, punishment, settlement, and slavery. The sexual violence of miscegenation was positively recast through Portuguese colonial endorsement of Lusotropicalism. Deployment as colonial intermediaries, in tandem with elevated status in colonial hierarchies, fostered problematic, often superior, Cape Verdean attitudes towards mainland Africans (Lobban Jr, 2019, pp. 8, 58, 60–61; Vale de Almeida, 2004, p. 113). All bequeathed 'imperial debris' (Stoler, 2013) in complex and weighty identity issues. DuBoisian 'double-consciousness'—the challenge of reconciling European and black identities—takes on enhanced complexity within Cape Verde's Creole society due to its colonial intermediary past (Vale de Almeida, 2004, p. 108). Indeed, despite post-independence efforts towards re-Africanization, a certain taboo maintains around being African in Cape Verde (Gorjão Henriques, 2018). There is much more than physical detachment from the continent. Rocha (2017) draws out how such sentiments contribute to contemporary othering of the West African immigrant. The '*mandjaku*', as they are termed, have emerged as contemporary folk-devils in Cape Verde. These legacies of colonialism have specific relevance to the policing sphere, not just as regards othering processes, but also as regards the quasi-schizophrenic police identity that has taken shape.

Morabeza for Transnational Policing?

As previously mentioned, the Creole term *morabeza*—conveying welcome and hospitality—has received criticism for having greater relevance to positive place-branding to market Cape Verde as a tourist destination than it does for accurately depicting its everyday security realities (Zoettl, 2016). However, insofar as addressing its police training, capacity, and resource deficiencies are concerned, foreign assistance to Cape Verde has consistently been very warmly received through successive historical phases. Across the five decades of its independence, Cape Verdean policing has been shaped by a series of foreign training arrangements that have evolved in alignment with fluctuations in geopolitics, development agendas, and international security priorities. As Steinberg (2020) has remarked, African police practices 'reveal an archaeology [of external influence] running several generations deep' and its 'police officers carry the burden of global history on their backs' (p. 136).

In the case of Cape Verde, a need for post-independence police training and capacity-building resulted in what one senior police officer termed 'a philosophy of openness' towards foreign assistance. He continued, 'Anyone who supports it [Cape Verdean policing] would be welcome and everyone supported it. And we benefit from that.' In terms of foreign policing engagement, therefore, Cape Verde has progressed through a variety of phases that can be conceptualized as follows: colonial instrument > grateful recipient > knowledgeable consumer > aspirant donor. PNCV officers across different levels were conscious of the need to tap into whatever police training or technical cooperation was available: 'the reasons were the necessity for [policing] knowledge'; 'We try to absorb the best experiences'; 'For us, everything to do with training is good'. The chronology of foreign police training for Cape Verde reveals an absorbent approach towards policing development in the archipelago.

Post-independence, foreign police assistance principally came from so-called *Paises Amigos* ('Friendly Countries'); those socialist countries such as Cuba, East Germany, and the Soviet Union that had lent support to the anti-colonial struggle and were ideologically sympathetic to the new Cape Verdean government of the PAIGC.[3] This resulted in the first cohort of post-independence Cape Verdean police officers being dispatched for training in locations such as the German Democratic Republic; one senior officer from that generation reminisced when interviewed about how technical lessons were accompanied by instruction in Marxist and Leninist theory—an aspect of training for which he had little interest. Such assistance faded with the fall of Communism and was followed by increased *rapprochement* towards the former Metropole in Lisbon. Whilst many Cape Verdean police officers have passed through Portugal for diverse police training, the dispatch of small cohorts of selected Cape Verdean officers to pursue a five-year degree programme in officer training at the Academy of Police Science and Internal Security was both important and symbolic. Not only had policing in Portugal also undergone post-dictatorship reform towards democratized and demilitarized policing, but there was clear intent to re-engage with former colonies, and provide training to small groups of officers brought to Lisbon (Durão and Lopes, 2015). For some cohorts, notably those from Cape Verde, those selected to be dispatched were seen to represent the future leadership cadre of the police. Echoing Metropolitan detachments of the past, the Lisbon training experience afforded enhanced capital for translation into career progression.

In tandem with training connections to Portugal, other channels opened up for European foreign police assistance; one officer interviewed ranked their strongest sources of support as Portugal, Spain, France, and then the UK. Emerging global insecurities—most notably drug and migrant smuggling—have also created new conduits for capacity-building and technical assistance (addressed later in the chapter). A noteworthy transatlantic connection has been forged between the PNCV and Boston Police Department that reflects both diaspora links to New England—there is a Cape Verdean Police Association in Boston—as well as connections around policing gang activity; criminal deportations from that US region back to the archipelago have opened up another route for lesson-drawing and police exchange.[4] Looking eastwards to the mainland African continent, the PNCV are now also forging training connections with the police academies of Angola and Mozambique to which PNCV officers have been dispatched (Pereira, 2021). Past pathways of transcolonial police circulation (Gonçalves and Cachado, 2017) have thus been replaced with new channels for police training mobilities between Luso-African postcolonial settings. Beyond these formal training connections, there are multiple smaller training visits and other technical support missions to Cape Verde. Reflecting its increased strategic interest and

[3] *Partido Africano para a Independência da Guiné e Cabo Verde* (African Party for the Independence of Guinea and Cape Verde).

[4] BPD in the Community, see: BPDNews (2018) 'BPD Chief Gross and BPD Cabo Verdean-American Police Officers Meet in Praia to Share Best Practices', 18 January. Available at: https://bpdnews.com/news/2018/1/18/bpd-in-the-community-bpd-chief-gross-and-bpd-cabo-verdean-american-police-officers-share-best-practices-in-policing (accessed 10 June 2022).

diplomatic presence within this Atlantic setting, China has also recently joined the ranks of donors to the PNCV, making significant financial contributions to support its training facilities.[5]

For Cape Verdean police officers—as with most recipients of foreign training or participants in transnational policing engagements—their positive representation of such experiences can be partially explained through motivated reasoning. By representing the contribution of such pedagogical experiences—organizationally and personally—in a highly favourable light, they enhance their own cultural, network, social, and symbolic capital upon their return. Selective and specialized police training programmes inevitably advance career prospects. However, these acquire even more prestige when obtained from the elevated transnational realm. Beek and Göpfert (2015) have drawn attention to how 'story-telling' is an important mechanism for African police officers to translate and make sense of their transnational experiences. In the case of Cape Verdean respondents, it was unsurprising that their reflections on participating in foreign training and transnational exchanges were overwhelmingly complimentary. Such experiences also afforded the opportunity to compare Cape Verdean policing's capacities and organizational structures against those of others; a benchmarking exercise for self-improvement that looks more to Europe than it does to Africa. One police officer felt that his five-year degree course at the Academy of Police Science and Internal Security in Lisbon had equipped him to serve anywhere in the world; whilst another felt that the operational practice of Cape Verdean policing was most similar to that of Portugal or France. However, unlike the multiple Western policing entrepreneurs and gurus who export policing *solutions* with hardwired conviction in those policing brands they promote (Ellison and Pino, 2013, p. 79), Cape Verdean police respondents—on the other side of such exports—displayed a degree of reflexivity and nuance, acknowledging the need for foreign lessons to be adapted to context.

Recognizing value within foreign training is, in itself, a *knowing* act; it makes sense to positively portray professional training that you have received. It also reflects *knowledgeable* engagement with transnational policing generally, and donor communities in particular. Decades of experience dealing with foreign police assistance creates institutional savviness for recipients within such arrangements: technical competences are increased where possible; crime-control policy initiatives and rhetoric are translated for local realities, often as symbolic expressions of modernization and professionalization; police training missions become integrated into wider diplomatic action; and, even flawed exports can be adapted to context. For example, in relation to that most ubiquitous (and most critiqued) of Western democratic police reform exports, community policing, one senior PNCV officer remarked how: 'We are trying to perfect things. There is no importation of a model ... There is no importation of a concrete model for us to introduce here.' This mixture of on the one hand recognizing value within foreign police training received, whilst on the other acknowledging local 'adaptation' (Beek and Gõpfert, 2015, p. 467) was a recurrent theme. Police training

[5] As well as having made a significant donation to the PNCV National Training Centre, China has also dispatched specialists to Cape Verde for residential training in areas including: anti-terrorism, strategic planning for police action, community policing, and tourism policing.

exports to Cape Verde thus exhibited patterns of translation and resistance (Blaustein, 2015). The way foreign police training and transnational exchange was discussed within interviews indicated agency and increased proficiency at harnessing training opportunities to both extract benefits and satisfy donors.

A growing body of scholars highlight how when policing expertise becomes mobile that it is transformed in the process, catalysing more complex effects than unidirectional export. Whether 'refined' (Hönke and Müller, 2012, p. 388) or 'translated' (Ellison and Pino, 2013, p. 77), undergoing processes of 'vernacularization' (Hönke and Müller, 2012, p. 395), 'non-linear reproduction' (Newburn et al., 2018, p. 570), or 'metamorphosis' (Sozzo, 2011, pp. 201–202), critical scholarship spotlights the need for nuanced examination of the translocation of policing knowledge/models. It is interesting to link these observations to decolonial thinking regarding lessons from elsewhere. Turning to the Cabralism of a half-century ago, Amilcar Cabral advocated 'critical assimilation' within cultural resistance, reiterating the need for selective and judicious adaptation of foreign technical and knowledge imports:

> a part of our struggle has been the constant application of the principle of critical assimilation, that is, availing ourselves of others, but criticizing what can be useful for our land and that which cannot. Accumulating and testing.
>
> (Rabaka, 2016, p. 137)

However, when the incoming flows of foreign police assistance and training are so diverse, so multi-sited, and so variegated, and indeed stretch across generations of the police corps, a certain schizophrenic police identity—*schizo-polícia*—and scope for conflicting police cultures and approaches can emerge. Steinberg (2020) has spoken of '[t]he ultimately schizophrenic composition of postcolonial policing' (p. 133) and Hills (2014) of the 'layers of knowledge comprising legacy issues, international influences, functional requirements and local norms and practices' (p. 773). Both were pronounced in Cape Verde. Individual police officers might have received formative police training in Cuba but studied for a law degree in Lisbon with multiple smaller training exchanges in addition to these. Generational difference was also manifest; the leadership cohort at the time of our fieldwork had mostly received training in sympathetic Communist settings during the post-independence era, whilst the younger generation of leadership aspirants had mostly received formative police training in Lisbon. Indeed, even the police training relationship with Portugal carried its own burdens; transitional policing processes across both former colony and Metropole had to wrestle with intersecting legacies of colonialism and dictatorship under new policing dispensations of independence and democratization (see Durão and Lopes, 2015). Certainly, PNCV respondents acknowledged the 'panoply of trainings' to which they were exposed, albeit that the collectively forged composite police culture still appeared decidedly Occidental. There was a strong orientation towards the West generally, and Portugal in particular. Such complexities of Cape Verdean police identity also rested upon an already complicated national psyche born of colonialism and geography (Gorjão Henriques, 2018; Vale de Almeida, 2004, p. 113).

Occidental 'Policeness' and Subaltern Global Cops

Drawing on the less recognisable experience of policing in Somalia, Hills (2014) has explored what it is to be recognized and to recognize oneself as police through the concept of *policeness*. The organizational structure, occupational culture, uniform appearance, and symbolic representation of the Cape Verdean state through the PNCV, all indicate an African police force that conforms to Western orthodox notions as to who the police are, what they should do, and when/where they should be doing it. Such Occidental commonality presents Cape Verde as a less problematic partner for transnational policing collaboration than might be found in some other West African contexts. However, in the same reflexive vein that acknowledged the necessary adaptation of foreign police training, senior PNCV figures were equally conscious of how 'cooperation has been, in fact, more directed towards the West, towards Europe', whilst 'exchange ... at the level of our sub-region [West Africa], I must admit that it is weak'. Whilst the Lusophone connection has facilitated police training links with Angola and Mozambique, connections with policing peers in the West African region were described as comparatively under-developed. A poignant example was given when a senior PNCV officer commented how he could readily pick up the phone to speak to the National Director of Policing in Portugal but would not have the same level of familiarity or access with his peer in Senegal; a much closer African neighbour with whom one might expect greater policing commonality.

Foremost within this Occidental policeness has been the reconstruction of policing links with Lisbon, where small groups of African police agents from the PALOPs (*Países Africanos de Língua Oficial Portuguesa*) are integrated into the police officer training cohort of the Academy of Police Science and Internal Security's five-year degree programme. Progressing beyond mere benevolent mentorship, and continuing long-standing practice of dispatching promising young Cape Verdeans to Lisbon for higher education, this officer-training programme symbolically aligns Cape Verdean and Portuguese policing realities. Indeed, statements that asserted proximity within the policing approaches adopted across these two settings were a recurrent refrain of fieldwork. This was not only a question of training at the Academy in Lisbon, or linguistic, cultural, and historical connections. It was also reflected in the particular importance placed upon criminal and penal law education within both policing contexts, as well as the fact that those Cape Verdeans officers selected for training in Lisbon were perceived as representing the future leadership cadre for policing back home. Indeed, the emphasis and the importance placed upon legal education came through strongly in the fieldwork with several respondents not only pointing to their legal training in Lisbon but also speaking of 'normative convergence' and proximity between these two countries' legal frameworks.

Within our project team, the research-lead from the Lisbon Police Academy (who played a fundamental role in facilitating the COPP-LAB project), approached policing research and education from a quite legalistic perspective; his work in police training across various Lusophone police settings communicated through what he termed a 'general theory of policing law' (Valente, 2014). Indeed, as a police officer and lawyer, his role as a diplomatic and legal bridge between police forces in the former colonies and the former Metropole furnished an important new cast member to the *dramatis personae* of global policing. Whilst Bowling and Sheptycki (2012, pp. 87–92) have set out an extremely useful typology of global cops, and Brogden and Ellison (2013, pp. 100–101) expose archetypal roles within police reform missions, these works place justifiable emphasis on identifying dominant transnational protagonists and critiquing Western actors who engage in more commodified policing transplants. A valuable addition here—not least from a decolonizing perspective—can be made by placing increased attention on archetypal subaltern and interlocutor roles that reformulate, and are integral to, global policing. This fieldwork provided some useful additions: *O policial jurídico neo-colonial*—the neo-colonial legal ace who returns to overseas territories to reanimate former colony–Metropole links through criminal justice processes and legal transplants; *O aspirante policial subalterno*—the subaltern officer candidate who travels abroad for training to later return with enhanced skills to translate into both police practice at home and enhanced leadership credentials for future career progression; *O intermediário do Sul*—the Southern broker who leverages postcolonial and subaltern status within efforts to combat global insecurities, increasing local agency within transnational policing. In short, by thinking more broadly, with increased attention to pluri-directional mobility in the co-constitution of global policing, we might (re)cast, or at least redefine, the roles within a more diverse and inclusive *dramatis personae* of global cops. One that better integrates subaltern, Southern, and postcolonial actors and perspectives into the story of global policing, as well as the diverse contributions they make to it. One that also challenges any suggestion of a global policing project with a coherent set of agendas or interests.

International Broker or Postcolonial Intermediary? Atlantic Policing of Global Insecurities

> It's the mid-Atlantic right? This is the crossing point for almost everything, right? ... Good and evil ... We are aware that the future of Cape Verde will depend on our actions, for better or for worse. But we are also aware of our vulnerabilities ... We don't have the means ... Just go to the Canary Islands. The police have more means in terms of naval resources than the whole of Cape Verde ... In this world of transnational crime, nobody can fight transnational crime just through the resources they have. And we feel that we also have an important role to play in combating this crime and we have been collaborating, with the resources we have, with the knowledge we have. We've been doing what we can to contribute to less crime, haven't we?

These comments from a senior PNCV officer demonstrate keen awareness of the threat that illicit mobilities pose not only to distant locations by transiting through Cape Verde, but also as regards future security and stability within the archipelago itself. The officer's comments reiterate their appreciation that transnational threats necessitate bilateral/multilateral action and that Cape Verde has an important role to play within such efforts. Indeed, whilst irregular migration from Africa and transatlantic drug trafficking present *'illicit' flows to be policed* by Cape Verdean authorities, it should also be recognized that these mobilities have also catalysed *flows of policing/ security technologies and trainings* into Cape Verde through a multitude of cooperative arrangements. The United Nations Office on Drugs and Crime (UNODC); the Economic Community of West African States (ECOWAS); the United States Africa Command (AFRICOM); Frontex—the European Border and Coast Guard Agency and wider European Mobility Partnership; support from powerful foreign governments through diplomatic missions—not least the USA and China: these represent just some of the auspices for transnational security governance in this increasingly securitized Atlantic space.

In this context, Cape Verde has emerged as a strategic hub for operationalizing both global prohibition regimes (against narco-traffic) and global mobility regimes (to combat irregular immigration and implement deportation) in the region.[6] The archipelago's security agencies now also act, in effect, as sentinels for those 'seigneurial states' which dominate transnational policing; those authorizing entities 'that seek, for instrumental or higher-minded reasons, to share or impose their conceptions of what appropriate regimes of law and order are upon other societies' (Goldsmith and Sheptycki, 2007, p. 21; see also, Sheptycki, 2007a, pp. 49–52). Consistently viewed as a good student of Western democracy, Cape Verde represents an important setting for the more nuanced examination of 'neo-colonial penality' advanced by Stambøl (2021b). The sheer volume, and diverse sources, of bilateral arrangements that endeavour to enlist Cape Verde's strategic advantage, also furnish 'brokering spaces in the transnational security field' (Qadim, 2014, p. 242). In essence, opportunities through which to assert agency within the asymmetric power arrangements of penal/ policing assistance and global mobility regulation. Opportunities also for Cape Verde, and its policing structures, to increase their standing and to earn respect within the global arena—not least from Western actors and international organizations perceived to be at the forefront of modern policing. However, Cape Verde's willing participation in externalized mobility–security arrangements also carries attendant risks; not only of reanimating aspects of its colonial intermediary past, but also of making its security arrangements complicit in processes of international othering in this postcolonial setting.

Stambøl's (2021a; 2021b) exploration of neocolonial penal transplants highlights how certain African criminal justice agencies harness their strategic location and importance to increase their bargaining power within the arrangements through which fortress continents conduct border control at a distance. In this way, 'penal aid to African countries may not only decrease or hollow out their sovereignty, but may also buttress it' (Stambøl, 2021b, p. 549). The situation is highly contextual and nuanced. In the case of Cape Verde's resource-poor policing and security apparatus, significant benefits can accrue through implementing the security arrangements of others. In this context of Occidental policeness, the *bons polícias* ('good police officers') of Cape Verde—as our ILO interlocutor referred to them—embrace the

[6] There is historical precedent for Cape Verde's strategic importance within global prohibition regimes. Under the Treaty of Washington of 1942, the US Navy was authorized to use the Cape Verdean archipelago as a base for their anti-slavery naval policing actions (Lobban Jr, 2019, p. 38).

opportunities for capacity-building, modernization, and professionalization afforded by foreign police assistance. For example, this was recognized in how participation within intelligence frameworks such as the Africa–Frontex Intelligence Community mitigated weak sub-regional policing links. One respondent described how such support 'had a huge impact, because Frontex allowed for various coordinations even with countries here in our sub-region that in operational terms did not have this connection, but which Frontex made work, in the fight against illegal immigration'. Additionally, Cape Verdeans are well aware of the risk that narco-trafficking poses through the experience of its Creole sister country, Guinea-Bissau—often referred to as Africa's first 'narco-state' (Kane, 2019). Shoring up domestic policing capacity, whilst also engaging with transnational crime control efforts, mitigates this risk.

The operationalization of foreign security priorities has catalysed criticism within Cape Verde. For example, a 2017 Statute of Forces Agreement which provided certain immunities for US military and contractors passing through the islands was challenged for undermining the islands' sovereignty (EFE, 2018). Other concerns resonate with the archipelago's colonial past and how it still weighs upon the mindset and outlook of its political elites. Varela and Lima (2018) consider its role within global mobility regimes as one of 'Foreman of the Empire'. For them, acquiescence to externalized border controls is symptomatic of an inability to break with the colonial past and has resulted in the forging of new suspect communities. Bowling and Sheptycki (2012) have observed how '"Othering" is integral to [policing] the space of flows' and creates categories of 'suitable enemies and folk-devils' (p. 115). In Cape Verde's intermediary redux for the twenty-first century, othering processes renew linkages between criminalization, deportation, immigration, and racialization in the transnational apparatus of mobility control. Priority targets of this discourse of insecurity reverberate in the public domain. A pejorative counterpoint to the cadre of subaltern global cops previously identified is furnished through the creation of *glocal* folk-devils for this transatlantic setting: the *mandjaku* African immigrant, the Latin American *narco* drug-trafficker, the *Americano* deportee, and the *thug* youth-gang member.

Transnational security assemblages may furnish emancipatory pathways towards greater agency if harnessed strategically. However, the power imbalances inherent within such arrangements, when combined with the selective priorities of transnational policing, can reactivate subordinate enlistments of the past. Whilst there is much still to uncover from attempts to mediate postcoloniality in the face of global insecurities in this islands setting, Cape Verde's transnational policing engagement reflects the need for the type of nuanced analyses advanced by scholars such as Qadim (2014) and Stambøl (2021a; 201b). At the nexus of colonial legacies, geopolitical interests, and illicit transnational flows, Cape Verde reflects how Southern settings can extract benefits from the multiple seigneurial suitors who covet their integration into mobility–security regimes. In terms of ambitions to decolonize criminological and policing scholarship, mapping Cape Verde's complex externalized security interactions in greater depth and engaging a wider range of its policing and security voices will yield further insights into how knowledge of the transnational policing environment is both accumulated and strategically repurposed.

'If They Build It, Will They Come?' An International Police Academy for Cape Verde

Policing in Cape Verde has recently displayed ambitions to progress beyond the status of serial recipient of foreign police assistance. It has emerged as an aspirant donor of policing knowledge and expertise through aspirations to establish an *Academia de Segurança Interna* (Academy of Internal Security) for the islands. This higher education facility would not only train Cape Verdean policing and security actors but would also welcome African police officers from other regional settings for training in Cape Verde. This objective has developed through domestic police and political mission statements (PNCV, 2014, p. 66), has been a feature of diplomatic exchange (PortugalDigital, 2013), and was formally committed to in 2017 when the Cape Verdean government recognized these institutional plans in programmatic law.[7] However, ambitions to construct this facility have yet to be realized. There are well-acknowledged challenges to these capacity-building objectives, not least its viability in terms of numbers and funding, as well as questions regarding external interest. However, the aspiration to construct this international police training facility is symbolic and a powerful metaphor. It reiterates how Cape Verdean policing wishes to 'flip the switch' on the direction of policing mobilities and progress towards greater agency within regional and transnational policing. To be clear, the plans envisaged are much more expansive than training new cohorts of Cape Verdean police officers at home, rather than dispatching them abroad. This facility could extend usage to the wider, pluralized penal and security fields of the archipelago; training prison guards and private security officers has been discussed. However, it is its potential role as a hub for inter-African police training and exchange that is of most interest. Those respondents interviewed saw an international police training facility as a site where the PNCV model for democratic and non-militarized policing could be shared with other police forces from across the region, not least other Luso-African police forces. As one senior police officer explained:

> I ... for example, think that Cape Verde possesses the conditions, at least in terms of geographic location, for a police institute to serve Western Africa ... I think that, even at the level of training ... the Cape Verdean Police ... Not only the Cape Verdean police, because not everything is done by the police. The very structure of learning in Cape Verde has the right conditions to provide training in our region.

The very notion of constructing an international police training facility signals a police force with self-confidence about its abilities and a keenness to receive regional and transnational recognition. It also sends a message about the quality and investment in policing being made in that particular setting. Certainly, there is *performative* value in signalling greater ambition within the transnational policing community, and public discourse around the academy *acts out* a leadership role. Whilst police officers have

[7] See the legal decree on the Academy of Internal Security: *O Decreto-Lei* n.o 49/2017 de 14 de novembro.

been held out as condensation symbols of the national character (Loader, 1997), this can also be extended to those police academies where they are trained. Whether it was establishing the ISCPSI in Lisbon after the demise of Portuguese dictatorship (Durão and Lopes, 2015), or grand ambitions for a new police college in Northern Ireland as part of transitional policing (Ellison, 2007), training institutions are important symbols within attempts to construct narratives of police reform and institutional prestige. In essence, they can *tell a story* about their particular police organizations (Beek and Göpfert, 2015). In the case of the plans for an Academy of Internal Security in Cape Verde, this story can be read both positively and more critically.

First and foremost, this higher education facility would enable the PNCV to create a training programme for its officers; one better tailored towards the contextual requirements of Cape Verde than inevitable compromises of formation abroad. Second, the PNCV would be able to receive and train police officers from other West African or Luso-African countries, showcasing its more democratic and less militarized brand of policing in the process. As previously noted, Cape Verde has already made significant progress in 'Marketing Good Governance' within its place branding and public diplomacy (Baker, 2006; 2009). For the PNCV to promote itself as a beacon of hope for democratic policing elsewhere in the region is a logical extension of such efforts. Whilst much academic attention has centred upon critiquing Western police exports to Africa, an international training facility in this Atlantic archipelago would open pathways for increased *inter-African* co-constitution of policing, potentially creating new police training networks and intra-continental mobilities.

However, from a more critical perspective, there is also the possibility that ambitions for an international police training facility in Cape Verde might also reflect a certain *learned behaviour* born from extensive engagement with (predominantly) Western foreign police assistance. In essence, Cape Verdean policing has, like many other African police forces, been exposed to multiple policing exports and can undoubtedly perceive the value added by forging export possibilities of its own. A 'geo-policial brand' (O'Reilly, 2017b) for Cape Verde could be forged around the more democratic and less militarized policing the PNCV delivers, the good governance credentials of Cape Verde, and also the archipelago's strategic importance for transnational policing action. To draw on the work of Ellison and Pino (2013), this push for protagonism within foreign police assistance seemingly replicates behaviour associated with Western police exporters; the Cape Verdean policing establishment 'Seeing like a *donor*' and 'Doing it the Western Way!' Consequently, ambitions for an enhanced role for Cape Verde within foreign police training must be set against its own (over)exposure to patterns of commodification, externalization, and promotionalism.

Considering the aforementioned Occidental policeness of the PNCV, and an outlook that can sometimes prioritize Portugal, Europe, Brazil, the United States, or even China, over its African neighbours, there is room for concern about underlying rationales for such ambition. The same questions that are raised regarding the Western export of police knowledge, training, and models must also be reflexively applied to Cape Verde. Is its policing model appropriate and translatable for other African contexts? Indeed, efforts to position itself as the best practice exemplar for democratic policing rest upon an implicit juxtaposition against *other*, seemingly tainted, African police forces. Colonial bequests again resurface in tacit superiority and distinction from their African counterparts as integral to the promotion of Cape Verdean policing. None of this is to suggest that there is not merit for an international police academy in Cape Verde, or that senior PNCV officers are entirely unreflexive regarding this proposal—they were quite aware of some of its limitations. Rather, it is to encourage that academy ambitions be viewed through a more critical lens. Engagement with the global policing mission has always been marked by a complex blend of 'self-interest as well as the desire to do good and to be seen to be doing good' (Goldsmith and Sheptycki, 2007, p. 7). There is much potential for Cape Verdean policing to play an important role in forging new cooperative arrangements for police training across the African continent, as well as in providing lessons in brokering benefits from transnational policing interaction. An islands nation that rests at the North–South interface, on the transit routes of illicit mobilities and which carries a heavy colonial legacy, it is a setting that presents both pathways and pitfalls for greater agency and ambition within the global policing web.

Conclusion

Ostensibly peripheral to the global policing web, this chapter has spotlighted how Cape Verdean policing is, in fact, highly integrated within transnational networks. Previously, a significant blind spot for policing scholarship, this Atlantic archipelago represents a rich setting through which to examine evolving subaltern roles within global policing mobilities. In this regard, it makes the following important contributions. First, through selective and critical absorption of foreign policing expertise, whilst also promoting its own policing brand externally, Cape Verdean policing challenges uncritical assumptions that subaltern actors are merely passive beneficiaries for knowledge flowing unidirectionally from North to South. Second, it offers insights into the policing nexus of postcolonial and transnational conditions; unpacking how policing in these islands carries heavy burdens of colonialism, as well as a schizophrenic identity born of multiple overlapping external influences. Third, it charts how this exemplary subaltern policing actor seeks to cultivate its own space in the transnational realm: by brokering its strategic location for policing global insecurities; by playing off multiple suitors for its policing attentions to extract capacity-building; and, by harnessing its own democratic policing credentials to cultivate a reputation as a Southern site for lesson-drawing. Fourth, by focusing on subaltern policing from this Atlantic context, possibilities can also be identified for the *worlding* of subaltern policing, practically and conceptually. By drawing out the experiences, roles, and ambitions of PNCV officers whose training and police work reaches beyond these islands, a deeper appreciation is advanced of subaltern action within the global policing web. Indeed, moving such, less acknowledged, roles centre stage reveals a more diverse *corpus* of transnationally engaged policing actors, and interactions, than previously recognized; one that better reflects evolving policing patterns throughout history and across the globe.

For subaltern settings such as Cape Verde, participating in transnational policing mobilities affords both *emancipatory pathways* towards greater agency and independence, as well as *postcolonial pitfalls* that risk reanimating problematic subordinate/

intermediary roles of the past. Certainly, Cape Verdean policing actors demonstrated knowledgeable and knowing engagement with transnational policing. This was evident: when critically assimilating foreign police imports to selectively adapt what was useful and discard what was not; when contributing to foreign policing agendas to avail of modernizing opportunities and be recognized as an international player; and, when cultivating their own policing brand and developing inter-African training links to enhance networks and credibility. However, a note of caution must be added to this discussion: *are such policing advances truly emancipatory*? Breaking from the yoke of colonial oppression has, in this chapter, been shown not to deliver a truly independent or protagonist place within the architecture of transnational policing or a policing organization free of external influence. We should be cautious not to conflate those important advances outlined earlier with emancipation from, or resistance to, powerful policing arrangements. It may prove that evolving towards increased status and recognition are very necessary precursor steps on the pathway towards ever greater independence. However, such progress will usually occur in compliance with established global policing power dynamics and will often be tied to the complex policing identity bequeathed to postcolonial settings. None of this is meant to dismiss the very real benefits for Cape Verdean policing that can derive from critically integrating foreign policing imports. Rather it is to reiterate that engagement with transnational policing is most often achieved within the constraints of pre-formatted power structures. Enhanced standing rarely equates to independent action on a level playing field. For both subaltern policing actors, and indeed for those who study them, articulating what emancipation really means within the context of transnational policing is a necessary next step in further advancing decolonizing agendas.

References

Agozino, B. (2007) *Counter-Colonial Criminology: A Critique of Imperialist Reason*. Bristol: Pluto Press.

Agozino, B. (2019) 'Humanifesto of the decolonization of criminology and justice', *Decolonization of Criminology and Justice*, 1(1), pp. 5–28.

Agozino, B. (2020) 'Africana Liberation Criminologies', in Agozino, B., Saleh-Hanna, V., Onyeozili, E. C., and Dastile, N. P. (eds) *The Routledge Handbook of Africana Criminologies*. London: Routledge, pp. 18–31.

Aliverti, A., Carvalho, H., Chamberlen, A. et al. (2021) 'Decolonizing the criminal question', *Punishment & Society*, 23(2), pp. 297–316.

Amar, P. (2013) *Global South to the Rescue: Emerging Humanitarian Superpowers and Globalizing Rescue Industries*. Abingdon: Routledge.

Baker, B. (2006) 'Cape Verde: The most democratic nation in Africa?', *Journal of Modern African Studies*, 44(4), pp. 493–511.

Baker, B. (2009) 'Cape Verde: Marketing good governance', *African Spectrum*, 44(2), pp. 135–147.

Beek, J. and Göpfert, M. (2015) 'Travelling police: The potential for change in the wake of police reform in West Africa', *Social Anthropology/Anthropologie Sociale*, 23(4), pp. 465–479.

Beek, J., Göpfert, M., Owen, O., and Steinberg, J. (2017) *Police in Africa: The Street Level View*. Oxford: Oxford University Press.

Bilgin, P. (2016) 'Unpacking the "Global"', in Hönke, J. and Müller, M.-M. (eds) *The Global Making of Policing: Postcolonial Perspectives*. Abingdon: Routledge, pp. 167–177.

Blanchard, E., Bloembergen, M., and Lauro, A. (2017) *Policing in Colonial Empires: Cases, Connections, Boundaries (ca. 1850–1970)*. Brussels: Peter Lang.

Blaustein, J. (2015) *Speaking Truths to Power: Policy Ethnography and Police Reform in Bosnia and Herzegovina*. Oxford: Oxford University Press.

Bordonaro, L. I. (2010) '"A Tiger That Wants to Become a Lion": Violent Forms of Agency Among Youth in Cape Verde', Paper presented to the 7th Congress of African Studies. Lisbon: Congresso Ibérico De Estudos Africano. Available at: http://hdl.handle.net/10071/2254 (accessed 10 June 2022).

Bowling, B. and Sheptycki, J. W. E. (2012) *Global Policing*. London: Sage.

BPDNews (2018) 'BPD Chief Gross and BPD Cabo Verdean-American Police Officers Meet in Praia to Share Best Practices', 18 January. Available at: https://bpdnews.com/news/2018/1/18/bpd-in-the-community-bpd-chief-gross-and-bpd-cabo-verdean-american-police-officers-share-best-practices-in-policing (accessed 10 June 2022).

Bretas, M. (1997) *Ordem na Cidade: O Cotidiano da Autoridade Policial no Rio de Janeiro,* 1907–1930. Rio de Janeiro: Rocco.

Brogden, M. (1987a) 'The emergence of the police: The colonial dimension', *British Journal of Criminology*, 27(1), pp. 4–14.

Brogden, M. (1987b) 'An act to colonise the internal lands of the island: Empire and the origins of the professional police', *International Journal of the Sociology of Law*, 15, pp. 179–208.

Brogden, M. and Ellison, G. (2013) *Policing in an Age of Austerity: A Postcolonial Perspective*. London: Routledge.

Ciocchini, P. and Greener, J. (2021) 'Mapping the pains of neo-colonialism: A critical elaboration of Southern criminology', *British Journal of Criminology*, 61(6), pp. 1612–1629.

Drotbohm, H. (2011) 'On the durability and the decomposition of citizenship: The social logics of forced return migration in Cape Verde', *Citizenship Studies*, 15(3–4), pp. 381–396.

Durão, S. S. B. and Lopes, D. (2015) 'Formação Internacional, Comunidades de Saberes e Mudança Institucional: Os Oficiais de Polícia Africanos Formados em Lisboa', *Fórum Brasileiro de Segurança Pública*, 9(1), pp. 122–139.

EFE (2018) 'Cape Verde ratifies controversial military agreement with the US', *Agencia EFE*, 20 September. Available at: www.efe.com/efe/english/world/cape-verde-ratifies-controversial-military-agreement-with-the-us/50000262-3755692 (accessed 10 June 2022).

Ellison, G. (2007) 'A blueprint for democratic policing anywhere in the world? Police reform, political transition and conflict resolution in Northern Ireland', *Police Quarterly*, 10(3), pp. 243–269.

Ellison, G. and O'Reilly, C. (2008) 'From Empire to Iraq and the War on Terror: The transplantation and the commodification of the (Northern) Irish policing experience', *Police Quarterly*, 11(4), pp. 395–426.

Ellison, G. and Pino, N. (2013) *Globalization, Police Reform and Development: Doing It The Western Way?* Basingstoke: Ashgate.

Foucault, M. (2003) *Society Must Be Defended: Lectures at the Collège de France,* 1975–76. London: Penguin.

Goldsmith, A. and Sheptycki, J. W. E. (2007) 'Introduction', in Goldsmith, A. and Sheptycki, J. W. E. (eds) *Crafting Transnational Policing: Police Capacity-Building and Global Policing Reform*. Oxford: Hart Publishing, pp. 1–27.

Gonçalves, G. R. (2014) 'Police reform and the transnational circulation of police models: The Portuguese case in the 1860s', *Crime, Histoire & Sociétés/Crime, History & Societies*, 18(1), pp. 5–29.

Gonçalves, G. R. and Cachado, R. A. (2017) 'Colonial Policing and the Portuguese Empire (c. 1870–1961)', in O'Reilly, C. (ed.) *Colonial Policing and the Transnational Legacy: The Global Dynamics of Policing Across the Lusophone Community*. Abingdon: Routledge, pp. 17–34.

Gorjão Henriques, J. (2018) 'To Be African in Cape Verde is Taboo', *BUALA*, 4 December. Available at: www.buala.org/en/to-read/to-be-african-in-cape-verde-is-a-taboo (accessed 10 June 2022).

Hills, A. (2000) *Policing Africa: Internal Security and the Limits of Liberalization*. Boulder, CO: Lynne Rienner.

Hills, A. (2014). 'What is policeness? On being police in Somalia', *British Journal of Criminology*, 54(5), pp. 765–783.

Hönke, J. and Müller, M.-M. (2012) 'Governing (in)security in a postcolonial world: Transnational entanglements and the worldliness of "local" practice', *Security Dialogue*, 43(5), pp. 383–401.

Hönke, J. and Müller, M.-M. (2016) *The Global Making of Policing: Postcolonial Perspectives*. Abingdon: Routledge.

Jones, T., Blaustein, J., and Newburn, T. (2021) 'Researching cross-national policy mobilities in crime control', *Criminology & Criminal Justice*, 21(3), pp. 408–426.

Kane, M. (2019) 'Drug Trafficking: Is Cape Verde Doomed to Become a Narco-State'? *ENACT*, 4 June. Available at: https://enactafrica.org/enact-observer/is-cape-verde-doomed-to-become-a-narco-state (accessed 10 June 2022).

Lima, R. (2018) 'De Gangues a Organizações de Rua: Grupos de Jovens Armados e a Construção de Uma Cultura de Resistência', *Revista Periferias*, 1(1), p. 1–25. Available at: http://revistaperiferias.org/materia/de-gangues-a-organizacoes-de-rua-grupos-de-jovens-armados-e-a-construcao-de-uma-cultura-de-resistencia/?pdf=173 (accessed 10 June 2022).

Loader, I. (1997) 'Policing and symbolic power: Questions of the social', *British Journal of Sociology*, 48, pp. 1–18.

Lobban Jr, R. (2019) *Cape Verde: Crioulo Colony to Independent Nation*. London: Routledge.

Mester, A. (2016) 'Iberian Atlantic Imperial Carcerality Vestiges of Colonial Disciplinary Violence in Cape Verde, Equatorial Guinea and Mozambique', PhD thesis, University of Michigan. Available at: https://deepblue.lib.umich.edu/bitstream/handle/2027.42/133180/amester_1.pdf?sequence=1&isAllowed=y (accessed 10 June 2022).

Newburn, T., Jones, T., and Blaustein, J. (2018) 'Policy Mobilities and Comparative Penality', *Theoretical Criminology*, 22(4), pp. 563–581.

O'Reilly, C. (2017a) *Colonial Policing and the Transnational Legacy: The Global Dynamics of Policing Across the Lusophone Community*. Abingdon: Routledge.

O'Reilly, C. (2017b) 'Branding Rio de Janeiro's Pacification Model: A Silver Bullet for the "Planet of Slums"?', in O'Reilly, C. (ed.) *Colonial Policing and the Transnational Legacy the Global Dynamics of Policing Across the Lusophone Community*. Abingdon: Routledge, pp. 227–252.

Pereira, N. (2021) 'A Formação Superior Policial da Polícia Nacional de Cabo Verde', Masters thesis in Police Science. Lisbon: ISCPSI. Available at: https://comum.rcaap.pt/handle/10400.26/37063 (accessed 10 June 2022).

Plácido dos Santos, G. (2014) 'Cape Verde and Drug Trafficking: A Major Challenge to the Rule of Law', *IPRIS Viewpoints*, 158, pp. 1–2.

PNCV (2014) *'Cabo Verde Disponível Para Acolher Uma Escola de Polícia da CPLP', Revista da Polîcia Nacional*, Praia: EME—Marketing e Eventos, Lda, p. 66.

PortugalDigital (2013) 'Angola Pretende Ajudar Cabo Verde Na Criação da Escola de Polícia da CPLP', 17 November. Available at: https://portugaldigital.com.br/angola-pretende-ajudar-cabo-verde-na-criacao-da-escola-de-policia-da-cplp/ (accessed 10 June 2022).

Qadim, N. E. (2014) 'Postcolonial challenges to migration control: French–Moroccan cooperation practices on forced returns', *Security Dialogue*, 45(3), pp. 242–261.

Rabaka, R. (2016) *Resistance and Decolonization: Amilcar Cabral*. London: Rowman & Littlefield.

Rocha, E. M. (2017) 'O Imigrante Oeste-Africano Como o Indesejável? Acerca do Processo de Racialização em Cabo Verde', *Mediações—Revista de Ciências Sociais*, 22(1), pp. 105–129.

Sheptycki, J. W. E. (2007a) 'The Constabulary Ethic and the Transnational Condition', in Goldsmith, A. and Sheptycki, J. W. E. (eds) *Crafting Transnational Policing: Police Capacity-Building and Global Policing Reform*. Oxford: Hart, pp. 31–71.

Sheptycki, J. W. E. (2007b) 'Criminology and the transnational condition: A contribution to international political sociology', *International Political Sociology*, 1(4), pp. 391–406.

Sinclair, G. and Williams, C. A. (2007) '"Home and away": The cross-fertilization between "colonial" and "British" policing, 1921–85', *Journal of Imperial and Commonwealth History*, 35(2), pp. 221–238.

Sozzo, M. (2011) 'Cultural Travels and Crime Prevention in Argentina', in Melossi, D., Sozzo, M., and Sparks, R. (eds) *Travels of the Criminal Question: Cultural Embeddedness and Diffusion*. Oxford: Hart, pp. 185–215.

Stambøl, E. M. (2021a) 'Borders as penal transplants: Control of territory, mobility and illegality in West Africa', *Theoretical Criminology*, 25(3), pp. 474–492.

Stambøl, E. M. (2021b) 'Neo-colonial penality? Travelling penal power and contingent sovereignty', *punishment & Society*, 23(4), pp. 536–556.

Steinberg, J. (2020) 'Ethnographies of global policing', *Annual Review of Law and Social Science*, 16, pp. 131–145.

Stoler, A. N. (2013) *Imperial Debris: On Ruins and Ruination*. Durham, NC: Duke University Press.

Tomás, A. (2021) *Amilcar Cabral: The Life of a Reluctant Nationalist*. London: Hurst & Co.

Vale de Almeida, M. (2004) *An Earth Coloured Sea*. London: Berghahn Books.

Valente, M. M. G. (2014) *Teoria Geral Do Direito Policial*. Lisbon: Almedina.

Varela, O. B. and Lima, R. W. (2017) 'Foreman of the Empire? Re-Analysis of the Readmission Agreement with the European Union and the Repatriation in the Archipelago of Cape Verde', Instituto Superior de Economia e Gestão, CesA/CSG. Available at: http://hdl.handle.net/10400.5/14492 (accessed 10 June 2022).

Zoettl, P. A. (2016) '*Morabeza*, cash or body: Prison, violence and the state in Praia, Cape Verde', *International Journal of Cultural Studies*, 19(4), pp. 391–406.

13
'Nothing is Lost, Everything is ... Transferred'
Transnational Institutionalization and Ideological Legitimation of Torture as a Neocolonial State Crime

Melanie Collard

Introduction

This chapter is not concerned with acts of torture as 'ordinary' crimes—that is, acts committed by private individuals or carried out by individual officials at their own initiative—but as state crimes: acts of torture that are explicitly prescribed, tacitly condoned, or at least tolerated by the authorities. It is focused on the 'institutionalization of torture' that took place in Argentina between 1976 and 1983. This analysis is, therefore, about great criminal power, namely that of the national (Argentine) and transnational (French) institutional perpetrators who were complicit in torture—a behaviour which violates human rights principles and is perceived as deviant by the international community and by domestic audiences.

Many academics have examined whether torturers, acting as agents of the state, were essentially different from the rest of the population (Arendt, 1965; Browning, 1998; Clarke, 2008; Gibson, 1990; Haney et al., 1973; Haritos-Fatouros, 1988; 2003; Huggins et al., 2002; Lankford, 2009; Lifton, 1986; Milgram, 1974; Staub, 1989; Zimbardo, 2007). Most of their findings seem to suggest that individual personality and its background information, by themselves, cannot distinguish individuals who will commit torture or other cruel acts from those who will not. If it is true that most torturers were not born, it follows that they must have been made. As to the 'making ingredients', some pointed at obedience to authority or ideological persuasion—processes which, in turn, require authorization, dehumanization, and routinization (Cohen, 2001; Crelinsten, 2003; 2007; Kelman and Hamilton, 1989; Osiel, 2004). Others suggested bureaucratization and its diffusion of responsibility (Bauman, 1989; Lifton, 1986). Others still thought that conformity to a violent group that promotes a culture marked by male domination assumes a more central role in the creation of official torturers (Browning, 1998; Huggins et al., 2002; Lankford, 2009; Staub, 1989). Sometimes, however, most agreed that would-be torturers must be taught to torture without question: training becomes necessary (Cohen, 2001; Crelinsten, 2007; Huggins et al., 2002; Haritos-Fatouros, 1988; 2003; Lankford, 2009; Gibson, 1990). Generally, this is a two-phase process: first, recruits must be made less sensitive to their own pain; and, second, they must be made less sensitive to the pain they inflict on others. This training is usually coupled with situationally specific temporary removals

Melanie Collard, *'Nothing is Lost, Everything is ... Transferred'* In: *Decolonizing the Criminal Question.* Edited by: Ana Aliverti, Henrique Carvalho, Anastasia Chamberlen, and Máximo Sozzo, Oxford University Press.
DOI: 10.1093/oso/9780192899002.003.0014

of moral constraint, better known as 'techniques of neutralisation' (Sykes and Matza, 1957), which imply an awareness of infringing a rule that the delinquent, at some level, accepts as legitimate, with perhaps 'denial of responsibility' being the most common modus operandi (Cohen, 2001, p. 9).

This chapter examines the transnational nature of this 'training' between France and Argentina. Whilst the United States played a pivotal role in the training of Latin American torturers particularly through Operation Condor and the School of the Americas as documented in the current literature on the subject (Aguila, 2010; Chomsky, 1991; Dinges, 2012; Fagen, 1992; Gareau, 2004; Hey, 1995; McClintock, 1992; Schirmer, 1998; Weschler, 1998) and torture was already a known technique to the military and police forces in Argentina before the transfer of the French expertise in the 1950s (Kalmanowiecki, 2000; Barreneche, 2019), a growing body of interpretative and qualitative research has provided compelling evidence of France's important role in this 'globalization of torture' and its prominent implication in the transformation of Argentine military into official torturers (Collard, 2018; Heinz, 1995; Llumá, 2002; Oliveira-Cézar, 2002; 2003; Périès, 1999; Ranalletti, 2005; Robin, 2004; Vidal-Naquet, 1963).[1] In the same line of arguments, this chapter suggests that the institutionalization and transnationalization of torture for political and ideological advantages are directly related to neocolonial settings.

This chapter will first examine how France came into conflict with its colonial inheritance[2] in Indochina (1946–1954) and Algeria (1954–1962). It will then explain that torture was central to the French army's defence of a waning colonial empire throughout most of the Algerian War. Its systematic use was the direct outcome of a methodology of warfare developed by the French in the 1950s which was intended to deal with both colonial and civil wars by not distinguishing 'insurgents' from 'population', and consequently merging civilians into a generic, dehumanized enemy. This chapter goes on to reveal that this methodology of warfare (as well as its underpinning ideology) became very attractive to other governments and allowed France to play an important role in the globalization of torture as French specialists in torture were able to pursue new careers well beyond the borders of Algeria[3] and, indeed, contributed to the culture of fear that developed between the 1960s and the 1980s in the Southern Cone of Latin America.[4] It will then engage in a reconstruction of the formation of the torture regime in Argentina (1976–1983), detailing the military relationship that France nurtured in Argentina and exploring especially the role of the French military advisors. Drawing on the case study, its suggests that an adequate explanation of torture perpetration requires looking beyond the level of the torture chamber, or even of the states in which torture is practised, to focus attention on the wider geopolitical context in which torture is embedded. It will

[1] This growing body of interpretative and qualitative research has involved the analysis of military and diplomatic government archives, public and private discourses, statements and reports of responsible government officials, autobiographies, army directives, documentary novels, newspaper articles, and letters.

[2] The term is used here to describe a set of unequal relationships between the colonial power and the colony itself.

[3] This is a comparable process to that of the global making of policing—see O'Reilly, this volume).

[4] See also the work of Huggins (1998) on the influence of the United States on police and military forces in the same period, including practices of torture.

conclude by arguing that a framework involving a layered analysis of torture perpetration offers an important lens through which to critique contemporary legacies of torture and state violence more generally.

The Algerian 'War of Decolonization' (1954–1962)

The institutionalization of torture in Algeria in the 1950s is well documented.[5] The renewed winds of democracy which blew in France after its liberation from the Germans very quickly came into conflict with its colonial inheritance, and outdated imperialism, first in Indochina (1946–1954),[6] followed by Algeria (1954–1962). By 1962, over 25,000 French soldiers had been killed and 60,000 wounded in Algeria, while on the Algerian side, over a million had died,[7] many of whom were also tortured (Lazreg, 2008, pp. 9–10).

In Algeria, torture was intimately linked to the nature of the colonial state—its use had begun in the aftermath of the French invasion in 1830, though it had not initially been institutionalized in the way that it was after 1954 (Le Cour Grandmaison, 2005, pp. 152–156). The war of decolonization (1954–1962) was the culmination of 'a long process of economic immiseration, political disenfranchisement, and colonial intolerance of Algerians' attempts to agitate for change within the system' (Lazreg, 2008, p. 4). At the time, the population of Algeria was mainly made up of two different cultural groups: on the one hand, there were the *Pieds-Noirs*—that is, nearly one million French nationals born on Algerian soil—and, on the other hand, the Muslim community.[8] The Algerian War saw the rise of a generation of young nationalists, many of whom joined the Front de Libération Nationale (FLN). These young people rejected their status as 'protected subjects' or 'French-Muslims', which they were accorded under a special legal system called the Code de l'Indigenat (Vaujour, 1985, p. 48). Algerian nationalism was subjected to fierce repression in which members of the *Pieds-Noirs* civilian population took part at times, exacerbating even more the ethnic nature of the conflict. With international decolonization processes under way in other latitudes, tensions also took on an ideological perspective. The FLN used the same techniques, followed the same gradual development, and based themselves on the same tactical principles as Viet Minh guerrillas had successfully utilized (Oliveira-Cézar, 2003, p. 71).[9] This was more than enough for the French military to believe at that time, and for a long time after Algerian independence in 1962, that communism had opened in Algeria a new front in its quest for world domination (Mazzei, 2002, pp. 110–111).

[5] See, e.g., Alleg, 1958; Branche, 2001; Fanon, 1963; Horne, 2006; Lazreg, 2008; Le Cour Grandmaison, 2005; MacMaster, 2004; Maran, 1989; Vaujour, 1985; Vidal-Naquet, 1963.

[6] In Indochina, the French army lost the war against the Viet Minh guerrillas who, led by Ho Chi Minh, had the support of Mao Tse-Tung's China and the Soviet Union (Grimal, 1985).

[7] More recently, some references (in Algeria) estimated that the figure is probably nearer two million (Horne, 2006, p. 538). This is an example of 'rewriting history'.

[8] See the work of Ghabrial (this volume) on Muslimness in the French empire.

[9] The Battle of Algiers was a focal point of the war, in which torture became systematic (Lazreg, 2008, p. 5), and it was conducted in an identical way to the 'Battle of Buenos Aires' (Abramovici, 2001, p. 28).

Or at least the 'threat of communism was used as a pretext to just a "colonial" war' (Collard, 2008, p. 81).[10]

Torture was central to the army's defence of a colonial empire in its waning years (Branche, 2001; Fanon, 1963; Lazreg, 2008; MacMaster, 2004; Maran, 1989; Vidal-Naquet, 1963). The systematic use of torture was the direct outcome of a methodology of counter-revolutionary warfare, the Doctrine of Revolutionary War—*Doctrine de Guerre Révolutionnaire*—that was developed by the French in the 1950s.[11] This French anti-subversive methodology was elaborated by several soldiers who were veterans of the Second World War and subsequent colonial wars as they saw in the Algerian War an opportunity for overcoming the humiliation of the loss of Indochina in May 1954 (Lazreg, 2008, pp. 3, 18). They studied the texts that nourished their adversaries in Indochina: Marx, Engels, Lenin, Lawrence of Arabia, and, most significantly, the one that summarized and surpassed them all: *Problems of Strategy in China's Revolutionary War*, written in 1936 by Mao Tse-Tung for the instruction of his officers in the Red Army. According to the latter, a guerrilla organization must permeate the population 'like fish in water' (Vidal-Naquet, 1963, p. 42). Indeed, during the Indochina war, guerrilla warfare[12] proved to be effective in confronting and defeating a stronger and more technically advanced army: that of France.

Consequently, the French Doctrine of Revolutionary War suggested that to combat and triumph over a revolutionary war, armies must adjust their conventional methods to their adversaries' subversive strategies (Branche, 2001, p. 326; Lazreg, 2008, p. 15). Since, according to this interpretation, the 'enemy' hides within and blends into the population with its support, an essential consequence is that any difference between combatants and civilians disappears: the entire population falls under suspicion, and everybody becomes a potential enemy. Accordingly, in the counter-revolutionary struggle, the key problem is that of obtaining intelligence—or *renseignement*—enabling one to know the enemy's organizational structure. Interrogation, in turn, is seen as the main tool for obtaining information, and recourse should be made to any means in order to get it, including the torture of those who are merely suspects (Mazzei, 2002, p. 125; Vidal-Naquet, 1963, p. 41).[13]

[10] This was exactly the same mistake as the Argentine military made at the start of the 1960s when they interpreted the insurrectional acts of the Peronist resistance as covert manifestations of international communism (Oliveira-Cézar, 2002, p. 27).

[11] Even though the theory did not initially advocate torture, it informed an anti-subversive warfare doctrine that could not be implemented successfully without its use (Lazreg, 2008, p. 15). Having set the theoretical and operational context, torture easily became institutionalized. Its use by the French military was not just an instance of violence committed by a few rogue individuals.

[12] Guerrilla, the diminutive of guerra, meaning 'little war', is actually an ancient military strategy used, for example, by the Carthaginians against the Romans and consolidated in modern times by the victory of Spanish irregular bands against the Napoleonic army in the early nineteenth century. The basic characteristics of a guerrilla war, which distinguish it from and permit it to confront effectively a regular army, are the following: the operation of small and highly mobile groups of armed persons; strategical reliance on the active and passive support of the civilian population; the waging of a war of attrition which over time inverts the relation of inferiority/superiority so that in its final stages the guerrilla force is able to transform itself into a regular army capable of defeating in open confrontation the weakened forces of the enemy (Aguilera, Peralta, and Beverly, 1980, p. 92).

[13] Torture, however, is not only inhuman but inefficient—it is frequently used against innocent people and the confessions extracted by it, if any, have no validity (Vidal-Naquet, 1963, p. 19). Beccaria summed up the ineffectiveness of torture as a truth-finding device with sarcasm: 'The strength of the muscles and the

The centrality of torture to the debate on the Algerian War resided not only in the horrors of the practices that took place, 'but rather in the extent to which it served as a symbol of a deeper corruption, both of the state and of the structures of military, administrative and judicial power that had made it possible' (MacMaster, 2004, p. 9). Some suggest that torture became established in Algeria at the behest of the government in France, which saw torture as necessary for the achievement of its war objectives, and its anti-torture rhetoric was just a way of keeping up democratic appearances (Carlson, 2000, p. 80; Maran, 1989, p. 57). The public outcry resulting from the systematic use of torture eventually contributed to the demise of the Fourth Republic, the re-entry of Charles de Gaulle into politics, the creation of the Fifth Republic, the recognition of Algerians' unconditional citizenship in 1958, and the signing of the Evian Accords in 1962, which led to the declaration of Algerian independence later in the year (Lazreg, 2008, p. 5; Peters, 1985, p. 133).[14] And yet for a long time no one was officially allowed to use the word 'war': one spoke only of the 'events in Algeria'. Only in October 1999 did the French National Assembly (parliament) decide to officially permit the term 'Algerian War'.[15]

The Argentine Dirty War (1976–1983)

An increasing amount of academic work has been undertaken concerning Argentina and its Dirty War (1976–1983).[16] On 24 March 1976, the powerful Argentine armed forces installed their dictatorship, launched the 'National Reorganisation Process'—*Proceso de Reorganización Nacional*—and initiated a phase of anti-insurgent warfare known as the 'Dirty War'—*Guerra Sucia*—that would last until 1983. During this period, Argentine soldiers kidnapped, tortured, and murdered between 9,000 and 30,000 people, according to the Comisión Nacional sobre la Desaparición de Personas (National Commission on the Disappearance of Persons) and human rights organizations (Abramovici, 2001; CONADEP, 1985; Feierstein, 2010; MacMaster, 2004). The torture techniques used included, but were not limited to: amputation; asphyxiation; attacks by animals; beatings; breaking bones; burnings, including roasting on a red-hot grill; cuttings; deprivation of food, water, sleep, or sanitary conditions; electro-shocks; *falacca* or *falanga*, blunt trauma to the soles of the feet with rods; genital mutilation, rape and other forms of sexual assault; injections or the use of chemicals to cause, for example, blindness; kickings; sensory deprivation or overload; stretchings; *submarino*, forced submersion of the victim into water, urine, vomit, blood, faeces, or

sensitivity of the nerves of an innocent person being known factors, the problem is to find the level of suffering necessary to make him confess to any given crime' (1963, p. 25).

[14] Whilst at the outbreak of the Algerian War most French people said that they preferred the maintenance of Algeria's departmental status, an arrangement which reflected the fiction that North Africa was no less French than France, on the eve of the opening of talks at Evian between the French government and the FLN, eight in ten of the French were in favour of granting independence to Algeria (Talbott, 1975, pp. 357–358).

[15] See Loi no. 99-882 du 18 octobre 1999, relative à la substitution, à l'expression 'aux opérations effectuées en Afrique du Nord', de l'expression 'à la guerre d'Algérie ou aux combats en Tunisie et au Maroc'.

[16] See, e.g., Aguila, 2010; Feierstein, 2010; Feitlowitz, 1998; Graziano, 1992; Heinz, 1995; Osiel, 2004; Perelli, 1990; Potash, 1980; Rouquié, 1978.

other matter until the point of suffocation is almost reached; suspension, including hangings and crucifixions; teeth or fingernail extraction; *teléfono*, boxed ears rupturing the tympanic membrane in the process; whippings; and psychological pressures such as forced nakedness, brainwashing, infected surroundings, confined isolation, mock executions, death threats, forced witnessing of others being tortured, or baby snatching right after delivery (Peters, 1985, pp. 169–171).

Although Argentina had been marked by the constant presence of armed forces in political life, be it through *coups d'état*, dictatorships, or exceptional regimes, the military government that settled itself between 1976 and 1983 exhibited new features which were distinct from those of prior authoritarian regimes in that country, in terms of both strategies and practices (Aguila, 2010, p. 137). Anti-communist ideology gave the Argentine armed forces a 'messianic mission to rebuild their societies by eliminating subversives'[17] (Feierstein, 2010, p. 44). Thus, the first necessary step would have been to update traditional military planning from a 'national defence' to a 'national security' military doctrinal approach by developing an operational capacity based on the hypothesis of 'Revolutionary War'. Yet, this 'concept was not new to the Argentine army' (Potash, 1980, p. 320). Indeed, the training in counterinsurgency techniques started much earlier. Willing to share its experience, the French military started advising the Argentine state in the ways and means of dealing with a 'new type of war' from the late 1950s. This influence would continue well into the establishment and organization of the 1976 dictatorship (Collard, 2018). Those contacts appeared mainly in two forms: on the one hand, the French *savoir-faire* (know-how) in Revolutionary War was taught at the École Supérieure de Guerre in Paris (the Paris Higher School of War) to an impressive body of international students, a quarter of whom came from Latin America, a further 22 per cent of whom were from Argentina; and, on the other, French assessors who had honed their torture skills in Indochina and in Algeria were invited from 1957 onwards, through the establishment of a French military mission into its Argentine equivalent, the Escuela Superior de Guerra of Buenos Aires (Abramovici, 2001; Carlson, 2000, p. 71; Collard, 2018; Feierstein, 2010, p. 45; MacMaster, 2004, p. 8; Périès, 1999, p. 709; Potash, 1980, p. 320; Robin, 2004, pp. 168–169; Rouquié, 1978, pp. 471–472).

As the Argentine government was looking for an effective way to stop rebellious Peronists who were supposedly taking part in the communist 'conspiracy' against the established order,[18] opportunities manifested themselves for the French military

[17] Subversives included not just the members of left-wing armed organizations (Lopez, 1987, pp. 137—148)—who together never numbered more than a thousand—but could be anyone 'with vaguely left-wing views, including labor union militants, students, doctors, lawyers, and social workers running soup kitchens and neighbourhood centers' (Feierstein, 2010, p. 46). According to Graziano, 80 per cent of Argentinian torture victims had no knowledge of subversive activities (1992, pp. 37–38).

[18] After the overthrow of General Perón in September 1955, Argentina entered a new phase. Perón's election in 1946 had introduced more economic and social rights to the working classes (Rouquié, 1978); the proscription and persecution of his political party triggered a spiral of violence that was, in reality, a confrontation between these classes and the upper/middle classes (James, 1990). The basic goal of Perón's opponents was the reversal of the redistribution of wealth that had taken place during his first two governments (from 1946 to 1955). A frightened bourgeoisie launched a frenetic anti-communist campaign with the aim of cracking down on the radical activism of the Peronists; little by little, this morphed into a tragic struggle in what the bourgeoisie saw as the defence of 'Western Christian civilisation' (Ranaletti, 2005, p. 297). This essentially local conflict then assumed international dimensions when Argentina joined the Cold War on the side of the regional bloc led by the United States (Rouquié, 1978, pp. 156–159).

advisors and veterans of Indochina and Algeria displaced by decolonization. Indeed, in Argentina, they found themselves in a 'society characterised by a state of tension over the social and financial advantages secured by the workers some years earlier, and by a state of agitation over what it thought were indicators of the presence of an internal enemy and the *expansion* of communist *subversion* within the social fabric' (Ranalletti, 2005, p. 296; Milanesio, 2013). This climate was familiar to them and they too believed in the same phantoms, interpreting colonial independence as the result of a manoeuvre orchestrated by international communism to destroy Western Christian civilization (Ranalletti, 2005, p. 298).[19] In this manner, the Doctrine of Revolutionary War—which possessed a 'transnational dimension' (Périès, 1999, p. 697; Oliveira-Cézar, 2002, p. 27)—managed to find in Argentina a 'fertile ground' early on as the French and Argentine militaries thought that 'Argentina and its people constituted an objective that was too important for international Marxism to overlook' (Robin, 2004, p. 202).

Through conferences, lectures, articles in military reviews, and technical training exercises, the French advisors, followed by their Argentine disciples (who would end up surpassing their masters), emphasized from 1957 onwards that the battlefield would now be the population itself and that information on potential subversives had to be gathered at all costs, even through the use of torture (Collard, 2018, p. 118; Robin, 2004, p. 201). The institution of the *disappeared*, the random searching of towns, the death flights, turning activists to infiltrate armed organizations and territorial division to 'control the population' were methods used by the French military in Algeria which were transferred to Argentina (Collard, 2018, p. 117). The fact that France had lost its colonial wars apparently did not matter. For the Argentine army, the French anti-subversive methodology of warfare provided a 'key for reading reality that made intelligible a complex and changing reality and enabled the armed forces, an institution that sinks its roots in medieval values, to cope with social complexity and change' (Perelli, 1990, p. 101). In turn, French specialists in torture were able—'with the authorisation of their superiors in the cabinet ministries and the military general staff' (Alleg, 2006, p. 101)—to pursue new careers well beyond the borders of Algeria.

For a long time, however, the French training of the Argentine military 'had no practical relevance for Argentina' (Heinz, 1995, pp. 75–76) and was, at least to some extent, 'out of place' since it was 'originally developed in the face of problems and in contexts different from those in relation to which [it was] subsequently implemented' (Aliverti et al., 2021, pp. 304–305; Sozzo, 2011, pp. 186–187; Newburn et al., 2018, p. 574). In fact, the 'new war' described by the French assessors did not exist in Argentina at that point: 'It was an anticipated war that the Argentine military would actually fight less than twenty years later' (Carlson, 2000, p. 73). This training in ideological extremism would ultimately function effectively in the reactionary education of the cadres—former Argentine 'students' of the French advisors—involved in Argentine state torture.[20]

[19] The 'civilising mission', the 'defence of national security', and the fight against 'international communism' were typically the main grounds for justification (Maran, 1989; Montero, 2008; Schirmer, 1998).

[20] The 'process of decontextualisation and adaptation' of the Doctrine of Revolutionary War in Argentina was, indeed, a two-stage operation: theoretical between 1958 and 1962, and practical between the end of the 1970s and the early 1980s (Périès, 1999, p. 768).

Neocolonialism as the Rationale Behind the Transnational Institutionalization and Ideological Legitimation of Torture

Gross human rights violations, such as torture, are frequently reinforced by the global economic system and connected to 'institutional structures of domination' (Herman, 1991, p. 91). Chambliss (1989) demonstrated how state networks can be crucial to the organization and support of activities that violate their own laws and international laws, and in so doing, fulfil their own broader political and economic objectives. By exporting torture equipment or torture expertise, *foreign* rather than *national* governments can also institutionalize torture in a given territory (Grewcock, 2008; Tomasevski, 1998). The 'West/North' seems to be leading this profitable business (Tomasevski, 1998, p. 199). The export of torture expertise to police, military, and security forces throughout the world is also undertaken through transnational transfers, via training manuals, courses, and practical instruction which are offered by 'Global North' professionals from the US, China, France, Russia, and the UK (Stanley, 2008). According to Amnesty International, 'much of this training occurs in secret so that the public and legislatures of the countries involved rarely discover who is being trained, what skills are being transferred, and who is doing the training' (2001, p. 41).

The question remains: why do democratic governments, such as France, become 'torture trainers' in authoritarian regimes, despite their claims that they take human rights seriously? Does democracy end at national borders? Facilitation and condemnation are sometimes exercised with astonishing ease by the same government at the same time, in relation to the same country (Tomasevski, 1998, pp. 183–184). According to Kelman, '[t]here are social conditions under which democratic cultures that ordinarily respect human rights may sanction torture, just as there are social conditions under which ordinary, decent individuals may be induced to take part in it' (2005, p. 128). The training in torture techniques and ideology may be a 'means by which more powerful states can tie weaker states into violence' (Stanley, 2008, p. 158). Indeed, torture does not happen in a vacuum: the geopolitical context is therefore key to understanding the motivation and opportunity behind the French involvement.[21]

The structures of the world of the 1960s, which took the form of two Western–Eastern blocs, capitalist imperialism and socialist imperialism, were so important to the ruling elites in the centre countries that they would have done almost anything to maintain them (Galtung, 1994, p. 130). Thus, to prevent changes in the geopolitical division of the world at the time, the central elites established their bridgeheads on the

[21] It has become received wisdom in criminology that all crimes require motivation and opportunity, an approach to crime that originated in the work of Cohen and Felson (1979). Furthermore, building on Merton's (1961) theory of anomie as extended to organizational crime by Passas (1990)—and on earlier work by Kramer and Michalowski (1990)—Kauzlarich and Kramer (1998) established an integrated analytical framework designed to indicate the key factors that contribute to, or restrain, various forms of state crime, among which is state torture. Taking into consideration the fact that states to some extent behave as rational actors, the authors argue that states' criminal behaviours result from the coincidence of pressure for goal attainment (*motivation*), availability, and perceived attractiveness of illegitimate means (*opportunity*), and an absence or weakness of social control mechanisms (*social control*) (Kauzlarich and Kramer, 1998, p. 148).

periphery and tied them closely to the centre so that they would carry out counterinsurgency in their own interests and in those of the centre (ibid, p. 131; Tomasevski, 1998, p. 199). These chains of repression across borders were created, for example, in Latin American and African armed forces, particularly in the former colonies. They can be defined as a process by which repression across borders is created through a kind of neocolonialism, defined as the 'last stage of imperialism' (Nkrumah, 1965).[22]

Neocolonialism results in the same kind of dependence of the colony upon the colonized as produced by colonialism, with the difference that neocolonialism does not use direct military force, but rather tools of soft power, such as the exchange of counterinsurgency know-how, as the latest bridge connecting the Global South to the Global North. Indeed:

> [t]hrough the long history of colonialism, in its various forms and moments, there have been constant importation processes from the metropoles to the colonies and ex-colonies. In some cases, they are simple dynamics of imposition and coercion that are based on the inequality, subordination and dependence that structure colonialism and neocolonialism. In others, they involve more complex dynamics in which actors from peripheral contexts play an active role promoting the adoption of crime control institutions, techniques and practices produced in central contexts as a form of incorporation into 'civilization', 'modernity' or 'development', but also as a way of obtaining benefits of various kinds.
>
> (Aliverti et al., 2021, p. 304)[23]

This notion of neocolonialism is key to understanding the transfer (or transplant) of violence through counterinsurgency strategies in the Global South (Jones and Newburn, 2019, pp. 16–20), and it is argued here that France's motivation for the transfer of expertise in Revolutionary War (which involved the use of torture) to Argentina was to maximize its military influence abroad.

One of the most important aspects of controlling the world military structure, in turn, is related to the 'development establishment' (Eide, 1977, p. 99). The French use of torture in Algeria was justified through the propaganda of the *mission civilisatrice*, 'civilizing mission', which was paradoxically founded on the Universal Rights of Man of 1789 (MacMaster, 2004, p. 5). France's colonial history was marked by the self-perception and notion of France as transmitter of the 'essence of French civilization, presumed to be the noblest in existence' (Confer, 1966, p. 3). The exercise of colonial

[22] In this context, this chapter differentiates between *imperialism* (a policy of forcefully extending a country's power and influence through (neo)colonization, use of military force, or other means), *colonialism* (a form of direct control over a territory and its people by an external power), and *neocolonialism* (a form of indirect control in which a dominating power uses newer and subtler modes of oppression and repression, such as economic, cultural, or military dominance). It adopts Nkrumah's (1965) definition of neocolonialism as the last stage of imperialism or *neo-imperialism*, which, in turn, can be defined as the domination and sometimes even hegemony over others primarily by way of formally free legal agreements, economic power, and cultural influence (see Koonings and Kruijt, 2002; Kuznetsov, 2006; Nkrumah, 1965).

[23] The commodification of torture through military and security training in counterinsurgency techniques can be linked to the research area of the 'transfer' or 'mobility' of institutions, techniques, and practices of crime control (Cohen, 1982; Jones et al., 2019; Jones and Newburn, 2019; Melossi et al., 2011; Newburn et al., 2018).

power is important in explaining the role of modern democratic states in the practice of torture (Peters, 1985, p. 138): in colonial settlements, torture presented a means by which economic and ideological control could be established, as it was used to 'encourage' productive bodies for labour (Fanon, 1963). Consequently, French initiatives abroad were justified on the basis of the understanding of its uniquely valuable contribution to the world: 'French culture' (Maran, 1989, p. 11). The peculiar inter-linkage of politics and culture led to the development of the 'civilizing mission ideology' (ibid, p. 12). The main assumption was that France—by virtue of its status as an enlightened civilization—had a duty to disseminate its *savoir-faire* widely. The ideology of the civilizing mission nurtured the Doctrine of Revolutionary War. It covered the field, motivating soldiers and generals, providing the government with another patriotic banner to wave, and slowing criticism of the policy on, and practice of, torture. Only with the end of colonialism did actions in the name of the civilizing mission dissipate, to be replaced by neo-imperialist and anti-communist ideologies in the discourse of 'development' (ibid, p. 12). Indeed, just as French trainers professed to believe that losing the war in Algeria would be 'synonymous with the decline of Christian civilization' (ibid, p. 16), the Argentine soldiers believed that if they were defeated within their own country 'world-wide communist domination would result' (Carlson, 2000, p. 74). This might be because the French Doctrine of Revolutionary War had its foundations in a range of historical components of the Catholic-military way of thought, most especially in the broad and all-inclusive conception of the 'enemy within' (Périès, 1999, p. 838; Ranalletti, 2005, p. 288). This ideological approach meant that the response to 'subversion' was generalized, and the use of torture became widespread (Carlson, 2000, p. 76; Ranalletti, 2005, p. 30).

In the postcolonial era, it remained a major concern that local forces should be equipped in order to help them to defend and expand imperial interests, increasingly in the context of the Cold War and the bipolar imperial confrontation between the United States and the Soviet Union (Collard, 2018, p. 69). For instance, the arming of the 'forward defense areas' (the very notion shows the continued impact of imperial thinking) by the United States in the 1950s and the 1960s was aimed at the containment of the Soviet Union and China (Galtung, 1994, p. 131). However, none of those 'forward defense areas' ever used the weapons provided to them for the purpose for which they had been intended—that is, defence against attack by the Soviet Union and China—but all the areas made use of their military training, directly or indirectly, for internal control (Eide, 1977, p. 102). It was in this context that the French military started advising the Argentine army in the ways and means of dealing with a 'new type of enemy'. The use of violence against the domestic population—such a prominent feature of the role of military in the Global South—was an outgrowth of counterinsurgency strategies developed in the West in the 1960s: 'A combination of a vast training program for officers from the ["]Third World["], and the pushing of weapons sales' (ibid, p. 99). Indeed, according to Eide, 'imperialism is the monopoly stage of violence' (ibid, p. 100). The period from the 'great' explorations, through the setting up of trading posts and missionary stations, to the establishment and exploitation of colonies, was characterized by violent European conquest. European conquest of the Global South during the history of colonialism meant the elimination of all its independent armed forces. These were replaced by subservient colonial armies, controlled by the colonial metropolis. Their main function was to suppress resistance to the accumulation of wealth through exploitation by the colonial powers (Grimal, 1985). It is easy to understand the psychological factors underlying the demand for independent armed forces by Global South regimes. Political independence, as a result of the elimination of colonialism, made it possible to break the monopoly of violence.

However, the process of militarization in the Global South did not lead to autonomy or to independence from the former imperial masters and from any new imperial pretenders: 'For this to be the case, it would require, first of all, that the armed forces being developed have as their prime function the defence of their country from external attack, primarily from the industrialised countries. But this is clearly not so' (Eide, 1977, p. 100). The notion that Argentina was developing its forces in order to prepare against external attacks in the early 1960s was ridiculous (Ranalletti, 2005). Studies of armed conflicts in the Global South show that most of them were internal, not international (Grimal, 1985). They were neo-imperial actions of expansion. Far from being used to protect their countries from imperial onslaughts, most Global South military forces served the same main function as the colonial army of the past: the repression of its own population.

It is therefore plausible to use a hypothesis which is the exact contradiction of the 'autonomy' assumption (Collard, 2018, p. 68). This would be that the militarization of the Global South *intensified* the domination by the Global North: 'It is possible that such militarization served to facilitate further penetration of external capital and technology, bringing the international and unequal division of labor to apply even to the remotest corners of the ["]Third World["]' (Eide, 1977, p. 100). On the political level, there might have been a façade of autonomy. On the economic level, however, there was an increasing subordination, not necessarily by serving some former colonialist industrialized metropolis, but rather 'by serving the totality of the old international economic order' (ibid, pp. 100–101). While it is true, however, that the personnel who actually carried out torture in the Argentine military were not French, these officers had been trained and influenced by France in their choice of techniques and strategies, as well as in the selection of targets (Collard, 2018, p. 69).

The motivations driving the French government were historical, political, and ideological factors that persisted from periods of colonization; the French neo-imperialist motives very obviously shaped patterns of criminal behaviour, both before and during the Argentine Dirty War. Such factors laid the foundations for the later state crime of transnational complicity in torture.

Conclusion

Torture is an individualized form of crime that tends to be 'embedded in entrenched structural violence' (Farmer, 2003, p. 219). Torturers are not born: they are nurtured, trained, and supported. In many countries 'they rely on the willingness of foreign governments to provide not only equipment but also personnel training and know-how' (Amnesty International, 2001, p. 41). The case study of the criminal cooperation between France and Argentina illustrated what Herman calls the 'institutional structure of domination built to violate human rights' (1991, p. 91). The French training in a methodology of anti-subversive warfare, which relied heavily on an ideology that promoted dehumanization, helped to justify the use of torture in Argentina during the Dirty War. France's motivation to become a 'torture trainer' after its own decolonization wars was to expand its neo-imperial interests by maximizing its military influence abroad through the development of militarization and, more specifically, counterinsurgency strategies. The French military *savoir-faire* was not transferred to help Argentina to protect its territory from potential threats, but rather served the same main function it did in Algeria: the repression of a state's own population. This type of transnational state crime, which illustrates the *persistence*—and not the *resurgence*—of torture, was directly related to neocolonial settings.

It follows that the use of torture amidst human rights dialogue must be discussed in its broader structural context, and not merely as an issue about the infraction of human rights in the country where it is employed. And if criminology is to offer a varied and useful set of perspectives to understand the politics of state torture, then it should 'revise its histories too' (Aliverti et al., 2021, p. 300). In line with the overall objective of this collection to 'reassess the premises and assumptions of theoretical and empirical perspectives in criminology by bringing to the fore the colonial effects in the production of such scholarship' (ibid, p. 299), this chapter suggests that the transnational institutionalization of torture as a form of social and political control could be better understood by looking at the broader picture and taking into account the global transfer of military knowledge and practices rooted in neocolonialism. This concept warns us of the potential regressive impact of unregulated and under-scrutinized exchanges of counterinsurgency know-how in relation to the Global South. The initiative of 'decolonizing the criminal question', of which the transfer of counterinsurgency expertise is a part, could also promote the denunciation of the commodification of torture through security and military training in counterinsurgency techniques for governing new global 'threats', such as terrorism and drug trafficking, by focusing on the broader structures enabling torture.

References

Abramovici, P. (2001) 'Comment la France a exporté la Torture en Argentine: L'Autre Sale Guerre d'Aussaresses', *Le Point*, 1500 (15 June), pp. 26–34.

Aguila, G. (2010) 'State Violence and Repression in Rosario during the Argentine Dictatorship, 1976–83', in Esparza, M., Huttenbach, H. R., and Feierstein, D. (eds) *State Violence and Genocide in Latin America: The Cold War Years*. London: Routledge, pp. 137–151.

Aguilera Peralta, G. and Beverly, J. (1980) 'Terror and violence as weapons of counterinsurgency in Guatemala', *Latin American Perspectives*, 7(2/3), pp. 91–113.

Aliverti, A., Carvalho, H., Chamberlen, A. et al. (2021), 'Decolonizing the criminal question', *Punishment & Society*, 23(3), pp. 297–316.

Alleg, H. (2006 [1958]) Lincoln, J. (trans.) *The Question*. Lincoln, NE: University of Nebraska Press Bison Books.

Amnesty International (2001) *Stopping the Torture Trade*. London: Amnesty International.

Arendt, H. (1965 [1963]) *Eichmann in Jerusalem: A Report on the Banality of Evil*. New York: Viking.

Barreneche, O. (2019) *De Brava a Dura. Policía de la Provincia de Buenos Aires. Una historia (1930–1973)*. Rosario: Prohistoria Ediciones.

Bauman, Z. (1989) *Modernity and the Holocaust*. Cambridge: Polity Press.

Beccaria, C. (1963) *On Crimes and Punishments*. New York: Bobbs-Merrill.

Branche, R. (2001) *La Torture et l'Armée Pendant la Guerre d'Algérie: 1954–1962*. Paris: Gallimard.

Browning, C. R. (1998) *Ordinary Men: Reserve Police Battalion 101 and the Final Solution in Poland*. London: Penguin.

Carlson, E. S. (2000) 'The influence of French "revolutionary war" ideology on the use of torture in the Argentine "dirty war"', *Human Rights Review*, 1(4), pp. 71–84.

Chambliss, W. (1989) 'State organized crime', *Criminology*, 27(2), pp. 183–208.

Chomsky, N. (1991) 'International Terrorism: Image and Reality', in George, A. (ed.) *Western State Terrorism*. Oxford: Polity Press, pp. 12–38.

Clarke, A. (2008) 'Creating a torture culture', *Suffolk Transnational Law Review*, 32(1), pp. 1–50.

Cohen, L. and Felson, M. (1979) 'Social change and crime rate trends: A routine activity approach', *American Sociological Review*, 44(4), pp. 588–608.

Cohen, S. (1982) 'Western Crime Control Models in the Third World: Benign or Malignant?', Research in Law, Deviance and Social Control, 4, pp. 85–119.

Cohen, S. (2001) *States of Denial: Knowing about Atrocities and Suffering*. Cambridge: Polity Press.

Collard, M. (2018) *Torture as State Crime: A Criminological Analysis of the Transnational Institutional Torturer*. London: Routledge.

Comisión Nacional sobre la Desaparición de Personas (CONADEP) (2006 [1985]) *Nunca Mas: Informe de la Comision Nacional sobre la Desaparicion de Personas*, 8th edn. Buenos Aires: Eudeba.

Confer, V. (1966) *France and Algeria: The Problem of Civil and Political Reform 1870–1920*. Syracuse, NY: Syracuse University Press.

Crelinsten, R. D. (2003) 'The world of torture: A constructed reality', *Theoretical Criminology*, 7(3), pp. 293–318.

Crelinsten, R. D. (2007) 'How to Make a Torturer', in Schulz, W. F. (ed.) *The Phenomenon of Torture: Readings and Commentary*. Philadelphia, PA: University of Pennsylvania Press, pp. 210–214.

Dinges, J. (2012) *The Condor Years: How Pinochet and His Allies Brought Terrorism to Three Continents*. New York: The New Press.

Eide, A. (1977) 'Arms transfer and Third World militarization', *Security Dialogue*, 8(2), pp. 99–102.

Fagen, P. W. (1992) 'Repression and State Security', in Corradi, J. E., Fagen, P. W., and Garreton, M. A. (eds) *Fear at the Edge: State Terror and Resistance in Latin America*. Berkeley, CA: University of California Press. pp. 39–71.

Fanon, F. (1963) Farrington, C. (trans.) *The Wretched of the Earth*. London: Penguin.

Farmer, P. (2003) *Pathologies of Power: Health, Human Rights and the New War on the Poor*. Berkeley, CA: University of California Press.

Feierstein, D. (2010) 'Political Violence in Argentina and its Genocidal Characteristics', in Esparza, M., Huttenbach, H. R., and Feierstein, D. (eds) *State Violence and Genocide in Latin America: The Cold War Years*. London: Routledge, pp. 44–63.

Feitlowitz, M. (1998) *A Lexicon of Terror: Argentina and the Legacies of Terror*. Oxford: Oxford University Press.

Galtung, J. (1994) *Human Rights in Another Key*. Cambridge: Polity Press.

Gareau, F. H. (2004) *State Terrorism and the United States*. London: Zed Books.

Gibson, J. T. (1990) 'Factors Contributing to the Creation of a Torturer', in Suedfeld, P. (ed.) *Psychology and Torture*. New York: Hemisphere, pp. 77–88.

Graziano, F. (1992) *Divine Violence. Spectacle, Psychosexuality and Radical Christianity in the Argentine 'Dirty War'*. Boulder, CO: Westview Press.

Grewcock, M. (2008) 'State Crime: Some Conceptual Issues', in Anthony, T. and Cunneen, C. (eds) *The Critical Criminology Companion*. Sydney: Hawkins Press, pp. 146–157.

Grimal, H. (1985 [1965]) *La Décolonisation*. Brussels: Editions Complexe.

Haney, C., Banks, C., and Zimbardo, P. G. (1973) 'Interpersonal dynamics in a simulated prison', *International Journal of Criminology and Penology*, 1(1), pp. 69–97.

Haritos-Fatouros, M. (1988) 'The official torturer: A learning model for obedience to the authority of violence', *Journal of Applied Social Psychology*, 18(13), pp. 1107–1120.

Haritos-Fatouros, M. (2003) *The Psychological Origins of Institutionalized Torture*. London: Routledge.

Heinz, W. S. (1995) 'The Military, Torture and Human Rights: Experiences from Argentina, Brazil, Chile and Uruguay', in Crelinsten, R. D. and Schmid, A. P. (eds) *The Politics of Pain: Torturers and their Masters*. Boulder, CO: Westview Press, pp. 65–97.

Herman, E. S. (1991) 'The United States versus Human Rights in the Third World', *Harvard Human Rights Journal*, 4, pp. 85–105.

Hey, H. (1995) *Gross Human Rights Violations: A Search for Causes. A Study of Guatemala and Costa Rica*. The Hague: Nijhoff.

Horne, A. (2006) *A Savage War for Peace*. New York: Review Books Classics.

Huggins, M. K. (1998) *Political Policing: The United States and Latin America*. Durham, NC: Duke University Press.

Huggins, M. K., Haritos-Fatouros, M., and Zimbardo, P. G. (2002) *Violence Workers: Police Torturers and Murderers Reconstruct Brazilian Atrocities*. Berkeley, CA: University of California Press.

James, D. (1990) *Resistencia e Integración. El Peronismo y la Clase Trabajadora Argentina 1946–1976*. Buenos Aires: Sudamericana.

Jones, T. and Newburn, T. (2019) 'Understanding transnational policy flows in security and justice', *Journal of Law and Society*, 46(1), pp. 13–30.

Jones, T., Blaustein, J., and Newburn, T. (2019) 'Researching cross national mobilities in crime control', *Criminology and Criminal Justice*, 21(3), pp. 408–426.

Kalmanowiecki, L. (2000) 'Origins and applications of political policing in Argentina', *Latin American Perspectives*, 27(2), pp. 36–56.

Kauzlarich, D. and Kramer, R. C. (1998) *Crimes of the American Nuclear State: At Home and Abroad*. Boston, MA: Northeastern University Press.

Kelman, H. C. (2005) 'The policy context of torture: A social-psychological analysis', *International Review of the Red Cross*, 87(857), pp. 123–134.

Kelman, H. C. and Hamilton, V. L. (1989) *Crimes of Obedience: Toward a Social Psychology of Authority and Responsibilities*. New Haven, CT: Yale University Press.

Koonings, K. and Kruijt, D. (2002) *Political Armies: The Military and Nation Building in the Age of Democracy*. London: Zed Books.

Kramer, R. C. and Michalowski, R. (1990) 'Toward an Integrated Theory of State Corporate Crime', Presented at the American Society of Criminology, Baltimore, MD.

Kuznetsov, Y. (2006) *Diaspora Networks and the International Migration of Skills: How Countries Can Draw on Their Talent Abroad*. New York: World Bank Publications.

Lankford, A. (2009) 'Promoting aggression and violence at Abu Ghraib: The U.S. military's transformation of ordinary people into torturers', *Aggression and Violent Behavior*. 14(5), pp. 388–395.

Lazreg, M. (2008) *Torture and the Twilight of Empire: From Algiers to Baghdad*. Princeton, NJ: Princeton University Press.

Le Cour Grandmaison, O. (2005) *Coloniser, Exterminer. Sur la Guerre et l'Etat Colonial.* Paris: Arthème Fayard.

Lifton, R. J. (1986) *The Nazi Doctors: Medical Killing and the Psychology of Genocide.* London: Macmillan.

Llumá, D. (2002) 'La Influencia Francesa en los Militares Argentinos: Los Maestros de la Tortura', *Todo Es Historia*, 422, pp. 6–16.

Lopez, E. (1987) *Seguridad Nacional y Sedición Militar.* Buenos Aires: Legasa.

MacMaster, N. (2004) 'Torture: From Algiers to Abu Ghraib', *Race & Class*, 46(2), pp. 1–21.

Maran, R. (1989) *Torture: The Role of Ideology in the French–Algerian War.* New York: Praeger.

Mazzei, D. H. (2002) 'La Misión Militar Francesa en la Escuela Superior de Guerra y los Orígenes de la Guerra Sucia, 1957–1962', *Revista de Ciencias Sociales*, 13, pp. 105–137.

McClintock, M. (1992) *Instruments of Statecraft: U.S. Guerrilla Warfare, Counterinsurgency, and Counter-Terrorism, 1940–1990.* New York: Pantheon.

Melossi, D., Sozzo, M., and Sparks, R. (2011) 'Introduction. Criminal Questions: Cultural Embeddedness and Diffusion', in Melossi, D., Sozzo, M., and Sparks, C. (eds) *Travels of the Criminal Question: Cultural Embeddedness and Diffusion.* Oxford: Hart, pp. 13–24.

Merton, R. (1961) *Social Theory and Social Structure.* New York: Basic Books.

Milanesio, N. (2013) *Workers Go Shopping in Argentina: The Rise of Popular Consumer Culture.* Albuquerque, NM: University of New Mexico Press.

Milgram, S. (1974) *Obedience to Authority.* New York: Harper & Row.

Montero, A. (2008) 'Las Policías y la Doctrina de la Seguridad Nacional en la Argentina. Primera Aproximación', in Bombini, G., Bergalli, R., and Rivera Beiras, I. (eds), *Violencia y Sistema Penal.* Buenos Aires: Editores del Puerto, pp. 265–290.

Newburn, T., Jones, T., and Blaustein, J. (2018) 'Policy mobilities and comparative penality', *Theoretical Criminology*, 22(4), pp. 563–581.

Nkrumah, K. (1965) *Neo-Colonialism: The Last Stage of Imperialism.* London: Thomas Nelson & Sons.

Oliveira-Cézar, M. (2002) 'Indonesia, Argelia, Argentina: Las Raices Francesas de la Guerra Antisubversiva', *Todo Es Historia*, 422, pp. 24–34.

Oliveira-Cézar, M. (2003) 'De los Militares Franceses de Indochina y Argelia a los Militares Argentinos de los Años 50 y 60: El Aprendizaje de la Guerra Contrarrevolucionaria', *Todo Es Historia*, 435, pp. 70–80.

Osiel, M. (2004) 'The Mental State of Torturers: Argentina's Dirty War', in Levinson, S. (ed.) *Torture: A Collection.* Oxford: Oxford University Press, pp. 129–141.

Passas, N. (1990) 'Anomie and corporate deviance', *Contemporary Crises*, 14, pp. 157–178.

Perelli, C. (1990) 'The Military's Perception of Threat in the Southern Cone of South America', in Goodman, L. W., Mendelson, J. S. R., and Rial, J. (eds) *The Military and Democracy: The Future of Civil-Military Relations in Latin America.* Lexington, MA: Lexington Books, pp. 99–106.

Périès, G. G. (1999) 'De l'Action Militaire à l'Action Politique. Impulsion, Codification et Application de la Doctrine de la "Guerre Révolutionnaire" au Sein de l'Armée Française (1944–1960)', Thèse de Doctorat, Université de Paris I-Sorbonne.

Peters, E. (1985) *Torture*, Philadelphia, PA: University of Pennsylvania Press.

Potash, R. A. (1980) *The Army and Politics in Argentina, 1945–1963.* Stanford, CA: Stanford University Press.

Ranalletti, M. (2005) 'La Guerra de Argelia y la Argentina. Influencia e Inmigración Francesa desde 1945', *Anuario de Estudio Americanos*, 62(2), pp. 285–308.

Robin, M. M. (2008 [2004]) *Escadrons de la Mort, l'Ecole Française.* Paris: Editions La Découverte.

Rouquié, A. (1978) *Pouvoir Militaire et Société Politique en République Argentine*. Paris: Presses de la Fondation Nationale des Sciences Politiques.

Schirmer, J. (1998) *The Guatemalan Military Project: A Violence Called Democracy*. Philadelphia, PA: University of Pennsylvania Press.

Sozzo, M. (2011) 'Cultural Travels and Crime Prevention in Argentina', in Melossi, D., Sozzo, M., and Sparks, C. (eds) *Travels of the Criminal Question. Cultural Embeddedness and Diffusion*. Oxford: Hart, pp. 185–216.

Stanley, E. E. (2008) 'Torture and Terror', in Anthony, T. and Cunneen, C. (eds) *The Critical Criminology Companion*. Sydney: Hawkins Press.

Staub, E. (1989) *The Roots of Evil: The Origins of Genocide and Other Group Violence*. Cambridge: Cambridge University Press.

Sykes, G. and Matza, D. (1957) 'Techniques of neutralization: A theory of delinquency', *American Sociological Review*, 22(6), pp. 664–670.

Talbott, J. (1975) 'French public opinion and the Algerian War: A research note', *French Historical Studies*, 9(2), pp. 354–361.

Tomasevski, K. (1998) 'Foreign Policy and Torture', in Dunér, B. (ed.) *An End to Torture: Strategies for its Eradication*. London: Zed Books, pp. 183–202.

Vaujour, J. (1985) *De la Révolte à la Révolution*. Paris: Albin Michel.

Vidal-Naquet, P. (1963) *Torture: Cancer of Democracy. France and Algeria 1954–62*. Harmondsworth: Penguin Books.

Weschler, L. (1998) *A Miracle, A Universe: Settling Accounts with Torturers*. Chicago, IL: University of Chicago Press.

Zimbardo, P. (2007) *The Lucifer Effect: How Good People Turn Evil*. London: Rider.

14

The Legacy of Colonial Patriarchy in the Current Administration of the Malaysian Death Penalty

The Hyper-Sentencing of Foreign National Women to Death for Drug Trafficking

Lucy Harry

Introduction

Of the fifty-five countries around the world that retain the death penalty (Amnesty International, 2021), many were, at one point in time, colonized by the British.[1] Whilst in some states the death penalty had a pre-colonial history, in many, the modern usage of the death penalty can be linked back to British rule. This is certainly the case in Southeast Asia, where British rule in what was known as 'Malaya' from 1824 to 1957 paved the way for the modern usage of the death penalty in Malaysia (and Singapore) through the transportation and establishment of a colonial penal code which has formed the basis of contemporary criminal laws.[2] As this book's editors urge, criminologists should 'more concretely and holistically locate colonial influences on our contemporary penal practices and rationales' (Aliverti et al., 2021, p. 301). Here, this is important for our understanding of why certain marginalized groups (namely, economically precarious foreign national women) are disproportionately sentenced to death for drug trafficking in present-day Malaysia.

With regards to capital punishment, historians—and to a lesser extent, criminologists—have explored the historical legacies of the death penalty for homicide in former British colonies—usually in Africa, the Caribbean, and white settler states such as the US, Canada, and Australia (Anderson, 2003; Hynd, 2008; 2012; Novak, 2014a; Malkani, 2018; Strange, 2003; 2020)—but the colonial ramifications of the contemporary use of the death penalty for the crime of drug trafficking have received inadequate attention. This is particularly true in the Asian context, where the death penalty for

[1] This includes: Antigua and Bermuda, Bahamas, Bangladesh, Barbados, Belize, Botswana, Gambia, Guyana, India, Jamaica, Lesotho, Malaysia, Nigeria, Oman, Pakistan, Qatar, Saint Kitts and Nevis, Saint Lucia, Saint Vincent and the Grenadines, Singapore, Trinidad and Tobago, Uganda, the US, and Zimbabwe.

[2] While there is archaeological evidence of a pre-colonial death penalty in what is now known as 'Malaysia', the basis of the modern use of capital punishment can be linked directly to British colonial rule and its accompanying legal system (Berrih and Ngeow, 2020, p. 28).

Lucy Harry, *The Legacy of Colonial Patriarchy in the Current Administration of the Malaysian Death Penalty* In: *Decolonizing the Criminal Question.* Edited by: Ana Aliverti, Henrique Carvalho, Anastasia Chamberlen, and Máximo Sozzo, Oxford University Press.
 DOI: 10.1093/oso/9780192899002.003.0015

drug trafficking is often treated in an ahistorical manner, or discussed in relation to the 'Asian War on Drugs' or is attributed to so-called 'Asian values' (Bae, 2008; Miao, 2017). Moreover, while the death penalty is a colonial-era punishment in Malaysia, and the drug regulation and criminalization legislation—the Dangerous Drugs Act 1952—was established during British rule, it was only after independence that drug trafficking became a capital offence in 1975, and later became the mandatory sentence in 1983. Therefore, the causal relationship between colonialism and the death penalty for drug trafficking is less straightforward, and might explain why it has been left relatively unexplored.

The research problem that this chapter seeks to address centres upon what the author deems a 'double colonial legacy' of the death penalty for drug trafficking in Malaysia: on the one hand, the death penalty is a legacy of British colonial rule and, on the other hand, the history of the criminalization of drugs is closely linked to colonization in this jurisdiction and elsewhere. This chapter draws on the author's research on foreign national women sentenced to death in Malaysia, consisting of forty-seven 'elite' interviews in early 2020 with stakeholders involved in the women's cases, including lawyers, prosecutors, judges, NGO activists, consular officials, religious counsellors, journalists, and researchers, as well as systematic reviews of legal and media sources to establish a database on 146 women's cases between the years 1983 and 2019.[3] And in so doing, this work provides a feminist analysis, considering how the link between 'colonial patriarchy' and penality (Cunneen and Baldry, 2013) takes on a new logic in a neoliberal, postcolonial era. As this chapter will argue, during British colonial times the death penalty was used as a tool of 'social control' and this logic has been reappropriated in a postcolonial era: the death penalty for drug trafficking has become a tool of domination deployed against marginalized, predominantly foreign national populations (who are often gendered and racialized) who have become the new 'other' of the postcolonial order.

This chapter will begin with an overview of the extant scholarship on capital punishment and colonization, highlighting the dearth of work on the death penalty for drug trafficking. To situate the present case study, it will then provide an overview of the current scope and application of the Malaysian death penalty, before considering the converging histories of the colonial death penalty alongside the criminalization of drugs in this jurisdiction. Finally, the chapter will consider the empirical data regarding the overrepresentation of foreign national women on death row for drug trafficking in Malaysia, and make the case that this trend can be understood with reference to the convergence of colonial-era penal logics and neoliberal economic structures.

Scholarship on Capital Punishment and Colonization

The existing historical analyses of the death penalty worldwide have mainly focused upon the death sentence for homicide in former British colonies, and are yet to analyse the colonial legacies embedded within the death penalty for drug trafficking. Historians such as Stacey Hynd (2008; 2012) and Clare Anderson (2003) have examined the usage of the death penalty in colonial Africa (including in Malawi, Kenya,

[3] Owing to ethical and access issues, the author did not attempt to interview any of the women on death row themselves.

and Mauritius) and argued that the use of capital punishment 'was not just a method of crime control or individual punishment, but an integral aspect of colonial networks of power and violence' (Hynd, 2008, p. 403). Accordingly, the purpose and use of the death sentence diverged between the 'metropole' and the colony, with the death penalty acting as a form of 'social control' in the latter, with public execution serving as 'the starkest display of the power of the colonial state' (Novak, 2014a, p. 24).

Scholars from within the criminological paradigm have examined the colonial and postcolonial death penalty in white settler colonies such as Ireland (Black, 2018), Canada (Strange, 2020), Australia (Strange, 2003), and the US (Malkani, 2018). Moreover, a current research project is exploring the relationship between the legacy of British colonialism and the global death penalty—as part of this, a preliminary comparison of the mandatory death sentence for homicide in Ireland and Trinidad and Tobago as well as Barbados finds that in post-independence Ireland the death sentence was used as a tool for repressing political opposition, whereas with the Caribbean examples, the authors found that the criminal justice apparatus (both during the time of slavery and post-slavery) were used as a 'means of emphasizing racial hierarchies' (Black et al., 2020, p. 14).

The existing literature on the historical and present ramifications of the colonial death penalty have successfully highlighted that particular subjugated and often racialized populations are disproportionately targeted by the colonial death penalty. But what is missing from this analysis is an exploration of how this punitive practice becomes embedded and thus has the potential of spreading beyond the remit of homicide—one example of which being the death penalty for drug trafficking in former British colonies.

An Overview of the Current Scope and Application of the Malaysian Death Penalty

A defining feature of the current scope and administration of the Malaysian death penalty is its disproportionate impact on foreign nationals. A recent Amnesty International (2019, p. 5) report revealed that of the 1,281 people on death row in Malaysia, 568 (44 per cent) are foreign nationals, and 73 per cent of all of those on death row were convicted for drug trafficking. The following nationalities—overwhelmingly from the Global South—were over-represented: Nigeria (21 per cent), Indonesia (16 per cent), Iran (15 per cent), India (10 per cent), the Philippines (8 per cent), and Thailand (6 per cent) (Amnesty International, 2019, p. 19). There is a higher over-representation of foreign nationals sentenced to death for drug trafficking on the female death row: disaggregated figures suggest that there are 141 women under sentence of death, 86 per cent of whom are foreign nationals, and 90 per cent of whom have been sentenced to death for drug trafficking (and 95 per cent of the total female death row population were sentenced to death for drug trafficking) (Amnesty International, 2019, pp. 19–20). This is one of the largest female death rows in the world (Cornell Center on the Death Penalty Worldwide, 2018).

Research and activists' efforts have shown that foreign national defendants experience intersecting forms of disadvantage when facing a capital charge in an alien criminal justice system (Hoyle, 2019). There is evidence to suggest that foreign nationals' rights under the Vienna Convention on Consular Relations (1963)—chiefly, the obligation on the side of the host state to notify the relevant embassy without delay in the event that a foreign national is arrested or detained—are not uniformly guaranteed (Hoyle, 2019). In the Malaysian context specifically, a report by Monash University revealed that foreign national capital defendants are only provided with interpreters in the courtroom, and not in the pre-trial stages; a violation of their right to a fair trial (Antolak-Saper et al., 2020, p. 22).

The death penalty for drug trafficking in Malaysia is governed by the Dangerous Drugs Act 1952. This legislation was inherited from British colonial rule; however, drug trafficking was not a capital offence until 1983, after independence (in 1957), when it was made the *mandatory* sentence. Under section 39B of the Act, drug trafficking does not necessitate movement across an international border, but is constituted based on the weight of drugs in the person's possession (based on the following thresholds: 15g or more of heroin and morphine; 1,000g or more of opium; 200g or more of cannabis; 40g or more of cocaine) and for amounts under this threshold, the accused is indicted on a lesser charge of 'possession', which, crucially, does not carry the death sentence. Some limited reforms to the Dangerous Drugs Act occurred in 2017 which give judges the discretion not to impose a death sentence on 'couriers'—whose role in the operation 'is restricted to transporting, carrying, sending or delivering a dangerous drugs'—when certification is provided by the Public Prosecutor attesting that the accused person had assisted in disrupting the wider drug trafficking activity (Hood, 2013, p. 3). However, this condition is very hard to satisfy, and so the death penalty still operates largely mandatorily in practice.

Significantly, the *mandatory* nature of the death sentence is an inheritance from British colonial rule: '[h]istorically, mandatory sentencing was a feature of English common law and was subsequently exported to other countries via colonialism' (Jabbar, 2019, p. 139). Therefore, we see the colonial logic of the mandatory death penalty for the 'most serious offences' being adopted in a post-independence Malaysia to combat the 'drug scourge' (a point we will return to later). In terms of executions, while statistics are hard to come by estimates from human rights groups indicate that 469 executions have occurred since independence in 1957 (229 of which for drug trafficking) and the last known execution occurred in 2017 (four persons were executed during that year) (Amnesty International, 2019, p. 5). But since then, there has been a moratorium on executions, as on 10 October 2018, World Day Against the Death Penalty, the former law minister Liew Vui Keong, announced the government's intention to abolish the death penalty, in part due to the recognition that the death sentence does not deter drug traffickers (Fortify Rights, 2018). There has been some delay in enacting this change, owing to political turmoil and the Covid-19 pandemic. In June 2022, the government stated it would abolish the *mandatory* death penalty only, reneging on the promise of total abolition made by their predecessors (Al Jazeera, 2022). In any event, despite the moratorium on executions, people are still being sentenced to death, and indeed in 2021 over fourteen people received death sentences (Amnesty International, 2022). Those sentenced to death face an indeterminate and protracted period of imprisonment; capital criminal proceedings can take as long as twenty-seven years (Berrih and Ngeow, 2020, p. 63). Alongside death-penalty abolition activism, there has been a growing civil society movement aimed at decriminalizing drugs in Malaysia and, indeed, the then Health Minister, Dzulkefly Ahmad, in 2019 announced plans to decriminalize drug use (Al Jazeera, 2019). However, legislative changes are yet to be made, and these proposals are unlikely to affect the offence of drug trafficking; rather, they aim to decriminalize the personal use of drugs.

Malaysia's use of the death penalty for drug trafficking is in keeping with regional trends. Indeed, an estimated over 90 per cent of the world's executions occur in the Asiatic region, and this is largely due to capital drug offences (Johnson and Zimring, 2006, p. 91). And four of the seven countries worldwide which have a 'high application' of the death penalty for drug trafficking are located in Southeast Asia (Indonesia, Malaysia, Singapore, and Vietnam) (Larasati and Girelli, 2021, p. 34). Importantly, the death penalty for drug trafficking is in contravention of international law: Article 6 of the International Covenant on Civil and Political Rights (ICCPR) stipulates that the death sentence should be reserved for the 'most serious offences' which is generally understood to mean crimes with lethal consequences—that is, intentional homicide.

Retentionist leaders have justified the use of the death penalty with reference to alleged 'Asian values' (Bae, 2008). Most infamously, the former Prime Minister of Singapore, Lee Kuan Yew, in 2002 asserted that 'the basic difference in our approach [to capital punishment] springs from our traditional Asian value systems which places the interests of the community over above that of the individual' (quoted in Johnson and Zimring, 2009, pp. 22–23). Yet, it would be culturally relativistic to suggest that we can speak of one unified value system which encompasses a heterogeneous continent. And so, more convincingly, scholars have shown that the 'Asian values' hypothesis is co-opted by authoritarian leaders to justify their draconian policies (Bae, 2008, p. 54; Zimring and Johnson, 2008). Moreover, the death penalty for drug trafficking is often explained away with reference to the so-called 'Asian War on Drugs' (Miao, 2017). However, not only could this framing be considered orientalizing, but it also disavows the British colonial influence on the current state of affairs, by making these punitive practices appear endemic to the region, and suggesting that the only outside influence has been the US 'War on Drugs'.

The Double Colonial Legacy: Two Converging Histories

One of the central arguments of this chapter is that the death penalty for drug trafficking in Malaysia is a 'double colonial legacy' due to it being the result of two converging histories: on the one hand, the colonial origins of the modern death penalty and, on the other, the criminalization of drugs. We will deal with each in turn, and towards the end of this section, see how the two converge.

Whilst there is evidence of a death penalty in the pre-colonial Malaysia states—for example, an inscription of Islamic law on a stone in Terengganu dating back to 1303 which discusses the death penalty for adulterous women (Berrih and Ngeow, 2020, p. 28)—the modern-day death penalty was inherited from the penal system instituted by the British colonizers. Starting in 1819, the British controlled the Malaysian territories of Malaya (now considered peninsular Malaysia), Singapore (which became independent from Malaysia in 1965), as well as the provinces of Sarawak and Sabah in Northern Borneo and Malaya became a British colony in 1824 (Berrih and Ngeow, 2020, p. 29). In 1871, the British established the 'Straits Settlement Penal Code' in

Penang and Malacca, which included the death penalty for crimes such as treason and murder (ibid, p. 20). Later, in 1936 a new penal code—based on the 1871 legislation—was introduced in all Federal Malay states (ibid, p. 31). This legislation was based on the 1860 Indian Penal Code, and included the death penalty for crimes like 'waging war against the Queen' (ibid, p. 30). Accordingly, the death penalty was mainly used as a 'political tool' during colonial times (ibid, p. 29).

Concurrently, with regard to drug use, regulation, and criminalization, opium has a long history in Southeast Asia—predating European colonialism—indeed, there is evidence that opium was traded with China as far back as the sixteenth century (Trocki, 2011). But, scholars believe that the first widespread use of drugs in what is now known as Malaysia occurred with British colonization in the early nineteenth century and, in particular, amongst the Chinese migrant labour force who the British employed for work in the tin mines in Malaya—these labourers would smoke opium in order to relieve aches and illnesses associated with their work, in addition to using it as a way to relax (Binti Md Isa, 2015, p. 30). During this time, it was also believed that cannabis was consumed by Indian migrant labourers and some of the Malay ethnic group (Arokiasamy and Taricone, 1992, p. 1301). Opium was a key commodity for the British colonial government, which, in the late nineteenth century, instituted a 'revenue farm system' where it contracted opium distribution out to Chinese merchants, who they taxed, and additionally, domestic poppy plantations were established at this time (Binti Md Isa, 2015, p. 31).

It was only by the late nineteenth century and early twentieth century that an anti-opium sentiment grew in the 'Straits Settlements' and 'Malay States' (Kenji, 2012). This movement was prompted by the Chinese community in Malaya, the international anti-opium movement (influenced by fellow colonial powers the US and Japan), and pressure back in Britain and from missionaries (Arokiasamy and Taricone, 1992, p. 1302; Kenji, 2012, p. 87). Consequently, an Opium Commission—to study the issue and provide recommendations—was established in 1907 (ibid). The colonial government viewed opium use in a racialized manner and indeed, the 'general and deep-rooted attitude then was to ascribe opium smoking to the inborn habit of the Chinese' (Kenji, 2012, p. 89). Following the international Geneva Convention on Drugs 1925, the colonial government instituted regulations on the use of opium, including mandating the registration of opium users, and later, in 1934, opium use was limited to those with a medical certification (Binti Md Isa, 2015, p. 35). During the Japanese rule of Malaya between 1942 and 1945, there were no restrictions on opium use; however, when the British assumed control again in 1945 the possession of opium and its smoking equipment was criminalized as part of the Opium and Chandu Proclamation in 1946 (ibid, pp. 37–38). And, in 1948, the colonial government announced a total ban on all drug dealings (ibid, p. 38). British efforts to regulate and criminalize drug use in Malaya culminated with the introduction of the Dangerous Drugs Act of 1952 which was modelled on the English Dangerous Drugs Acts of 1920 and 1925 (ibid, p. 39)—crucially, this legislation is what now governs the death penalty for drug trafficking.

Following independence in 1957, the government of the new state of Malaysia retained the Dangerous Drugs Act of 1952. It should be noted here that Singapore seceded in 1965 and became an independent state from Malaysia, but its government likewise passed the Misuse of Drugs Act 1973 that was also influenced by British colonial policy. In Malaysia, during the late 1960s and early 1970s, there was a national panic about a new trend in drug misuse amongst young men, who, it was thought, were influenced by 'hippy culture' and the Vietnam War (as American soldiers who were stationed in Malaysia for 'rest and recreation' were influencing local youth culture), and the types of drugs used diversified to include cannabis, heroin, and psychotropic drugs such as amphetamines (Kamarudin, 2007, pp. 6–7). In response to the increase in drug use, tougher penalties were enforced, including the death penalty for drug trafficking which was added to the Dangerous Drugs Act in 1975 (Harring, 1991).

The way that this 'drugs crisis' was framed is of critical importance here. It was believed that the drugs scourge was the 'main threat to national security', as during the 1980s it was thought that roughly 65 per cent of those 'addicted' to drugs were young men, who 'represented the backbone and the hope of the nation's future' and thus drug trafficking was framed as a threat to the newly independent state's development (Harring, 1991; Kamarudin, 2007, p. 8). Drug trafficking was seen as an 'external' problem, and the death sentence was designed 'to rid Malaysia of foreigners using Malaysia, particularly Penang, as a trafficking center' (Harring, 1991, pp. 403–404). Consequently, the death penalty became mandatory in 1983, and suspected drug offenders were also detained under the Internal Security Act 1960, which had traditionally been reserved for the detention of political insurgents (Harring, 1991). The following statement from former Prime Minister Mahathir Mohamad in 1986 is revealing:

> Malaysia views the drug problem as a major threat to the security and well-being of the country. Drugs have been used in the past to subjugate a country. We do not wish to be colonised once again or have our security and economy undermined. Accordingly we have promulgated the death penalty against drug traffickers.
>
> (Cited in Berrih and Ngeow, 2020, p. 41)

In this way, we can start to see the relationship between colonialism and the death penalty for drug trafficking, as the 'drugs issue' was seen as an immediate threat to the socio-economic fabric of postcolonial Malaysia and, it was thought, drugs threatened the ability of the new state to prosper following British subjugation. By acknowledging the framing of drug use as a political issue and political threat, we can see how the death penalty—which historically, under British colonial rule was used to suppress political insurgencies—was viewed as the most appropriate response to this perceived threat to the nation's security.

The Research Problem: The Death Penalty for Drug Trafficking as a Modern Manifestation of Colonial Patriarchy and Penality

Critiques of the mandatory death penalty focus on its arbitrariness (Jabbar, 2019). And, indeed, here it will be argued that the mandatory[4] death sentence for drug trafficking affects *specific* gendered, racialized, foreign national populations and this can

[4] Or a death sentence that operates in a mandatory fashion, as does the Malaysian death penalty for drug offences.

be explained by reference to the concept of 'colonial patriarchy' and penality (Cunneen and Baldry, 2013). Chris Cuneen and Eileen Baldry (ibid, p. 6) write, in the context of the over-incarceration of Indigenous women in Australia, that:

> contemporary penal culture, and in particular its severity and excess *directed* against particular subjects, can be understood within the specific dynamics of colonialism. Indeed we argue further that a colonial mode of penality has underpinned racialised/gendered crime control in late modern states with their internal colonised Others.

They link coloniality and patriarchy, as the former 'was and is an economic and political manifestation' of the latter (ibid, p. 7). This relates to penality as the colonial patriarchal logic dictated who was deemed 'high risk, dangerous and marginalised' and, in turn, who was subjected to differentiated forms of punishment (ibid, pp. 3, 6). Here, we see that marginalized, predominantly foreign populations (who are often gendered and racialized) are the new 'other' of the postcolonial order in Malaysia, who are subjected to the harshest criminal sanction.

As mentioned earlier, there are a disproportionate number of foreign national women on death row in Malaysia. According to the author's review of 146 women's cases between the years 1983 and 2019, 90 per cent of the women were foreign nationals, predominantly from the Global South, including the following nationalities: Thailand (18 per cent), China (11 per cent), Indonesia (11 per cent), Iran (11 per cent), and the Philippines (9 per cent). We will explore the trend of the 'hyper-incarceration' of foreign national women for drug trafficking in Malaysia later (Anthony and Blagg, 2020).

The hyper-sentencing of foreign national women for drug trafficking

Related to the concept of 'colonial patriarchy' is '*hyper*-incarceration', a term first coined by Loic Wacquant (2010) who shows that instead of referring to 'mass incarceration' in the US we should instead think of '*hyper*-incarceration' as penal policies have been highly 'targeted' towards '(sub)proletarian African American men from the imploding ghetto' (p. 74). And this concept has since been applied to the over-incarceration of Indigenous women in Australia and explains how 'particular penal strategies and social policies more generally, have resulted in specific groups being defined as suitable penal subjects' (Cunneen et al., 2013, p. 91). We find racialized women from the Global South hyper-imprisoned for drug offences worldwide, as a result of being constructed as the punishable 'Other' (Sudbury, 2005). And, indeed, statistics attest to this phenomenon: from 2000 to 2017, the female prison was the fastest growing carceral population—it increased by over 50 per cent (to 714,000) as compared to a 20 per cent increase of the overall world prison population—and this is largely attributed to harsh drug policies (Heard, 2017).

The data from Malaysia show that the death penalty for drug trafficking disproportionately impacts economically precarious foreign national women. While most existing studies of women and drug trafficking highlight that women engage in drug couriering as a result of the 'feminization of poverty' (Del Olmo, 1986; Huling, 1995; Green, 1996; Sudbury, 2005; Fleetwood, 2014; Jeffries and Chuenurah, 2019), here the issue is economic insecurity rather than abject poverty per se (albeit at times the two may overlap). The author's interviewees frequently recited that women engage in drug trafficking for a 'quick buck', 'fast money', 'easy money'. Often it was not a sustained survival strategy, but instead women would courier items in order to supplement income from other forms of insecure employment—as one international NGO worker interviewed described: 'it's not a career as such; it's just to fill a present need'. Often the economic needs were gendered: several of the interview participants cited cases involving single mothers, divorcees, or pregnant women in need of money to take care of 'family problems', including supporting their children or paying for a family member's medical bills.

The author's review of legal documents pertaining to 146 women's cases between the years 1983 and 2019 found that of those who stated their employment in their legal defence, many were employed in feminized and precaritized industries: so, for example, 29 per cent were working in the retail, hospitality, and beauty industries (in roles such as waitress, hairdresser, bartender, beautician, cleaner); 13 per cent stated that they were primarily working as a courier (either for someone else or couriering goods for their own small business); 17 per cent were unemployed or did not have any official employment; 9 per cent were working in healthcare or as domestic workers; and 8 per cent in the entertainment and sex industry (the majority of whom stated that they were working as masseuses). More still stated that they had 'no specific work' or 'did odd jobs', held down multiple jobs that changed over time—an indictment of the precarious job market. In many ways, this finding is somewhat unsurprising given that precarity is gendered, and disproportionately affects women in the Global South (Standing, 1989). The concept of 'precarity' can be understood as follows:

> work for remuneration characterized by uncertainty, low income, and limited social benefits and statutory entitlements. Precarious employment is shaped by the relationship between *employment status* (i.e. self- or paid employment), *form of employment* (e.g. temporary or permanent, part-time or full-time), and *dimensions of labour market insecurity*, as well as *social context* (e.g. occupation, industry, and geography) and *social location* (or the interaction between social relations, such as gender, and legal and political categories, such as citizenship).
>
> (Vosko, 2009, p. 2)

And, indeed, we see this labour dynamic play out in Southeast Asia both historically and at present: during the postcolonial economic growth and structural adjustment process that occurred from the 1960s to the 1980s in the ASEAN region, there was an unprecedented increase in women's participation in the labour market (Lim, 1993). This 'feminization of labour' occurred alongside the 'flexibilization' of labour, which meant that women were moved into peripheral, temporary, and part-time positions (Gills, 2001, p. 9). This was prevalent in textiles and electronics manufacturing on the 'global conveyor belt' (Kaur, 2000) and was underscored by orientalist and misogynist discourses where women were considered to be 'naturally' more 'docile' and 'nimble' (Elson and Pearson, 1981, p. 93). And, more recently, since the 1990s we have witnessed the 'feminization' of intra-regional migration in Southeast Asia, whereby an increasing number of Asian women are migrating to work in feminized industries—such as healthcare, domestic work, entertainment, and the manufacturing and/or textiles sectors—in more affluent Asian countries such as Hong Kong, Singapore, and crucially, Malaysia (Piper, 2008, p. 1291).

The latter trend helps us to make sense of the finding that many of the women claimed they were travelling to Malaysia in search of employment when they were allegedly duped into smuggling drugs by an unscrupulous recruiter (who was usually male), as one lawyer recounts about his female client on death row:

> She worked in a factory, and she was divorced with two children. She was given a work opportunity to come to Malaysia to work as a masseuse. She had never travelled before. She didn't even own a suitcase; she turned up at the place where she would collect a ticket with just plastic carrier bags with clothes in them. The person who offered her a job as the masseuse gave her a bag to take with her to Malaysia, and once she arrived in Malaysia she was supposed to drop that bag off at a particular address to a particular person. She had all of this information in a text message. So, she accepted the bag, put her clothes into it, and travelled to Malaysia. When she arrived, the x-ray showed something suspicious in the bag, and drugs were found in the lining.
>
> (Lawyer)

As a religious counsellor working with women on death row revealed when interviewed, for many living in less affluent Southeast Asian nations, Malaysia is seen as 'the land flowing with milk and honey where anyone can come and get work'. And there is a large transnational feminized labour force to account for the growing Malaysian middle class and more women entering the labour force, with migrant domestic workers amounting to roughly 300,000–400,000 of the Malaysian population (Miles et al., 2019).

Moreover, from the author's review of 146 cases, of the women arrested at the airport, 65 per cent claimed in their legal testimony that they had been paid to courier a bag across an international border at the behest of another—albeit, the majority claimed that they did not realize they were smuggling drugs, but instead thought they were transporting 'legal' items such as clothing, cosmetics, or electronics as part of their personal suitcase allowance in order to avoid custom duties, as the following quotation from a court defence highlights:

> The defence of the appellant was that she was carrying the luggage as instructed by her employer John (a Nigerian) from Guangzhou, China to Malaysia. John had offered her a job with a salary of 10,000 Chinese Yuan to transport children's things and clothes to places outside of China.
>
> (Court testimony)

This practice is referred to elsewhere as 'suitcase trading' or 'parallel trading' and research has shown that many women in the Global South engage in this economic activity as an agentic response to exclusion from the globalized economy (Desai, 2009; Garni, 2014; Laidler and Lee, 2014).

Most pertinently, the research revealed that many of the women were viewed as 'disposable' by Malaysian law enforcement (Wright, 2006). As many of the lawyers interviewed attested, once law enforcement have arrested a female drug courier, they make no effort to conduct follow-up investigations into the wider drug operations that the couriers may be a part of:

> It is just a case of KPI [Key Performance Indicators] really ... So maybe one month you have to make ten arrests, another month five arrests ... Because you know sometimes when we cross-examine the police officers and we say, 'why don't you follow up? You have access to all this information, why don't you investigate further to try to get to the real trafficker?' and they will always say, 'oh, what we have is sufficient to convict this person'.
>
> (Lawyer)

This finding accords with research from England and Wales, where commentators have noted that the 'drug courier' 'has become an expressive target in the State's offensive against illegal drugs ... the courier provides a cheap, expendable, diversionary scapegoat' (Green, 1996, p. 18). Overall, we see that foreign national women are exposed to these punitive practices as a consequence of neoliberal restructuring and the feminization of precarity and migration in the region.

'Securitization' in response to the 'foreign threat' of drug trafficking

To understand why we are currently witnessing the 'hyper'-sentencing of foreign national women to death in Malaysia, we must review the government's approach to drug trafficking. As mentioned earlier, during the 1980s especially, drugs were viewed as the greatest threat to the newly independent nation (Kamarudin, 2007, p. 8). While attitudes towards drugs and the death penalty have changed over time amongst segments of Malaysian society—for example, there is currently an anti-death penalty movement as well as advocates of harm reduction and the decriminalization of drugs—the legislative changes of the 1980s have set this punitive approach in stone (Novak, 2014b). The 'threat' of drug trafficking has largely been framed as an external one. And this punitive logic has been appropriated in recent times, and has led to a 'securitization' approach to drugs, and the conceptualization of 'drug trafficking as an external predation' caused by foreigners (Martel, 2013, pp. 27, 31). This 'securitization' process has a gendered dimension and, indeed, was largely prompted by growing concerns throughout Southeast Asia that West African drug-trafficking syndicates are entrapping local women and using them as drug couriers (Martel, 2013).

During the author's research interviews, when discussing the cases of women who claimed to have been coerced or tricked into couriering drugs to Malaysia, a persistent racist and xenophobic theme that recurred was the involvement of West African—and more specifically, Nigerian—men who allegedly recruited the women and were the 'masterminds' behind the trafficking operations. Indeed, as one lawyer recounted, 'in almost 99 per cent of cases, there's a Nigerian or West African man involved'. The prevailing, problematic stereotype was that these West African/Nigerian men would be living in Malaysia (or elsewhere in Southeast Asia) and they would have a 'local' girlfriend who they would dupe into couriering drugs for them.

And, from the review of media files, there was plenty of evidence of articles warning about the dangers of Nigerian drug-trafficking syndicates exploiting women as couriers:

> Two Iranians and a Nigerian have been employed as Casanovas by an international drug syndicate to entice Malaysian women into smuggling drugs abroad... Nineteen Malaysian women have been arrested this year in Argentina, Brazil, Peru and China for drug trafficking ... They were believed to be victims of the Casanovas, aged between 30 and 35, who had swept the women off their feet by showering them with expensive gifts, lavish dinners and shopping sprees before sending them off on all-expenses-paid holidays overseas.
>
> (The Associated Press, 2007)

However, the author's research revealed that only local Malaysian women benefited from this sympathetic stance and frame of victimhood, as one lawyer explained with reference to the media coverage of these cases:

> It depends on who the victims are. If it's a Malay girl and the community say, 'look at how she was tricked', they can connect, because it could be one of your sisters, or could be one of your family members ... It's very different if it is a Nigerian girl and you portray her, and then they don't relate.
>
> (Lawyer)

When it came to foreign national women caught up in drug couriering, the author's research interviews revealed a perception that women of certain nationalities were under constant suspicion at the airport but did not engender sympathy nor were viewed through the frame of 'victimhood'. This finding fits with other research which has shown that racialized women are increasingly surveilled and criminalized at the securitized border (Pickering and Ham, 2014).

However, in the Malaysian context, in a region where there is a significant flow of migrant labour, race and ethnicity become conflated with citizenship (Hoyle, 2019). Other research on migrant domestic workers in Taiwan has shown that there is a 'construction of racialized differences among migrant workers by national divides' (Lan, 2006, p. 60). For example, in Taiwan, Hong Kong, and Singapore there has been a decline in recruitment of Filipina migrant workers who are considered 'smart but unruly', in favour of the recruitment of Indonesians who are seen as 'stupid yet obedient' (Lan, 2006, p. 60). Pei-Chia Lan (2006) discusses how there has been a process of 'stratified otherization' among foreign national workers, so white-collar foreigners are welcome, whereas for those in manual or domestic work, '[t]he fusion of an occupational categorization with an ethnic classification implies that these nationals are "naturally suited" to these dirty, dangerous, and demeaning jobs' (pp. 59–60).

In Malaysia, we see that there is a conflation of racialization, citizenship, and criminalization. According to the lawyers interviewed, the 'suspicious' countries and nationalities include women from mainland China, Iran, Indonesia, the Philippines,

Nigeria, India, and more recently, Ukraine and Uzbekistan. In particular, the following stereotype of a risky' female traveller prevailed:

> There is a profile of a travel-savvy Chinese woman, of perhaps no known sources of income, who then is a professional drug mule, and she gets away with it because she is good looking; she is attractive; she dresses well; she looks professional ... [Border control] are also looking out for high-class prostitutes, and tall, lanky, good-looking Mainland Chinese women could also be high-class prostitutes.
>
> (Lawyer)

As well as for drug trafficking, this stereotype is used to single out women who are deemed at risk of being human trafficked for sex work, yet due to their 'savviness' they do not fit the 'passive' and sympathetic female 'victim' frame and thus are represented as a 'vamp' through 'linking women's trafficking to her sexuality, her body, or her improper womanhood in ways that shore up neo-colonial heterosexualities and state power' (Schemenauer, 2012, p. 95). Thus, overall, the securitization process reveals a paternalistic logic—in keeping with the concept of 'colonial patriarchy'—which determines which deviant women, caught at the border, are in need of 'saving' and which are in need of 'punishing'—often occurring along the lines of racialized citizenship.

Conclusion

This chapter has sought to address the notable lack of research on the historical and present legacies of colonization as it relates to the mandatory death penalty for drug trafficking in former British colonies—here Malaysia—and how this results in the 'hyper'-sentencing of precarious foreign national women to death. Whilst there is much scholarship that appraises the historical and enduring features of the death penalty for homicide in former British colonies, little has been written about the history of the death penalty for the crime of drug trafficking. It is likely that this is because of the fact that, under British colonial rule, drug trafficking was not a capital offence, and thus there is not a clear causal relationship between colonialism and capital drug offences. However, this chapter has shown, with reference to the author's primary research in Malaysia, that colonization has affected the death penalty for drug trafficking in more insidious ways. There is a 'double colonial legacy' at work here: the death penalty in modern, contemporary form is introduced as a colonial tool of domination in Malaysia, and simultaneously the 'drug problem' is introduced in Malaysia through colonization, through British incentivization of drug production and trade at first, and then British and US transformation of drugs into a 'threat' to society. After independence, these instruments of repression are preserved (and conjoined) by the Malaysian state and they are reappropriated through a new rhetoric ('the drugs issue is a threat to our autonomy and independence') and hence the mandatory death sentence for drug trafficking is introduced in post-independence Malaysia. This new, postcolonial tool of domination is then deployed against marginalized, predominantly foreign national populations who are the new 'other' of the postcolonial order, as we saw with the disproportionate number of economically precarious foreign national women on death row for drug trafficking in Malaysia.

What does this case study reveal about decolonizing the criminal question? This chapter has shown how colonial punishments take on new forms in a postcolonial world yet within these, the colonial logic is reappropriated. In so doing, the chapter also underscores the importance of considering feminist perspectives as part of the decolonizing project; something that has previously been overlooked. Colonial legacies have a gendered character—as we saw with reference to 'colonial patriarchy' and penality (Cunneen and Baldry, 2013)—and particular policies, laws and penalties that survive in postcolonial settings affect women, especially racialized, poor women, in unique ways due to the mixing of postcolonial, neoliberal patriarchies that make women especially precarious and thus vulnerable to punitive practices. Another important contribution this chapter makes is a blurring of the Global North/Global South binary with the case of Malaysia—a previously colonized nation in the Global South that enacts penal policies that are especially targeted at punishing and criminalizing foreign nationals from neighbouring nations that are economically more deprived. So while the logics survive, they take on new forms and structural dynamics. Ultimately, the chapter alerts us that criminologists ought to look at the complexities of how these surviving forms of colonial patriarchal penality operate in the post-colony and that doing so requires a historically aware and intersectionally attuned account.

References

Aliverti, A., Carvalho, H., Chamberlen, A. et al. (2021) 'Decolonizing the criminal question', *Punishment & Society*, 23(3), pp. 297–316.

Al Jazeera (2019) 'Malaysia to decriminalise drug use, says health minister', *Al Jazeera*, 28 June. Available at: www.aljazeera.com/news/2019/6/28/malaysia-to-decriminalise-drug-use-says-health-minister (accessed 1 June 2022).

Al Jazeera (2022) 'Malaysia to abolish mandatory death penalty', *Al Jazeera*, 10 June. Available at: www.aljazeera.com/news/2022/6/10/malaysia-to-abolish-mandatory-death-penalty (accessed 4 July 2022).

Amnesty International (2019) *Fatally Flawed: Why Malaysia Must Abolish the Death Penalty*. London: Amnesty International.

Amnesty International (2022) *Global Report: Death Sentences and Executions 2021*. London: Amnesty International.

Anderson, C. (2003) 'The Execution of Rughobursing: The Political Economy of Convict Transportation and Penal Labour in Early Colonial Mauritius', *Studies in History*, 19(2), pp. 185–197.

Antolak-Saper, N. et al. (2020) *Drug Offences and the Death Penalty in Malaysia: Fair Trial Rights and Ramifications*. Clayton: Monash University.

Arokiasamy, C. M. V. and Taricone, P. F. (1992) 'Drug rehabilitation in West Malaysia: An overview of its history and development', *International Journal of the Addictions*, 27(11), pp. 1301–1311.

Associated Press (2007) 'Report: Casanvoas hired to lure Malaysian women to smuggle drugs abroad', Associated Press, 18 August. Retrieved from Factiva database.

Bae, S. (2008) 'Is the death penalty an Asian value?', *Asian Affairs*, 39(1), pp. 47–56.

Berrih, C. and Ngeow, C. Y. (2020) *Isolation and Desolation: Conditions of Detention of People Sentenced to Death Malaysia*. Paris: Ensemble contre la peine de mort (ECPM).

Binti Md Isa, Y. (2015) *Harm Reduction in the Context of Drug Use in Malaysia: A Critical Analysis of its Justification and its Compatibility with the Criminal Justice Approach*. Lancaster: Lancaster University.

Black, L. (2018) '"On the other hand the accused is a woman . . ." Women and the death penalty in post-independence Ireland', *Law and History Review*, 36(1), pp. 139–172.

Black, L., Seemungal, F., and Seal, L. (2020) 'British legacy and the global legacy', *Amicus Journal*, 15, pp. 11–14.

Cornell Center on the Death Penalty Worldwide (2018) *Judged for More Than Her Crime: A Global Overview of Women Facing the Death Penalty*. Ithaca, NY: Cornell Law School.

Cunneen, C. and Baldry, E. (2013) 'Contemporary Penality in the Shadow of Colonial Patriarchy', in Coventry, G. and Shircore, M. (eds), *Proceedings of the 5th Annual Australian and New Zealand Critical Criminology Conference: July 7 and 8, 2012*. Cairns: James Cook University, UNSW Law Research Paper No. 2013-4. Available at: https://ssrn.com/abstract=2196709 (accessed 10 June 2022).

Cunneen, C., Baldry, E., Brown, D. et al. (2013) *Penal Culture and Hyperincarceration: The Revival of the Prison*. Farnham: Ashgate.

Del Olmo, R. (1986) 'Female Criminality and Drug Trafficking', in Morales, E. (ed.) *Drugs in Latin America*. Williamsburg, VA: College of William and Mary, Department of Anthropology.

Desai, M. (2009) 'Women cross-border traders: Rethinking global trade', *Development*, 52, pp. 377–386.

Elson, D. and Pearson, R. (1981) '"Nimble fingers make cheap workers": An analysis of women's employment in Third World export manufacturing', *Feminist Review*, 7, pp. 87–107.

Fleetwood, J. (2014) *Drug Mules: Women in the International Cocaine Trade*. Basingstoke: Palgrave Macmillan.

Fortify Rights (2018) 'Malaysia: Abolish Capital Punishment, Deterrence Argument Unfounded', *Fortify Rights*, 14 November. Available at: www.fortifyrights.org/mly-inv-2018-11-14/ (accessed 1 June 2022).

Garni, A. (2014) 'Transnational traders: El Salvador's women couriers in historical perspective', *Sociological Forum*, 29(1), pp. 165–188.

Gills, D.-S. S. (2001) 'Neoliberal Economic Globalisation and Women in Asia', in *Women and Work in Globalizing Asia*. London: Routledge.

Green, P. (1996) 'Drug Couriers: The Construction of a Public Enemy', in Green, P. (ed.) *Drug Couriers: A New Perspective*. London: Quartet Books.

Harring, S. (1991) 'Death, drugs and development: Malaysia's mandatory death penalty for traffickers and the international war on drugs', *Columbia Journal of Transnational Law*, 29, pp. 365–405.

Heard, C. (2017) 'Why are Women Prisoner Numbers Rising So Rapidly?', Penal Reform International, 9 November. Available at: www.penalreform.org/blog/why-are-women-prisoner-numbers-rising-so-rapidly/ (accessed 1 June 2022).

Hood, R. (2013) *The Death Penalty in Malaysia: Public Opinion on the Mandatory Death Penalty for Drug Trafficking, Murder and Firearms Offences*. London: The Death Penalty Project.

Hoyle, C. (2019) 'Capital Punishment at the Intersections of Discrimination and Disadvantage: The Plight of Foreign Nationals', in Steiker, C. and Steiker, J. (eds) *Comparative Capital Punishment*. Northampton, MA: Edward Elgar.

Huling, T. (1995) 'Women drug couriers—sentencing reform needed for prisoners of war', *Criminal Justice*, 9(4), pp. 15–62.

Hynd, S. (2008) 'Decorum or deterrence? The politics of execution in Malawi, 1915–66', *Cultural and Social History*, 5(4), pp. 437–448.

Hynd, S. (2012) 'Murder and mercy: Capital punishment in colonial Kenya, ca. 1909–1956', *International Journal of African Historical Studies*, 45(1), pp. 81–101.

Jabbar, P. (2019) 'Imposing a Mandatory Death Penalty: A Practice Out of Sync with Evolving Standards', in Steiker, C. and Steiker, J. (eds) *Comparative Capital Punishment*. Northampton, MA: Edward Elgar.

Jeffries, S. and Chuenurah, C. (2019) 'Vulnerabilities, victimisation, romance and indulgence: Thai women's pathways to prison in Cambodia for international cross border drug trafficking', *International Journal of Law, Crime and Justice*, 56, pp. 39–52.

Laidler, K. J. and Lee, M. (2014) 'Border Trading and Policing of Everyday Life in Hong Kong', in Pickering, S. and Ham, J. (eds) *The Routledge Handbook on Crime and International Migration*. New York: Routledge.

Johnson, D. T. and Zimring, F. E. (2006) 'Taking capital punishment seriously', *Asian Journal of Criminology*, 1(1), pp. 89–95.

Johnson, D. T. and Zimring, F. E. (2009) *The Next Frontier: National Development, Political Change and the Death Penalty in Asia*. Oxford: Oxford University Press.

Kamarudin, A. R. (2007) 'The misuse of drugs in Malaysia: Past and present', *Jurnal Antidadah Malaysia (Malaysian Anti-Drugs Journal)*, 1(2), pp. 1–24.

Kaur, A. (2000) 'Working on the global conveyor belt: Women workers in industrialising Malaysia', *Asian Studies Review*, 24(2), pp. 213–230.

Kenji, T. (2012) 'Anti-opium movement, Chinese nationalism and the Straits Chinese in the early twentieth century', *Malaysian Journal of Chinese Studies*, 1, pp. 85–100.

Lan, P.-C. (2006) *Global Cinderellas: Migrant Domestics and Newly Rich Employers in Taiwan*. Durham, NC: Duke University Press.

Larasati, A. and Girelli, G. (2021) *The Death Penalty for Drug Offences: Global Overview 2020*. London: Harm Reduction International.

Lim, L. L. (1993) 'The Feminization of Labour in the Asia–Pacific Rim Countries: From Contributing to Economic Dynamism to Bearing the Brunt of Structural Adjustments', in Ogawa, N., Jones, G. W., and Williamson, J. G. (eds) *Human Resources in Development along the Asia–Pacific Rim*. Oxford: Oxford University Press.

Malkani, B. (2018) *Slavery and the Death Penalty: A Study in Abolition*. Abingdon: Routledge.

Martel, S. (2013) 'The recruitment of female "mules" by transnational criminal organizations: Securitization of drug trafficking in the Philippines and beyond', *Social Transformations*, 1(2), pp. 13–41.

Miao, M. (2017) 'The penal construction of drug-related offenses in the context of "Asian values": The rise of punitive anti-drug campaigns in Asia', *International Comparative, Policy and Ethics Law Review*, 1(1), pp. 46–76.

Miles, L., Lewis, S., Tend, L.W. et al. (2019) 'Advocacy for women migrant workers in Malaysia through an intersectionality lens', *Journal of Industrial Relations*, 61(5), pp. 682–703.

Novak, A. (2014a) *The Death Penalty in Africa: Foundations and Future Prospects*. Basingstoke: Palgrave Macmillan.

Novak, A. (2014b) *The Global Decline of the Mandatory Death Penalty: Constitutional Jurisprudence and Legislative Reform in Africa, Asia, and the Caribbean*. Farnham: Ashgate.

Pickering, S. and Ham, J. (2014) 'Hot pants at the border: Sorting sex work from trafficking', *British Journal of Criminology*, 54(1), pp. 2–19.

Piper, N. (2008) 'Feminisation of migration and the social dimensions of development: The Asian case', *Third World Quarterly*, 29(7), pp. 1287–1303.

Schemenauer, E. (2012) 'Victims and vamps, madonnas and whores: The construction of female drug couriers and the practices of the US security state', *International Feminist Journal of Politics*, 14(1), pp. 83–102.

Standing, G. (1989) 'Global feminization through flexible labor', *World Development*, 17(7), pp. 1077–1095.

Strange, C. (2003) 'Masculinities, intimate femicide and the death penalty in Australia, 1890–1920', *British Journal of Criminology*, 43(2), pp. 310–339.

Strange, C. (2020) *The Death Penalty and Sex Murder in Canadian History*. Toronto: University of Toronto Press.

Sudbury, J. (2005) 'Mules, Yardies and Other Folk Devils: Mapping Cross Border Imprisonment in Britain', in Oparah, J. C. (ed.) *Global Lockdown: Race, Gender, and the Prison-Industrial Complex*. London: Routledge.

Trocki, C. A. (2011) 'Opium as a Commodity in the Chinese Nanyang Trade', in Tagliacozzo, E. and Chang, W. (eds) *Chinese Circulations: Capital, Commodities, and Networks in Southeast Asia*. Durham, NC: Duke University Press.

Vosko, L. (2009) *Managing the Margins: Gender, Citizenship, and the International Regulation of Precarious Employment*. Oxford: Oxford University Press.

Wacquant, L. (2010) 'Class, race & hyperincarceration in revanchist America', *Daedalus*, 139 (3), pp. 74–90.

Wright, M. (2006) *Disposable Women and Other Myths of Global Capitalism*. London: Routledge.

Zimring, F. E. and Johnson, D. T. (2008) 'Law, society, and capital punishment in Asia', *Punishment & Society*, 10(2), pp. 103–115.

PART 5
MOVING FORWARD: NEW METHODS AND APPROACHES

15
Criminal Questions, Colonial Hinterlands, Personal Experience
A Symptomatic Reading

Rod Earle, Alpa Parmar, and Coretta Phillips

Introduction

In this chapter we consider the challenges and opportunities that a postcolonial practice might allow for a criminological analysis of offending, punishment, and desistance. While categorical, experiential links between colonial dynamics and contemporary experiences of criminal justice may be challenging to verify empirically, we argue that there is methodological and theoretical merit in seeking to understand contemporary individual experiences through the lens of race and colonialism. We suggest that analysis of the relationship between race and crime is enriched by connecting criminological analysis with historical colonial experience and personal biography in the present. It is by tracing how patterns of race and crime extend into lived experience of colonial legacies, despite the formal historical abeyance of such regimes, that a clearer understanding may emerge of how they shape our sensibilities, social interactions, narratives, and institutions.

A wide variety of cultural and social theorists have repeatedly drawn attention to the way wilful ignorance of, or selective amnesia about, Britain's colonial past impoverishes an understanding of how its footprints step steadily through the present day (Gilroy, 2004). Criminology is either a slow learner or has been particularly myopic towards the colonial and imperial foundations of penal institutions, concepts of order and governance, and categorization of different racial groups (Brown, 2005; Agozino, 2003; Brown, 2017). We are concerned that the almost insatiable appetite for criminology in the UK that we see in burgeoning undergraduate applications to study crime-related subjects stems, at least in part, from prospective students seeing in criminology the exciting figure of the murderous deviant, the threatening 'other', and the prospects of control, without recognizing their colonial and racist implications. We are not convinced that on graduating their vision will be any clearer.

While accepting that criminology in the UK is a diverse and vibrant discipline, it cannot be said that confronting the colonial origins of these imaginary figures and the ensuing centralization of criminal justice as a response, are as dynamic as they need to be. Instead, criminology tends towards an exclusive and instrumental focus

Rod Earle, Alpa Parmar, and Coretta Phillips, *Criminal Questions, Colonial Hinterlands, Personal Experience* In: *Decolonizing the Criminal Question*. Edited by: Ana Aliverti, Henrique Carvalho, Anastasia Chamberlen, and Máximo Sozzo, Oxford University Press.
 DOI: 10.1093/oso/9780192899002.003.0016

on its traditional problematics of control, with questions of policing, street crime, and managing prison populations leading the discipline. Despite the orthodox focus on cops, courts, and corrections, the three 'C's, being subject to continual critical scrutiny, there remains a relative silence surrounding the structuring violence of colonization (Agozino, 2003) and wider failures to engage consistently with race, racialization, and racism (Phillips et al., 2019).

In this chapter we seek to develop and demonstrate a way of centralizing rather than marginalizing the colonial dynamics of race in criminological analysis. As Leonardo (2009) has argued, to get beyond race, it is necessary to go through race. There are no shortcuts and the current vogue in denying the salience of race, whether it is in attacks on critical race theory in the USA and Australia or the Sewell report (CRED, 2021) in the UK, is intended to constrain, obstruct, or divert the liberatory potential of making the longer journey.

Trying to tease out some of the connections and routes through which we can appreciate the durability of colonialism and racism in the present is not an easy undertaking. References to traces of empire can be misleading if they simply seek to evoke mechanistic causal chains. Stoler (2016) emphasizes the importance of tracing enduring fissures in imperial relations, rather than assuming there are convenient 'historical shortcuts to show that every contemporary injustice can be folded into an originary colonial tale' (Stoler, 2016, p. 169). At the same time, of course, racial identities are constantly made and remade, always in relation, always in flux or unstable (Gunaratnam, 2003) in sharp and ironic contra-distinction to their original characterization as fixed in nature.

In this chapter we try to emphasize and expose the ways in which race is historically recursive rather than routinely repetitive. The patterns that emerge in criminal justice systems are not built on fixed racial identities or straightforward colonial legacies but on dynamic social practice. We use three case studies from our empirical research to explore how the colonial hinterlands of everyday experience might inform their social practice in relation to criminal justice. Our intention is to demonstrate how criminological research might develop further possibilities for richer and more nuanced accounts of the intersection of criminal justice systems with lived experience of coloniality. Our argument with criminology is the extent to which such possibilities are neglected.

Methodological Approach—Symptomatic Reading

We are mindful of the need to be alert to discontinuities as well as continuities in the colonial past and the postcolonial present (Brown, 2017). Our aim is to develop and enable stronger narratives that can account for the complexities and exigencies of the ways in which colonial history is discernible in contemporary personal experience. Colonial and postcolonial linkages are rarely self-evident or easily traced (Stoler, 2016) and we need better ways and more experience of recognizing how they may remain implicit, just out of view (Parma et al ., 2022). We need to be more alert to the ways they are allowed to slip out of view and, significantly, are often only retrieved by a minority of scholars and minority ethnic scholars. It is frequently relatively clear, for example, that ontological proxies of race can often surface through stories about family, culture, migration, belonging, nationality, and in how research participants explain what constitutes home(s) (Gunaratnam, 2003; Bloch, 2018). There is then the dual task of interpretive excavation to understand how individuals negotiate and articulate the racialized social locations in which they find themselves and acknowledging their salience. This involves appreciating the textures of how race is told or indeed, not told, or how it might be referenced in opaque terms in individual narratives.

Interviews inevitably entail joint construction, negotiation, and interaction, and we have found Althusser's ideas about symptomatic reading (Althusser and Balibar, 2009) to be particularly valuable in the approach we are adopting. Symptomatic reading is a strategy for interpreting the 'latent content' behind the 'manifest content' of a text. The intention of our symptomatic reading is to identify synonyms and substitutes for race and racialized experience. Our concern is with the way race works ideologically in the Althusserian sense that ideology offers people a way to live through the various contradictions and tensions in the conditions of their existence. These take shape in daily practice and in the form of the lives our respondents refer to in biographical interviews. Our interest in ideology seeks to problematize the sociological appreciation of race as an innocent social construct, as an aspect of social 'diversity', and emphasize the way race operates as an ideological force in society securing division and hierarchy in the interest of some people and at the expense of others.

If we want to appreciate the magnitude of race and racism in questions of crime, social order, and disorder, and draw out implications that appear to have been missed or are simply missing, a simple or 'innocent' reading of the criminal question (Aliverti et al., 2021) is not enough. This is particularly the case in a discipline as 'white' as criminology when questions of 'white innocence', the predispositions that white people have to neglect race, miss race, or otherwise deny the salience of race, are only just beginning to be identified (Smith and Linnemann, 2015; Phillips et al., 2019).

Our argument revolves around the life stories narrated by men entangled in a convergence between racialization and criminalization and where both have become thoroughly entwined in the general modalities of government. These involve the most powerful and potentially violent of state agencies, the criminal justice system, becoming increasingly proximate to a person's everyday life. These agencies carry with them all the racializing force of their colonial history. To illustrate these dynamics, we draw from a series of qualitative interviews. These are deliberately selective in that they seek perspectives from men variously involved in criminal justice and whose ethnicities align with the categories of 'black', 'Asian', and 'white'. In doing so, we take seriously Aliverti et al.'s (2021, p. 307) invocation towards acts of political recognition that centralize 'those most often invisibilized, silenced and side-lined in contemporary criminal justice practices and in knowledge constructions'.

The first two case studies emerge from a life history study with minority ethnic young men. They are of black Jamaican origin (Cairo) and Bangladeshi Muslim (Rafan) origin. They capture some of the processual interactions between structural positionings and internal, subjective worlds. Cairo and Rafan were research participants in a study drawing from a purposive sample of twenty young, minority ethnic Londoners, examining how racial orders are mobilized and contested in everyday life. Both were from a volunteer pool in contact with community development and sports organizations, mosques, and other youth groups, in four London boroughs in 2017. To specifically address the hidden presence of whiteness, we include a symptomatic reading of material from a prison study conducted by Phillips and Earle in 2006–2008. The research centred on examining the construction and negotiation of ethnic and masculine identities in prisoners' lives, particularly as they intersected with faith, nationality, and locality. This third interview provides insight into an adaptive repertoire among white identities in the postcolonial period that emerged after the end of the Second World War as national independence movements secured some separation from pre-war colonial domination. Taken together, the interviews offer illustrations of how we can become more alert to enduring colonial traces that operate in a person's life, materially, symbolically, culturally, and psychically. The analysis uses an approach which seeks out, through a close reading, reflection, and collaborative discussion between us, the sentiments, feelings, ambiguities, silences, and controversies, that animate race in postcolonial everyday experience. While the analysis of each case study is led by a single author, it is the result of extensive collaboration underpinned by our respective ethnic identities and positioning within the racial hierarchies of the colonial order. The specific contribution of this chapter, then, is to supplement and encourage diverse approaches to decolonizing criminology through revisiting empirical studies, developing teamwork, and collaborative analysis to better inform our understanding of challenging and obscured postcolonial dynamics (Agozino, 2003; Carrington et al., 2016; Carrington et al., 2019; Aliverti et al., 2021). By tracing the way in which empire extends beyond history and reappears in personal lives, our own as well as those of our research subjects, we become more appreciative of the instability and persistence of racial stereotypes as well as their inherent malleability both in imperial times and now. Our approach follows Stoler (2016) in finding durable and harmful patterns in the debris of empire scattered through the biographies of our respondents.

Cairo's Jamaican Excursions and Versions

At the time of interview, Cairo was seventeen and living with his parents and siblings in London. He was interviewed by Coretta Phillips, a black/mixed race Londoner. Asked about his nationality, Cairo was emphatic: 'I'm Jamaican ... Yes, I've got British passport ... I'm Jamaican by blood.' Cairo's narrative throughout the interview is infused with a deep sense of love, affection, and loyalty to his Jamaican-born parents. He credited his father with providing him with a moral upbringing. As the only 'boy child' there was a strong sense of familial responsibility in Cairo's narrative, as he understood the paternal expectation that he would portray himself in a respectful matter in the local community, never diminishing the family name.

Taking Stoler's (2016) lead, we acknowledge that colonial remnants can 'be there' and then 'not there', activated, reactivated, and then receding from view and effect. More helpful, she suggests, is to think in terms of 'processes of partial reinscriptions, modified displacements, and amplified recuperations' (ibid, p. 27). Cairo was aware that his mother would contact the police or send him 'back home' for informal social control, 'Jamaican-style', if she found out he was involved in anything illegal. The option of informal social control for school misbehaviour or offending are often routine and transnational in scope for children with familial ties to Britain's former colonial territories in Africa and the Caribbean (Bailey et al., 2014). Cairo's behaviour at school radically improved when he believed he was at risk of being sent 'back home' to Jamaica for physical chastisement. Describing his school experiences, he describes his anger at teachers who he believed deliberately provoked his temper to test him—'They'd press my button for me to have a reaction.' Cairo recounts that his troublesome behaviour at school, provoked or otherwise, was effectively halted when the prospect of 'back home' social control became an imminent possibility. The threat Cairo sensed of being sent to relatives in Jamaica and of being beaten with a cane in their secondary schools was enough to motivate him to moderate his behaviour in school, whatever the provocations.

Imperializing Merton?

Cairo always assumed he would encounter the racial hierarchies and poverty that frames the lives of many young black Londoners. In relation to employment and financial security, he observed that 'if he's [a black man] saying the same thing as a white man first, the white man is still going to make more money'. Recognizing the impact of colonialism on global as well as local inequalities, as Aliverti et al. (2021) urge, we must more comprehensively unpack how persistent racialized differentials unravel or are threaded through a person's life. When Cairo's mum was ill and bedridden and his dad was only intermittently employed and bringing money into the house, Cairo describes his predicament:

> A few ceilings were leaking, it wasn't that bad but obviously food-wise it was bad … We went through this rough patch. My mum developed thyroids in here, she had a problem with her back so she basically in bed every day … my dad, he's trying. It's not only him that can look after the whole house but he was trying. It got to a point where literally like we were scraping looking for food inside the cupboards to see what we can make up … It's like I got to a point where your belly is hurting you … You feel like your belly is eating itself.

Cairo goes on to describe how his illicit solutions involving fraudulent online credit-card scams 'literally fed me, put food in my mouth'. By 'frauding it out', as he put it, he was able to supplement the family's budget to provide food and household essentials. Using his computer skills, Cairo used the dark web to hack credit-card accounts, then bought iPhones that were sold on locally through a network of friends and associates. While subsistence might have provided the spur to Cairo's offending, he was candid that he went much further. The proceeds were also about underwriting a desired lifestyle involving the designer labels associated with wealth and success, and extravagant quantities of cash.

There is no easy divide between his 'noble cause' offending and the casual acquisition of unearned consumer goods. His interview includes numerous stories of how widely his predicaments and solutions are shared among his peer group. Sometimes he is 'putting food in their mouths' but it is noticeable how easily this vocabulary of necessity and survival slips across to the provision of material 'luxuries' and accessorizing a lifestyle. Cairo's descriptions of his peer group's 'starving' appetites refers deliberately and explicitly to designer labels as much as it does food and household necessities. In Mbembe's (2017) work, there is a powerfully evocative reflection on the aesthetic and cultural violence of colonialism alongside its economic and political dimensions. His analysis describes the seductive activation of desires that infused relations between African elites, traders, and Europeans, all variously positioned in the transatlantic slave trade. Disconcertingly, Mbembe maintains that it was not just bodies that were stolen as the colonized people were captured by the fantasy of wealth, enchanted by the possibilities of access to objects and goods sold by Europeans. In this sense, Africans drawn into colonial relations were compulsively invested in a potent logic of consumption that saw material goods within an emotional and affective economy created by a climate of enviable wealth. For Mbembe, the contemporary 'erotics of merchandise' should be understood as a kind of symbolic fetishization, a materialistic cult, in which desires for commodities penetrated deep into the core of imperial subjectivity.

For Mbembe (2017, p. 103), it is in 'mobilizing the memory of the colony' and the ways this produces psychic images that have a motive force even to those who have not witnessed colonialism directly that we find particularly helpful. It is this history of colony in the lived-present, background, foreground, and underground, that is so invisible, so unfelt, among white people, but that so insistently frames black people's subjectivity. There was certainly a vivid sense of this in Cairo's talk, if you looked.

There is much more to learn about the phenomenology of subjection—the existential and psychic costs of ongoing racializing practices for black male bodies—which has so far escaped criminological attention (Yancy, 2017). The affective content of both criminalization and racialization is far more pervasive, destructive, wearing, injuring to the psychic self on an ongoing basis, than is recognized within mainstream criminology. 'The Black Man is also the name of a wound' is how Mbembe (2017, p. 18) puts it. While we may not recommend a full detour through the Afropessimism literature, criminologists cannot entirely neglect it.

Rafan's Criminal Justice Rejections and Recreations

Rafan, a twenty-year-old young man, was interviewed in East London by Alpa Parmar and was of Asian Bangladeshi Muslim background. He had been caught up in the criminal justice system for a violent episode at school and had also tried dealing drugs, although without any great success or relish. He had himself been the victim of crime on various occasions, including having been robbed in his local neighbourhood. At the time of the interview, Rafan was focusing on his work as a security guard and sought meaning, purpose, and achievement in life through this employment. His work in security and his aspiration to progress to become a professional bodyguard aligned with his bold and ambitious aspirations, as revealed in the interview: he was in the process of setting up an events company which specialized in security.

While at school, Rafan had been involved in a fight which left the other boy seriously injured. Rafan described it as 'the stupidest thing he'd ever done' and was remorseful about the incident, although felt unfairly blamed as the sole perpetrator in an incident that he felt involved more people. He said other pupils of the school were also 'to blame' but that no one supported him, and no witnesses came forward in the ensuing police investigation and court case. Rafan was excluded from school and referred to what he called a 'behaviour' school from which he largely withdrew his engagement.

Violence was a relatively normal part of Rafan's life, and he admitted to having 'punch-ups and scuffles' on a regular basis. During the interview, Rafan seemed intent on presenting an idealized version of himself, adopting what appeared to be a highly mannered and staged thoughtful demeanour. His responses seemed to lack spontaneous authenticity but, as the interview unfolded, it became more apparent that what appeared as a contrived self-presentation was, in fact, likely to be Rafan's preferred mode of self-presentation. It was an approach to life in which he liked to project an image of a 'perfect ideal' of himself. From Alpa's point of view, it seemed to operate as a defence mechanism upon which he learned to convince himself that he was moving forward and beyond the snare of the criminal justice system into which he had so nearly fallen. The court case against him was discontinued but not before he had felt the force of its capacity to define his future. Taking back control of his future thus had a full presence in Rafan's life.

The postcolony

In Rafan's self-conscious performance of himself there are echoes of the kinds of psycho-social postcolonial analysis developed by Homi Bhabha (1994). Bhabha's essay on 'sly civility' in *The Location of Culture*, advances an argument about the way the colonized adapt to the force and expectations of the coloniser by adopting certain mannerisms that reflect those expectations, while simultaneously indicating and rejecting their false authority. In Bhabha's analysis, the colonizer is always asking 'the native' to provide a narrative of themselves, but 'the native's' recognition that this demand is always also a plea by the colonizer for the native to 'tell us why we are here' is profoundly unsettling of the colonial hierarchy. The exposure of colonial uncertainty and the existential insecurity of the colonizer is subversive because it triggers, according to Bhabha, the inevitable paranoia at the heart of the colonial relationship—'why don't they love us? why are they trying to kill us? why do they hate me?' While Bhabha's arguments sometimes tend towards a reductive essentialism that pitches the 'historical native' as a conveniently two-dimensional figure, his determination to unpack the enduring psychic load within the 'colonial scene' has contributed much to postcolonial theory and may have unexplored potentials in criminological settings and analysis.

In discussions about the relationship between race and crime, Rafan suggested there was a relatively uncomplicated and unproblematic racial hierarchy. When asked why, as he had suggested, black boys might be caught up in the criminal justice system more than Asian and white boys, Rafan's response was straightforward and simple:

> I don't know. Because they're black... It is what it is, to be honest.

His casual acceptance of the racialized order within the context of offending was stark and matter of fact. He did, however, appear to recognize the racial disparagement that lingered in the observation he had just made, and sought to qualify it with an immediate and corresponding reference to the Asian boys:

> It's just the way... it's probably the way they act or... See, even that is not right, saying 'the way they act'. Look at the way Asian boys act.

In Rafan's response, there is a restatement of conventional racial categorization that fixes criminality to black people, a categorization usually suppressed or avoided in public discourse on race and crime, but Rafan licenses his use of it by referring to his own minority and racialized status, implying without explicitly stating a correspondence that is felt but remains less than intelligible. Rafan seeks to temper his dismissive characterization of black people and to draw some of its poison by implicitly placing himself within the same racializing dynamic: 'look at the way Asian boys act'.

Rafan clearly felt marked by the violent incident he was involved in and his constant references throughout the interview to his parents being 'perfect' and having not done anything wrong seemed to be an attempt to disassociate his own wrongdoing from his family and wider relatives. He talked of how his dad was 'really well known... and really respected' underlining how Rafan's behaviour had ripple effects on his dad's reputation and business as he was a minicab driver who drew on his standing in the community for local custom. In this vein, Rafan seemed keen to convey how his family were 'normal' rather than in any way contaminated by the deviant status associated with criminal justice:

> Well you've got to remember something. A father's a grafter, he's outside. A mother's at home, mother brings up the kids. All of us, my brothers and sisters, everyone's fine. Everyone's completely perfect and happy with their life. No one's doing anything wrong, so it just says that my mum brought us up perfectly.

While the stigmatizing effects of criminal labelling are widely felt and generally recognized, there are imperial antecedents that may pull discretely and implicitly on Rafan's personal experience. The idea of being guilty by association was embedded in colonial constructions of criminality in India and were an important element in establishing the authority of white colonial power. Identifying collective pathological deviance was a formal project of government in Britain's Indian and African colonies where concepts of hereditary criminality were attributed in different ways. Colonial practices towards South Asians, for example, marked the criminal for such a reading through the use of penal tattoos (Anderson, 2004) and latent criminality was seen as an extended feature of whole groups of people. As Brown (2017, p. 188) observes, 'by the late 1940s... somewhere between three and 13 million Indians were subject to penal control' in India as a result of the criminal tribe's policy. This policy, enacted through Criminal Tribes Act 1924, established colonial ways of thinking about criminality, and 'seeing' and 'not seeing' Indian people's lives that are historically consequential. While conventional colonial narratives and critiques have tended to focus on the larger violence of events, such as those of the Thugee campaigns in the 1830s or the Jallianwala

Bagh massacre of 1919, the diffuse impact of the criminal tribe's policy is far less well known and underappreciated (Brown, 2017). Modes of surveillance towards whole tribes and the practice of making individuals guilty by association were established and played out in colonial India as was the practice of biometric identification through fingerprinting (Sengoopta, 2003). The fine threads and filaments of everyday lived experience that are woven into colonial institutions and processes are only now beginning to be gathered into the historical record and may inform better understandings of the way life is lived in the present. Identifying and situating these colonial traces in people's daily lives in Britain offers new and richer ways of making sense of their experiences of criminal justice and government.

These features of colonial rule in India on people's everyday lives and the image of a collective, 'tribal' criminality passed around and down hereditary lines of descent became a dominant organizing mentality of colonial India. And they did not stay in India. As in all features of coloniality, the experiences travelled to and fro between metropole and colony. Metaphorical and literal baggage assembled and shaped people's lives, influencing their sense of themselves, their place in society, and their prospects (Hall, 2002). Rafan might not be schooled in colonial history but the image he deploys of black criminality emerges from the colonial optics that regarded people of African descent as pathological criminals whose behaviours stemmed directly and inevitably from their biology (Anderson, 2004). Rafan's fatalistic comment that 'It is what it is' may be a throwaway remark but is also a succinct rephrasing of the 'born criminal' trope attached to black people by colonial powers.

In his interview, Rafan at various points either talked directly about or alluded to the exclusion he had been subject to, because of his involvement in crime and because of his ethnic background. Rafan also felt the force of being labelled and marked by his involvement in the fight and despite the court case not resulting in his prosecution he did not feel vindicated. The potential stain on his character remained a looming presence in his life. He felt as though his whole family were marked by the incident and was working hard to redeem himself in his family's and community's eyes. He had internalized a sense that he had let his family down and seemed to overcompensate by presenting an ideal version of himself to Alpa whenever he could. The stain of an enduring criminality had begun to shape his life from that moment on and haunted the decisions he went on to make. Our work is an attempt to pull these colonial threads, follow where they might lead, and explore how they may reach back into the past.

Warren: Transnational Whiteness Refusing to be Seen

Warren is an older white prisoner from Essex, a county on the north-eastern margins of London where he has worked for some years in the print industry. The interview was conducted in HMP Maidstone, Kent in 2007 by Rod Earle.

In his postcolonial studies of classical literature, Edward Said points to the 'dead silence' around race and identifies the imperial assumptions about the Atlantic slave trade to be found in, for example, Jane Austen's novel *Mansfield Park* (Said, 1993). Even in everyday life, the recurring silences around race generate troubling omissions and gaps in life experience that correspond to its animating, but simultaneously denied, apparently dead, presence. They combine to reproduce a sense of the unintelligibility of race, and its inevitable return. Using contemporary theorization of whiteness as an analytical frame, a symptomatic reading reveals more of the dynamics of race stirring below the surface of the interview. In it, Warren clings covertly to the classic racial understanding of whiteness as superiority. It is a defiant but fugitive whiteness that dare not speak its name out loud in the prison, the interview or, for that matter, much of the wider world. As the interview unfolds, this carefully hidden identification gradually leaks through on the back of his South African accent. This audible but un-transcribed data becomes central to the symptomatic reading that explores the implications of Warren's silences about race and whiteness. The interview provides an opportunity for exploring how a symptomatic reading may expose the work that must be done to make postcolonial critiques of whiteness matter more in criminological research.

'Don't get me white'? racial routes in and out of Zimbabwe, London, and Essex

In part of the interview, Warren tells Rod that he spent nineteen years of his life in Zimbabwe. Rod picks this up and mentions to Warren the slight hint of a South African accent in his voice. This leads Warren to tell Rod he speaks 'Dutch' and also 'some African languages', though he doesn't specify which ones. In fieldnotes, Rod recalls wondering if Warren really means he speaks Afrikaans, the South African derivative of Dutch that is such a powerful signifier of the imperial legacy of European struggles to own Africa and Africans. Perhaps Warren was concerned that it might disclose too much about himself too soon. He knows the research is concerned with race, and Afrikaans is a language uniquely and inescapably associated with apartheid, the paradigmatic pariah racial order of the postcolonial period. Re-listening to the interview some years later reveals how this unexpected linguistic disclosure seems to set off a tangential narrative that weaves uneasily through the rest of the interview. Rod notes how clumsily (perhaps leadingly) he asks Warren about his years in Zimbabwe, asking if he was 'raised there'. Warren responds defensively: 'Absolutely not, I spent 19 years of my adult life there, working', insisting he was born and brought up in Barking, Essex. He declares 'I'm an Englishman' and, as he does so, Rod hears again the South African/Afrikaans under-accent and Warren's alertness to its ambiguous, dislocating signals: 'I may not sound like one but believe me I am'. Warren willingly presents detailed vignettes from a 'colourful' life in London living with various women and of his travels around the world, but volunteers nothing at all of the substantial section of his life, the nineteen years spent in Zimbabwe that account for his accent and tension his assertion of being 'an Englishman'.

Unsettled by various aspects of the interview, Rod's post-interview fieldnotes record his impression of Warren's evasive need to talk in code and euphemism about race. It surfaces in inferences about the supposed drug-taking habits of his neighbours: 'I have no wish to associate with neighbours of that type' and that 'when they try to get to know you too intimately, that is a no-no as far as I am concerned'. He seems to deliberately avoid using any of the conventional ethnic terminology. With misgivings rising in the interview that Warren is dissembling around his feelings about race, Rod presses the point and asks specifically and perhaps a little provocatively about whether any of the people and communities he is referring to are white. Warren appears to register Rod's provocation and responds by erasing it with the classic assertion of 'race-blindness', with all its characteristic cognitive dissonance:

> As far as black people are concerned ... their colour of their skin is not in my vision, for want of a better expression. I accept everybody. I don't care what colour they are, I don't care what religion they are. As long as they don't do me any harm, I treat them with all the respect they deserve.

The interview transcripts read-as-text and as repeat-listening-recordings reinforce Rod's impression that Warren is saying almost the opposite of what he means. In the interview itself and over several listenings, Rod's suspicions grow that Warren, somewhat unusually for a white person, 'owns' rather than disowns a white racial identity, and that his orientation is actively rather than passively pro-racism. Rod mentions that racism is often a feature of life within communities and Warren responds, 'I am fully aware of the racial aspect, especially in London. I have always been aware and tried to convince people to see things my way, rather than their way. In the print business there has tended to be a lot of racial animosity, people belonging to the BNP and the likes'. He declares himself as 'non-racist' and speculates about the origins of racist feelings in an account that tumbles quickly into the logics of post-racial reverse as he appears to attribute the source of racist sentiments arising from within minority and immigrant communities: 'are they indoctrinated? Is it inbred in them or is it total resentment because they are in our country or whatever, I have no idea?'

In the interview, Rod pursues the Zimbabwe connection. Warren says he went there to work on a farm with his brother but states that he didn't like farming, that he has always seen himself as a printer, 'since I left school'. Rod asks if he worked as a printer in Zimbabwe and Warren says he did 'a bit', but pointedly doesn't expand. The gaps in his account seem to widen. He has a south African accent and has said he spent a third of his life in Zimbabwe but will tell nothing of it. The silences are symptomatic of an unspoken but almost self-evident racial story anchored in white English nationalism.

Accents of colonial hierarchy, evidence of whiteness

Because of their accents, white South Africans enjoy less of the conventional comforts associated with white invisibility and innocence. In a post-apartheid context, they tend towards a covert, fugitive whiteness as out of place in a post-apartheid Africa as they are in multi-cultural London or a multi-cultural prison (Phillips, 2012). The evasions and toxic ambiguity of Warren's account are consistent with those that emerge in research about white people in South Africa who consciously select, edit, and borrow their whiteness according to the circumstances under which it is exposed to question (Steyn, 2001). Inevitably, they are more aware of their whiteness and have become more self-conscious of its variable implications. If they leave South Africa for Europe, for example, they know that when they speak, their accent projects not just an 'interesting' national or regional identity but an ideology (Vestergaard, 2001). This is because the Afrikaans language around which their accent forms became central to an explicit white nationalist project in which the construction of white supremacist identities would enable and justify the national boundaries of the whole continent of Africa.

In contrast to most white identities in which the construction and presence of whiteness is profoundly implicit, discretely positioning whiteness at the centre of racial discourse as the marker against which difference will be drawn, South African white identities are unavoidably aligned with apartheid's white supremacist ideology. They cannot so easily pass as innocent beneficiaries of whiteness (Robbins, 2017). Aware of the institutional whiteness of the apartheid regime signalled in their accent, white South Africans adopt a variety of biographical caveats. As with white people in the UK, they find some refuge in forms of 'secondary whiteness' (Alexander, 2017) that establish an ethnic whiteness at a suitable distance from the racial whiteness of apartheid and Empire. For Warren, however, it seems that there is no need for this kind of prevarication around ethnic difference because he remains loyal to the primary whiteness of 'his race' and its place in his imagined nation, England.

Race is thus part of a structuring set of relations making Warren the man he is and the world he moves through, from Zimbabwe to Barking. A symptomatic reading attends to silences, tension, absences, and contradictions around race and includes them in the analysis. Focusing more closely on the dynamics of race tangled in the criminological net in which Warren is caught and through which racism often slips unacknowledged can be revealing and rewarding for criminological analysis. By stressing the ideological valence of race in imperial and colonial projects, we are led to explore the ways in which it manifests in the personal experience of our respondents. Focusing on Warren's life as a white man situates race and coloniality as shaping his biography just as much as they might do Rafan's and Cairo's, even though their racialization is usually more open to critical scrutiny and criminological capture.

Conclusions: Colonial Violence, White Innocence, Criminal Questions

In outlining their experiences of crime, criminal justice, and injustice, Cairo, Rafan, and Warren lay bare some of the ongoing dimensions of coloniality. Their stories speak to traces and remnants of colonial practices that are not sequestered in the past but instead can take shape and matter in the world today. Racial hierarchies are writ large in their experiential realities, albeit sometimes subtly in the background and at other times their narratives reveal colonial presence in the foreground. Cairo, Rafan, and Warren's biographical connections to Jamaica, Bangladesh (and India), and Zimbabwe segue into the pervasive but sometimes elusive coloniality in the present. In so doing, they enable us to centralize race as an organizing logic of contemporary societies in ways that are more consistent with the analysis and approach of Saidiya Hartman (2008). Hartman's work aligns with Mbembe's to identify how the legacies of slavery and the ongoing colonial shape of the modern world flow through everyday life. Slavery, insists Hartman, established a racial calculus that fundamentally discounts and devalues black life. This deadly and death-dealing calculus remains active in modern society as the 'afterlife of slavery' and accounts for the persistence of 'skewed life chances, limited access to health and education, premature death, incarceration and impoverishment'. Paul Gilroy's (1987) seminal contributions to criminology are among the few that consistently and systematically centralize the legacies of colonialism and develop the implications of this 'afterlife of slavery'. This stands in stark contrast to the seeming erasure of coloniality and critical analysis of race at the centre of criminology. Gilroy's (2004) more recent work on postcolonial melancholia is less related to criminological questions than his earlier work but clearly signposts criminologists on the direction they must travel to redress this critical absence. Stoler's (2016, p. 342) argument for more work on the 'less perceptible effects of imperial interventions that settle into the social and material ecologies in which people dwell, and survive' is an argument we have tried to engage with in this chapter by deploying a particular methodological apparatus: symptomatic reading, collective analysis, and collaborative endeavour.

The tell-tale signs of the erasure of race and its consequences are not exclusive to criminology and in attending to them criminology might learn much from the way postcolonial studies identify absence and silence in the classical canon of literary studies (Morrison, 1993). For example, when the Covid-19 pandemic reanimated interest in Albert Camus's 1947 novel *The Plague*, a few alert critics highlighted the painful irony of neglecting the significance of Camus's erasure of colonized Arab experience (the novel is set in Algeria), at exactly the time that there was the same apparent indifference towards ethnic differentials in the impact of the Covid-19 'plague' in the UK (Rose, 2020; Earle, 2020). This tendency towards an exclusively white optic is not new, but often goes unmarked and unremarked. It reappeared, for instance, in a criminal justice context in 2021 when a judge offered an unusual bargain to a young white supremacist, neo-Nazi sympathizer he was sentencing for downloading an encyclopaedic collection of inflammatory racist material from the internet. The judge suspended a two-year custodial sentence, insisting instead that the man work through the judge's all-white recommended reading list: 'Have you read Dickens? Austen? Start with *Pride and Prejudice* and Dickens' *A Tale of Two Cities*. Shakespeare's *Twelfth Night*. Think about Hardy. Think about Trollope' (Earle, 2021; Tickell, 2021).

Inattention to race is a persistent feature of white writing in criminology (Phillips et al., 2019; Parmar, 2016). Whether it is apathy, an unconscious or even a conscious turning away from race, it is made possible by a lack of accountability and empathy towards those people most consistently impacted by racial capitalism and the white supremacist dynamics that unfold so reliably through criminal justice systems. It is a silence that is sustained in the social experience of many white people and comprehensively theorized by Gloria Wekker (2016) as a form of white innocence. White innocence in academic life embraces what black philosopher Charles W. Mills (1997, pp. 188–189) described as a 'conceptual tokenization, where a black perspective is included but in a ghettoized way that makes no difference to the overall discursive logic of the discipline, or subsection of the discipline, in question: the framing assumptions, dominant narratives, prototypical scenarios'.

White innocence denies the salience of race in everyday life through the assumption that contemporary societies are post-racial meritocracies. Thinking of race with under-theorized sociology and without considering it as ideology seriously limits our understanding of the traction it can have in real life, the work it does for white people, and the violence it does to those who are not white. Their whiteness is not an epidermal fact about the colour of their skin but refers to their position in a set of social relations established by colonialism. These positions offer access to, dividends from, and benefits accorded to the accumulated cultural capital that colonialism provides to a small minority of the global population.

Making connections: coloniality and criminology

In the UK, the effort to qualify British racism as 'less bad', 'less violent', 'less extreme' than the South African or the US variant has secured significant traction because it offers white people in the UK a familiar and comforting sense of elevation and erasure. It conveniently ignores Britain's pivotal role in securing, by the middle of the twentieth century, the global presumption that 'the white race' was superior to all others and that the British Empire was not only the prime example but actual proof of its qualities. As Stuart Hall warns, 'it is only as the different racisms are historically specified—in their difference—that they can be properly understood' (Hall, 1980, p. 337). What we have tried to do in this chapter is to establish the possibility of exploring more fully how historical specificities and differences make race and racism such a powerful force in the criminal justice system. Interviewing Cairo, Rafan, and Warren and seeking out the racial threads that are woven through the way they experience the world and talk about the world reveals the coloniality of the present. We do not seek to become ventriloquists projecting our voices through theirs, but we are interested in excavating connections between their experiences, our experiences, and the unavoidability of colonial history. James Baldwin's remark that 'people are trapped in history and history is trapped inside them' (Baldwin, 1958/1985) is a plea to use our knowledge of colonial history to free us from the traps its sets. Each of us, like Cairo, Rafan, and Warren, are differently positioned in those traps but attending carefully to them we might find the language and the narratives to decolonize at least some of the criminal questions they pose. To do so, we may need to abandon the old, white criminology and its habits of 'booming loudly with knowledge of the other' (Mykhalovsky, 1996), a noise that silences voices less often heard but with so much to say. We might follow Bhambra's (2014) lead in sociology and attend to connections that link the new black criminologies, Southern criminologies, and indigenous criminologies. These suggest that resistance and change often begin in new methodologies, art, and especially the art of words. In that spirit we end with a poet's angry warning:

> I am fed up with documentations of my grief ... researchers claiming to record history when all they do is pick my wounds ... This is my story, not yours. Long after you turn off your recorder I stay indoors and weep. Why don't people understand? ...
> (Choman Hardi, 'The Angry Survivor', in *Considering the Women* (2015))

References

Agozino, B. (2003) *Counter-Colonial Criminology: A Critique of Imperialist Reason.* London: Pluto Press.

Alexander, C. (2017) 'Breaking Black: The Death of Ethnic and Racial Studies in Britain', *Ethnic and Racial Studies*, 41(6), pp. 1034–1054.

Aliverti, A., Carvalho, H., Chamberlen, A. et al. (2021) 'Decolonizing the criminal question', *Punishment & Society* 23(3), pp. 297–316.

Althusser, L. and Balibar, E. (2009) *Reading Capital*. London: Verso.

Anderson, C. (2004) *Legible Bodies: Race, Criminality and Colonialism in South Asia*. New York: Berg.

Bailey, C., Robinson, T., and Coore-Desai, C. (2014) 'Corporal Punishment in the Caribbean: Attitudes and practice', *Social and Economic Studies*, 63(3/4), pp. 207–233.

Baldwin, J. (1958/1985) 'Stranger in the Village', in Baldwin, J. (ed.) *Notes of Native Son*. London: Pluto Press.

Bhabha, H. (1994) *The Location of Culture*. London: Routledge.

Bhambra, G. (2014) *Connected Sociologies*. London: Bloomsbury.

Bloch, A. (2018) 'Talking about the past, locating it in the present: The second generation from refugee backgrounds making sense of their parents' narratives, narrative gaps and silences', *Journal of Refugee Studies*, 31(4), pp. 647–663.

Brown, M. (2005) 'Colonial History and Theories of the Present: Some Reflections upon Penal History and Theory', in Godfrey, B. and Dunstall, G. (eds) *Crime and Empire 1840–1940*. Cullompton: Willan.

Brown, M. (2017) 'Postcolonial penality: Liberty and repression in the shadow of independence, India c. 1947', *Theoretical Criminology*, 21(2), pp. 186–208.

Carrington, K., Hogg, R., and Sozzo, M. (2016) 'Southern criminology', *British Journal of Criminology*, 56(1), pp. 1–20.

Carrington, K., Dixon, B., Fonseca, D. et al. (2019) 'Criminologies of the Global South: Critical reflections', *Critical Criminology*, 27(1), pp. 163–189.

Commission on Race and Ethnic Disparities (CRED) (2021) *Commission on Race and Ethnic Disparities: The Report*. UK Government. Available at: www.gov.uk/government/publications/the-report-of-the-commission-on-race-and-ethnic-disparities (accessed 12 May 2022).

Earle, S. (2020) 'How Albert Camus's *The Plague* Became the Defining Book of the Coronavirus Crisis', The New Statesman, 27 May. Available at: www.newstatesman.com/long-reads/2020/05/the-plague-albert-camus-coronavirus-resurgence (accessed 12 May 2022).

Earle, R. (2021) 'A racist, a judge and a clear case of white privilege', The Guardian, 2 September. Available at: www.theguardian.com/world/2021/sep/02/a-racist-a-judge-and-a-clear-case-of-white-privilege (accessed 11 May 2022).

Gilroy, P. (1987) *Ain't no Black in the Union Jack*. London: Routledge.

Gilroy, P. (2004) *After Empire: Melancholia or Convivial Culture?* London: Routledge.

Gunaratnam, Y. (2003) *Researching 'Race' and Ethnicity: Methods, Knowledge and Power*. London: Sage.

Hall, C. (2002) *Civilizing Subjects: Metropole and Colony in the English Imagination 1830–1867*. Cambridge: Polity Press.

Hall, S. (1980) 'Race, Articulation and Societies Structured in Dominance', in *Sociological Theories: Race and Colonialism*. Paris: United Nations Educational, Scientific and Cultural Organization (UNESCO).

Hardi, C. (2015) 'The Angry Survivor', in *Considering the Women*. Hexham: Bloodaxe Books.

Hartman, S. (2008) *Lose Your Mother: A Journey Along the Atlantic Slave Route*. London: Farrah, Straus and Giroux.

Leonardo, Z. (2009) *Race, Whiteness and Education*. London: Routledge.

Mbembe, A. (2017) *Critique of Black Reason*. Durham, NC: Duke University Press.

Mills, C. (1997) *The Racial Contract*. Ithaca, NY: Cornell University Press.

Morrison, T. (1993) *Playing in the Dark: Whiteness and the Literary Imagination*. New York: Vintage.

Mykhalovskiy, E. (1996) 'Reconsidering table talk: Critical thoughts on the relationship between sociology, autobiography and self-indulgence', *Qualitative Sociology*, 19(1), pp. 131–151.

Parmar, A. (2016) 'Race, Ethnicity and Criminal Justice: Refocussing the Criminological Gaze', in Bosworth, M., Hoyle, C., and Zedner, L. (eds) *Changing Contours of Criminal Justice*. Oxford: Oxford University Press, pp. 55–68.

Parmar, A., Earle, R., and Phillips, C. (2022) 'Seeing is believing: How the layering of race is obscured by "white epistemologies" in the criminal justice field,' Journal of Criminal Justice Education, 33(2), pp. 289–306.

Phillips, C. (2012) *The Multicultural Prison*. Oxford: Oxford University Press.

Phillips, C., Earle, R., Parmar, A. et al. (2019) 'Dear British criminology: Where has all the race and racism gone?' *Theoretical Criminology* 24(3), pp. 427–446.

Robbins, B. (2017) *The Beneficiary*. Durham, NC: Duke University Press.

Rose, J. (2020) 'Pointing the finger: Jacqueline Rose on "The Plague"', *London Review of Books*, 42(9). Available at: www.lrb.co.uk/the-paper/v42/n09/jacqueline-rose/pointing-the-finger (accessed 12 May 2022).

Said, E. (1993) *Culture and Imperialism*. London: Vintage.

Sengoopta, C. (2003) *Imprint of the Raj: How Fingerprinting was Born in Colonial India*. London: Macmillan.

Smith, J. and Linneman, T. (2015) 'Whiteness and Critical white studies in crime and justice', Issues in Criminal Justice, Social and Restorative Justice, 18(2), pp. 101–104.

Steyn, M. E. (2001) *Whiteness Just Isn't What it Used To Be: White Identity in a Changing South Africa*. New York: State University of New York Press.

Stoler, A. L. (2016) *Duress: Imperial Durabilities in our Times*. Durham, NC: Duke University Press.

Tickell, A. (2021) 'English Literature, Racism and Rehabilitation', The Open University, 8 September. Available at: www.open.edu/openlearn/history-the-arts/literature/english-literature-racism-and-rehabilitation (accessed 11 May 2022).

Vestergaard, M. (2001). Who's got the map? The negotiation of Afrikaner identities in post-apartheid South Africa, *Daedalus: Journal of the American Academy of Arts and Sciences*, 130(1), pp. 19–44.

Wekker, G. (2016) *White Innocence: Paradoxes of Colonialism and Race*. Durham, NC: Duke University Press.

Yancy, G. (2017) 'The Violent Weight of Whiteness: The Existential and Psychic Price Paid by Black Male Bodies', in Zack, N. (ed.) *The Oxford Handbook of Philosophy and Race*. Oxford: Oxford University Press.

16

Ayllu and *Mestizaje*

A Decolonial Feminist View of Women's Imprisonment in Peru

Lucia Bracco Bruce

Introduction

In this chapter, I am positioning my theoretical stance on issues of imprisonment from a Southern perspective. I specifically focus on the debates of Latin American decolonial theorists who coined the modernity/coloniality project in dialogue with decolonial feminists. Linked to this, the relational dynamics of Peruvian women's prisons are the epicentre of my reflections in this chapter. Drawing on ethnographic research in the largest women's prison in Peru, colloquially called Santa Monica, I will discuss two concepts, *Ayllu* and *Mestizaje*, to account for intermingled political and social dynamics inside Santa Monica that aid a better understanding of prisons' governance and women prisoners' intersubjective relationships in their everyday lives. My intention is to identify the long-standing modern/colonial/patriarchal structure of prisons, while recognizing the potential of the *praxis* of individuals and collectives. In this case, I explore how women prisoners organize and interrelate, and through their experience, what they may teach us about incarceration and prison organization.

The chapter is divided into two sections. In the first one, I offer a brief account of the main arguments of Latin American decolonial theorists, particularly Anibal Quijano and Maria Lugones. Then I link their theoretical approach to the emergence and configuration of Latin American creole states with the modern penitentiary, particularly Peruvian women's prisons. I suggest that in order to consider a decolonial criminology or to decolonize the criminal question, as premised in this book, it is necessary to recognize the historical patterns of the region. That is, to elaborate embodied and localized knowledge that problematizes universal readings of the sociopolitical phenomenon based on situated and regional Western experiences (Carrington et al., 2019; Curiel, 2009; Espinosa, 2016). Therefore, it is not possible to formulate a proper understanding of the processes of criminalization, punishment, and incarceration in Latin America without an analysis of coloniality and the colonial heritage (Segato, 2007; Zaffaroni, 1989).

In the second section, I analyse the concepts of *Ayllu* and *Mestizaje* to account for women prisoners' political and social dynamics inside Santa Monica. I explore these concepts with the aim of producing categories that are rooted in the core concerns of our realities, which may offer other venues for understanding processes globally

Lucia Bracco Bruce, Ayllu *and* Mestizaje In: *Decolonizing the Criminal Question.* Edited by: Ana Aliverti, Henrique Carvalho, Anastasia Chamberlen, and Máximo Sozzo, Oxford University Press.
DOI: 10.1093/oso/9780192899002.003.0017

(Bautista, 2014);[1] and to think on those actions and resistances that are performed within the gerund of oppression and resistance (Lugones, 2008b). I think it is important to emphasize that the analysis in this chapter is not a finished reflection but an avenue to create more contextual analysis about how modern-colonial-patriarchal institutions, such as prisons, have historical baggage that are imprinted in the contemporary lived experiences of men and women prisoners. Thus, I distance binary and dichotomous analyses that focus on the division of colonial legacies on one side and resistances on the other (Lugones, 2008b) and focus on the agencies and resistances within oppressive circumstances, centring on the nuances, ambivalences, and tensions between those spectrums and their implications on women prisoners' everyday performances.

The Modern-Colonial-Patriarchal Structure

To analyse the processes of criminalization, punishment, and incarceration in Latin America it is necessary to draw upon its historical background. The decolonial turn proposes a new paradigm that centres on the analysis of global power that found its base in the modern-colonial-patriarchal world-system. Two of their representative authors, Anibal Quijano and Maria Lugones, offer a meta-narrative explanation of power relationships during the colonial expansion and its implications on political, social, cultural, and subjective processes that are currently reproduced (Castro-Gómez, 2019).

The conquest of America is the milestone that configured the modern-colonial-patriarchal world-system and, in spite of the fact that colonial expansion started at the end of the fifteenth century, its asymmetrical force and its impact is reproduced through our colonial heritage up until the present day. Anibal Quijano focuses on the concept of 'coloniality of power'. For Quijano, colonial expansion configured a new social classification and categorized individuals and collectives according to specific biological marks and phenotypic racial characteristics. Phenotypical racial attributes were used to determine a person's place and labour in the social structure and their possibility of accessing wealth and power, and configured new geo-cultural identities and hierarchical intersubjective relationships of domination between the conquerors and the colonized populations (Quijano, 1992; 2000; Mignolo, 2000a; Escobar, 2000).[2]

Quijano assumes race as being cultural and gender as being a natural characteristic of human beings, where sexual difference had been present long before the colonial expansion of Spain and Portugal. Nonetheless, the decolonial feminist Maria Lugones strongly questions this argument as it is framed within the structure of

[1] As Juan Jose Bautista (2014) suggests, it is clearer for observing the perverse consequences (and resistances) of the modern-colonial (and I include patriarchal) world pattern founded in 1492 in Latin America, but it does not mean that similar processes have not occurred in other regions or within other countries globally.

[2] Quijano argues that power struggles are apparent in five dimensions of social experience: labour, nature, sex, subjectivity, and authority. Therefore, the dispute about power will also include such dimensions and the redistribution of resources associated with labour, sexuality, and subjectivity.

heteronormative patriarchy. In this regard, Lugones (2008a) addressed Quijano's concept of the coloniality of power, and coined the term 'coloniality of gender' (p. 73). For Lugones, gender and sex are colonial impositions. Specifically, she refers to a modern/colonial gender system imposed by European colonizers. Hence, the colonial expansion set a new social organization in terms of gender which established a Westernized gender system, following the mandates of the Christian bourgeois Western family (Mignolo, 2005). The new emphasis meant the abandonment of communities, which unravelled the marriage and kinship patterns that guided social life before the colonial period.[3]

The social fragmentation configured during the colonial period moulded the construction of the Republican state in Peru (Cotler, 2005). As a legal and political process, colonialism ended, but exclusionary actions were transformed into subtler but no less racist strategies (Dussel, 2000), thus demonstrating Peru's colonial heritage (Quijano, 2000). The formation of Creole nation-states was a key element in the naturalization/perpetuation of a global power pattern, and the validation of progress as the reproduction of 'modern' Western societies in the former colonies.

For decolonial authors, coloniality is modernity's obscure feature and the other side of the same coin (Escobar, 2003). As Castro-Gómez and Grosfoguel (2007) note, modernity is a political–economic process that intermingles with an epistemic, cultural one. Thus, as Castro-Gómez (2005) explains, modernity is the ideological belief that propels the geopolitical division of the world between centres and peripheries (with different hegemonic powers and different peripheries throughout the centuries), and the epistemic base of global power patterns. For the Peruvian historian Carlos Aguirre, chronologically, modernity in Latin America is often linked to the early nineteenth century, which followed the colonial period and the constitution of an independent nation-state. In particular, in Peru it also refers to an economic process that intermingles with a symbolic–cultural one which produced internal power patterns. In that sense, it is a period where a small number of families controlled economic and political growth, intending to reform the institutional arena, but in a restricted participatory system (Aguirre, 2019). These reforms had an ideological, symbolic background. In other words, during this period the primary aspiration and self-perception of the political and social elites was to be 'modern' (Aguirre, 2009; 2019), following the myth of reproducing the alleged superior European standards.

Consequently, the construction of nation-states in the Americas resulted in the conversion of colonial power to an 'internal colonialism' (Mignolo, 2000b, p. 303). As decolonial jurist Armando Guevara (2009) explains, once independence from Spain was established, Peruvian Euro-centred elites embarked on ethnocidal projects with the aim of building a new, modern nation-state that reproduced idealized European

[3] There is a current debate about gender systems before and after colonial expansion. As mentioned, Maria Lugones suggests that the sex–gender dimension was not a variable that configured social classification before colonization. However, communitarian and decolonial feminists such as Rita Segato, Julieta Paredes, and Maria Galindo problematize this idea. All of them suggest the existence of gender systems, but note that these gender systems operated differently to those in Europe. For more on this topic, see Segato, 2013; Paredes, 2010; and Mannarelli, 2018.

models. As Nugent (2015) notes, the state proposed universalist, egalitarian principles as the legitimate basis of national community. However, everyday practice was still based on hierarchy, privilege, and social exclusion.

In that sense, coloniality-modernity became an internal process, where the North was found in the South (Espinosa, 2016)—and the South was also found in the North (Blagg and Anthony, 2019), thus creating geopolitical and epistemic global patterns of power that are still reproduced in the present. In that regard, the decolonial turn provided new horizons for understanding the re-functionalization of long-standing colonial structures. This shows how internal colonialism resulting from a colonial heritage propels mechanisms of exclusion, discrimination, and structural violence by Latin American's social, political, and governmental institutions (Rivera Cusicanqui, 2012) as well as how internal colonialism has marked the customs of subjective composition and configuration of intersubjective relations in the Latin American region (Quijano, 2000).

Race, Gender, and Imprisonment: The Modern-Colonial-Patriarchal Penitentiary

According to Salvatore and Aguirre (2017), it was between 1830 and 1940 that the modern penitentiary was born in Latin America. In other words, prisons as institutions are the products of the modern/colonial/patriarchal nation-state. Hence, prisons in the region were moulded by ideals imported from liberalism and republicanism, and functioned based on modern/patriarchal/colonial mandates (Aguirre, 2009; Constant, 2016; Salvatore and Aguirre, 2001). In a highly hierarchical and discriminatory society, such as that of Peru, this has led to prisons being used to control those seen as the masses of uncivilized and immoral populations, primarily associated with indigenous communities or impoverished groups (Aguirre, 1988; 2003; 2009; García-Basalo, 1954). Those deprived of their freedom, who were seen as immoral and undisciplined, were involved in an alleged process of resocialization in order for them to reflect on their actions in isolation from society and to become honest and industrious citizens through the means of work, education, and religion (Aguirre, 2009; Constant, 2016; García-Basalo, 1954).

During the configuration of the creole 'modern' states, the management of women's prisons, in particular, had a solid Catholic and moral component and women prisoners were sent to convents and religious congregations (Constant, 2016; Vega, 1973). As already discussed, the colonial period introduced a Westernized gender system, configured around binary and asymmetrical gender roles. Therefore, women were expected to be affectionate and more docile than men, were confined to the private sphere (religious or familial), and transgression from these social norms was defined as deviant (Oliart cited in Constant, 2016).

Although it cannot be denied that the experience of imprisonment is always gendered, as Lugones (2008a) suggests, the rationality of categorical separation distorts the understanding of a social phenomenon. To analyse the complexity of lived experience, then, we should distance ourselves from categorical thinking. In that regard, decolonial feminists such as Ochi Curiel (2009) or Yuderkys Espinosa (2016) follow

Lugones's argument and use the concept of 'matrix of oppression'.[4] Therefore, an understanding of women prisoners' experiences must consider how colonialism and patriarchy are intertwined, and how different systems of oppression create imbrications that shape internal hierarchies among women. Consequently, in relation to women, particularly indigenous women, prisons had aimed to inculcate obedience and compliance in their caring role and social reproduction, not only as mothers or wives but mainly as servants. Many poor Andean migrant women were hired as workers during the late nineteenth century, maintaining and reproducing class and racial hierarchies and stereotypes in society. So, after completing their time in the confinement of the institutions and having assumed alleged, civilized, religious norms, these women were sent to high- and middle-class families as servants to be monitored and exploited in the fulfilment of their feminine role (Aguirre, 2003; Boutron and Constant, 2013).

The birth of the modern-colonial-patriarchal prison came hand in hand with the diffusion of modern-colonial-patriarchal discourse on dangerousness, criminalization, and punishment. Therefore, the story of the configuration of the nation-states in Latin America is ancient and continuous. Imprisonment is still a selective device which naturalizes the suffering and death of men and women who are not considered 'white' (Aniyar de Castro, 1981; Bergalli, 1982; Del Olmo, 1981; Segato, 2007; Zaffaroni, 1989). Our colonial heritage, then, shaped discriminatory processes. It also gave rise to practices of resistance in our society within the same collectives. Prison organization and the interrelations among women prisoners may provide examples of this.

Ayllu and *Mestizaje*: Women in Contemporary Prisons in Lima, Peru

In the previous sections, I applied some ideas from the theoretical project of modernity/coloniality in dialogue with decolonial feminists, and how their ideas may provide an understanding of the configuration of prisons as colonial-modern-patriarchal institutions in Latin America, focusing on Peruvian women's prisons. In this section, I propose an analysis of contemporary prison dynamics and how internal colonialism in Peru still configures problematic socio-political dynamics that make invisible other organizational systems and racist discourses that produce internal hierarchies among women prisoners. I will discuss two concepts: first, *Ayllu*, as an Andean category that may be helpful for understanding women's surreptitious communitarian organization within prisons; and, second, *Mestizaje*, as a non-clear-cut identity/self-identification which hides a racist discourse. To provide examples of these concepts, I draw on an

[4] The concept of a 'matrix of oppression' was introduced by Patricia Hill Collins (1999). Curiel (2009) utilizes the term 'matrix of oppression' in contrast to the idea of intersectionality (Crenshaw, 1989) to provide a lens that enables us to see how power structures collide or intersect. Although Crenshaw had provided a valuable concept, Curiel suggests that the idea of intersectionality is not enough for understanding the complexity of women's experiences as it leaves out how these systems of domination were and are configured. In that regard, it is not only important to identify and describe the intersections, but also to account for their origins and history and, in the case of Latin America, their modern-colonial-patriarchal basis.

ethnography I conducted between December 2018 and May 2019 in Santa Monica, the largest women's prison in Peru which is located in Lima (Bracco, 2022).

Ayllu: A Communitarian Organizational System within Santa Monica

It cannot be denied that, structurally, prisons are punitive and violent institutions that foster individualization and mistrust between prison actors (between staff and prisoners, and among prisoners). Moreover, in the last few decades, there has been an increase in incarceration rates that has resulted in overcrowded prisons characterized by precarious and inhumane living conditions (Bergman, 2020). For example, in the case of Santa Monica, the overcrowding rate is more than 50 per cent (Instituto Nacional Penitenciario, 2021). Having said this, the main focus on violence and punishment may make invisible the complex interpersonal dynamics and the construction of other forms of relationships between women deprived of their liberty.

In this section, I engage in an exercise to analyse the relational dynamics of prison using a Southern category, particularly an Andean conceptualization, of communitarian organization and affective networks: *Ayllu*. *Ayllu* is a social organization for the production and reproduction of life based on a kinship system, which has been extensively studied in the social sciences, particularly in anthropology (Sendon, 2016). At the same time, it is possible to discuss the law of the *Ayllu* and its normative structure, which is not based on the modern state nation-law but on the law of kinship and effective bonds (Portugal, 2009). This way of being, doing, living, and organizing has been referred to as pre-modern from the perspective of coloniality.

From that perspective, I do not mean to indicate that women prisoners in Santa Monica necessarily have an Andean identity structure at their core or that Peruvian prisons deliberately and formally operate within an Andean communitarian organization. I intend to engage in what Mignolo (2008) conceptualized as 'border epistemology'; in other words, to be able to produce knowledge from more than one system of knowledge. Thus, I consider that the incorporation of the category *Ayllu* and the Andean epistemology may shed new light on the relational dynamics in our contexts, in this case in particular, in the prison of Santa Monica.

With the category *Ayllu*, I seek to broaden the analysis of co-governance dynamics in Santa Monica (Bracco, 2022). In brief, I propose that Santa Monica operates through two juxtaposed legal systems. This means that in the prison there is a convergence of two legal systems, which are interrelated and interdependent, generating an inter-legal encounter that operates in tension with collaborative and confrontational dynamics. On the one hand, there is the so-called 'formal' normative-legal system that responds to written national laws and operates by providing the framework for the prison that positions formal roles for the actors in the prison. On the other hand, in everyday life, there is a customary normative-legal system classified as 'informal' that regulates the coexistence of all those inside the prison (both prisoners and staff).

By incorporating the category of *Ayllu*, I intend to recreate it in an urban prison context, and to rename this second, generally considered informal, legality. As already noted, *Ayllu* is an Andean economic–political communitarian management of agrarian societies, particularly for *Aymaras* and *Quechuas*, and for Patzi Paco (2004), the core form of indigenous organization.[5] Moving away from a static and stereotypical vision of *Ayllu*, in more contemporary analysis, *Ayllu* refers to a communitarian–social fabric. It is traditionally linked to a common territory (Mignolo, 2008), but research has demonstrated that it may be a symbolic territory which links people with a common past and a shared future project, creating a system of kinship based on collaborative networks (Neira 2021, personal communication, 15 June 2021). *Ayllu* is a form of conviviality and, consequently, a type of collaborative governance that produces a safety net, knowledge management, and community practices that contribute to the managing of life (ibid).

I will refer to the prison of Santa Monica as the symbolic and geographical territory which brings together a collective of women and provides a 'home' for those living in it. In this case, the common past of women prisoners is linked to the experience of being criminalized and punished by the Peruvian state, and the joint project is to survive and face their imprisonment. Therefore, women do not necessarily have a communitarian approach to life but enter an informal and legitimized communitarian organization that enables them to survive and live in the best possible way that they are able, given the circumstances of their incarceration. This approach does not mean that women do everything through a communitarian organization, but only those activities that require collective action, for example the organization of daily activities for the management of a convivial existence.[6] It is possible to observe five interrelated elements that support the communitarian organization as a macro-structure: power, economy, labour, festivities, and an effective safety net.

With regard to communitarian power, Santa Monica prison is divided into eight blocks. Each one has a group of internal-prisoner authorities called delegates, elected in a subtle negotiation between staff and prisoners in an assembly organized in each block. Moreover, among those selected to represent their blocks, two of them are elected to fulfil the roles of General Delegate of Santa Monica and General Treasurer. Therefore, Santa Monica operates with centralized governance and simultaneously decentralized units. The delegation of each block includes: a General Delegate, a Treasurer, and seven more delegates (each responsible for an area of conviviality: Cleaning, Food and Microwave, Disciplinary, Telephone, Judicial, Health, Culture, and Sports). General delegates have frequent meetings with the prison authorities and staff to decide on the prison's activities. They are responsible for transmitting the information and organizing prisoners to act on those decisions inside their blocks. A delegate's role is not formalized, and their position operates through an ambiguous grey area of authority. Thus, their work is not officially included in their

[5] Feliz Patzi Paco is a Bolivian sociologist who has discussed indigenous identities and communitarian organization in depth. For him, there is too much attention paid to the symbols of the indigenous (e.g. clothes, costumes, etc.), and a lack of interest in indigenous organization. He distinguishes 'communitarian' from the 'common' usually linked to Marxist socialism (Patzi Paco, 2004).

[6] A communitarian organization does not mean that every action is created collectively, since there are also familial and individual actions. The same occurs in Santa Monica; for example, women prisoners also have smaller *Ayllus*, symbolic families, with whom they create more trusting relationships as well as finding intimate support and exchanging food, basic products, etc. Also women prisoners act individually for other activities inside prison.

legal files (therefore, invalid for their applications for parole and transitory release benefits). The formal authorities expect them to empower and act on their role and to simultaneously be submissive to the formal power. Thus, delegates have a fragile, even surreptitious yet legitimized, power to co-administrate (in conjunction with prison staff) order, conviviality, and the daily life of the prison.

In sum, delegates act as intermediaries between prison authorities, staff, and women prisoners, and also among prisoners. They perform their power in the manoeuvring of potential situations of conflict and learn how to mediate to ensure equilibrium between the needs of order and security from prison authorities, and the urge for autonomy and better conditions for prisoners (Bracco, 2022). For example, as Isabel, a General Delegate, notes, delegates need to know how to inform prisoners about formal decisions made by the authorities and how to calm the prison population. The way they notify the prison population, the selection of the words they use, is critical. As she says, 'I have to talk to the population about the decisions taken. If something is not good, they can go to a riot. That is why you need to know how to say things.'[7] Moreover, in the case of mediation among prisoners, if a conflict arises between cellmates, the delegate can move the allegedly 'conflictive' prisoner to a different cell, the common room, or the corridor.

In relation to the communitarian economy, each block administrates a communitarian fund with each prisoner paying a daily quota to the block's Treasurer.[8] To produce more funds, the blocks use a rotational system to rent chairs and tables on visitor days, and sell boiled water to prisoners. With the communitarian funds, each block pays for its cleaning products, the maintenance of common areas, the decoration of the blocks, and the purchase of collective goods such as microwaves, televisions, or DVD players (installed in the block's corridors). Moreover, the communitarian fund is also used to cover expenses for producing institutional events that are part of the activities, such as celebrations on Mother's Day or, as Tatiana recalls, Christmas celebrations. Prisoners organize by blocks, and as Tatiana notes, each block buys the materials (from the communitarian fund) to create products which are presented at institutional events:

> Of course, we work here to pay for the budget. What is paid by them [referring to the authorities], if the event is big, they put up the sunshade, because that is very expensive. The scenery, in some cases when the event is really big, or the costumes. But not for everything, sometimes. For example, for Christmas once, we all worked with recycled goods, it costs a lot, we worked very much for that. It was, for example, the nacimientos with recycled bottles, all the pavilions collaborated, we invested a lot.

In relation to communitarian labour, inside each block delegates organize a structured labour routine with standards and procedures. For example, in the case of Cleaning

[7] For delegates, the problem with riots is not necessarily the collapse of order and control, but the consequences it may have for women prisoners. For example, some women may be transferred to other prisons thus breaking interpersonal relationships and taking them far away from their relatives and visits.

[8] The quota may vary per block, and women prisoners referred to payments that oscillated between 1.5 and 20 soles (US$0.40 and US$5.5) weekly. The money was not used to cover bedding and food. Women prisoners clearly distinguished themselves from men's prisons where there may be a quota for basic nourishment, which did not occur in Santa Monica at the time of my fieldwork.

and Food delegates, they organize a rota to ensure prisoners' participation in the cleaning and delivery of food to the prisoners in their block. These activities do not seek to discipline and control prisoners' mobility, but to ensure adequate conditions of conviviality during their term of imprisonment. For example, Patricia, a prisoner, suggest that if she fails to fulfil her responsibility for delivering the *paila* (prisons' food) to the pavilion, it could create internal conflict and the daily schedules would then be affected thus delaying any planned activities.

Prisoners also undertake responsibilities for maintaining the prison's infrastructure, such as repairing the bathrooms, installing electrical connections, among other repairs. Moreover, they organize administrative, security, and communitarian activities and produce institutional events, such as those mentioned previously. In those cases, prisoners not only cover the expenses but also help to organize the block's team and participation. As Fenix recalls when she was a Sport delegate: 'You have to motivate the compañeras to participate. You are in charge of creating a team, and the rehearsals. Then, the day of the championship, you are responsible that everything works OK with your team.'

What I refer to as 'communitarian festivities' are activities that promote social bonds and provide distraction. In these cases, delegates also negotiate with authorities to organize centralized and decentralized celebratory activities for all the women prisoners. For example, that was the case for the Christmas celebrations for the prisoners in Santa Monica: from the communitarian funds, the General Delegates bought 200 kilos of pork; bought gas; coordinated with external suppliers and negotiated with prison authorities for permission for the goods to enter the prison; organized the use if formal labour hours and the equipment for cooking the pork; and arranged to celebrate Christmas inside their blocks without being formally restricted during the night by security staff. As many women prisoners recalled, Christmas is particularly a difficult time, where many of them feel more nostalgic about their homes and families. Communitarian festivities are intended to create emotional support among the women, are seen as a partial truce for any possible conflicts among prisoners, and create a secure place to share their feelings and thoughts about their families outside prison.

Finally, regarding an effective communitarian safety net, as I have detailed, imprisonment is not lived in isolation (which is not even possible due to the organization of the prison) or as an individual self. From a psychological perspective, it is not a sum of multiple individualized *Yos*/selves, but the recognition of diverse and various (hierarchized) *Nosotras*/us. In that sense, although prison may be regarded as a violent and coercive space for women prisoners, it also has cracks and tunnels that oblige women to interrelate and, in many cases, it may lead to the construction of trusting and emotionally safe networks to cope psychologically with imprisonment. As I will detail in the next section when discussing *Mestizaje*, social groups for women prisoners also have hierarchies and conflicts, but the aim is to focus on the spaces within the system of oppression system where women prisoners are able to find an affective network to feel socially and psychologically content in a precarious environment. As Fenix suggests:

> We had made a very strong group. Imagine that we have reached the point that Julio [her husband] didn't bring me anything because he had expenses and I didn't even

> have toilet paper. People from outside don't know, our husbands or our mothers, we get into debt, in food, in clothes... So, among us, we say: 'Hey, how was it? Who came today?' For example, Sully's husband sends her money. When someone's husband doesn´t come, but the other one did and gave her toilet paper, his dad sends big packages, or maybe he brought chicken. Now we are in the obligation that if Julio brings food, we have an obligation to give her a Tupperware, and she has an obligation to bring it up.

The creation of this communitarian social-political-economic-affective organization is not sustained contractually but through the customary and through *praxis*. I have detailed the macro-structure of this organization, but women prisoners also establish relationships at different dimensions (meso and micro) that forge prison's operability and create an adequate affability inside the prison. In general, this communitarian organization remains a surreptitious dimension of the prison, and is barely recognized by the authorities (while simultaneously expecting the women to act upon their roles).[9] In turn, its non-recognition enables prisons to be regarded as functional 'modern' institutions where the formal dimension is the only one which keeps the prison functioning, and where the performance of power and control within a prison is confined to the formal authorities. Focusing on women's collective organizational aids to decolonize the prison also recognizes the other forms of organization that exist (with their tensions and ambivalences) within modern/colonial/patriarchal institutions.

In other words, from a decolonial perspective, the existence of these forms of relationships resist the capitalist-modern-colonial-patriarchal nation-state order. Within the formal structure of prison that individualizes subjects, another communitarian network operates on a daily basis. This community, then, should not be seen only as a way of dealing with the economic precariousness of prisons but also as the recognition of another political-social-affective system of organization among women. This reading does not imply romanticizing the relationships between women deprived of their liberty but aims to recognize their communitarian organization and to incorporate the Southern category of *Ayllu* in the understanding of the complex relational dynamics in Santa Monica. That said, there are also hierarchies, conflicts, and violence which I will detail in the next section. The matrix of power and internal colonialism also traverses women prisoners' subjectivities, reinforcing colonial and gendered legacies and creating internal hierarchies among women prisoners.

[9] Darke (2018) explores the co-governance between authorities and prisoners in Brazilian prisons. In his research, he suggests that prisoners and staff form reciprocal relations of mutual aid and protection. Therefore, the author discusses prisoners enacting strategies of survival, such as solidarity, reciprocity, and negotiations to ensure conviviality. Following his line of conceptualization, I also propose that Santa Monica functions as a co-governance institution between the authorities and the prisoners, but I suggest some particularities in this instance. First, I do not focus on the interdependency between authorities and prisoners, but in the inter-relations and communitarian organization (that moves between solidarity and conflict) among prisoners. Second, by introducing the concept of *Ayllu*, my intention is to emphasize that communitarian organization is, in fact, a strategy for surviving the conditions in a failed nation-state's modern institution, which is at the same time, from a decolonial perspective, a different form of organization that operates in Peru even beyond the prison. It is in this sense, in recognizing other forms of organization, that it is possible to discuss the decolonization of prisons or criminology.

Mestizas and *Mestizaje*: About the 'Race'-Ethnic-Cultural Dimension in Prison

This section will discuss the ethnic–racial self-identification of women prisoners and the impact of colonial legacies on women's relationships during imprisonment.[10] As Phillips (2012) suggests, prison life is racialized. Phillips (2012) in her analysis of UK prisons refers to how a nation's historical macro-political and social dynamics impact on the experience of the prisoner and the culture of prisoner society.

Phillips (2012) highlights that racial identities in UK prisons are fluid and flexible within the confines of the prison and how prisoner interactions refer to cultural fusion, multicultural amicability, and racialized tensions. Even though race and ethnicity are not essentialized features but plural and dynamic categories (Phillips, 2012), researchers of Northern prisons have analysed racialized social communities in prisons. Within the prison confines and in the struggles of symbolic or material power, race tends to become reified and essentialized (Phillips, 2012). Therefore, race, ethnicity, and ethnoreligious identities may become defining dimensions of segregation and loyalty among prisoners (Crewe, 2009; Goodman, 2008; Irwin, 2004; Pollok, 2004). For example, in the case of women, Trammel (2012), who conducted her research on women's prisons in California, referred to these tensions and found ample evidence that some women construct social relationships based on race, and racial segregation among prisoners, particularly between white and Hispanic women.

Following that line, in Latin America in general and Peru in particular, the analysis of racialized communities and racial–ethnic hierarchies within prison must incorporate the macro-historical process of colonization described earlier. To contextualize the analysis is vital for addressing the concept of Mestizo. In 2017, the Peruvian government conducted a national census that included a question about racial–ethnic self-identification for the first time. The historical delay in introducing racial and ethnic features into the census also tends to highlight the state and society's difficulty in discussing these issues (Villasantes, 2017).[11] Beyond that, the results of the census show that 60 per cent of the national population self-identified as Mestizo. Similarly, the first census of the prison population conducted a year earlier (2016) in Peruvian prisons at a national level reproduces the national statistics: 56 per cent (56.3 per cent of men and 54.4 per cent of women prisoners) consider themselves Mestizos.[12]

[10] As Breny Mendoza (2001) suggests, the terms *Mestiza* and *Mestizaje* are defined and redefined according to the historical, social, and cultural context. Traditionally, in Latin America, they have referred to the racial mix between Spanish and indigenous groups, more specifically the 'product' of a relationship between a Spanish man and an indigenous woman. Although this reference creates an archetypical notion of the idea of *Mestizaje*, it may also be seen as a monolithic one. In this chapter, I focus on this definition, but it may also be problematized and broadened through the concept of the *Mestiza* consciousness, as referred by Gloria Anzaldúa (1987), which will be addressed in further research.

[11] The census included the possibility of self-identify in the following racial–ethnic identities: Quechua, Aymara, Native or Indigenous from the Amazon; Other Native or Indigenous community; Black, *zambo, mulato, moreno*, Afro-peruvian; White; *Mestizo*; Other (do not know, do not respond).

[12] The census on the penitentiary population indicated the following statistics on male and female prisoners: 12.6 per cent Quechua; 1.3 per cent Aymara; 0 per cent Native or Indigenous from the Amazon; 0 per

While there seems to be a correspondence between the percentage of people who consider themselves Mestizo outside and inside prison, we must also bear in mind that most people deprived of their liberty are also those who have the least access to education, health, and formal labour. Most of the prisoners lived in poverty or extreme poverty prior to imprisonment. They are members of social groups who have historically been denied access to our society's supposed 'modernizing process'. In her article 'The Colour of Prisons in Latin America', Segato (2007) reflects on the concept of race in Latin America and the difficulty of analysing this dimension in our prison population. As Segato (2007) points out:

> The 'colour' of the prisons I refer to here is the mark on the body of an indigenous or African family past, a reality that remains unanswered statistically but has generated some testimonial responses ... What I wish to emphasise is that a prison can be 90% inhabited by non-white prisoners without any of them considering themselves to be members of an indigenous society or part of a political, religious or self-declared African-American or Afro-descendant political, religious or popular culture entity.
> (Author's translation, p. 149)

Thus, to analyse the dimension of 'race'-ethnicity is to un-shell what is not being said and to unravel the category of Mestizo/a. As Oscar Espinosa (n.d.), a Peruvian anthropologist, acknowledges, in Peru the term Mestizo involves the intersection between racial, ethnic, and cultural characteristics. It is a non-precise or unclear self-identification that involves a hybrid identity. Considering the decolonial arguments and the relational dynamics that still operate in postcolonial societies, Espinosa (ibid) argues that to identify as a Mestizo/a is to not identify as white or indigenous. To be white is to identify with the foreigner, the conqueror; to be indigenous is to be subject to historical discrimination, exploitation, and abuse. Consequently, to self-identify as a Mestizo is to engage in an identity of 'mixture', to allegedly be distanced from hierarchical power relationships, and locate oneself in a desired and utopian positionality where we are all homogeneous and equal citizens.

Nonetheless, as Peruvian scholars suggest (Espinosa de Rivero, n.d.; Manrique, 1999; Portocarrero, 2007), the concept of Mestizo arguably reproduces racist dynamics and hidden social conflicts. It is an ideology because it creates the illusion of homogenization and equality among citizens and, at the same time, it justifies a system of hierarchical relationships between groups. Following Espinosa, the main difference between *Mestizaje* and racism is that the latter explicitly relies on a domination system of discrimination and exploitation. It is not that racism does not exist in *Mestizaje*, but it is invisible. In Peru, racism has been deeply interiorized, it is an ensemble of hidden values embedded in our practices, but silent in our explicit discourses (Portocarrero, 2007). Indeed, *Mestizaje* preserves the system of domination, but it is hidden, pretending to ignore and silence racial–ethnic differences (Espinosa de Rivero, n.d.). Thus, the racialized–colour line in Latin America is more complex

cent Other Native or Indigenous community; 10.9 per cent Black, *zambo, mulato, moreno*, Afro-peruvian; 11 per cent White; 0.7 per cent Other; 7.4 per cent do not know, do not respond.

where 'whiteness' is not just about phenotypical features. Therefore, it is not a phenotypical question, but a question of access to power, to territory, to property, education, or wealth.

Hence, like women outside prisons, women prisoners are not a homogenous group but are traversed by the matrix of oppression, and dimensions such as class, race, and ethnicity intersect and permeate their experience of imprisonment. Thus, although most of the prison population consider themselves as Mestiza, women prisoners are a racialized population with internal hierarchies. Therefore, racial identification in Santa Monica is not straightforward and explicitly segregated, reproducing the silence and difficulty in discussing racial identities outside the prison and within Peruvian society. However, *Mestizaje* processes silence explicit racist dynamics. In fact, racist dynamics may be reinforced in the context of prison conviviality.

These dynamics are possible to observe in Santa Monica when women prisoners refer to the colloquial phrase, '*Ella es más como yo*'/'She is more like me'. When participants refer to other women as more like them, they refer to the imbrication of racial-ethnic-cultural-class dimensions (and therefore, access—or not—to power, to territory, to property, education, or wealth) to create identification and construct a possible trustful relationship. The phrase does not explicitly refer to a racial–ethnic dimension, even though it does so implicitly. It relates to racial-ethnic-cultural characteristics: the neighbourhoods or regions they lived in before imprisonment, their education level, their economic status, their allegedly 'superior' moral values (usually linked to Catholic morality), or physical-embodied aspects. For example, Isabel[13] constantly said she preferred to relate with prisoners with 'a certain level of education' that she defines as 'educated women capable of engaging in reflective conversation'. Hence, by introducing education level as a distinctive characteristic among prisoners, Isabel associates formal education with the possibility of being reasonable, and consequently, civilized. In a country with significant inequalities, access to formal education is determined by class, and in postcolonial societies this relates to race–ethnicity.

Similarly, Talia says that she prefers to 'hang out' with her two friends because she feels a connection with them; they are 'alike' in age and 'similarly looking', but mainly because the three of them 'like to laugh and make jokes, because they can't cry all day for being imprisoned'. Nonetheless, she is surprised that other prisoners criticize them for 'living in a bubble', being 'distant', and defining them as prisoners who 'think they are better than others'. Talia implicitly says that her group of friends are young and considered beautiful women (considered *Mestizas* but also 'whiter' than other women prisoners), related to medium- and high-income families in Peruvian society, which provide the economic resources to pay prison expenses and for 'luxuries' inside Santa Monica.

Once again, the *Mestizaje* process commonly positions women prisoners as racially and ethnically homogeneous, where racial discrimination or segregation disappeared from their social dynamics. Nonetheless, in both examples, participants distinguish between 'them' and 'others', allocating a hierarchical differentiation between the groups and alleging their superiority in these cases in terms of reflexiveness

[13] Isabel and Talia (named in the next paragraph) are women prisoners at Santa Monica and were research participants.

and coping strategies to face imprisonment. In that sense, considering how racism is deeply interiorized (Portocarrero, 2007), this discourse is subtly expressed throughout other socio-demographic and embodied characteristics.

Following Segato (2007), I argue that we need to consider the political significance of the idea of 'race' and *Mestizaje* in Latin America to destabilize the profound colonial structure and our colonial legacies that have traversed identities and social relationships. As Segato suggests, the carceral order has an intermingled and dynamic relationship with the colonial racial order. Indeed, the criminal justice system reinforces and reproduces pre-existing labelling taking into account the idea and power relationships of race. She argues that formal prison institutions reinforce and duplicate racial hierarchies that already exist, such as those configured in the world-system explained by decolonial authors. Segato's understanding of race aids reflection on the concept of *Mestizaje*. She suggests that her definition of race also alludes to an embodied 'footprint'. In other words, racism is not automatically directed at those who self-identify or are seen as indigenous or African-American, but at those whose bodies are historically 'marked' by subordination and represent the disposed population. While I agree with her argument, I also expand on it to include the racist–classist dynamics within the prison, in this case in particular, between women prisoners.

Conclusion: Final Reflections

The perspective analysed in this chapter does not seek to legitimize imprisonment but to put forward an agenda employing a decolonial feminist epistemology. To propose a decolonial feminist perspective means explicitly recognizing the historical patterns of the region. Such a perspective should lead us to acknowledge how the configuration of the modern-colonial-patriarchal matrix of power configured during the European colonial expansion in Latin America still reproduces through internal colonialism and has moulded our political, economic, social, and subjective spheres in the present day. In this case in particular, it has shaped the configuration of prison as a 'modern' institution, centring the analysis of prisons and imprisonment in the so-called 'formal' structures while making invisible complex dynamics like those discussed in this chapter.

Likewise, the decolonial turn aims to make visible resistances to the modern-colonial-patriarchal project. However, as portrayed in this chapter, the idea is not to construct fixed or closed categories that create fictional dichotomies of colonial legacies-resistances. On the contrary, the focus is on fluid movements, nuances, ambivalences, and tensions. In this chapter, I have proposed analysing women's imprisonment dynamics through the intermingled concepts of *Ayllu* and *Mestizaje*. Women's communitarian (yet surreptitious) organization in prison in Peru is akin to *Ayllu* whilst it also reflects *Mestizaje* features. To decolonize the prison implies the recognition of the communitarian organization that creates the illusion of a 'modern' functioning institution. It also makes visible the colonial legacies of the colonial-modern-patriarchal matrix of power that traverses women prisoners' relationship, thus to break free of the myth of *Mestizaje*, which makes internal hierarchies among women prisoners invisible. The incorporation of these categories, I have argued, may provide new lenses for future research.

I have centred on a Peruvian women's prison and focused on how the macro colonial-modern-patriarchal legacies and resistances have impacted the contemporary inner organization of the prison and gendered and racialized social relationships. Nonetheless, this analysis can also be observed in other prisons in the Global South and even the Global North. With this idea, I should emphasize that it is necessary to focus on the local particularities but also on how localized knowledge may be helpful in understanding and transforming global phenomena. There are Norths in the South, and Souths in the North. Thus, more than a geographical dimension, colonial-modern-patriarchy is geopolitical and has cultural dimensions potentialized by globalization. Therefore, the analysis of prisons in the South and the theoretical perspectives propelled by Southern criminologists should also enter into dialogue with Northern theories and may help to understand the North.

Finally, to engage in a decolonial feminist epistemology is to legitimize women prisoners as knowledge producers. In this case, it is to propose that women prisoners and their everyday life experiences may have much to teach us about incarceration. The aim is not to consider the colonial heritage only in coercive and domination terms. From a decolonial feminist perspective, the objective is to focus on the colonized subjects' capacity to strategically incorporate and use to their benefit discourses and practices of resistance. In this task, a decolonial feminist perspective is a way to introduce new lenses to put onto the agenda the resistances as localized praxis within oppressive circumstances in order to recognize and potentialize them.

References

Aguirre, C. (1988) 'Violencia, castigo y control social: esclavos y panaderías en Lima', *Pasado y Presente*, pp. 27–37.

Aguirre, C. (2003) 'Mujeres delincuentes, prácticas penales y servidumbre doméstica en Lima (1862–1930)', in O'Phelan, S., Muñoz, F., Ramón, G. et al. (eds) *Familia y vida cotidiana en América Latina, siglos XVIII–XX*. Lima: Fondo Editorial de la Pontificia Universidad Católica del Perú.

Aguirre, C. (2009) 'Cárcel y sociedad en América Latina: 1800–1940', in Kingman, E. (ed.) *Historia social urbana: Espacios y flujos*. Quito: FLACSO.

Aguirre, C. (2019) *Donde se amansan los guapos. Las cárceles de Lima 1850–1935*. Lima: Fondo Editorial de la Universidad del Pacífico.

Aniyar de Castro, L. (1981) *Conocimiento y Orden Social: criminología como legitimación y criminología de la liberación. Proposiciones para una criminología latinoamericana como teoría crítica del control social*. Maracaibo: Instituto de Criminología de la Universidad del Zulia.

Anzaldúa, G. (1987) *Borderlands/La Frontera: The New Mestiza*. San Francisco, CA: Aunt Lut Books.

Bautista, J. J. (2014) *¿Qué significa pensar desde América Latina?* Madrid: Editores Akal.

Bergalli, R. (1982) *Crítica de la Criminología*. Bogotá: Temis.

Bergman, M. (2020) 'Insights from new studies on violence in Latin American prisons', International Criminal Justice Review, 30(1), pp. 5–7.

Blagg, H. and Anthony, T. (2019) *Decolonising Criminology.* Imagining Justice in a Postcolonial World. London: Palgrave Macmillan.

Boutron, C. and Constant, C. (2013) 'Gendering transnational criminality: The case of women's imprisonment in Peru', *Signs: Journal of Women in Culture and Society*, 39(1), pp. 177–195.

Bracco, L. (2022) *Prison in Peru: Ethnographic, Decolonial and Feminist Perspectives.* London: Palgrave Macmillan.

Carrington, K., Hogg, R., Scott, J. et al. (2019) *Southern Criminology.* Abingdon: Routledge.

Castro-Gómez, S. (2005) *La hybris del punto cero: ciencia, raza e ilustración de la Nueva Granada (1750–1816).* Bogotá: Pontificia Universidad Javeriana.

Castro-Gómez, S. (2019) *El tonto y los canallas. Notas para un republicanismo transmoderno.* Bogotá: Pontificia Universidad Javeriana.

Castro-Gomez, S., and Grosfoguel, R. (2007) 'Prólogo. Giro decolonial, teoría crítica y pensamiento heterárquico', in Castro-Gómez, S. and Grosfoguel, R. (eds) *El giro decolonial: reflexiones para una diversidad epistémica más allá del capitalismo global.* Bogotá: Siglo del Hombre Editores.

Constant, C. (2016) 'Pensar la violencia de las mujeres. La construcción de la figura delincuente', *Política y Cultura*, 46, pp. 145–162.

Cotler, J. (2005) *Clases, Estado y Nación.* Lima: Instituto de Estudios Peruanos.

Crenshaw, K. (1989) 'Demarginalizing the intersection of race and sex: A black feminist critique of antidiscrimination doctrine, feminist theory and antiracist politics', *University of Chicago Legal Forum*, 1(8), pp. 139–167.

Crewe, B. (2009) *The Prisoner Society: Power, Adaptation, and Social Life in an English Prison.* Oxford: Oxford University Press.

Curiel, O. (2009) 'Descolonizando el feminismo: Una perspectiva desde América Latina y el Caribe', Paper presented at the first Latinamerican colloquium about praxis and feminist thought, Grupo Latinoamericano de Estudios, Formación y Acción Feminista (GLEFAS) y el Instituto de Género de la Universidad de Buenos Aires.

Darke, S. (2018) *Conviviality and Survival. Co-producing Brazilian Prison Order.* London: Palgrave Macmillan.

Del Olmo, R. (1981) *América Latina y su criminología.* Mexico: Siglo XX1.

Dussel, E. (2000) 'Europa, modernidad y eurocentrismo', in Lander, E. (ed.) *La colonialidad del saber: eurocentrismo y ciencias sociales. Perspectivas latinoamericanas.* Buenos Aires, Argentina: CLACSO.

Escobar, A. (2000) 'El lugar de la naturaleza o la naturaleza del lugar: ¿globalización o postdesarrollo?', in Lander, E. (ed.) La *colonialidad del saber: eurocentrismo y ciencias sociales. Perspectivas latinoamericanas.* Buenos Aires: CLACSO.

Escobar, A. (2003) 'Mundos y conocimientos de otro modo. El programa de investigación de modernidad/colonialidad latinoamericano', *Tabula Rasa*, 1, pp. 51–86.

Espinosa, Y. (2016) 'De por qué es necesario un feminismo descolonial: diferenciación, dominación co-constitutiva de la modernidad occidental y el fin de la política de identidad', *Solar*, 12(1), pp. 141–171.

Espinosa de Rivero, O. (n.d.) 'Desafíos a la ciudadanía multicultural en el Perú: El "mito del mestizaje" y la "cuestión indígena"'. Available at: www.luc.edu/media/lucedu/dccirp/pdfs/articlesforresourc/Article_-_Espinosa,_Oscar.pdf (accessed 12 May 2022).

García Basalo, J. (1954) *San Martín y la reforma carcelaria. Aporte a la historia del derecho penal argentino y americano.* Buenos Aires: Ediciones AraYÚ.

Goodman, P. (2008) '"It's just black, white, or Hispanic": An observational study of racializing moves in California's segregated prison reception centers', *Law and Society*, 42(4), pp. 735–770.

Guevara, A. (2009) *Diversidad y complejidad legal: aproximaciones a la antropología e historia del derecho*. Lima: Pontificia Universidad Católica del Perú.

Instituto Nacional Penitenciario (2021) 'Población Penal Intramuros por Situación Jurídica y de Género'. Available at: https://siep.inpe.gob.pe/form/reporte (accessed 12 May 2022).

Irwin, J. (2004) *The Warehouse Prison: Disposal of the New Dangerous Class*. Los Angeles: Roxbury.

Lugones, M. (2008a), 'Colonialidad y Género', *Tabula Rasa*, 9, no. jul-dic, pp. 73–101.

Lugones, M. (2008b) 'From within Germinative Stasis: Creating Active Subjectivity, Resistant Agency', in Keating, A. (ed.) *Entre Mundos/Among Worlds*. London: Palgrave Macmillan.

Mannarelli, M. (2018), *La Domesticación de las mujeres: Patriarcado y género en la historia peruana*. Lima: La Siniestra Ensayos.

Manrique, N. (1999) *La piel y la pluma: escritos sobre literatura, etnicidad y racismo*. Lima: SUR Casa de Estudios del Socialismo.

Mendoza, B. (2001) 'La desmitologización del mestizaje en Honduras: Evaluando nuevos aportes', *Mesoamérica*, 42, pp. 256–278.

Mignolo, W. (2000a) 'La colonialidad a lo largo y a lo ancho: el hemisferio occidental en el horizonte colonial de la modernidad', in Lander, E. (ed.) La *colonialidad del saber: eurocentrismo y ciencias sociales. Perspectivas latinoamericanas*. Buenos Aires: CLACSO.

Mignolo, W. (2000b) *Local Histories/Global Designs*. Princeton, NJ: Princeton University Press.

Mignolo, W. (2005) 'Prefacio', in Walsh, C. (ed.) *Pensamiento Crítico y Matriz (De)colonial*. Quito: Ediciones Abya-Yala.

Mignolo, W. (2008) 'The communal and the decolonial', Ideas for movement turbulence. Available at: www.turbulence.org.uk/turbulence-5/decolonial/ (accessed 12 May 2022).

Neira, E. (2014) 'Dos formas de arder: alegorías de género y episteme poiético', Paper presented at the II Congreso de Estudios Poscoloniales—III Jornadas de Feminismo Poscolonial 'Genealogías Críticas de la Colonialidad', 9–11 December 2014.

Nugent, D. (2015) 'Appearances to the Contrary: Fantasy, Fear and Displacement in Twentieth-Century Peruvian State Formation', in Krupa, C, and Nugent, D. (eds) State *Theory and Andean Politics: New Approaches to the Study of Rule*. Philadelphia, PA: University of Pennsylvania Press.

Paredes, J. (2010) *Hilando fino desde el feminismo comunitario*. La Paz: CEDEC y Mujeres Creando Comunidad.

Patzi Paco, F. (2004) *Sistema communal: una propuesta alternativa al sistema liberal. Una discusión teórica para salir de la colonialidad y del liberalismo*. La Paz: Comunidad de Estudios Alternativos.

Phillips, C. (2012) *The Multicultural Prison: Ethnicity, Masculinity, and Social Relationships among Prisoners*. Oxford: Oxford University Press.

Pollock, J. (2004) *Prisons and Prison Life: Costs and Consequences*. Los Angeles: Roxbury.

Portocarrero, G (2007) *Racismo y mestizaje y otros ensayos*. Lima: Fondo editorial del congreso del Perú.

Portugal, A. (2009) *O ayllu andino nas crônicas quinhentistas*. Sao Paulo: UNESP.

Quijano, A. (1992) 'Colonialidad y modernidad/racionalidad', in Bonilla, H. (ed.) *Los conquistados: 1492 y la población indígena de las Américas*. Quito: Libri Mundi.

Quijano, A. (2000) 'Colonialidad del poder, eurocentrismo y América Latina', in Lander, E. (ed.) *La colonialidad del saber: eurocentrismo y ciencias sociales. Perspectivas latinoamericanas*. Buenos Aires: CLACSO.

Rivera Cusicanqui, S. (2012) 'Violencias (re)encubiertas en Bolivia', *Otramérica, Santander*.

Segato, R. (2007) 'El color de la cárcel en América Latina: Apuntes sobre la colonialidad de la justiciar en un continente en deconstrucción', *Nueva Soceidad*, 208, pp. 142–161.

Segato, R. (2013) *La crítica de la colonialidad en ocho ensayos*. Buenos Aires: Prometeo Libros.

Trammel, R. (2012) *Enforcing the Convict Code: Violence and Prison Culture*. Boulder, CO: Lynne Rienner.

Salvatore, R. and Aguirre, C. (2001) 'Introduction. Writing the History of Law, Crime, and Punishment in Latin America', in Salvatore, R., Aguirre, C., and Joseph, G. (eds) *Crime and Punishment in Latin America: Law and Society Since Late Colonial Times*. Durham, NC: Duke University Press.

Salvatore, R., and Aguirre, C. (2017) 'Revisitando el nacimiento de la penitenciaria en América Latina', *Historia de las Prisiones*, 4, pp. 7–42.

Sendon, P. (2016) *Ayllus del Ausangate: Parentesco y organización social en los Andes del sur peruano*. Lima: Pontificia Universidad Católica del Perú/Centro Bartolomé de las Casas.

Vega Santa Gadea, F. (1973) 'La Evolución de la pena privativa de la libertad en el Perú. Consideraciones generales acerca de la punición Incaica, La Cárcel en la Colonia y la Administración Penitenciaria durante la República', *Derecho PUCP*, 31, pp. 163–194.

Villasantes, M. (2017) 'Censo étnico peruano: ¿cómo conciliar la diversidad étnica y la ciudadanía nacional?', *Revista Ideele*, 290. Available at: https://revistaideele.com/ideele/content/censo-%C3%A9tnico-peruano-%C2%BFc%C3%B3mo-conciliar-la-diversidad-%C3%A9tnica-y-la-ciudadan%C3%ADa-nacional (accessed 12 May 2022).

Zaffaroni, E. (1989) *En busca de las penas perdidas. Deslegitimación y dogmática jurídico-penal*. Buenos Aires: Ediar.

17
An Alternative Spotlight
Colonial Legacies, Therapeutic Jurisprudence, and the Enigma of Healing

Amanda Wilson

Introduction

This chapter takes as its focus the as yet understudied colonial dynamics of therapeutic jurisprudence. Colonial thinking and practices continue to permeate criminal justice systems in colonial jurisdictions. The detrimental impacts of this on Indigenous persons are well documented (Nielsen and Robyn, 2003; Cunneen, 2014; Tauri and Porou, 2014; Monchalin, 2016; Blagg and Anthony, 2019). The leading hallmark of colonialism in jurisdictions, such as Australia and Canada, is the shameful yet persistent overrepresentation of Indigenous persons in prison.[1] While addressing the plight of colonial subjects ensnared by settler–colonial criminal justice systems is not an *explicit* concern of therapeutic jurisprudence, three claims have been made that suggest it may have something important and beneficial to offer to Indigenous persons who come into contact with the system, and efforts to decolonize criminal justice more broadly. First, in addition to its general orientation towards the promotion of well-being, therapeutic jurisprudence has a claimed emphasis on healing. Proponents suggest that law can be 'an instrument of healing and rehabilitation' (Winick, 2011, pp. 3–4), and that law has an 'enormous potential to heal' (Wexler, 2008, p. 20). A 'therapeutic orientation' is said to be 'one that promotes healing through law' (Winick and Wexler, 2002, p. 485). Second, it is claimed that therapeutic jurisprudence provides a challenge to 'the hegemony of an *individualistic* legal world view', instead proffering 'one which is more connected and relationally based' (Brookbanks, 2001, p. 331). Third, it is claimed that therapeutic jurisprudence provides 'common principles for the development' of various legal reforms that seek to 'eradicate systemic, monocultural bias in postcolonial criminal justice systems which tend to lead to intractable, carceral overrepresentation' (Stobbs, 2020).

These claims sound promising, but whether therapeutic jurisprudence does (or indeed can) deliver on them has received scant attention.[2] It is also the case that,

[1] Indigenous women are more over-represented than Indigenous men and are the fastest growing prisoner population. For a discussion of the enduring impact of colonial patriarchy on Indigenous women's imprisonment, see Baldry and Cunneen, 2014; Marques and Monchalin, 2020.

[2] A further claim, which I do not have the space to interrogate fully here, is that the 'roots' of the judicial approach in problem-solving courts 'can be traced back to Indigenous and tribal justice systems' (Winick and Wexler, 2003, p. 3). As we shall come to see, there are compelling reasons to be sceptical of such a claim.

Amanda Wilson, *An Alternative Spotlight* In: *Decolonizing the Criminal Question*. Edited by: Ana Aliverti, Henrique Carvalho, Anastasia Chamberlen, and Máximo Sozzo, Oxford University Press.
DOI: 10.1093/oso/9780192899002.003.0018

compared to other so-called 'alternatives' or 'innovations' in the criminal justice field,[3] the colonial dynamics of therapeutic jurisprudence have largely eluded the purview of criminologists and criminal justice scholars (but see Kwaymullina, 2007; Larsen and Milnes, 2011; Bartels and Richards, 2013). I seek to address these lacunae through a critical examination of the drug court—the most widely recognized institutional setting for the application of therapeutic jurisprudence. Drawing on observational fieldwork and interview data, I explore the ways in which the structure and operations of these courts perpetuate colonial legacies. The implications of these findings are then discussed in the light of the above claims made by proponents of therapeutic jurisprudence—in particular, the extent to which therapeutic jurisprudence can deliver healing for Indigenous persons. Despite the centrality for healing to its assumptions and claims, precisely what proponents mean by 'healing' remains unclear (Wilson, 2021). In considering whether therapeutic jurisprudence can provide healing for Indigenous persons, this chapter will, in the process, shed light on what healing means. Before I proceed, however, I want to briefly outline the therapeutic jurisprudence approach in the drug court setting.

The therapeutic jurisprudence approach

In the criminal justice realm, therapeutic jurisprudence has come to be constitutive of three interconnected dimensions: (1) a philosophical dimension; (2) an empirical dimension; and (3) a practical dimension (for more, see Wilson, 2021). The present chapter is concerned with the practical application of the therapeutic jurisprudence approach to drug court participants. The approach, informed by its philosophical and empirical dimensions,

> does not discount the weaknesses that [drug court] participants have shown in that they have committed offences as a result of a substance abuse problem that hitherto they have not been able to overcome. But it suggests that these participants are also the source and strengths and possible solutions for their problems. The court should acknowledge both aspects of their nature, involving participants' strengths in aid of the change process and facilitating them addressing their weaknesses ... the participant is respected as a source of solutions and as the primary change agent, supported by the team and external agencies.
>
> (Wexler and King, 2013, p. 35)

Therapeutic jurisprudence also suggests a range of tools and techniques that are drawn from cognitive behavioural research to maximize the 'therapeutic potential' (Winick, 2013, p. 219) of the drug court including behavioural contracting and motivational interviewing, and insights from the scholarship on stages of change, such as 'strength-based approaches' that are claimed to 'bolster the individual's sense of self-esteem and self-efficacy' (Winick, 2013, p. 222). Proponents argue that judicial officers in these

[3] Restorative justice, for instance, has been the subject of long-standing postcolonial and settler colonial critique (see especially Tauri, 2022; Cunneen, 2002; Blagg, 2017).

courts should be alive to their role as 'therapeutic agents' and how their interactions with participants 'will have inevitable consequences for the ability of those individuals to achieve rehabilitation' (Winick, 2013, p. 221). Thus, they need to 'understand how to convey empathy, how to recognize and deal with denial, and how to apply principles of behavioral motivation theory' (Winick and Wexler, 2002, p. 482). The 'coercive power of the court' is also regarded as an important tool for encouraging 'the offender to succeed in completing the treatment program' (Hora et al., 1999, pp. 475–476). As Wexler and King (2013, pp. 33–34) assert:

> Practices that are regarded as coercive in mainstream courts—such as the use of imprisonment—are seen to be worthwhile and therapeutic when used by a DTC as they are seen to promote obedience in relation to program conditions which participants have consented to upon entering the DTC program.

Space precludes me from an in-depth critique of this approach here, but suffice to say that incarcerating drug court participants for failing to abstain from drugs as a means by which to promote their commitment to drug rehabilitation calls into question the suggestion that drug courts offer a 'therapeutic', 'healing' alternative to the conventional 'punitive approach' to drug-dependency and crime (Winick and Wexler, 2002, p. 485). In the next section, I explore the colonial dynamics of the institutional setting of the drug court and the way in which particular structures and operations perpetuate colonial legacies. The findings coalesce around three themes: cultural tokenism; assimilation through subjugation; and colonial consciousness.

Colonial Legacies: A Case Study of Therapeutic Jurisprudence Applied

The data drawn on in this section comes from a larger comparative study of four drug court case study sites (two in Australia and two in Canada) that took place between 2013 and 2017.[4] The larger study involved mixed methods including analysis of quantitative programme data and qualitative semi-structured interviews (with drug court professionals and women participants) as well as non-participant observation of drug court team meetings and court sessions/report-backs. A total of fifty-one interviews with drug court professionals were conducted, of which the majority were women (67 per cent) and all of whom were white with the exception of a peer-support worker who identified as 'native' (her word choice).[5] Demographic programme data revealed that 15 per cent of the total number of drug court participants across the four sites were Indigenous.

[4] The case study sites included the two oldest drug courts in each jurisdiction (the Drug Court of New South Wales and the Toronto Drug Treatment Court) as well as two smaller sites (the South Australian Drug Court and the Edmonton Drug Treatment and Community Restoration Court). To preserve the anonymity of participants, quotations will only identify the job title/role of participants.

[5] This make-up reflects the broader demography of the drug court team workforce across the sites.

Like most other programmes and interventions in the criminal justice system, drug courts have been designed to meet the needs and interests of white men. Given that the majority of crime is committed by white men, this is perhaps not surprising. The consequence, however, is that most programmes and interventions fail to take difference on board, or, if they do, they are ill-equipped to respond appropriately. Drug courts are no exception (see Beckerman and Fontana, 2001; O'Hear, 2009; Morse et al., 2014). As we shall come to see, although various accommodations for Indigenous persons in drug courts do exist, these are perfunctory at best. Little thought has been given to the disproportionate impact particular structures and operations have on Indigenous participants, nor to the extent to which the strict regimens of the court work to further subjugate this population; stripping them of opportunities for self-determination. The therapeutic jurisprudence approach to drug court participants outlined in the previous subsection compounds these issues by framing drug misuse and criminalization as the product of internal 'weaknesses' that a participant has failed to 'overcome'. In so doing, the approach shuts out systemic and structural explanations for drug use and lawbreaking, instead favouring simplistic assumptions and solutions (*qua* cognitive behavioural psychology) that are grounded in modernity's fiction of abstract individualism. This is especially problematic for Indigenous peoples, for as Brady has identified, culture is significant to 'indigenous interpretations of the etiology of drug and alcohol abuse', and many express substance abuse as being rooted in the 'deprivation and the erosion of cultural integrity... as a result of colonization' (Brady, 1995, p. 1489; see also Phillips, 2003; Chenhall, 2007).

Cultural tokenism

Before I discuss this theme, I want to address an anticipated objection to my use of the term 'culture' in what follows. Edward Said's *Orientalism* (1978), a seminal text in postcolonial theory, draws attention to the practice of socially constructing the 'Other' by the 'Occident'. Othering, racializing, and orientalizing are irrefutably wrong. At the same time, there is a need to talk about real difference in the world, and that includes cultural difference. This is significant to Indigenous peoples because the 'assertion of indigenous culture' is an 'important part of decolonization' (Cunneen, 2014, p. 400). The challenge for the postcolonial scholar is how to recognize difference in such a way that it does not reproduce cultural domination and essentialism. As Leti Volpp (1996, p. 1611) attests, there is no easy way to do this: '[i]t is indeed difficult to talk about culture... [and] it is a project that requires constant contextualization and mediation'. If this is what is required, then what follows is limited as I am unable to thoroughly interrogate the invocations of culture in the confines of this subsection. What I am able to do, however, is to bring to the fore the reproduction (albeit in subtler formations) of colonial suppression of culture—to show how Indigenous culture is tokenized, and how cultural needs and interests are often denied—all while acknowledging that Indigenous culture is neither fixed nor homogenous and that it can be (and is) negotiated and experienced differently.

Despite many drug court professionals across the four sites claiming that drug courts were 'culturally sensitive' and/or responsive, the structure and operations of the drug courts were devoid of any recourse to Indigenous culture.[6] In each case study site, so-called 'culturally appropriate' accommodations merely equated to the provision of various external services and supports that participants could be referred to provided they supported their rehabilitation. These were not typically offered as a matter of course (though at one Australian drug court, special efforts were made to place Indigenous participants in Indigenous-specific residential rehabilitation provided there was capacity). The onus was on participants to express an interest in reaching out to their culture and to garner the support of relevant drug court professionals in order for them to be linked to services and supports. As a psychotherapist explained:

> if a participant really wants to incorporate Aboriginal spirituality or they want to go to a powwow or they want to have a ritual around you know when they're menstruating, if they want to do things like that they can but they have to get support ... so it's on like a special needs basis ... if there is enough support on board and if I advocate ... they do make exceptions ...

Given the coercive nature of a drug court and the racialized (and gendered) norms and expectations it promotes, it is a tall order to expect Indigenous persons to be comfortable to advocate for these sorts of accommodations, especially considering that historically, Indigenous peoples have been denied and deprived of their cultural practices (indeed, some practices were even criminalized).

In the drug court setting (a 'white space' (Ahmed, 2012)), access to culturally oriented services, supports, activities, and practices was found to require justification—that is, it needed to be justified on the basis that it worked in the service of the participant's rehabilitation. As a case manager explained, 'if someone wants to smudge or anything like that ... that's totally fine ... that doesn't interfere with their recovery at all and if it's important to them then it's totally fine and acceptable' (case manager). But not all professionals were convinced of the merits of these accommodations. One case manager suggested that some Aboriginal participants 'use their spirituality as an excuse to get out of things ... there's a fine line between being sensitive and allowing ... versus letting someone manipulate you ...' The courts would also often deny requests from Indigenous participants for accommodations that (in their view) either did not work in the service of their rehabilitation and recovery, or had the potential to interfere with it. For instance, an Aboriginal participant from one of the Australian courts wanted to go to a funeral that was outside the area they were confined to living in while on the programme, but the case manager said 'they just can't be taking off and going somewhere at such a distance; they can't get their dose and can't see their counsellor and that becomes really problematic'. Another case manager stated that she did not allow an Indigenous participant to visit her family because they lived too far away:

> When they say they want to see their sister it's like a couple [of hours] trip. Then you're stuck. It's like well that's two hours there. Then you've got the background of

[6] None of the courts observed involved the participation of Indigenous Elders. The participant report-backs to the judicial officer occurred in white spaces—formal courtroom settings with standard layouts. Indigenous spirituality and healing activities and practices were formally absent.

> history there. 'I know you need to see your sister you know [but] I can't let you see your sister because of these reasons.' You explain it all to them; in the end sometimes they just cut and go anyway.

Moreover, it was observed that an Aboriginal woman being released from custody tried to advocate that, if she did well in her residential treatment, she be allowed to go to her sister's place because her father was sick and needed looking after. The judicial officer replied: 'I'm not going to suddenly change your treatment plan . . . do some hard work at recovery.' Despite relationships, connections, and family (including extended family) being critical to the well-being of Indigenous persons (King et al., 2009, p. 77), as these examples illustrate, the courts often denied them this need.

Some drug court professionals disclosed that they would 'take advantage' of participants' interest in Aboriginal culture, using it as a carrot to engage them in the programme. The tragic irony of this practice (which comes perilously close to the manipulation/commodification of culture to serve particular ends) was noted by a case manager: 'it used to be you had to take them away from that [culture] whereas we try to integrate them back into that and into everybody else's world'.[7] Reaching out to Indigenous culture is permissible, provided it aids the broader (colonial) project of civilizing. Commodifying culture in this way is tokenistic; its value is conditional on the extent to which it can bolster the hegemonic culture's values and mandates. It is also the case that the concepts that give cultural practices like powwows or sweats meaning have been eroded by colonialism. So while participants can take part in sweats and the like, their lives are simultaneously structured in such a way that render these practices tokenistic.

Because the structure and operations of the drug court do not take cultural difference into account, its capacity to meet Indigenous needs and interests is limited. As a probation officer articulated; 'the follow up is lacking . . . they get in touch with their culture, then they get out of the treatment and they're not really connecting with it anywhere else'. As these findings show, drug courts draw on culture in tokenistic ways. Indigenous culture is mobilized to serve the 'therapeutic' interests of the dominant non-Indigenous culture, rendering it a limited add-on that is only permitted to be drawn on—or, in the case of cultural practices, made accessible—if it can be demonstrated that doing so works in the service of the Indigenous person's rehabilitation and recovery. When this cannot be demonstrated, access to culture is denied and the charge of propagating the colonial legacy of cultural suppression looms large.

Assimilation through subjugation

Indigenous participants often struggled to comply with the demands and expectations of the court. Some professionals suggested that this might be due to the regimens of

[7] Note the problematic phrasing concerning the person being expected to integrate back into 'everybody else's world'.

the court being discordant with their values and beliefs. For instance, a case manager mentioned that some Indigenous participants found the cognitive behavioural treatment offered difficult—that they 'find it a bit shaming that they have to talk about themselves in a group, culturally'. They went on to say that 'they might look at a word and think differently, different values and beliefs'. On the one hand, this could be read as an acknowledgement of real cultural difference. On the other, it could be read as orientalizing. The broader point, however, is that the ideology of Western cognitive behaviouralism that underlies the therapeutic jurisprudence approach to drug court participants excludes other approaches to healing. As Hays (2014, p. 18) notes, cognitive behavioural approaches are limited by the:

> dominant-culture emphasis on individual independence (over family and social interdependence), assertiveness (over subtle forms of communication, talking (over the use of non-verbals, listening, and the deliberate use of silence), a linear cognitive style (over storytelling and less linear forms), and a secular world view (over a spiritual world view).

The expectation that Indigenous participants distance themselves from family was also difficult to comply with:

> family expectations really work against drug court you know. If you're on home detention, you cannot have the family come round. If they want to come round and want to stay it's just culturally unacceptable [to say no]. And they'll come around and drink and that's just impossible ... the whole family thing makes it very hard.
>
> (Defence counsel)

Leaving aside the problematic way this is expressed ('the whole family thing'), what is being drawn attention to here is a real difference that the court not only fails to account for but also expects to be overcome.

Some drug court professionals used offensive, salvationist language with respect to Indigenous participants. These statements were generally preceded by generalizations that rendered the lives of Indigenous peoples 'chaotic', 'shambolic', 'dysfunctional', or 'dislocated' and therefore in need of intervention. For instance, a judicial officer remarked that while it is a 'tragedy that so many of our participants are Aboriginal ... I think it is great that we've managed to provide a program for them'. One defence counsel even went so far as to proclaim that they had 'saved' an Indigenous participant. Others noted how the court 'kept' Indigenous participants on the programme much longer than non-Indigenous participants in the hope that they could turn their lives around. For instance, defence counsel at one Australian court said:

> as far as Aboriginals in general are concerned ... I mean I could name three or four cases just off the top of my head of [Aboriginal] women who have survived just outrageously longer than you'd expect; given lots of opportunities, made bugger all progress (or apparently made bugger all progress) and [the judicial officer] just keeps having them back.

They went on to recount that on one occasion an Aboriginal woman:

> was trying to self-terminate from the program for months before and [the judicial officer] just wouldn't let her go. [The judicial officer] said: 'I want you to succeed. And she didn't succeed as far as graduation is concerned but eventually she . . . self-terminated or [got] terminated. But you know, just bending over backwards to keep her.

On the one hand, this could be seen as positive inasmuch as the judicial officer is trying to keep the Aboriginal woman from going to prison, but the programme is clearly not equipped to meet her needs and interests (hence the woman wanting to self-terminate). Not allowing her the choice to terminate her programme is deeply problematic. Even if one takes the motive to be benevolent or well meaning, this does not negate the fact that the participant's capacity for self-determination is being denied. The example also highlights the interplay between colonial dynamics and gender—the woman in the above example is patronized and infantilized (for more on intersectionality, see Wilson, 2014). This intersection reinforces colonial patriarchy.

The intensive structuration of Indigenous participants' lives[8] can be seen to reflect both past (and present) assimilationist policies that seek justification in the figment that Indigenous peoples are 'primitive and barbaric' and thus in need of civilizing (Cunneen, 2007).[9] This flawed and racist logic leaves participants with no choice but to subscribe to the norms and expectations imposed on them by the court. Though as Cunneen (ibid, p. 42) notes of assimilationist policies, this is not a 'choice' to be made by Indigenous people: instead, assimilation can be achieved through the force of law. This is certainly true of institutional settings for therapeutic jurisprudence. In drug courts, social norms and expectations are enforced through punitive sanctions. Participants who persistently fail to conform are terminated or expelled from the programme and imprisoned. This assimilative predicament is reflected in the following remarks of a probation officer:

> one of the Indigenous women I've worked with kind of looked at it [drug court] . . . as white man's law even though . . . essentially she came from . . . I think she's got an Aboriginal mother and an Anglo-Australian father but she identified strongly as Aboriginal, and she didn't really recognise . . . white man's law that sort of thing. That's not to say that she didn't do her requirements but she kind of did them begrudgingly.

What the above example illustrates is the way in which Indigenous participants are denied authentic experiences. Instead, their experience is governed and shaped by the court (white man's law) through various requirements and conditions that they must abide by. The only 'alternative' is prison (white man's cage).

[8] It is true that the lives of non-Indigenous participants are also heavily structured, but this structuration has a disproportionate impact on Indigenous persons.

[9] The practice of civilizing Indigenous peoples stemmed from the need for colonizers to justify the concept of private property which, in turn, 'legitimated' the dispossession of Indigenous peoples from their lands (see Locke, 1988; Arneil, 1994).

While all drug court participants are subject to exhaustive surveillance, this has a disproportionate impact on Indigenous participants, putting both them and their families at greater risk of criminalization and other state interventions. Several drug court professionals disclosed that Indigenous participants had had their children taken away from them in the course of their drug court programme. Others noted that Indigenous participants were 'picked up' by the police more often than their non-Indigenous counterparts for minor offences, especially Indigenous women. For instance, an Aboriginal woman who had shoplifted a small sum of items was on an 'honesty warning', meaning that if drug use was not admitted and it was detected by a drug test then she would face termination. She and her partner were adamant that she had not used (and the numbers detected in the urine screen were very low), but because she denied the drug use and the test came back positive, she was automatically in breach of the 'honesty warning' even though there was good reason to doubt its accuracy. She was subsequently terminated from the programme and imprisoned. The woman had one child and was pregnant with another when she was terminated from the programme. She ended up having her baby in prison.

White settlers invaded every aspect of the lives of Indigenous peoples. The colonial state sanctioned legislation and policies that restricted their movements, regulated their marriages and relationships, controlled their employment, forcibly removed children from their families, stamped out their culture, and attempted to 'civilize' them by assimilating them into white ways of living (see Cox et al., 2009; Woolford, 2009). Some unsettling parallels can be drawn between these colonial intrusions and the intrusions that drug courts make in the lives of Indigenous participants.

Colonial consciousness

As the previous subsections have highlighted, colonial consciousness evidently informs many of the structures and operations of the drug court. It also came across in the way drug court professionals interacted with and perceived Indigenous participants.

In keeping with the protectionist rhetoric of colonialism, some were of the view that the lives of Indigenous participants needed to be recalibrated. In a pre-court team meeting, the team was discussing an Aboriginal woman with a schizophrenic mother who 'slits her wrists in front of her' and how her partner had recently taken off with another drug court participant while she was serving sanctions in prison. The judicial officer remarked: 'she needs new parents, a new partner'. Other professionals stereotyped Indigenous participants. For instance, defence counsel at an Australian drug court proclaimed that every day their client came in 'there was some other Aboriginal disaster story'. The family life of Indigenous participants was described by many as 'dysfunctional' as the following quote from a judicial officer (confusingly) exemplifies:

> it's just the long-term history of chaos and dysfunction; it is just clearly there to see. Their partners and family and children are often families and brothers and mothers of fathers; [it's] very chaotic.

Some made blatant racist remarks about the appearance of Indigenous participants—'she's not obviously Aboriginal'—and their abilities—'some of them don't even speak English amazingly'. Disturbingly, one programme manager blamed Indigenous peoples' reluctance to participate in 'alternative' programmes for their over-representation:

> it's easier to just go to gaol which is why we have such a high incarceration rate because they're very welcome to do any of our programs but a lot of them elect not to.

These examples speak to a colonial consciousness that privileges the worldview of the colonizer; Othering the colonized in a negative way that frames them as uncivilized and therefore deserving of an interventionist response.

There was another form of colonial consciousness at play in drug courts that was more progressive insofar as it reflected a conscious awareness of the impacts of colonialism in the lives of Indigenous participants. The overwhelming majority of drug court professionals interviewed were cognizant of the enduring impacts of colonialism. Some expressed this when discussing the needs of Indigenous participants. For instance, they mentioned 'traumatic histories', 'generational trauma', the experience of 'discrimination or prejudice throughout their life', children having been removed and placed in care, and/or a persistent 'fear of losing custody of children', and more general comments about 'disadvantage' and 'marginalization'. Others made reference to specific colonial practices such as the residential schools in Canada and other ways in which Indigenous people had been cut off from their culture. But as a programme manager from one of the Canadian courts noted, drug court programmes don't 'specifically address' the legacies of colonialism:

> we understand the needs of the aboriginal people are different and we understand there's a legacy of colonialism and residential schools and we understand those barriers. We also understand enough about those barriers that we understand we are probably not the type of people that they need to be talking to so we connect them with Elders or native friendship centres or other services that we have …

Overall, many were of the view that it is difficult for Indigenous participants to succeed in terms of what the court expects of them because of their marginalization and disadvantage:

> our Aboriginal people have been so marginalised for so long it takes a long time for them to … more than a year for them to come back and be productive and whatever … somebody in drug court told me once it's really hard to habilitate somebody whose never been habilitated or to rehabilitate somebody whose never been habilitated in the first place … it takes an awful lot more extra.
>
> (Case manager)

> [I]t's hard for them, it's hard to make up for 200 years of disadvantage in a short period of time. You sometimes see them you know getting off the ground and doing well, but the weight of all those problems just can pull them back down again … so yeah enormous weight of disadvantage, chaotic kids, chaotic family, family in gaol [*sighs*] … so we push our Aboriginal women and men you know … especially when

> they've got kids themselves ... I will say, 'someone's got to stand up, someone's got to stop this cycle/intergenerational cycle and we'll help you stand on your own feet, help break this'. And they often feel very you know proud of their success, but I/we do see the weight of disadvantage ... you know just dragging the chains behind you all the past and they're just too heavy to ... they're very heavy and it's very tiring to carry them along for a long time you know.
>
> (Judicial officer)

There is much that warrants critical scrutiny in the above-mentioned statements—possessive references, patronizing and racist sentiments, question-begging responsibilization, to name but a few—but suspending that critique for now, the main point to emphasize is that while compounding disadvantage was recognized, these professionals could not see a way forward. Indeed, only one drug court professional that I spoke to was able to suggest ways in which the treatment offered by drug courts could be more responsive to the needs of Indigenous peoples:

> the grief which the Aboriginal people are going through hasn't been looked through. The addiction which is related to the Aboriginal people is also ... we have to understand it in the context of colonisation too. So if we are to take care of the Aboriginal people's needs, we need to start from that perspective; to first look at, like, what are their needs? Have we had some reconciliation or not? Have they got a chance of grieving? And have we [been] allowed to serve them ... within their way of understanding what treatment should be like, rather than treating them within the medical model. Because when we look at most of the treatments we provide, they are within the medical models so if somebody says, 'no, I'm not willing to take that one', are we looking at that—their belief in their spirituality? How do we integrate their spirituality within the service we provide? ... [I]s the staff reflective of the different populations? ... no. The staff doesn't ... reflect at all the people we're trying to serve.

By exploring the themes of cultural tokenism, assimilation through subjugation, and colonial consciousness, this section has attempted to shed light on the various colonial dynamics of drug courts and the way in which they perpetuate colonial legacies.[10] In the next section, I discuss the implications of these thematic findings for therapeutic jurisprudence in relation to its healing claims.

The Enigma of Healing

The Royal Commission on Aboriginal Peoples (1996, pp. 100–101) states that, in Aboriginal terms, healing:

> refers to personal and societal recovery from the lasting effects of oppression and systematic racism experienced over generations. Many aboriginal people are suffering

[10] Future work could build on the analysis presented here by considering the extent to which the culture of the institutional setting as a white space might shape racist practices and sentiments. For more on race and institutional life, see Ahmed, 2012.

> not simply from disease and social problems, but also from a depression of spirit resulting from 200 or more years of damage to their cultures, languages, identities and self-respect. The idea of healing suggests that to reach 'whole health', Aboriginal people must confront the crippling injuries of the past.

Indigenous conceptions of health and healing extend beyond the individual; requiring 'that an individual live in harmony with others, their community and the spirit worlds' (King et al., 2009, p. 76). For Indigenous persons, social and emotional well-being 'is a complex, multidimensional concept encompassing connections to land, culture, spirituality, ancestry, family, and community' (Dudgeon and Walker, 2015, p. 278). The self is 'inseparable from, and embedded within a range of interconnected domains', thereby rendering well-being a 'collectivist' phenomenon (ibid). In contrast, therapeutic jurisprudence—anchored in the assumptions of Western cognitive psychology and behavioural science—proffers an individualistic conception of well-being. The incompatibility between therapeutic jurisprudence's individualistic perspective and a collectivist perspective poses a significant challenge for therapeutic jurisprudence, casting doubt on the extent to which it is able to maximize the well-being of Indigenous persons. As we have seen, this tension plays out on Indigenous participants in the way that the court attempts to govern and shape their lives in ways that do not reflect their authentic experience of the world.

As for what healing entails, the Aboriginal Healing Foundation (2006, p. 3) states that healing from historical trauma 'involves truth-telling; a remembering and re-telling of personal, family and social history from an Aboriginal perspective; and also involves connecting and reconnecting with one's culture and traditions'. Culture is inextricably linked to healing such that '[c]ultural activities are, in fact, a type of healing intervention: both culture and tradition contribute to and result in healing' (ibid, p. 3). Ambelin Kwaymullina (2007, p. 5), an Indigenous lawyer from the Bailgu and Njamala peoples of the Pilbra region in Western Australia, offers this perspective on healing and therapeutic jurisprudence:

> Perhaps the most important thing all those interested in the practice of therapeutic jurisprudence can do is to recognise the significance of country. To understand that in order for a process to be [a] therapeutic one it must be holistic, it must repair and renew connections, and it must recognise that for Indigenous peoples, land is not just where we live, it is who we are. And recognising the broader web of connections within which we all exist is also to recognise a larger responsibility—a responsibility to value the stories of creation and suffering that are part of country, a responsibility for the Western legal system to acknowledge its place in causing that suffering; and for all of us to find a way not just of living together in country, but of healing together in it.

In the light of the above, the sort of healing that therapeutic jurisprudence offers Indigenous persons is evidently limited. In the drug court setting, what takes precedence over all else is the rehabilitation of the participant, the success of which is measured by abstinence from drugs and crime, and 'positive' activities like securing gainful employment, education/training, or volunteer work. The end goal is for participants to become responsibilized, productive citizens who lead 'pro-social' lives. Following the therapeutic jurisprudence approach, problems of drug use and criminalization are the product of internal weaknesses that participants have failed to overcome. The solution to these problems rests within the individual who is 'supported' by the court to address their weaknesses. It is the individual who is deemed wholly responsible for their drug-dependency and criminalization. Despite structural and systemic factors being acknowledged by those who work in institutional settings for therapeutic jurisprudence, neither the therapeutic jurisprudence approach nor the key tools and techniques that proponents advocate for take into account the influence of structural and systemic factors.[11] This significantly narrows the scope of healing in therapeutic jurisprudence. At best, healing is merely analogous to individual rehabilitation and thus can offer little to Indigenous persons (or to anyone else for that matter).

It is also the case that the therapeutic jurisprudence approach and particular techniques that proponents advocate for, such as behavioural contracting and the use of coercion and imprisonment, was found to contribute to the reproduction of colonial dynamics and the perpetuation of colonial legacies. This casts an even greater shadow of doubt over therapeutic jurisprudence's healing claims, and its therapeutic orientation more broadly.[12] As Kwaymullina argues, '[a]ny process that disempowers and dispossesses, no matter how lofty the aim, is an anti-therapeutic one that can never lead to a therapeutic result' (Kwaymullina, 2007, p. 5).

Conclusion

It would be simplistic to say that because therapeutic jurisprudence is embedded in the law, it is doomed to fail Indigenous peoples—that because law and its institutions have been and continue to be tools of colonial violence, therapeutic jurisprudence is destined to reproduce colonial legacies, never delivering healing and meaningful justice for Indigenous persons. It is possible to challenge law from within; to identify and to push latent features and forms that could work in the service of a different kind of justice, one that was 'decolonized' proper and that took healing seriously (see also Cunneen, 2009, p. 335). My argument is that therapeutic jurisprudence fails for another reason: it does not challenge the status quo. There is no challenge to criminalization, let alone the hyper-criminalization of Indigenous persons. There is no challenge to imprisonment—the single, most effective means (both historically and presently) of governing Indigenous populations in colonial jurisdictions (Brown, 2002; Baldry and Cunneen, 2014). Indeed, proponents unashamedly draw on oppressive mechanisms

[11] E.g. King et al. (2014, pp. 157–158) argue that '[i]n the main, problem-oriented courts focus on the individual. Though broad economic or social factors may be the roots of poverty, addiction, or homelessness, the courts seek primarily to address the defendant's immediate problems, and only secondarily, the wider socio-political structures.'

[12] One might want to claim that the failure of therapeutic jurisprudence to deliver meaningful healing for Indigenous persons does not lie with it per se—that it is curtailed by the dominant, cognitive behavioural rehabilitative ethos that pervades the broader criminal justice system. However, as I have argued elsewhere (Wilson, 2021), proponents actively promote the central tenets of cognitive behaviouralism and 'what works'. For them, healing is inextricably linked to these frameworks.

of punishment including imprisonment as means through which to achieve what they deem to be therapeutic outcomes for Indigenous peoples. In practice, what therapeutic jurisprudence offers is a suite of tools and techniques designed to promote compliance with the law, and an approach that responsibilizes Indigenous persons for their drug-dependency and criminalization and attempts to reform their lives in so-called 'pro-social' ways.

A question, then, for proponents is: why not take a more radical standpoint? One answer might be that it is not the remit of therapeutic jurisprudence to challenge law, only to find better or more 'therapeutic' ways to the support the status quo's law and order regimen. Another answer might be that therapeutic jurisprudence is acutely aware of its tenuous tenure; it wants to keep its seat at the table and therefore cannot afford to 'rock the boat' too much. But if that is so, then one might reasonably question whether the therapeutic jurisprudence vessel is seaworthy—that is, whether it is good enough to make any meaningful headway with respect to justice or healing for Indigenous peoples. So long as proponents insist that therapeutic jurisprudence pursuits play handmaiden to dominant, racialized justice interests, what therapeutic jurisprudence offers will remain severely limited (see also Arrigo, 2004). This problematic stance manifests in its practices. As the findings of this chapter have demonstrated, the therapeutic jurisprudence approach and its associated tools and techniques reproduce colonial legacies and contribute to colonial dynamics that continue to marginalize and oppress Indigenous persons.

Returning to Stobbs's claim that 'principles' of therapeutic jurisprudence can assist in the development of legal reforms designed to attend to systemic issues that contribute to the over-representation of Indigenous persons in postcolonial criminal justice systems—if there was any truth to this claim, then we would expect there to be some gesture (either in theory or in practice) towards emancipation and/or sociopolitical transformation. I have not been able to locate evidence of any such gesture. On the contrary, what I have found is that the way in which therapeutic jurisprudence is applied in its most well-known institutional setting serves to compound the marginalization and oppression of Indigenous peoples. This should be a cause for concern for its proponents, given therapeutic jurisprudence's claimed emphasis on healing, the promotion of well-being, and the minimization of anti-therapeutic impacts. This finding should also be of concern for criminologists and criminal justice scholars. As mentioned in the introduction, to date there has been very little critical engagement with therapeutic jurisprudence compared to other 'alternatives' like restorative justice. I hope this chapter will serve as a reminder that therapeutic jurisprudence warrants interrogation.

I want to end with a cautionary note. Recently, there has been a push to consider the merits of swift and certain punishments (see especially Bartels, 2015; 2017; 2019). There is not the space to consider the problematics of this development here, but there are two brief points I want to make. The first is that this approach (*qua* the HOPE court model) has been conceptually grounded in therapeutic jurisprudence (Bartels 2017; 2019). The second is that little thought has been given to the disproportionate impact that such punishments are likely to have on Indigenous peoples. While Bartels (2017, p. 175) makes cursory references to reservations about 'subjecting Indigenous people to SCF [swift, certain, and fair] sanctions' and 'the need to ensure any HOPE program adopted in Australia is culturally appropriate for Indigenous people',[13] precisely what a 'culturally appropriate' approach to the imprisonment of Indigenous persons with swift and certain gusto would entail remains unclear.[14] Therapeutic jurisprudence has been a feature of Western criminal justice thinking and practices for over twenty-five years. Swift and certain developments and other projects designed to mainstream therapeutic jurisprudence beyond the problem-solving court context are chomping at the bit. The time to take therapeutic jurisprudence, its colonial dynamics, and the colonial legacies it perpetuates seriously is not just overdue: it is urgent.

References

Aboriginal Healing Foundation (2006) *Final Report of the Aboriginal Healing Foundation: Vol. III Promising Healing Practices in Aboriginal Communities*. Ontario: Aboriginal Healing Foundation.

Ahmed, S. (2012) *On Being Included: Racism and Diversity in Institutional Life*. Durham, NC: Duke University Press.

Arneil, B. (1994) 'Trade, plantations, and property: John Locke and the economic defense of colonialism', *Journal of the History of Ideas*, 55(4), pp. 591–609.

Arrigo, B. A. (2004) 'The ethics of therapeutic jurisprudence: A critical and theoretical enquiry of law, psychology and crime', *Psychiatry, Psychology and Law*, 11(1), pp. 23–43.

Baldry, E. and Cunneen, C. (2014) 'Imprisoned indigenous women and the shadow of colonial patriarchy', *Australian & New Zealand Journal of Criminology*, 47(2), pp. 276–298.

Bartels, L. (2015) 'Swift and certain sanctions: Is it time for Australia to bring some HOPE into the criminal justice system?', *Criminal Law Journal*, 39(1), pp. 53–66.

Bartels, L. (2017) *Swift, Certain and Fair: Does Project HOPE Provide a Therapeutic Paradigm for Managing Offenders*. Cham: Palgrave Macmillan.

Bartels, L. (2019) 'HOPE-ful bottles: Examining the potential for Hawaii's opportunity probation with enforcement (HOPE) to help mainstream therapeutic jurisprudence', *International Journal of Law and Psychiatry*, 63, pp. 26–34.

Bartels, L. and Richards, K. (2013) 'Talking the talk: Therapeutic jurisprudence and oral competence', *Alternative Law Journal*, 38(1), pp. 31–33.

Beckerman, A. and Fontana, L. (2001) 'Issues of race and gender in court-ordered substance abuse treatment', *Journal of Offender Rehabilitation*, 33(4), pp. 45–61.

Blagg, H. (2017) 'Doing Restorative Justice "Otherwise": Decolonising Practices in the Global South', in Aertsen, I. and Pali, B. (eds) *Critical Restorative Justice*. Oxford: Bloomsbury Collections, pp. 61–78.

Blagg, H. and Anthony, T. (2019) *Decolonising Criminology: Imagining Justice in a Postcolonial World*. London: Palgrave Macmillan.

[13] Elsewhere, Bartels (2015, p. 65) notes that 'the implications for Indigenous persons would need to be considered carefully, although the program may have the potential to reduce their over-representation in custody'. In support of the latter, Bartels cites Don Weatherburn's (2014) book *Arresting Incarceration* which has been the subject of pointed critiques (see especially Cunneen and Tauri, 2016; Tauri, 2018). Bartels (2015, p. 65) also notes that programmes with 'significant numbers of Indigenous offenders should be developed in consultation with relevant community representatives'. But these remarks are superficial; they neither concretely nor robustly consider the impacts such programmes might have on Indigenous persons.

[14] On this, Bartels (2017, p. 175) offers that 'participation in a cultural awareness program could be used as a response to non-compliance and might help to reduce incarceration' yet, at the same time, acknowledges 'the challenges of making sure such a response is delivered in such a way that is both swift and certain'.

Brady, M. (1995) 'Culture in treatment, culture as treatment. A critical appraisal of developments in addictions programs for indigenous North Americans and Australians', *Social Science & Medicine*, 41(11), pp. 1487–1498.

Brookbanks, W. (2001) 'Therapeutic jurisprudence: Conceiving an ethical framework', *Journal of Law and Medicine*, 8(3), pp. 328–341.

Brown, M. (2002) 'The politics of penal excess and the echo of colonial penality', *Punishment & Society*, 4(4), pp. 403–423.

Chenhall, R. D. (2007) *Benelong's Haven: Recovery from Alcohol and Drug Abuse within an Aboriginal Australian Residential Treatment Centre*. Melbourne: Melbourne University Press.

Cox, D., Young, M., and Bairnsfather-Scott, A. (2009) 'No justice without healing: Australian Aboriginal people and family violence', *Australian Feminist Law Journal*, 30(1), pp. 151–161.

Cunneen, C. (2002) 'Restorative Justice and the Politics of Decolonization', in Weitekamp, E. G. M. and Kerner, H.-J. (eds) *Restorative Justice: Theoretical Foundations*. Cullompton: Willan, pp. 32–49.

Cunneen, C. (2007) 'Assimilation and the re-invention of barbarism', *Australian Indigenous Law Review*, 11, pp. 42–45.

Cunneen, C. (2009) 'Criminology, criminal justice and indigenous people: A dysfunctional relationship?', *Current Issues in Criminal Justice*, 20(3), pp. 323–336.

Cunneen, C. (2014) 'Colonial Processes, Indigenous Peoples, and Criminal Justice Systems'. in Bucerius, S. and Tonry, M. (ed.) *The Oxford Handbook of Ethnicity, Crime, and Immigration*. New York: Oxford University Press, pp. 386–407.

Cunneen, C. and Tauri, J. (2016) *Indigenous Criminology*. Bristol: Policy Press.

Dudgeon, P. and Walker, R. (2015) 'Decolonising Australian psychology: Discourses, strategies, and practice', *Journal of Social and Political Psychology*, 3(1), pp. 276–297.

Hays, P. (2014) 'An international perspective on the adaptation of CBT across cultures', *Australian Psychologist*, 49(1), pp. 17–18.

Hora, P. F., Schma, W. G., and Rosenthal, J. T. A. (1999) 'Therapeutic jurisprudence and the drug court movement: Revolutionizing the criminal justice system's response to drug abuse and crime in America', *Notre Dame Law Review*, 74(2), pp. 439–538.

King, M., Smith, A., and Gracey, M. (2009) 'Indigenous health Part 2: The underlying causes of the health gap', *The Lancet*, 374(9683), pp. 76–85.

King, M., Freiberg, A., Batagol, B. et al. (2014) *Non-Adversarial Justice*. Leichhardt: Federation Press.

Kwaymullina, A. (2007) 'Country and Healing: An Indigenous Perspective on Therapeutic Jurisprudence', in Reinhardt, G. and Cannon, A. (eds) *Transforming Legal Processes in Court and Beyond*. Perth: Australian Institute of Judicial Administration, pp. 1–7.

Larsen, A.-C. and Milnes, P. (2011) 'A cautionary note on therapeutic jurisprudence for Aboriginal offenders', *Murdoch University Electronic Journal of Law*, 18(1), pp. 1–27.

Locke, J. (1988 [1689]) *Two Treatises of Government*. Cambridge: Cambridge University Press.

Marques, O. and Monchalin, L. (2020) 'The Mass Incarceration of Indigenous Women in Canada: A Colonial Tactic of Control and Assimilation', in George, L., Norris, A. N., Deckert, A. et al (eds) *Neo-Colonial Injustice and the Mass Imprisonment of Indigenous Women*. Cham: Palgrave Macmillan, pp. 79–102.

Monchalin, L. (2016) *The Colonial Problem: An Indigenous Perspective on Crime and Injustice in Canada*. Toronto: University of Toronto Press.

Morse, D. S., Cerulli, C., Bedell, P. et al. (2014) 'Meeting health and psychological needs of women in drug treatment court', *Journal of Substance Abuse Treatment*, 46(2), pp. 150–157.

Nielsen, M. O. and Robyn, L. (2003) 'Colonialism and criminal justice for indigenous peoples in Australia, Canada, New Zealand and the United States of America', *Indigenous Nations Journal*, 4(1), pp. 29–45.

O'Hear, M. M. (2009) 'Rethinking drug courts: Restorative justice as a response to racial injustice', *Stanford Law & Policy Review*, 20(2), pp. 463–500.

Phillips, G. (2003) *Addictions and Healing in Aboriginal Country*. Canberra: Aboriginal Studies Press.

Royal Commission on Aboriginal Peoples (1996) *Vol. 3: Gathering Strength: Report of the Royal Commission on Aboriginal Peoples*. Ontario: Canada Communication Group.

Said, E. (1978) *Orientalism*. London: Routledge & Kegan Paul.

Stobbs, N. (2020) 'Therapeutic Jurisprudence in International and Comparative Perspective', in *Oxford Research Encyclopaedia of Criminology and Criminal Justice*. Oxford: Oxford University Press, pp. 1–30.

Tauri, J. M. (2018) 'The master's tools will never dismantle the master's house: An indigenous critique of criminology', *Journal of Global Indigeneity*, 3(1), pp. 1–18.

Tauri, J. M. (2022) 'What exactly are you restoring us to? A critical examination of indigenous experiences of state-centred restorative justice', *Howard Journal of Crime and Justice*, 61(1), pp. 53–67.

Tauri, J. M. and Porou, N. (2014) 'Criminal justice as a colonial project in settler-colonialism', *African Journal of Criminology and Justice Studies*, 8(1), pp. 20–37.

Volpp, L. (1996) 'Talking "culture": Gender, race, nation, and the politics of multiculturalism', *Colombia Law Review*, 96(6), pp. 1573–1617.

Weatherburn, D. (2014) *Arresting Incarceration: Pathways Out of Indigenous Imprisonment*. Canberra: Aboriginal Studies Press.

Wexler, D. B. (2008) 'Two decades of therapeutic jurisprudence', *Touro Law Review*, 24(1), pp. 17–29.

Wexler, D. B. and King, M. S. (2013) 'Promoting Societal and Juridical Receptivity to Rehabilitation: The Role of Therapeutic Jurisprudence', in Cooper, C., Chisman, A. McG., and Lomba Maurandi, A. (eds) Drug Treatment Courts: An International Response for Drug Dependent Offenders. Inter-American Drug Abuse Control Commission (CICAD) and Secretariat for Multidimensional Security of the Organization of American States (OAS), pp. 21–43.

Wilson, A. (2014) 'Putting therapeutic jurisprudence on edge: A gendered engagement', *University of British Colombia Law Review*, 47(3), pp. 1185–1217.

Wilson, A. (2021) 'Therapeutic jurisprudence in criminal justice: The price of letting one hundred flowers bloom', *European Journal of Current Legal Issues*, 25(1).

Winick, B. J. (2011) 'Therapeutic Jurisprudence and Victims of Crime', in Erez, E., Kilchling, M., and Wemmers, J.-A. (eds) *Therapeutic Jurisprudence and Victim Participation in Justice: International Perspectives*. Durham, NC: Carolina Academic Press, pp. 3–14.

Winick, B. J. (2013) 'Problem Solving Courts: Therapeutic Jurisprudence in Practice', in Weiner, R. L. and Branks, E. M. (eds) *Problem Solving Courts: Social Science and Legal Perspectives*. New York: Springer, pp. 211–236.

Winick, B. J. and Wexler, D. B. (2002) 'Drug treatment court: Therapeutic jurisprudence applied', *Touro Law Review*, 18(3), pp. 479–486.

Winick, B. J. and Wexler, D. B. (2003) 'Introduction', in Winick, B. J. and Wexler, D. B. (eds) *Judging in a Therapeutic Key: Therapeutic Jurisprudence and the Courts*. Durham, NC: Carolina Academic Press, pp. 3–10.

Woolford, A. (2009) 'Ontological destruction: Genocide and Canadian Aboriginal peoples', *Genocide Studies Prevention*, 4(1), pp. 81–97.

18

In Our Experience

Recognizing and Challenging Cognitive Imperialism

Kwan-Lamar Blount-Hill and Ahmed Ajil

Introduction: Colonization and Cognitive Imperialism

Colonization is intricately connected to intellectual control. Two primary psychologies are of paramount concern within any process of colonization involving invasion and displacement of other peoples. First, colonizers must construct an ideological framework that justifies subjugation of another people and mollifies any moral discomfort with conquest (Macoun, 2016). Second, colonizers must neutralize colonized peoples' motivations for physical rebellion (Dugassa, 2011). Kurtz (1996, p. 106) describes essential processes of governance:

> [L]eadership of a complex political formation of any ideological persuasion . . . engages in two complementary practices. In one, domination, it uses coercion and force . . . In the other, hegemony, it uses intellectual devices to infuse its ideas of morality to gain the support of those who resist or may be neutral, to retain the support of those who consent to its rule . . .

These apply with perhaps more urgency in colonial government. Once established, colonial control is accomplished both by threat of force and a hegemonic ideology that construes colonial authority as rightful, legitimate, and, most importantly, superior (Dimou, 2021). In line with Marxist–Gramscian discussions of hegemony (Gramsci, 1971), ideas reinforcing the colonial status quo are so embedded throughout day-to-day life that they become taken-for-granted, practically invisible truths even to the oppressed and colonized. Under a colonial regime, hegemonic claims are forced upon all colonial subjects, including members of the dominant class, subjugated natives, and subordinated others imported or permitted into colonized lands.

The zenith of colonial success is subconscious acceptance by the colonized of their dominated position, refusing to resist it or even choosing to defend it ('false consciousness'; Heywood, 1994, p. 85), demonstrating the insight of historian Carter G. Woodson (2009) in 1933: 'When you control a man's thinking, you do not have to worry about his actions . . . He will find his "proper place" and will stay in it' (p. 4). Fanon emphasized the scope of historical colonial powers' enforced displacement of

Kwan-Lamar Blount-Hill and Ahmed Ajil, *In Our Experience* In: *Decolonizing the Criminal Question.*
Edited by: Ana Aliverti, Henrique Carvalho, Anastasia Chamberlen, and Máximo Sozzo, Oxford University Press.
 DOI: 10.1093/oso/9780192899002.003.0019

physical bodies and territory but also of cultures, worldviews, collective memories, and ways of thinking:

> Colonialism is not satisfied with snaring the people in its net or draining the colonized brain of any form or substance. With a kind of perverted logic, it turns its attention to the past of the colonized people and distorts it, disfigures it, and destroys it.
>
> (Fanon, 2005 [1963], p. 149)

Ngugi wa Thiong'o argues that indoctrination through education and erasure of native histories is facilitated perhaps most effectively through linguistic dominance by European tongues (especially, English) and elimination of indigenous languages. At Wits University, he noted, 'In colonial conquest, language did to the mind what the sword did to the bodies of the colonised' (Willis, 2017, n.p.). Dispossessed of self-determination, cultural traditions, and languages, colonized and enslaved peoples experienced what he calls a 'colonization of the mind'.

Colonization of the mind occurs because of cognitive and socio-psychological oppression that we refer to as *cognitive imperialism*. The notion resonates with the *coloniality of power* concepts developed by Latin American social theorists (Mignolo, 2007; Quijano, 2000; Quijano, 2007 [1992]) who posit that hierarchies established during early European colonization are perpetuated by Eurocentric systems of knowledge. Cognition, simply defined, is the act of thought—'the neuronal processes concerned with the acquisition, retention, and use of information' (Dukas, 2004). Here, we parse more precisely the character of the systems enacting colonial dominance (i.e. coloniality), emphasized in Quijano and others, from the logical structure undergirding colonization and the process of socializing colonial subjects into accepting that logic (i.e. cognitive imperialism) ending in colonization of the mind.

Decolonial theorists recognize Western/Eurocentric universalism as an imperial project which centralizes power, advances one group and location over others, delineates hierarchies by culture and ethnicity (if not by intention, nonetheless in effect), and claims universal legitimacy (Deckert and Tauri, 2019). Assertions that Western theories of criminology and criminal justice (CCJ) are 'context-free, post-ideological, and, therefore, universal' (Ajil and Blount-Hill, 2020, p. 87; also Maldonado-Torres, 2007) legitimate and justify the displacement and subordination of alternative epistemes produced in the Global South (Carrington, Hogg, and Sozzo, 2016). Critical race theory, queer theory, feminist theory, critical theory, decolonial perspectives, and Southern perspectives, among others, each arose as a critique of hegemony that advances white, heterosexual, male bourgeoisie as an academic archetype. Still, scholars have documented hegemony within academe at large (Kim, 2012; Rowlands, 2015) and CCJ in particular (Carson and O'Malley, 1989; Kim, 2020). An academic education and professionalization process that indoctrinates acceptance of the universality of Western theorizing is, de facto, cognitive imperialism.

We argue alongside others (e.g. wa Thiong'o, 2011 [1986]) that knowledge-making is as important as war-making for imperial expansion, displacement, colonization, and subjugation of the indigenous.[1] This may be particularly true within CCJ departments, which often collaborate with criminal justice systems that control black, brown, foreign, dissident, and 'deviant' populations (Agozino, 2003; Kitossa, 2012). For important reasons, analyses of cognitive imperialism within CCJ are necessary for a fuller appreciation of the effect of cognitive imperialism more so than any other social science. To start, the foci of CCJ form central questions of empire. In answering, 'Why do individuals or groups disregard laws?' criminologists supply the science of disobedience. Armed with its insights, those studying the criminal 'justice' question of 'How do societies react to criminal behaviour?' supply a complementary science of control. Together, these tools provide empires with the ability to refine their control using 'cutting-edge' knowledge about the nature of disobedience. As such, even where cognitive imperialism operates within CCJ exactly as elsewhere, it has unique relevance in the CCJ context. Furthermore, cognitive imperialism creates a barrier to more critical, less colonial system-supportive considerations of 'the criminal question' (Aliverti et al., 2021).

In general, the project of decolonization 'describes the "undoing of colonialism" by granting former colonies independence and self-governance', and, where 'ideologies and power structures that justified and maintained colonial projects continue', it involves action that 'highlights, questions, resists and fights this matrix of power on political, economic, social and epistemic levels' (Ajil and Blount-Hill, 2020, p. 87). Our work has centred on decolonization of CCJ, liberation of the *othered* within CCJ, and attacking philosophies of imperialism along with the processes and systems intended to support, uphold, and propagate the aims of such philosophies. Echoing other works lamenting a homogenously white Western academic workforce (Philips and Bowling, 2003), this work has centred on arguments for greater inclusion of othered scholars (Blount-Hill et al., 2022).[2] However, colonization of the mind resulting from cognitive imperialism blunts the impact of incorporating subjugated group members into the colonial power structure. In almost too perfect a show of power, the effect of cognitive imperialism is that even demographic diversity often fails to bring the diversity of thought that would challenge coloniality.

In the remainder of this chapter, we explore the nature of Western/Eurocentric cognitive imperialism in CCJ. We analyse our experience and that of CCJ scholars-in-training to explore cognitive imperialism, colonization of the mind, and *de*colonization of the mind as both praxis and countervailing philosophy. We argue that early career academics' (ECA) engagement with this imperialist project is especially pertinent to understanding its impacts and workings.

[1] We understand 'Western' to encompass those nations whose populations are predominantly descended from European peoples, no matter where they now reside (including North America and Oceania), and 'Eurocentric' to encompass the intellectual and cultural progeny of those peoples as developed in their continental homeland and as exported and evolved in colonized places to make sense of their experiences and perspectives.

[2] Otherness is 'the result of a discursive process by which a dominant in-group ("Us", the Self) constructs one or many dominated out-groups ("Them", Other) by stigmatising a difference—real or imagined—presented as a negation of identity and thus a motive for potential discrimination' (Staszak, 2009, n.p.).

Experiencing criminal justice academe: the data

We draw on several bodies of data to discuss how cognitive imperialism acts upon academics. Our framework is inspired by a collaborative autoethnography completed in February 2020 and published elsewhere (Ajil and Blount-Hill, 2020), in which we analysed our experiences as CCJ doctoral students. We will use its material to develop our conceptualizations here. Second, we will analyse the results of a 'reaction study' from a convenience sample of ECAs. Finally, we draw upon ongoing analyses of published autoethnographic/biographic material on the lived experiences of othered scholars in CCJ scholarship, across seniority, conducted for work developing what we call *inclusive criminology* (Blount-Hill et al., 2022).

Generally, autoethnography is construed as the examination of one's own experience of social phenomena common and familiar to at least a subset of others. Autoethnographers 'study their life stories to reveal sociological phenomena at work within their own lived experiences' (Ajil and Blount-Hill, 2020, p. 90). The method shares the same limitations as all small-*n* case studies, though it might be expected to provide similar benefits (e.g. a more comprehensive view of the subject, more contextualized sense of the data, and less reliance on preconceptions and a priori hypotheses). Like traditional ethnography—wherein researchers immerse themselves in foreign experiences—autoethnography offers a richly contextualized view of the studied phenomenon, though is limited, like all ethnography, by having that experience mediated through the interpretations and understandings of the researcher. Autoethnographers face another, unique, challenge: in blending researcher-subject positionalities, they risk a heightened potential for bias. Autoethnographers justify this risk with a unique reward: as researchers, we have the ability to access contextual, psychological, physical, and social data simply impossible or infeasible for others to acquire through conventional means. Moreover, training in social scientific analyses allows us to convey experience with nuance and precision, in ways resonant with social scientists, to a degree few, if any, research subjects can match. On these metrics, we aver that we are worthy research subjects, though we invite the scrutiny and caution of interpretation that all scientific methods require, whether statistical studies, interviews, or ethnography.

Qualitative study of cognitive imperialism requires a study participant to recognize their experience of the phenomenon, explain these experiences and the meanings ascribed by the participant, and to do so with context in mind and truthfully. If this work is collaborative, multiple autoethnographers can analyse each other's experience along with one's own, and can challenge each other's interpretations of those experiences, providing at least some check on individualistic subjectivity. In February 2020, we engaged in this type of work, completing a four-week journaling and reflection exercise using structured prompts to reflect on our past and current experience as othered scholars while also responding to each other's journaling (Ajil and Blount-Hill, 2020).

Overlap in our respective personal experiences in academe converged significantly on othering and little else. Reflecting on the diversity of our experience, Blount-Hill (2021, p. 97) notes:

> My work with Ajil benefitted from the diversity of our perspectives, including differing nationalities (Swiss versus American), ethno-racial backgrounds (Arab versus Black), religious upbringings (Muslim versus Christian, leaning secular versus very religious), sexualities (heterosexual versus homosexual), epistemologies (decolonization versus critical race and mainstream social psychological theories), and areas of expertise (politico-ideological violence versus perceptions of justice), inter alia. We also differed in our career paths. As he has thrown himself evermore into the role of scholar-activist, I have burrowed deeper and deeper into what might be considered the colonial state.

Our identity is common primarily with respect to our difference from the hegemonic archetypical academic (e.g. white, Christian, male, heterosexual, able-bodied, cisgendered), the colonial referent from which divergence creates a point for othering. Ajil publicly documented personal reflections on his research and experience on the web log 'mesopaq'. Blount-Hill published a collaborative autoethnography (Blount-Hill and St. John, 2017a) and a subsequent reflection (Blount-Hill and St. John, 2017b), as well as a reflection on his work with Ajil on 'Writing the Other as Other' (Blount-Hill, 2020). To explore whether themes from our experience extend beyond us, we conducted a *reaction study*, requesting that participants read our collaborative autoethnography and subsequently answer questions focused on the resonance of three identified themes with their personal experiences. The study was meant to be neither explanatory nor generalizable, but rather an exploration of other narratives to determine by corroboration the themes' suitability for further study. We used the findings, along with other literature, to develop a framework for cognitive imperialism, its effects, and responses to it.

The reaction study was conducted online between September and December 2020, using LimeSurvey. Five individuals participated. Samantha, a Swiss female, aged thirty-three, was a criminologist four years into a Swiss doctoral programme, who reluctantly associated herself with a form of epistemic otherness which arose from her choice of working outside CCJ mainstream topics, paradigms, and methods. She provided responses totalling approximately 1,200 words. Aubrey was a twenty-nine-year-old American female who was two and a half years into a US doctoral programme, who identified otherness in race, gender, and sexuality (910 words). Rashon was a twenty-seven-year-old male, two years into a US doctoral programme whose response focused on his othered racial identity (1,277 words). Likewise, Teddy—a twenty-six-year-old third-year Ugandan American doctoral student in a US doctoral programme—also focused on an othered racial identity and invisible disability (696 words). Zoé was a thirty-two-year-old Spanish–Swiss criminologist and sociologist three years into a Swiss doctoral programme at the time of the survey, whose otherness centred on her female gender and lower class upbringing (2,917 words). All five spoke of epistemological othering due to their work in one or another critical perspective (e.g. feminist theory, queer theory, critical race theory). Where othered racial identity was mentioned, it was uniformly some variant of Black American (e.g. descendants of Africans arriving as slaves or immigrants to the United States).

Recognizing and Reflecting on Cognitive Imperialism

In our collaborative autoethnography, we found that we use our otherness as a world-view and perceptual framework (a 'lens') to reflect upon and critically analyse our research and that of others for 'fair and accurate representations of all members of the society' (recognitional justice; Mathiesen, 2015, p. 207). As a second theme, we noted that experiences of othering caused feelings of stress, insecurity, anger, and disconnect. We found that, to cope with these feelings and to combat being othered, we often engage in impression management ('self-policing'), seek ways to justify our work within the bounds of colonial standards ('seeking legitimacy'), and pursue goals designed to outmatch our non-othered colleagues in a bid to demonstrate the equality (or superiority) of our othered intellectual capacity ('overachieving'). A third theme was our tendency to seek connections with other othered scholars, both within and outside specific othered identities ('otherness solidarity') (Ajil and Blount-Hill, 2020).

Obtaining reactions of other ECAs was especially important to us. Recently, Kidman (2020) published a study of twenty-nine senior Māori academics working in New Zealand's higher education system and taking a decolonial, activist approach. From this cohort was 'a concern that younger Māori scholars would ultimately be assimilated into the colonial logic of academy and the threat this posed to the role of Māori critic and conscience of society' (ibid, p. 255). If colonial imperialism occurs predominantly through socialization processes, these processes are at their peak at the inception of identity formation closer to the beginning of a career and relatively stable throughout. As individuals become invested in current identities, they are less likely to change or adapt these identities and more likely to interpret their worlds in support of current identities. Thus, the study of ECA experience allows us to consider colonial socialization at its apex while also directing focus to those most open to post-, anti-, or de-colonial perspectives. A chance meeting between us is responsible for such a shift in the first author's perspective, an outcome that would have been less likely had we first met now when our careers have advanced.

Based on our analysis of ECAs' stories, we found that, when asked, our colleagues identified similar aspects of cognitive imperialism as we had. Each had moments of *recognition* when they became consciously aware of hegemony at work. They *reflected* to understand the scope of hegemonic power, which led to *reorientation*, a commitment to adjust their thinking and behaviour to avoid propagation of coloniality, and to identify it when encountered. Finally, there was a *response*, through which they found ways both to *recover* and to seek *reform* (including de- and re-construction or even abolition) of present-day power structures to rid them of coloniality. We noted earlier that an underappreciated feature of cognitive imperialism is that it concerns the psychologies of *both* the colonized as well as others in the colonizer's own national and/or social groups. Perspectives of our colleagues who identify racially as white allowed us to discover similarities in their process of decolonizing the mind with that of our participants of colour.

Recognition is a ubiquitous start to decolonizing one's mind. Zoé, identifying as white, attested to a moment of recognition regarding the othering of people of colour in academic spaces:

> At a seminar, during informal discussion, one of the professors recounted that he and his wife were writing a book on slavery. The publisher made demands which they considered exaggerated. He insisted that 'You can't even say slave, you have to say an enslaved person'. Then he lamented that one couldn't use the word 'n*****. It is getting ridiculous!' He added that 'trigger warnings' were infantilizing. This man was white, old, straight and there as a speaker. He had everything to feel and be perceived as legitimate. Six others (all white) present did not react.

This particular reflection recalled Blount-Hill and St. John's (2017a) work, wherein they outlined specific aspects of academic culture that conflicted ('clashed', they said) with their conception of Black American culture. They used the term *cultural incongruence* for a condition 'where two cultures differ such that coming together causes stress, strain or all-out clash' (Blount-Hill, 2017b, n.p.). Extending beyond Black American experience, we adapted their language of 'clash' to elaborate a set of 'clashes' between othered identities and imperialist academic institutions faced by scholars at any career point but especially ECAs.

First, we interpreted a *clash of identity*, in which the interests of the academy are directly adverse to communities of othered identities (Kitossa, 2012). For example, Western scholarship on terrorism that fails at nuance or balanced points of view imperils the quality of life for Muslim and brown-skinned communities (Ajil, 2020; Al-Kassimi, 2017). Zoé described a similar reaction to her female gender: 'There are many stereotypes about women—less competent, less of a place in academia—we are often reminded of that.' She recounted a colleague's comment when she won a prestigious award, 'Well done for your scholarship! You were lucky since they favor women now.' Zoé's reflection on gender illustrates an important discussion in decolonial literature that bears mention. While Quijano (2000) explains the racial construct as a means to found arguments about colonized peoples' inferiority as natural and inherent, he also explains the pairing of this construction with previous ideologies of dominance in a comprehensive doctrine of capitalist profit through extraction of labour and resources. Grosfoguel (2011) identifies four additional hierarchies, including 'A global gender hierarchy that privileged males over females and European Judeo-Christian patriarchy over other forms of gender relations' (p. 98). 'Traditional' academic socialization would mean acceding to these assumptions of identity-based hierarchy. For criminologists, this would lead to particularly odious results. We seek to answer 'the criminal question,' that is, 'What is the nature of crime, its control, and interrelations between the two?' What answers may be expected to spring forth from a mind giving home to the thought that women and racial minorities were, on average, inherently less deserving and less skilled?

Others also lamented the lack of place for their identity. *A la* Russell-Brown (2021), Aubrey declared, 'White academia was never meant for me.' Rashon ascribed intentionality to the clash between his identity and academe—it was 'orchestrated': 'It is the deliberate act of anyone who stands in support of white, heterosexual, male, Eurocentric, and status-quo ideology.' This clash led to a second, a *clash of experience*, in which the academy makes no space for the unique experiences associated with non-hegemonic identities. This is a circumstance with which more senior scholars are all too familiar. Richardson (2021) recounts being arrested, jailed, and later harassed by a police officer employed by the same university at which he served as a faculty member, and how this experience was silenced and dismissed by his academic department. Short of intellectual assault on othered identity, a subtler form of othering occurs when academic spaces communicate the message that some are not welcome, and their experiences do not matter. Zoé described being discounted:

> My Spanish-speaking family immigrated directly from Northern Africa, a working-class family. Intellectuals have always been feared or laughed at in my family. Arriving at university, my vocabulary, postures, questions were often perceived as a little 'uncultivated.' I am sometimes criticised for not using words that are 'sophisticated' instead of the hearer reacting to the substance of my remark or question.

Teddy spoke of similar othering due to economic class, as did Samantha regarding a non-traditional journey into academe. These experiences are not unique to CCJ. Scholars across the social sciences have noted their experience of othering, discrimination, and/or marginalization based on gender (Savigny, 2014), class (Langhout, Drake, and Rosselli, 2009), sexuality (Giddings and Pringle, 2011), and race (Patton, 2004). However, in CCJ, the centring of male, middle-class, heterosexual, white experience as the normative ideal invites labelling as 'deviant' those lives diverging from these experiences. Surely, given the variety of human experience, we need answers to the criminal question from more open and inclusive minds.

Third, we found in participants' responses a *clash of perception*, wherein the worldview of othered individuals is structured by assumptions in conflict with those around them, leading to contrary interpretations of the same thing. Rashon had 'seen professors attempt to convince their students that they could be overthinking when they experience inequality and should "not think too highly of themselves"', alluding that perceiving inequitable treatment was evidence of undue self-importance. Zoé recounted being dismissed in a public forum by a postdoctoral researcher. Her narrative illustrated the essential dilemma of differential experience where one is privileged as more legitimate than another and those closer to, or emulating, the hegemonic archetype are held to have unique access to a supposedly universal truth. In discounting Zoé's position unequivocally, 'being in a dominant position, he did not even feel the need to justify his "criticism"'. 'What's violent,' she explained, 'is censorship, that feeling of not having a say.' This once again invokes major debates existing across the social sciences, including the epistemic destruction wrought by European man's replacement of the Christian God as sole perceiver of universal and omnipotent truth (Castro-Gómez, 2005). That Zoé's story involves abuse of power by a postdoctoral researcher, and not tenured faculty, illustrates not only the complexity of academic power dynamics but also the extent to which coloniality pervades the lowest rungs of academic authority—a mark of successful cognitive imperialist strategy.

Finally, there is a *clash of connection*, in that othered CCJ scholars have a connection to our subjects of study that may not be shared by our colleagues. For most academics, those they study are indeed Other. In contrast, many othered academics (though not all) study those groups they identify as Us (i.e. their own social groups).

Identification with the study subject is present in Blount-Hill and St. John's (2017a, p. 120) autoethnographic study:

> Imbued with religious meaning, I was told that the gifts given to me by God required my gratitude through service to others . . . I have sought to bring more minorities into the field, to work with, publish with, teach and mentor others who have struggled like me.

Connection to our subjects, though, is not always a healing experience. Reflecting on racialized events throughout 2020, McCoy's (2021) personalization and internalization of numerous tragedies produced 'a myriad of emotions including anger, exhaustion, sadness, frustration' (p. 5). After the Paris tragedy in November 2015, Ajil (2015a) composed 'Tears of Wrath', documenting trepidation at the coming Islamophobia and the negative consequences that would befall Europe's Muslims, of which he was one. Identification with the subject inherently comes with deeply felt and personalized frustration with injustice.

Disjuncture between the cognitive, affective, cultural, and experiential proximity of othered scholars to their subjects of study versus their peers is a difference in positionality that, when situated as a zero-sum preference, necessitates either conflict or assimilation (e.g. Tapia and Martinez, 2017). For criminologists called on to answer the criminal question, we propose at least causes for concern. First, many simply will not endure. Clashes between othered academics and CCJ hegemony often cause those othered to withdraw to themselves and their allies, disconnecting from those closer to the hegemonic archetype (Crichlow, 2017). Social distance creates conditions for further clash. Zoé reported 'what I might call "petty bourgeois violence": A colleague and I were criticised for spending too much time on our paid jobs outside of school because this could undermine the work of our study groups. It was "irresponsible on our part"'. Furthermore, a choice between marginalization or assimilation will inhibit rigorous consideration of what criminologists study and how societies use their scholarship. Kidman's (2020) cohort of senior Māori scholars paint the picture of careers stalled and under-resourced, of constrained influence on important aspects of university life, let alone larger social or political spheres. In the alternative, they bemoan the plight of Māori ECAs 'under increasing pressure to set aside decolonising research agendas in favour of more compliant forms of intellectual labour that do not place their careers at risk or challenge the status quo' (p. 258). As authors, we do not claim to have a resolution for this circumstance, but we present, in the following sections, how we, our respondents, and other scholars navigate them.

Reorienting and Responding to Cognitive Imperialism

Reflecting on cognitive imperialism provided insight into our responses to hegemony in academe and society. Among the first was a collage of negative emotions. Ajil and Blount-Hill (2020) reported 'frustration and helplessness' (p. 96), 'indignation, destabilization, and frustration' (p. 97). Zoé reported anger: 'Most of the time, I am angry. I know things will "come out badly" if I speak when angry, so I say nothing, let nothing show, and feel bad afterwards.' Such sentiments are reflective of emotions described throughout the literature: 'angry and defensive' (Pizarro, 2017); '[e]xasperated' (Sykes, 2021, p. 7); 'anger . . . disillusionment and frustration' (Hawkins, 2021, p. 2). Loneliness and isolation are common reactions to othering, as Zoé confirms: 'The worst part is obviously feeling alone; there is never a [supportive] reaction [from others], neither during nor after [an incident]' (also Crichlow, 2017; Mitchell, 2021).

Chief among emotional responses was fear. Fighting cognitive imperialism can be detrimental to one's professional aspirations. Zoé noted: 'I have a certain activist orientation in my research, which is sometimes discrediting. I am not "a real" scientist because I have political ideas.' Blount-Hill and St. John (2017a, p. 120) reported of their subjects, J and Z:

> Z found it 'disheartening to have to worry about the appeal of my career simply because I desire to address [racial disparity in the criminal justice system] with my time and energy', and J testified that '[t]here were moments this priority caused tension with my colleagues and professors'.

Aubrey also:

> I've often not tweeted [i.e. published via the social media mobile phone application and website Twitter] or even liked or retweeted certain thoughts in fear of being labeled a complainer, too radical, or leftist. There's this conscious and unconscious decision-making that prohibits me from speaking candidly in professional (read: White) spaces. Any perceived indiscretion will tank any possibility in landing a job, especially when also researching less mainstream topics.

Zoé provided a narrative supporting this fear:

> I was at a table and a professor criticized researchers who see domination relationships everywhere, who 'oppress others with their politicized research.' Shortly before, it had been remarked that I was 'too politicized.' Nobody else reacted; on the contrary, people nodded, 'Yes, it is painful. These politicized people do not do good science because they are not objective.' When I responded, an unconstructive quarrel ensued and my credibility was damaged because I am seen as politicized.

Rashon wrote of 'many instances where I have been perceived as too defensive or too much like a "victim" '.

We also found support for the coping behaviours noted by Ajil and Blount-Hill (2020). Respondents and others (e.g. Sykes, 2021; Warren, 2021) self-policed so as not to show their emotions. Notably, Zoé's story shows that this strategy denies one's voice and leads to disconnection from one's colleagues. She wrote, '[I] speak only when I am 100% sure what to say', supporting Ajil's (2015b) assessment that 'The fundamental right to err is not equally distributed.' Teddy wrote, 'I found myself choosing when to speak up, since it was draining responding to all of them and seemed to have no effect.' Zoé went on: 'Another strategy I put in place is not to talk about my private life, especially the perceived feminine aspects of my private life, at work.' Teddy took a similar stance, writing that one way of coping was 'tuning out certain people or keeping non-Black students at armlength'. Not sharing with those around you the joy of a new birth, an exciting personal achievement, interesting hobby, or day-to-day ups and downs, we presume protects the individual from the assault of cognitive imperialism but also precludes support from their social environment. Inhibited by fear, disturbed by anger, and exhausted of disappointment, how can we hope to innovatively answer the criminal question under such conditions?

As we had, others sought legitimacy and defended their right to be in academic space. Zoé wrote: 'I spend more time justifying myself than speaking about my research. It is a HUGE waste of time, which could be spent on improving with constructive criticism.' She provided an example: 'I wanted to do research on sexism in policing. People I spoke to at the time told me I couldn't be objective. So, I avoided this subject to protect the perceived scientificity of my work.' The notion of an 'objective' social science, much less one whose topic of study is as morally situated as crime and punishment, has been challenged by significant portions of the global academic and global CCJ community (e.g. Aas, 2011). Yet our respondents spanned the United States and Switzerland and converged on this critique, illustrating the still quite prevalent view that ours is an objective science. Even if limited in scope, this standard is used to police the possibilities of creative answers to the criminal question from a significant number of emerging and continuing scholars. In this environment, we found that othered academics felt the burden to overachieve. While virtually all ECAs struggle with so-called 'imposter syndrome' (Wilkinson, 2020)—a sense that they are not as qualified as others in their profession—many of our respondents spoke of an externalized version of the feeling. They felt that *their colleagues* did not believe them to be as qualified as others in their profession. Rashon wrote: 'I have to bring a work ethic that dispels myths about students similar to me.' 'I would say a lot of my drive comes from my parent's desire to disprove stereotypes of their (my) race and socio-economic class', Aubrey agreed, which tracked closely with similar statements by Teddy. Zoé confessed that, '[t]o compensate, I try to work a lot; I know that I am "behind" because of my background, something that will haunt me'.

In retrospect, these mechanisms were widespread but not necessarily healthy. Zoé wrote: 'It would be easier if I didn't have to struggle with my own perception of my legitimacy and the image the academic world constructs of me.' She continued:

> It makes me very aggressive, always trying to convince people that, despite my ovaries, my daughter, lack of bourgeois references, and my attraction to anarchism, I know how to do science. I find myself not wanting to listen or being harder on people from the dominant group. I don't really know what to do with that. I was talking with a friend who has the same feeling. We are so used to putting on boxing gloves to defend ourselves that suddenly we wear them all the time, even when perhaps we shouldn't.

Recover and Reform: Seeking Constructive Ways Forward

Two healthier means of coping were the search for community among other othered and the empowerment that comes with challenging othering in its many guises—'cathartic processes through which we regain our rightful agency and can be our true empowered selves' (Blount-Hill, 2021, p. 94). By far the most common reprieve was reliance on 'community'. Samantha argues, 'Being on the margins is a force for forging and strengthening ties with "other" people.' Zoé described these as 'people with whom I get along, who show a certain kindness'. Rashon creates 'my own space, which allows me to stay authentic. By that, I mean surrounding myself with other people who understand (or at least give the extra effort to) and respect my walk of life.' Teddy found community with Black scholars-in-training in his doctoral programme. 'Not having to codeswitch or deal with white people when we're together has been a source of relief', he bluntly admitted. Aubrey described a similar strategy:

> I find solace in other scholars similar to me. I seek comrades in online academic spaces such as Twitter and Instagram [both social media mobile applications and websites] who amplify their marginalized experience in academia. Finding spaces that are understanding, accepting, and believing of your experience assists with not only keeping my mental health in check, but finding potential collaborators and building a network.

Communities feature mentors, individuals who provide scholarly or professional guidance in encouraging and reassuring ways. Teddy took advantage of two types. Junior scholars naturally seek mentorship from more senior faculty members, those with, as Aubrey explained, 'the most power to help us minoritized students succeed'. Teddy mentioned, 'A Black faculty advisor has been good. Being first author on a project is something I doubt would have happened with non-Black professors.' Teddy also related experience with a *peer* mentor, a not-so-senior scholar who nonetheless provided guidance and support:

> Our first published collaboration came at a time when I thought the idea for it was irrelevant because a faculty member I talked with said my reference theory was insignificant in CJ. Having my peer mentor vindicate my idea did make me feel better; that it became a publication was even more rewarding.

Regarding mentors, though, Rashon was careful to manage expectations and take account of what they could offer and what they could not. 'Each of my mentors serves a different role in my life. Coming to terms with that has saved me from a lot of disappointment.'

These practices led, for our respondents, to a state we call *recovery*. Often a temporary outcome and recurrent need, we use this term to denote those periods when marginalized scholars feel rejuvenated, excited once again about opportunities to achieve 'success' in their academic careers. Only, after deeper contemplation of their experience, scholars tended to shift their definitions of 'success' to encompass instead resistance and reform: 'Having found our own healing, we may then turn our attention to liberating still more of the colonized other and fighting this colonising system' (Blount-Hill, 2021, p. 94). Key to this was the development of what Ajil has called an *indigenous eye*, the *othered lens* described earlier. Zoé noted 'a sensitivity developed by having experienced dispossession of legitimacy; this allows one to begin to imagine the experiences of others'. She continues, 'Having been "the other" makes me vigilant (I hope!) to various forms of violence the dominant hegemony tries to pass off as harmless.' Aubrey thought her otherness made her:

> hypervigilant of the oppressive structures inherent in academic spaces. I practice personal self-reflection and a trained eye to reflexivity and positionality within my own scholarly work and teaching. People who possess marginalized identities are the most qualified for not only speaking on their lived experiences, but also [on] how institutions of oppression affect others.

Aubrey's suggestion that the lived experience can itself become a vector of decolonial thought and practice resonates with existing scholarship (Earle, 2016; Goddard-Durant et al., 2021; Mbaki et al., 2021). Moreover, a desire to dismantle imperialist structures appears responsible for a significant portion of othered scholars' work in perspectives like decolonization. Rashon's work provided an apt illustration, echoing sentiments found in the story of others throughout the literature (e.g. Brooms and Brice, 2017; Brown, 2021):

> My discipline focuses on Black and Brown offending and other negative issues. I believe this is limiting. To ultimately help the people in this population, we need more research that highlights what works in these communities and how marginalized populations have historically come together to resist structural inequality. I do not give voice to, but rather amplify the voices of marginalized groups. It is imperative that we show people that knowledge is not produced only by people with degrees, but also by people with firsthand experience of the issues that we research. I also implement different classroom activities that challenge the assumptions of my students. We often have assumptions not grounded in anything other than bias. Pointing that out in my classroom is important and gives me hope that I am preparing my students to be less discriminatory once they are in the field [i.e., employed within the criminal legal system].

Conclusion

We set out to write this chapter based on the premise that while colonization includes undeniably—and most importantly (Tuck and Yang, 2012; Chandrashekar, 2018)—the physical oppression and subordination of indigenous peoples, special attention must also be given to the ways that colonial power advances and maintains itself by producing hegemonic knowledge to legitimate and consolidate its authority and discredit challenges to the status quo. Hegemonic dominance can come through sheer intellectual 'force', dominating discussion and silencing other voices. However, it may also be more insidious as it permeates from nation- and group-levels to the individual. The goal of colonizing structures is to colonize their subjects' minds. Colonization of the mind is *what happens* (or, rather, what can happen) to the colonized. The *justification* and *doing* of colonizing is what we refer to as *cognitive imperialism*. Our thoughts on this concept are ongoing and still being refined, but our intent is to bring attention to the socialization and other processes that cause individuals and groups of *both* the colonized and colonizing classes to internalize hegemonic discourses. We caution that this process is likely particularly intensive during the first years of an academic's professional identity-formation.

Based on an analysis of data collected in different contexts—primarily our own published and non-published autoethnographic work and a reaction study involving five graduate students from the United States and Switzerland—we explore the ways in which the Other in academia engages with cognitive imperialism. We found evidence of several recurring themes. Although certainly overlapping, iterative, and far from linear, there is recognition of and reflection on instances of exposure to hegemonic knowledge. There are moments of reorientation and response, where we develop strategies of coping with or avoiding cognitive imperialism. Finally, there are instances where we recover and seek reform, usually as a long-term endeavour, so that our everyday efforts challenge the status quo and mitigate the impacts of oppressive knowledge structures.

Engaging with the plurality of ways in which cognitive imperialism affects all researchers, othered or not, and how they, in turn, engage with it is, in our view, of crucial importance to the decolonization of academic scholarship and was precisely the aspiration of this chapter. The project of decolonization is multifaceted but must, as one prong in such efforts, include expanding the circle of perspectives considering the criminal question. To conclude, it may be worthwhile dwelling on the fact that this work is, per se, part of our ongoing effort to recover and seek reform. After all, 'becoming a post-[or de-] colonial autoethnographer is not a ceremonial moment that signifies the complete departure from colonizing research; it marks the beginning of and a pledge for our continuous labor of self-reflective interrogation . . .' (Toyosaki, 2018, p. 35; brackets added). We have found that combining forces and exchanging with others who negotiate otherness in their daily scholarly work has been a way to build strength, give hope, and co-construct a vision for a better future. As Samantha puts it: 'These strengths and resources put together are certainly the key to making the voices that tend to be relegated, silenced, discredited, etc., *heard*.' Let these words drive us in our efforts towards more inclusive, more respectful, and more sustainable scholarship.

References

Aas, K. F. (2012) '"The Earth is one but the world is not": Criminological theory and its geopolitical divisions', *Theoretical Criminology*, 16(1), pp. 5–20.

Agozino, B. (2003) *Counter-Colonial Criminology: A Critique of Imperialist Reason*. London: Pluto Press.

Ajil, A. (2015a) 'Tears of wrath', Mesopaq blog, 13 November. Available at: https://mesopaq.wordpress.com/2015/11/15/tears-of-wrath/ (accessed 10 June 2022).

Ajil, A. (2015b) 'Where I am from', Mesopaq blog, 28 March. Available at: https://mesopaq.wordpress.com/2015/03/28/where-i-am-from/ (accessed 10 June 2022).

Ajil, A. (2020) 'Politico-ideological violence: Zooming in on grievances', *European Journal of Criminology*, 19(2), pp. 304–321.

Ajil, A. and Blount-Hill, K. (2020) '"Writing the other as other": Exploring the othered lens in academia using collaborative autoethnography', *Decolonizing of Criminology and Justice*, 2(1), pp. 83–108.

Al-Kassimi, K. (2017) 'The U.S. informal empire: US African Command (AFRICOM) expanding the US economic-frontier by discursively securitizing Africa using exceptional speech acts', *African Journal of Political Science and International Relations*, 11(11), pp. 301–316.

Aliverti, A., Carvalho, H., Chamberlen, A. et al. (2021) 'Decolonizing the criminal question', *Punishment & Society*, 23(3), pp. 297–316.

Blount-Hill, K. (2020) 'Advancing a social identity model of system attitudes', *International Annals of Criminology*, 57(1–2), pp. 114–137.

Blount-Hill, K. (2021) 'Writing another as other: A retro-inro-extrospection', Decolonization of Criminology and *Justice*, 3(1), pp. 92–102.

Blount-Hill, K. and St. John, V. J. (2017a) 'Manufactured "mismatch": Cultural incongruence and Black experience in the academy', *Race and Justice*, 7(2), pp. 110–126.

Blount-Hill, K. and St. John, V. J. (2017b) '"Manufactured" mismatch: Cultural incongruence and Black experience in the academy', John Jay Research, 18 April. Available at: https://johnjayresearch.commons.gc.cuny.edu/2018/04/18/manufactured-mismatch-cultural-incongruence-and-black-experience-in-the-academy/ (accessed 10 June 2022).

Blount-Hill, K., St. John, V. J., Moton, L. et al. (2022) 'In their experience: a review of racial and sexual minority experience in academe and proposals for building an inclusive criminology', *Race and Justice*, 12(3), pp. 457–480.

Brooms, D. R. and Brice, D. A. (2017) 'Bring the noise: Black men teaching (race and) white privilege', *Race and Justice*, 7(2), pp. 144–159.

Brown, R. A. (2021) 'There can be more than one: A black man's journey through the academy', *Race and Justice*, 11(3), pp. 276–287.

Carrington, K., Hogg, R., and Sozzo, M. (2016) 'Southern criminology', *British Journal of Criminology*, 56(1), pp. 1–20.

Carson, K. and O'Malley, P. (1989) 'The institutional foundations of contemporary Australian criminology', *Journal of Sociology*, 25(3), pp. 333–355.

Castro-Gómez, S. (2005) *La hybris del punto cero: Ciencia, raza e ilustración en la Nueva Granada (1750–1816)*, 2nd edn. Bogotá: Pontificia Universidad Javeriana.

Chandrashekar, S. (2018) 'Not a metaphor: Immigrant of color autoethnography as a decolonial move', *Cultural Studies ↔ Critical Methodologies*, 18(1), pp. 72–79.

Crichlow, V. J. (2017) 'The solitary criminologist: Constructing a narrative of Black identity and alienation in the academy', *Race and Justice*, 7(2), pp. 179–195.

Deckert, A. and Tauri, J. (2019) 'Editorial', *Decolonization of Criminology and Justice*, 1(1), pp. 1–4.

Dimou, E. (2021) 'Decolonizing Southern criminology: What can the "decolonial option" tell us about challenging the modern/colonial foundations of criminology?', *Critical Criminology*, 29, pp. 431–450.

Dugassa, B. F. (2011) 'Colonialism of mind: Deterrent of social transformation', *Sociology Mind*, 1(2), pp. 55–64.

Dukas, R. (2004) 'Evolutionary biology of animal cognition', *Annual Review of Ecology, Evolution and Systematics*, 35, pp. 347–374.

Earle, R. (2016) *Convict Criminology: Inside and Out*. Bristol: Policy Press.

Fanon, F. (2005 [1963]) Philcox, R. (trans.) *The Wretched of the Earth*. New York: Grove Press. Available at: https://grattoncourses.files.wordpress.com/2019/12/frantz-fanon-richard-philcox-jean-paul-sartre-homi-k.-bhabha-the-wretched-of-the-earth-grove-press-2011.pdf (accessed 10 June 2022).

Giddings, L. S. and Pringle, J. K. (2011) 'Heteronormativity at work: Stories from two lesbian academics', *Women's Studies Journal*, 25(2), pp. 91–100.

Goddard-Durant, S., Sieunarine, J. A., and Doucet, A. (2021) 'Decolonising research with black communities: Developing equitable and ethical relationships between academic and community stakeholders', *Families, Relationships and Societies*, 10(1), pp. 189–196.

Gramsci, A. (1971) Hoare, Q. (ed.) and Smith, G. N. (trans.). *Selections from the Prison Notebooks of Antonio Gramsci*. New York: International Publishers. Available at: https://ia800503.us.archive.org/17/items/AntonioGramsciSelectionsFromThePrisonNotebooks/Antonio-Gramsci-Selections-from-the-Prison-Notebooks.pdf (accessed 10 June 2022).

Grosfoguel, R. (2011) 'Decolonizing post-colonial studies and paradigms of political-economy: Transmodernity, decolonial thinking, and global coloniality', *Transmodernity*, 1(1), pp. 1–37.

Hawkins, D. F. (2021) 'A racism burnout: My life as a black academic', *Race and Justice*, 11(3), pp. 301–317.

Heywood, A. (1994) *Political Ideas and Concepts: An Introduction*. London: Macmillan.

Kidman, J. (2020) 'Whither decolonisation? Indigenous scholars and the problem of inclusion in the neoliberal university', *Journal of Sociology*, 56(2), pp. 247–262.

Kim, J. (2012), 'The birth of academic subalterns: How do foreign students embody the global hegemony of American universities?', Journal of Studies in International Education, 16(5), pp. 455–476.

Kim, M. E. (2020) 'Anti-carceral feminism: The contradictions of progress and the possibilities of counter-hegemonic struggle', *Affilia*, 35(3), pp. 309–326.

Kitossa, T. (2012) 'Criminology and colonialism: Counter colonial criminology and the Canadian context', *The Journal of Pan African Studies*, 4(10), pp. 204–226.

Kurtz, D. V. (1996) 'Hegemony and anthropology: Gramsci, exegeses, reinterpretations', *Critique of Anthropology*, 16(2), pp. 103–135.

Langhout, R. D., Drake, P., and Rosselli, F. (2009) 'Classism in the university setting: Examining student antecedents and outcomes', *Journal of Diversity in Higher Education*, 2(3), pp. 166–181.

Macoun, A. (2016) 'Colonising White Innocence: Complicity and Critical Encounters', in Maddison, S., Clark, T., and Costa, R. de (eds) *The Limits of Settler Colonial Reconciliation: Non-Indigenous People and the Responsibility to Engage*. Singapore: Springer.

Maldonado-Torres, N. (2007) 'On the coloniality of being: Contributions to the development of a concept', *Cultural Studies*, 21(2–3), pp. 240–270.

Mathiesen, K. (2015) 'Informational justice: A conceptual framework for social justice in library and information services', *Library Trends*, 64(2), pp. 198–225.

Mbaki, Y., Todorova, E., and Hagan, P. (2021) 'Diversifying the medical curriculum as part of the wider decolonising effort: A proposed framework and self-assessment resource toolbox', *The Clinical Teacher*, 18(5), pp. 459–466.

McCoy, H. (2021) 'What do you call a black woman with a PhD? A n*****: How race trumps education no matter what', *Race and Justice*, 11(3), pp. 318–327.

Mignolo, W. D. (2007) 'Introduction: Coloniality of power and de-colonial thinking', *Cultural Studies*, 21(2-3), pp. 155–167.

Mitchell, O. (2021) 'Tokenism in criminology and criminal justice departments: Problems and solutions', *Race and Justice*, 11(3), pp. 338–346.

Patton, T. O. (2004) 'Reflections of a black woman professor: Racism and sexism in academia', *Howard Journal of Communications*, 15(3), pp. 185–200.

Phillips, C. and Bowling, B. (2003) 'Racism, ethnicity and criminology. Developing minority perspectives', *British Journal of Criminology*, 43(2), pp. 269–290.

Pizarro, J. (2017) 'The uncivil Latina', Race and *Justice*, 7(2), pp. 160–178.

Quijano, A. (2000) 'Coloniality of power, Eurocentrism, and Latin America', Nepantla: Views from the *South*, 1(3), pp. 533–580.

Quijano, A. (2007 [1992]) Therborn, S. (trans.) 'Coloniality and modernity/rationality', *Cultural Studies*, 21(2), pp. 168–178.

Richardson, J. (2021) '"No CAP": Reflections on the intersectionality, positionality and the experiences of navigating race as a black male criminologist', *Race and Justice*, 11(3), pp. 260–275.

Rowlands, J. (2015) 'Turning collegial governance on its head: Symbolic violence, hegemony and the academic board', *British Journal of Sociology of Education*, 36(7), pp. 1017–1035.

Russell-Brown, K. (2021) 'Black Lives Matter in criminology? Let's prove it', *Race and Justice*, 11(3), pp. 328–337.

Savigny, H. (2014) 'Women, know your limits: Cultural sexism in academia', *Gender and Education*, 26(7), pp. 794–809.

Sykes, B. L. (2021) 'Academic turning points: How microaggressions and macroaggressions inhibit diversity and inclusion in the academy', *Race and Justice*, 11(3), pp. 288–300.

Tapia, M. and Martinez, R. O. (2017) 'Ethics review and the minority ethnographer: A case study in racialized invalidation', *Race and Justice*, 7(2), pp. 127–143.

Toyosaki, S. (2018) 'Toward de/postcolonial autoethnography: Critical relationality with the academic second persona', Cultural Studies ↔ Critical *Methodologies*, 18(1), pp. 32–42.

Tuck, E. and Yang, K. W. (2012) 'Decolonization is not a metaphor', *Decolonization: Indigeneity, Education & Society*, 1(1), pp. 1–40.

wa Thiong'o, N. (2011 [1986]) *Decolonising the Mind: The Politics of Language in African Literature*. Melton: James Currey Ltd.

Warren, P. Y. (2021) 'The room where it happens: Reflections on being a black woman in the academy', *Race and Justice*, 11(3), pp. 347–354.

Wilkinson, C. (2020) 'Imposter syndrome and the accidental academic: An autoethnographic account', *International Journal for Academic Development*, 25(4), pp. 363–374.

Willis, A. (2017) '9 of the most powerful quotes from Ngũgĩ wa Thiong'o's public lecture', HuffPost, 3 March. Available at: https://www.huffingtonpost.co.uk/2017/03/03/9-powerful-things-ngugi-said-at-his-public-lecture_a_21872421/ (accessed 10 June 2022).

Woodson, C. G. (2009 [1933]) *The Mis-Education of the Negro*. Fresno, CA: *Journal of Pan African Studies*. Available at: www.jpanafrican.org/ebooks/3.4eBookThe%20Mis-Education.pdf (accessed 10 June 2022).

Conclusion

Teasing Out the Criminal Question, Building a Decolonizing Horizon

Ana Aliverti, Henrique Carvalho, Anastasia Chamberlen, and Máximo Sozzo

Overview

As we pointed out in the Introduction, the project of decolonizing the criminal question is ambitious. The identification of colonial and neocolonial effects in such a vast and complex field of actors and institutions, discourses, and practices, all of which constitute the criminal question in contemporary societies, is a complex and multifaceted task. Therefore, pursuing such ambition can only be the result of a collective effort on the part of committed social researchers working both in the Global North and in the Global South. As we also highlighted in the Introduction, such effort has been undertaken with greater intensity in recent years and we hope this collective book contributes to this ongoing effort.

In this final chapter, we assess the achievements of such decolonizing efforts so far, dialoguing with the different chapters that make up the book and, more generally, with the recent literature on the subject. We also seek to map an agenda for future work within the framework of this collaborative and collective project. In this sense, we understand decolonization as both a work of tearing apart (and teasing out), and building up, which involves intellectual, political, and ethical dimensions. The structure of this chapter broadly follows the three axes that we defined as crucial for this decolonizing project in the Introduction. First, it addresses the relationship of colonialism with the production and circulation of knowledge regarding the criminal question. Then, the chapter discusses how to approach the issue of the influence and embedment of coloniality on institutions and practices of criminal justice and social control. Third, through a reflection on methodology, we scrutinize the possibility and manifestations of struggle and resistance against colonial legacies, matrices, and logics. The chapter ends with an analysis of the political and ethical dimensions involved in the effort of decolonizing the criminal question.

Ana Aliverti, Henrique Carvalho, Anastasia Chamberlen, and Máximo Sozzo, *Conclusion* In: *Decolonizing the Criminal Question.*
Edited by: Ana Aliverti, Henrique Carvalho, Anastasia Chamberlen, and Máximo Sozzo, Oxford University Press.
 DOI: 10.1093/oso/9780192899002.003.0020

Problematizing and Dismantling Dynamics of Hierarchization, Subordination, and Dependency in Knowledge Production and Circulation

Criminology, in its original foundation from a positivist matrix, emerged in the last quarter of the nineteenth century as a 'scientific discipline' whose object was the 'criminal'—understood as a manifestation of otherness, of a biological and psychological nature, strongly racialized and classed. Born in the European context, this construction immediately spread globally, including vast regions of the Global South. It was based on the broader dynamics of exporting and importing allegedly 'scientific' problems, methods, concepts, and arguments, and to a large extent was used to justify practices of exploitation and domination. The birth and development of criminology, and the forms of governance that it advocated for were embedded in the broader processes of colonization and (neo)colonization, in their various forms, which simultaneously reproduced and deepened their effects (Agozino, 2003; 2004; Carrington and Hogg, 2017; Carrington et al., 2019, pp. 17–19; Moore, this volume; Rodrigues Santos, this volume).

Since that moment of emergence of positivist criminology, profound inequalities between different parts of the world in the production and circulation of knowledge on the criminal question articulated in the strong predominance of a handful of national contexts from the Global North, of the imperial metropolises, of the central countries, in relation to the Global South, the colonies and ex-colonies, the peripheral countries. This hierarchy implied subordination and dependence of disadvantaged contexts and intellectuals. It prioritized and naturalized a style of intellectual production in the Global North, which postulated the universality of its problems, methods, concepts, and arguments, hiding their particularity and specificity (Chakrabarty, 2000; Connell, 2007). In turn, this was articulated with the uncritical importation of these intellectual artefacts by researchers from the Global South, who committed to apply them to their own contexts, generating local empirical data that reinforced the appearance of universality, the 'context-free', timeless and placeless, character of that intellectual production of the Global North. As Iturralde (this volume) shows, such knowledge has been consequential in the design and implementation of public policies around crime control and punishment.

This hierarchy, subordination, and dependency between different regions of the world in the production and circulation of knowledge on the criminal question, built during the 'golden age' of positivist criminology between the end of the nineteenth century and the beginning of the twentieth century, did not disappear despite the subsequent decline of this paradigm. Notwithstanding the great theoretical mutations that emerged out of alternative criminological perspectives developed in the United States during the first half of the twentieth century—particularly within the Chicago School of Sociology—the dynamics of hierarchization, subordination, and dependency were not questioned. Indeed, since the second half of the twentieth century, the criminological 'boom', especially in the United States and the UK (and, to some extent, in other English-speaking countries, with different depth and periodicity), with its impressive process of institutionalization—departments, scientific journals, full-time positions for professors and researchers, undergraduate and postgraduate programmes, etc. (Loader and Sparks, 2011; 2013)—has only consolidated and deepened these global inequalities in this field of knowledge.

Rather paradoxically, these global inequalities in the production and circulation of criminological knowledge deepened at the time in which critical theories in this field of study, with their different orientations—'labelling', 'radical', 'feminist', 'abolitionist', etc.—emerged, putting social inequality and injustice at the centre of debates on the criminal question. However, these critical perspectives—in their majority—did not problematize the 'geographical applicability' (Aas, 2012, p. 6) of their own theoretical and normative constructions, reproducing the long-term phenomenon of taking their universal character for granted, thus replicating approaches from which they sought to separate themselves (Cunneen, 2011, p. 250; Moosavi, 2019, p. 259). Now, as we pointed out in the Introduction, it is also true that such critical approaches gave impetus to the development of 'Southern', 'counter-colonial', 'decolonial', 'postcolonial' perspectives that have emerged, first in a more isolated way but, especially in the last decade, with an extraordinarily wide level of strength and diffusion. These perspectives have decidedly problematized this hierarchy, subordination, and dependency in the production and circulation of knowledge on the criminal question between various regions of the world under contemporary conditions (Agozino, 2003; 2004; Cunneen, 2011; Medina, 2011; Aas, 2012; Carrington, Hogg, and Sozzo, 2016; Zaffaroni and Codino, 2015; Carrington et al., 2018; 2019; Moosavi, 2019; Travers, 2019; Aliverti et al., 2021).[1]

Decolonizing the criminal question implies questioning this state of affairs within this field of study (as well as the dynamics that sustain it) and generating concrete steps for its dismantling. To this end, we identify some of these steps, raised in recent literature and conveyed in this book. Before delving into these, we note that any steps to democratize the study of the criminal question should understand the production of academic knowledge as being in part the outcome of the material and structural conditions that enable or thwart it. Indeed, the inequalities in the production and circulation of knowledge between central and peripheral contexts are based not only on ways of thinking that are constructed in the academic worlds of both types of scenarios, following established historical trajectories, but are also anchored in the radical disparity of the material conditions for social research on the criminal question between these areas. In vast underprivileged regions of the world, academics and researchers have a pervasive experience of low wages, lack of funds for the development of empirical research, difficulties in accessing intellectual production that is published in commercial media (books, academic journals, etc.), lack of access to data, and state actors and institutions related to social control, lack of specialized postgraduate programmes, and limited career paths (Medina, 2011, pp. 14–17; Carrington et al., 2019, pp. 185–186; Moosavi, 2019, pp. 259–260). To all this, we may add the consolidation of English as the lingua franca of the communication of academic production in this field, generated from the central countries, which produce various effects of exclusion for researchers who live and work in non-English-speaking countries and face a whole

[1] In dialogue with the more general, similarly growing scholarship in the social sciences (among many others, Connell, 2006; 2007; Comaroff and Comaroff, 2012; Mignolo, 2011; 2012; Sousa Santos, 2014; 2018).

series of difficulties in writing and publishing in this language (Medina, 2011, pp. 17–18; Faraldo Cabana, 2018; Moosavi, 2019, p. 260). For all this, it is no coincidence that it is easier to plan programmatically than to carry out these crucial steps towards decolonizing the production and circulation of knowledge on the criminal question (Moosavi, 2019, p. 258; Travers, 2019, p. 11; Sozzo, 2021, p. 80). Any decolonizing effort should place these structural inequalities centre stage, but it should do so not just to highlight limitations in achieving 'Northern standards'. Importantly, we can also understand the character of these structural conditions as a springboard to develop certain methodological sensibility and theoretical innovation upon questions of social injustice and marginalization (see Bracco Bruce and Bandyopadhyay, this volume).

An important task in this direction is the construction of a historical research agenda on criminology in peripheral contexts, rescuing the crucial authors and texts, especially when they have moved beyond the uncritical importation of problems, methods, concepts, and arguments generated in central contexts (Carrington et al., 2019, p. 6). Even during the 'golden age' of positivist criminology, it is possible to find episodes and moments of resistance, which involved various forms of theoretical inventiveness. In Latin America, for instance, examples have been identified, ranging from the problematization of the relationship between immigration and crime beyond readings that were based on 'individual factors', to the reconstruction of the aetiology and classification of crime, challenging in some measure the thinking of Lombroso and Ferri, in the work of José Ingenieros (Sozzo, 2006, pp. 358–384; 2011; 2017; 2022a). Again, in the Latin American scenario, important original contributions have recently been excavated in the work of critical criminologists of the 1970s and 1980s in relation to the problematization of environmental damage and its links with the extractivism of peripheral capitalism in the research of Rosa del Olmo (Rodríguez Goyes, 2019; 2022). So, too, in the work of Eugenio R. Zaffaroni (Sozzo, 2006, pp. 407–411; Fonseca, 2018, pp. 721–724; García and Sozzo, forthcoming), we can trace efforts to build a dialogue between Southern and Northern criminologists which avoids reproducing an uncritical importation of concepts and theories from the North to the South. This work of remembrance and restoration is an important avenue for contestation of the hegemony of Northern knowledge production, and is still an ongoing process. These exercises not only allow a better understanding of the past, avoiding 'amnesia' (Rodríguez Goyes and South, 2017), but also provide tools to think about the present in peripheral scenarios, as sources of inspiration for contemporary research.

Another central step consists in interrogating the attitude of researchers, both from the peripheral and central contexts, with respect to the uncritical circulation and consumption by the former of knowledge generated in privileged scenarios. Rather than dismissing this knowledge, we advocate revealing the limits of its scope for reconstructing its 'situated' character in a time and place (Aas, 2012, p. 11; Carrington et al., 2019, p. 4). As Mark Brown (2018, pp. 95–97) has stated, rescuing the work of Dipesh Chakrabarty (2000), it is necessary to 'provincialize' this intellectual production (see also, Medina, 2011, p. 19; Carrington et al., 2019, pp. 5–6). Now, this 'provincialization' is only possible from a deep immersion in the peripheral contexts themselves, accounting for an 'embeddedness' of the criminal question in its past and present (Melossi, 2001; Nelken, 2011; Melossi, Sozzo, and

Sparks, 2011) through plural methodological ways, an exercise which a number of the chapters of this book effectively pursue. Through this immersion, it becomes possible to 'decentre' the methods, concepts, and arguments conceived in central contexts and actively reject an attitude of 'application', of uncritical importation, of reproduction of subordination and dependency (Medina, 2011, p. 19; Carrington et al., 2019, pp. 19–20; Bracco Bruce and Cunneen, this volume). Through this kind of 'thick approach', that implies 'looking from the periphery', 'looking from the margin' (Zaffaroni, 1988, p. 3; 1989, pp. 170–172; Aas, 2012, p. 11; Brown, 2018, p. 96), we can painstakingly build a more equitable dialogue with the intellectual productions of the central contexts, carefully subjecting them to an exercise of auscultation, in which it is possible to select and adapt various elements, while at the same time contesting and setting aside others (Aas, 2012, pp. 8, 16; Carrington, Hogg, and Sozzo, 2016, pp. 2–3; Carrington et al., 2019, pp. 2, 5–6, 184; Carrington et al., 2019b, p. 165; Moosavi, 2019, pp. 260–261, 267; Sozzo, 2022b, pp. 375–385; Bandyopadhyay, Bracco Bruce, and Iturralde, this volume). Within the framework of Latin American critical criminology of the 1980s, Zaffaroni argued that this theoretical dialogue between the centre and the periphery is not only 'inevitable' but also 'desirable'. However, this requires overcoming intellectual dependency and subordination, to enable the emergence of what he calls 'syncretic criticism' (Zaffaroni, 1984, p. 75; 1988, p. 4; 1989, p. 175; see García and Sozzo, forthcoming).

At the same time, in this 'syncretic' search, there is extraordinarily fertile ground for the exploration of alternative ways of making sense of dimensions of the contemporary criminal question that have been developed beyond what is recognized as 'scientific' in the Global North, in the traditions and knowledges generated in the Global South, despite the processes of colonization and neocolonization in its various forms (Zaffaroni, 1988, pp. 76, 99; 1989, pp. 173–174; Cunneen, 2011; 2018; this volume; Cunneen and Tauri, 2016; Mehta, 2018; 2023). In this direction, the contribution of Lucia Bracco Bruce (this volume) stands out, who, in order to interpret certain dimensions of the collective life of women in Peruvian prison contexts, rescues and uses the traditional local concepts of *Ayllu* and *Mestizaje*. Likewise, Amanda Wilson's (this volume) exploration of the different meanings of 'healing' in 'therapeutic jurisprudence' language for indigenous peoples, is a compelling illustration of this approach (see also, Cunneen, 2011, pp. 261–263; this volume). 'Doing theory from the South' also involves unsettling and questioning concepts and frameworks which are unfit and inadequate to study the criminal question in the North, subjecting to scrutiny theoretical frameworks premised on North–South differences, and foregrounding global connections linking places, institutions, and people fostered through colonial conquer (Carrington et al., 2016; 2019; Aliverti, 2021; Mehta and Aliverti, 2023; Sozzo, 2022; Harry, O'Reilly, Super, Wassem, this volume).

It is essential to recognize that this is a complex path, which is fraught with the risk of falling into the reproduction of what is established in this field of knowledge and the co-optation of new perspectives and concepts, and thus of failing to realize the radical and critical character of these ideas. Noticing these difficulties, though, is not the same as warding them off.

Finally, one of the main insights of decolonization approaches (and into which many chapters of this book delve) is the exploration of the multiple and persistent effects of colonialism in the institutions and practices of social control, both in central and peripheral contexts in our present. This type of exploration, per se, produces a decolonizing impact, innovating with respect to the repeated neglect by a good part of the intellectual production of the Global North. We now turn to the exploration of such contributions.

Continuities, Discontinues, Permutations, and Erasures in the Colonial Matrix of the Criminal Question

One important issue in decolonial scholarship, which this collection highlights, is how to trace and understand the development of colonial legacies and their influence on contemporary conditions and dynamics. It is now uncontroversial (except perhaps in the most conservative confines of academia, politics, and the media) that the violence and subjection perpetrated through colonialism are not simply matters of historical interest, as they continue to have a lasting effect on contemporary societies in both interpersonal and international relations (Bhattacharyya et al., 2021; Lentin and Lentin, 2006). However, the precise character and shape of these effects can vary significantly depending on the context and also of the perspective applied to examine it.

Perhaps the main trope in scholarship in this field is that of persistence, as it seeks to uncover and highlight the enduring influence of a colonial or imperial past on contemporary conditions and dynamics. The focus here is primarily on tracing the debris left by colonialism, and on uncovering the colonial and imperial formations (Stoler, 2016) that inhabit and condition the present, whose influence is often obscured, if not actively denied by dominant discourses and representations. In so doing, this approach seeks to expose the deep roots of the criminal question and thus challenge the idea that it is possible to properly understand contemporary problems without a significant and critical engagement with their colonial underpinnings. Rodrigues Santos's chapter in this volume offers a compelling illustration of this kind of archaeological work, depicting the persistent othering and subjugation of black and indigenous populations in Brazil in spite of shifts in politics, law, and policy. He argues that this structural violence is likely to be perpetuated unless proper efforts are made to uproot its bases, a problem which is aptly captured by the common saying which he uses as the title of one of the chapter's sections, 'Brazil has a Huge Past Ahead' (see also Phoenix Khan, this volume; Darke and Phoenix Khan, 2021). This theme can also ground a genealogical approach, evidencing how issues that are deemed to be new and contemporary reveal themselves as reiterations of practices and processes with a much longer history (see also Moore, 2015; de Noronha, 2019). For instance, Ghabrial's chapter insightfully discusses how the notion of 'border criminality', which has become one of the defining aspects of crime control in the twenty-first century, can be linked to colonial practices as far back as the nineteenth century.

This predominant theme, in this book as well as in scholarship more broadly, presses us to see coloniality as a living and in many ways dominant force shaping contemporary power relations, structural inequalities, and lived experiences, not just in so-called postcolonial societies but also in the former colonial metropolises, both in relation to marginalized populations (see Earle, Parmar, and Phillips, this volume) and elite settings (see Blount-Hill and Ajil, this volume). It also urges us to recognize the partial, limited, and exclusionary character of hegemonic understandings of historical and contemporary conditions and dynamics, rescuing what has been omitted and suppressed by dominant discourses and narratives (Mignolo, 2011). It thus highlights the need for counter-narratives as part of a decolonial project, as exemplified by Agozino's intervention in this volume.

While a focus on persistent elements and structures is necessary for an understanding of coloniality, a different but equally valuable approach calls our attention to shifts and transformations in colonial matrices of power (Quijano and Ennis, 2000; Iturralde, this volume), scrutinizing how coloniality can take different shapes and lead to new relations of exploitation and subjection. Several contributions in the collection illustrate different ways in which this insight can be mobilized. For instance, Collard shows how techniques of torture developed in a colonial setting can then be exported as a form of expertise to ground new forms of exploitation and subjection in postcolonial scenarios. Harry's chapter, in turn, explores how a colonial legacy can be transformed in a postcolonial setting, permutating in ways that blur the lines between colonized and colonizer in Malaysia. Similar insights can be found in O'Reilly's examination of Cape Verde's strategic use of colonial ties and geopolitical position to craft its leadership in policing matters in Africa, or in Waseem's elaboration of the postcolonial condition of policing in Pakistan and Nigeria and its interrogation in the light of social unrest and public protest. This theme of the transmutation of colonial features, as exemplified by the aforementioned interventions, highlights how colonial legacies are replete with new connections and discontinuities. In this sense, it adds a significant new dimension of enquiry to the theme of persistence, as it analyses not only what has remained the same but also and mainly what has changed, but in a way that nevertheless remains related to and conditioned by colonial and imperial formations.

A decolonial project needs to be keenly attentive to these metamorphoses and permutations of coloniality, to be fully aware of the pervasiveness and, in many ways, the inescapability of colonial and imperial duress in contemporary structures and institutions, particularly those related to the criminal question. This also points to the issue of specificity: although this pervasiveness implies a certain level of universality to the influence of coloniality, awareness of this complexity highlights how there are very different kinds of colonial legacies, each with their own context and peculiarities. While they may certainly share many traits, no two colonial experiences are the same. There are fundamentally different forms of colonialism whose specificity needs to be acknowledged, lest we run the risk of reducing the concept to that of 'original' or 'primitive' colonialism, linked to the long era of European empires from the fifteenth century onwards. Instead, we need to be attentive to the ways in which colonial experiences not only persist after processes of independence, but also how such processes give rise to new, different forms of (neo)colonialism which cannot be understood simply by reference to a colonial past (on this, see Carrington et al., 2016; Stambøl, 2021; Collard and Iturralde, this volume). The allure of essentialism is always present, especially given the influence of universalistic and totalizing perspectives in fields such as criminology. A decolonial effort therefore requires an inherently dialectical lens, which can recognize the uniqueness of experience at the same time as it can acknowledge the connections and relations embedded in it. In order to excavate and appreciate these complexities, a reflection on methodologies is critical, which is the focus of the following section.

To some extent, the choice of which approach to prioritize—whether one that highlights continuities or one that emphasizes transformations and detours—will depend on the context or issue under analysis; some studies will require a better understanding of complexities and nuances, while others might demand a more sustained effort on uncovering linearities and permanence. Nevertheless, an important point of caution that needs to be kept in mind is that not everything is a colonial legacy. Attention to the enduring and forceful influence of coloniality should not itself result in a reductive assumption that every aspect of the criminal question has its roots in the colonial matrix. Rather, it should guide us to locate and explore how coloniality is part of a complex and fluid tapestry in which colonial and imperial legacies react against and interact with other tendencies, structures, and processes. For instance, both Harry's and Waseem's chapters show how colonial debris can fuse with nationalism in postcolonial settings to give rise to new dynamics of criminalization, racialization, and exclusion. In contrast, the chapters by Phoenix Khan, Super, Ravid, and Wilson articulate the cultural dynamics and (neo)liberal penal logics that infiltrate and transmute remnants of the past. Even the most persistent colonial debris suffers transformations and becomes part of new configurations which significantly, even fundamentally, alter their character and effects. Decolonization therefore raises the question not only of how we can think about these legacies, but also how we can rethink them in the light of their multifaceted histories and their interconnected, interrelated, contemporary conditions.

Methodological Approaches: Reflexivity, Narratives of Resistance and Enduring Struggles

For us, the future of decolonizing efforts requires a clear commitment towards a set of methodological lessons we can derive from the studies covered in this collection. These approaches can pave the way for a more robustly critical glance at penal power and injustice and can cast light on their impacts on racialized and marginalized communities. Several authors in this book offer clear guidance as to how to develop and apply such lessons, pointing to vital skills and practices scholars in the field ought to take seriously (e.g. Cunneen, Earle, Parmar, and Phillips, and Moore, in this volume). At a most fundamental level, commitment to methodological alertness would have us regularly revisit *what*, *how*, and *where* to decolonize. Later, we briefly take each of these questions in turn.

First, scholars in this collection have sought to highlight and challenge the conceptual limits and frontiers of the project of criminology as a field of study (e.g. Moore on crime and Super on punishment) and showed that looking at the criminal question, from a Southern lens or from a subaltern context, opens horizons and futures that can enable a rethinking of practices and institutions not only in the periphery but also in the centre. These and other efforts found in the broader scholarship have illustrated that a decolonizing project puts into question the hegemony of established narratives and ideas that have dominated this field of study (Mpofu and Ndlovu-Gatsheni, 2020).

These works have demystified and demythologized Eurocentric theories and epistemologies (Bhambra and Holmwood, 2021) and invite us to 'get a grip' by looking at social problems within a wider frame, allowing the travel of knowledge production which is attentive to local, cultural, discursive, and geopolitical nuance, but is also historically accountable.

Second, in different ways, all the chapters in this collection remind us that the political project of decolonizing is one that first starts by acknowledging reflexively our own status (and privilege) not only professionally, as Blount-Hill and Ajil show in their chapter, but also in the research we conduct and in our relationship with the people we research. Those of us with the academic capital to reach a wider audience—due to geopolitical reasons or institutional or personal status—have a responsibility to promote a more inclusive, collaborative critical criminology that seeks to unsettle established narratives and hegemonies; those with the power to do so need to initiate this effort and have a duty to keep it alive.

But questions of how to decolonize and about the sorts of methodologies most well suited to doing so also alert us to the limits of the fields we research. In large part, our efforts to incorporate in the collection research from underexplored areas and contexts has led us to collaborate with scholars who work at the margins of the field (e.g. historians like Ghabrial, legal scholars like Rodrigues Santos, or anthropologists like Bandyopadhyay) and with criminologists who are comfortable and skilled in engaging with transdisciplinary ideas. Thus, a methodological way forward involves being prepared to go beyond the narrow confines of what has so far been considered criminology (in its institutionalized form in the academic world in some contexts, particularly of the Global North) and engage in dialogue with areas and perspectives more critically advanced elsewhere (culturally, geographically, and intellectually).

Questions of reflexivity about what we study and how we study it also extend to how we speak about and relate with research participants. The chapter by Earle, Parmar, and Phillips clarifies how positionality and biography can impact both research practices as well as the analysis that emerges from the data we collect. Arguably, this is particularly important for decolonizing efforts where often the dynamics between researcher and researched are shaped by colonial legacies and imbalances, and bear the marks of the ongoing oppressive structures that confine knowledge in the hands of some. Questions of power dynamics and structural and biographical categories of race, class, and gender have long been acknowledged as central to reflexive sociology and criminology (Bourdieu and Wacquant, 1992). Likewise, feminist scholars have articulated the relevance of developing research tools that allow us to empathize with and humanize the people we research without essentializing and denying them their agency. Researchers should remain activist, politically attuned, thus pursuing structural change and equality as a core purpose for doing research (Potter and Alcoff, 1993; Gelsthorpe, 1992). As the chapters in this collection show, such approaches can range from archival to ethnographic research and can take many epistemological forms. What matters is how much we are willing to listen to the complex experiences we are recounting and doing so with humility and care (Back, 2007), which is related to the ethical aspect of the decolonizing project which we will consider in the next section.

As the chapters in this collection show, methodologies matter and are critical for highlighting the nuance and complexity when carving out stories of colonial legacies and injustices, as well as for progressing emancipatory aims through scholarship. In so doing, we ought to advance the skills needed to encourage decolonial research that is more phenomenological, more intersectional, more feminist, and from the standpoint of the oppressed. As Bracco Bruce alerts us to in her study of Santa Monica prison in Peru, discursive, cultural, but also intersectional nuance are imperative for advancing decolonial narratives. Her broader work on this subject (Bracco Bruce, 2022) also reminds us that creative, arts-based methods have the capacity to reach, visibilize, and communicate in ways that traditional, Eurocentric, empiricist, and positivist methods cannot achieve, particularly in spaces of control and confinement and in postcolonial settings (see also Back and Puwar, 2013; Chamberlen, 2018).

Agozino, Bracco Bruce, and Harry highlight in this collection the intimate connections between feminist and decolonial approaches; their common political goals and parallel histories. The dialogue between these two perspectives needs to be further invested in and advanced in this field of study; if these are employed together, they hold the promise to concretize, visualize, embody, and voice untold stories, lived experiences, and complex, contradictory accounts that ought not be essentialized or boxed into binary categories and normative thinking. As Hoagland (2012) noted, a hegemonic methodological approach from the metropole is inherently Cartesian, 'inward-turning, promoting cognitive dismissal of all that lies outside its bounds of sense, and resulting in a highly sophisticated Eurocentrism' (p. 101) that reinforces and legitimizes practices of ignorance (Sullivan and Tuana, 2007).

The dialogue between decolonial and feminist theories and methodological approaches can bear many fruitful outcomes, not least their capacity to showcase the struggles and resistances forged in postcolonial settings. They can tell these stories of survival and resistance without orientalizing or infantilizing people and communities. As the studies in the book show, beyond mapping enduring colonial legacies, we also ought to be cognizant of the ways in which these are resisted, opposed, and used as organizing principles for the development of social movements. These movements often go unnoticed by mainstream media and discussions in the Global North, but they can teach us much about the promise of organizing, activism, community care, and solidarity. As the chapters by Bracco Bruce, Ghabrial, and Waseem show, resistance to oppressive structures is ongoing and central to peripheral contexts and is critical to bringing about incremental but radical change. In rescuing the agentic capacity of postcolonial states to leverage their global influence, O'Reilly's chapter also remarks the importance of not falling into patronizing narratives that devoid colonized actors of power. Attention to these is imperative for a decolonial criminology that is also able to offer methodological and theoretical tools.

Finally, a decolonial methodology needs to be nuanced about the 'where' of research, about space and temporal relations within the settings we observe. Many of the authors in this collection have sought to study the jurisdictions they focus on by being part of the postcolonial contexts they research—we have thus sought to include as many chapters as possible that not only theoretically decolonize the criminal question, but empirically investigate how this is done. Many of the authors in this collection are native to the cultures, legal systems, and discourses they engaged with and thus their research can offer insights from the South challenging the long history of criminological work on the 'Other' and questioning the traditional anthropological allure to exceptionalize, exoticize, patronize, and caricature non-European and non-Western contexts. They achieve this by providing needed nuance and detail about their research settings, and by being careful to comprehensively reject the tendency to perpetuate, as Wilson has warned, the saviour mentality. This attention to positionality and proximity is instrumental for a decolonial project on the criminal question.

Politics and Ethics

Throughout the volume, we highlighted the politics and ethics of decolonization. Decolonizing is not a metaphor, but it is concrete and grounded. It is both an intellectual approach and a political movement, thus it is concerned with theory and praxis, and as such shares with other radical traditions, most notably abolitionism and feminism, a deontological concern about social justice. One important aspect is, then, to rescue what has been said in previous sections, acknowledging and interrogating power both in the operation of systems of control and oppression, but also in the production of knowledge about them.

As contributors to this volume have argued, the 'state' is a critical complex site or field to understand the circulation, the enabling, and the operation of penal power. They reject a priori, normative formulations of the '(colonial) state' (in its various forms) as separated from the social and economic fields, static and monolithic, linking its foundations to the people in power (particularly the local elites and foreign actors), and offering an account of it as contextually and historically specific, and in perpetual mutation. Its historical formations and contemporary configurations point to the intricacies between capital accumulation, racial subjugation, colonial expansion, and penal power (Taussig, 1987; Hay and Craven, 2004; Astudillo and Jamieson, 2021).

From Brazil and Colombia to South Africa and Israel, the foundations of the modern state in colonial settings were tightly anchored to corporative interests, in a way that renders contemporary distinctions between state and corporation artificial and inadequate (Stern, 2011; Hibou, 2004; Iturralde and Rodrigues Santos, this volume). Such historical criss-crossing between the public and private, as Super and Waseem (this volume) demonstrated, shaped practices of punishment and policing infusing them with distinct features, including its extra-legal and informal nature. Postcolonial crime control remains closely linked to the establishment of the modern nation-state in colonial settings in other important aspects. In the case of Israel, as Ravin shows, its establishment as an 'imagined community' (Anderson, 2016) (i.e. European, modern, white, and Jewish) 'relied on processes of othering and exclusion of both "Oriental" Jews and Palestinians' that still permeates criminal and border control practices. As Waseem argues in her contribution to this book, in the case of Pakistan and Nigeria, the formation of the state to enable colonial domination remains important for examining the role of the police in quelling popular dissent against the background of police forces tarnished by allegations of brutality and corruption. Such historical scrutiny of the complex politics underpinning the configuration of the contemporary criminal question, she suggests, are critical for its interrogation and decolonization.

The complex historical interface between modern state formation, capital accumulation, and processes of social control necessarily entails that decolonization is a broader political process that seeks to dismantle the global, material, and cultural inequalities which social control institutions and practices contribute to sustaining. It is about tearing apart but also building up. Although portrayed as a utopia, these 'decolonizing futures' are already being crafted and rehearsed through mundane but creative and inventive practices of care and solidarity by ordinary people around the world and transnationally. Such 'politics of life' emerge out of the necessities of everyday life in the most unexpected spaces to support livelihood in the context of disenfranchise and dispossession. They bear important promises for disrupting conceptions of national and individual identity based on fixity, dualism, and homogeneity, opening up new avenues of social and cultural interaction, collaboration, and contestation from below. Some of the chapters of this book attest and speak directly to these grassroots radical interventions (Agozino, Bracco Bruce, and Cunneen, this volume). More research is needed to better document the conditions for the flourishing and fortification of these practices, as a way to build bridges between academia and activism.

So, too, as we argued in the Introduction, academic knowledge forms part of the shaping of the criminal question, and therefore is an object of enquiry in its own right. Decolonization thus involves dissecting and laying bare how academic power operates to silence certain voices and suppress knowledge about actors, places, practices, and histories. The task of revealing academic complicities in the matrix of colonial power on the criminal question demands sustained attention to how criminological knowledge is produced, who produces it, and about what and whom. As contributors in this collection argue, such task requires profound changes to the way criminological knowledge is constructed. It is not about adding 'books to a reading list' (Moore, this volume), or glittering healing in the criminal apparatus and the criminological lexicon (Wilson, this volume). This is a task demanding systemic change on the geographies and identities in and of criminology, as well as the way knowledge is produced, communicated, and circulated (or not) while remaining alert to the politics of (in)visibilities and (un)evenness of such processes. As the volume shows, the politics of knowledge production should not be relegated to a footnote, but rather play a central part in our understanding of the criminal question as itself a site of reproduction and contestation of power forces and relations. It also demands acknowledgement of our active engagement in the inequalities that produce this field and that this field produces. It requires a political and ethical commitment to change these conditions through sustained efforts to include silenced voices and advocate for academic models of funding and collaborations that lead to more democratic production and communication of criminological knowledge.

This brings us to the ethics of producing and communicating this knowledge. To a certain extent, ethical and moral discomforts and dilemmas are inescapable and unavoidable in the academic field, given the disparities of power inherent in the production of knowledge. They are even more marked in criminology. As a field founded on the premise of distinction (social, biological, racial) between the researcher and the researched (Aliverti et al., 2021), as Blount-Hill and Ajil, and Cunneen (this volume) explain, we need to be mindful of this deep epistemological baggage and the 'cognitive imperialism' that characterized (and, to a large extent, still characterizes) the field, and the ethical implications of engaging in it. At the very least, academic ethics demands acknowledging our positionality and privilege (class, education, gender, linguistic, racial, geopolitical status) and adopting theoretical and methodological frameworks that strive to ameliorate such inequalities without orientalizing or romanticizing crime (Cain, 2000), or falling into the white savour trap (León, 2021; Tuhiwai Smith, 1999). In their contribution, Earle, Palmar, and Phillips provide a fascinating example of the interactions between racialization and criminalization on the one hand, and individual biographies and narratives on the other. Most importantly, they present these interactions as rich conversations, that convey at once the relational nature of academic research and shed light on both sides of it. This is a brave and honest form of conducting research which can bear key insights on ethical ways of doing criminological research. So, too, by knitting together rich archival material, Ghabrial describes the subversive nature of the *harraga* who by their mere presence made evident the fictions of law and the fabrication of reality that ensues from it through the reordering of spaces, relationships, and affects.

Academic ethics is also crucial when embarking on collaborative projects with collaborators at both sides of the colonial tide, to avoid reproducing the very same colonial logics and relationships we are critiquing in our writing. Importantly, as Mark Brown rightly points out in his Foreword to this volume, such ethical awareness is crucial when teaching our students. The call to decolonize the curriculum and the classroom involves us all—teachers and students—at a deeply ethical level in terms of our conceptions and assumptions about the criminal question, and the extent to which we are prepared to challenge the spatial, temporal, and subjective boundaries that shape criminology as a field, and be challenged. We hope that this volume goes some way in progressing such political and ethical engagement.

As we previously indicated, despite our best efforts, we struggled to fully realize the political aspirations of this project. Although we aimed at including more chapters by scholars not only from, but living and working in, the Global South and which express perspectives from so-called peripheries, we found that global academic imbalances and structures of inequality as well as linguistic limitations conditioned the availability of the kind of dialogue and 'syncretic criticism' we aimed at stimulating with this project. While we feel our efforts to be inclusive have, in the end and for the most part, paid off, we also feel that there is still much more to be done to advance a global conversation on coloniality and the criminal question that would be crafted from marginal, peripheral, and Southern viewpoints. Since the project of decolonizing is active and political—and should not be only a theorical stance—we hope that the chapters in this collection have invited readers to see it as an ongoing process—something we might call, using an abolitionist's term, a 'decolonizing horizon', one that needs to evolve and advance constantly until global inequalities, epistemic injustice (Fricker, 2007), the coloniality of knowledge (Quijano and Ennis, 2000; Keating, 2019; Bendix, 2018), and enduring legacies of oppression begin to be redressed.

References

Aas, K. F. (2012) '"The Earth is one but the world is not": Criminological theory and its geopolitical divisions', *Theoretical Criminology*, 16(1), pp. 5–20.

Agozino, B. (2003) *Counter-Colonial Criminology: A Critique of Imperialist Reason*. London: Pluto Press.

Agozino, B. (2004) 'Imperialism, crime and criminology: Towards the decolonisation of criminology', *Crime, Law and Social Change*, 41, pp. 343–358.

Aliverti, A., Carvalho, H., Chamberlen, A. et al. (2021) 'Decolonizing the criminal question', *Punishment & Society*, 23(3), pp. 297–316.

Anderson, B. (2016) *Imagined Communities: Reflections on the Origin and Spread of Nationalism*. London: Verso.

Astudillo, F. J. and Jamieson, R. W. (2021) 'The Galápagos as penal colony: Exile, peonage, and state control at the Hacienda El Progreso, 1878–1904', *Punishment & Society*, 25(1), pp. 42–59.

Back, L. (2007) *The Art of Listening*. Oxford: Berg.

Back, L. and Puwar, N. (2013) *Live Methods*. Hoboken: NJ: Wiley-Blackwell.

Bendix, D. (2018) *Global Development and Colonial Power: German Development Policy at Home and Abroad*. London: Rowman & Littlefield.

Bhambra, G. and Holmwood, J. (2021) *Colonialism and Modern Social Theory*. Cambridge: Polity Press.

Bhattacharyya, G., Elliot-Cooper, A., Balani, S. et al. (2021) *Empire's Endgame: Racism and the British State*. London: Pluto Press.

Bourdieu, P. and Wacquant, L. (1992) *An Invitation to Reflexive Sociology*. Chicago, IL: University of Chicago Press.

Bracco Bruce, L. (2022) *Prison in Peru: Ethnographic, Feminist and Decolonial Perspectives*. London: Palgrave Macmillan.

Brown, M. (2018) 'Southern Criminology in the Post-Colony: More than a 'Derivative Discourse'?', in Carrington, K., Hogg, R., Scott, J. et al. (eds) *The Palgrave Handbook of Criminology and the Global South*. London: Palgrave Macmillan.

Cain, M. (2000) 'Orientalism, occidentalism and the sociology of crime', *British Journal of Criminology*, 40(2), pp. 239–260.

Carrington, K., Hogg, R., and Sozzo, M. (2016) 'Southern criminology', *British Journal of Criminology*, 56(1), pp. 1–20.

Carrington, K. and Hogg, R. (2017) 'Deconstructing criminology's origin stories', *Asian Journal of Criminology*, 12(3), pp. 181–197.

Carrington, K., Hogg, R., Scott, J. et al. (2019). *Southern Criminology*. New York: Routledge.

Chakrabarty, D. (2000) *Provincializing Europe. Postcolonial Thought and Historical Difference*. Princeton, NJ: Princeton University Press.

Chamberlen, A. (2018) *Embodying Punishment: Emotions, Identities, and Lived Experiences in Women's Prisons*. Oxford: Oxford University Press.

Comaroff, J. and Comaroff, J. (2012) *Theory from the South: Or, How Euro-America is Evolving Toward Africa*. Abingdon: Routledge.

Connell, R. (2006) 'Northern theory: The political geography of general social theory', *Theory and Society*, 35, pp. 237–264.

Connell, R. (2007) *Southern Theory*. Cambridge: Polity.

Cunneen, C. (2011) 'Postcolonial Perspectives for Criminology', in Bosworth, M. and Hoyle, C. (eds) *What is Criminology?* Oxford: Oxford University Press, pp. 249–262.

Darke, S. and Phoenix Khan, O. (2021) 'Coloniality, just war & carceral injustice in Brazil', *Punishment & Society*, 23(5), pp. 723–740.

Faraldo Cabana, P. (2018) 'Research Excellence and Anglophone Dominance: The Case of Law, Criminology and Social Science', in Carrington, K., Hogg, R., Scott, J. et al. (eds) *The Palgrave Handbook of Criminology and the Global South*. London: Palgrave Macmillan.

Fricker, M. (2007) *Epistemic Injustice: Power and the Ethics of Knowing*. New York: Oxford University Press.

Garcia, N. and Sozzo, N. (forthcoming) 'For a "marginal criminological realism". Zaffaroni and the birth of a critical perspective on the criminal question from the Global South', *Justice, Power and Resistance*.

Gelsthorpe, L. (1992) 'Response to Martin Hammersley's paper "On Feminist Methodology"', *Sociology*, 26(2), pp. 213–218.

Hay, D. and Craven, P. (eds) (2004) *Masters, Servants and Magistrates in Britain and the Empire, 1562–1955*. Chapel Hill, NC: University of North Carolina Press.

Hibou, B. (ed.) (2004) *Privatising the State*. London: Hurst.

Hoagland, S. L. (2012) 'Denying Relationality', in Sullivan, S. and Tuana, N. (eds) Race and *Epistemologies of Ignorance*. New York: State University of New York Press, pp. 95–118.

Keating, C. (2019) 'Coloniality of knowledge, Ch'ixinakax Utxiwa, and intercultural translation: The (im)pertinence of language and discourse studies', *Language, Culture and Society*, 1(1), pp. 141–146.

Lentin, A. and Lentin, R. (eds) (2006) *Race and State*. Cambridge: Cambridge Scholars Publishing.

León, K. (2021) 'Critical criminology and race: Re-examining the whiteness of US criminological thought', *The Howard Journal of Crime and Justice*, 60(3), pp. 388–408.

Loader, I. and Sparks, R. (2011) *Public Criminology?* London: Sage.

Loader, I. and Sparks, R. (2013) 'Knowledge Politics and Penal Politics in Europe', in Daems, T., Van Zyl Smit, D., and Snacken, S. (eds) *European Penology?* Oxford: Hart.

Medina, J. (2011) 'Doing Criminology in the "Semi-Periphery" and the 'Periphery', in Arberet, R., Smith, C. J., and Zhang, S. X. (eds) *Routledge Handbook of International Criminology*. New York: Routledge.

Mehta, R. (2023) 'A Southern feminist take on border criminologies', *International Journal of Crime, Justice, and Social Democracy* (forthcoming).

Mehta, R. and Aliverti, A. (2023) 'Introduction to Special Issue: Southerning border controls', *International Journal of Crime, Justice, and Social Democracy* (forthcoming).

Melossi, D. (2001) 'The cultural embededness of social control. Reflections on the comparison of Italian and North American cultures concerning punishment', *Theoretical Criminology*, 5(4), pp. 403–424.

Melossi, D., Sozzo, M., and Sparks, R. (2011) 'Introduction. Criminal Questions: Cultural Embeddedness and Diffusion', in Melossi, D., Sozzo, M., and Sparks, C. (eds) *Travels of the Criminal Question: Cultural Embeddedness and Diffusion*. Oxford: Hart.

Mignolo, W. (2011) *The Darker Side of Western Modernity*. Durham, NC: Duke University Press.

Mignolo, W. (2012) *Local Histories/Global Designs: Coloniality, Subaltern Knowledges and Border Thinking*. Princeton, NJ: Princeton University Press.

Moore, J. M. (2015) 'The 'New Punitiveness' in the context of British Imperial History', London: Centre for Crime and Justice Studies. Available at: www.crimeandjustice.org.uk/sites/crimeandjustice.org.uk/files/09627251.2015.1080938_0.pdf (accessed 22 September 2022).

Moosavi, L. (2019) 'A friendly critique of "Asian Criminology" and "Southern criminology"', *British Journal of Criminology*, 59(2), pp. 257–275.

Mpofu, B. and Ndlovu-Gatsheni, S. (eds) (2020) *The Dynamics of Changing Higher Education in the Global South*. Newcastle upon Tyne: Cambridge Scholars Publishing.

Nelken, D. (2011) 'Theorising the Embeddedness of Punishment', in Melossi, D., Sozzo, M., and Sparks, C. (eds) *Travels of the Criminal Question: Cultural Embeddedness and Diffusion*. Oxford: Hart.

Noronha, D. L. (2019) 'Deportation, racism and multi-status Britain: Immigration control and the production of race in the present', *Ethnic and Racial Studies*, 42(14), pp. 2413–2430.

Potter, E. and Alcoff, L. (1993) *Feminist Epistemologies*. New York: Routledge.

Quijano, A. and Ennis, M. (2000) 'Coloniality of power, Eurocentrism, and Latin America', Nepantla: Views from *the South*, 1(3), pp. 533–580.

Rodriguez Goyes, D. (2019) *A Southern Green Criminology: Science Against Ecological Discrimination*. Bingley: Emerald.

Rodriguez Goyes, D. (2022) 'Green criminological dialogues: Voices from Asia', *International Journal for Crime, Justice and Social Democracy*, 11(1), pp. 1–10.

Rodriguez Goyes, D. and South, N. (2017) 'Green criminology before "green criminology": Amnesia and absences', *Critical Criminology*, 25(2), pp. 1–26.

Souza Santos, B. (2014) *Epistemologies of the South: Justice against Epistemicide*. London: Routledge,

Souza Santos, B. (2018) *The End of Cognitive Empire. The Coming of Age of Epistemologies of the South*. Durham, NC: Duke University Press.

Stambøl, E. (2021) 'Neo-colonial penality? Travelling penal power and contingent sovereignty', *Punishment & Society*, 23(4), pp. 536–556.

Stern, P. (2011) *The Company-State: Corporate Sovereignty and the Early Modern Foundations of the British Empire in India*. New York: Oxford University Press.

Stoler, A. L. (2016) *Duress: Imperial Durabilities in Our Times*. Durham, NC: Duke University Press.

Sullivan, S. and Tuana, N. (eds) (2007) *Race and Epistemologies of Ignorance*. New York: SUNY Press.

Taussig, M. (1987) *Shamanism, Colonialism, and the Wild Man*. Chicago, IL: Chicago University Press.

Travers, M. (2019) 'The idea of a Southern criminology', *International Journal of Comparative and Applied Criminal Justice*, 43(1), pp. 1–12.

Tuhiwai Smith, L. (1999) *Decolonizing Methodologies: Research and Indigenous Peoples*. London: Zed Books.

Zaffaroni, E. R. (1988) *Criminologia, aproximación desde un margen*. Bogota: Temis.

Zaffaroni, E. R. (1989) *En busca de las penas perdidas*. Buenos Aires: Ediar.

Zaffaroni, E. R. and Codino, R. (2015) 'Notas para una criminología del sur', Revista de Derecho Penal y Criminologia, V, 11, pp. 17–27.

Index

For the benefit of digital users, indexed terms that span two pages (e.g., 52–53) may, on occasion, appear on only one of those pages.

Introductory Note

References such as '178–79' indicate (not necessarily continuous) discussion of a topic across a range of pages. Wherever possible in the case of topics with many references, these have either been divided into sub-topics or only the most significant discussions of the topic are listed. Because the entire work is about the 'criminal question', the use of this term (and certain others which occur constantly throughout the book) as an entry point has been restricted. Information will be found under the corresponding detailed topics.

Figures are indicated by *f* following the page number